Municipal Magdeburg Law (*Ius municipale Magdeburgense*)
in Late Medieval Poland

Medieval Law and Its Practice

VOLUME 30

The titles published in this series are listed at *brill.com/mlip*

Municipal Magdeburg Law (*Ius municipale Magdeburgense*) in Late Medieval Poland

A Study on the Evolution and Adaptation of Law

By

Maciej Mikuła

Translated by

Andrzej Branny

BRILL

LEIDEN | BOSTON

This book is made open access with funding suport from the Jagiellonian University under the Excellence Initiative – Research University programme (the Priority Research Area Heritage).

This English edition is a revised translation from the Polish of *Prawo miejskie magdeburskie (Ius municipale Magdeburgense) w Polsce XIV – pocz. XVI wieku. Studium o ewolucji i adaptacji prawa*, Kraków: Jagiellonian University Press, 2017 (1st ed.), 2018 (2nd ed.).

The translation of this volume has been financially supported by the Faculty of Law and Administration, Jagiellonian University in Kraków.

Cover illustration: Page from the *Iura civilia Magdeburgensis civitatis*. The National Library (Warsaw), Shelfmark 12600 III. https://polona.pl/item/iura-civilia-magdeburgensis-civitatis,MTAyNzkzOTIx/164/#item(102793921) (Accessed 5 November 2020).

The Library of Congress Cataloging-in-Publication Data is available online at http://catalog.loc.gov
LC record available at http://lccn.loc.gov/2021001988

Typeface for the Latin, Greek, and Cyrillic scripts: "Brill". See and download: brill.com/brill-typeface.

ISSN 1873-8176
ISBN 978-90-04-42967-3 (hardback)
ISBN 978-90-04-45619-8 (e-book)

This book is printed on acid-free paper and produced in a sustainable manner.

Contents

Acknowledgements

In the course of writing this book, I have become indebted to a number of wonderful persons for all their support and encouragement. I am especially grateful to my wife Monika and my daughter Celinka. Their patience and understanding were of great help when I was struggling my way through the manuscripts of the *Weichbild*. I also owe a debt of gratitude to my colleagues from the Chair of History of Polish Law and the Chair of Church Law and Law on Religious Denominations at the Faculty of Law and Administration of the Jagiellonian University. In a series of academic meetings chaired by Professor Wacław Uruszczak, I was able to present my research and discuss research in progress. I would like to thank Professor Uruszczak in particular for reading the manuscript of my book and offering valuable comments and counsel in his pre-publication review. In the course of my work I could always count on professional assistance, useful advice, and friendly guidance from Dr Krzysztof Fokt and draw fresh inspiration from conversations with Dr Władysław Pęksa. I would like to thank them both.

I made up my mind to embark on this project after talking it over at some length with Professor Zygfryd Rymaszewski, a leading authority on the Saxon-Magdeburg Law who had spent years studying the manuscripts of the *Sachsenspiegel*. I found his comments and advice highly motivational and of great help in the course of my research.

I would also like to thank Professor Marian Mikołajczyk for taking so much of his time to discuss and aid with all kinds of problems that cropped up at every stage of my research.

I would also like to express my deep gratitude to Ms Jagoda Marszałek for her help in the field of Latin and the collation of Latin texts. I am grateful Professor Martin Langner for a linguistic consultation concerning sources in German.

To view the extant manuscripts of the *Weichbild*, I had to visit libraries and archives in Poland, Austria, Germany, and Russia. In each of those institutions, I was offered all the help and cooperation I could possibly need. This is why I would like to thank all the librarians and archivists for their kind assistance. Without their generous help, I would not have been able to get hold of the primary and secondary material for my analyses and comparative studies. My special thanks go to Dr Wieland Carls from Leipzig.

This book was completed during a six-month postdoctoral fellowship at the Max Planck Institute for European Legal History in Frankfurt am Main. I would like to express my thanks to Professor Heiner Lück, Dr Heinz Mohnhaupt, and

Professor Laurent Waelkens for their help in preparing the initial draft of my project, and, finally, I would like to thank the Heads of Institute, Professor Thomas Duve and Professor Stephan Vogenauer, for endorsing the project and providing excellent working conditions for its completion.

Frankfurt am Main, 7 September 2017

Acknowledgements to the English Edition

The English version of this book owes its existence to the encouragement and support of a number of people. I would like to thank Professor John Hudson and the Editorial Board of the Brill Series Medieval Law and Its Practice for accepting it for publication. I am deeply grateful to Professor Piotr Górecki for his reviewer comments which helped me to improve and clarify my argument. My special thanks go to Dr Andrzej Branny for his dedication and care in preparing the English translation of my book. I am very grateful Ms Marcella Mulder for her constant help, support and patience, and to Ms Cory Hitt for the detailed copy-editing.

Kraków, 15 October 2020

Note on the English Edition

The English edition of this book is a partially abridged version of the Polish original, with the exception of the Introduction, which has been expanded to include a section on the sources and the history of urban law in the medieval Kingdom of Poland. The revised Introduction stresses the connection between the evolution of the text of the Magdeburg *Weichbild* and the objective demand for an adaptation of an originally foreign law code (the Magdeburg Law) to the needs of Poland's urban population. That this interaction determined the reception of the Magdeburg Law in the Kingdom of Poland is, incidentally, the principal claim advanced in my study. The final sections of the Introduction are devoted to a comprehensive synopsis of the content of the Magdeburg *Weichbild*. As far as the main body of the work is concerned, brief summaries have been added at the end of some sections in Chapters 1–5. Also, the Conclusion has been slightly expanded. In this new version, Chapter 2 is much shorter: the original, detailed analysis of the *versio Sandomiriensis* manuscripts is left out. Also Appendixes 2 and 3 have been trimmed down. While working on the English version of my study, I took another careful look at my sources. There are therefore certain corrections and revisions, the aim of which is to present my points with greater clarity.

Tables and Illustrations

Tables

Figures

Photos

Abbreviations

1261Wr.	*Magdeburg's Legal Instructions for Wrocław* (*Rechtsmitteilungen Magdeburgs für Breslau*) of 1261
1295Wr.	*Magdeburg's Legal Instructions for Wrocław* (*Rechtsmitteilungen Magdeburgs für Breslau*) of 1295
951b (Leipzig MS)	MS in the University Library in Leipzig, Shelfmark 951b
AJG (Częstochowa MS)	MS in the Archives of the Pauline Monastery in Częstochowa, Shelfmark AJG II-3
Baworowscy MS	see BN 12607
BJ 168 (Wawel MS)	MS of High Court of German Law at the Royal Castle of Wawel, in the Jagiellonian Library, Shelfmark 168
BJ 169 (Cracow MS)	MS of the Cracow City Council, in the Jagiellonian Library, Shelfmark 169
BJ 170a	MS in the Jagiellonian Library, Shelfmark 170a
BJ 170b	MS in the Jagiellonian Library, Shelfmark 170b
BJ 399	MS in the Jagiellonian Library, Shelfmark 399 (unsystematic German collection of judgements of the Magdeburg Bench)
BJ 4405 (Żegota Pauli's MS)	Żegota Pauli's MS in the Jagiellonian Library, Shelfmark 4405
BN 12600 (Mikołaj of Smogorzewo's MS)	MS in the National Library in Warsaw, Shelfmark 12600 III
BN 12607 (Baworowscy MS)	MS in the National Library in Warsaw, Shelfmark 12607 III
BN 3068 (Tomasz of Bydgoszcz's MS)	MS in the National Library in Warsaw, Shelfmark 3068 III
BOZ (Marcin Zabowski's MS)	MS in the National Library in Warsaw, Shelfmark BOZ 90
Commune incliti	see *Statutes*
Cracow MS	see BJ 169
Częstochowa MS	see AJG
D.	*Digesta*
Decreta I, II	Ludwik Łysiak, Karin Nehlsen-von Stryk, eds., *Decreta iuris supremi Magdeburgensis castri Cracoviensis. Die Rechtssprüche des Oberhofs des deutschen Rechts auf der Burg zu Krakau, 1456–1481; 1481–1511* (Frankfurt am Main, 1995, 1997)

Dział. I (Działyńscy Codex I)	MS in the Library of the Polish Academy of Sciences at Kórnik, Shelfmark 801
Dział. IV (Działyńscy Codex IV)	MS in the Library of the Polish Academy of Sciences at Kórnik, Shelfmark 800
Działyńscy Codex I and IV	see Dział. I, Dział. IV
F 143 (St Petersburg MS)	MS in the Library of the Russian Academy of Sciences in St Petersburg, Shelfmark F 143
Flor. (St Florian MS)	MS in Sankt-Florian Abbey in Austria, Shelfmark 551/II
Gn. (Gniezno MS)	MS in the Archdiocesan Archives at Gniezno, Shelfmark 104
Henryków MS	see II F 8
II F 8 (Henryków MS)	Henryków MS called also Wrocław MS, in the Library of the University of Wrocław, Shelfmark II F 8
II Q 3	MS in the Library of the University of Wrocław, Shelfmark II Q 3, including *Magdeburg Bench Law* (*Das Magdeburg Schöffenrecht*) edited by Paul Laband
II Q 4 (Żagań MS)	MS in the Library of the University of Wrocław, Shelfmark II Q 4
IM	*Ius municipale Magdeburgense, Weichbild*
JIM	Mikołaj Jaskier, *Iuris Municipalis Maideburgensis Liber vulgo Weichbild nuncupatur* ... (Samosci, 1602)
JSSp.	Mikołaj Jaskier, *Iuris Provincialis quo Speculum Saxonum vulgo nuncupatur Libri tres* ... (Samosci, 1602)
Kiel. (Kielce MS)	MS in the Library of the Diocesan Seminary in Kielce, Shelfmark RK 45/28
Kielce MS	see Kiel.
Leipzig MS	see 951b
Liber Legum	see Przem.
Marcin Zabowski's MS	see BOZ
MFr.	*Die Magdeburger Fragen*
MGH	*Monumenta Germaniae Historica*
Mikołaj of Smogorzewo's MS	see BN 12600
MSR	*Magdeburg Bench Law* (*Das Magdeburger Schöffenrecht*)
NS	Zygfryd Rymaszewski, *Nieznany spis prawa chełmińskiego z przełomu XIV i XV wieku* [A Newly Discovered Manuscript of Chełmno Law from the Late 14th–Early 15th Century] (Łódź, 1993)

NTO	Józef Reczek and Wacław Twardzik, *Najstarsze staropolskie tłumaczenie ortyli magdeburskich* [The Earliest Polish Translation of the Magdeburg ortyle], 1–3 (Warszawa, 1970)
Opatów MS	see Oss.
Oss. (Opatów MS)	MS in the Ossoliński National Institute, Shelfmark Oss. 832/II
Petersburg MS	see F 143
PL	*Patrologia Latina*
Plesz.	Witold Maisel, ed., "Prawo magdeburskie miasta Pleszewa" [The Magdeburg Lawbook of Pleszew], *Studia i Materiały do Dziejów Wielkopolski i Pomorza* 9/1 (1963)
Przem. (Przemyśl MS)	*Liber legum*, in the State Archive in Przemyśl, Archives of Przemyśl City, Shelfmark 428
Przemyśl MS	see Przem.
PS	*Old Chełmno Law* (*Der Alte Kulm*)
Q II 157 (1)	the first text of *Weichbild* in MS St.P. Lat. Q II 157 in the Russian National Library in St Petersburg
Q II 157 (2)	the second text of *Weichbild* in MS St.P. Lat. Q II 157 in the Russian National Library in St Petersburg
RGV	*Constitution of Courts* (*Rechtsbuch von der Gerichtsverfassung*)
SSp	*Speculum Saxonum* (*Sachsenspiegel*)
St Florian MS	see Flor.
Statutes, or Łaski's *Statutes*	*Commune incliti Poloniae Regni privilegium constitutionum et indultuum publicitus decretorum approbatorumque ...*, ed. Jan Łaski (Cracoviae, 1506)
SzIM	Paweł Szczerbic, *Ius Municipale, to jest prawo miejskie majdeburskie nowo z łacińskiego i z niemieckiego* na *polski język* z *pilnością* i *wiernie przełożone* [*Ius Municipale* [The Magdeburg Municipal Law]: A New and Meticulously Accurate Translation from the Latin and the German], ed. Grzegorz M. Kowalski, Bibliotheca Iagellonica. Fontes et Studia 20 (Kraków, 2011).
Tomasz of Bydgoszcz's MS	see BN 3068
Vulg.	the *Weichbild* vulgate
Warsaw MS	see Warsz.

Warsz. (Warsaw MS)	MS in in the Library of the University of Warsaw, Shelfmark 5
Wawel MS	see BJ 168
Żagań MS	see II Q 4
Żegota Pauli's MS	see BJ 4405

Introduction

1 The Towns and Cities of 'Younger Europe'

It is no exaggeration to say that the intellectuals and theologians of the Middle Ages were firmly committed to a vision of a harmonious and static society, divided into three, mutually dependent segments, that is, those who pray, those who fight, and those who work (those who are responsible for communal food production). However, in the 12th–13th century, this simple model came under pressure, not least because of the rise of a new class of wealthy burghers and merchants.[1] The compilers of the *Ius municipale Magdeburgese* sought to address this difficulty by declaring in one of the articles of the *Constitution of Courts* (*Rechtsbuch von der Gerichtsverfassung*)[2] that the urban law originated in ancient Babylonia and was reinstated upon a plea from the Magdeburg merchants by the Holy Roman Emperor.[3] Another paragraph of that *Constitution* invokes a vision of the Magdeburg Law spreading in the north-eastern periphery of the Empire – that is, in the Marches of Meissen and Lusatia, the Lands of the Bohemian Crown and Poland – where it was adopted as a model for the emerging urban communities.[4] The territorial expanse of the new law indicated in this passage contains a vital historical clue. In the territories inside the *limes* of the ancient Roman Empire nearly all post-Roman cities (*coloniae*) went through a phase of dramatic decline, but the lines of continuity with the past were rarely broken off completely. In Italy, Southern France, and Catalonia, the legacy of Roman law was alive and well when the universities rediscovered the Justinian Code in the late 12th century. The situation was different in the new states in West Slavic Central Europe, with no existing tradition of Roman urban life. As local and international trade began to pick up from the 11th–12th century onwards, this part of Europe saw a dynamic growth of new settlements of a proto-urban character. Unlike the traditional farming settlements, their economy depended on trade (often institutionalized in the

1 Jacques Le Goff, *Medieval Civilization*, trans. Julia Barrow (Blackwell Publishing: 1991), pp. 255, and 261–262.

2 For a comprehensive survey of the sources of the Saxon-Magdeburg Law in Poland, see Wieland Carls, "Rechtsquellen Sächsisch-magdeburgischen Rechts", in: Inge Bily, Wieland Carls, and Katalin Gönczi, *Sächsisch-magdeburgisches Recht in Polen. Untersuchungen zur Geschichte des Rechts und seiner Sprache*, (Ivs Saxonico-Maidebvrgense in Oriente) 2 (Berlin, 2011), p. 84.

3 Cf. Appendix 4, Article 110 of the Magdeburg *Weichbild*.

4 *Ibid.*, Article 113.

form of regular market days) and artisan production.[5] It should be made clear, however, that they were not towns in the sense in which the term was used after the adoption of the Magdeburg Law.

With the conversion of Mieszko I to Christianity in 966, Poland became one of the key nations of 'Younger Europe'.[6] Two centuries later, when Europe entered a period of vigorous social and economic expansion, Poland was a monarchy in the midst of a process of feudal fragmentation. The idea of the unity of the Kingdom of Poland – formally established by the royal coronation of Bolesław I the Brave in 1025, and reaffirmed by the subsequent coronations of his son Mieszko II in 1025 and Mieszko's grandson, Bolesław II the Bold, in 1076 – was never called into question, although the royal princes of the Piast dynasty ruled their provinces independently of the Senior Prince, who nominally was to have supreme power over the rest. The restoration of the unity of the realm under a crowned monarch remained a distant objective until the end of the 13th century, when coronation was brought back as a trump card in the political power play. In the end, centralized monarchy was restored for good by Władysław I Łokietek (literally, Władysław I the Elbow-High), and from his coronation in Cracow in 1320 until 1795, Poland was ruled by a succession of crowned kings. However, the newly restored Kingdom of Poland did not include Silesia, which was divided into numerous principalities whose Piast rulers had become vassals of the King of Bohemia.

The emergence of 'new' towns (i.e. communes striving for self-rule) in Poland under the Piasts was no doubt enhanced by the influx of migrants from Western Europe, a process that reached massive proportions in the 12th and 13th century. The settlers brought with them a law code that at first applied only to them, but was soon found to be so attractive as to be worth adopting for the townspeople at large. In the Kingdom of Poland, the legal status of urban settlements under Polish law was inadequate to address the new realities. The new settlers, accustomed to greater personal freedom, were not fond of such a model. It was also made obsolete not only by the changing demographics, but also as a result of the development of markets and the rise of a money economy (the old system was based on rents in kind and labour or

5 Maria Bogucka and Henryk Samsonowicz, *Dzieje miast i mieszczaństwa w Polsce przedrozbiorowej* [A History of Towns and the Urban Middle Class in Poland until 1795] (Wrocław – Warszawa – Kraków – Gdańsk – Łódź, 1986), pp. 24–25, 27 and 37.

6 The term 'Younger Europe' was coined by Jerzy Kłoczowski for the peoples and nations of Central and Eastern Europe that joined Latin Christendom in the 10th–11th centuries. See Jerzy Kłoczowski, *Młodsza Europa. Europa Środkowo-Wschodnia w kręgu cywilizacji chrześcijańskiej średniowiecza* [The Younger Europe: Central and Eastern Europe and the Civilization of the Christian Middle Ages] (Warszawa, 2003), pp. 11 and 13.

military service). Yet another factor which accelerated the pace of transition in the 12th and 13th centuries was the fragmentation of the kingdom and the growing role of the Church and local elites. The fragmentation made it easier for Church institutions, local landlords, and towns to obtain more grants and privileges from their territorial liege lords (the princes) – most importantly, judicial rights. While the landlords profited from having a share in the fines and fees imposed by courts, they had to ensure the functioning of a system of justice that was fit for purpose.

The law code brought by the new settlers appeared to be the best solution to this problem. The choice of the so-called German law (*ius Theutonicum*) was only natural given the proximity of Magdeburg, the most dynamic centre of the new urban law in Eastern Germany. The successful expansion of the Magdeburg Law in Central and Eastern Europe is due to its three key characteristics: 1) guarantees of personal freedom, including the right to move elsewhere as long one has paid one's taxes; 2) a detailed, written catalogue of duties of both parties of the contract, the owner and the residents, including the burghers' hereditary right to their plots of land; and 3) a collegiate court system, in which the owner delegated his feudal rights at first to a magistrate invested with judicial powers (Pol. *wójt*, Ger. *Vogt*, Lat. *advocatus*) and jurymen, and later to the Town Council, which was a fully self-governing body.[7] These principles constitute the essence of *ius Theutonicum*, yet, in the historical realties of the 13th century, in many places it took a long time after the foundation of a town under Magdeburg Law until it was absorbed into the provisions of civil and criminal law and judicial procedure.

In Poland, the first town founded under German law was Złotoryja (Goldberg, 1211). From that date onwards, chartered towns sprang up one after another, first in Silesia and then in other Piast principalities. In the 14th

7 See Kazimierz Tymieniecki, "Prawo niemieckie w rozwoju społecznym wsi polskiej" [German Law and the Social Development of the Polish Village], *Kwartalnik Historyczny* 37 (1923), 39, 41, 60–64, and 68–70; Kazimierz Tymieniecki, "Prawo czy gospodarstwo?" [The Law or the Household?], *Roczniki Dziejów Społecznych i Gospodarczych* 8/2 (1946), 289–291; Benedykt Zientara, "Das Deutsche Recht (*ius teutonicum*) und die Anfänge der städtischen Autonomie", in: *Autonomie, Wirtschaft und Kultur der Hansestädte*, eds. Konrad Fritze, Eckhard Mueller-Mertens, Walter Stark (Weimar 1984), pp. 94–100; Józef Matuszewski, "Prawo sądowe na wsi polskiej lokowanej na prawie niemieckim" [Law in Polish Villages Founded under German Law], *Studia z Dziejów Państwa i Prawa Polskiego* 2 (1995), 54–59; Józef Matuszewski, "Rodzaje własności gruntu we wsi lokowanej na prawie niemieckim" [Types of Land Ownership in Villages Founded under German Law], in: *Parlament, prawo, ludzie. Studia ofiarowane Profesorowi Juliuszowi Bardachowi* [Parliament, the Law and the People: A Festschrift in Honour of Professor Juliusz Bardach], eds. Katarzyna Iwanicka, Maria Skowronek, Kazimierz Stembrowicz (Warszawa, 1996), pp. 158, 160–162, and 164.

century, after the kingdom was reunited by Władysław Łokietek (1306–1333) and during the reign of his son Kazimierz the Great (1333–1370), the influx of new settlers from the West into the newly founded towns dropped off markedly. The 'colonization' continued, but its character changed. Now, the new settlements were usually built in underdeveloped areas, *de cruda radice*, and the settlers were recruited from Poland; alternately, existing settlements with a Polish population were chartered under Magdeburg Law. Meanwhile, the process of setting up new towns and villages under Magdeburg Law disseminated to other parts of the Kingdom of Poland and to other countries of Central and Eastern Europe.[8]

2 The Saxon-Magdeburg Law and the Municipal Law in the Kingdom of Poland in the 13th–16th Centuries

The foundation of a town under Magdeburg Law doesn't meant that the new legal order was adopted immediately or in its entirety by the new community. The implementation of specific regulations that – by modern standards – belong to the sphere of civil and criminal law, judicial procedure, and the constitution of courts typically took quite a long time. Moreover, municipal law in its advanced form (although, to be fair, it did not reach that stage until the turn of the 15th century) was a conglomerate of heterogeneous elements of which the provisions of the Saxon-Magdenburg Law was a vital part, but not the only one.

2.1 *Municipal Law: Sources of Polish Provenance*

Irrespective of the owner of a town (e.g. the crown, members of the nobility, or the Church), all towns remained under royal jurisdiction. The right to establish a new town under German law belonged exclusively to the king (who issued the appropriate royal charters on an individual basis, as *privilegia*).[9] His consent had to be sought for the right to hold fairs and fix market days, collect road tolls, and impose compulsory depot (whereby travelling merchants had to offer

8 Heiner Lück, "Urban Law: The Law of Saxony and Magdeburg", in: *The Oxford Handbook of European Legal History*, eds. Heikki Pihlajamäki, Markus D. Dubber, and Mark Godfrey, Published online: August 2018, DOI: 10.1093/oxfordhb/9780198785521.001.0001.

9 See monographs: Stanisław Kuraś, *Przywileje prawa niemieckiego miast i wsi małopolskich XIV–XV wieku* [German Law Privileges for Towns and Villages in Małopolska in the 14th–15th Century] (Wrocław – Warszawa – Kraków – Gdańsk, 1971); Krystyna Kamińska, *Lokacje miast na prawie magdeburskim na ziemiach polskich do 1370 r. Studium historyczno-prawne* [Incorporation of Towns under Magdeburg Law in Poland until 1370: A Study in Legal History] (Toruń, 1990).

their cargo for sale during a specified number of days).[10] By the 15th century, towns had also come under the jurisdiction of the Polish Parliament (*Sejm*). For the most part, parliamentary legislation dealt with fiscal matters and military service, although it also includes certain regulations concerning trade and criminal law.[11] The town owners, too, retained the right to make law. Statutes issued in their name dealt primarily with the town's economic life; occasionally they amended some provisions of the existing civil and criminal law. The towns – that is, the town councils – enacted their own statutes (*wilkierze*, Ger. *Willküren*), chiefly to regulate trade and the functioning of guilds. Apart from written law, custom and customary law still played a considerable role in the daily practice of the municipal courts.[12]

2.2 *Sources of the Saxon-Magdeburg Law in Poland*

As it was shown, sources of Polish provenance played an important role in the shaping of urban law in medieval Poland. However, its basic structure was made up of the Magdeburg Law,[13] whose reception was by no means straightforward. Its more systematic adoption, expansion, and adaptation took place in a number of mutations and phases. In general, we can distinguish four variants of the Magdeburg Law functioning in the Kingdom of Poland. Three of them stemmed directly or indirectly from the judgments (the case law) of the Magdeburg lay judges' bench: the Magdeburg Law, the Law of Środa, and the Chełmno Law (a.k.a. *Der Alte Kulm*). The Chełmno Law was common in the north of Poland (although a handful of Northern towns adopted the Lübeck Law). The trajectory of the Chełmno Law begins with the incorporation of Chełmno (Kulm) in 1223. Its charter stipulated the creation of a bench of lay judges, a collegiate institution of justice, with competences similar to those of the Magdeburg Bench. A distinctive feature of the history of the Chełmno Law was the striving for collating and codifying the various updates and amendations. The product of these efforts was a law code known as the *Old Chełmno Law* (*Der Alte Kulm*), which included, among others, the case law of the Magdeburg Bench. That case law can also be found at the heart of the Law of Środa, which

---

10 Maciej Mikuła, *Prawodawstwo króla i sejmu dla małopolskich miast królewskich (1386–1572). Studium z dziejów rządów prawa w Polsce* [Royal and Parliamentary Legislation for the Royal Towns of Małopolska (1386–1572): A Study in the History of the Rule of Law in Poland] (Kraków, 2014), chapter 3.

11 *Ibid.*, chapter 2.

12 Grzegorz M. Kowalski, *Zwyczaj i prawo zwyczajowe w doktrynie prawa i praktyce sądów miejskich karnych w Polsce XVI–XVIII w.* [Custom and Customary Law in Legal Doctrine and Practice of Municipal Criminal Courts in Poland 16th–18th Century] (Kraków, 2013), p. 174.

13 For a systematic review of the sources of the Saxon-Magdeburg Law in Poland, see Carls, "Rechtsquellen Sächsisch-magdeburgischen Rechts", pp. 69–109.

spread out into Southern Poland, even though it was not borrowed directly from Magdeburg. The intermediary was Halle, a town in the Archbishopric of Magdeburg, which supplied the founders of Środa (Neumarkt in Schlesien/ Novum Forum, 1235) with a model to copy in *Halle's Legal Instruction for Środa Śląska* (*Hallische Rechtsmitteilung für Neumarkt*).[14] In the 14th century, as the town received a new charter, the Law of Środa was supplanted by a modernized version of the Magdeburg Law, which provided for the creation of a town council.

At the core of the Magdeburg Law, which by the late Middle Ages had disseminated from the Elbe to the Dnieper and from the Baltic to Transylvania (Siebenbürgen), was the case law of the Magdeburg Bench.[15] The Magdeburg Bench was the lay court to which the towns incorporated under German law turned for explication and interpretation of the law in difficult cases. In Polish, the rulings of that court were commonly referred to as *ortyle* (Ger. *Urteile*). While in some regions this practice continued until the first half of the 16th century, in Poland, King Kazimierz the Great sought to weaken the dependence on Magdeburg by establishing a High Court of German Law in Cracow in 1356. However, the new court did not succeed in completely displacing the traditional practice, as some Polish towns are known to have kept up the Magdeburg connection well into the 15th century. In their rulings, the lay jurors of Magdeburg depended primarily on the *Sachsenspiegel* (*Speculum Saxonum*), a record of Saxon law written in Latin (the original has not survived) and translated into Middle Low German around 1220–1235 by Eike von Repgow. Although the *Sachsenspiegel* covers only common and feudal law, and its suitability for matters of urban law is limited, it came to be regarded as the authoritative legal code in all towns chartered under Magdeburg Law.

---

14 Krystyna Kamińska, "Prawo średzkie jako instrument polityki osadniczej i gospodarczej w Polsce od XIII do początku XVI wieku" [The Środa Law as an Instrument of Settler Policy and Economic Development in Poland in the 13th and Early 14th Century], in: *Historia integra. Księga pamiątkowa ofiarowana prof. Stanisławowi Salmonowiczowi w siedemdziesięciolecie urodzin* [Historia integra: A Festschrift in Honour of Professor Stanisław Salmonowicz on His 70th Birthday], eds. Danuta Janicka and Ryszard Łaszewski (Toruń, 2001), pp. 147–160.

15 Heiner Lück, "Wirkungen des *Sachsenspiegels* und des Magdeburger Rechts in Ostmitteleuropa", in: *Legal Transitions. Development of Law in Formerly Socialist States and the Challenges of the European Union/Rechtsentwicklung in den ehemaligen sozialistischen Staaten und die Herausforderung der Europäischen Union*, eds. Elemér Balogh, Andrea Hegedűs, Péter Mezei, Zsolt Szomora, and Julianna S. Traser, (A Pólay Elemér Alapítvány Könyvtára) 17 (Szeged, 2007), pp. 274–278; Heiner Lück, "Die Anfänge des Magdeburger Stadtrechts und seine Verbreitung in Europa. Strukturen, Mechanismen, Dimensionen", *Sachsen und Anhalt* 27 (2015), 189–95.

Its reception was rapid and widespread, as shown by a significant number of extant copies in Germany, the Kingdom of Poland, and other countries of Central Europe. This fact justifies the use of the term 'Saxon-Magdeburg Law'.

The jurors of the Magdeburg Bench not only answered questions on specific legal points, but also compiled and sent out legal instructions. Thus, for instance, they sent two sets of such instructions (*Rechtsmitteilungen*) to Wrocław, one in 1261 and the other in 1295. Wrocław (Breslau) was just one of the many places where the Magdeburg instructions and judgments were combined with regulations from other sources, including the *Sachsenspiegel*, to produce an astonishing variety of compilations and adaptations. At the earliest stage of the process of compilation and consolidation of the law's text, we can identify three landmark compilations: 1) the *Constitution of Courts* (*Rechtsbuch von der Gerichtsverfassung*, c. 1257–1262), a relatively short text which on the whole retained its integrity when copied; 2) the *Magdeburg Bench Law* (*Magdeburger Schöffenrecht*, c. 1270), an open-ended collection which was re-edited by copyists and used selectively during the process of transmission; and 3) the *Weichbild*, a comprehensive compilation meant to fix the law – which it generally did – while in fact spawning hundreds of manuscript copies which, it seems, never reproduced the received text without altering it, however slightly.

The end of the 13th century saw the creation of an important mutation of the Magdeburg Law that appears to have spread in Silesia and then to southern Poland (hence term 'the Silesian-Małopolska compilation', used in this study) even before it was incorporated in the Latin compilation by Konrad of Opole in 1306. Also known as *Ius municipale Magdeburgense*, *Liber primus iuris municipalis*, the *Magdeburger Weichbild*, and the *das Sächsische Weichbildrecht* it became, thanks to the Latin translation, one of the key sources of the Saxon-Magdeburg Law adopted by Polish towns. In fact, the *Weichbild*, the *Sachsenspiegel*, and the Magdeburg lay judges' case law (*ortyle*), in either version (i.e. the Latin or the vernacular), constituted a trio of prime sources of law in the Kingdom of Poland. The most dynamic element of the system, the Magdeburg Bench case law, was given no less attention than the other two, as shown by the circulation of the German-language collection *Die Magdeburger Fragen*.

In collections of the Saxon-Magdeburg Law which contained all three of those source texts, the *Weichbild* was usually called *liber primus* and given pride of place.[16] This should come as no surprise. The *Weichbild* contains a

16 In his *History of the Sources of Old Polish Law*, Stanisław Kutrzeba states that the *Weichbild* was the most important code of Magdeburg Law in the urban communities of medieval Poland (Stanisław Kutrzeba, *Historia źródeł dawnego prawa polskiego*

body of regulations concerning urban institutions and their competences, the structure of municipal courts, judicial procedure, the normative framework of commerce and trade, and practical points of criminal and civil law. Along with the *Sachsenspiegel*, the Lübeck Law, a handbook of Roman and canon law, and the treatise *Summa legum levis, brevis et utilis* by Raymundus Parthenopaeus, it found its way into the definitive edition of Poland's laws – *Commune incliti*, compiled by Jan Łaski, Grand Chancellor of King Alexander Jagiellon. Published in 1506 with a royal imprimatur, it was the first authoritative version of both the *Weichbild* and the *Sachsenspiegel* to be printed in Poland.

[History of the Sources of Old Polish Law], 2 (Lwów – Warszawa – Kraków, [1926]), p. 208). Zygfryd Rymaszewski, however, argues that the Polish towns looked to the Land Law of the *Sachsenspiegel* as the most authoritative text of law (Zygfryd Rymaszewski, *Łacińskie teksty Landrechtu Zwierciadła Saskiego w Polsce* [Latin Texts of the Landrecht of the *Sachsenspiegel* in Poland] (Łódź, 1975), p. 6). For a discussion of the content of the Magdeburg *Weichbild*, see Chapter 1.1. In German legal history, medieval collections of laws are referred to as *Rechtsbücher*. For a comprehensive modern study of the medieval law books, see Heiner Lück, "Rechtsbücher als 'private' Rechtsaufzeichnungen?", *Zeitschrift der Savigny-Stiftung für Rechtsgeschichte: Germanistische Abteilung* 131 (2014), 432–3. See also Hiram Kümper, *Sachsenrecht. Studien zur Geschichte des Sächsichen Landrechts in Mittelalter und früher Neuzeit*, (Schriften zur Rechtsgeschichte) 142 (Berlin, 2007), esp. Chapter A.2 'Die Quellen: Deutsche Rechtsbücher des Mittelalters', p. 16ff. The term 'law book' is also employed by historians elsewhere, for example in the Czech Republic (see for example Naďa Fiedlerová and Lenka Šmídová Malárová, "The Earliest Law Books of the City of Brno and Their Relation to the Contemporary Legal Practice", *Krakowskie Studia z Historii Państwa i Prawa* 10/2 (2017), with a bibliographical list of earlier studies), Slovakia (Adriana Švecová, "Die Stadtrechtsbücher in der mittelalterlichen Slowakei und Ungarn als Beispiel des eigenen Selbstbewusstseins im Rahmen der europäischen Rechtskultur", *Krakowskie Studia z Historii Państwa i Prawa* 9/3 (2016), 327–43) and Hungary (Katalin Gönczi, "Stadtbücher aus dem Königreich Ungarn im Spiegel der städtischen Schriftkultur – Überlegungen zum Stand der Forschung", *Krakowskie Studia z Historii Państwa i Prawa* 9/3 (2016), 313–26). The term 'law book' is not much used in Polish studies of the reigns of the late Piasts and the Jagiellons, although occasionally it can even appear in the title as in this edition of the laws of Poznań and the title of a collection of the Magdeburg and canon laws of Przemyśl. See Witold Maisel, ed., *Poznańska księga prawa magdeburskiego i miśnieńskiego* [The Poznań Book of Magdeburg-Meissen Law] (Wrocław, 1964); Witold Maisel, "Die Quellen des deutschen Rechts im mittelalterlichen Posen", in: *Studien zur Geschichte des sächsich-magdeburgischen Rechts in Deutschland und Polen*, eds. Dietmar Willoweit and Winfried Schich, (Rechtshistorische Reihe) 10 (Frankfurt am Main, 1980), p. 116; Dietlinde Munzel, "Posener Rechtbuch", in: *Handwörterbuch zur deutschen Rechtsgeschichte*, 1st ed., 3 (Berlin, 1984), col. 1831–1832; Anna Łosowska, *Kolekcja liber legum i jej miejsce w kulturze umysłowej późnośredniowiecznego Przemyśla* [The Liber legum MS and Its Place in the Intellectual Culture of Late-Medieval Przemyśl] (Warszawa – Przemyśl, 2007).

3 The Magdeburg *Weichbild* in Poland: A Reassessment and a New Research Agenda

The Magdeburg *Weichbild* is perhaps the only major medieval legal text which has not been the subject of a comprehensive monographic study in Poland.[17]

---

17 The most comprehensive description of the *Weichbild* can be found in Stanisław Kutrzeba's *Historia źródeł* (pp. 208–211). The *Weichbild* is also discussed in Zygfryd Rymaszewski's studies of the *Sachsenspiegel*, especially *Łacińskie teksty Landrechtu Zwierciadła Saskiego w Polsce* and "*Forum commune* and *forum liberum*" (in *Studia z Dziejów Państwa i Prawa Polskiego* 2 (1995), 76–91). The latter traces the history of the two terms that occur in Łaski's *Statutes* by going through a number of Latin and German sources, and, in effect, challenges Stanisław Estreicher's claim about the evolution of the marketplace ("*Freimarkt* and *Frymark*", *Czasopismo Prawnicze i Ekonomiczne* 25 (1929), 337ff.). Cf. also Emil Kałużniacki, "Die polnische Recension der Magdeburger Urtheile und die einschlägigen deutschen, lateinischen und czechischen Sammlungen", *Sitzungsberichte der phil.-hist. Classe der Kaierischer Akademie der Wissenschaften* 111 (1886), 156–60; Stanisław Estreicher, "Nieznane teksty ortyli magdeburskich" [Recently Discovered Texts of the Magdeburg *ortyle*], in: *Studia staropolskie. Księga ku czci Aleksandra Brücknera* [Old Polish Studies: A Festschrift in Honour of Aleksander Brückner] (Kraków, 1928), pp. 112–126. Recently, a new approach to the interpretation of textual evidence which is at centre of this debate has been presented by the author of this monograph in three articles. The first of them stresses the importance of categorizing the textual variants that are employed in further analyses: Maciej Mikuła, "Modyfikacje łacińskich tekstów Weichbildu magdeburskiego a ewolucja prawa w średniowiecznych miastach polskich. Uwagi wstępne" [Modifications of Latin Texts of the Magdeburg *Weichbild* and the Evolution of Law in Medieval Polish Towns: An Introduction], in: *Acta Iuridico-Historica Pilsnensia*, 2012–2013 (published 2014; ed. Vilém Knoll), 137–52. The second article calls for examining the consequences of modifications of the text of the law in legal practice (Maciej Mikuła, "Die Modifizierung des Erb- und Familienrechts im Magdeburger Weichbildrecht (Einführung zum Thema)", in: *Judiciary and Society Between Privacy and Publicity*, ed. Danuta Janicka, 8th Conference on Legal History in the Baltic Sea Area, 3rd–6th September (Toruń, 2015), pp. 329–343); the third points to importance of users' glosses in the assessment of the functioning of the *Weichbild* in legal practice (Maciej Mikuła, "*Weichbild* magdeburski w rękopisie Biblioteki Jagiellońskiej nr 4405" [The Magdeburg *Weichbild* in MS BJ 4405], in: *Nil nisi veritas. Księga dedykowana Profesorowi Jackowi Matuszewskiemu* [*Nil nisi veritas*. A Festschrift Dedicated to Professor Jacek Matuszewski], eds. Marcin Głuszak and Dorota Wiśniewska-Jóźwiak (Łódź, 2016), pp. 151–157). A number of illuminating insights can also be found in Grzegorz M. Kowalski's introduction to his critical edition of Paweł Szczerbic's Polish translation of the *Weichbild*: Paweł Szczerbic, *Ius Municipale, to jest prawo miejskie majdeburskie nowo z łacińskiego i z niemieckiego* na *polski język* z *pilnością* i *wiernie przełożone* [*Ius Municipale*, or the Magdeburg Municipal Law: A New and Meticulously Accurate Translation from the Latin and the German], ed. Grzegorz M. Kowalski (Bibliotheca Iagellonica. Fontes et Studia) 20 (Kraków, 2011). The literature on this subject will be examined in greater detail in Chapter 1 of this monograph. For a general survey of research into Magdeburg Law in Poland, see *Danuta* Janicka, "Wkład polskich historyków prawa w badania nad prawem magdeburskim w

Nor has research outside Poland shown more sustained interest in the *Weichbild* texts used in this country;[18] important work in this field comes from the 19th century, and – for all its worth – it has become outdated in numerous

XX w. (1945–2010)" [The Contribution of Polish Law Historians to the Study of Magdeburg Law in the 20th Century (1945–2010)], *Studia Iuridica Toruniensia* 10 (2013), 46–75; and Danuta Janicka, "Neuere Rechtsgeschichte in Polen in den Jahren 2002–2014", *Zeitschrift für Neuere Rechtsgeschichte* 37 (2015), 130–42.

18 The presence of the *Weichbild* in Polish towns is discussed in Wieland Carls's "Rechtsquellen Sächsisch-magdeburgischen Rechts", in: Inge Bily, Wieland Carls, and Katalin Gönczi, *Sächsisch-magdeburgisches Recht in Polen. Untersuchungen zur Geschichte des Rechts und seiner Sprache*, (Ivs Saxonico-Maidebvrgense in Oriente) 2 (Berlin, 2011), pp. 86–88. At this point due *acknowledgement* must also be given to Ulrich-Dieter Oppitz's authoritative and continually updated catalogue of manuscripts of German law, esp. *Deutsche Rechtsbücher des Mittelalters*, 1, Köln – Wien 1990, pp. 47–48 and supplementary material in Ulrich-Dieter Oppitz, "Ergänzungen zu „Deutsche Rechtsbücher des Mittelalters und ihre Handschriften", *Zeitschrift der Savigny-Stiftung für Rechtsgeschichte. Germanistische Abteilung* [henceforth *ZRG GA*] 128 (2011), 452. Supplementary material concerning other *Weichbild* compilations (i.e. not the Silesian-Małopolska branch), see *ZRG GA* 120 (2004), 371–5; *ZRG GA* 131 (2014), 400–17; *ZRG GA* 132 (2015), 463–78; and *ZRG GA*, 133 (2016), 484–7. Basic information on the *Weichbild* and its key versions (the so-called Konrad of Opole compilation, Konrad of Sandomierz's Latin translation, and the printed versions by Jan Łaski, Mikołaj Jaskier and Paweł Szczerbic) can be found in standard reference books, especially Peter Johanek's entry "Magdeburger Rechtsbücher", in *Die deutsche Literatur des Mittelalters: Verfasserlexikon*, eds. Kurt Ruh, Gundolf Keil, *et al.*, Supplementary 11, 2nd ed., 2004, col. 950–953; and Ruth Schmidt-Wiegand's entry "*Weichbild*", in *Handwörterbuch zur deutschen Rechtsgeschichte*, 1st ed., 5 (Berlin, 1998), col. 1209–1212. Cf. also the bibliographical entry "Weichbildrecht, Das Sächsische" in the source catalogue *Geschichtsquellen des deutschen Mittelalters* (http://www.geschichtsquellen.de/repOpus_04593.html, accessed 8 July 2017). The latter mistakenly identifies the text reprinted by Jacob Friedrich Ludovici (*Das Sächsische Weichbild in der lateinischen und jetzo gebräuchlichen hochteutschen Sprache aus alten bewährten Codicibus ...*, Halle 1721), and by Alexander v. Daniels and Franz v. Gruben (*Das Saeschsische Weichbildrecht. Ius municipale Saxonum. Erster Band. Mit Weltchronik und Weichbildrecht in XXXVI mit Glosse*, Berlin 1858) as Konrad of Sandomierz's version; in fact it is the *Weichbild* vulgate.

The problems of adoption of the Magdeburg judgments (*Urteile*) into the *Weichbild* gloss are discussed by Gerhard Buchda, "Enthält die Glosse zum sächsischen Weichbild echte Schöffensprüche?", in: *Festschrift Heinrich Demelius zum 80. Geburtstag. Erlebtes Recht in Geschichte und Gegenwart*, ed. Gerhard Frotz (Wien, 1973), pp. 25–50. For a broader analysis of the relationship between the Magdeburg judgments and the *Weichbild* vulgate, see Renate Schelling "Magdeburger Schöffensprüche und Magdeburger Weichbildrecht in urkundlicher und handschriftlicher Überlieferung", in: *Hanse, Städte, Bünde. Die sächischen Städte zwischen Elbe und Weser um 1500. Ausstellung Kulturhistorisches Museum Magdeburg 28. Mai bis 26. August 1996. Braunschweigisches Landesmuseum. Ausstellungszentrum Hinter Aegidien 17. September bis 1. Dezember 1996*, 1, ed. Matthias Puhle, (Magdeburger Museumsschriften) 4/1 (Magdeburg, 1996), pp. 118–128. See also Kümper, *Sachsenrecht*, pp. 395–397; Christine Magin, *'Wie es umb der iuden recht stet.' Der Status der Juden in Spätmittelalterlichen deutschen Rechtsbüchern* (Göttingen, 1999), pp. 56–58.

ways.[19] In recent studies, while the importance of the *Weichbild* for the expansion of the Magdeburg Law is fully acknowledged,[20] it is usually assumed

19 See Ernst Theodor Gaupp, *Das alte Magdeburgische und Hallische Recht. Ein Beitrag zur deutschen Rechtsgeschichte* (Breslau, 1826; repr. Aalen, 1966), pp. 119–156; Paul Laband, ed., *Magdeburger Rechtsquellen. Zum akademischen Gebrauch herausgegeben* (Königsberg, 1869; repr. Aalen, 1967), especially pp. 96–100; Paul Laband, "Eine bisher unbekannte Rechtshandschrift", *Zeitschrift für Rechtsgeschichte* 11 (1873), 44–52; Ferdinand Bischoff, "Beiträge zur Geschichte des Magdeburgerrechts", *Sitzungsberichte der Kaiserlichen Akademie der Wissenschaften. Philosophisch-Historische Classe* 50/4 (1865), 333–70; Ferdinand Bischoff, "Über einen deutschen Rechtscodex der Krakauer Universitäts-Bibliothek", *Sitzungsberichte der Kaiserlichen Akademie der Wissenschaften. Philosophisch-Historische Classe*, 48/1–2 (1864), 269–97; Carl Gustav Homeyer, *Die Extravaganten des Sachsenspiegels* (Berlin, 1861), especially pp. 238–239 and 251–259; and Carl Gustav Homeyer, *Die deutschen Rechtsbücher des Mittelalters und ihre Handschriften*, New Edition, eds. Conrad Borchling, Karl A. Eckhardt and Julius von Gierke (Weimar, 1931–1934), pp. 31–33.

20 Wieland Carls, "Überlieferungsgeschichtliche Beobachtungen zum Verhältnis von Schwabenspiegel und Sächsisch-magdeburgischem Recht", in: *Schwabenspiegel-Forschung im Donaugebiet. Konferenzbeiträge in Szeged zum mittelalterlichen Rechtstransfer deutscher Spiegel*, ed. Elemér Balogh, (Ivs Saxonico-Maidebvrgense in Oriente) 4 (Berlin – Boston, 2015), p. 130; Katalin Gönczi, "Städte des Magdeburger Rechts in Osteuropa", in: *Städtische Räume im Mittelalter*, eds. Susanne Ehrich and Jörg Oberste (Regensburg, 2009), pp. 185–186; Jolanta Karpavičienė, "Das sächsisch-magdeburgische Recht in den Kleinstädten Litauens", in: *Grundlagen für ein neues Europa. Das Magdeburger und Lübecker Recht in Spätmittelalter und Früher Neuzeit*, eds. Heiner Lück, Matthias Puhle and Andreas Ranft (Köln – Weimar – Wien, 2009), pp. 102–103; Dirk Heirbaut, "Sachsenspiegel or Sassen Speyghel (Saxon Mirror)c.1220–1235, ed. pr. 1474 Eike von Repgow (c.1180–c.1235)", in: *The Formation and Transmission of Western Legal Culture. 150 Books that Made the Law in the Age of Printing*, Serge Dauchy, Georges Martyn, Anthony Musson, Heikki Pihlajamäki, Alain Wijffels, eds., coop. Naoko Seriu (Studies in the History of Law and Justice) 7, series eds. Georges Martyn, Mortimer Sellers (New York – Berlin – Heidelberg, 2016), pp. 29–30; Heiner Lück, *Über den Sachsenspiegel. Entstehung, Inhalt und Wirkung des Rechtsbuches, mit einem Beitrag zu den Grafen von Falkenstein im Mittelalter* (Halle an der Saale, 1999), p. 70; Rolf Lieberwirth, "Einführung oder Rezeption? Mittelalterlich deutsches Recht in slawischen Herrschaftsgebieten. Das Beispiel: Polen", in: *Rechts- und Sprachtransfer in Mittel- und Osteuropa. Sachsenspiegel und Magdeburger Recht. Internationale und interdisziplinäre Konferenz in Leipzig vom 31. Oktober bis 2. November 2003*, eds. Ernst Eichler, Heiner Lück, and Wieland Carls, (Ivs Saxonico-Maidebvrgense in Oriente) 1 (Berlin, 2008), pp. 171 and 176; Heiner Lück, "Die Verbreitung des Sachsenspiegels und des Magdeburger Rechts in Osteuropa", in: *Der sassen speyghel. Sachsenspiegel – Recht – Alltag*, Vol. 2: *Aus dem Leben gegriffen – ein Rechtsbuch spiegelt seine Zeit. Beiträge u. Katalog zur Ausstellung 'Aus dem Leben gegriffen – ein Rechtsbuch spiegelt seine Zeit'*, ed. Mamoun Fansa, 2nd ed., Archäologische Mitteilungen aus Nordwestdeutschland, 10 (Oldenburg, 1996), pp. 43–44; Heiner Lück, *Sachsenspiegel und Magdeburger Recht. Europäische Dimensionen zweier mitteldeutscher Rechtsquellen*, (Adiuvat in itinere) 5 (Hamburg, 1998), pp. 30, 37, 45 and 48–49; Lück, "Wirkungen des *Sachsenspiegels*", p. 276; Heiner Lück, "Prawo magdeburskie jako czynnik identyfikacji europejskiej rodziny miast", in: *Europejskie miasta prawa magdeburskiego: tradycja, dziedzictwo, identyfikacja.*

that it was due solely to the spread of the vulgate and its direct textual offspring.[21]

This claim, which, I believe, is an unfounded assumption, can in fact be verified – provided that the relevant evidence is gathered and thoroughly examined. This study is an attempt to do just that. Its aim is to demonstrate that the single-line-with-deviations model of the Polish reception of the *Weichbild* is untenable. I will focus on a selection of 21 Latin texts which, I believe, hold vital cues both to the expansion and use of the Saxon-Magdeburg Law and to the number and characteristics of their German-language antecedents, both extant and presumably lost. A close analysis of the Latin texts is crucial for

---

Sesja komparatystyczna Kraków, 13–15 października 2006. Materiały konferencyjne, ed. Anna Biedrzycka and Agnieszka Kutylak-Hapanowicz (Kraków, 2007), p. 48; Heiner Lück, "Das sächsich-magdeburgische Recht als kulturelles Bindeglied zwischen den Rechtsordnungen Ost- und Mitteleuropa", in: *Rechts- und Sprachtransfer in Mittel- und Osteuropa. Sachsenspiegel und Magdeburger Recht. Internationale und interdisziplinäre Konferenz in Leipzig vom 31. Oktober bis 2. November 2003*, eds. Ernst Eichler, Heiner Lück, and Wieland Carls, (Ivs Saxonico-Maidebvrgense in Oriente) 1 (Berlin, 2008), p. 12; Heiner Lück, "Zur Verbreitung des *Sachsenspiegels* und des Magdeburger Rechts in den baltischen Landern", in: *Baltische-europäische Rechtsgeschichte und Lexikographie*, eds. Ulrich Kronauer and Thomas Taterka (Heidelberg, 2009), pp. 28–29; Heiner Lück, "*Sachsenspiegel* und Magdeburger Recht. Grundlagen für Europa", *Denkströme. Journal der Sächsischen Akademie der Wissenschaften zu Leipzig* 4 (2010), 81–104 (http://www.denkstroeme.de/heft-4/s_81-104_lueck, accessed 8 July 2017); Lück, "Die Anfänge des Magdeburger Stadtrechts", p. 194; Heiner Lück, "Aspects of the Transfer of the Saxon-Magdeburg Law to Central and Eastern Europe", *Rechtsgeschichte – Legal History* 22 (2014), 84; Mikola M. Kobilec'kij, *Magdeburz'ke prawo v Ukraïnì*, [The Magdeburg Law in Ukraine (14th–Early 19th Century)] (L'vìv, 2008), p. 72; Rolf Lieberwirth, *Eike von Repchow und der Sachsenspiegel* (Berlin, 1982), pp. 43–46; Clausdieter Schott, "Magdeburger Recht und *Sachsenspiegel* – Stadtrecht und Landrecht", in: *Das Burger Landrecht und sein rechtshistorisches Umfeld. Zur Geschichte der Landrechte und ihrer Symbolik im Mittelalter von Rügen bis Niederösterreich*, eds. Dieter Pötschke, Gerhard Lingelbach, and Bernd Feicke, co-ed. by Ulrich-Dieter Oppitz (Berlin, 2014), p. 145.

21 See more recent monographs, for example, Ludwig Meuten, *Die Erbfolgeordnung des Sachsenspiegels und des Magdeburger Rechts. Ein Beitrag zur Geschichte des sächsich-magdeburgischen Rechts* (Frankfurt am Main, 2000); Margret Obladen, *Magdeburger Recht auf der Burg zu Krakau: Die güterrechtliche Absicherung der Ehefrau in der Spruchpraxis des Krakauer Oberhofs* (Berlin, 2005); Adrian Schmidt-Recla, *Kalte oder warme Hand? Verfügungen von Todes wegen in mittelalterlichen Referenzrechtsquelle*, Forschungen zur deutschen Rechtsgeschichte, 29 (Köln, 2011), pp. 423–424; Jana Pacyna, *Mittelalterliche Judenrechte. Norm und Anwendung im Magdeburger Rechtskreis (1250–1400)* (Halle/Saale, 2015), Chapter 3.2.2. In her study of the legal status of women in the towns of Małopolska Nataliia Ivanusa uses the 16th century editions of the *Weichbild* (Jan Łaski's, Mikołaj Jaskier's and Paweł Szczerbic's). Cf. Nataliia Ivanusa, *Frauen im Sächsisch-Magdeburgischen Recht. Die Rechtspraxis in kleinpolnischen Städten im 16. Jahrhundert*, (Studien zur Ostmitteleuropaforschung) 38 (Marburg, 2017), *passim*.

tracing the network of variants which form the true history of the *Weichbild* in Poland. The number of extant German manuscripts is relatively small, and only four of them comprise the full text of the Silesian-Małopolska compilation, previously also known as Konrad of Opole's compilation.[22] For this reason, I do not focus on the vulgate *Weichbild* popularized in Poland by the Latin translation by Mikołaj Jaskier in 1535. My approach is justified by the fact that Jaskier worked with a vernacular text that differed considerably from the text that had been the basis of the Silesian-Małopolska compilation and was continually modified by its medieval copyists. In so far as his translation breaks with the traditional chain of a transmission, it marks an important fault line in the early history of sources of urban law in Poland. My study explores the terrain on the other side of this divide.

4 Sources and Periodization of Urban Legal Studies

The history of urban law in medieval and early-modern Poland can be divided into periods with a somewhat fluid border line in the early 16th century. The pioneers of change are Mikołaj Jaskier, whose revised Latin edition of the Saxon-Magdeburg Law began to displace older legal texts,[23] and Bartłomiej Groicki, the author of the first compilation of municipal law in Polish. Paweł Szczerbic's translation of Jaskier's books in 1581 sealed the transition at the heart of legal apparatus from Latin to Polish. The process of change started with an overhaul of the sources of law in the early 16th century and proceeded rapidly after 1535 (the date of publication of Mikołaj Jaskier's glossed editions of the Magdeburg *Weichbild* and the *Sachsenspiegel*), reaching out gradually from

22 Maciej Mikuła, "Das Magdeburger Weichbildrecht in seiner schlesisch-kleinpolnischen Fassung. Anmerkungen zur Autorschaft und Textevolution", in: *Kulturelle Vernetzung in Europa. Das Magdeburger Recht und seine Städte. Wissenschaftlicher Begleitband zur Ausstellung »Faszination Stadt«*, eds. Gabriele Köster, Christina Link, Heiner Lück (Sandstein Kommunikation, 2019), pp. 147–165.

23 In his studies, Zygfryd Rymaszewski employs the term 'version' exclusively for translations. With regard to Mikołaj Jaskier's edition of the *Sachsenspiegel*, he argues that rather than a new translation, it was a new compilation based on the 1528 Leipzig edition, manuscripts of the Wrocław version (or, to use his terminology, 'redactions of the *versio Vratislaviensis*'), and *Commune incliti* (Jaskier's *versio vulgata*). Cf. Zygfryd Rymaszewski, *Łacińskie teksty Landrechtu Zwierciadła Saskiego w Polsce. Jaskier – tekst główny i noty marginesowe*, [Latin Texts of the Sachsenspiegel Landrecht in Poland: Jaskier – the Main Text and the Marginal Glosses] (Łódź, 1985), pp. 25, 33, 217–218. Cf. also Heiner Lück, "Jaskier Mikołaj", in: *Handwörterbuch zur deutschen Rechtsgeschichte*, 2, 2nd ed. (Berlin, 2012), col. 1355–1356.

the sphere of codification to the practical application of the law by the courts. At the same time, the traditional, medieval compilations of Saxon-Magdeburg Law fell into *desuetudo* (they were not longer in use), not least because the pace of social and economic change made them increasingly obsolete. That may perhaps be the reason why the arrival of the mass-produced copies of a standard normative text (whose uniformity was guaranteed by print) did not stifle demand for codes of law other than a refurbished *Weichbild* or *Sachsenspiegel*. Arguably, there was more to the rising demand for Groicki's treatises than their handy format and the fact that they were written in Polish. After all, Paweł Szczerbic was the first to publish the Saxon-Magdeburg Law in Polish and to arrange its contents in alphabetical order, and yet his book had not gained as much popularity or respect as Groicki's treatises, which went through several reprints by the end of the century. What may have contributed to their extraordinary popularity was the inclusion of legal acts supplementing and amending the Saxon-Magdeburg Law, that is, the municipal statutes of the Cracow Town Council (*wilkierze*), a broad selection of royal legislation, and an adapted version of the *Constitutio criminalis Carolina*. The latter offered the legal practitioners a model of criminal procedure in keeping with times; it stood in sharp contrast to the *Sachsenspiegel* and *Weichbild*'s privileging of judicial combat and oaths.[24] The claim that the 16th century saw a radical break with an earlier form of urban legal culture – characterized by manuscript transmission of sources of law, the proliferation of differing compilations of the Saxon-Magdeburg Law, and the absence of the Polish language in the court records – was convincingly argued by Stanisław Estreicher.[25] This study looks back to that earlier phase which, however, continues beyond 1506, which marks the publication of Jan Łaski's *Commune inciliti*. In fact, the ousting of handwritten texts of law by the uniform printed text proceeded gradually for the following thirty years, that is, until the publication of Jaskier's edition of the *Weichbild*. The year 1535 is thus a natural *terminus ad quem* of this study, even

24 Cf. Lotar Dargun, "O źródłach prawa miast polskich w wieku szesnastym. II. O źródłach porządku sądowego spraw miejskich Prawa Magdeburskiego przez Bartłomieja Groickiego" [Sources of Urban Law Used in Polish Towns in the 16th Century: II. Sources of Judicial Procedure in Urban Matters in Accordance with Bartłomiej Groicki's Magdeburg Law], *Rozprawy Akademii Umiejętności. Wydział Historyczno-Filozoficzny* 25 (1891), 120–56. For a discussion of the rules of evidence in criminal procedure under *ius municipale*, see Marian Mikołajczyk, *Proces kryminalny w miastach Małopolski XVI–XVIII wieku* [Criminal Procedure in the Towns of Małopolska in the 16th–18th Century], (Prace Naukowe Uniwersytetu Śląskiego w Katowicach) 2979 (Katowice, 2013), especially Chapters 6–9.

25 Stanisław Estreicher, *Kultura prawnicza w Polsce XVI wieku* [Legal Culture in Poland of the Sixteenth Century] (Kraków, 1931), *passim*.

though Jaskier's book will still have to wait for its own monograph. It requires separate treatment because – unlike earlier versions of the Saxon-Magdeburg Law used in the medieval Kingdom of Poland – its chief source is the vulgate *Weichbild* from Germany. Moreover, it includes glosses that are not to be found in any medieval Latin text of Polish provenance.

5 The Evolution of the Legal Text and the Process of Adaptation of the Magdeburg Law

A thorough, comparative study of the *Weichbild* corpus should not only help to clear up various text-critical points, but should also help to seek answers to some important questions that are normally not raised in analytical research of the kind. What were the reasons for the wide discrepancies between the texts in use? What were the consequences of the lack of a standard normative text for contemporary legal practice? What was the impact of the appearance of the normative text in a standard printed form[26] for the evolution of legal culture?[27] After all, the *Weichbild*, as any legal text, can be regarded as a reality-creating instrument in the sense that a change in a normative text – once it is implemented in practice – has an impact on the extratextual reality.

26 See: "Preface", in: *The Formation and Transmission of Western Legal Culture. 150 Books that Made the Law in the Age of Printing*, Serge Dauchy, Georges Martyn, Anthony Musson, Heikki Pihlajamäki, Alain Wijffels, eds., Naoko Seriu, coop. (Studies in the History of Law and Justice) 7, series eds. Georges Martyn, Mortimer Sellers (New York – Berlin – Heidelberg, 2016), p. 1.

27 I use the term 'legal culture' to mean a group of individual and collective attitudes towards law; see: Krzysztof Pałecki, "O użyteczności pojęcia kultura prawna" [About the Utility of the Concept of Legal Culture], *Państwo i prawo* 2 (1974), 73–4; also: Adam Podgórecki, *Prestiż prawa* [The Prestige of Law] (Warszawa, 1966), p. 180: "These general habits and values related to acceptance, evaluation, criticism and implementation of the applicable legal system can be defined as the general legal culture of a given society"). A review of issues related to this concept: Mateusz Stępień, "Kultura prawna" [Legal Culture], in: *Lexicon of sociology of law*, eds. Anna Kociołek-Pęksa, Mateusz Stępień (Warszawa, 2013), pp. 120–124 and Anna Kociołek-Pęksa, Władysław Pęksa, "Between History and Sociology – Remarks on Differences in Percussion 'Legal Culture', Particularly Sociology of Law and the Disciplines of the History of Law", *The Lawyer Quarterly* 4 (2016), 209–25 (there is also literature on the subject, note 29). Cf. the term 'local legal culture': Tom Johnson, *Law in Common. Legal Cultures in Late-Medieval England* (Oxford, 2020), pp. 7–8. On the historical aspect, see considerations of Stanisław Estreicher, Stanisław Grodziski, and Wacław Uruszczak (Estreicher, *Kultura prawnicza*; Stanisław Grodziski, *Z dziejów staropolskiej kultury prawnej* [From the History of the Old Polish Legal Culture] (Cracow, 2004); Wacław Uruszczak, *Historia państwa i prawa polskiego* [History of Polish State and Law], 1: 966–1795, 1st ed. (Warsaw, 2010), pp. 185–186).

Consequently, these questions focus our attention on a broader issue connected with the development of Polish urban law, namely, the process of adaptation of originally foreign imports. The continual evolution of the legal text in medieval culture is beyond question. What requires explanation, however, is the character of that evolution, especially as there is a plethora of apparently random differences between individual manuscripts. It seems that a careful comparative study of these, often relatively small, differences, may shed light on the evolution of the *Weichbild* in Poland in its true complexity. An initial stage of such research necessitates cataloguing the extant texts, establishing their distinctive characteristics, identifying the leading Latin translations, and establishing the differences among the texts. The results of such research could then be used to trace the history of the *Weichbild* texts in Poland by mapping their lines of transmission from the German base texts to the point where that diversity was streamlined into a single authoritative printed text (that of Jan Łaski's *Commune inciliti*, a.k.a. Łaski's *Statutes*). A key premise of this investigation is the indisputable fact that the earliest German-language manuscript of the *Weichbild* (dated 1308) believed to be the base of the Silesian-Małopolska compilation is markedly different from the Latin text of *Commune inciliti*.

While committed to the idea of an evolving *Weichbild* in the course of its reception in Poland, this study challenges a tacit assumption that the evolution of the *Weichbild* text of the Silesian-Małopolska compilation was unilinear. First of all, there are very few extant copies of the *Weichbild* itself. Most of them have probably been damaged due to heavy use, and those that did outlive their time were probably discarded after the arrival in the 16th century of the new text in print. In effect, the dearth of extant manuscripts makes the construction of a credible stemma (i.e. a manuscript pedigree chart) impossible. Secondly, no pairs of the manuscripts in our database are perfectly identical. The differences that conferred on each of them their individual profiles could have been either deliberate/intentional or accidental/unintentional (e.g. a scribal error replicated by successive copyists). Over time, as new manuscripts were produced, these differences created an endlessly permutating body of texts, so numerous and diverse that Łaski and his collaborators would in no way be able to get hold of them, let alone collate them for his edition. So much for the claim that Łaski stands at the end of a tradition, bringing together and enveloping all that went before him. Nevertheless, I will argue that he and his team did find and recognize the importance of two texts representative of two branches of the Latin version of the Silesian-Małopolska *Weichbild*. Another claim raised in this study is that a considerable portion of lexical variants of the Magdeburg *Weichbild* is intentional. They should be interpreted as evidence of the adaptation of the *Weichbild* to its new historic environment and its needs, or, more broadly, as opening an insight into the interaction of an evolving legal text and a society (or at least part of society, i.e. the urban community) in the process of change.

6 The Trap of Legal Positivism, or the Instruments of Historical Legal Studies

The study of manuscripts containing legal texts involves not only a careful comparison and explanation of textual variants, but also reckoning with two important issues: the potential practical effect of any significant revision of the parent text and the reasons which may have prompted the introduction of such modifications. Probing those issues can be difficult and problematic. To begin with, it is not always possible to decide whether an omission was deliberate or whether it should be put down to scribal error. Furthermore, the use of methods of modern grammatical interpretation for the exegesis of medieval texts is open to all kinds of doubt. Can we be sure that any particular revision of the parent text, which to the modern reader looks like an attempt to amend the law, was indeed seen in this way by its author? Why not assume that the copyist had no intention of influencing the functioning of a legal institution at large, even if his copy has numerous amendations, albeit of little significance? These are tough questions, but they are legitimized by the assumption that the copyists (who were often editors and compilers, as well) were intelligent graduates of the *trivium* (grammar, logic, and rhetoric).[28] They would therefore know the difference between *non plus quam tres solidos* (no more than three *solidos*) and *minus quam tres solidos* (less than three *solidos*) – a pair of phrases that crop up in the derivative texts of the *Weichbild*. Indeed, for many of those in charge of the administration of justice, this distinction would simply mean that petty theft committed at night was to be punished 'in skin and hair', but when the value of the stolen property was considerable, the culprit should be sentenced to death. The point of this observation is that even in interpreting an obvious amendation, we must not jump to conclusions about its practical effect. At the same time, relying on common sense does not absolve the researcher from a scrupulous collation of all the textual variants which may have affected the construing of the underlying legal provision. The questions of whether and how a given provision was used in practice cannot be answered

28 See Maria Kramperowa and Witold Maisel, "Księgozbiory mieszczan poznańskich drugiej połowy XVI w". [Book Collections of Poznań Burghers (Late 16th Century)], *Studia i Materiały do Dziejów Wielkopolski i Pomorza* 11/1 (1960), 257–9.

without a point of reference, that is, a 'standard' version which is then subject to a series of modifications. Medieval law is usually treated as a body of rules that were fuzzy because their precise meaning was not fixed until the trial, that is, when the construal of legal provisions would depend on circumstances or the tribunal taking into account some special considerations (like blunting the tools of criminal justice in the interest of peace and reconciliation).[29] This study, however, deals with the ambiguity, or malleability, of medieval law at the stage of transmission (i.e. the copying of manuscripts).

The problem of preserving the integrity of the original text and its copies was crucial to all spheres of medieval written culture, from law through theology and philosophy to religion.[30] In the case of law, the multiplicity of texts can be accounted for by the adage *habent sua fata leges* (laws have their destiny), in which the *fata* refers to the fortunes of the text after its creation regardless of its composition and the establishment of the base text, for example, by writing down customary law or by an imprimatur granted by an official authority. However, whereas the text of a book published under official licence cannot be changed (just as in the continental system it is not possible to change the law without going through clearly defined procedures), the legal text recorded in the manuscript was subject to continual modifications which were not necessarily authorized by institutions vested with significant legislative authority.[31] To some extent, the endless stream of modifications of received texts resulted from the need to interact with customary law – whose hold was still considerable. But in the main, the proliferation of variants was an inevitable part of the process of copying manuscripts, correcting an existing text, producing syncretic compilations, or starting translation projects aimed at making a legal text more accessible in another language. If the function of the normative text is to have an impact on reality, the effected changes must have consequences

29 For a review of the debates about the medieval understanding of the nature of the law, see Pacyna, *Mittelalterliche Judenrechte*, pp. 16–21.

30 Cf. the Theme Issue of *The Medieval Translator* (Vol. 16: *Translation and Authority – Authorities in Translation*, eds. Pieter De Leemans and Michèle Goyens, Brepols: 2017), and especially Igor Fillipov's analysis of the use of legal terms *proprietas* and *possessio* in Latin translations of the Bible ("*Vulgate* versus *vetus Latina:* The Choices of Caesarus of Arles", pp. 324–327). For an introduction to this particular problem, see the entry "Selected Texts Disseminated Internationally through Translation: The Bible", in: *Translation. An International Encyclopedia of Translation Studies*, 3, eds. Harald Kittel, Armin P. Frank, Norbert Freiner, Theo Hermans, Werner Koller, José Lambert, and Fritz Paul (Berlin – Boston, 2011), pp. 2340–2408.

31 They have an individual character, but it would be wrong to call them 'private'. Cf. Heiner Lück, "Rechtsbücher als „private" Rechtsaufzeichnungen?", *Zeitschrift der Savigny-Stiftung für Rechtsgeschichte: Germanistische Abteilung* 131 (2014), 432–433.

for the effect and implementation of the law. While in a positivist legal culture, lawmaking has to go through three separate stages – enactment, entry into force, and application of law – in the medieval world, there was a lot of feedback. The legal text was modified while being copied, and the law was implemented almost as soon as it was written down, each new copy claiming no less authority than the one it replaced.

Not only jurists, but also all who rely on the law, have a deep interest in its stability and integrity. A good illustration of this *basso continuo* of the history of law and institutions that depend on a legal code is the case of the Catholic Church, with its striving to safeguard the integrity of theological doctrine and canon law. In the history of the canon law, no work has been as important as the twelfth-century *Decretum Gratiani.* It was a concordance aimed at harmonizing a thicket of contradictory rules which had grown uncontrollably during the early Middle Ages, a period when the Church in Western Europe found it hard to contain the forces of decentralization.[32] One aspect of the effort to codify and unify canon law was the overcoming of territorial divisions; another was the establishment of an authentic base legal text and the authorization of its exclusive use. In practice, the latter objective could only be achieved after the invention of print, which guaranteed the uniformity of all the copies of the text (in this case, the incunable edition of *Corpus Iuris Canonici* in the late 15th century).[33] The supersession of manuscripts by print put an end to the

32 The original *Decretum Gratiani* exists in two recensions; Gratian himself is certainly the author of the earlier version. This view was first presented 60 years ago by Adam Vetulani, and restated by Anders Winroth. Cf. Anders Winroth, *The Making of Gratians's Decretum* (Cambridge University Press: 2000), pp. 12–14, 193 and 195; and Adam Vetulani, "Nouvelles vues sur le *Décret de Gratien*", in *La Pologne au Xe Congrès international des sciences historiques à Rome* (Warszawa, 1955; repr. Aldershot, 1990, ed. Wacław Uruszczak), pp. 96, 100–101.

33 We should bear in mind that the introduction of print created new hazards. One such hazard concerned printers, some of whom would take liberties with the text, e.g. would not print it in its entirety (cf. António M. Hespanha, "Form and Content in Early Modern Legal Books Bridging the Gap between Material Bibliography and the History of Legal Thought", *Rechtsgeschichte* 12 (2008), 12–50, esp. pp. 19–21, and 48–49). For that reason the authorities had to keep an eye on the printers who received the official commissions (cf. Maria Cytowska, *Bibliografia druków urzędowych XVI wieku* [Bibliography of 16th Century Legal and Government Documents] (Wrocław, 1961), *passim*). The problem of interpretation and adaptation of the written text for print is discussed by Julia Boffey, "Banking on Translation: English Printers and Continental Texts", in: *In principio fuit interpres*, ed. Alessandra Petrina, (The Medieval Translator) 15 (Brepols: 2013), especially pp. 328–329. In her book, Maria Cytowska notes that the uniformity of the text in the printed editions must not be taken for granted: "in the first batch of documents distributed through official channels by the royal chancery we can find numerous hand-written revisions and corrections. These notes were then collected by the editors who revised the text of the

practice of introducing informal alterations to the text of the law. However, it would be wrong to think of this development as a one-time event. This was a process that took decades everywhere, and the Kingdom of Poland was no exception. To explore the complexities of the transition from law in manuscript to law in print, it may be helpful to draw on Reinhard Koselleck's concept of 'sediments of time' (*Zeitschichten*), or spatial time warps which are not engulfed by the tide of innovation,[34] and to add a third to the two familiar dichotomies (customary law vs statute law and oral law vs written law)[35] – that is, law in manuscript form vs printed law.

7 The Contents of This Study: An Outline

Chapter 1 presents the Silesian-Małopolska compilation against the background of other sources of the Magdeburg Law. Using earlier research as a starting point for a series of analyses of the German texts, I try to trace the dynamics of their evolution, never losing sight of the fact that this compilation – from the moment of its creation – was addressed to towns in Poland. In this respect, the Silesian-Małopolska compilation differed from the *Weichbild* vulgate, which was in use in Saxony and in other parts of Germany. However, this problem is of little consequence, as the legal practice of Polish towns relied on Latin rather than German texts. Manuscripts with the matching Latin text are discussed in the remainder of the chapter. As this book is principally a legal-historical study of the *Weichbild*, only minimal attention is paid here to the heuristic and hermeneutical critique of the source, let alone to the problems of authorship or provenance. Occasionally, however, interest in the circumstances of the text's production can become quite keen, as in the case of the binding of the quires, scribal hands, or other details of the polymorphic manuscripts. All such information is necessary to ascertain whether the quire with the Magdeburg Law functioned prior to being bound into a given codex. Knowing this will bring us closer to the answer to the next question: what was the point or purpose of writing down collections of the Magdeburg Law?

---

following print runs. It means that the printer who started work on another print run of a given legal document would follow the revised text sent to him from the chancery" (Cytowska, *Bibliografia druków urzędowych XVI wieku*, p. 15).

34 Reinhart Koselleck, "Sediments of Time", in: Reinhart Koselleck, *Warstwy czasu. Studia z metahistorii* [Sediments of Time: On Possible Histories], transl. Krystyna Krzemieniowa and Jarosław Merecki (Warszawa, 2012), p. 6.

35 Helmut Coing, *Europäisches Privatrecht*, 1: *Älteres Gemeines Recht (1500 bis 1800)* (München, 1985), p. 86.

Chapter 2 traces the evolution of the Latin text on the basis of a series of analyses. Their results are presented in three Appendices, containing a concordance table with the formal characteristics of the texts (*inter alia*, a list and the sequence of the articles), a table of variants in the Latin texts, and a comparison of the Latin and the German texts. Chapter 2 tries to answer the following questions: 1) what groups of texts can be distinguished within the pool of Latin translations of the *Weichbild*? 2) How did the Latin text evolve? 3) What drove the evolution of the Latin texts? 4) Which German texts acted as base texts for the Latin translations? 5) What are the distinctive markers (i.e. the signatures) of the individual translations? 6) What was the role of the German texts in the evolution of the Latin *Weichbild*? 7) What are the characteristic features of the extant Latin texts of the *Weichbild*? A series of detailed analyses in this chapter will provide the evidentiary basis for a reconstruction of the evolution of the Latin *Weichbild* in Poland.

Chapter 3 opens with an analysis of the *Weichbild* in *Commune incliti*. The goal of this analysis is to prepare a comprehensive assessment of the grand œuvre of Jan Łaski and his collaborators. The list of variants in the Latin text (Appendix 2) shows the relative proximity of other manuscripts to the authorized text of the *Weichbild* from in the *Statutes*. Łaski's *Weichbild* is a culmination of the evolution of the medieval legal text and therefore can be used as a reference point for that evolution. In this chapter, this evolutionary process is traced within four thematic blocks (a similar arrangement can be found in any of major collections of the Magdeburg Law, such as the Magdeburg-Wrocław lay judges' case law, the municipal law of Chełmno (*Der Alte Kulm*), and the *Poznań Book of the Magdeburg and Meissen Law*). The four thematic units are gathered under the following headers: 1) The town and its residents; 2) Crime and the process of proving it; 3) The family and family property; and 4) Debtor and creditor. While the discussion in Chapter 1 laid the groundwork for a reconstruction of the evolution of the Latin text in Chapter 2, Chapter 3 examines the consequences of amendments aimed at adapting the provisions of the Magdeburg Law to the needs of local legal practice.

Chapter 4 deals with various additions to the main text by its users, such as instructions, glosses, links, cross-references, and other annotations which indicate that the text was used in practice. They can be treated as evidence of the practical application of the *Weichbild*, although it is usually difficult to make out its intended purpose (i.e. to formulate the normative basis of a judgment, or to help the litigant in his argument). The clue may sometimes be offered by the provenance of the manuscript. In this way, the analyses of Chapter 4 link up with the general descriptions of the *Weichbild* manuscripts in Chapter 1. The bulk of the chapter is devoted to the analysis of glosses collected not only from medieval manuscripts, but also from several copies of Łaski's *Commune incliti*. Without reaching out to the latter source, it is impossible to ask the question about the effect of print on the medieval legal culture.[36]

The concluding chapter recapitulates the findings of the preceding chapters and, using the story of the Polish *Weichbild* as a case in point, draws a broader picture of transition and historical change. One of main themes in this appraisal is the change of legal culture caused by the print-guaranteed standardization of the legal text. The Conclusion takes another look at the extraordinary trajectory of the Latin translation of the *Weichbild* in medieval Poland and reflects on the role of Cracow in the evolution of urban law and on the meaning of the terms 'reception' and 'adaptation'.

The data which illustrate and underpin the argument of the book are collected in four Appendices. Appendix 1 is a concordance table matching the Latin and German texts examined in this study, including the primary sources of the Weichbild, namely, the *Rechtsmitteilungen Magdeburgs für Breslau* of 1261 and 1295; the *Magdeburg Schöffenrecht*; and the *Constitution of Courts*. Appendix 2 lists all the significant variants of the Latin texts using the earliest extant text as a reference. A comparative analysis of the Latin texts revealed that 220 records showed changes of legal provisions or modifications that were tantamount to distortion. The number of the records varies a great deal, depending on the feature used as the criterion. This could be the omission of a merely single word or, at the other extreme, the addition of a large chunk of text from a collection of the Magdeburg judgments (*ortyle*). Appendix 3 contains over 200 records selected for comparison of three Latin texts with their German matches. The point of the comparison is to assess the level of

36 This study, focused on the complexities of the normative text, is less interested in confronting the provisions of the law with practical realities. The question about the use of the Saxon-Magdeburg Law by municipal courts in the late Middle Ages is still unresolved, although we know a great deal about their functioning (Cf. Obladen, *Magdeburger Recht*, p. 205 ff.). We know a great deal, too, about the practical implementation of law by criminal courts in the Early Modern Age, see: Marian Mikołajczyk, *Przestępstwo i kara w prawie miast Polski południowej XVI–XVIII w.* [Crime and Punishment in the Law of Southern Polish Towns in the 16th–18th Century] (Katowice, 1998); Mikołajczyk, *Proces kryminalny*, *passim*; Marian Mikołajczyk, "'Stosując się do prawa wyraźnego …' Podstawy prawne wyroków kryminalnych grodziskiego sądu miejskiego w latach 1702–1756" ['Following the Law Clearly …' The Legal Basis of Criminal Convictions Grodzisk City Court during 1702–1756], *Studia Iuridica Lubliniensia* 19 (2013), 202; Kowalski, *Zwyczaj i prawo zwyczajowe* [Custom and Customary Law], p. 121ff., p. 167. Due to differences in the nature our sources and changes in the country's legal culture – a problem mentioned earlier – the findings and conclusions about the 17th and 18th centuries must not be projected onto medieval and early 16th-century Poland.

accuracy in translation. The reasons why those three texts were chosen rather than certain others are discussed in Chapter 2 (in brief, the choice was determined by the observation that the Latin texts could be classed into different groups). Appendices 2 and 3 are closely interconnected. The initial plan was to provide only one additional appendix. However, as the mass of data would have made it look rather clumsy and forbidding, the appendix was reframed and split into two.

As things stand, we are still missing a critical edition of the complete text of the Latin *Weichbild* that was used in the medieval Kingdom of Poland. This study attempts to repair this gap, if only partially, by publishing the earliest Gniezno manuscript. Moreover, by matching the text of the Gniezno manuscript with textual variants from other texts in Appendix 2, it offers the reader the basic corpus of the Latin *Weichbild*, a body of texts related to – but markedly different from – the vulgate. That being said, the appearance of this book does not obviate the need for the publication of a critical edition of the *Weichbild*, one that would be based on all its texts in their entirety (here, they are represented only by their textual variants, selected according to criteria adopted for this study alone). The need for a complete edition has not been abandoned – its time has simply not yet come.[37]

A recent trend in narrative and legal textual studies is the use of dedicated information technology (IT) tools and programs. In France, this kind of software was successfully employed in a research project whose aim was to compare the first edition of Machiavelli's *Il Principe* to its 16th-century French translations.[38] The software tool HyperMachiavel enabled the researchers to analyse the contextual meaning of the key words and phrases in the original and its French counterparts with extraordinary precision and thoroughness. The findings of this project also shed light on the causes and reasons that led to the production of several translations of the same book in the course of one century.[39] Meanwhile, researchers at the University of Halle (Germany) have developed the software package LERA (*Locate, Explore, Retrace and Apprehend*

37 Maciej Mikuła, "Edycje źródeł do dziejów prawa miejskiego w Polsce XIV–XVI w.: propozycja elektronicznej metaedycji źródeł normatywnych" [Editions of Sources for the History of Municipal Law in Poland (14th–16th Century): A Proposal for an Electronic Metaedition of Normative Source Material], *Krakowskie Studia z Historii Państwa i Prawa* 9/4 (2016), p. 499, English edition: *Krakowskie Studia z Historii Państwa i Prawa*, special issue (2018).

38 http://hyperprince.ens-lyon.fr (Accessed: 6 February 2021).

39 Jean-Claude Zancarini, "*Uno Picolo Dono*: A Software Tool for Comparing the First Edition of Machiavelli's *The Prince* to Its Sixteenth Century French Translations", in: *The Radical Machiavelli. Politics, Philosophy and Language*, eds. Filippo Del Lucchese, Fabio Frosini, and Vittorio Morfino (Leiden – Boston, 2015), pp. 39–55.

complex text variants) to analyse multiple versions of the same text. At the time when this book was being completed, the range of LERA's applications was broadened to include comparing texts in a number of modern languages.[40] The use of such digital tools to compare textual variants in one language or in the field of translation studies surely paves the way for new perspectives for research on the evolution of legal texts. A prerequisite of a successful application of the new technology is, however, the availability of formatted (i.e. encoded) source texts. As the tide of innovation is advancing rapidly, this study may well be one of the last research projects carried out with no input from the new sophisticated digital tools. Just after preparing this study, the project "IURA: Sources from Laws of the Past" was begun at the Faculty of Law and Administration at Jagiellonian University in Cracow (www.iura.uj.edu.pl). This repository of legal texts from the past includes a special tool for a comparison of texts.

8 In Search of Method

This study of the *Weichbild* comes more than forty years after the publication of Professor Zygfryd Rymaszewski's monograph on the *Sachsenspiegel*. His trailblazing work, which brought to light the Latin texts of the *Sachsenspiegel* which were used in Kingdom of Poland, is the fruit of painstaking dedication, and the thoroughness and soundness of his research were met with respect and admiration. In his monograph, Rymaszewski asks two key questions: 1) to what extent does the Latin translation of the Wrocław version of the *Sachsenspiegel* and two recensions of the *versio Sandomiriensis* follow the German text? 2) What are the characteristic features of the *Sachsenspiegel* in Jan Łaski's *Statutes*? To answer the former question, he compared two texts representative of the Wrocław version and two recensions of the Sandomierz version with Karl A. Eckhardt's edition of the *Sachsenspiegel* in the *Monumenta Germaniae Historica*. His comparative study of the *Statutes* is also based on the same choice of manuscripts. However, his findings were not received with unanimous approval. In his review, Josef J. Menzel finds fault with Rymaszewski's research

40 http://lera.uzi.uni-halle.de (Accessed: 8 July 2017). Cf. Thomas Bremer, Paul Molitor, Marcus Pöckelmann, Jörg Ritter, and Susanne Schütz, "Zum Einsatz digitaler Methoden bei der Erstellung und Nutzung genetischer Editionen gedruckter Texte mit verschiedenen Fassungen. Das Fallbeispiel der *Histoire philosophique des deux Indes* von Guillaume-Thomas Raynal", *Editio* 29/1 (2015), 29–51.

strategy – namely, the use of only a small number of selected manuscripts.[41] In particular, Menzel points out that the comparison of the Latin manuscripts with Eckhardt's text cannot reveal the true scale of the modifications introduced by the translators, because the version of the *Sachsenspiegel* they used was not identical with the text of the critical edition. Menzel does seem to have a point, but to assess the validity his objections, we need to take a closer look at Rymaszewski's monograph. Sure enough, Eckhardt's standard edition is of primary importance for Rymaszewski, yet he also makes frequent references to the German text of the Henryków and the Cracow manuscripts. Moreover, he treats with great care the supplementary material which appears first in those manuscripts and then finds its way into the Latin version. Rymaszewski certainly takes a broad view of his subject matter. If he had not done so, he would not have been able to confirm Carl G. Homeyer's observation that the text of *Sachsenspiegel* in those manuscripts is very close to the base text of both the Wrocław and the Sandomierz versions.[42]

The choice of approach and method in this study is in a way determined by the fact that the text of the German *Weichbild* used in the Kingdom of Poland has never been edited and published. The material available in print includes only incunabula and 19th-century editions of the vulgate and editions of sources which are included in the *Weichbild*. For that reason, the first point on my research agenda was to go back to the extant manuscripts of the German Silesian-Małopolska compilation, previously known by the name of Konrad of Opole. As a result of their cross-comparison and confrontation with the sources of *Weichbild*,[43] it was possible to identify and list the variants of the German text. That list enabled me to proceed to the next phase of the investigation, that is, identifying the base text of each of *Weichbild*'s Latin translations. In total, I was able to locate 21 extant Latin texts of the *Weichbild* in the archives and libraries of Poland, Austria, Germany, and Russia, including a fragment copied into the Municipal Records of Pleszew and published

41 Josef J. Menzel, Review of Zygfryd Rymaszewski, *Łacińskie teksty Landrechtu Zwierciadła Saskiego w Polsce* [Lateinische Texte des Landrechts des Sachsenspiegels in Polen]: *Versio Vratislaviensis, Versio Sandomiriensis, Łaski, Zeitschrift der Savigny-Stiftung für Rechtsgeschichte: Germanistische Abteilung* 93/1 (1976), 383.

42 Rymaszewski, *Łacińskie teksty. Versio*, p. 11.

43 The principal sources are *Magdeburg's Legal Instructions for Wrocław* (*Rechtsmitteilungen Magdeburgs für Breslau*), *Magdeburg Bench Law* (*Das Magdeburg Schöffenrecht*), and the *Constitution of Courts* (*Rechtsbuch von der Gerichtsverfassung*) as reproduced in Paul Laband's *Magdeburger Rechtsquellen* and Friedrich Ebel's *Magdeburger Recht*, Vol. II: *Die Rechtsmitteilungen und Rechtssprüche für Breslau*, Part 1: *Die Quellen von 1261 bis 1452*, Mitteldeutsche Forschungen, 89/II/1 (Köln – Wien, 1989).

by Witold Maisel.[44] In my search, I was guided by the monumental catalogue *Deutsche Rechtsbücher des Mittelaters*, compiled by Ulrich-Dieter Oppitz.[45]

The next step was to compare the Latin texts. As a point of reference, I took the earliest manuscript (the Gniezno MS) from 1359 (with the caveat that we do not know how close it was to the autograph of the *versio Sandomiriensis*). An extensive cross-comparison of the Latin texts enabled me to identify and list the variants of the Latin texts, and then to try and reconstruct the stages in the evolution of the Latin *Weichbild*. I relied on the same database to select the most appropriate Latin manuscripts for comparison with their German counterparts. This, in turn, enabled me to correlate the base text of the individual translations and to assess the role of the German texts in the generation of variants in the Latin manuscripts. The table of variants in the Latin text was then used to assess the scope of the adaption (i.e. the degree of novelty) of the *Weichbild* in Jan Łaski's *Statutes* and for further analysis of the practical consequences of the alterations entered into that text.

While this study is concerned primarily with differences that are substantive (i.e. matters of law), it is also interested in clarifying the editorial and linguistic aspects of those differences. This means paying due attention to the arrangement of articles (chapters), the use of rubrics, the arrangement of the text within an article (sequence of words and phrases), synonyms and paraphrases, abbreviations and interpolations, and supplements and glosses. Due to the bewildering number of such variants in the manuscripts, less attention was paid to changes in grammar and spelling.

9 Editor's Note

In this book, you will find four key terms. They are presented here with a short explanation.

1) Compilation. This refers to texts with similar contents and structure. Of all the terms listed here, 'compilation' has the broadest scope. In this

44 Witold Maisel, "Prawo magdeburskie miasta Pleszewa" [The Magdeburg Lawbook of Pleszew], *Studia i Materiały do Dziejów Wielkopolski i Pomorza* 9/1 (1963), 66–82.

45 For a detailed discussion of these texts, see Chapter 1.3. Their list is not identical with that in U.-D. Oppitz's catalogue. For example, MS 817 from the Polish Academy of Sciences Library at Kórnik does not contain the *Weichbild*, but has a selection of the Magdeburg *ortyle* on f. 31–34 (cf. Kałużniacki, *Die polnische Recenzion*, pp. 219 and 259–260; No. 838 in U.-D. Oppitz's catalogue). Marcin Zabowski's MS from the National Library in Warsaw, listed as No. 1457 in U.-D. Oppitz's catalogue contains in fact both the *Sachsenspiegel* and the *Weichbild*.

study, the term is used about two types (branches) of the *Weichbild*: the vulgate and the Silesian-Małopolska compilation.

2) Version. This term refers to any group of manuscripts within a compilation, for example, the Sandomierz version (alternatively, *versio Sandomiriensis*). All versions of a compilation have very similar contents and structure; the individual versions are differentiated by the presence or absence of certain annotations, the sequence of articles (chapters), the wording of the provisions, the presence of supplements, and minor omissions. The changes may have been made for various reasons, but most often, the changes are made by the author of a new translation.
3) Variant. 'Variant' refers to a subgroup of texts (or sometimes a single text) within a version on account of their having certain characteristic features than make them distinct. When the term 'variant' is used in this sense, it should be clear from the context that it refers to a text or manuscript as a whole (e.g. the Wawel variant). Variant is also used in its accustomed sense of *textual variant* – that is, any minor variation (deletion, rearrangement, repetition, or replacement of one or more words) entered by the editor or copyist into the text that was being reproduced.
4) Group. The term 'group' is used in a general sense about any class of objects in an undifferentiated way. Where precision is called for, 'group' is replaced with terms like 'version' or 'variant'.

The article numbers follow the numbering in the earliest Latin manuscript, that is, the Gniezno manuscript, unless indicated otherwise. The concordance tables in Appendix 1 can be used to find the matching article number in other texts, whether Latin or German. The numbering of articles in the *Rechtsmitteilungen Magdeburgs für Breslau* (1261) follows the new scheme of Friedrich Ebel's 1989 critical edition.[46] Unaware readers should note that Ebel's edition differs from its 19th-century predecessors. The old § 64 is now split into two smaller units (§ 64 and § 65), while the old §§ 66–69 are now amalgamated into § 67. As a result of these changes, the number of articles was reduced from 79 to 77.

Passages from German manuscripts are reproduced in accordance with the instruction written by the editors of *Liber Vetustissimus Gorlicensis* (*Das älteste Görlitzer Stadtbuch*),[47] while Latin texts, including the *Weichbild* from

46 Friedrich Ebel, ed., *Magdeburger Recht*, Vol. II: *Die Rechtsmitteilungen und Rechtssprüche für Breslau*, Part 1, pp. 1–16.

47 Krzysztof Fokt, Christian Speer, Maciej Mikuła, eds., *Najstarsza zgorzelecka księga miejska 1305–1416 (1423). Edycja i komentarz*, cz. 1 [*The Earliest Book of Municipal Court Records of Zgorzelec (Görlitz) 1305–1416 (1423): A Critical Edition and Commentary*, Part 1] (Fontes Iuris Polonici) 5 (Kraków, 2017).

the Gniezno manuscript, are reprinted according to the guidelines prepared by Adam Wolff.[48]

10 A Synopsis of the Contents of *Ius municipale Magdeburgense*

Before moving on to a detailed discussion of my argument, I would like to present here a synopsis of the contents of the *Weichbild* from the Gniezno manuscript, the full text of which is reprinted in Appendix 4. The Magdeburg *Weichbild* is short and concise in comparison with its companion piece, the *Sachsenspiegel*. However, its appeal, it seems, lay not in brevity or fine formulas, but in its focus on problems of urban life and in its pragmatic directness. Judging by the earliest Latin translation (the Gniezno MS, 1359), the original text of the *Weichbild* – together with the provisions of the *Constitution of Courts* – consisted of 117 articles. Their number and indices vary in other manuscripts – an issue that will be discussed at a later point. This synopsis is not intended to serve as an analysis, but merely as an overview and summary of the points covered in the *Weichbild* and thus give the reader an idea of its scope and substance.

10.1 *Municipal Institutions, Legislation, and Trade*

The *Weichbild* opens with a prologue saturated with religious invocations. It is followed by a handful of articles (following the Gniezno MS, 1359) dealing with the election of municipal officials (jurors and aldermen), their oaths of office, and the aldermen's capacities to regulate trade and supervise weights and measures (Article 1). The aldermen had the right to mete out punishment in skin and hair (by implication, he could not pronounce the death sentence, Article 2) for violating urban statutes (*wilkierze*), and impose fines for all kinds of deception in buying and selling (tampering with measures and weights, Article 3). Right at the outset, the *Weichbild* pulls back the curtain to reveal a typical urban scene. The urban setting returns in the final section, the *Constitution of Courts*, where it is said that urban law was created for merchants (Article 112).

48 Adam Wolff, "Projekt instrukcji wydawniczej dla pisanych źródeł historycznych do połowy XVI w". [A Blueprint Guide to Publishing Written Historical Sources from before the Mid-16th Century], *Commentationes: Studia Źródłoznawcze* 1 (1957), 155–88.

10.2 *The Courts*

The courts are mentioned in a number of articles, but they are referred to for the first time in Article 4, where we are told that the castellan (Lat. *castellanus*, Ger. *Burggraf*) presides as judge in his high court. As in many new Polish towns, that arrangement simply did not work, and it was therefore reconfigured. The honorific legal formula remained unaltered, but the person in the judge's seat was now the town owner, or an alderman officiating as his deputy. The *Burggraf* was to hold three grand courts every year: the first on the Feast Day of St Agatha [February 5th]; the second on the Feast Day of Saints John and Paul [June 26th]; and the third in the octave of St Martin's [November 11]. If any of these days were to fall on holidays, the court was put off. The *Burggraf*/*castellanus*/town owner had jurisdiction over the most serious public order crimes, like rape, assault, and house-breaking. Should he be unable to preside over the court, the burghers may appoint someone else in his place (Articles 5, 11, 103). The *Weichbild* specifies in detail the penalties and time limits for their payment. After the *Burggraf*'s court was dissolved, the administration of justice fell to the court of the *Schultheiss* (Lat. *scultetus*, Pol. *sołtys*). These courts were to sit for 14 days, three times every year: the first on the day after the Epiphany; the second on the first Tuesday after Easter week; and the third on the first Tuesday after Trinity Sunday (Article 6). In Polish towns, these courts were presided by the *Vogt* (Lat. *advocatus*, Pol. *wójt*). The court could not proceed without the *Schultheiss* being present, except in an emergency, for example, when an offender was brought before the court who had been taken in the act of committing a crime. At that point, someone else could take over the function of the judge. The *Weichbild* enumerates the situations which justified the emergencies or proceeding without the *Schultheiss*. These included grievous bodily harm and theft *in flagrante delicto* (Articles 9 and 34), as well as debt cases that did not require oath-swearing by compurgators (Article 83) and debt cases involving non-residents (Article 9). The presence of jurors guaranteed the collegiate character of the courts. In the *Burggraf*'s court, too, the chief judge (the *Burggraf* or town owner) had to have the *Vogt* at his side. The *Weichbild* says explicitly that those courts and their jurisdiction were established especially for the residents of towns incorporated under Magdeburg Law (Articles 21 and 82).

10.3 *The* Schultheiss [sołtys], *the* Vogt [wójt], *and the Jurors*

In Poland, the offices of the *Schultheiss* [*sołtys*] (in villages) or the *Vogt* [*wójt*] (in towns) were usually entrusted to a pioneer settler who committed himself to bring in more settlers and run the new settlement. He was to receive the authority and the fief of the settlement from the lord of the land (Article 6).

This meant, at least in the medieval Kingdom of Poland, that the relationship between the lord and the fief-holder fell under feudal law. The *Weichbild*'s formulas of judicial powers sanctioned this dependence. While both the *Burggraf* and the *Schultheiss* were responsible for the administration of justice, the latter participated in the revenue generated by fines imposed by his court (Article 5 and 117), including fines for offending jurors both during and after the trial (Articles 22 and 90). More fines were in store for those who interfered with the court proceedings or questioned the court's judgments (Article 99). The *Weichbild* also had penalties for *Schultheissen* (and presumably, by implication, *Vögte*) who failed to obey the summons to a *Burggraf*'s court (Article 4). Finally, in two long articles, the *Weichbild* denounces all forms of corruption and bias in the work of courts and prescribes stiff penalties for such offences (Articles 100 and 101).

10.4 *Criminal Procedure*

Like many other topics, criminal procedure was presented in the *Weichbild* in an unsystematic manner. At the same time, evidentiary procedure was absolutely central to the provisions dealing with criminal law. It seems that other vital elements of the criminal procedure were introduced as supplements for a evidentiary procedure – such as, for example, the rule that legal action is initiated by the complaint of the wrong party or the affirmation of the *res iudicata* principle in Article 67.

According to the *Weichbild*, criminal procedure was based on two principled modes of proof: oaths sworn by the litigant together with a number of oath-helpers (the ceremony is also known as compurgation or wager of law); and ordeal (also called trial by combat, wager by battle, or *iudicium Dei*, Article 103).[49] These methods of establishing facts, truth, and guilt were increasingly at odds with the times, and their use in the legal practice of medieval courts was on the wane. In the municipal courts, they were all but superseded by trial by jury, and by the 16th century, they were completely obsolete – a dead letter of the law. A key element of the procedure described in the *Weichbild* was the order of presenting proof, that is, a purgatory oath by the defendant or an accusatorial oath by the plaintiff.[50] The court's decision about the order

49 Cf. Chapter 3.3.4.

50 In the *Weichbild* of the Gniezno MS, the standard compurgation involved the presence of six oath-helpers (*metseptimus*); the oath *mettercius*, i.e. with two oath-helpers, appears only once in connection of the false claims (Article 49). The oath-helpers were to be freemen (Article 95) of good repute with a clean court record (Article 32, 49 and 102). A man who promised to come forth as an oath-helper could not be released from his promise by anybody other than the judge (Article 97).

of proceedings depended on a casuistic examination of circumstances of the case. At all events, the right to speak first was immensely advantageous, as the judges could decide that there was no need to continue and declare the case closed.

The first of those circumstances was the formal condition of instant reaction, that is, the order of proceeding depended on whether a complaint action was initiated immediately after the crime.[51] If a hue and cry was made, but the injured person did not appear in court until the following day, he lost the advantage of being first to the assailant, who, if he appeared in court on the same day, could clear himself under oath *metseptimus* (Article 10). In the case of the most serious crimes (rape, highway robbery, house-breaking), the formal condition of instant reaction was lifted provided a hue and cry had been made and the perpetrator had been caught red-handed. However, if the latter conditions were not met, the assailant could claim precedence and clear himself under oath *metseptimus* (Article 11). However, another provision trumped this complex protocol by giving unconditional priority to the party in the accusatorial role (Article 72). In the case of the most serious crimes against public order, the victim (who, presumably, because of his wounds, was unable to come to court) could appoint an attorney (Lat. *prolocutor*, Ger. *Fürsprech*). The court could, however, then order a check as to whether the victim's condition prevented him from appearing in court to make his complaint (Articles 53 and 55). The casuistic exceptions from the requirement that the victim of a crime should bring a complaint before the court immediately shed intriguing light on the *Weichbild*'s treatment of the defence of necessity. If, for example, the assault took place on the highway, a public place protected by the king's peace, and the injured assailant reached the court with his demand for justice ahead of the victim, the judges were to allow the latter to present his case first in the order of precedings. However, that privilege was lost if the victim waited to make his complaint until the following day (Article 27). The accused had, as a rule, the right to answer the charges (Articles 28 and 32). If he rejected them, he could ask the court to establish a surety (Lat. *satisdatio*, Pol. *gwar*, Ger. *gewere*) until the time at which he would prove his innocence. That surety was not only a form of bail, but also a guarantee that the text of the complaint would not be altered (Article 56 and, with regard to property litigation, Article 80). In the case when injuries were inflicted on both sides, the right to be first in

51 The provisions concerning criminal procedure usually formulate the complaint with due care (Articles 38, 51, 52, 53, 54, and 55). The *Weichbild* also contained the text of the Jewish oath and a description of the manner in which it was to be delivered, including the participants' dress and gestures (Articles 108 and 109).

presenting proof should belong to the party that had accused the other of having started the conflict. If there was no agreement on that point, the truth was be established by oath *metseptimus*, six oath-helpers who had been present at the scene (Article 87).

The second of those circumstances was the hue and cry, an alarm raised by locals for the purpose of pursuing and catching a felon or robber. The right to be first in presenting proof belonged to the victim who started the hue and cry that led to the capture and arrest of the alleged criminal. The victim could bring with him oath-helpers who had taken part in the hue and cry (Articles 7, 30, and 32). If no such witnesses could be found and the suspect was a man of good repute, he had the right to clear himself by a purgatory oath *metseptimus* (Article 8).

The third factor determining the right to be first in presenting proof was the case when the criminal was caught red-handed (*in facto manifesto*). This was significant in cases of house-breaking (Article 102), robbery and rape (Article 54), and wounding (Article 49). The phrase 'caught while committing the act' appeared in Article 51 and was repeated in Article 81 with regard to pilferage or burglary; it is connected with hue and cry, the arrest of an armed criminal, and breach of the public peace. A separate provision dealt with the case of a woman caught in the act of committing murder or wounding. The same rules would apply here: the right to be first in presenting proof belonged to the plaintiff, who would the swear the accusatorial oath *metseptimus.* If the plaintiff merely had seen the woman at the scene of the crime, but she had not been apprehended and he came to court on the following day, the right to be first in presenting proof passed on to her (Article 88).

The *Weichbild* also contained the right to be first in presenting proof based on the circumstances of who received the complaint. In the case of wounding inflicted by both parties, if one party went to the judge and the other to four jurors (in another version of the *Weichbild*, their number rose to 11, Article 113, though in Poland it was usually seven), showing them the wounds and demanding that the judge be sent for, the right to be first in presenting proof went to the latter party (Article 30). There were more provisions that introduced further points which made the rules of granting the right to be first in presenting proof even more complex. For example, if a defendant accused of wounding was released on bail and killed before the opening of the trial, the suspected murderer had the right to be first in bringing action (Article 36). Article 37 outlined another scenario in which that right was to be given to the wounded person unless an agnate relative of the dead victim had already been granted wager by battle.

The fifth of the circumstances that played a role in the granting of the right to be first in presenting proof was the good character and trustworthiness of the accused. If the fray took place in broad daylight and the accusation was levelled at a man of good character who had not been seen at the scene of the crime, he has the right to be first in presenting a proof in the form of a purgatory oath *metseptimus*, with six oath-helpers, took precedence over his accuser's right to wager by battle (Article 92). If, however, the crime was committed during the hours of darkness, the accused could clear himself on one condition: he had to muster reliable oath-helpers who were ready to give him an alibi under a purgatory oath *metseptimus*. This latter case shows a creeping redefinition of the role of the compurgators: what they are expected to contribute to the trial is circumstantial evidence, rather than an asseveration of their faith in the character of principal oath-swearer.

For the *Weichbild*, ordeal or wager by battle was as important an instrument of obtaining proof as oaths. It could be used in cases involving severe injury – for example, grievous wounding (battle wounds 'deserve' to be repaid) or bruising in the back and the belly area caused by blows from a club or stick (Article 63, as well as Articles 31 and 35) – and breach of public order (robbery, rape, or house-breaking, Article 103). Should one of the litigants in a case of mutual wounding die of his wounds before the day appointed for wager by battle, his adversary faced the punishment for wounding, namely, his hand would be cut off (Article 31). If all the conditions attached to a case of mutual wounding were met (i.e. hue and cry and the right to be first in presenting proof), the victim could challenge to a wager by battle as many of his assailants as was the number of his wounds. If, however, there were more assailants than the number of wounds the victim was able to show, his assailants could clear themselves by a purgatory oath *metseptimus*. The procedure of administering wager by battle described in Article 56 was evidently borrowed from the *Sachsenspiegel*. It provided for the appointment of a deputy in wager by battle and a deferment in case a stand-in could not be found, or in case the challenged party was unable to accept the challenge (for various reasons, e.g. inequality of the combatants' social status). It also prescribed in detail the manner in which the battle (duel) was to be fought (the weapons, etc). Obviously, such regulations were completely out of place in a late medieval urban community.

If a person accused of murder or wounding escaped, his property could be seized and confiscated to cover the impending compensation for the damage incurred by the victim and to pay the fees and fines imposed by the court (Article 91). Deputizing was the subject of another provision with a strikingly complex set of rules. The father could stand in on three occasions for his son (provided he lived in the father's house and was not married) if the latter was accused of a capital crime and caught red-handed. If the son was allowed to present a purgatory oath *metseptimus*, his father could come in his stead; however, if the father was accused of the same crime, he had to go through the purgation ritual first (Articles 24 and 87).

10.5 *Crime and Punishment*

In general, serious crimes like murder, rape, highway robbery, and housebreaking were punished by death (Articles 7, 11, 32, 49, and 102). There was one exception to this rule. In the case of mutual wounding, the use of the sword was punished by cutting off the hand, and the use of the dagger (Lat. *cultellus*, Ger. texts *Messer*) was punished by death, because the dagger was treated as a murderer's weapon (Article 33). The punishment for larceny depended on the value of the stolen goods and on whether it took place in daytime or at night. Hanging was the standard method of capital punishment. The court could spare a man of good repute if the crime was committed in daytime and the stolen object was worth less than three shillings. He would then qualify for punishment 'in skin and hair' (Lat. *ad cutem et crines*, Ger. *zu Haut und Haar*), prescribed for petty larceny (Article 39). It was possible for the felon to purchase a pardon (i.e. the remission of the death sentence or the amputation of the right hand), but he still forfeited all his rights and his property (Article 58). A burgher guilty of robbery and plundering his neighbours was to forfeit his own house, and the house in which a woman was raped was to be torn down (Article 107).

The *Weichbild* provided for an amicable settlement (Lat. *concordia*, Ger. *Einigung*) of disputes both in and out of court. The reconciliation could be attested by the judge and jurors or by oath sworn by the witnesses of the out of court settlement (*metseptimus*). A breach of the settlement agreement was punished by mutilation or death, or, alternately, whatever price was to be paid for the original crime (Article 23). Once a dispute was settled *extra curiam*, it should not be brought before the court again (Article 29). If a complaint were to be lodged, even though the settlement agreement had been made, the court should order the offending party to pay a judicial fine (Articles 70 and 104).

10.6 *Transfer of Property under Municipal Law*

Apart from being in charge of criminal justice, the municipal authorities also had the right to oversee property transfers in the area of their jurisdiction. To ensure the legal validity of all transfers of property, it was necessary to obtain the approval of the municipal court. The *Weichbild* regulated that sphere not only with regard to purchase and donation, but also security interests (pledges), that is, the establishment of a pledge to guarantee repayment of debt (Article 13). The creation of a dower, that is, the husband's marital gifts or donations, including property rights, had to be announced in open court (*iudicium bannitum*, Articles 14 and 25). After a year and a day, the grant became irrevocable (Articles 16 and 45). Claims concerning rights of possession could be brought before the court, and if the jurors who had heard the case died, the court should admit the testimony of witnesses that were still alive. Such a fact-finding procedure must have looked obsolete in medieval towns which kept a written record of all official business in municipal record books. Less vulnerable to ravages of time were the provisions concerning fees charged by the court (Articles 13 and 19).

10.7 *Hereditary Property versus Gifted Property*

The dividing line between hereditary assets (including rents) and gifts (acquired property) was determined primarily by the rules concerning alienation. The general rule was that hereditary property could not be alienated (sold or given away) without the heirs' consent (Articles 14 and 46). The only reason for introducing in this version of the *Weichbild* a clause declaring all deathbed dispositions of property whose value exceeds three shillings invalid – unless it is approved by the heirs (Article 17) – must have been a high vigilance for the protection of family interest. However, an heir pressing his claim in court for the recovery of hereditary property had to desist if the defendant was able to show that he had held it for at least a year and a day and if the defendant could name the person from whom he had obtained it (Article 46). Moreover, the possessor was to enjoy the primary right to argue his case (Article 96). If the recovery claim involved rent (*bona censualia*, Ger. *Zinsgut*), the parties were to validate their rights by summoning six compurgators (Article 41).

10.8 *Marital Property, Inheritance Rules, and Guardianship*

Generally, the Magdeburg Law assumed that marital property was divisible. According to the Latin translation of the *Weichbild* in the Gniezno manuscript, the bride entered into marriage with a dowry which usually consisted of household goods, clothes, and personal jewellery (Lat. *supellectilia*, Ger. *Gerade*, Pol. *gerada*, *szczebrzuch* Article 14). The husband could assign some of his property (dower) to his wife as a gift (Lat. *dos*, Ger. *Morgengabe*, from the custom of the husband offering his wife a morning-gift after the nuptials) or as a share in his property if she were to be widowed. The latter was to revert to the heirs of her husband upon her death unless they decided otherwise (Articles 45 and 46). The dower settlement had to be made in open court, but if the handover took place outside of the legal protocol and the heirs contested the widow's title, she could validate her claim by swearing an oath together with six compurgators (Article 14). She forfeited the right to keep her late husband's dowry upon remarriage.

Since spouses as a rule did not inherit from each other (Article 25), the entire inheritance fell to their children, unless one or more of them had been in any way excluded (e.g. had received their portions before their father's death). If one of the heirs died childless, his portion should pass, first, to his siblings, or, second, should be distributed equally between his relatives within the same degree of kinship (Articles 14, 18, and 89). However, if that death occurred while the widow was in possession of the estate, the share of the deceased child passed to her under the same conditions that applied to the dower (Article 73). The question of inheritance became more complicated when a widower married a widow and both had children from former marriages. On the assumptions that the widow brought no property into the marriage and the inheritance was acquired during the course of marriage, her husband's son was first in order of succession – before her children or his sister's children and grandchildren, provided the son's social status was on a par with that of his father (Article 44). The *paris conditionis* (equal in status) clause means that illegitimate offspring (bastards) had no automatic right to inherit. If there were no male heirs, and the daughter had already been endowed with a dowry and given birth to a son, he inherited his grandfather's estate. If an heir joined a monastic community as a minor and left it after coming of age, he retained his right to inherit. An adult son who decided to become a monk would lose that right (Article 61). The property of an individual who died without heirs was to be forfeited to the king (Article 66). The property of a person sentenced to death was not automatically confiscated; it passed to his descendants in the order of succession (Article 72). Finally, the will as a unilateral testamentary disposition of property was unknown to the *Weichbild*.

The deceased person's heritable property, according to the *Weichbild*, consisted of weapons of war (Ger. *Hergewet*, Lat. *arma bellica*), things customarily used by women (Lat. *supellectilia*, Ger. *Gerade*, Pol. *gerada*), and the estate (Ger. *Erbe*, Lat. *res hereditaria*, Pol. *dziedzictwo*). The *Hergewet*, which was to be inherited by a male heir, consisted not only of arms and armour, but also war horses, men's clothing, and linen (Articles 61 and 25). Obviously, this provision reflected a world that was rather remote from the urban way of life. It was a world of warriors and knights in which men entered into marriage with substantial property and women would bring in a cartload of household goods, clothes, personal items, and ornaments. They made up the *gerada*, property that belonged to the wife and could be inherited exclusively by her female relatives or, alternately, by relatives in holy orders (Article 18). It seems simple enough, and yet it was the very enumerative definition of the *gerada* that caused problems.

As the estate of a deceased wife was being devolved, some assumed that it comprised no more than the objects that she originally brought into the marriage, while others insisted that the enumeration referred to classes of objects that qualified as the *gerada*. The disagreement had practical consequences. Was it fair, for example, for the daughters to inherit all of their mother's jewellery (which she may have acquired during the course of her marriage)? The *Weichbild* supplied ammunition for both sides of the argument (Articles 14, 25, 26, 60, 61, and 94). The disposition of the deceased spouse's property is the subject of a provision concerning alimentation and food stored in the household. After the husband's death, a month's supply of provisions (Ger. *Mußteil*) fell to his heirs and the widow (Article 25). Long-lasting food (*pulmenaria*), like grain, pork-cuts, and lard, should be divided between them equally (Article 25 and 26). However, after the wife's death, her female relatives were not admitted to share in the *pulmenaria*: the widower, as per the letter of law, was the sole owner of that food (Article 60).

The *Weichbild* contained a few rules about minors and their guardians. An orphaned minor *in pupillari aetate*, that is, one that had not yet reached puberty, and his estate was to be taken care of by the nearest male agnate as soon as the *hergewet* was released (Articles 50 and 61). Minors could not be restored and legally own their inherited property until they came of age (Article 96). A minor over the age of 12 could choose his guardian (curator), who was obliged to render account of his management of the minor's property to the minor and his mother (Articles 50 and 74).

10.9 *Obligations Founded on Contract and on Tort*

The *Weichbild* did not formulate any systematic law of obligations. The norms regulating that sphere of life were fragmentary, though by no means useless or unfair. Several provisions addressed the problem of debt and contractual obligations. To prove the payment of debt, the litigant had to swear an oath with six compurgators, trustworthy persons who faced no criminal charges themselves, and if the court action involved property, they had to live in the vicinity (Articles 42, 43, 79, and 82). If goods or immovable property were offered in court as security against the payment of debt, and the debtor missed the time limits imposed by the court on three occasions, the expiry of the fourth limit gave the creditor full rights to the pledge, while the debtor could no longer reclaim it (Article 13). The value of the pledged goods should not be greater than the debt (Article 91). If a plaintiff went to court and obtained a writ of execution, the defendant had to pay the debt on the same day (unless he was a guest/*hospes*), but if he confessed to the debt, he was given fourteen days to pay it (Articles 9 and 20). The failure to do so resulted ultimately in the confiscation of the debtor's property and declaring him an outlaw (Article 20). The creditor who started legal action to seize the debtor's property had the right to go to the debtor's house and eat and drink there as he pleased; if the debtor still refused to follow the court order, his property was to be sold to pay off the debt, and the remaining sum given over to his heirs (Article 42). The confiscation order involved banning the debtor from entering his property; each time he defied the ban, he was ordered to pay a fine (Article 15). The proof set by the *Weichbild* in an action of debt brought by a servant against his master were the oaths of the plaintiff and his two oath-helpers (*mettertius*); if the court ruled in his favour, the master had to pay the debt on the same day (Article 24). The *Weichbild* also mentions sureties, persons who promised on behalf of the principal debtor that the debt would be paid on time. When things went wrong, a surety could either pay the debt himself or try to prove in court that the payment did take place. Ultimately, the obligation could be voided by the surety's death; his children did not inherit it (Article 64). This was not the case with debt incurred by the principal debtor. His heirs could either rid themselves of this burden by paying off the debt or proving under oath *metseptimus*, that is, with six oath-helpers, that it had already been paid (Articles 86 and 105). Some provisions addressed the obligations of buyers and sellers in remarkable detail. The seller of a horse was obliged to promise solemnly that the animal is free from faults or blemishes and that the transaction is perfectly legal (Article 38). Should it be alleged that the horse had been stolen, the buyer must point out the man from whom he bought the animal, or else it may be taken away from him (Article 69). The proof of theft was established by oath-taking, although in this case the legal ritual was far more elaborate. The presumable owner was to say the oath while holding the horse's left ear with his right hand and pushing his right leg against the horse's forelegs (Article 85). The liability for any damage done by the animal rests with the owner unless he denies his property (Article 106). One could abjure any liability for damage caused by objects or animals that were on loan or deposited for safe-keeping by declaring under oath that the damage occurred through no fault of his own. However, this form of clearing oneself was not allowed in the case of pledged objects and animals, except horses and cattle. In the latter case, if he proved by oath that he was not guilty of the animals' death, he did hot have to pay back the price of the lost animals, but merely the sum that had made up the pledge (Article 77). Debts incurred by gambling were not enforceable (Article 76).

As this review shows, the scope of regulations in the *Weichbild* was fairly broad. Moreover, many of the regulations addressed problems of urban life, which made the *Weichbild* more popular than the *Sachsenspiegel*. The Latin text presented above belongs to the so-called Sandomierz version, because its author and translator was a Polish burgher – Konrad of Sandomierz. The evolution of the text of the *Weichbild* in the Silesian-Małopolska compilation in connection with the process of adaptation to practical needs will be the subject of the following analyses.

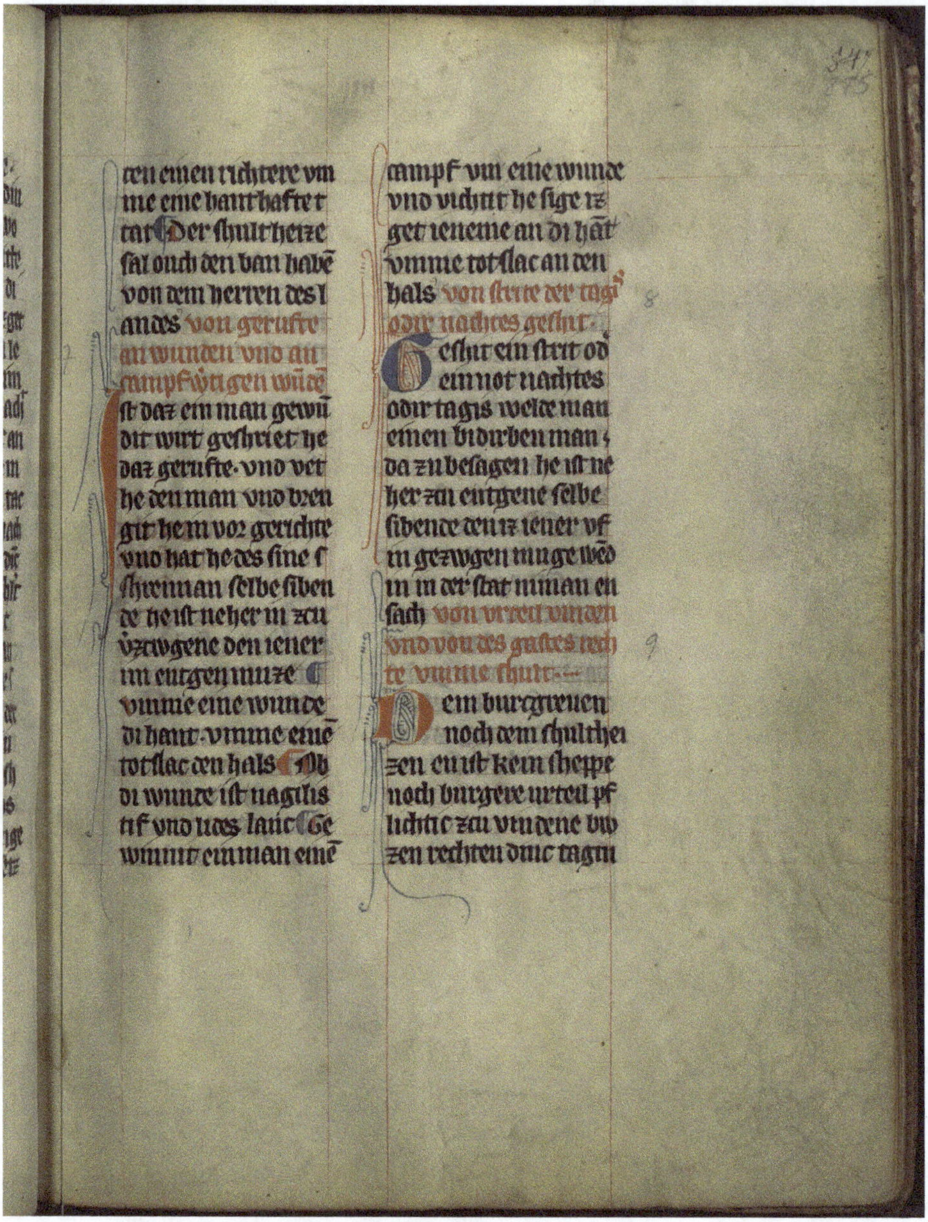

PHOTO 1 Cracow City Council manuscript, Jagiellonian Library in Cracow, Shelfmark 169 III, f. 275r

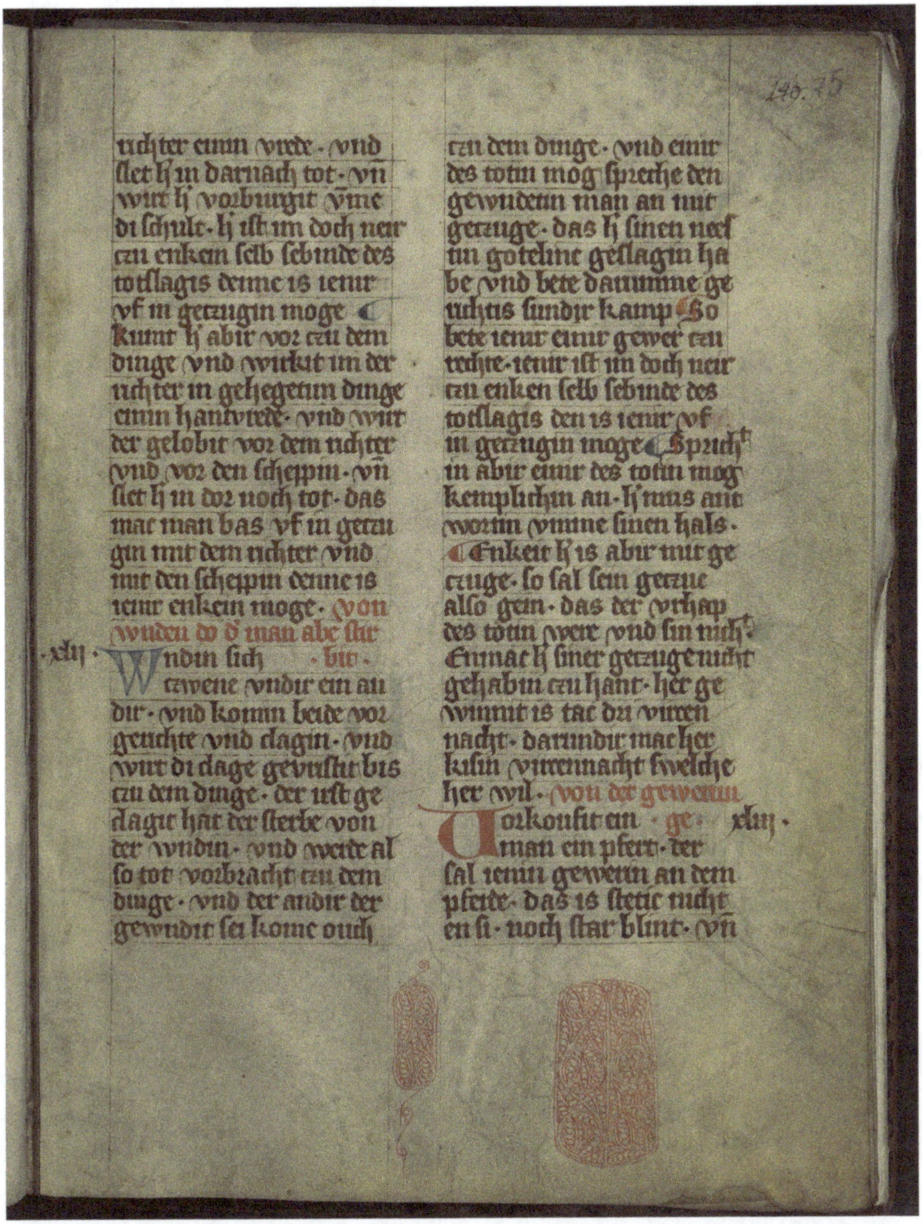

PHOTO 2 Manuscript of High Court of German Law at the Royal Castle of Wawel, Jagiellonian Library in Cracow, Shelfmark 168 III, f. 75r

CHAPTER 1

Manuscripts and Printed Texts of the Silesian-Małopolska Compilation

1 Sources and Contents of the *Weichbild*

This project begins with a closer look at the sources of the Magdeburg *Weichbild*. As we know it to be a compilation, the first step will be to mark out its components. In general, it is possible to distinguish two major branches of the *Weichbild*, the vulgate used in Eastern Germany and a version prepared for users in the Kingdom of Poland. Traditionally, the latter has been referred to as Konrad of Opole's compilation. In this study, however, I will refer to it as *the Silesian-Małopolska compilation*, in order to make a clear distinction between that source and *Weichbild*'s Polish branch as a whole, which, as I will argue, does not rely exclusively on Konrad of Opole's autograph.

1.1 *Konrad of Opole's Compilation or the Silesian-Małopolska Compilation: A Question of Terminology*

Although this study deals primarily with the Latin *Weichbild*, it would be unwise to ignore the corresponding German sources. This raises the problem of terminology, that is, naming the compilation which comprises all of the manuscripts of that group. Most scholars believe that the compilation is the work of Konrad of Opole.[1] However, the text in the Cracow manuscript (BJ 169), attributed to Konrad of Opole, cannot be the archetype of the compilation. This is proven by the fact that some passages (provisions) of the Henryków MS (II F 8), also of Silesian provenance, are slightly closer to the

1 Ernst Th. Gaupp, *Das alte Magdeburgische und Hallische Recht. Ein Beitrag zur deutschen Rechtsgeschichte* (Breslau, 1826), pp. 193–199; Paul Laband, ed., *Magdeburger Rechtsquellen. Zum akademischen Gebrauch herausgegeben* (Königsberg, 1869), p. 38; Wacław Korta, "Rola kulturalna średniowiecznej kancelarii" [The Cultural Role of the Medieval Chancery], in: *Studia z dziejów kultury i ideologii ofiarowane Ewie Maleczyńskiej w 50 rocznicę pracy dydaktycznej i naukowej* [Studies in History and Ideology: A Festschrift in Honour of Professor Ewa Maleczyńska to Mark 50 Years of Her Academic and Teaching Career] (Wrocław – Warszawa – Kraków, 1968), p. 69; Zygfryd Rymaszewski, *Łacińskie teksty Landrechtu Zwierciadła Saskiego w Polsce. Versio Vratislaviensis, versio Sandomiriensis, Łaski* [Latin Texts of the Sachsenspiegel Landrecht in Poland: Versio Vratislaviensis – versio Sandomiriensis – Łaski] (Łódź, 1975), p. 9, Notes 3 and 4, p. 10.

earlier sources of the *Weichbild*.[2] If that is the case, how certain can we be that Konrad of Opole was indeed the author of the compilation preserved in the manuscripts dedicated to Cracow (1308) and to Henryk Gusvelt (the Henryków MS of 1306)?[3] That claim is corroborated by the following argument. First, it is pointed out that the *Weichbild* compilation is a companion piece to the *Sachsenspiegel*, which was written (*hat gesriben*) by magister (Master) Konrad (Henryków MS), and – more precisely – by Konrad of Opole (Cracow MS). Those are the names mentioned in the Prologues. Second, as Ernst Th. Gaupp points out, the *ortyl* (*Urteil*) appended to the *Weichbild* has the names 'Konrad' (of Opole?) and 'Henryk' (Gusvelt?) inscribed for the litigants, while they are not mentioned in the text of that *ortyl* in the Brzeg (Brieg) Codex.[4] The two names are clearly suggestive of Konrad of Opole and Henryk Gusveld, but that is not sufficient evidence to draw the firm conclusion that Konrad of Opole was actually the author of the *Weichbild*, not merely a copyist. The Silesian provenance of the Henryków MS has been established beyond any doubt (see Section 2.1). The same can be said about other key 14th-century texts, like the *Magdeburg's Legal Instructions for Wrocław* (*Rechtsmitteilungen Magdeburgs für Breslau*) and the *Sachsenspiegel*. The Silesian origin of the *Weichbild* compilation in the Cracow MS has been firmly established.[5] Therefore, the term 'Silesian-Małopolska' seems to be the most appropriate designation, as it refers

2 The argument rests on three pieces of evidence: 1) Article 1 in the Cracow MS contains the phrase: *Di ratman legen ir burtdinc uz swenne so si wellen mit der wizzegisten rate*. It is missing in the Henryków MS and in the *Magdeburg's Legal Instructions of 1261*, and in *Magdeburg Bench Law*; 2) Article 80 of the Cracow MS leaves out the reference to the *Burggraf* of Magdeburg: *In des borchgreuen dinge* zů Meydeburch *mac ein man* ..., whereas this information can be found in the Henryków MS and in the *Magdeburg's Legal Instructions of 1295* (in F. Ebel's edition of 1295Wr.); and 3) Article 88 of the Cracow MS leaves out the detail of the juryman being exposed to insults, which can be found in the Henryków MS and in *Magdeburg's Legal Instructions of 1295*: *Ob ein schepphe in gehegeteme dinge uf der bank* mit vnbillichen worten van einem manne *misshandelet worde* ... (in F. Ebel's edition). See Maciej Mikuła, "Das Magdeburger Weichbildrecht in seiner schlesisch-kleinpolnischen Fassung. Anmerkungen zur Autorschaft und Textevolution", in: *Kulturelle Vernetzung in Europa. Das Magdeburger Recht und seine Städte. Wissenschaftlicher Begleitband zur Ausstellung »Faszination Stadt«*, eds. Gabriele Köster, Christina Link, Heiner Lück (Sandstein Kommunikation, 2019), pp. 147–165.

3 The Henryków MS itself is of a later date, see Chapter 1.2.1.

4 Gaupp, *Das alte Magdeburgische und Hallische Recht*, pp. 198–199; and Johann E. Böhme, ed., *Diplomatische Beyträge zur Untersuchung der schlesischen Rechte und Geschichte*, 2.2 (Berlin, 1775), p. 123 (3).

5 On the role of Silesia in the dissemination of the Saxon-Magdeburg Law, see Elisabeth Nowak, *Die Verbreitung und Anwendung des Sachsenspiegels nach der überlieferten Handschriften*, Dissertation zur Erlangung der Doktorwürde der Philosophischen Fakultät der Universität Hamburg (Hamburg, 1965) [typescript], pp. 323–324.

both to the origin of those texts (Silesia) and the territorial scope of their reception and subsequent evolution (Małopolska). The German *Weichbild* from that compilation became the basis for the Latin translation, whose author – Konrad of Sandomierz – is named explicitly in the sources.[6] Taking into account the translator's background and – as I will attempt to demonstrate in the following discussion – the crucial role of Cracow in the evolution of the Latin *Weichbild*, the term 'Silesian-Małopolska compilation' can be extended to cover the Latin progeny of the Silesian German-language corpus (associated with Konrad of Opole) – in particular, the *versio Sandomiriensis*.

Of crucial significance to the history of the *Weichbild* in Poland is the Cracow MS, or – more precisely – the Cracow City Council MS (BJ 169), whose text is representative of the Silesian-Małopolska compilation. It is markedly different from the vulgate because its author draws on a range of sources besides the *Weichbild* itself: namely, the *Magdeburg's Legal Instructions for Wrocław* (*Rechtsmitteilungen Magdeburgs für Breslau*) of 1261 and 1295; the *Magdeburg Bench Law* (*Magdeburger Schöffenrecht*); the *Constitution of Courts* (*Rechtsbuch von der Gerichtsverfassung*); and the *Sachsenspiegel*. The *Weichbild* vulgate had never been popular in the Kingdom of Poland, at least not until 1535 when Mikołaj Jaskier published a new, authorized version of the Magdeburg Law based mainly on the German vulgate. The differences between the contents of the two compilations are presented in Table 1.

1.2 Magdeburg Bench Law (Magdeburger Schöffenrecht) *and* Magdeburg's Legal Instructions for Wrocław (Rechtsmitteilungen Magdeburgs für Breslau) *of 1261*

As Paul Laband has demonstrated, the author of the Silesian-Małopolska compilation gave the pride of place in his *Weichbild* to the *Magdeburg Bench Law* (MSR). It consists of 52 articles,[7] enhanced by numerous revised provisions from *Magdeburg's Legal Instructions for Wrocław* of 1261, borrowings from the *Sachsenspiegel*,[8] and a group of original entries. The text of the Cracow MS

6 Stanisław Kutrzeba, *Historia źródeł dawnego prawa polskiego* [A History of the Sources of Old Polish Law], 2 (Lwów – Warszawa – Kraków, [1926]), p. 210.

7 52 articles in the manuscript form the Wrocław University Library shelfmark II Q 3.

8 In his edition of the *Weichbild*, based on the vulgate, Mikołaj Jaskier glossed with references to the *Sachsenspiegel*, see: Zygfryd Rymaszewski, *Łacińskie teksty Landrechtu Zwierciadła Saskiego w Polsce. Jaskier – tekst główny i noty marginesowe*, [Latin Texts of the Landrecht of the Sachsenspiegel in Poland: Jaskier – the Main Text and Marginal Notes] (Łódź, 1985), p. 205 ff. His intention was to enable his readers to consult both law sources and to indicate which regulations are identical and which are complementary. However, all too often, the cross references are inaccurate. This is true both of the references from the *Sachsenspiegel* to the *Weichbild* (*ibid.*, p. 207) and the other way round, as illustrated by the examples in Table 2.

TABLE 1 The contents of *Magdeburg's Legal Instructions for Wrocław* (1261 and 1295), *Magdeburg Bench Law*, and the *Constitution of Courts* in selected texts of the *Weichbild*

Text	*Magdeburg Bench Law* (MSR)	*Magdeburg's Legal Instructions for Wrocław* of 1261	*Magdeburg's Legal Instructions for Wrocław* of 1295	*The Constitution of Courts* (RGV)
BJ 169 and II F 8	missing: 30, 50	missing: 65, 72[a]	23 Articles transposed into 17 Articles	6–15; 16 § 3; 17–8
BJ 168	missing: 30[b]	missing: 44 § 2, 45, 55–68[c]	23 Articles transposed into 17 Articles[d]	6–15; 16 § 3; 17–8[e]
Weichbild vulgate: ed. Daniels & Gruben	missing: 3, 15, 20, 30, 32, 34, 38–39[f]	missing: 44 § 2, 45–50, 52, 63–69, 75, 76 § 1, 77;[g] plus Articles 6, 22, 53, 54 (due to gaps in the MSR)	Articles 1–4, 6–8, 13, and 16	Articles 1–27 (all)

a In the German texts the contents of Article 72 appear only in an abbreviated and thoroughly modified version in Article 53. Article 65, set apart in F. Ebel's edition, comprises no more than the address and signature of the Magdeburg lay judges. For E.Th. Gaupp this is further proof of the two-stage formation of the *Legal Instructions*, in 1261 and 1283 (cf. Gaupp, *Das alte Magdeburgische und Hallische Recht*, pp. 48–49).

b Article 50 of the *Magdeburg Bench Law* is missing from the Cracow MS; it appears, though, as Article CIX in the Wawel MS.

c These are Articles 55–70 following the numbering scheme in Paul Laband's *Magdeburger Rechtsquellen. Zum akademischen Gebrauch herausgegeben* (Königsberg, 1869), Gustav Adolf Tzschoppe and Gustav Adolf Stenzel's *Urkundensammlung zur Geschichte des Ursprungs der Städte und der Einführung und Verbreitung deutscher Kolonisten und Rechte in Schlesien und der Oberlausitz* (Hamburg, 1832), No. LVI, pp. 351–363); and Gaupp's *Das alte Magdeburgische und Hallische Recht*, pp. 230–249.

d Article 14 duplicated in Article CVII.

e Articles 6–15 removed and placed ahead of *Sachsenspiegel*.

f Article 29 of the *Magdeburg Bench Law*, missing from the Cracow MS, reappears as Article 43 of the vulgate. Meanwhile, Article 50 of the Magdeburg Bench Law, missing from the Cracow MS, is mirrored by Article 62 of the vulgate.

g They are Articles 63–71, 77, 78 § 1, 79 according to the numbering scheme in P. Laband's, G.A. Tzschoppe, and G.A. Stenzel's, and E.Th. Gaupp's editions.

TABLE 2 References to the *Sachsenspiegel* in the marginal glosses of Mikołaj Jaskier's edition of the *Weichbild*

BJ 169	MSR	JIM	Reference to JSSp	Type of reference
13	35	LXIII	II 24, III 5	regulations broadening the scope of lien and alienation of property
14	14	LVII	II 21, 24	additional regulations concerning land rent (II 21), incorrect reference II 24
25	45	LVIII	I 14	other regulations concerning family property
29	44	LI	I 8	incorrect reference
31	8	LXXXIII	I 49	additional regulations concerning trial by combat
36	13	LXXXVII	I 68	incorrect reference
37	14	LXXXVIII	I 64	additional reference: in SSp I 62 reference to JIM Article XXXVIII
38	31	XCIX	I 9	additional reference: in SSp I 9 reference to JIM Article XCIX and CXL
40	49	LXIX	II 43	regulations matching JIM
45	36	LX	III 83	additional reference
46	37–38	LXI	I 21, 52	complementary regulations concerning dower (I 21; in II 21 it is similar to JIM); identical to the regulations concerning consent of close relatives to the alienation (I 52)

JIM – Mikołaj Jaskier, *Iuris Municipalis Maideburgensis Liber vulgo Weichbild nuncupatur …* (Samosci, 1602); JSSp – Mikołaj Jaskier, *Iuris Provincialis quo Speculum Saxonum vulgo nuncupatur Libri tres …* (Samosci, 1602).

includes Articles 1–29, 31–49, and 51–52 of the *Schöffenrecht* – that is, 94 per cent of the *Magdeburg Bench Law* content. A significant number of the regulations of the *Magdeburg Bench Law* have their origin in the 1261 *Magdeburg's Legal Instructions for Wrocław*. When these are added to the articles taken over directly from the latter, it is revealed that 75 out of 76 (77)[9] chapters of the Cracow manuscript (i.e. 99 per cent) reproduce the provisions of the *Legal*

9 This calculation does not include § 65 (in Friedrich Ebel's edition) because it contains only a list of names of Magdeburg officials; cf. Friedrich Ebel, ed., *Magdeburger Recht*, Vol. II: *Die Rechtsmitteilungen und Rechtssprüche für Breslau*, Part 1: Die Quellen von 1261 bis 1452 (Köln – Wien, 1989), p. 12.

Instructions. By comparison, the author of the manuscript of the High Court of German Law at the Royal Castle of Wawel (BJ 168) borrowed more material directly from the *Magdeburg Bench Law* (even though Article 50 was removed to the so-called *partes extravagantes* of the *Weichbild*,[10] the rate is it still at 96 per cent), but left out more provisions from the 1261 *Legal Instructions* (i.e. used 77 per cent). The fact that most of the provisions came from the *Sachsenspiegel* may have been the reason for this type of revision in a manuscript volume that contained both the *Weichbild* and the *Sachsenspiegel*. Eight provisions of the *Magdeburg Bench Law* are missing from the vulgate (those provisions that are taken over from the *Magdeburg Bench Law* make up 85 per cent), while material from the 1261 *Legal Instructions* amounts to 71 per cent. However, as already noted, much of the 1261 *Magdeburg's Legal Instructions for Wrocław* had already been absorbed into the *Magdeburg Bench Law*. Unfortunately, the sources in Paul Laband's edition offer little that would help us to ascertain which version was actually used by the author of the Silesian-Małopolska compilation.

1.3 Constitution of Courts (Rechtsbuch von der Gerichtsverfassung), Magdeburg's Legal Instructions for Wrocław (Rechtsmitteilungen Magdeburgs für Breslau) *of 1295, and Other Sources*

As the research of Paul Laband has shown, the original core of the *Constitution of Courts* (RGV) were Articles 6–15 (as numbered in the later, complete version), supplemented by Articles 16–18. Laband points out that the latter (or more precisely, Articles 17 and 18, plus 16 § 3–18) were of greater practical importance. They were incorporated into the Silesian-Małopolska *Weichbild*, while the more theoretical points concerning *translatio imperii*, the accountability of the emperor, and the question of appealing the judgements of the *Magdeburg Lay Bench* in Articles 6–15 are relocated to the end, after the formula of the Jewish oath (that material amounted to 42 per cent of the complete *Constitution of Courts*). The *Weichbild* vulgate contains the whole of Articles 1–27 of the *Constitution of Courts*, and was later expanded to include Articles 28–41 from the *Sachsenspiegel*.[11] In addition, the Silesian-Małopolska

10 This is a section added to the main text by the copyist just ahead of the Jewish oath. In this way, he probably wanted his manuscript to have nearly as many chapters as the basic text after some provisions from the *Sachsenspiegel* had been removed from Wawel MS (BJ 168). Cf. Ferdinand Bischoff, "Beiträge zur Geschichte des Magdeburgerrechts", *Sitzungsberichte der Kaiserlichen Akademie der Wissenschaften. Philosophisch-Historische Classe* 50/4 (1865), 335–41.

11 Renate Schelling, "Magdeburger Schöffensprüche und Magdeburger Weichbildrecht in urkundlicher und handschriftlicher Überlieferung", in: *Hanse, Städte, Bünde. Die sächischen Städte zwischen Elbe und Weser um 1500. Ausstellung Kulturhistorisches Museum Magdeburg 28. Mai bis 26. August 1996. Braunschweigisches Landesmuseum.*

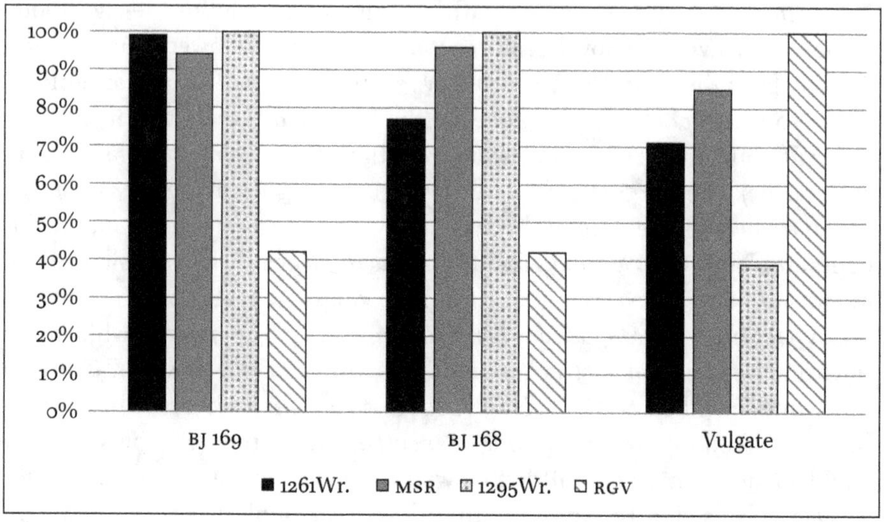

FIGURE 1 Borrowings from *Magdeburg's Legal Instructions for Wrocław* of 1261 and 1295, the *Magdeburg Bench Law* (MSR) and the *Constitution of Courts* (RGV) in the *Weichbild* manuscripts

compilation includes all of the 1295 *Legal Instructions for Wrocław*, whereas only nine articles in the vulgate come from that source (39 per cent).[12] In the Silesian-Małopolska compilation, there are also a number of articles whose provenance is unclear, including three with procedural formulas that can also be found in the Berlin manuscript, published by Hermann Wasserschleben.[13] Both the Weichbild vulgate as well the Silesian-Małopolska compilation include the formula of the Jewish oath (Article 108).[14]

The extent of the borrowings between the sources under discussion are shown graphically in Figure 1.

Ausstellungszentrum Hinter Aegidien 17. September bis 1. Dezember 1996, 1, ed. Matthias Puhle, (Magdeburger Museumsschriften) 4/1 (Magdeburg, 1996), p. 118.

12 This does not include § 24 (in F. Ebel's numbering scheme) as it contains only the address and a list of names of Magdeburg officials, i.e. a kind of content that for obvious reasons was edited out of the *Weichbild* (Ebel, *Magdeburger Recht*, Vol. II: *Die Rechtsmitteilungen und Rechtssprüche für Breslau*, Part 1, p. 20).

13 Article 52 matches Article LXXVI, and Article 54 – Article LXXVIII. Moreover, whereas the opening of Article 51 in the Cracow MS (BJ 169) is a borrowing from the *Magdeburg Bench Law*, the final section is identical to Article LXXVII of the Berlin MS. Cf. Hermann Wasserschleben, ed., *Sammlung deutscher Rechtsquellen*, 1 (Giessen, 1860), pp. 125–126. According to F. Bischoff (*Beiträge zur Geschichte*, p. 282), the procedural formulas of Article 51, 52 and 54 can also be found in the Brzeg Codex (a collection of *ortyle*). Cf. Böhme, *Diplomatische Beyträge*, p. 122, No 7; p. 123, No. 2 and 3; p. 124, No. 1.

14 Cf. Jana Pacyna, *Mittelalterliche Judenrechte. Norm und Anwendung im Magdeburger Rechtskreis (1250–1400)* (Halle/Saale, 2015), pp. 151–163.

1.4 *The Impact of the* Sachsenspiegel

The dependence of the *Weichbild* on the *Sachsenspiegel* is a matter of considerable complexity and has to be analysed in light of two categories: indirect borrowing (via the *Legal Instructions*, the *Magdeburg Bench Law*, and the *Constitution of Courts*) and direct borrowings.[15] At this point, let it be noted that the Cracow MS contains no passages taken over directly from the *Sachsenspiegel* (SSp); it has plenty of the SSp regulations handed down by the 1261 *Legal Instructions*. The extent of those borrowings is presented in Table 3.

TABLE 3 Provisions of the *Sachsenspiegel* incorporated into Cracow MS (BJ 169) via *Magdeburg's Legal Instructions for Wrocław* of 1261

Cracow MS (BJ 169)	Wawel MS (BJ 168)	*Weichbild* vulgate	*Magdeburg's Legal Instructions for Wrocław* of 1261 (1261Wr.)	*Sachsenspiegel* (Spp)[a]
56[b]	–	–	1261Wr. 68 *in fine* [70][c]	SSp I 63 § 4 *in fine*., 64, 65 § 1
57	–	–	1261Wr. 69 [71]	SSp I 65 § 2
58	–	–	1261Wr. 70, 71 [72, 73]	SSp I 65 § 3; 68 § 1
59	–	–	1261Wr. 55–61	SSp I 22 § 4–5; 23, 24, 25 § 1–3[d]
60	–	–	1261Wr. 62	SSp I 62 § 8, 9
61	–	–	1261Wr. 63	SSp I 62 § 10, 11

a Following the numbering scheme of Karl A. Eckhardt's edition: Eike von Repgow, *Sachsenspiegel. Landrecht*, (*Monumenta Germaniae Historica. Fontes iuris Germanici antiqui*. Nova Series) I.1 (Göttingen – Frankfurt, 1973).

b In his edition of the Magdeburg Lawbook of Pleszew, Witold Maisel observes that Article 52 includes a sentence that is very similar to SSp I 63 § 1 (cf. Witold Maisel, ed., "Prawo magdeburskie miasta Pleszewa" [The Magdeburg Lawbook of Pleszew], *Studia i Materiały do Dziejów Wielkopolski i Pomorza* 9/1 (1963), p. 81, Note 16). However, that provision of the Sachsenspiegel is actually incorporated into Article 56.

c In brackets the numbers of the scheme employed in the critical edition of P. Laband, G.A. Tzschoppe, and G.A. Stenzel, as well as that of E.Th. Gaupp.

d Contrary to the assertion of P. Laband (in *Magdeburger Rechtsquellen*, p. 94), Article 23 SSp was fully incorporated into 1261Wr.

15 According to Rolf Lieberwirth, the Magdeburg lay judges often drew on various sections of the *Sachsenspiegel*. See Rolf Lieberwirth, "Magdeburger Recht;" in: *Hanse, Städte, Bünde. Die sächsischen Städte zwischen Elbe und Weser um 1500*, ed. M. Puhle, 1, (Magdeburger Museumsschreiben) 4 (Magdeburg, 1996), p. 116.

The copyist of the Wawel manuscript (for the use of the High Court of German Law at Wawel, MS BJ 168) informs the readers about the omission and directs them to the text of the *Sachsenspiegel* reproduced in the same volume. However, he does copy some of *Sachsenspiegel* provisions in the so-called *partes extravagantes* of the *Weichbild* (I 66 § 3, I 69, in Article CV and III 39 § 1 in Article CX), presumably to fill the gap left after the removal of material referring to the *Constitution of Courts* from the main body of the *Weichbild*.

The impact of the *Sachsenspiegel* on the *Weichbild* vulgate is quite different. Owing to the complete incorporation of the *Constitution of Courts*, numerous provisions of the SSp found their way into the *Weichbild*. As Paul Laband has demonstrated, large chunks of the *Weichbild* (i.e. Articles 19, 28–41, and 109–125) can also be traced back to the *Sachsenspiegel*.[16] As Table 3 shows, due to the omission of some provisions of *Magdeburg's Legal Instructions for Wrocław* of 1261, which came originally from *Sachsenspiegel*, the vulgate does not contain some of the *Sachsenspiegel* material that can be found in the *Weichbild* of the Silesian-Małopolska compilation.

1.5 *Practical Consequences of the Differences between the Silesian-Małopolska Compilation and the* Weichbild *Vulgate*

There are three major consequences of the differences between various compilations of the German-language *Weichbild*. First, the Silesian-Małopolska compilation comprises the complete text of *Magdeburg's Legal Instructions for Wrocław* of 1295.[17] It addresses a wide range of issues, the following of which are not treated by the vulgate (numbers according to 1295 Wr.): confiscation of property (Article 5); accusations in connection with injuring an assailant in self-defence (Articles 9–10); the accusation of a woman of killing or wounding (Article 11); the division of inheritance among sons (Article 12); killing and wounding (Articles 14–15)l proxies in judicial procedure (Article 17); elements of the *gerada*[18] (Articles 18–19); exclusion of evidence (Article 20); liability of minors under guardianship (Article 21); oaths in cases of insults (Article 22); and the jurisdiction of municipal courts (Article 23).

---

16 Schelling, *Magdeburger Schöffensprüche*, p. 118; Laband, *Magdeburger Rechtsquellen*, pp. 94, and 110–111. Cf. also comparative analyses of the Weichbild vulgate and the *Sachsenspiegel* in: Wilhelm von Thüngen, ed., *Das sächsische Weichbildrecht nach dem Codex Palatinus Nro. 461. Mit einer Einleitung als Inaugural-Dissertation* (Heidelberg, 1837), pp. 23–25; and Gaupp, *Das alte Magdeburgische und Hallische Recht*, pp. 115–116.

17 Ferdinand Bischoff, "Über einen deutschen Rechtscodex der Krakauer Universitäts-Bibliothek", *Sitzungsberichte der Kaiserlichen Akademie der Wissenschaften. Philosophisch-Historische Classe* 48/1–2 (1864), 292.

18 See Chapter 3.4.4.

Second, the Cracow MS acknowledges to a much greater extent the *Magdeburg Bench Law* (MSR) and *Magdeburg's Legal Instructions for Wrocław* of 1261. Although of the two articles of the *Magdeburg Bench Law* missing from the Cracow MS, the *Weichbild* vulgate has one (concerning inheritance left to children; Article 50 of the MSR in Article 62 of the vulgate), it does not include a number of important provisions from the MSR that are mentioned in the Cracow MS. These provisions are concerned with: the use of false weights and measures (numbering scheme of the *Magdeburg Bench Law*; Article 3); accusations in connection with injuring or killing (Article 15); the division of the *gerada* between women and clergymen (Article 20); theft (Article 32); deposits (Article 34); consent of family members to a donation (Article 38); and the effect of second marriages on rules of inheritance (Article 39). Similarly, a considerable number of the provisions of the *Legal Instructions* of 1261 were not adopted by the vulgate. These include (barring those that were omitted because of their origin in the *Magdeburg Bench Law*) provisions concerning judicial sentencing (Article 44 § 2–45); presentation of charges (Article 46); inheritance rights of family members of a man sentenced to death (Article 47); inheritance rights of children and widows (Article 48); the right of minors to choose their guardian (Article 49); the testimony required in cases in which a man has to prove his freedom (Article 50); inheritance debts (Article 52); judicial proceedings and sentencing (Articles 63 and 62); forfeiture of rights in the case of the death penalty having been commuted to a fine (Article 69); seizure of livestock found trespassing (Article 74); debts (Article 76 § 1); and compensation (Article 77).

Third, whereas the Cracow and other manuscripts tap into the earliest sources of Magdeburg Law, the vulgate is oriented primarily towards the *Sachsenspiegel*. The publication in tandem of the *Sachsenspiegel* and a pruned *Weichbild* by Mikołaj Jaskier in 1535 made the two legal collections equally accessible. However, the assumption that the publication of a complete, authoritative edition of the *Sachsenspiegel* would make up for its fragments embedded in the *Weichbild* does not take into account the fact that the latter owed its worth to the unique blend of the *Magdeburger Schöffenrecht* and the *Legal Instructions* of 1261 and 1295. There remains the unresolved question of the provenance of the final section (Articles 126–135) of the vulgate. Paul Laband does not refer it back to the *Sachsenspiegel*,[19] which makes the assess-

19 Laband, *Magdeburger Rechtsquellen*, p. 111. The provisions of this section are concerned with attempted wounding (Article 126), non-payment of wergild (Article 127), standard width of public roads (Article 128), sequestration of horses (Article 129), reprieve and commutation of executions (Article 130), payment claims (Article 131), vindication of stolen

ment of the practical value of the competing compilations of the *Weichbild* all the more difficult.

1.6 *Summary: The Silesian-Małopolska Compilation as an Urban Law Code*

The foregoing analysis shows that the authorship attribution of the *Weichbild* used in medieval Poland to Konrad of Opole is essentially conjecture, with no firm evidence to back it up. Konrad of Opole's text is certainly part of the picture, but it is in no way identical to the compilation which began to be disseminated in both German and Latin versions from Silesia and Małopolska in the 13th century. Even if its origin was in Silesia, it was given its distinctive shape in Małopolska – hence the term 'Silesian-Małopolska compilation'. A comparative analysis of sources and texts of the two major compilations – the vulgate and the Silesian-Małopolska manuscripts – shows that the latter was highly receptive to the Magdeburg case law. The Cracow MS therefore absorbed 99 per cent of the regulations from *Magdeburg's Legal Instructions for Wrocław* of 1261, 94 per cent of the *Magdeburg Bench Law* judgments, and 100 per cent of the *Magdeburg's Legal Instructions for Wrocław* of 1295, while the vulgate took in 71 per cent, 85 per cent, and 39 per cent of those texts, respectively. The vulgate, on the other hand, was more receptive to the legal material from the *Sachsenspiegel* and the *Constitution of Courts* (*Rechtsbuch von der Gerichtsverfassung*). The role of practical demand in the process of modification of the received text in either of the two branches of the *Weichbild* is not easy to assess or compare. Nevertheless, what can be said with certainty about the Silesian-Małopolska compilation is that it had its origins in the Magdeburg Law; its popularity was connected with the rise of towns; and, finally, it was already subject to modifications at its earliest stage, that is, the appearance of German-language manuscripts.

---

goods (Article 132), court fees (Article 133), and litigation between Christians and Jews (Articles 134 and 135). These problems are tackled in the *Sachsenspiegel*, but its approach is different, as shown by the provision concerning the width of public roads. See: SSp II 59 § 3 in Karl A. Eckhardt's edition of 1973; and in: Eike von Repgow, *Sachsenspiegel. Die Dresdner Bilderhandschrift Mscr. Dresd. M 32. Textband*, ed. Heiner Lück, coop. Thomas Haffner, Marion Perrin, and Jörn Weinert (Graz, 2006), p. 164, f. 2. Cf. also Mikołaj Jaskier's Latin redaction in *Iuris Provincialis quo Speculum Saxonum vulgo nuncupatur Libri tres ...* (Samosci, 1602), f. XCII; and the Polish translation of Paweł Szczerbic, *Speculum Saxonum, albo prawo saskie i majdeburskie, porządkiem obiecadła z łacińskich i niemieckich egzemplarzów zebrane. A na polski język z pilnością i wiernie przełożone* [Speculum Saxonum or Saxon and Magdeburg Law, in Alphabetic Order, from Latin and German Copies Collected. A New and Meticulously Accurate Translation into Polish], ed. Grzegorz M. Kowalski, 1, (Bibliotheca Iagiellonica. Fontes et Studia) 29 (Kraków, 2017) p. 218.

2 Dynamics of the German Text

To form a better understanding of the evolution of the Latin texts of the *Weichbild*, it is necessary to consider its background, the dynamic development of its German prototype within the Silesian-Małopolska compilation.

2.1 *Studies of the* Weichbild *in the Cracow MS (BJ 169) and the Henryków MS (II F 8).*

The Cracow MS of 1308,[20] also known as Konrad of Opole's manuscript, is made up of 309 leaves. It contains a selection of Latin and German texts, namely, the *Sachsenspiegel Landrecht* and *Lehnrecht* and the Lübeck Law (in Latin), as well as two parts of the *Sachsenspiegel* and the *Magdeburger Weichbild* (in German).[21] In his major study of the Cracow City Council MS, Ferdynand Bischoff compared the Cracow MS (BJ 169) with the text of the *Legal Instructions for Wrocław*, the *Magdeburg-Görlitzer Law of 1304*, and the *Weichbild* vulgate.[22] He notes that the Cracow manuscript not only reproduces the contents of the *Legal Instructions* (1261), but that it also retains – with a few exceptions – the sequential order of the provisions from the sources. He concludes – in my opinion, rightly – that the divergences from the wording of some of the articles in *Magdeburg's Legal Instructions for Wrocław* of 1261 result from the author's use of a different version of that basic text. Paul Laband identified that missing

20 In his *A History of the Sources of Old Polish Law*, S. Kutrzeba questioned the dating of the Cracow MS and attributed its authorship to a Cracow notary (1337?–1354) (Kutrzeba, *Historia źródeł*, 2, p. 210). His argument, which called for a revision of established dating of the Cracow MS (BJ 169) by 30 years to 1338, was refuted by Rymaszewski in *Łacińskie teksty Landrechtu Zwierciadła Saskiego w Polsce. Versio* [Latin Texts of the Landrecht of the Sachsenspiegel in Poland. Versio], p. 10, Note 12). The problem was also raised in Theodor Goerlitz's study "Das flämische und das fränkische Recht in Schlesien und ihr Widerstand gegen das sächsische Recht", *Zeitschrift der Savigny-Stiftung für Rechtsgeschichte. Germanistische Abteilung* 57 (1937), 156. Goerlitz sets down the *terminus ad quo* at 1292 and the *terminus ad quem* at a time shortly before 1310 without opting for a more precise date.

21 For a meticulous description of its contents, see Zofia Włodek, *Catalogus Codicum Manuscriptorum Medii Aevi Latinorum qui in Bibliotheca Jagellonica Cracoviae Asservantur*, 1 (Wrocław, 1980), pp. 155–159; see also the description by Władysław Wisłocki in *Inwentarz rękopisów Biblioteki Jagiellońskiej* [Inventory of Manuscripts in the Jagiellonian University], 1 (Kraków, 1877–1881), p. 67. For more recent descriptions, see Oppitz's Catalogue, No. 845, pp. 613–614, and Friedrich Ebel and Renate Schelling's "Das lateinische lübische Recht in der schlesisch-polnischen Fassung des 13. Jahrhunderts", *Zeitschrift der Savigny-Stiftung für Rechtsgeschichte. Germanistische Abteilung* 110 (1993), 95.

22 Bischoff, "Über einen deutschen Rechtscodex", pp. 276–297.

link as the *Magdeburg Bench Law*.[23] Ferdinand Bischoff reacted by reaffirming his claim that the Cracow MS reproduced all of the *Legal Instructions* of 1295, while compressing some of its provisions into single articles. Furthermore, he contends that the text of the Cracow MS has its closest match in the Uffenbach MS and that the differences between the two are not sufficiently significant to undermine their inherent affinity. In other words, it is highly unlikely that both texts are independent of one another. They share exactly the same oath formulas (Articles 51–53) and nearly the exact same Jewish oath. While Bischoff rules out the dependence of the Cracow MS on the *Weichbild* vulgate,[24] he insists that the Cracow manuscript, the *Legal Instructions for Zgorzelec* (Görlitz), the Naumburg Codex, and the Uffenbach MS are all related. He does not rule out that the *Weichbild* of the Cracow MS was composed c. 1304 (or slightly later) in Silesia or in Cracow, but he expresses doubt about his official character.[25] In his view, it did not possess that status until it was adopted by the Cracow City Council (in the form of the Cracow MS).

The composition of that text at the beginning of the 14th century can be explained by reference to the following events. By 1304, an expanded version of *Magdeburg's Legal Instructions* was already in use in Zgorzelec; one year later, the town started its own book of court records. Głogów (Glogau) acquired its own manuscript of Magdeburg Law in 1314. In Cracow, a book of court records was started c. 1300,[26] rendering the need for a handy copy of the law more pressing than ever. This need was met by Cracow MS, which, as Zygfryd Rymaszewski observes, contains the full corpus of the Saxon-Magdeburg Law.[27]

As was mentioned in Section 1.1, the text of the *Weichbild* in the Cracow MS is not identical to the archetype of compilation – if only because it contains passages that are closer to the Henryków MS. The latter, Wrocław University

23 Laband, *Magdeburger Rechtsquellen*, p. 93ff.

24 Bischoff, "Über einen deutschen Rechtscodex", p. 269.

25 *Ibid.*, p. 297.

26 Bożena Wyrozumska, *Kancelaria miasta Krakowa w średniowieczu* [Chancellery of the City of Cracow in the Middle Ages] (Kraków, 1995), p. 56; and Piotr Okniński, "Uwarunkowania początków rozwoju kancelarii miejskich. Przykład Krakowa (do 1312 r.)" [The Origins of Municipal Chancelleries: The Case of Cracow (until 1312)], in: *Loca scribendi. Miejsca i środowiska tworzące kulturę pisma w dawnej Rzeczypospolitej XV–XVIII stulecia* [Loca scribendi: Sites and Communities Involved in the Creation of the Culture of Writing in the Old Polish Commonwealth in the 15th–18th Century], eds. Anna Adamska, Agnieszka Bartoszewicz, and Maciej Ptaszyński (Warszawa, 2017), pp. 39–40.

27 Rymaszewski, *Łacińskie teksty Landrechtu Zwierciadła Saskiego w Polsce. Versio*, p. 10; and Edward Potkowski, *Książka rękopiśmienna w kulturze Polski średniowiecznej* [The Hand-written Book in the Culture of Medieval Poland] (Warszawa, 1984), p. 176.

Library MS II F 8, is a collection of German sources of municipal law.[28] It dates back to the turn of the 14th century, or the early 15th century at the latest, and its Silesian provenance is beyond any doubt.[29] As both texts are closely related, they must have had a common base.

2.2 *The Impact of the Cracow City Council* Weichbild*: the Wawel MS (BJ 168) and MS BJ 170a*

It has been said that the Wawel MS (BJ 168) was granted by King Kazimierz the Great to the Mayor (*wójt* / *Vogt* / *advocatus*) and aldermen of the High Court of German Law at the Royal Castle in Cracow.[30] It is certainly true that the manuscript was used by the Court. That is attested by, among others, an entry made by Andrzej Czarnisza, mayor and president of the High Court in 1392–1416.[31] The contents of the manuscript show the pre-eminently practical bias of this law book.[32] The first detailed description of the manuscript

28 1) The Latin *Landrecht* of the *Sachsenspiegel* in the Wrocław version (f.1–38); 2) the Lübeck Law (in Latin) (f. 39–43); 3) *Das Lehnrecht* in the Wrocław version in Latin (f. 45–67); 4) *Das Landrecht* (f. 68–125); 5) *Die Weichbildchronik* (f. 126–134); 6) *Das Lehnrecht* (f. 129–157); 7) the *Weichbild* in the Silesian-Małopolska version (f. 158–180); 8) *Magdeburg's Legal Instructions for Wrocław* (f. 181–190); and 9) the Magdeburg judgments (*ortyle*) (f. 190–194).

29 Rymaszewski, *Łacińskie teksty Landrechtu Zwierciadła Saskiego w Polsce. Versio*, p. 11. This manuscript has been the object of intense scrutiny as shown by the bibliographical list compiled by Oppitz (No. 261, p. 409). However, it should be noted that his list also includes publications that merely mention the Henryków MS. For a supplementary bibliography and a digitized copy of the manuscript, see the website of the Wrocław University Library, see http://dk.bu.uni.wroc.pl/cymelia/displayDocument.htm;jsessionid=0C8E4EBBFF0E78C07ADFC0E96B1FB74B?docId=5002000234 (Accessed: 22 May 2017). Cf. also Ebel and Schelling, *Das lateinische lübische Recht*, p. 97.

30 Similarly, e.g. F. Bischoff, "Beiträge zur Geschichte", p. 333.

31 Mark Munzinger, "The Text and Textualization of Codex BJ 168: Legal Culture in Transition at the High Court of Magdeburg Law at the Castle of Kraków", *Krakowskie Studia z Historii Państwa i Prawa* 4 (2011), 30–2.

32 Its list of contents is as follows: 1) Kazimierz the Great's royal charter establishing the High Court of German Law at the Royal Castle in Cracow (f. 1r i v); 2) indices (*regesta*) of the *Landrecht* and the *Weichbild* (f. 2r–8r); 3) an extract from the *Weichbildchronik* (f. 9r i v); 4) an extract from the *Constitution of Courts* (f. 9v–12v); 5) the *Sachsenspiegel* in the Silesian-Prussian version (f. 13v–66v); 6) *partes extravagantes* of the *Sachsenspiegel* (f. 66v–68v); 7) the *Weichbild* (f. 68v–87v); 8) three pages of short supplements: a) an entry made by Andrzej Czarnisza, president of the High Court of German Law at the Royal Castle in Cracow (f. 87v); b) an extract from the Decretals of Gregory IX (Articles 3, 52 and 2 – f. 87v); c) an extract from the *Weichbild* (f. 87v); d) an extract from *Codex Justinianeus* (Articles 8, 17 and 12 – f. 88r); e) a note concerning the size of the Frankish *łan* (*Fränkische Großhufe*) (f. 88r); f) an extract from St John's Gospel (John 1, 1–15 – f. 88v); g) the lay judge's oath in Polish and in German (f. 88v). This list of contents follows Włodek,

was published by Ferdinand Bischoff.[33] There, he also made the case for the Cracow MS being older than the Wawel MS. Although this conclusion has been generally accepted, some of his other claims are debatable. For example, Bischoff assumes that Kazimierz the Great, aware of the need of the newly created High Court for its own codex of the Saxon-Magdeburg Law, asked the Cracow City Council for help, as the City of Cracow already possessed of a copy of the law, that is, the Cracow MS (BJ 169). In effect, a new copy, a somewhat modified version of MS BJ 169, was prepared and designated, by the authority of the Cracow High Court, as a basis for a Latin translation,[34] preserved in the Opatów MS. Later, the text in that manuscript, he argues, provided the model for Łaski's *Statutes*.[35] A table where assorted similarities and differences between the texts in question are put side-by-side appears to prove his point. Yet, ultimately, Bischoff's argument fails to convince. The evidence indicates that a large number of provisions in the Wawel MS are closer to the original sources of the *Weichbild* (i.e. *Magdeburg's Legal Instructions for Wrocław*) than to the *Weichbild* in the Cracow MS.[36] This means that the latter could not be the only basic text for the Wawel MS. Its more complex origin is further indicated by the fact that the *Sachsenspiegel* in the Wawel MS belongs to the so-called Silesian-Prussian version, with the addition of *partes extravagantes*,[37] while the *Sachsenspiegel* of the Cracow MS represents the *versio Vratislaviensis*. Moreover, there are some clear hints that the text in the Wawel MS was at least partly collated with the Cracow MS. The wording of Article 27 offers a strong proof of the dependence of the Wawel MS on the Cracow MS. It shows Table 4.

Bischoff's claim about the affiliation of the Opatów MS (MS Oss., see Section 3.13) and the text of Łaski's *Statutes* was challenged by Emil Kałużniacki.[38] Another of his points, the alleged dependence of the Latin translation on the Cracow MS, will be discussed in greater detail in this study (see Chapter 2). What may also prove to be significant in this discussion is the omission in the

Catalogus Codicum, pp. 151–155, which has supplanted the summary enumeration of Wisłocki (*Inwentarz*, pp. 66–67). See also the catalogue of Oppitz, No. 844, pp. 612–613.

33 Bischoff, *Beiträge zur Geschichte*, pp. 335–339.

34 See also Laband, *Magdeburger Rechtsquellen*, p. 99.

35 Bischoff, "Beiträge zur Geschichte", p. 333,

36 For an overview of passages that overlap in the Wawel MS and the *Magdeburg Bench Law* (or *Magdeburg's Legal Instructions for Wrocław* of 1295) and at the same time indicate points of departure of the Cracow MS from the *Magdeburg Bench Law*, see Appendix 3, Nos. 340, 342, 347, 348, 351, 352, 354, 355, 358, 360, 361, 455, 475.

37 Carl G. Homeyer, *Die Extravaganten des Sachsenspiegels* (Berlin, 1861).

38 Emil Kałużniacki, "Die polnische Recension der Magdeburger Urtheile und die einschlägigen deutschen, lateinischen und czechischen Sammlungen", *Sitzungsberichte der phil.-hist. Classe der Kaiserischer Akademie der Wissenschaften* 111 (1886), 157, Note 1.

TABLE 4 Comparison of the text of Article 27 in Cracow MS (BJ 169) and the matching passages in *Magdeburg's Legal Instructions for Wrocław* of 1261 (1261Wr.), *Magdeburg Bench Law* (MSR), and Wawel MS (BJ 168)

1261Wr. (following F. Ebel's edition)	Cracow MS (BJ 169)	Wawel MS (BJ 168)[a]
... vnde recht vnde vnvorklaget, **vnde diesilbe man, die gewundet is, komet zů were vnde wundet ienen wider vnde schriet daz ruochte vmbe den vriede, den her an ime gebrochen hat**, vnde ne mach her doch vůr gerichte nicht komen vnde klagen van vnkraft sines libes oder von angeste sines libes, **vnde komet iene man, die inc erst wundete, mit einer vrevele** vore vnde klage: Die ander, an deme die vriede erst gebrochen wart, kome na vnde klage desselben tages in der hanthaften tât ...	... sines libis daz in iener slet odir wundit und shriet he daz gerufte, **und kumit iener vor mit der vrevele,** *und clagit dem richtere, und disser en mac noch en tat vor uncreften sines libis denne nicht vorkumen, und kume dar nach des selbin tages vor, und clage dem richtere und den sheppfen ...*	**... und der selbe man der gew[u]ndit ist kome czu were und w[u]nde ienin wedir, und schrie das gerufte, umme den vrede den her an im gebrochin hat, und kumt ienir man der in irst hat gew[u]n[di]t mit einim vrevele,** *und clagit dem richt[er] und desir enmac vor unkreftin sinis libis noch en tat, dennoch nicht vorkomin und kumt dar noch des selbin tagis dar, und clage dem richter und den scheppin ...*

a The text in the Wawel MS is a synthesis of 1261Wr. (or MSR, as edited by P. Laband) and the Cracow MS.

Wawel MS of a few articles from the *Sachsenspiegel*. Although the reader is informed about the omission, the compiler fills the gap, apparently with a mind to preserve the numbering sequence of the Cracow MS, with an equal number of articles before the Jewish oath at the end of the text.[39] The origin of the *partes extravagantes* is mixed – two of them mirror the already incorporated provisions of the *Magdeburg's Legal Instructions for Wrocław*, another pair have their counterparts in the *Sachsenspiegel*, while the rest can be matched with passages in the *Weichbild* vulgate and the *Legal Instructions for Zgorzelec* (Görlitz) of 1304.[40] This patchwork combination is not known to exist in any other single text. Apart from the *partes extravagantes* of the *Weichbild*, the

39 In print: Bischoff, "Beiträge zur Geschichte", pp. 354–355.

40 *Ibid.*, p. 345.

Wawel MS also contains the *partes extravagantes* of the *Sachsenspiegel* published by Carl G. Homeyer (Nos. 31–56). In his commentary, Homeyer stressed their distinctly urban character; some of them have been taken directly from the provisions of the Magdeburg Law.[41]

At this point, it is necessary to consider MS BJ 170a, as it may also have had an impact on the text of the Latin *Weichbild*. The paper manuscript from the third quarter of the 14th century contains 175 leaves.[42] A comprehensive description, more detailed than that in Homeyer's study of the *Sachsenspiegel* or Władysław Wisłocki's catalogue of manuscripts in the Jagiellonian Library, can be found in Emil Kałużniacki's study of the Magdeburg *ortyle*.[43] However, more recently, that description has been superseded by a critical account of MS BJ 170a in a Jagiellonian Library catalogue of medieval manuscripts written by Zofia Włodek and Ilpo Tapani Piirainenen, as well as Winfried Waßer's introduction to their edition of the *Sachsenspiegel* from that manuscript.[44] The texts in MS BJ 170a are – without exception – sources of German law.[45]

A careful comparative analysis shows that the provisions of the Magdeburg *Weichbild* are part of two collations in MS BJ 170a (Cf. the concordance in Appendix 1). While one contains almost exclusively provisions of the *Magdeburg Bench Law* (MSR), the other complements that collation by an ordered sequence of the *Weichbild* articles that have not found their way into

41 Homeyer, *Extravaganten*, p. 236; Laband, *Magdeburger Rechtsquellen*, p. 100; and Kutrzeba, *Historia źródeł*, p. 205.

42 Art historians have backdated the origin of the manuscript to the first quarter of the 14th century. Cf. Zofia Ameisenowa, *Rękopisy i pierwodruki iluminowane Biblioteki Jagiellońskiej* [Manuscripts and Illuminated Incunabula in the Jagiellonian University Library] (Wrocław – Kraków, 1958), pp. 109–110; and Dariusz Tabor, *Malarstwo książkowe na Śląsku w XIV wieku* [The Art of Book Illustration in Silesia in the 14th Century] (Kraków, 2008), p. 265.

43 Kałużniacki, "Die polnische Recension", pp. 270–271, Note 1.

44 Wisłocki, *Inwentarz*, pp. 67–68; Włodek, *Catalogus Codicum*, pp. 159–162; Oppitz, *Deutsche Rechtsbücher*, No. 846, p. 614; Ebel and Schelling, *Das lateinische lübische Recht*, pp. 95–96; and Ilpo Tapani Piirainen, Winfried Waßer, eds., *Der Sachsenspiegel aus Oppeln und Krakau*, (Schriften der Stiftung Haus Oberschlesien. Landeskundliche Reihe) 10 (Berlin, 1996), pp. 13–15. See also Ilpo Tapani Piirainen, "Der *Sachsenspiegel* von Conrad von Oppeln und Rechtshandschriften in Breslau", in: *Die Anfänge des Schrifttums in Oberschlesien bis zum Frühhumanismus*, ed. Gerhard Kosellek, (Tagungsreihe der Stiftung Haus Oberschlesien) 7 (Frankfurt am Main *et al.*, 1997), pp. 241–244.

45 It contains: 1) Indices (*regesta*) (f. 1–5); 2) *Das Landrecht* in Latin (k. 6r–47v), 3) *Das Lübische Recht* (the Lübeck Law in German) (f. 47v–53v); 4) *Das Lehnrecht* in Latin (f. 54r–78r); 5) an extract from the German *Weichbild* (f. 80r–87r–Articles 6–18 (the *Constitution of Courts*); 6) *Das Landrecht* in German (f. 87r–114r); 7) an extract from the *Weichbildchronik* about the creation of the world (*Weichbildchronik*, f. 114r and v); 8) the *Weichbild* (f. 114v–133v); 9) and *Das Lehnrecht* in German (f. 133v–158v).

the MSR. The preparation of the compilations would have been impossible without access to a source other than the *Weichbild* – in all likelihood, a copy of the *Magdeburg Bench Law*. There can also be little doubt about the key role of the Cracow MS, given the identical rubrics in the provisions borrowed first from *Magdeburg's Legal Instructions for Wrocław* of 1295 and a characteristic amplification of Article 1.[46] Taking these clues into account, it can be argued that the Cracow MS was the base of a text (which no longer survives) used later to produce the compilation of MS BJ 170a – probably in Silesia, possibly in Opole.[47] This scenario cannot be ruled out, even though it envisages the *Weichbild* being taken back from Małopolska to Silesia. Yet a u-turn of this kind was not without precedent. After all, the Magdeburg *ortyle* – originally addressed to Cracow – ended up in compilations used outside Małopolska,[48] and equally, the path of the *Weichbild* of the Żagań MS was far from straight.

2.3 *The Amplified* Weichbild*: Baworowscy MS (BN 12607) and the Żagań MS (II Q 4)*

In his studies of the history of *Weichbild*, Laband stresses the importance of the bilingual 15th-century Żagań MS (II Q 4) from the Wrocław University Library. However, it is not the only bilingual legal codex produced in the late Middle Ages. Manuscript BN 12607, held by the National Library, also hails from the 15th century and contains an assortment of Magdeburg *ortyle* in both German and Latin, as well as a bilingual *Sachsenspiegel*.

In fact, MS BN 12607, which used to be part of the Baworowscy Collection in Lviv', contains an array of legal texts in addition to the staple rule books – the *Weichbild* and the *Sachsenspiegel*.[49] So far, the most accurate list of MS BN 12607 contents has been presented by Friedrich Ebel and Renate Schelling. It is reproduced with minor corrections[50] and additional information about the structure of the manuscript in Table 5.

46 Appendix 3, No. 301.

47 Piirainen and Waßer, *Der Sachsenspiegel aus Oppeln*, pp. 13 and 27.

48 Laband, *Magdeburger Rechstsquellen*, pp. 98–99; and Jacob F. Behrend, *Die Magdeburger Fragen* (Berlin, 1865), p. x.

49 Oppitz's Catalogue, No. 1454, p. 823. Cf. Ebel and Schelling, *Das lateinische lübische Recht*, p. 102; and Jerzy Kaliszuk and Sławomir Szyller, eds., *Inwentarz rękopisów do połowy XVI wieku w zbiorach Biblioteki Narodowej* [Inventory of Manuscripts (until the Mid-16th Century) in the National Library Collections] (Inwentarze Rękopisów Biblioteki Narodowej) 3 (Warszawa, 2012), pp. 193–194.

50 The authors make no distinction between the *Weichbild* and the *Sachsenspiegel*.

TABLE 5 Contents of Baworowscy MS (BN 12607)

No.	Current folio numbering	Notes
1.	1r	instructions in Polish and German
2.	1v	judgments of the High Court of German Law at the Royal Castle in Cracow
3.	2r–11v	'Oaths of guilds and members of the City Council; some records of the church authorities'[a]
4.	12ra–14vb	digest (*regesta*) of the articles of the Meißen Law
5.	15ra–26rb	digest (*regesta*) of the articles of the *Weichbild* and the *Sachsenspiegel*
6.	26va–26vb	German *ortyl* (*Urteil*) concerning *gerada*
7.	27ra–61vb	the *Weichbild*
8.	62ra–158vb	the *Sachsenspiegel*
9.	158vb–167vb	Magdeburg judgments (*ortyle/Urteile*)
10.	168ra–217rb	the *Decretum Gratiani*
11.	217rb–255ra	Decretals of Gregory IX, *explicit*: taken down on 17 June 1437
12.	255ra–256va	Digest of the Decretals
13.	256va–258v	the Lübeck Law (das Lübische Recht)
14.	258v	*recepta*
15.	258v–260v	Treatise on Inheritance and Marriage Law
16.	262r–263r	Joannes Andreae, *Lectura arboris consanguinitatis*
17.	263r–263v	two cases of consanguinity
18.	264ra–360vb	*Blume des Sachsenspiegels* (legal manual)

a Jerzy Kaliszuk and Sławomir Szyller, eds., *Inwentarz rękopisów do połowy XVI wieku w zbiorach Biblioteki Narodowej* [Inventory of Manuscripts (until the mid-16th Century) in the National Library Collections] (Inwentarze Rękopisów Biblioteki Narodowej) 3 (Warszawa, 2012), p. 193.

The Baworowscy MS (BN 12607) is a patchwork of texts written in more than one hand. It includes a digest (*regesta*) of the articles of the Meißen Law, a digest (*regesta*) of the articles of the *Weichbild* and the *Sachsenspiegel* in Latin translation, and a group of texts made up of the *Weichbild*, the *Sachsenspiegel*, and the *ortyle* written by three copyists. According to Ebel and Schelling, the sequence of the *ortyle* in the Baworowscy MS is nearly identical to their arrangement in the Opatów MS (Oss.) and can be connected with the Cracow collection of manuscripts of the Jagiellonian Library Shelfmark 399 (BJ 399).[51] The composition date of the *Weichbild* in the Baworowscy MS is unknown. The *explicit* on the last leaf of the Decretals of Gregory IX (1437) is not telling in this regard, as it belongs to a different quire than the one with the *Weichbild*, the *Sachsenspiegel*, and the *ortyle*.

The Baworowscy MS is a superb collection, one part of which – namely, a bilingual *Weichbild*, the *Sachsenspiegel*, and German-language *ortyle* – used to function separately as a manuscript of at least 140 leaves. It was then supplemented with a dedicated digest (*regesta*) written exclusively in German and, successively, with other texts, up to the point at which the manuscript gained its present bulk. One of the most eye-catching items of this collection is a Latin index of the articles of the *Weichbild* and the *Sachsenspiegel*. Contrary to the common practice of citing rubrics, it lists with exemplary precision the initial phrase of each article, together with the number of the leaf where it can be found (f. 15ra–26rb). This pagination, which starts with the first *Weichbild* leaf and ends with the *ortyle*, is an additional, conspicuous marker of the initially independent functioning of this part of the codex. The index is heavily glossed and cross-referenced: the information about the content of individual articles is compressed into headline phrases. Since this indexing does not cover the *ortyle*, we may surmise that the glossator did not know German well enough to do the job.

This may also have been a factor in his handling of the *Weichbild*. He put the Latin text first and had the matching article in the original German follow it. There are, however, some inconsistencies: for example, Article 3 is missing from the German text. That may have been caused by the copyist's error: he divided Article 2 into two and placed those parts after the Latin Articles 2 and 3. Another irregularity can be found around Article 48. The copyist added to it a Latin translation of the relevant Magdeburg *ortyl* and left some room below for the original German text. However, instead of then filling that gap, he decided to refer the reader to Folio XXI (f. 47v). There, in an annex to Article 74, we do find a German *ortyl* concerning inheritance, but it is hardly pertinent to the matter in hand (Article 48 is about inheritance law). Moreover, the Latin translation of the *ortyl* attached to Article 74 matches the adjacent German text, but differs from the Latin text appended to Article 48. Yet another editorial

51 Friedrich Ebel, "Nachträge zu Homeyer – Borchling – Gierke – Eckhardt: Die deutschen Rechtsbücher des Mittelalters und ihre Handschriften", *Zeitschrift der Savigny-Stiftung für Rechtsgeschichte. Germanistische Abteilung* 99 (1982), 312; Ebel and Schelling, *Das lateinische lübische Recht*, p. 102, Note 26.

intervention made for no apparent reason is the shortening of Article 90 in the German text.[52] At no point, however, can there be any doubt that the Latin text was the author's (or rather, the copyist's) primary concern and that he took great care to preserve its integrity. If his preference for Latin is taken as an indication of the manuscript's provenance, Poland under the Jagellons rather than Silesia is a more fitting place of origin. At the same time, the omissions suggest that the compiler (copyist) of the manuscript could not have been the author of the Latin translation of the *ortyle* annexed to the *Weichbild*.

The Żagań (Sagan) MS is a massive codex of 539 leaves. It is made up of several parts which are dated back to the 15th century.[53] The first such part, which is of particular interest to this study, is written in a rather careless cursive hand and is the work of one scribe (f. 1–134). The uniform hand and its distinct foliation are clear indications that it used to function separately from the rest of the codex. What has also attracted attention is the arrangement of its constituent texts. Laband was the first to note that the three key texts of the Saxon-Magdeburg Law appear in this manuscript in the same order as in Łaski's *Statutes*.[54] Under the heading Liber I, the collection opens with the *Weichbild* (f. 1r–36r), immediately followed on the verso of the first quire by the *Landrecht* from the *Sachsenspiegel* (f. 36v–95v). The third section, the *Lehnrecht* from the *Sachsenspiegel* (f. 98r–125v), is separated from the *Landrecht* by two short texts, 'Von der Herren Geburt' (f. 96) and the *Weichbildchronik*, detached from the text of the *Weichbild* itself (f. 96–97). These are followed by Pope Gregory XI's bull *Salvator humani generis* and an alphabetical subject index. It is worth noting that other monuments of German law, like the *Meißen Law* and the *Sachsenspiegel* (*regesta*), can be found in other parts of the Żagań MS.

The author of the first part of the Żagań MS arranged the Latin and German text of the *Weichbild* in parallel, giving the Latin version pride of place. The German articles are often curtailed or even left out. In the whole manuscript, there is only one instance of a German text standing alone. This error of omission is most likely due to inattention on the part of the copyist (Article 9 with a Magdeburg *ortyl* attachment; in this section, article numbering is according to Żagań MS), but it can also serve as proof that the compiler of the Żagań *Weichbild* MS was not the translator of the attached *ortyle*. Moreover, in a number of cases, he made considerable alterations to the German text. Some articles are omitted (Articles 72, 73, 78, and 79, following the MS Gn. pagination); some are excerpted (Articles 1, 66, and 107); and a significant number of

52 Cf. Appendix 2, No. 193.

53 In Oppitz's *Catalogue*, No. 268, pp. 411–413.

54 Laband, *Magdeburger Rechtsquellen*, pp. 96–98.

them appear in the manuscript in a severely curtailed form (Articles 2, 4, 6, 14, 33, 70, 75, 76, 83, 86, 88, 90, 91, 93, 97, 100, 103, and 105).[55] Occasionally, important details do not match up (Articles 14, 26, 28, and 106). More often, there are minor differences between the German and the Latin texts, such as, for example, the addition of *Daz selbe hat der man seyn teil dem, der ym ebin burtig ist* in Article 28. The phrase neither occurs in the Latin translation nor in other German texts (see Nr. 342 in Appendix 3). Another notable feature of this part of the Żagań MS is the composition of the rubrics. The German rubrics seem to have been in place first, while the Latin ones have the appearance of being filled in later (and the job has not been completed). The primacy of Latin in Part I of the Żagań MS is a strong indication that its place of origin should be sought outside Silesia – probably in Małopolska, but possibly in Cracow. If this conjecture is allowed to stand, the follow-up argument is incontrovertible: the manuscript must have been *brought to* Silesia and eventually deposited at the Augustinian Abbey Library at Żagań.

At any rate, there can be no doubt about the features that the two manuscripts (Baworowscy, BN 12607 and Żagań MS II Q 4) have in common – that is, parallel arrangement of the Latin and the German text, the primacy of Latin, and the use of the *ortyle* in conjunction with the articles of the Saxon-Magdeburg Law. Laband notes that the arrangement of the texts in the Żagań MS is identical to that of the Cracow MS, and for the difference in the number of articles, Laband offers the explanation that the compiler of latter simply divided one of them into three (cf. the Concordance Table in Appendix 1). He also points out that the Latin articles are glossed with notes that reappear in Łaski's *Statutes*, although not all of the alterations acknowledged in the latter can be found in the Żagań MS. These observations led him to formulate a thoroughly justified conjecture that the Żagań MS was an intermediary between the so-called Konrad of Opole's compilation and Łaski's *Statutes*. Laband has no problems with explaining the origin of some of the supplementary material in the Żagań MS and the statutes – it comes from collections of Magdeburg judgments (*ortyle*), like the Dresden or the Toruń MS. Moreover, nearly all of them can be found in the *Magdeburger Fragen* and certain other manuscripts. In fact, only one of them is missing from the German-language collection of *ortyle* in MS BJ 399.[56] Laband reiterates Jacob Friedrich Behrend's argument that

55 For example, the following passage is missing from the German counterpart of Article 88: … *quod facere potest incontinenti si vult, aut per sex ebdomadas in iudicio sculteti. Sin autem vir iuramentum unica manu prestare debet, quod in eodem oportet facere iudicio.*

56 Laband, *Magdeburger Rechtsquellen*, p. 98.

all those collections contain *ortyle* addressed to Cracow[57] and concludes that they all stem from the Cracow collection of the Magdeburg judgments. This would mean, in effect, that the *Weichbild* was augmented with *ortyle* from that very collection.[58]

This also means that further studies of the Latin manuscripts of the Saxon-Magdeburg Law have to address the following questions: 1) does the German text of the *Weichbild* in Baworowscy and Żagań manuscripts stem from the Cracow MS? 2) Can Laband and Behrend's argument about the origin of the *ortyle* attached to the *Weichbild* be corroborated by more precise evidence? 3) What are the reasons for the augmentation of the *Weichbild*, and what were the circumstances in which the augmentation took place?

2.3.1 Problems of Filiation of the Cracow MS

The *Weichbild* in the Baworowscy MS (BN 12607) is fairly close to the text in the Cracow MS (BJ 169). However, the extensive alterations in the German text of the Żagań MS (II Q 4) render comparisons with other sources extremely difficult. Nevertheless, it is possible to identify passages in which a characteristic feature of the Cracow MS is mirrored by the Żagań MS and Baworowscy MS (exclusively). One such example is provided by a phrase from Article 22 of the Cracow MS (for an in-depth comparison, see Table 6).

Moreover, in none but these three manuscripts (Cracow MS, Baworowscy MS and Żagań MS) does the text of Article 88[59] leave out the exemplification of the offence, that is, insulting a member of the jury (the Bench).[60] Article 80[61] about the *Burggraf*'s judicial powers leaves out the wording of the original source, which mentions exclusively the *Burggraf* of Magdeburg.[62] Manuscripts BJ 169 and BN 12607 also share a passage about the aldermen's right to convoke an assembly (*burding*): "Di ratman legen ir burtdinc uz swenne so si wellen mit der wizzegisten rate". This is a highly significant addition to the original German text; its counterpart can be found solely in the corresponding Latin texts.[63]

These examples show that the Cracow MS indeed influenced the Żagań and the Baworowscy manuscripts, although it was not alone in that role. The impact of other sources is manifested in the numerous differences between the

57 Behrend, *Die Magdeburger Fragen*, pp. X–XI.
58 Laband, *Magdeburger Rechtsquellen*, p. 99.
59 Numbering of MS BJ 169.
60 Cf. Appendix 3, No. 475.
61 Numbering of MS BJ 169.
62 Cf. *ibid.*, nr 455.
63 Due to the thorough revision of Article 1 in the Żagań MS, that text cannot be included in this comparison.

TABLE 6 Comparison of Article 22 with matching phrases in German manuscripts. Numbering of articles follows the MS BJ 169

Legal Instructions for Wrocław of 1261	Cracow MS BJ 169	Baworowscy MS BN 12607	Żagań MS II Q 4	Henryków MS II F 8	BJ 170a	Wawel MS BJ 168
[32] Swer so einen *schephenen* beschildet uf der banc, *her gewinnet sine bůze,* drizich schillinge, vnde die richtere sin gewette.	[22] Swer so einen *scheppfen* shildit uf der banc, *der muz dem selbin sheppfen buze geben* drizic shillinge und der richter gewinnet sin gewette.	[28] Wer so einen *scheppen* schildet off der banc, *der muß dem salbin scheppin busse geben* dreizig schillinge und der richter gewinnet sein gewette.	[24] *in initio.* Wer einen schildet off der banck, *der muß dem selbigen scheppen busse gaben* XXX schilli[n]g[e] undderrichter gewynet seyn gewette.	[22] Wer so eynen *scheppen* schildet uff der bank, *der scheppe gewynnet seyne busse* dreisig Schillinge und der Richter sein gewette.	XX. Swer so einen *scheppen* beschildet uf der bank, *der gewinnet sine buze* drizic schillinge, und der richter sin gewette.	[24] *in initio.* Swer so einin *scheppin* beschildit uf der banc, *h*[*er*] *gewinnit sine buse* drisic schillinge und der richter sin gewette.

Cracow MS and the text of the other two manuscripts. Not all the alterations in 'junior' texts are due to borrowing – many of them could well have been corrections and revisions that are part of a natural evolution of a text. Nevertheless, there are passages in the latter that can be traced to the old sources of the *Weichbild*, the *Magdeburg Bench Law*, and the Henryków MS. The Henryków MS is independent of the Cracow MS, although they both have a common base. Two examples of such an alternate affiliation are listed in the concordance in Appendix 3.[64] They show up against the backdrop of omissions in the Cracow MS, probably caused by scribal error. Although the slips are quite inconspicuous, they are not copied. The fact that the correct version appears both in the Baworowscy MS and the Żagań MS 4 is clear sign that these manuscripts rely on a source that is closer to the *Weichbild* prototype than the Cracow MS. That prototype must have functioned in the territory of the Kingdom of Poland by the middle of the 14th century at the latest, or otherwise the defects of the

64 Cf. Appendix 3, Nos. 348 and 355.

Cracow MS would have left their mark on the Latin *Weichbild*. In other words, the Cracow MS could not have been the sole base of the Latin translation of the *Weichbild*. The evidence examined here provides proof of the indebtedness of both the Baworowscy MS and the Żagań MS to the Cracow MS; it also points to the functioning in early 14th-century Poland of another German text, independent of and closer to the 'original' *Weichbild* than the Cracow MS.

2.3.2 Provenance of the Supplements

The key role in establishing the provenance of the *ortyle* is played by Article 14 of the *Weichbild*, which concerns itself with the material circumstances of wives and widows.[65] It is supplemented with two *ortyle*, one after the other – an arrangement which is by no means insignificant. Laband's research demonstrates that the same pair of judgments appear in the Dresden and the Toruń manuscripts,[66] whereas the second *ortyl* is absent from all other texts except MS BJ 399. The latter manuscript, however, could not have been the source of the augmentation, because it does not feature the first of the two texts. One way to solve this riddle would be go through non-systematic collections of *ortyle*, as well as those that are included in Jacob F. Behrend's *Die Magdeburger Fragen*, and check them for the presence of the 'control pair'.

While Old Chełmno Law had to be ruled out as a likely source,[67] the two *ortyle* did appear in some other manuscripts. One such manuscript is the *Poznań Book of Magdeburg and Meißen Law* (in German), edited and published by Witold Maisel.[68] Another is the Latin translation of the collection of the *ortyle* in the Żegota Pauli's MS (BJ 4405).[69] However, the translation does not match the text of the *ortyle* in the Latin *Weichbild*. It is therefore impossible that the compiler of the *Weichbild* took advantage of that earlier Latin translation. What can also be said with great certainty is that the Żegota Pauli's MS is closely associated with Cracow, and it is highly likely that both the translation of the *ortyle's* collection as well as the writing of this manuscript took place in

65 Cf. Appendix 2, No. 44.

66 Laband, *Magdeburger Rechtsquellen*, p. 99. The collection of texts from the Dresden MS was published by Wasserschleben, *Sammlung*, pp. 80–120.

67 The Chełmno Law can offer hardly any material to supplement the text of the *Weichbild*. I have reached this conclusion after consulting the 1838 German edition of *Der Alte Kulm*: Karl Ch. Leman, ed., *Das Alte Kulmische Recht, mit einem Wörterbuche* (Berlin, 1838); and the Polish translation from 1985: Witold Maisel and Zbigniew Zdrójkowski, eds., Andrzej Bzdęga and Anna Gaca, trans., *Prawo starochełmińskie 1584 (1394)*, (Teksty Pomników Prawa Chełmińskiego w Przekładach Polskich) 2 (Toruń, 1985), p. 8.

68 Witold Maisel, ed., *Poznańska księga prawa magdeburskiego i miśnieńskiego* [The Poznań Book of Magdeburg-Meißen Law] (Wrocław, 1964), IV.150 and 151, pp. 144–145.

69 See Chapter 1.3.14.

Cracow.[70] But the base of the *ortyle's* translation in the Żegota Pauli's MS could not be MS BJ 399. Yet in spite of indisputable similarities, noted by Stanisław Estreicher,[71] the two manuscripts differ considerably. One of the differences is the lack in MS BJ 399 of the second of the two 'control' *ortyle*. Yet it could not be a redaction of German *ortyle* that is annexed to the Baworowscy MS at the back of the *Sachsenspiegel*, because it has none of the supplements that we find in the *Weichbild*. In effect, we have to assume the existence of another base text, possibly a prototype of the Pilzno Codex of German-language *ortyle*, edited by Władysław Wisłocki. That collection contains both 'control' *ortyle* (Articles cxxxxv and cxxxxvi, numbering in Wisłocki's edition).[72] It can be taken for granted that Pilzno received its collection of *ortyle* from Cracow. It should be noted that all the *ortyle* attached to the *Weichbild* are included in the earliest Polish translation of *ortyle* published by Józef Reczek and Wacław Twardzik. This Polish translation follows the arrangement of the Latin translation of the *ortyle* in the Żegota Pauli's MS,[73] which also includes all the ortyle from the *Weichbild*.

As a conclusion, it can be assumed that the *ortyle* in the *Weichbild* came from the German-language collection associated with Cracow, which could be the base for the German-language Pilzno Codex and for the oldest Polish translation. This collection was also close to the Latin collection of *ortyle* in MS BJ 4405. In all, a complete list of *ortyle* incorporated into the *Weichbild* includes – in addition to those identified by Laband, that is, the *ortyle* annexed to Articles 7, 14, 48, 68, 73, 74, 90, 95, and 97 of the *Weichbild* (numbers following the Gniezno MS, see Chapter 1.3.1.)[74] – those *ortyle* that are supplemented to Articles 4, 9, 13, 48, 58, 90, and 105.[75] In this way, Laband's broad conjecture that the augmentation of the *Weichbild* is connected with the creation of collections of Magdeburg *ortyle* in Cracow is proven correct.

70 See Stanisław Estreicher, "Nieznane teksty ortyli magdeburskich" [Recently Discovered Texts of the Magdeburg *ortyle*], in: *Studia staropolskie. Księga ku czci Aleksandra Brücknera* [Old Polish Studies: A Festschrift in Honour of Aleksander Brückner] (Kraków, 1928), *passim*.

71 Estreicher, "Nieznane teksty", p. 121. It is also worth noting that the compiler of this Weichbild did not use the Latin translation of the *ortyle*, known from the Działyńscy Codex I and based on a shorter German-language collection, which has been preserved in MS BJ 170b.

72 Władysław Wisłocki, "Kodeks pilzneński ortylów magdeburskich" [The Pilzno Codex of Magdeburg *ortyle*], *Rozprawy Akademii Umiejętności* 2 (1874), 159.

73 Józef Reczek and Wacław Twardzik, *Najstarsze staropolskie tłumaczenie ortyli* magdeburskich [The Earliest Polish Translation of the Magdeburg ortyle] 1 (Warszawa, 1970), p. 18.

74 Appendix 2, Nos. 24, 44, 107, 158, 163, 165, 198.

75 Appendix 2, Nos.15, 29, 30, 38, 142, 193, 200, 217.

2.3.3 The Reasons and Circumstances of the Augmentation of the *Weichbild* with Sample *ortyle*

Before we answer the question of why a law code like the *Weichbild* came to be augmented with supplementary material (*ortyle*), it is worth taking a closer look at the thematic range of this innovation. As it happens, some provisions seem to be more susceptible to augmentation than others. Such provisions are those that are concerned with: surety in cases of killing and wounding (Article 7); the legal status of guests (aliens) (Article 9); pledge (Article 13); dower (Article 14); representation of heritable grandchildren (Article 48); time limits in oath taking (Article 68); inheritance rules (Article 73); duty of care (Article 74); aldermen's court (Article 90); inheritance of goods hidden away from the taxman (Article 95); and dropping charges (Article 97).[76] It is no accident that most of those situations were regarded as key issues in the administration of justice and were subject to regulations in 14th-century municipal by-laws (*wilkierze*, Ger. *Willküren*) and royal privileges for Cracow.[77] As the *ortyle* appeared at those points where such problems were addressed, it is only reasonable to assume that the augmentation of the *Weichbild* was driven by pragmatic concerns.

The time at which the augmentation occurred is unknown. We do not even know whether the *ortyle* were attached first to the German or the Latin text, or whether it happened simultaneously. Apart from Łaski's *Commune incliti*, there are five extant *Weichbild* texts augmented with Magdeburg *ortyle*, three of which are only in Latin (two of them in Latin and German). The circumstances in which the process of expanding the *Weichbild* began are very difficult to make out, as there is no manuscript with an unalloyed body of an augmented German text. Yet, the fact that we do not have such a source is no

76 Laband, *Magdeburger Rechtsquellen*, p. 98; and Bischoff, "Beiträge zur Geschichte", pp. 360–362. Cf. the following records in Appendix 2: cf. *supra* notes 73 and 74. Numbers of articles according to the MS Gn.

77 Michał Patkaniowski, *Krakowska rada miejska w średnich wiekach* [The Cracow City Council in the Middle Ages] (Kraków, 1934), pp. 42–46 and Chapter 9 (Legislative Functions of the Cracow City Council); Marcin Starzyński, *Krakowska rada miejska w średniowieczu* [The Cracow City Council in the Middle Ages] (Kraków, 2010), pp. 100–120 and Appendix 2 "Medieval by-laws (wilkierze) of the City of Cracow"; Maciej Mikuła, *Prawodawstwo króla i sejmu dla małopolskich miast królewskich (1386–1572). Studium z dziejów rządów prawa w Polsce* [Royal and Parliamentary Legislation for the Royal Towns of Małopolska (1386–1572): A Study in the History of the Rule of Law in Poland] (Kraków, 2014), *passim*; and Maciej Mikuła, "Statuty prawa spadkowego w miastach polskich prawa magdeburskiego (do końca XVI wieku)" [Inheritance Statutes in Polish Towns under Magdeburg Law (until the End of the 16th Century)], *Z Dziejów Prawa* 7 (15) (2014), 33–63.

proof of it never having existed. At any rate, this situation leaves us in the realm of speculation and hypotheticals.

The augmentation of the Latin text could have been done by juxtaposing the German text – already supplemented with *ortyle* – and the Latin *Weichbild*, as had happened in the case of the Baworowscy and the Żagań manuscripts. Another possible scenario would have the augmentation take place simultaneously. The author had at hand both the German and the Latin *Weichbild*, put matching portions of either text next to each other, and attached to some of them the appropriate *ortyle*, which he had to translate into Latin. Although we know of no extant German-language manuscript with an augmented text, its existence cannot be ruled out. A third scenario in which the *ortyle* would have been initially attached to the Latin text is utterly implausible for one simple reason: the Latin translations of the collections of *ortyle* in the Żegota Pauli's MS and in the Działyńscy Codex I do not fit the adjacent passages in the *Weichbild*. In short, they could not have been used to supplement the text of *Ius municipale Magdeburgense*. For the third scenario to work, one person would have to translate the German *ortyle* into Latin and attach them to the Latin *Weichbild*, and then another person would have to go through the whole body of text again to adjust its Latin and German parts, to find the right German-language *ortyle* and fit them in the German-language *Weichbild*. This is too complicated and frankly, does not make a great deal of sense.

Both the tracing of the origin of the *ortyle* to an unknown Cracow collection and the fact of their being attached to a German-language *Weichbild* associated with the Cracow City Council manuscript give weight to the conjecture that Cracow was the place where the augmentation of the *Weichbild* began. Let me also note that if an interest in a practice-oriented German law book was limited to just a few bigger Polish towns, in that circle, Cracow would be the most likely sponsor of such an ambitious initiative.

2.4 *Summary: Evolution of the German Text and the Problem of Adaptation of the Magdeburg Law in the Kingdom of Poland*

Let me now recapitulate the main points of the argument. The German *Weichbild* representative of the Silesian-Małopolska compilation was produced in Silesia in 1295–1308. The earliest extant text in the manuscript is not identical to the archetype which was the base of both the Cracow and the Henryków manuscripts. Patterns of filiation link the Cracow MS to the next generation of German texts, like the extant Wawel MS, MS BJ 170a, the Baworowscy MS, and the Żagań MS. At some point, one of those texts was augmented with a selection of Magdeburg judgments from a collection of *ortyle* created in Cracow. These judgments were also translated into Latin and added to the Latin *Weichbild*. The circumstances of this momentous development remain obscure. Of the various scenarios, only one can be definitely ruled out, namely, that the Latin *Weichbild* was the first to be augmented, and the German *Weichbild* followed suit.

Although the dynamics of the German-language texts of the Silesian-Małopolska compilation were driven by the inclusion of selected Magdeburg *ortyle*, which most likely took place in Cracow, the main axis of the evolution remained in the area of Latin texts. The following sections of this chapter will analyse those texts, offering not only a detailed description of their characteristics, but also trying to deduce who may have used them.

3 Latin Manuscripts and Jan Łaski's Printed Text

Studies of manuscripts with Latin texts of the Magdeburg *Weichbild* began more than 150 years ago, and their number has been growing steadily. Most of research effort is focused on in-depth analyses of the sources and the creation of new descriptive catalogues. I have relied primarily on a catalogue of manuscripts of German law compiled by Ulrich-Dieter Oppitz. Nearly all of the manuscripts discussed here are listed either in Oppitz's main work or its supplements. The two items that are outside the scope of Oppitz's catalogue are MS RK 45/28 from the Library of the Catholic Seminary at Kielce[78] and MS BOZ 90 from the National Library in Warsaw.[79] In the course of my research, I have built a database of 18 manuscripts, with 19 copies of the Silesian-Małopolska *Weichbild*, one digest (*regesta*) from the *Pleszew City Council Records* published by Witold Maisel, and one printed text: Jan Łaski's *Commune incliti*. Unfortunately, a significant number of manuscripts were destroyed during the Second World War, especially in 1944, during the suppression of the Warsaw Rising (the losses are duly acknowledged in Oppitz's catalogue).[80] One important source, the Sanok

78 Jerzy Wolny, "Inventaire des manuscrits théologiques médiévaux de la bibliothèque du chapitre à Kielce", *Mediaevalia Philosophica Polonorum* 16 (1971), 43–85; Maciej Mikuła, "Das sächsisch-magdeburgische Recht in den Manuskripten der Bibliothek des Priesterseminars in Kielce, Signatur RK 45/28 – Ergänzung zu Deutsche Rechtsbücher des Mittelalters", *Zeitschrift der Savigny-Stiftung für Rechtsgeschichte: Germanistische Abteilung* 1/137 (2020), 505–510.

79 Kaliszuk and Szyller, *Inwentarz rękopisów*, p. 52.

80 Some of the lost manuscripts from the National Library collection are listed in Oppitz's Catalogue. Cf. records 1463, 1466, 1470, 1472, 1473 and 1480. Monographic studies: Jerzy Kaliszuk, *Codices deperditi. Średniowieczne rękopisy łacińskie Biblioteki Narodowej utracone w czasie II wojny światowej*, [Codices deperditi: Medieval Latin Manuscripts of the National Library Lost during World War II], Vol. 1: *Dzieje i charakterystyka kolekcji*

MS, has vanished without trace. However, as a fairly detailed description of its contents can be found in the Proceedings of the Academy of Sciences in Vienna from the year 1886, I have decided to include that manuscript in my overview.

3.1 *Gniezno MS (1359) in the Archdiocesan Archives of Gniezno, Gn. 104*[81]

The Gniezno MS is one of the documents analysed closely by Zygfryd Rymaszewski in his studies of the *Sachsenspiegel*.[82] Dated 1359, it is a fairly close copy of Konrad of Sandomierz's autograph, though not identical to it (see below in this section). It is the work of scribe the Mikołaj of Cieszyn, who makes it explicitly clear (on three occasions) that this translation of the Magdeburg Law from German into Latin was conducted by Konrad of Sandomierz at the request of Mikołaj of Pacanów, a burgher of Sandomierz. A meticulous description of the manuscript by Stanisław Estreicher can be found in Father Tadeusz Trzciński's catalogue of medieval manuscripts in the Chapter Library at Gniezno.[83] The manuscript is written in a neat hand in two columns. The articles are headed by rubrics in red and numbers. In his account of the contents of this manuscript, Stanisław Estreicher lists seven items. The volume begins with an incipit to *Iuris provincialis* (*Sachenspiegel*, f. 1–2v), followed by the Prologue and the main text of the Latin *Sachsenspiegel – versio Sandomiriensis* (up to f. 80v). The next four items in Estreicher's description are in fact constituent parts of the Magdeburg *Weichbild*: the incipit to *Ius*

[A History and Description of the Collection] (Wrocław, 2016), p. 105, 192 and 520; 2.2: *Katalog rękopisów utraconych* [A Catalogue of the Lost Manuscripts] (Wrocław, 2016), No 1153, 1207 [series: Dziedzictwo Kulturowe po Skasowanych Klasztorach (Cultural Heritage of the Dissolved Monasteries), ed. Marek Derwich, 8/1, 8/2.2]. See also Alexander Rogatchevski's account of his search for the lost manuscripts of the Saxon-Magdeburg Law in the archives and libraries of St Petersburg: Alexander Rogatchevski, "Das sächsisch-magdeburgische Rechtsdenkmäler und verwandte Quellen in den St. Petersburger Handschriftensammlungen", in: *Grundlagen für ein neues Europa. Das Magdeburger und Lübecker Recht in Spätmittelalter und Früher Neuzeit*, eds. Heiner Lück, Matthias Puhle, and Andreas Ranft, Quellen und Forschungen zur Geschichte Sachsen-Anhalts, 6 (Köln – Weimar – Wien, 2009), pp. 268–269.

81 Hereafter referred to as Gn.; Oppitz, *Deutsche Rechtsbücher*, No. 573.

82 Rymaszewski, *Łacińskie teksty Landrechtu Zwierciadła Saskiego w Polsce. Versio*, pp. 76–77; and Oppitz, *Deutsche Rechtsbücher*, No. 573.

83 [Tadeusz] Trzciński, *Średniowieczne rękopisy biblioteki kapitulnej w Gnieźnie* [Medieval Manuscripts in the Cathedral Chapter Library at Gniezno], (Rocznik Towarzystwa Przyjaciół Nauk Poznańskiego) 35 (Poznań, 1909), pp. 307–310. The manuscript is mentioned in Jadwiga Rył, "Biblioteka katedralna w Gnieźnie" [Cathedral Chapter Library at Gniezno], *Archiwa, Biblioteki i Muzea Kościelne* 33 (1976), 278; and Jadwiga Rył, "Biblioteka katedralna w Gnieźnie. Aneks" [Cathedral Chapter Library at Gniezno. Appendix], *Archiwa, Biblioteki i Muzea Kościelne* 36 (1978), 238.

municipale (f. 82r–283v); articles of the *Weichbild* (83v–115v); the Jewish oath added to the *Weichbild* (f. 115v–116); and a fragment about the *Constitution of Courts* (f. 116v–121r), separated by *explicit* – the ending of the Book of Magdeburg Law (f. 116v). The whole text ends with *Conclusio libri*, which again mentions Konrad of Sandomierz. The scribe Mikołaj of Cieszyn added in the date on which he completed his writing, marked as the vigil of the Feast of the Holy Trinity A.D. 1359 (f. 121r–121v). This collection contains exclusively texts of urban law.

So far, the *Weichbild* in this manuscript has not been the subject of in-depth analysis. The need for such research was voiced by Laband.[84] Zygfryd Rymaszewski mentioned the Gniezno MS several times in his study of the *Sachsenspiegel*.[85] Some of its provisions dealing with issues of private law have been analysed in two recent articles.[86] As the earliest extant text of legal interest, it provides an important point of reference for other Latin sources. Its main text is glossed in what looks like 15th-century hand; the glosses are scant but not insignificant. Their presence indicates that the text of the Gniezno MS it is not identical to Konrad of Sandomierz's archetype. As has been recently observed, it is only in this manuscript and in the Działyńscy Codex I (MS Dział. I) that the text of Article 24 does not contain certain phrases which clarify the meaning of the provision concerning the validity of claims made by servants for payment for performance of services.[87] Moreover, in most texts, except MS Gn. and MS Dział. I, Articles 79 and 105 require the proof of the oath of one rather than seven individuals in claims regarding debt payment. A commentator on the Działyńscy Codex I amended that gloss, as did a user of the Gniezno MS (who added in the correct number of compurgators). This variant is peculiar to the two manuscripts, and it does not occur in other German texts.[88] It

84 Paul Laband, "Eine bisher unbekannte Rechtshandschrift", *Zeitschrift der Rechtsgeschichte* 11 (1873), pp. 50–51.

85 Rymaszewski, *Łacińskie teksty Landrechtu Zwierciadła Saskiego w Polsce. Versio*, esp. Table 6, p. 222.

86 Maciej Mikuła, "Modyfikacje łacińskich tekstów Weichbildu magdeburskiego a ewolucja prawa w średniowiecznych miastach polskich. Uwagi wstępne" [Modifications of Latin Texts of the Magdeburg *Weichbild* and the Evolution of Law in Medieval Polish Towns: An Introduction], in: *Acta Iuridico-Historica Pilsnensia*, 2012–2013 (published 2014; ed. Vilém Knoll), pp. 142–147; and Maciej Mikuła, "Die Modifizierung des Erb- und Familienrechts im Magdeburger Weichbildrecht (Einführung zum Thema)", in: *Judiciary and Society Between Privacy and Publicity*, ed. Danuta Janicka, 8th Conference on Legal History in the Baltic Sea Area, 3rd–6th September (Toruń, 2015), pp. 336–342.

87 Records 60, 174, and 216 in Appendix 2.

88 Rekords 341, 453, and 501 in Appendix 3.

was probably the copyist Mikołaj of Cieszyn who changed the wording of a faithful Latin translation of the German text (see Chapter 2.4.3.).

3.2 *St Petersburg MS (1367–1368) in the Library of the Russian Academy of Sciences in St Petersburg, F 143*[89]

The second earliest text of the *Weichbild* is part of MS F 143, dated 1367–1368. Its description can be found in a number of catalogues;[90] Laband included it in his preliminary analysis of landmark texts of German law.[91] In his earlier studies, of the *Weichbild* Laband made use of German texts and three Latin texts supplemented with *ortyle* (Opatów MS, Żagań MS, and Łaski's *Statutes*). After discovering MS F 143, he located its *Weichbild* in between the Cracow MS 169 and the complete text in Jan Łaski's *Statutes*.[92]

In its present form, the St Petersburg MS is a composite of two separate manuscripts, as shown by the collation of quires, the change of hand, and the size of margins. The first part contains a German-language *Sachsenspiegel*, copied by Franczek Lemberk from Lviv' and completed by 22 June 1367 (f. 1r–126v). The *Sachsenspiegel Landrecht* and *Lehnrecht* are preceded by rubric indices. Work on the *Sachsenspiegel* must have taken a long time, since the copying of Book II was not finished until 6 December 1367. The second part of the codex consists of two quires of 12 leaves each. It is written in a different hand, and the writing is very dense and fills all the available space on the page. The different origins of the two parts are indicated in a most conspicuous manner by the width of their margins. For example in Part One, folium 61 – with the first page of Book III of the *Sachsenspiegel* – the width of the left margin is in the range of 4.4–4.7 mm, the right margin (3.8–4.3 mm), the upper margin (3.4–3.8 mm), and the lower margin (5.2–5.3 mm); the irregularities are the effect of uneven edge cuts. Folium 127r with the first page of the *Weichbild* has narrower margins – the left margin – 3.2–3.4 mm; the right margin – 2.5–2.7 mm; the upper margin – 2.4–2.5 mm, and the lower margin – 4.9–5.1 mm. It is written in a neat hand, even though the script is small and dense. Each article, excepting

89 Hereafter referred to as F 143.

90 Oppitz, *Deutsche Rechtsbücher*, No. 931, pp. 647–648; Oppitz, "Ergänzungen zu *Deutsche Rechtsbücher des Mittelalters und ihre Handschriften*", *Zeitschrift der Savigny-Stiftung für Rechtsgeschichte: Germanistische Abteilung* 128 (2011), 448; and Alexander Rogatchevski, "Die sächsisch-magdeburgische Rechtsdenkmäler und verwandte Quellen in den St. Petersburger Handschriftensammlungen", in: *Grundlagen für ein neues Europa. Das Magdeburger und Lübecker Recht in Spätmittelalter und Früher Neuzeit*, eds. Heiner Lück, Matthias Puhle, and Andreas Ranft, Quellen und Forschungen zur Geschichte Sachsen-Anhalts, 6 (Köln – Weimar – Wien, 2009), p. 248, Note 29.

91 Laband, "Eine bisher unbekannte Rechtshandschrift", pp. 44–51.

92 *Ibid.*, pp. 50–51.

the first one, is rubricated in red ink, and the initials are two lines in height. At the top of Article 1, a space is left blank for an initial that was to be eight lines in height.

The first quire of Part Two contains the *Weichbild* (f. 127–134v) and a digest of the *Sachsenspiegel* (f. 135–138). The digest spills over to the pages of second quire, which also contains provisions of the Lübeck Law (f. 141) and a note concerning debt, written in another hand (f. 141). These are followed by *auctoritates legistice*, that is, legal maxims (f. 141v–142) and some official documents from Słupca. Notes dated 1455, 1459, 1466, and 1468 make reference to two mayors of Słupca: Marcin and Andrzej.[93] After a few pages which were left blank (f. 144–149v), there follows a note about the diversification of the punishment for theft depending on the circumstances of the case. As this overview suggests, the second part of volume functioned over a fairly long period as a repository of texts used for practical purposes. The copying of the *Weichbild* was completed on the *Invocavit* Sunday (16 February) of 1368 (f. 134v). Possibly, the fact that both parts of the manuscript were completed at about the same time was not accidental, and as the copying of the *Weichbild* was finished, the two manuscripts could be bound into one volume. Be that as it may, Part Two remains an autonomous collection of regulations assembled around the slightly trimmed *Weichbild* (Articles 31, 48, 55, 71, 94, 95, and 98 are left out) and digests of *Sachsenspiegel* and the Lübeck Law. The level of coherence of the two parts is hard to assess. Checking the cross-references added to some provisions of the *Weichbild* (Articles 3, 4, 10, 90, 97, 99, and 106) is not of much help, either. They all refer the reader to Book II or Book I (*II libro registro*), but only in the first three cases does the reference include the number of the relevant article – presumably of the *Sachsenspiegel*. And out of these, only one link connects provisions that have something in common (the reference from Article 10 of the *Weichbild* to Article 66 Book I of the German-language *Sachsenspiegel* in Part One).

3.3 *Mikołaj of Smogorzewo's MS (1421) in the National Library in Warsaw, BN 12600 III*[94]

Manuscript BN 12600 III, which used to be part of the Baworowscy Collection (MS 998) and is now held by the National Library (Acc. 9862), was compiled by

93 The catalogue of medieval manuscripts held in the Library of the Russian Academy of Sciences in St Petersburg refers to Słupsk, correct: Słupca (Ludmila I. Kiseleva, *Catalogue des manuscrits médiévaux en écriture latine de la Bibliothèque de l'Académie des Sciences de Russie de Saint-Pétersbourg* (Paris, 2005), p. 128).

94 Hereafter referred to as BN 12600; Oppitz, *Deutsche Rechtsbücher*, No. 1453.

Mikołaj of Smogorzewo. Dated 1421, it contains exclusively landmark texts of German law,[95] which include: 1) digests (*regesta*) of the *Sachsenspiegel*[96] and the Lübeck Law (f. 1ra–4rb); 2) the *Sachsenspiegel* (f. 4rb–56ra); 3) the Lübeck Law (f. 56ra–64ra); 4) the *Weichbild* (f. 64rb–89rb); and 5) an article from the Chełmno Law (89va) written in smaller script by a later hand. So far, the *Weichbild* from this manuscript has not been the subject of a critical analysis. The text, which is very neatly written, is laid out in two columns. The incipits, two lines in height, are preceded by rubrics in red ink. An assortment of legal acts concerned exclusively with municipal law – all written in the same hand (apart from an entry on the last page) – indicates that the manuscript was to function in legal practice in the urban context.

3.4 *Częstochowa MS (1423) in the Archives of the Pauline Fathers in Częstochowa, AJG II-3*[97]

The Częstochowa MS was given a brief description by Bolesław Ulanowski in the second volume of the *Archives of the Law Commission*.[98] Ulanowski dated it to 1423, in accordance with the date entered in the manuscript itself (f. 107). However, the realization that the quires are not assembled in the correct order led to disagreements over the proper description of the contents of the manuscript. Ulanowski argued that the quires were bound in the wrong order, a mistake that resulted in the separation of two major texts. A landmark source of Magdeburg Law was affected by the division (Ulanowski did not identify it; f. 12–36 and 139–149), as was the treatise *Summa Henrici* (f. 37–50 and 108–138). However, for Oppitz, the binding error resulted in the splitting of the *Sachsenspiegel* by a fragment of the *Summa Henrici* (the misplaced f. 108–138 should have occupied an earlier slot in the codex). In his opinion, the text of the Magdeburg Law on f. 138–145 is in fact the second half of the *Sachsenspiegel*, cut off from its other half on f. 70–107. He also identified the long text on f. 12v–36v as the Magdeburg *Weichbild*. As a result, in his catalogue

95 In descriptions of this manuscript, the list and sequence of legal acts that make up its contents are either incomplete or flawed. See Oppitz, *Deutsche Rechtsbücher*, No. 1453; Ebel and Schelling, *Das lateinische lübische Recht*, pp. 101–102; and Kaliszuk and Szyller, *Inwentarz rękopisów*, p. 192.

96 The catalogues name this this body of text *Weichbild*, yet in fact it is the *Sachsenspiegel* which begins with the phrase *Deus iudex iustus*. It is followed by the Lübeck Law.

97 Hereafter referred to as AJG; Oppitz, *Deutsche Rechtsbücher*, No. 351.

98 Bolesław Ulanowski, "Opisy rękopisów" [Descriptions of Manuscripts], ed. Stanisław Kutrzeba, in: *Archiwum komisji prawniczej*, 2 (Kraków, 1921), pp. XVII–XVIII. The author of the description published in *Archiwum Komisji Prawniczej* is named incorrectly in Oppitz's *Deutsche Rechtsbücher*, No. 351, p. 441. Cf. also Rymaszewski, *Łacińskie teksty Landrechtu Zwierciadła Saskiego w Polsce. Versio*, Table 6, Item 17.

the Częstochowa MS is said to contain two texts of the *Weichbild* and one text of the *Sachsenspiegel*.

After taking a careful look at the manuscript itself, I have come to the conclusion that while Ulanowski's account of the consequences of the binding error is essentially correct, his description could do with some extra details. Let me present what – in my opinion – is a definitive list of contents of the Częstochowa MS. It contains: 1) The Statutes of Kazimierz the Great (f. 1–12v); 2) a digest of the *Sachsenspiegel* (f. 12v–14); 3) the *Sachsenspiegel* (*versio Vratislaviensis*), which begins with the phrase *Deus iudex iustus*[99] (f. 12v–36v, f. 139–145); 4) *Summa Henrici* (f. 108–138, f. 37–50v); 5) the Latin *Weichbild* (f. 53v–70); 6) a digest of the *Sachsenspiegel* (f. 70–72); 7) the Latin *Sachsenspiegel Landrecht* (*versio Sandomiriensis*), which begins with the phrase *Duos gladios* (f. 72–107); and 8) users' notes (f. 149v). The manuscript thus contains two different Latin translations of the *Sachsenspiegel* and not, as Oppitz's catalogue would have it, two texts of the *Weichbild*. All the texts are written in one hand; the script is fairly neat; and the initials are outlined in red ink.

The contents of the Częstochowa MS offer no clear clues about its intended functioning. Although the key texts of the Saxon-Magdeburg Law are given prominence, the manuscript also contains some miscellaneous texts. While the inclusion of *Summa Henrici* does not sway it in any particular direction, its date of composition (1423) may explain why Polish land law is represented in this collection solely by the Statutes of Kazimierz the Great. At that time, the Statutes of Cracow and Warta were still in the making (1421–1423).[100] Nonetheless, we are not left completely in the dark about the manuscript's use. A handful of notes on the last leaf points to the municipal court at Sieradz and the High Court of German Law at Kalisz (f. 149v). This is a clear hint that the

99 See Rymaszewski, *Łacińskie teksty Landrechtu Zwierciadła Saskiego w Polsce. Versio*, p. 21.

100 See Wacław Uruszczak's studies into the dating of the Statutes of Warta and Cracow: "Z badań nad Statutem Warckim z 1423 roku" [Studies of the Statutes of Warta], in: *Parlamentaryzm i prawodawstwo przez wieki* [Parliamentarism and Legislation over the Centuries], eds. Jerzy Malec and Wacław Uruszczak (Kraków, 1999), pp. 135–147; Wacław Uruszczak, "Nowelizacja Statutów Kazimierza Wielkiego w statucie warckim z 1423 roku. Z badań nad ustawodawstwem w dawnej Polsce" [Amendment of the Statutes of Kazimierz the Great in the Statute of Warta of 1423: Studies in Polish Legislation until the Late 18th Century], in: *Studia z Dziejów Państwa i Prawa Polskiego* [Studies in the History of Polish State and Law], 9/1, eds. Jacek S. Matuszewski and Wojciech Witkowski (Lublin – Łódź, 2006), pp. 93–108; Wacław Uruszczak, "Rękopisy Statutu krakowsko-warckiego z 1421/1423" [Manuscripts of the Statutes of Cracow and Warta, 1421/1423], in: *Nil nisi veritas. Księga dedykowana Profesorowi Jackowi Matuszewskiemu* [Nil nisi veritas: A Festschrift in Honour of Professor Jacek Matuszewski], eds. Marcin Głuszak and Dorota Wiśniewska-Jóźwiak (Łódź, 2016), pp. 99–114.

manuscript, regardless of the circumstances of its creation, eventually found its way into the hands of legal practitioners administering municipal law. Thus far, there has been no detailed study of the *Weichbild* in the Częstochowa MS.[101]

3.5 *MS Lat. Q II 157 (1427) in the National Library of Russia in St Petersburg*[102]

MS Lat. Q II 157 has survived the ravages of history. According to the provisions of the Treaty of Riga, signed in 1922, it should have been returned to Poland,[103] but in fact, it never left St Petersburg (Leningrad). In Poland, after the war, it was assumed that it had been handed over, but then destroyed in the Warsaw Rising in 1944.[104] It resurfaced in 1996 in connection with the publication of Alexandr Rogachevski's monograph *The Sword of Roland*. Rogachevski also made reference to the manuscript, long thought lost, in another article.[105]

The manuscript deserves an extended description if only because it is a composite made up of three distinctly different parts, written in three hands. The first part consists of four quires, and the next part consists of six. Part I contains a Latin *Weichbild* (contrary to earlier descriptions, it is neither the

101 For more references, see my articles mentioned in the footnotes to this study.

102 Hereafter referred to as MS Q II 157 (1) and (2).

103 The presence of the manuscript in St Petersburg was confirmed in the 19th century catalogues of Beda Dudík ("Historische Forschungen in der keiserlichen öffentlichen Bibliothek zu St. Petersburg", *Sitzungsberichte der kaiserlichen Akademie der Wissenschaften, philosophisch-historische Classe* 95/1 (1879, published 1880), p. 362, No. 114) and Alfred Blumenstock ("Wiadomość o rękopisach prawno-historycznych Biblioteki Cesarskiej w Petersburgu. Sprawozdanie z poszukiwań" [Latest Information about Legal History Manuscripts in St Petersburg Imperial Library], in: *Archiwum Komisji Historycznej. Collectanea ex Archivo Collegii Historici*, 6 (Kraków, 1891), pp. 437–438, No. 339).

104 Oppitz, *Deutsche Rechtsbücher*, No. 1471; Ebel and Schelling, *Das lateinische lübische Recht*, pp. 102–103.

105 Alexander Rogatchevski, *Mech Rolanda: pravovye vzgli͡ady nemet͡skikh gorozhan XIII–XVII vv.* [The Sword of Roland] (St. Petersburg, 1996), pp. 46, 136–137 and 154; Alexander Rogatchevski, "Das Magdeburger Recht auf dem heutigen Territorium Rußlands. Forschungsstand und Forschungsperspektiven", in: *Rechts- und Sprachtransfer in Mittel- und Ostmitteleuropa. Sachsenspiegel und Magdeburger Recht. Internationale und interdisziplinäre Konferenz in Leipzig vom 31. Oktober bis 2. November 2003*, eds. Ernst Eichler and Heiner Lück, (Ivs Saxonico-Maidebvrgense in Oriente) 1 (Berlin, 2008), p. 249, Note 31. Cf. also Oppitz, *Ergänzungen*, p. 542. See also: Kaliszuk, *Codices deperditi*, 1, p. 192; Olga Bleskina, *Katalog sobraniâ latinskih rukopisej: pravo, filosofiâ, nauka, literatura i iskusstvo / Catalogus codicum manuscriptorum latinorum, qui in Bibliotheca Publica Petropolitana asservantur: jurisprudentia, philosophia, scientia, monumenta litterarum* (Sankt-Petersburg, 2011), No. 73, pp. 47–48.

Weichbild vulgate[106] nor the German version known as Konrad of Opole's compilation), the Latin *Sachsenspiegel* (*versio Vratislaviensis*), and *Halle's Legal Instruction for Środa Śląska* (*Hallische Rechtsmitteilung für Neumarkt*) (f. 1–53v). This is followed by a homily written by the second hand (f. 54r–55r). The second part, written in the third hand, begins with a new quire. It consists of the Latin *Sachsenspiegel* (*versio Vratislaviensis*) and a Latin *Weichbild* (f. 56r–123v). The text of each of the two *Weichbilds* represents the *versio Sandomiriensis*, but they are not identical.

If the reasons for combining two sets of texts of the Saxon-Magdeburg Law are not clear, it is certain that each one had had its own history. The first one, as shown by the inclusion of *Halle's Legal Instruction for Środa Śląska* and the replacement of 'burgers of Magdeburg' by 'burghers of Novum Forum [i.e. Neumarkt/Środa Śląska] or of Magdeburg',[107] had been used in a town founded under a local variant of the Magdeburg Law called in Latin *ius Novi Fori* or *ius Sredense*. One consequence of having a compound of two sets of texts like MS Q II 157 (1) and (2) is that only the second (the later) of the two *Weichbilds* can be used for reliable dating.[108] The writing in both sets is somewhat careless; decorated initials appear only in Part I (as far as f. 43r), and elsewhere, the spaces provided for such decorations remain blank. There can be little doubt that both parts of this compound manuscript were created for practical purposes.

3.6 *Kielce MS (1429) in the Library of the Diocesan Seminary in Kielce, RK 45/28*[109]

Manuscript RK 45/28, held in the collections of the Diocesan Seminary Library in Kielce, is a combination of liturgical and legal texts. Its contents are listed in an inventory published by Jerzy Wolny.[110] A set of texts of Saxon-Magdeburg Law (f. 95–140v) was compiled by Piotr *pauperus*, parish priest (*rector*) of

106 More on the vulgate in: Ebel and Schelling, *Das lateinische lübische Recht*, pp. 102–103, and Oppitz, *Ergänzungen*, p. 542. Rymaszewski goes so far as to claim that the text of the first *Weichbild* in this manuscript is a German version of Konrad of Opole's compilation (*Łacińskie teksty Landrechtu Zwierciadła Saskiego w Polsce. Versio*, Table 6, Item 13).

107 Cf. Appendix 2, No. 201.

108 *Anno Domini millesimo quadringentesimo vicesimo septimo die Sabbathi proxima ante Letare.*

109 Hereafter referred to as MS Kiel.; cf. also Andrzej Kwaśniewski, "Księgozbiory prywatne zachowane w Bibliotece Kapituły Kieleckiej (XV–XVIII w.)", [Private Collections Held in the Chapter Library in Kielce (15th–18th Century)], *Biuletyn Biblioteki Jagiellońskiej* 62 (2012), 69.

110 Wolny, *Inventaire des manuscrits*, p. 74. This manuscript is also mentioned by Anna Łosowska in her *Kolekcja liber legum i jej miejsce w kulturze umysłowej*

Potok. According to the *explicit*, he completed the writing of the *Weichbild* on 4 August 1429. In addition to the Saxon-Magdeburg Law, the manuscript contains a legal manual entitled *Processus iudiciariis* and a short legal disquisition. The *Processus* is written in a hand very similar to that of parish priest Piotr. As the liturgical and the legal texts appear on leaves that belong to different quires and the legal set is written in one hand, it can be assumed that they functioned separately before being bound in this codex. The homilies (f. 36–88v) are written in what could be the same hand; moreover, the second Piotr's *explicit* is situated in folio 86va – parish priest Piotr copied some of the non-legal texts of the manuscript, as well. What also links the homilies and the legal text is the form of their decorative initials penned in red ink. The remaining liturgical texts (e.g. fol. 89–94) are written by various hands. The texts of Saxon-Magdeburg Law in this manuscript have not yet been studied. It is a fair guess that MS Kiel. was used by officials looking after the landed property of the Church.

3.7 *Baworowscy MS (First Half of the 15th Century) in the National Library in Warsaw, BN 12607 III*[111]

This collection of unknown provenance, formerly in the Baworowscy Collection (No. 1014) and at present held by the National Library in Warsaw (as Acc. 9869), contains a set of legal acts and treatises on urban and canon law, including judgments of the of the High Court of German Law in Cracow (for a description of this bilingual manuscript, see the overview of the German-language texts in Section 2.3). So far, no study has been made of the *Weichbild* in this manuscript.

3.8 *St Florian MS (1453) in Sankt-Florian Monastery Library in Austria, 551/II*[112]

A description of the St Florian MS was published by Bolesław Ulanowski.[113] The Codex used to belong to Tyniec Abbey; in the 19th century, it was sold to the Bishop of Tarnów, Gregor Ziegler. He donated it to the Augustinian Abbey at Sankt-Florian in Austria, from which it took its name.[114] According to Ulanowski, the St Florian MS, written by two scribes, one of whom copied just the beginning of the Statutes of Kazimierz the Great, consists of two parts.

późnośredniowiecznego Przemyśla [The Liber legum MS and Its Place in the Intellectual Culture of Late-Medieval Przemyśl] (Warszawa – Przemyśl) 2007, p. 205.

111 Hereafter referred to as MS BN 12607; cf. also Oppitz, *Deutsche Rechtsbücher*, No. 1454.

112 Hereafter referred to as MS Flor.; cf. also Oppitz, *Deutsche Rechtsbücher*, No. 1367.

113 Ulanowski, "Opisy rękopisów", pp. XIX–XXI; and Albin Czerny, *Die Handschriften der Stiftsbibliothek St. Florian* (Linz, 1871), pp. 187–188.

114 Ulanowski, "Opisy rękopisów", p. XIX.

Part I, made up of 40 leaves, consists of: (1) the Statutes of Kazimierz the Great, and (2) the Statute of Warta. Part II contains the key texts of the Magedburg Law: (3) the Magdeburg *Weichbild* (f. 41–58), (6) the *Sachsenspiegel* (f. 59v–96v), (7) a digest of the *Weichbild* (f. 96v–98), (8) a digest of the *Sachsenspiegel* preceded by *Explicit prologus, incipit ius provinciale* (f. 98–102); and the following supplements: (4) *De numero ponderum et mensuarum ac diversorum* (f. 58–59), (5) two articles from the Statutes of Kazimierz the Great (f. 59), and (9) *vocabula libri municipalis* (f. 102–102v), that is, a lexicon of the Magdeburg Law.[115] In his commentaries, Ulanowski places significant stock on the similarities between the texts of Magdeburg Law in the Flor. MS and the Gn. MS, shown in particular by the presence in both of the fragment *Explicit prologus.* He notes also a number of formal differences, such as the removal of identical rubrics from the main text to the digests (*regesta*). This composite codex brings together two key texts of Polish land law and a set of 'urban' regulations. Its provenance and function are obscure. It was probably not intended for use by a municipal court. The small octavo format,[116] careless handwriting, and blank spaces left for incipits set it apart from 'quality' manuscripts that are known to have functioned in medieval communes. Stanisław Kutrzeba, who edited Ulanowski's description of the Flor. MS, picked out the date 1453 inscribed next to the text of the Statutes of Kazimierz the Great and decided that it marked the completion of the entire manuscript.[117]

3.9 *MS Dział. 801 (Działyńscy Codex I, 1455) in the Kórnik Library of the Polish Academy of Sciences*[118]

The polymorphic Działyńscy Codex I held at the Kórnik Library contains an assortment of historiographical[119] and legal texts. In his description, Antoni Zygmunt Helcel distinguishes six parts of the codex. Part I contains miscellaneous materials of various provenance; Part II contains a prose narrative of the Trojan War by Guido delle Colonne; Parts III and IV are comprised for the most part text of German law; Part V contains collections of land and feudal law (including the *Lehnrecht* from the *Sachsenspiegel*); and Part VI contains a

115 The lexicon was published by Ulanowski (*ibid.*, pp. XX–XXI).

116 The leaves in this manuscript: width 15.2 cm, height 21 cm.

117 Stanisław Kutrzeba, "Opisy rękopisów", in: *Archiwum komisji prawniczej*, 2 (Kraków, 1921), p. XXI.

118 Hereafter referred to as MS Dział. I; cf. also Oppitz, *Deutsche Rechtsbücher*, No. 837.

119 Jacek Wesołowski, *Kolekcje historyczne w Polsce średniowiecznej XIV–XV wieku* [Historical Collections in Medieval Poland (14th–15th Century)] (Wrocław – Warszawa – Kraków, 1987), pp. 136–138.

handful of narrative works and a collection of the Magdeburg *ortyle* (f. 331–343) published in the form of a homographic reprint by Michał Bobrzyński.[120]

There is no point in presenting the whole codex here, as its many constituent elements represent different classes of texts, practically independent of one another, that belong to different socio-cultural contexts. It is written in many different hands using various kinds of writing materials.[121] Stanisław Budka's analysis shows that the writing in quires 13–22 (f. 141–235) predates 1455,[122] whereas quires 12 (f. 129–140) and 21 (f. 236–247) were assembled in 1466. On the basis of Jerzy Zathey's excellent extended description of MS Dział. I and the critical observations of Bolesław Ulanowski, I have compiled a detailed survey of the contents of the fourth part of this multiple-text manuscript (see Table 7).

It is worth noting that the *Weichbild* is written in two hands. The change from one to the other coincides with the opening of another quire. Another aspect of this shift was brought to light by Stanisław Budka. His research shows that the first three leaves of the *Weichbild* are 11 years older than the other leaves. However, I am convinced that the red rubrics in both parts of the *Weichbild* are in the same hand. That would indicate that the creation of the Działyńscy Codex I proceeded gradually and that the copyists at work on the texts of the Saxon-Magdeburg Law were simultaneously copying texts of Polish land law and miscellaneous narratives. Zathey links this codex with the university community and the Benedictine Abbey at Łysa Góra, but also notes some of its characteristics that would suggest a rather different provenance.[123] Unfortunately, there is not a shred of evidence that could offer a clue as why S[tanisław] of Opatów decided to make a copy of the *Weichbild* at that very time (1455) and in the village of Solec, of all places.

120 Michał Bobrzyński, ed., *Ortyle magdeburskie. Przedruk homograficzny z kodeksu Biblioteki Kórnickiej* [The Magdeburg Ortyle: A Homographic Reprint of the Kórnik Library Codex] (Poznań, 1876).

121 Antoni Z. Helcel, *Starodawne prawa polskiego pomniki poprzedzone wywodem historyczno krytycznym tak zwanego Prawodawstwa Wiślickiego Kaziémirza Wielkiego w texcie ze starych rękopism krytycznie dobranym* [Ancient Monuments of Polish Law with a Critical-Historical Introduction to the Legislation Known as Kazimerz the Great's Statute of Wiślica: A Critical Edition of Its Text Collected from Old Manuscripts] (Warszawa, 1856), p. XXVIII. Helcel's description of this manuscript is far more comprehensive than that of Jan W. Bandtkie in his *Jus Polonicum, codicibus veteribus manuscriptis et editionibus quibusque collatis* (Varsaviae, 1831, p. XV). Both have been superseded by the detailed analyses of Jerzy Zathey (*Katalog rękopisów średniowiecznych Biblioteki Kórnickiej* [A Catalogue of Medieval Manuscripts in Kórnik Library] (Wrocław, 1963), p. 449).

122 Zathey, *Katalog*, pp. 449–450.

123 *Ibid.*, p. 453.

TABLE 7 Contents of Part IV of Działyńscy Codex I

Folium number	Contents	Hand[a]	Notes
129	rules concerning the size of the Frankish *łan* (*Hufe*)	A	–
129	excerpt from a Latin-Polish lexicon of legal terms of German law	A	–
129v	oath formulas according to German law	A	–
129v	sample legal formulae	A	–
130–132	a brief digest of the *Weichbild*	A	–
132v–137	a brief digest of the *Sachsenspiegel*	A	–
137v–170v	The Magdeburg *Weichbild*	B[b] and C from 141 onwards	Hand C (autograph): S[tanisław] of z Opatów,[c] f. 170v, job completed 22 November 1455, Solec; in the same hand – the text of the Polish translation of the Statutes of Kazimierz the Great (f. 265–298, except 296–298)[d]
171–174v	varia	D and E	–
175–238	The *Sachsenspiegel*	F; G from 227v onwards; and H 236	Hand H f. 238 (autograph): 1466; (inscribed by H) *summa* of the Statutes of Kazimierz the Great and the Statute of Warta,[e] and (f. 296–298) the translation of the Statutes of Kazimierz the Great, *Lehnrecht* from the *Sachsenspiegel* (1469), the *Story of Apollonius King of Tyre* and the final part of the collection of Magdeburg *ortyle*
239v–246	A compendium of German law in essential rules	I	–

a The hands in Part IV are labelled A – I.

b Helcel's reference to a change of hand on f. 133v. must be a printer's error. The change occurs on f. 132v.

c Jerzy Zathey does not rule out that this entry may refer to Stanislaus Martini Institoris de Opathow, enrolled at the University of Cracow in 1424 (Zathey, *Katalog*, p. 451).

d Helcel, *Starodawne prawa polskiego pomniki*, p. XXXIII.

e *Ibidem*, p. XXXIII.

Zygmunt Rymaszewski used the texts of the Działyńscy Codex I and the Gniezno MS in his analysis of the Sandomierz version of the first redaction of the Latin *Sachsenspiegel*. Interestingly, the *Weichbild* in MS Dział. I is closest to the text in the oldest surviving manuscript MS Gn., and its importance as source is greatly enhanced by its gloss, evidently written by a user (see Chapter 4.2 of this study).

3.10 *MS Dział. 800 (Działyńscy Codex IV, after 1472) in the Kórnik Library of the Polish Academy of Sciences*[124]

The first extended description of the Działyńscy Codex IV from the Kórnik Library was published by Antoni Z. Helcel in Volume I of his *Ancient Monuments of Polish Law*; a precise analysis of the manuscript was recently written by Jerzy Zathey.[125] MS Dział. IV contains a sizable collection of acts of Polish law, the *Weichbild* (f. 102–145), and the *Sachsenspiegel Landrecht* (f. 146–240) – all of which are in one hand. Helcel claims that the provenance of the Działyńscy Codex IV must be Mazovia, because the Magdeburg *Weichbild* in this manuscript contains a few quotations from the Chełmno Law (*Der Alte Kulm*).[126] However, this argument fails to persuade. Moreover, none of the key texts of Polish law, a significant number of which have survived, ever mentions the statutes or customs of Mazovia. In effect, the provenance of this text needs to be re-examined (see Chapter 2.6 and 4.2.5 of this study). Zygfryd Rymaszewski observes that the *Weichbild* and the *Sachsenspiegel* in the Działyńscy Codex IV are in a way distinct, but he stops short of postulating the presence of another Latin translation to account for the difference. His solution is to classify the *Weichbild* of MS Dział. IV as the second redaction of the *versio Sandomiriensis*.[127] He argues that the author of the Działyńscy Codex IV stripped the *Weichbild* of provisions that can be found in the *Sachsenspiegel* for reasons of economy (however, this is stated explicitly in the text).[128] Although, as this discussion demonstrates, the *Weichbild* of the Działyńscy Codex IV has attracted some scholarly attention, so far it has not been the object of systematic, in-depth analysis. Finally, allow me to correct an incorrect piece of information in the Catalogue of Medieval Manuscripts in the Kórnik Library. The *Weichbild* from

124 Hereafter referred to as MS Dział. IV. Cf. also Oppitz, *Deutsche Rechtsbücher*, No. 836.

125 Helcel, *Starodawne prawa polskiego pomniki*, pp. XLII–XLV; and Zathey, *Katalog*, pp. 445–449. Cf. also Bandtkie's introductory note to *Jus Polonicum* (p. XVI).

126 Helcel, *Starodawne prawa polskiego pomniki*, pp. XLII–XLIII; Rymaszewski, *Łacińskie teksty Landrechtu Zwierciadła Saskiego w Polsce. Versio*, pp. 73, 76; and Zathey, *Katalog*, p. 448.

127 Rymaszewski, *Łacińskie teksty Landrechtu Zwierciadła Saskiego w Polsce. Versio*, pp. 73 and 76.

128 *Ibid.*, p. 71.

the Działyńscy Codex IV did not go to print in Jan Łaski's *Statutes*; he used a different text.[129]

3.11 **Liber legum** *of Przemyśl (1473–1474) in the State Archive in Przemyśl, AMPrzem. 428*[130]

The *Liber legum* (*Law Book*) of Przemyśl, held in the Przemyśl State Archive (Acts of the Town Przemyśl, Shelfmark 428), is the subject of a monograph by Anna Łosowska.[131] She divides the texts of that codex into three groups: the Saxon-Magdeburg Law collection, texts of Roman and canon law, and historiographical works. The catalogue of documents in the category of German law is exceedingly long. The codex opens with the Magdeburg *Weichbild*, preceded by an index of rubrics and followed by a note marking the completion of this copying job on 5 March 1473 (f. 13r–27r). It also contains the Sandomierz version of the *Sachsenspiegel*, followed by a note marking the completion of this copying job in 1474 (f. 27v–61r). Both texts are written in one hand (we are told that the scribe's name is Stanisław).[132] The *Law Book of Przemyśl* also contains the Wrocław version of the *Sachsenspiegel* (the *Landrecht* with the Lübeck Law and the *Lehnrecht*, f. 118r–149r and f. 168r–190r, respectively); a collection of the Magdeburg *ortyle*, including some translated in Przemyśl (f. 63r–68r, 70r–74v);[133] the *Law Book of Środa Śląska* (*Das Rechtsbuch der Stadt Neumarkt in Schlesien*) (f. 102r–103v);[134] a manual of canon and Roman, law *Summa legum levis, brevis et utilis*, by Master Raymundus (Parthenopaeus), used as an auxiliary law book in urban courts (f. 312–388); a digest of the *Sachsenspiegel* with supplementary material from Roman law (f. 68r–69v and 76r–102r); a lexicon of legal terms of Magdeburg Law (f. 162–163); and Gregory XI's and Urban VI's bulls condemning certain provisions of the *Sachsenspiegel*.[135] Łosowska notes

---

129 Zathey, *Katalog*, p. 448.

130 Hereafter referred to as MS Przem. Cf. also Oppitz, *Deutsche Rechtsbücher*, No. 1296; Ebel and Schelling, *Das lateinische lübische Recht*, pp. 99–100.

131 Łosowska, *Przemyska Liber legum*. For earlier studies, see the bibliography in Łosowska's monograph. The first extended description of this manuscript was written by Kałużniacki, "Die polnische Recension", pp. 220–226.

132 Łosowska ventures the conjecture that the copyist of the *Weichbild* and the *Sachsenspiegel* in the Przemyśl *Liber legum* and the scribe of MS Dział. are one and the same person, Stanisław of Opatów. Cf. Łosowska, *Liber legum*, pp. 186–187.

133 *Ibid.*, p. 225.

134 *Iura que dicuntur Withbilde* (*ibidem*, pp. 210 and 228–230). *Law Book of Środa Śląska* is dated to c.1335/1337; at its core is *Halle's Legal Instruction for Środa Śląska* (*Hallische Rechtsmitteilung für Neumarkt*) of 1235. Cf. also Oppitz, *Deutsche Rechtsbücher*, 1, p. 60.

135 Łosowska, *Liber legum*, p. 173.

that the codex is an agglomeration of elements that at least partially functioned as separate manuscripts:

> Some quires have their own numbering scheme which additionally sets off the texts thus marked from the rest of the codex. This is another piece of evidence to support the argument that the individual texts used to function separately. Those texts are *Speculum Saxonum*,[136] *Ius feodale*,[137] the Przemyśl redaction of the Magdeburg *ortyle*, a treatise on canon law [*Defesorium iuris*] by Gerardus Monachus, *Summa legum* by Raymundus Parthenopaeus and the *Decretalia*.[138]

The orderly arrangement of quires, she insists, should be treated as proof that the composition of codex was well planned by its author, Szymon of Jaworów.[139]

An important implication of this discussion is that the copyist of the Latin *Weichbild* and *Sachsenspiegel* (representing the *versio Sandomiriensis*) must not be identified with the author of the codex or any of its various parts. While Feliks Kiryk links the creation of the *Liber legum* with the growth and rising status of Przemyśl's urban community,[140] Łosowska is convinced that "the origin, or at least the use, of the Przemyśl collection [was connected] with the local ecclesiastical elite".[141] Yet she does not rule out that the former owners of some books in the codex were members of the urban elite, connected with the town chancery. As the municipal records have not survived, the claim that the judgments of the High Court of German Law in Cracow were translated into Latin by a local man, "former town clerk of Przemyśl" (*per quendam notarium*

136 I.e. *versio Vratislaviensis*.

137 *The Sachsenpiegel-Lehnrecht*.

138 Łosowska, *Liber legum*, pp. 170–171

139 *Ibid.*, pp. 168–170, 175, 177, 184, and 337.

140 Feliks Kiryk, "Przyczynki do dziejów szkolnictwa i stosunków kulturalnych późnośredniowiecznego Przemyśla" [Some Highlights of the History of Education and Cultural Relations in Late-Medieval Przemyśl], in: *Cracovia, Polonia, Europa: studia z dziejów średniowiecza ofiarowane Jerzemu Wyrozumskiemu w sześćdziesiątą piątą rocznicę urodzin i czterdziestolecie pracy naukowej* [Cracovia, Polonia, Europa: A Festschrift Dedicated to Professor Jan Szymczak on His 65th Birthday Anniversary and 40 Years of Academic Work], eds. Krzysztof Baczkowski, Waldemar Bukowski, Mariusz Markiewicz, Krzysztof Ożóg, Maciej Salamon, Franciszek. Sikora, and Stanisław Szczur (Kraków, 1995), pp. 361–371; Feliks Kiryk, "Ze stosunków ustrojowych w późnośredniowiecznym Przemyślu", in: *Parlamentaryzm i prawodawstwo przez wieki*, eds. Jerzy Malec, Wacław Uruszczak (Kraków, 1999), pp. 271–282.

141 Łosowska, *Liber legum*, p. 188.

civitatis Przemisliensis), cannot be dismissed out of hand.[142] Nor can we simply reject the old story which credits Szymon of Jaworów with collecting all the books of urban law he could find, and no doubt a place where they could be found was the town chancery. In this study, at least one part of the story is confirmed, namely, the *Weichbild* of the Przemyśl *Liber legum* does come from a chancery background.

Łosowska also compared the *Weichbild* of the Przemyśl *Liber legum* with that of the Działyńscy Codex IV.[143] Her conclusion is that both texts were written in the 15th century by anonymous authors and that in both collections, the *Weichbild* is followed by the *Sachsenspiegel*. Although this sequence is peculiar to these two manuscripts, she does not believe they have a common ancestor (and neither do I).[144] Her analysis focuses on the differences between the two texts, such as the divergences in the wording and the arrangement of some articles from the beginning of the *Weichbild*, in Article 43, the formula of the Jewish oath, and the phrasing of the rubrics.[145] The asymmetry between the two texts is visibly heightened by errors in article numbers, the adoption of lumps of the Chełmno Law (MS Dział. IV), and the insertion of 14 articles without numbers after the Jewish oath (MS Dział. IV).[146] Łosowska also compared the *Weichbild* of the Przemyśl *Liber legum* with Łaski's *Statutes*. In this case, her conclusion is that the two texts do not share a common base and that Łaski's *Weichbild* begins with a long introduction which is missing in Przemyśl MS.[147]

There is little to disagree with in terms of her findings. After all, each of the three texts belongs to a different branch of the *Weichbild* filiation tree: Przemyśl MS; the Działyńscy Codex IV; and the *Statutes*.

3.12 *Pleszew MS in the Acts of the Town of Pleszew I/2 (until 1498) in the State Archives in Poznań*[148]

The Book of Pleszew Town Council opens with the first 54 articles of the *Weichbild*. Their sequence corresponds with that of the Gniezno MS (f. 51–55). To this batch, two more articles are added of unidentified provenance, each in a different hand. The *Weichbild* text from the Pleszew MS was published

142 *Ibid.*, p. 185.
143 *Ibid.*, pp. 205–206.
144 *Ibid.*, p. 206.
145 *Ibid.*, pp. 207–209.
146 *Ibid.*, p. 209. Actually, the 14 articles are a supplement to the *Weichbild* known as the *Constitution of Courts*.
147 *Ibid.*, p. 209.
148 Hereafter referred to as MS Plesz. Cf. also Oppitz, *Deutsche Rechtsbücher*, No. 1219.

by Witold Maisel;[149] the *Book of Pleszew Town Council* was published in two instalments, with Part I edited by Tomasz Jurek, and Part II edited by Adam Kozak.[150] Maisel's description embraces all the characteristic features of the Pleszew *Weichbild* extract (hand, ductus, initials, rubrics). On the subject of filiation, he merely notes that the Pleszew text shows some similarities with one of the texts in Łaski's *Statutes*,[151] and in a footnote, he refers the reader to Mikołaj Jaskier's *Iuris Municipalis*. While Maisel dates the writing of the Pleszew *Weichbild* to 1519/1520, Adam Kozak makes a strong case for dating it back to the 15th century, before 1483.[152] The reasons why only the first part of the *Weichbild* was copied are not clear. Agnieszka Bartoszewicz notes that the practice of copying legal texts into municipal records was not uncommon and cites the cases of Krzywin and Radziejów, whose town council books contain judgments of the High Court of German Law at Kościan (Kosten) and provisions of the Chełmno Law, respectively.[153]

3.13 *Opatów MS (1488) in the Ossoliński National Institute, Oss. 832/II*[154]

According to a sketchy description by Wojciech Kętrzyński, the Opatów MS is a 15th-century paper codex written carelessly in one hand.[155] Its date of origin, 1488, is mentioned in a summary in the last part of the manuscript. It proclaims that:

> ... here end the books of Magdeburg and Saxon Law authorized by Emperor Otto, written and completed by one Mikołaj, cleric of the

149 Witold Maisel, "Prawo magdeburskie miasta Pleszewa" [The Magdeburg Lawbook of Pleszew], *Studia i Materiały do Dziejów Wielkopolski i Pomorza* 9/1 (1963), 67–82.

150 Tomasz Jurek, ed., "Najdawniejsze zapiski z księgi miejskiej Pleszewa (1428–1444)" [The Earliest Records in the Book of Pleszew Town Council (1428–1444)], in: *Wielkopolska dawniej i dziś. Studia, źródła i materiały* [Wielkopolska in the Past and Today: Studies, Sources and Materials], ed. Andrzej Gulczyński, (*Kwartalnik Historii Kultury Materialnej*) 60/3 (2012) (Poznań, 2011) and Adam Kozak, transl. and ed., *Najstarsza pleszewska księga radziecka: zapiski z lat 1485–1519* [The Oldest Volume of the Book of Pleszew Town Council: Records 1485–1519], (Wielkopolska Dawniej i Dziś) 4 (Poznań, 2014).

151 Maisel, "Prawo magdeburskie", pp. 68–69.

152 Adam Kozak, "Introduction", in: *Najstarsza pleszewska księga radziecka*, p. 8.

153 Agnieszka Bartoszewicz, *Piśmienność mieszczańska w późnośredniowiecznej Polsce* [Urban Literacy in Late Medieval Poland] (Warszawa, 2012), p. 114.

154 Hereafter referred to as MS Oss.

155 See description of the manuscript: Bischoff, "Beiträge zur Geschichte", pp. 341–345; Wojciech Kętrzyński, ed., *Catalogus Codicum Manuscriptum Bibliothecae Ossolinianae Leopoliensis. Katalog rękopisów Biblioteki Zakładu Nar. Im. Ossolińskich*, 3 (Lwów, 1898), pp. 276–277; Oppitz, *Deutsche Rechtsbücher*, nr 281.

> Gniezno diocese and court clerk, in A.D. 1488 on the Friday before the carnival, *dies Veneris*, 15th February at Opatów.

The codex opens with the *Weichbild* (f. 1ra–17ra as *capitula* 51–157), followed by the *Sachsenspiegel* in *versio Sandomiriensis* (f. 17ra–57va, *capitula* 158–439). The pagination is continuous, with the exception of the third text in this set, that is, a Latin translation of the *Sachsenspiegel, versio Vratislaviensis*, divided into 237 *capitula* (f. 57va–104va). The codex also comprises the acts of the town of Jihlava (German Igel) in Bohemia[156] (*Iura seu statuta Iclaviae civitatis*, f. 105–117r) and two legal collections, *Breviloquus liber de iure valde utilis* – a Latin translation of Magdeburg judgments (*ortyle/Urteile*) (f. 117r–128v); and *De propositionibus actoris et responsionibus rei* (f. 128v–129v), addressed to the aldermen of Lwów. These are clearly separated from the texts of Saxon-Magdeburg Law. The last item in this collection is a short treatise, *Modus vivendi* (f. 129v–132r). The rubrics are outlined in red, at times too sparsely. As a result, some headers run over to the outer margin or the inner margins between two columns of text. Unfortunately, the first five leaves of the manuscript have been damaged. In his description, Ferdinand Bischoff claims that the texts in the Opatów MS are closest to those in Łaski's *Statutes*.[157] This claim will be examined in Chapter 2 of this study. Let me add that the various attempts to trace the filiation of Łaski's texts cannot be verified. This is the case with the alleged similarities between the *Statutes* and the Sanok MS (see 3.19 below) and the so-called MS Petersburg III.[158] The former has been written off as lost, and the latter was destroyed in a blaze.

3.14 *Żegota Pauli's MS (Second Half of the 15th Century) in the Jagiellonian Library, BJ 4405*[159]

Stanisław Estreicher wrote a description of the Żegota Pauli's MS while he was working on his study of the Magedburg *ortyle*.[160] There was never any

156 Incorrectly identified as *Illaviae* in Kętrzyński's catalogue. The acts are in Latin translation.
157 Cf. Bischoff, "Beiträge zur Geschichte", p. 333.
158 Helcel, *Starodawne prawa polskiego pomniki*, p. XLV. This manuscript was kept until 1924 in the Imperial Library in St Petersburg Shelfmark Lat. F II 124. Oppitz, *Deutsche Rechtsbücher*, nr 1466. Description: Helcel, s. XLV–XLVII.
159 Hereafter referred to as BJ 4405. Cf. also Oppitz, *Deutsche Rechtsbücher*, No. 860.
160 Estreicher, "Nieznane teksty ortyli", pp. 118–126; Maciej Mikuła, "*Weichbild* magdeburski w rękopisie Biblioteki Jagiellońskiej nr 4405" [The Magdeburg *Weichbild* in MS BJ 4405], in: *Nil nisi veritas. Księga dedykowana Profesorowi Jackowi Matuszewskiemu* [*Nil nisi veritas.* A Festschrift Dedicated to Professor Jacek Matuszewski], eds. Marcin Głuszak and Dorota Wiśniewska-Jóźwiak (Łódź, 2016), pp. 147–159.

doubt about the intentions of the author of the Żegota Pauli's MS (BJ 4405).[161] If it is judged it by its contents, the purpose of creating this collection was unabashedly practical. One part of the manuscript, written in late 15th-century hand, contains:[162] 1) a register of 281 *ortyle* (f. 1–5), Hand A; 2) a compendium of German law in the form of key legal rules (the same work can be found in Działyńscy Codex I, f. 239–246) (f. 5v–9v), Hand B; 3) a digest of the privileges issued by Kazimierz the Great in 1336, 1342, 1358, and 1363, Hand B; 4) Magdeburg *ortyle* (f. 11–88); 5) a handful of legal maxims and two prescriptions (f. 89v); and 6) the *Weichbild* – in the same hand as the *ortyle*, except the passage *de imperio et terra Saxonum*, which is written in a different hand (f. 89–107v). A special feature of this codex is the digests of the four royal privileges addressed to Cracow, which are concerned with the competences of the city council; inheritance and family law; criminal law; and other important subjects. The new legislation in the form of royal statutes and confirmations of Cracow's own statutes (by-laws, *wilkierze/Willküren*) supplemented or amended the Saxon-Magdeburg Law, which remained the mainstay of Cracow's legal order. Additionally, the contents of the second part of Żegota Pauli's MS bear witness to the codex's practical intent. It includes: a digest of 13 articles of the Chełmno Law (f. 108r–108v); a digest in Polish of the privileges (including the most recent one from the year 1521, f. 114r–137v); and three normative acts adopted by the Cracow goldsmiths (including the most recent one from the year 1549, f. 140–142). The special connection of MS BJ 4405 with Cracow is all too obvious.

3.15 *Warsaw MS (Second Half of the 15th Century) in the University of Warsaw Library, Warsz. 5*[163]

The Warsaw MS has survived in incomplete form. The lost leaves at the beginning of the codex contained the first 74 articles of the Magdeburg *Weichbild*.[164] The remaining articles, Articles 75–110, are written on f. 1–7v. The next batch (f. 8–40) contains the second redaction of the Sandomierz version of the Latin *Sachsenspiegel*. It is followed by the first nine articles of the German-language *Sachsenspiegel* (*versio Vratislaviensis*), (f. 41–43), the Jewish oath (f. 79v–80v), and Book I of *Summa legum brevis, levis et utilis* by Master Raymundus (f. 46,

161 Żegota Pauli was the owner of the MS in 19th Century.

162 Estreicher, "Nieznane teksty ortyli", pp. 119–121.

163 Hereafter referred to as MS Warsz. Cf. also Oppitz, *Deutsche Rechtsbücher*, No. 1481.

164 Helena Kozerska and Wanda Stummer, eds., *Katalog rękopisów Biblioteki Uniwersyteckiej w Warszawie* [A Catalogue of Manuscripts in the University Library in Warsaw], 1 (Warszawa, 1963), pp. 7–9.

82r–97v).[165] After a number of articles of the *Sachsenspiegel* and following the first part of the *Summa legum*, several leaves have been left blank, probably to be filled in later. However, for an unknown reason, this gap was never resolved, and the leaves remain blank. Whereas the manuscript as a whole is written in a number of hands, the *Weichbild* and the Latin *Sachsenspiegel* are the product of just one copyist. His hand is exceptionally neat. The initials, three lines in height, are executed in red; the text in the rubrics is in red ink, too.

3.16 *Żagań MS (15th Century) in the Wrocław University Library, II Q 4*[166]

The profile of the bilingual Żagań MS retained in the Library of the University of Wrocław is presented in Section 2.3

3.17 *Leipzig MS (15th/16th Century) in the University Library in Leipzig "Albertina", 951b*[167]

Written in one hand, the Leipzig MS contains the following texts of Saxon-Magdeburg Law:[168] 1) the *Sachsenspiegel-Landrecht* (Konrad of Sandomierz's version) (f. 1–78); 2) *Capitulum de electione consulum* (f. 78v); 3) Konrad of Sandomierz's Magdeburg *Weichbild* (f. 84–129v, f. 130 blank); 4) a brief digest of the *Sachsenspiegel* (f. 131); and 5) a brief digest of the *Weichbild*, which lists two articles that do not appear in the text above (f. 132–134). The catalogue also mention as a separate item a block of 14 non-numbered articles of the *Weichbild*, which match Articles VI–XIV in Alexander von Daniels and Franz von Gruben's edition of the *Weichbild* vulgate.[169] These provisions come from the *Constitution of Courts*, usually appended to the *Weichbild* after the Jewish oath. The displacement of Articles 89–93 from their correct slot to a position after Article 56 is due to a binding error. The Leipzig MS has been dated to the late 15th/early 16th century for no better reason than its affinity to other sources from that period, such as the Marcin Zabowski's MS (BOZ) and Łaski's *Statutes* (see Chapter 2.2.3). The history of the Leipzig MS is unknown, but some additional notes in the text itself include Polish equivalents of words in the main body (e.g. *inducie vulgariter rokÿ*),[170] which suggests a strong Polish connection. A note in 19th-century hand pencilled in on the margin says that

165 Rymaszewski, *Łacińskie teksty Landrechtu Zwierciadła Saskiego w Polsce. Versio*, Table 6.
166 Hereafter referred to as MS II Q 4. Cf. also Oppitz, *Deutsche Rechtsbücher*, No. 268.
167 Hereafter referred to as MS 951b. Cf. also Oppitz, *Deutsche Rechtsbücher*, No. 890.
168 Rudolf Helssig, *Die lateinischen und deutschen Handschriften der Universitätsbibliothek Leipzig*, 3: *Die juristischen Handschriften* (1926, repr. Wiesbaden, 1996), pp. 88–89; Oppitz, *Deutsche Rechtsbücher*, p. 632.
169 Helssig, *Die lateinischen und deutschen Handschriften*, p. 89.
170 Articles 21 and 53.

the manuscript was bought by the University Library in Leipzig for the price of 10 marks. It is just a possibility that the book was brought to Leipzig from the Congress Kingdom of Poland after the defeat of the November Rising (1830–1831).

3.18 *Tomasz of Bydgoszcz's MS (Early 16th Century) in the National Library in Warsaw, BN 3068 III*[171]

Manuscript BN 3068, now held in the National Library, was returned to Poland from Leningrad (St Petersburg) after the end of World War I. It had been seized by the Russians with other books from the Załuscy Library in Warsaw after the Third Partition of Poland in 1795 and transferred to the Imperial Public Library in St Petersburg. There, it had the shelfmark Lat. F II 191. Dated to the early 16th century, BN 3068 is a late arrival and may have been completed after the publication of Jan Łaski's *Statutes* (see Chapter 2.2.3). There is no uncertainty about the scribe, however. His name is Tomasz of Bydgoszcz (f. 227ra).[172] The volume contains the key texts of the Saxon-Magdeburg Law and a miscellany of excerpts and short notes. The most comprehensive list of its contents can be found in a description by Ebel and Schelling. The following list is based on that record supplemented with information from the National Library inventory of medieval and early 16th-century manuscripts: 1) an astrological treatise (f. 1r–1v); 2) a systematic digest of the *Sachsenspiegel*, arranged according to subject – the beginning of the text is missing (f. 2ra–19va); 3) the *Weichbild*, rubricated as Book I (f. 20ra–45vb) plus a series of provisions on f. 42–45 listed in the National Library inventory as an extract from the *Weichbild* – in fact it is a quasi-separate text called the *Constitution of Courts*, often appended to the *Weichbild* after the Jewish oath; 4) the *Sachsenspiegel* (*versio Vratislaviensis*), rubricated as Book II, together with the Lübeck Law (f. 45vb–102vb) – note that the sequence *Weichbild* – *Sachsenspiegel* – Lübeck Law is identical in *Commune incliti*; 5) an extract from *versio Sandomiriensis* of the *Sachsenspiegel*, mainly provisions concerning family law (f. 103ra–108rb); 6) a compilation of

---

171 Hereafter referred to as MS BN 3068. Cf. also Oppitz, *Deutsche Rechtsbücher*, No 1459. In Oppitz's catalogue and Ebel and Schelling's article, the manuscript's shelfmark is cited incorrectly as BN III 3065.

172 Kaliszuk and Szyller, *Inwentarz rękopisów*, p. 90; *Dziedzictwo kulturowe po klasztorach skasowanych na ziemiach dawnej Rzeczpospolitej oraz Śląsku w XVIII i XIX w.: losy, znaczenie, inwentaryzacja* [The Cultural Heritage of Monasteries Dissolved on the Territory of the Polish-Lithuanian Commonwealth and in Silesia in the 18th and 19th Century: History, Significance, Stock-taking], a data base sponsored by the Ministry of Science and Higher Education in the framework of the National Programme of the Development of the Humanities in 2012–2016, http://pw.kasaty.pl/rekopis/Scroll/4384.html?search=bydgoszcz (Accessed: 18 March 2015).

materials from the *Sachsenspiegel*, Roman and canon law – the text is of Polish provenance (f. 108rb–146rb); 7) a treatise in 24 books for practitioners of urban law (f. 146va–221vb); 8) extracts from the *Weichbild* (223vb–224rb); 9) coin conversion tables (f. 224rb–226va); 10) a lexicon of legal terms of Magdeburg Law (f. 224vb–226va); 11) oath formulas (f. 226vb–227va); and 12) a prescription (228vb). The *Weichbild* is flanked with numerous glosses and annotations (for a more detailed analysis, see Chapter 4 of this study).

3.19 *Marcin Zabowski's MS (1513) in the National Library in Warsaw, BOZ 90*[173]

This paper manuscript, completed in 1513 by Marcin Zabowski of Lwówek,[174] used to be held in the collection of the Library of Zamoyski Estate.[175] It contains the Sachsenspiegel (*versio Sandomiriensis*) (f. 1ra–45va) and the *Weichbild* (f. 45va–69va). The third text, which is introduced in the text by the rubric *Incipit De imperio terre Saxonie ius suum ab inicio statutum fuerit et confirmatum*, is in fact the *Constitution of Courts*, often appended to the *Weichbild* (f. 66vb–69va). The contents and thematic scope (see Chapter 2.2.3) of the MS BOZ position it very closely to the earliest extant Latin *Weichbild* from Gniezno MS. Among the things they have in common are certain phrases that refer to the *Sachsenspiegel* and the *Weichbild* and the special treatment of the provisions of the *Constitution of Courts*.

3.20 *Sanok MS (Early 16th Century) in the Central National Archives of Ukraine in Lwów (Fonds Sanok 438) – Now Lost*[176]

The Sanok MS is known exclusively from descriptions, including one by Emil Kałużniacki.[177] The paper manuscript had been held in the Central Historical Archives of Ukraine in Lviv' until its disappearance, which may have predated 1982, the year when the loss was discovered.[178] So far, all efforts to explain the circumstances of its disappearance or to ascertain its whereabouts have failed. According to Kałużniacki, the manuscript contained the Magdeburg *Weichbild* (pp. 3b, 19–44), Konrad of Sandomierz's version of the *Sachsenspiegel*, a fragment of the Latin translation of the *Sachsenspiegel-Lehnrecht*, *Rechtsbuch nach*

173 Hereafter referred to as MS BOZ. Cf. also Oppitz, *Deutsche Rechtsbücher*, No. 1457. Oppitz's catalogue mentions only the *Sachsenspiegel*.

174 See the explicit (f. 69v): *Iste liber est finitus per Martinum Zabowskÿ de Lwowek in vigilia Sancte Crucis Anno Domini millesimo quingentesimo tredecimo. Cantor.*

175 Kaliszuk and Sławomir Szyller, *Inwentarz rękopisów*, p. 52.

176 Oppitz, *Deutsche Rechtsbücher*, No. 929.

177 Kałużniacki, "Die polnische Recension", pp. 155–159.

178 Oppitz, *Deutsche Rechtsbücher*, No. 929.

Distinctionen (i.e. the Law Book of Meißen), the Magdeburg *ortyle*, digests of the *Sachsenspiegel-Landrecht*, and the *Weichbild*.[179] According to Oppitz's Catalogue, the contents of the Sanok MS were as follows: 1) *versio Sandomiriensis* of the *Sachsenspiegel*; 2) the *Weichbild*; 3) the *Sachsenspiegel-Lehnrecht*; 4) *versio Vratislaviensis* of the *Sachsenspiegel*; 5) the Law Book of Meißen; and 6) the Magdeburg *ortyle*. Kałużniacki believes that the *Weichbild* of the Sanok MS was even closer to Łaski's *Statutes* than MS Oss., whose description was provided by Ferdinand Bischoff.[180] Kałużniacki even goes so far as to claim that in preparing his edition of the *Weichbild*, Łaski relied heavily on the text of the Sanok *Weichbild*. Needless to say, none of these claims can be verified.

3.21 *Jan Łaski's* Statutes (Commune incliti Poloniae Regni privilegium, *1506*)[181]

Zygfryd Rymaszewski writes that one of the main objectives of his monograph of the *Sachsenspiegel-Landrecht* was to examine and profile the text of the *Landrecht* in Łaski's *Commune incliti*. His research has established that the *Sachsenspiegel* in the *Statutes* is an imaginative compilation of the *versio Vratislaviensis* and the two redactions of the *versio Sandomiriensis*. As Łaski's collection of laws enjoyed the status of an official document, the texts that were included in it acquired enormous importance. In his latest study of the *Commune incliti*, Wacław Uruszczak shows that the official authorization elevated both the rank of the land law (or, more broadly, Polish common law) in the first part of the book, as well sources of the second part.[182] The latter (Part II) contains: 1) an alphabetical index of subjects covered by the provisions

179 In his survey, Rymaszewski does not mention the *Lehnrecht* and identifies the text of the *Sachsenspiegel* as Konrad of Opole's version (Rymaszewski, *Łacińskie teksty Landrechtu Zwierciadła Saskiego w Polsce. Versio*, Table 6. Cf. also Kałużniacki, "Die polnische Recension", pp. 157–159).

180 Kałużniacki, "Die polnische Recension", p. 157, Note 1.

181 Hereafter referred to as the *Statutes*. Cf. Karol Estreicher, *Bibliografia polska* [Polish Bibliography], General Series, 21 (Kraków, 1906), pp. 79–80; Maria Cytowska, *Bibliografia druków urzędowych XVI wieku* [A Bibliography of Official Documents of the 16th Century] (Wrocław, 1961), No. 1, pp. 53–54; Ebel and Schelling, *Das lateinische lübische Recht*, pp. 97–98; and Wieland Carls, "Rechtsquellen Sächsisch-magdeburgischen Rechts", in: Inge Bily, Wieland Carls, and Katalin Gönczi, *Sächsisch-magdeburgisches Recht in Polen. Untersuchungen zur Geschichte des Rechts und seiner Sprache*, IVS SAXONICO-MAIDEBVRGENSE IN ORIENTE, 2 (Berlin, 2011), pp. 102–103.

182 See Wacław Uruszczak, '*Commune incliti Poloniae Regni privilegium constitutionum et indultuum*: O tytule i mocy prawnej Statutu Łaskiego z 1506 roku' [*Commune incliti Poloniae Regni privilegium constitutionum et indultuum*: The Title and Legal Validity of Łaski's *Statutes* (1506)], in: *Prace poświęcone pamięci Adama Uruszczaka* [Studies in Honour of the Late Adam Uruszczak], eds. Jan Halberda, Michał Hosowicz, and Anna.

of the Saxon-Magdeburg Law (5 non-foliated leaves, after f. 175v); 2) Book I – the Magdeburg *Weichbild* (f. 176r–197r); 3) Book II – the *Sachsenspiegel-Landrecht* (f. 197v–239r); 4) provisions of the Lübeck Law (its title separates it clearly from the *Sachsenspiegel*, but the shift is not indicated by the page header (f. 239r–245r);[183] 5) the *Sachsenspiegel-Lehnrecht* (f. 245v–263r); and 6) *Summa legum brevis, levis et utilis* by Master Raymundus, with a separate pagination. It is by no means insignificant that Łaski decided to include in his book texts of feudal law (the *Sachsenspiegel-Lehnrecht*) rather than any of the collections of *ortyle*. One way of explaining this decision is to point out that a selection of *ortyle* formed part of the *Weichbild* and there was no need for more. It is, however, less easy to find any reasons for the inclusion of the *Lehnrecht*. Admittedly, offices like *wójt* (*Vogt, advocatus*) or *sołtys* (*Schultheiß, scultetus*) could be defined in terms of feudal law, and the jurisdiction over those who held such offices belonged to provincial feudal courts, appropriately named *sądy leńskie* (*Lehngerichte*). Yet the number of hereditary office-holders in this category had been falling steadily.[184] Łaski's choice is all the more puzzling as Konrad of Sandomierz had decided to omit the section on feudal law from his translation. It is estimated that in addition to 12 parchment copies of the *Statues*, around 150 copies were printed (those that were published in 1507 with a supplement containing statutes (*constitutiones*) recently adopted by the Sejm). They were to be distributed among provincial courts and cathedral chapters all over Poland.[185]

3.22 *Summary: Destination of Latin Texts of Magdeburg* Weichbild

A review of the state of research on the Latin *Weichbild* is part of the following discussion of the characteristic features of the individual manuscripts and Łaski's *Commune incliti*. In fact, what we know about texts of the *Weichbild* consists of partial insights that can be gathered from studies of other problems and often surprisingly imprecise information from inventories and catalogues

---

Karabowicz, (Prace Instytutu Prawa Własności Intelektualnej UJ) 96 (Zakamycze, 2006), pp. 115–135 For information on earlier research, see the bibliography in this text.

183 Rymaszewski writes: "All the indications suggest that Lübeck Law found its way into Łaski's collection by chance, due to the scribe's mechanical carrying on with his job of copying a manuscript in which it was so to say concealed". (Rymaszewski, *Łacińskie teksty Landrechtu Zwierciadła Saskiego w Polsce. Versio*, p. 148).

184 See Ludwik Łysiak, *Własność sołtysia (wójtowska) w Małopolsce do końca XVI wieku* [Property of the sołtys (wójt) in Małopolska until the End of the 16th Century] (Kraków, 1964), p. 108 ff.

185 Piotr Tafiłowski, *Jan Łaski (1456–1531) kanclerz koronny i prymas polski* [Jan Łaski (1456–1531): Grand Chancellor of Poland and Primate of Poland] (Warszawa, 2007), p. 296. Cf. also Potkowski, *Książka rękopiśmienna*, p. 176.

of medieval manuscripts. Unfortunately, many manuscripts have been destroyed or lost. In the case of the Sanok MS, all we have is a helpful description by Emil Kałużniacki. In general, the extant manuscripts can be sorted into the following groups as far as their contents are concerned:

1) Eight manuscripts contain texts of the Saxon-Magdeburg Law only.[186] The St Petersburg MS consists of two distinct parts; the date of their amalgamation remains unclear. MS Q II 157 is also a composite of two sets of the Saxon-Magdeburg Law, and the time at which they were put together is also unknown.
2) Five manuscripts, each written in a single hand, contain texts of the Saxon-Magdeburg Law and other legislative acts, for example, the municipal laws of Jihlava (the Opatów MS), canon law (Tomasz of Bydgoszcz's MS), and Polish land law (the Częstochowa MS, the St Florian MS, the Działyńscy Codex IV).
3) Six manuscripts are made up of blocks which contain texts of diverse provenance,[187] though in each case, the corpus of the Saxon-Magdeburg Law is a uniform set which predates the volume into which it was bound.

This preliminary survey shows that collections that originally included the text of the Saxon-Magdeburg Law alongside other codes of law were an exception. Why the land law block was added to the Częstochowa MS, the St Florian MS, and the Działyńscy Codex IV is a matter of speculation. It may also be speculated whether it is somehow connected with their monastic provenance, especially the Częstochowa MS and the St Florian MS[188] – hence the practical needs of an institution often involved in property litigation. Speculations aside, one thing can be said with great certainty: in practically every case, the *Weichbild* is accompanied by other collections or codes of the Saxon-Magdeburg Law. This means that the *Weichbild* was not regarded as the sole and complete source of urban law. Unfortunately, it is impossible to unequivocally identify the sponsors of the great majority of the manuscripts. It is a fair guess, however, that they were owned not only by institutions (e.g. the town councils), but also by individual owners of private libraries that included books of law.[189]

186 They are MS Gn., MS F 143, MS BN 12600, Q II 157, MS BJ 4405, MS Plesz., MS 951b, and MS BOZ.

187 They are MS Kiel., MS BN 12607, MS Dział. I, MS Przem., MS II Q 4, and MS Warsz.

188 Earlier, of the Abbey of Tyniec near Cracow.

189 Potkowski, *Książka rękopiśmienna*, pp. 195 and 210. A study by Maria Kramperowa and Witold Maisel of 20 library collections that belonged to Poznań burghers of the second half of 16th century lists several volumes featuring Saxon-Magdeburg Law, among them Jan Cervus Tucholczyk (2), Bartłomiej Groicki (4), the Sachsenspiegel in German (3), the Sachsenspiegel edited by Paweł Szczerbic (2). See Maria Kramperowa and Witold

4 Conclusions

'The Silesian-Małopolska compilation' is an umbrella term which encompasses the German texts of the *Weichbild*, also known as Konrad of Opole's compilation, and various Latin texts that descended from German sources. The *Weichbild* of this compilation differs a great deal from the vulgate used in Eastern Germany. The differences result principally from the fact that each branch of the *Weichbild* developed a dependence on its own source of borrowings. Whereas users of the vulgate had a clear preference for the *Sachsenspiegel*, the *Weichbild* community further East found their bearings in *Magdeburg's Legal Instructions for Wrocław* (*Rechtsmitteilungen Magdeburgs für Breslau*) of 1261 and 1295. The near-total absorption of the latter lent the Silesian-Małopolska compilation its distinctive character. The compound name by which I propose to designate this family of texts has the advantage of indicating their origin (Silesia) and the region where they were adopted and modified (Małopolska). The Silesian origin of the compilation is suggested by the fact that the Henryków MS (II F 8), whose Silesian provenance is established beyond any doubt, is closer to the original *Weichbild* than the Cracow City Council MS (BJ 169), attributed to Konrad of Opole. The extraordinary similarity of those two texts indicates that they must have a common base. The key texts of the Silesian-Małopolska compilation are contained in two groups of manuscripts. The first set includes the Cracow MS, the Henryków MS, the Baworowscy MS, and the Żagań MS; the second is made up of the German-language the Wawel MS used by the High Court of German Law at Wawel and a compilation shelfmarked BJ 170a. The latter has certain characteristics that exclude their complete dependence on the *Weichbild* known from the other four manuscripts. These features appear not only in the aforementioned articles and compilations; in many cases, they are closer to the original sources of the *Weichbild* than the Cracow Council manuscript or the Henryków MS. There is also additional evidence that points to the links between the Wawel MS and MS BJ 170a and a text characteristic of Cracow MS – a fact which proves the impact of that manuscript or a text very close to it on the wording of the *Weichbild* in the Wawel MS and MS

Maisel, "Księgozbiory mieszczan poznańskich drugiej połowy XVI w". [Library Collections of Poznań Burghers of the Second Half of the 16th Century], *Studia i Materiały do Dziejów Wielkopolski i Pomorza* 11/1 (1960), 304, 305, and 307. Cf. "Law Books During the Transition from Late-Medieval to Early-Modern Legal Scholarship", in: *The Formation and Transmission of Western Legal Culture. 150 Books that Made the Law in the Age of Printing*, Serge Dauchy, Georges Martyn, Anthony Musson, Heikki Pihlajamäki, Alain Wijffels, eds., Naoko Seriu, coop. (Studies in the History of Law and Justice) 7, series eds. Georges Martyn, Mortimer Sellers (New York – Berlin – Heidelberg, 2016), pp. 18–19.

BJ 170a. Whereas these two manuscripts contain just two different variants of the German text, the other four texts underwent an evolution which consisted of the addition to the received text of a selection of Magdeburg *ortyle* in the Baworowscy MS and the Żagań MS. The Baworowscy MS contains a *Weichbild* which is clearly dependent on the Cracow Council manuscript, and its assortment of the *ortyle* is of Cracow provenance. Moreover, both the Baworowscy and the Żagań manuscripts are bilingual: Latin and German. This means that the *ortyle* were added to both versions of the *Weichbild* independently from each other – that is, it can be ruled out that it affected the Latin *Weichbild* first.

However, it was the Latin rather than the German *Weichbild* that became more popular in the Kingdom of Poland, if the proportion of extant manuscripts in either language are anything to go by. At the same time, it may be surmised that a great deal more manuscripts have been lost, as those that have survived are parts of blocks which include other legal texts such as the *Sachsenspiegel*, Polish land law, or canon law. A close study of those volumes shows that in many of them, each section was written in a different hand, which could indicate that they were made up of heterogeneous manuscripts. Blocks of monastic provenance, like the Częstochowa MS or the St Florian MS, which contained texts of the municipal law and Polish land law, were written in one hand. However, manuscripts of the Magdeburg Law seem to have functioned as separate units, dedicated to the needs of the urban communities and their legal practice. Unfortunately, the evidence is too scant to decide whether they were used in municipal courts (with the exception of Cracow MS and Pleszew MS, which surely were used in such a way, and the Przemyśl MS, which probably was); whether they were used in High Courts of German Law (like the Wawel MS); or whether they were simply private property.

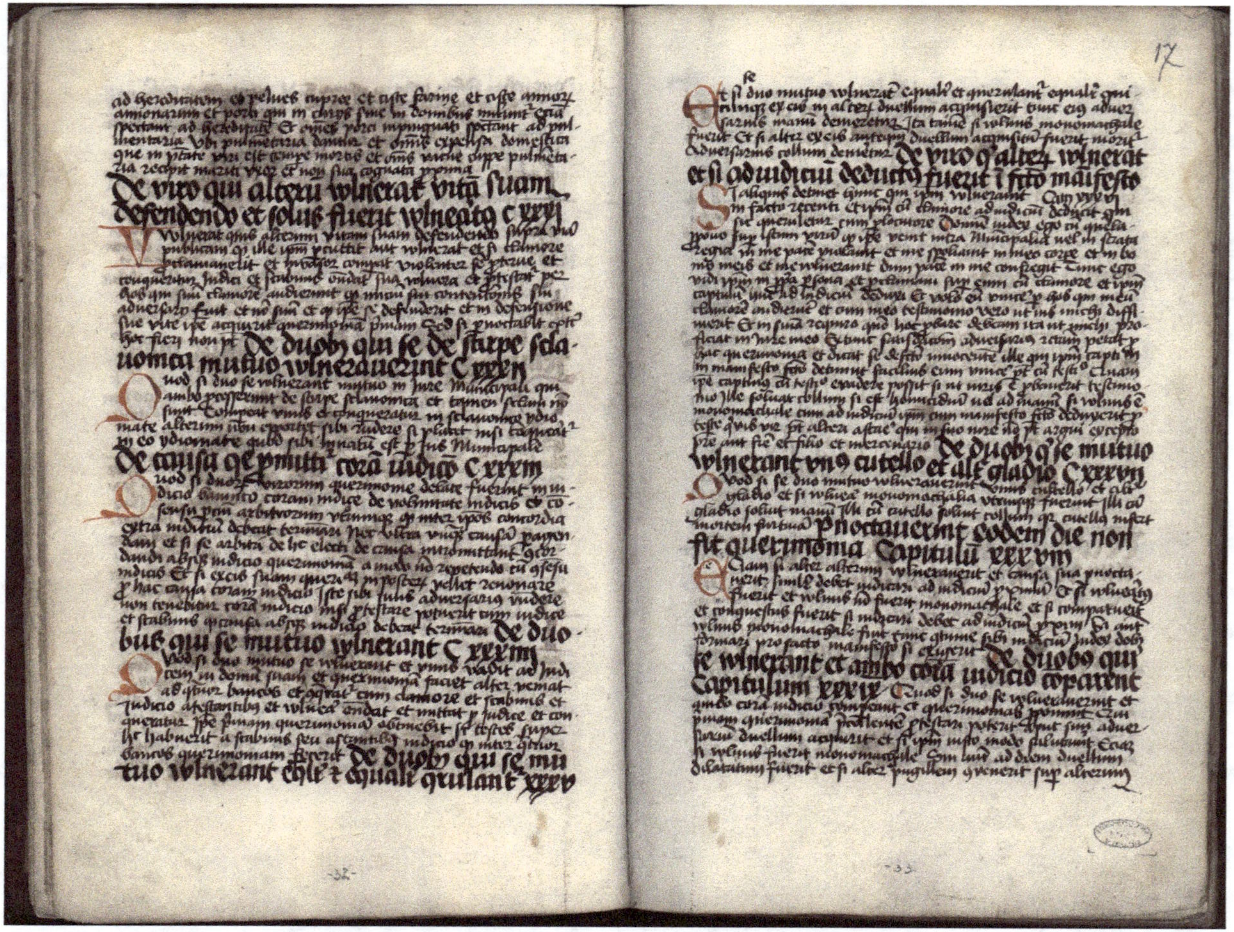

PHOTO 3 *Liber legum* – the book of law of Przemyśl, State Archive in Przemyśl, Acts of the Town Przemyśl, Shelfmark 428, f. 16v–17r

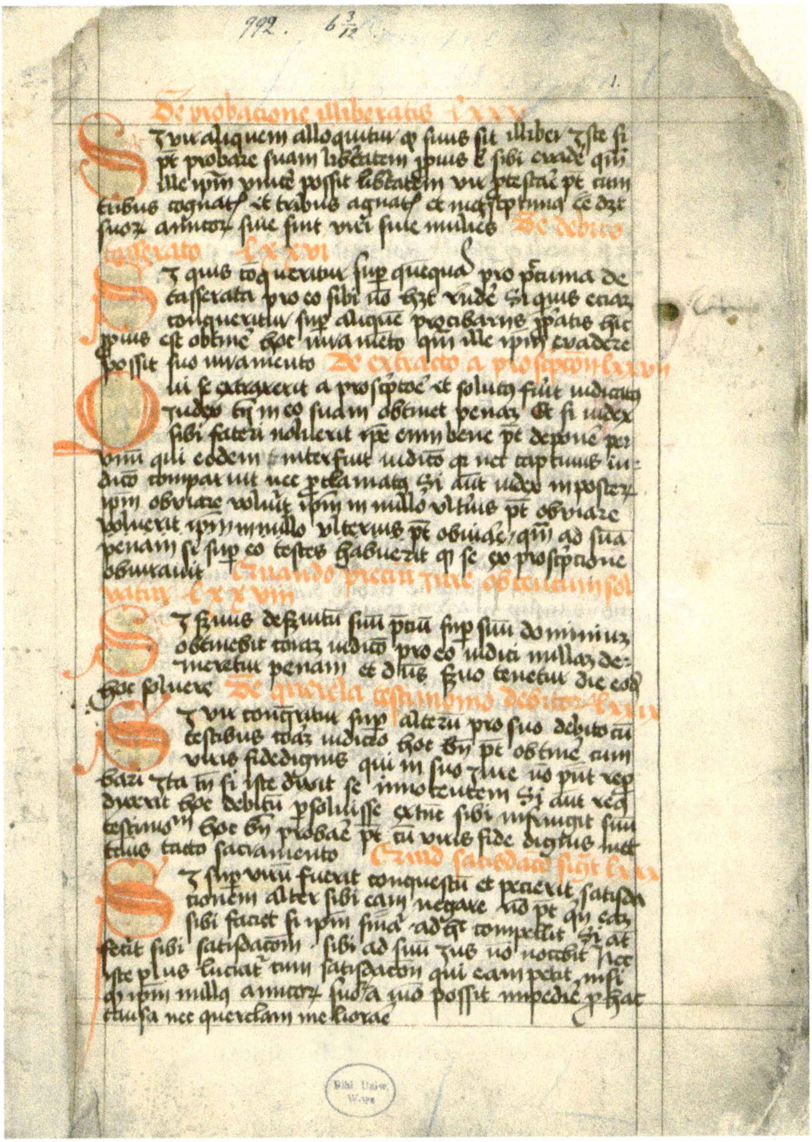

PHOTO 4 Warsaw manuscript, University of Warsaw Library, Shelfmark 5, f. 1r

CHAPTER 2

Dynamics of the Latin Text of the *Weichbild*: The Sandomierz and the Cracow Versions

In order to explain the dynamics of the Latin texts, a number of questions need to be answered: how did the Latin texts evolve before being consolidated in the definitive edition of the *Weichbild* in Jan Łaski's *Statutes*? What are the relations between the German and the Latin texts? What are the specific characteristics of the texts in the extant Latin manuscripts? Was there only one, or were there possibly two medieval Latin translations of the *Weichbild*? In order to answer these questions, it is necessary to make a series of comparisons of both the formal features (the structure) of the text and its contents.

1 Formal Features of the Latin Texts

1.1 *The Ordering of Articles in the Latin Texts*

There is a distinct set of formal features that recurs, although not in its entirety, in all Latin texts. First, some of them contain additional regulations in the form of separate provisions or extensive supplements. While additions taken over from the German texts are present in the earliest Latin texts (e.g. the Gniezno MS; Articles 55, 57, 76 § 1, 3 and 77), the corpus of the Magdeburg *ortyle* is a source of important supplementary passages in provisions that echo the German text of the Baworowscy MS (BN 12607) and the Żagań MS (II Q 4). Second, some Latin texts leave out the same articles as does the Wawel manuscript, even though they are included in the Cracow manuscript (Articles 56 and 81, according to the numbering scheme of the Gniezno MS). Third, some Latin texts skip a provision. The omission can only be detected when the translation is compared to the German text, as in the case of Article 76 (according to the numbering scheme of the Cracow MS BJ 169). Fourth, the *Constitution of Courts*, which, as a rule, follows the Jewish oath, can appear either in an abridged or an extended form, or can be left out altogether.

Fifth, only a portion of the Latin texts reproduces the articles from the Cracow MS or the Wawel MS (BJ 168) consistently in the same order. Notable among the differences are two provisions concerning the *gerada* and *hergewet* (in the Gniezno MS, Articles 60 and 61).[1] In many Latin manuscripts, they were included next to each other. The change of order also concerns Articles 96 and 97, as well as Articles 102 and 103 of the Gniezno MS. The order in which the articles are arranged is naturally not an argument with the same strength as the presence or absence of an article.

The distribution of features discussed above are presented in Table 8.

TABLE 8 Formal features of the Latin texts of the *Weichbild* as compared with that of Cracow MS (BJ 169) and Wawel MS (BJ 168)

	Gn.	F 143	Dział. I	BJ 4405	Przem.	BOZ	157 (1)	157 (2)	BN 12600	Plesz.	BN 12607	Oss.	II Q 4	Dział. IV	Warsz.	AJG	Kiel.	Flor.	951b	BN 3068	Statutes
Article 55 (as designated in MS Gn.)	+	–	+	+	+	+	+	+	+	–	–	–	–	–	o	+	+	–	+	+	+
Article 57 (as designated in MS Gn.)	+	+	+	+	+	+	+	+	+	–	–	–	–	–	o	–	–	+	+	+	+
Article 76 § 1 and 3 (as designated in MS Gn.)	+	+	+	+	+	+	+	+	+	–	–	–	–	–	–	+	+	+	+	+	+
Article 77 (as designated in MS Gn.)	+	+	+	+	+	+	+	+	+	–	–	–	–	–	–	+	+	+	+	+	+
No additions from the *ortyle*	+	+	+	+	+	+	+	+	+	+	–	–	–	+	+	+	+	+	–	–	–
Articles 56, 81 (as designated in MS Gn.) but not included in MS BJ 168	+	+	+	+	+	+	+	+	+	–	+	+	+	–	–	+	+	+	+	+	+
Absence of Article 76 of MS BJ 169 in the matching place in the German text	+	+	+	+	+	+	+	+	+	–	–	–	–	–	–	–	–	+	–	–	–
Shorter version (+), extended version (–), or missing (B) RGV	+	B	+	B	B	+	+	+	+	B	–	–	–	–	–	–	–	+	+	+	–
Sequence of Articles 52–54 in MS Gn. different from that in MS BJ 168	+	+	+	+	+	+	+	+	+	+	–	–	–	–	o	–	–	–	+	+	+

1 For an explanation of terms *gerada*, *hergewet*, and principal inheritance, see Chapter 3.4.4.

TABLE 8 Formal features of the Latin texts of the *Weichbild* (*cont.*)

	Gn.	F 143	Dział. I	BJ 4405	Przem.	BOZ	157 (1)	157 (2)	BN 12600	Plesz.	BN 12607	Oss.	II Q 4	Dział. IV	Warsz.	AJG	Kiel.	Flor.	951b	BN 3068	Statutes
Articles on the *gerada* and the *hergewet* positioned next to each other	+	+	+	+	+	+	+	+	+	–	–	–	–	–	o	–	–	±	+	+	+
Sequence of Articles 96–97 in MS Gn. different from that in MS BJ 169	+	–	+	+	+	–	–	–	–	–	–	–	–	–	–	–	–	+	–	–	–
Sequence of Articles 102–103 in MS Gn. different from that in MS BJ 169	+	–	+	+	+	–	–	–	–	–	–	–	–	–	–	–	–	+	–	–	–
Article on the Jewish Oath split up	+	+	+	+	+	+	+	+	+	–	–	–	–	–	–	–	–	+	+	–	–

'o' denotes an absence of an article due to damage to the manuscript; '±' denotes that the provision on the *gerada* was included twice, together with the provision on the *hergewet*, in a slot matching the sequential arrangement of the Cracow MS.

In effect, taking their formal features as the only criterion, the extant Latin texts can be divided into the following groups:

I) MSS Gn., F 143, Dział. I, BJ 4405, Przem., BOZ, Q II 157 (1), Q II 157 (2) and BN 12600 show either all or a clear majority of the features indicated in Table 8. It is no coincidence that some of them (and certainly the Gniezno MS and the Działyńscy Codex I) are present in manuscripts which include the *Sachsenspiegel* in its Sandomierz version (*versio Sandomiriensis I* according to Zygfryd Rymaszewski's classification). The texts in this group do not contain any additions from the *ortyle*, and in those cases where they do include an extract from the *Constitution of Courts* after the Jewish oath, it is its abridged version. The texts of this group form the Sandomierz version of the Latin Silesian-Małopolska compilation of the *Weichbild*, produced originally by Konrad of Sandomierz. It is also worth noting that the author of the Pleszew MS copied less than half of the complete set of provisions.

II) Group II includes texts that lack a number of the features that are characteristic of the Gniezno MS. The compliance of the Baworowscy MS (BN 12607), the Opatów MS (Oss.), and the Żagań MS (II Q 4) with the

Gniezno manuscript is limited exclusively to the inclusion of provisions that are omitted in the Wawel manuscript. In particular, they contain additions from the *ortyle*, as does the German text in the Baworowscy MS and the Żagań MS. The texts of the Działyńscy Codex IV (Dział. IV) and the Warsaw MS (Warsz.), which also include the *Sachsenspiegel* in its Sandomierz version (*versio Sandomiriensis II* according to Zygfryd Rymaszewski's classification), do not contain any *ortyle*. However, the two manuscripts have some formal features in common with the German text of the Wawel MS.

III) Group III comprises manuscripts that show some features characteristic of the Gniezno MS and of Group II. The texts of this group are not uniform. Although formally the St Florian MS (Flor.) is not much different from MS Gn., it is in fact a compilation. This is testified by the recurrence of the provision on the *gerada* in places that match its position in the manuscripts of Groups I and II. The claim that it belongs to the class of compilations will be reinforced in the subsequent discussion. The formal features of the Tomasz of Bydgoszcz's MS (BN 3068) and the Leipzig MS (951b) leave no doubt that they belong to Group I and Group II, respectively. They, too, contain an abridged version of the *Constitution of Courts* from Group I, supplementary material from the *ortyle*, and additional provisions characteristic of the Gniezno MS Gn. The status of the Częstochowa MS and the Kielce MS is unclear. Like the Gniezno MS, they ignore the *ortyle*, but contain the provisions that are omitted in the Wawel manuscript. Furthermore, they feature three of the four articles characteristic of the Gniezno manuscript. In the main, the Częstochowa MS and the Kielce MS seem to depend on the text found in the manuscripts of Group I; but, given the presence of numerous features typical of Group II, its domination is by no means total.

Jan Łaski's *Statutes* deserves special attention, if only because of its official status. For this reason, it will be the focus of the third chapter, but at this stage (analysis of formal features), it can already be said that it is a composite of texts from Group I and II.

While considering the issue of formal features, it is worthwhile to explain the origin of the articles added to the Gniezno MS and other manuscripts in Group I. They are concerned with establishing a proxy for an injured person (Article 55 of MS Gn.), accusations of wounding or murder (Article 57), and the master's liability for his servant's debts (Article 76 § 1 and 3), as well as liability for damage to property, which was deposited for safe-keeping, handed over for use, including the liability for damages caused by animals (Article 77). Obviously these concerns were anything but petty. The source of Article 55 is

TABLE 9 Articles 56, 57, 76, and 77 of the *Weichbild* and their origin

	Gracow MS (BJ 169)		Gniezno MS (Gn.)		Baworowscy MS (BN 12607)	Działyńscy Codex IV (MS Dział. IV)	
	Sachsenspiegel	***Weichbild***	***Sachsenspiegel***	***Weichbild***	***Weichbild***	***Sachsenspiegel***	***Weichbild***
Numbering in MGH[a]	Wrocław version	German text	Sandomierz version I	Group I	Group II	Sandomierz version II	MS Dział. IV
SSp I 49 and 69	+	–	+	+ [57]	–	+	–
SSp III 6 § 1–3	+	–	+	+ [76]	–	+	–
SSp III 5 § 3–5	+	–	+	+ [77]	–	+	–
SSp I 63–65 § 1	+	+	–	+ [56]	+	+	–

a Karl A. Eckhard's edition.

Article 72 of *Magdeburg's Legal Instructions for Wrocław* of 1261. This regulation was included, in a much amended form, in Article 53 of the Cracow MS; that fact probably prompted the compilers who used that text to go back to its full wording. The text of the other articles falls back on the *Sachsenspiegel*, as presented in Table 9.

Thus, the texts of Group I reinstate a handful of important *Sachsenspiegel* provisions (Articles 57, 76, and 77 of the MS Gn.) that are missing in Group II. However, while drawing this conclusion, we need to take note of a string of baffling annotations which begin with a reference to the provisions of the *Weichbild* in the Gniezno MS *Sachsenspiegel* at a place where Articles 63, 64, and 65 § 1 of SSp I are left out.[2] The content referred to can be found subsequently in Article 56 of the *Ius municipale*. It is the other way around in the Działyńscy Codex IV, where the reader looking for missing Articles 55, 56, and 57 (as designated in MS Gn.) is referred to the matching section of the *Sachsenspiegel*. It is worth noting that these articles are also missing in the Wawel MS, where they are replaced with a note in Latin *Hoc capitulum continuetur in iure, quod dicitur landrecht*.

2 Rymaszewski, *Łacińskie teksty Landrechtu Zwierciadła Saskiego w Polsce. Versio Vratislaviensis, versio Sandomiriensis, Łaski* (Łódź, 1975), p. 71.

The presence of a complete set of regulations in the *versio Vratislaviensis* of the *Sachsenspiegel* is a well established fact: it was a translation of the entire text of the law code which predates the Silesian-Małopolska compilation of the *Weichbild*. The availability of the complete text may well have been prompted by Konrad of Sandomierz's decision not to include said regulations from his translation of the *Weichbild* (i.e. the contents of Article 56). Yet, if we assume that that was his reasoning, why did he expand the size of his *Weichbild* by adding other articles from the *Sachsenspiegel* without editing them out from the latter to preserve balance? There is no solution to this inconsistency. As Table 9 shows, the Latin text of the Group II manuscripts follows the German base. Only the author of the Działyńscy Codex IV clears up the redundancies from the *Weichbild* and restores the complete text of the *Sachsenspiegel*.

On the diachronic level, the problem of this structural inconsistency can be reformulated in terms of the following alternatives: 1) either Konrad of Sandomierz's extended version came first (Group I), but some of his successors (Group II), after consulting the German base, decided to trim down his text; or 2) it all began with an (original) version of the text in the Cracow MS which was first expanded by Konrad of Sandomierz and later cut back by the author of the Działyńscy Codex IV (which belongs to Group II). This will discussed in the following sections.

1.2 *Summary: The Division of the Latin* Wechbild *Texts into Groups on the Basis of Their Formal Characteristics*

This comparative analysis, which is based principally on a concordance of the content of the texts collected in Appendix 1 and focused on their general characteristics (content and sequence), shows that one of the aspects of the differentiation of texts is the way in which they were edited. Some texts (Group I) were augmented with provisions from the *Sachsenspiegel*, which made them more rounded than the texts of another group (designated Group II), which were augmented with Magdeburg judgments (*ortyle*), which made them more suited for practical use. The thematic rearrangement of the sequence of provisions in Group I indicates that their editor(s) sought to introduce some order into a fragmented text, although its product fell far short of a systematized law code. The analysis has also identified a group of texts in which the two types of augmentation are combined. Now that the manuscript texts have been divided into clearly defined groups and the differentiation can be associated with an intention or purpose, the next stage in the investigation would be to seek further proof of this profiling at the level of content, namely, editorial modification of the substance of individual provisions.

2 Divergences in the Latin Texts of the *Weichbild*

2.1 *Quantitative Analysis of the Latin Texts of the* Weichbild

Appendix 2 contains a list of variants in the Latin texts. Account has been taken of the modifications which essentially amended the regulations, that is, made them more precise – or, quite the opposite – clouded the originally clear wording of a regulation. For this reason, thousands of linguistic variants and minor editorial amendments are omitted.[3] It was deliberately decided not to include variants in the list of items that make up the *gerada* and the principal inheritance (*dziedzictwo*), because these discrepancies concern relatively marginal details, such as types of fabrics and household vessels. The appendices do not include the final articles appended to the Jewish oath. They come from the *Constitution of Courts* and contain regulations that can be deemed irrelevant in the Polish context (except the provision concerning the number of jurors). This is confirmed by the fact that some manuscripts omit those provisions.

Statistical calculations have turned out to be a useful tool. They require certain introductory explanations, however. Out data pool is the records of Appendix 2 with all the amendations, defined as divergences from the text of the Gniezno MS, the earliest extant manuscript.[4] As each record includes a fairly exhaustive catalogue of variants, some of them tend to be quite large, especially those that take stock of the borrowings from the *ortyle*, while others are relatively small (in cases where the comparison offers only minor omissions or copyists' errors). Due to peculiarities of the individual texts, the irregularities detected in the course of a statistical review must be treated with great caution.[5] The results of the comparisons are presented in Figure 2.

---

3 For a more extensive categorization of the variants, see the Introduction to Annex II.

4 This seems more important than the departure from a presumed Konrad of Sandomierz's archetype (cf. the discussion in Chapter 1 (2.1). The second-oldest text, the Petersburg MS (F 143), was heavily modified.

5 If a given manuscript leaves out one or more articles in a legal text, we have assumed – for the purpose of the statistical calculations – that it does not conform with the Gniezno MS. The texts of MS Q II 157 (2), the Warsaw MS, and the Opatów MS have not been preserved in their entirety. This study has addressed this issue by developing a statistical method to estimate the number of possible divergences from MS Gn. in the missing passages. It proceeds in three stages: 1) calculation of average number of amendations per page for each text; 2) the determination of the number of missing pages; 3) determination of the estimated number of amendations with regard to the text of the Gniezno MS in the missing passages. In determining the number of pages of the *Weichbild* missing from the Warsaw MS and the Opatów MS (each of them opens with the *Weichbild*), we have used the Działyńscy Codex IV and the Baworowscy MS, respectively, because other comparisons show a significant similarity between those pairs. In the Działyńscy Codex IV, the portion of the text which corresponds to the preserved part of the Warsaw MS makes up approx. 26 per cent of the whole.

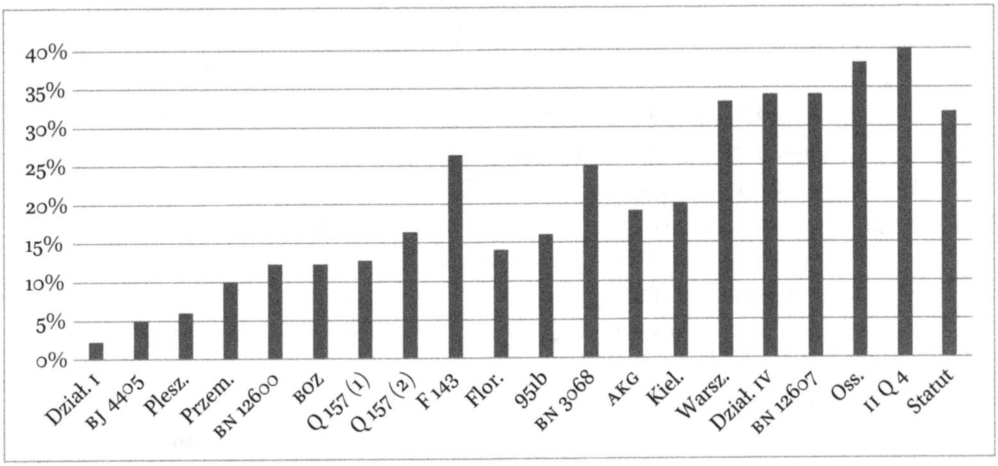

FIGURE 2 Quantitative analysis of divergences from the text of Gniezno MS in subsequent Latin texts on the basis of data collected in Appendix 2 (in per cent)

The results presented in Figure 2 correspond to the classification of the texts based on their formal features. The highest degree of consistency with the Gniezno MS can be found in manuscripts of Group I: deviation rates ranging between 2 per cent and 16 per cent, with the exception of the St Petersburg MS (F 143) with a score of 26 per cent (see Table 10 below). The furthest removed from the Gniezno MS are the Żagań manuscript (II Q 4; 40 per cent) as well as other Group II texts, such as the Baworowscy MS (BN 12607; 34 per cent), the Opatów MS (Oss.; 38 per cent), the Warsaw MS (Warsz.; 33 per cent), and the Działyńscy Codex IV (Dział. IV; 34 per cent). With a score of 25 per cent, Tomasz of Bydgoszcz's MS (BN 3068) stands out from Group I not only because of its amount of *ortyle*, but also due to the profuse amendations introduced into the text by the copyist. Positioned in the middle ground between Group I and Group II are compilations like the St Florian MS (Flor.; 14 per cent) and the Leipzig MS (951b; 16 per cent), as well as the Częstochowa MS (MS AJG; 19 per cent) and the Kielce MS (Kiel.; 20 per cent), both of which contain neither the

So, proportionally, the 8.5 pages of the extant text of the *Weichbild* (for the calculation, the provision ending with the Jewish oath is included) amounts to c. 26 per cent of the text. This means that about 22 pages are lost. In the case of the Opatów MS and MS Q II 157 (2), the estimate takes into account a leaf torn out of the middle of the codex. MS Pleszew, whose author copied fewer than half of the provisions, presents an altogether different challenge than physical damage to the manuscript. Nevertheless, in this case, a workable estimator has also been devised. I am grateful to Dr Marcin Suder from the AGH University of Science and Technology in Kraków, Department of Applications of Mathematics in Economics for his assistance in finding the appropriate statistical tools.

case law of the *ortyle* nor the additional provisions of the Gniezno MS. Finally, the deviation rate for the *Statutes* is 32 per cent.

2.2 *Group I: MSS Gn., F 143, BN 12600, Q II 157 (1), Q II 157 (2), Dział. I, BJ 4405, Przem., Plesz. and BOZ*

Direct proof of the indebtedness of Group I manuscripts to the *versio Sandomiriensis* of the *Weichbild* is an annotation reproduced in four manuscripts naming Konrad of Sandomierz as the author of the translation.[6] Mikołaj of Cieszyn, the author of the Gniezno MS, states that: *Iste liber finitus et de Teutunico translatus in Latinum per Conradum scriptorem.* An equally unequivocal statement can be found at the beginning of MS Q II 157 (2): *Incipit ius municipale per Cunradum civem Sandomiriensem de Theutonico translatum in Latinum.*[7] The divergences between the texts of this group are not profound (see Chapter 2.4.3), with the exception of MS Q II 157 (2) (16 per cent) and the St Petersburg MS (26 per cent). While the differences between MSS Gn. and Q II 157 (2) were caused by the copyist's omissions, the origins of the divergences in MS F 143 are illustrated in Table 10, below.

TABLE 10 Petersburg MS (F 143): Quantitative analysis of textual divergences from Gniezno MS (Gn.)

	Number of records
Omission of seven articles	10[a]
Individual textual divergences	28[b]
Absence of faults found in MS Gn. (see Section 4.3)	4[c]
Textual divergences unique to Group I	4[d]
Textual divergences unique to Group II	7[e]
Textual divergences common to Groups I and II	5[f]

a No. 72, 106, 107, 161, 195, 196, 197, 198, 201, and 202.
b No. 1, 7, 8, 9, 14, 20, 21, 23, 26, 32, 34, 36, 53, 57, 63, 65, 66, 86, 116, 117, 122, 125, 126, 127, 148, 149, 150, and 189.
c No. 60, 175, 201, and 216.
d No. 4, 181, 182, and 187.
e No. 3, 22, 28, 45, 91, 151, and 172.
f No. 49, 53, 93, 102, and 179.

6 MS Gn., MS Q II 157 (2), MS BN 12600, and MS BOZ.
7 Identical wording in MS BN 12600.

Can the high degree of compatibility between the St Petersburg MS and Group II manuscripts be regarded as conclusive proof of a close relationship between the two? In seeking to answer this question, we need to bear in mind that the medieval copyist saw nothing wrong in selecting and adapting his material, including the content of the provisions. The author of the St Petersburg MS left out 12 passages (clauses), some of which match the omissions peculiar to Group I, such as, for example, the provisions that municipal legislation must not contravene God's law, that in no circumstances can an heir be deprived of his portion of the inheritance, and that the *sołtys* (*scultetus*) should be a free-born local man.[8] This brings the St Petersburg MS closer to Group II. Yet, if the size and nature of additions rather than omissions is crucial in demonstrating filiations between texts, making a case for a close relationship between MS F 143 and Group II texts becomes very hard indeed. The additions and modifications that the St Petersburg MS shares with the texts of Group II are on the whole too scanty for a compelling argument. Having said that, there are other ways of addressing the issue:

1) First, only Group II manuscripts and the St Petersburg MS contain an extensive appendix confirming the plaintiff's right to take precedence in presenting proof in cases concerning the price and quality of food, which corresponds to Article 76 in the German text of MS BJ 169.[9]
2) Second, at the end of Article 1, there is a passage resembling that in Article 3. Crucially, the punishment for a breach the councillors' rulings with regard to measures and weights is set at 36 shillings (*szeląg*), and not 30, as is the case in Article 3. Thirty-six shillings is an amount consistent with the wording of the German texts and with Group II manuscripts, while the fine of 30 shillings occurs only in some Group I manuscripts.
3) Third, exclusively in MSS F 143, AJG, Kiel., Flor., Dział. IV, BN 12607 and II Q 4, the wording of Article 16 includes the term 'objection', which matches the German text, and not the term 'arrest' (*contradicione, arrestacione*).[10]

I argue that these conformities with Group II manuscripts are due to the copyist's use of the St Petersburg MS from one of the Group II manuscripts. Despite the presence of some Group II features, the decision to qualify MS F 143 as a Group I text and treat it as a compilation depends largely on the fact that it features nearly all of the additional provisions characteristic of the Group I text, which must have been the copyist's main source. It is worth noting that some of the divergences in the text of the St Petersburg MS from the Gniezno MS also

8 No. 1, 91, and 22.
9 No. 173.
10 No. 45.

occur in Group I manuscripts.[11] The persistence of this bunch of variants is an important clue which justifies a distinction of two subsets within Group I (see Section 4.3). What is more, the accurate dating of the St Petersburg MS strongly suggests that the origins of Group II should be sought prior to 1368.

2.3 *Group II: MSS BN 12607, Oss., II Q 4, Dział. IV, and Warsz.*

Close similarities can be found in the following two pairs: MS Dział. IV / MS Warsz.; and MS BN 12607 / MS Oss. The text of the *Weichbild* in the Żagań MS (II Q 4) is close to that in the latter pair of manuscripts, principally due to its intermix of *ortyle*, although, admittedly, it has a number of individual features of its own. Let us, at this point, map the filiations that emerge on the basis of comparison of the formal features of the texts:

1) The first pair, which contains the Sandomierz version of the *Sachsenspiegel* (in its second redaction), matches other Group II manuscripts, with the exception of the provisions that are also missing in the Wawel manuscript MS (BN 168).
2) The Baworowscy MS (BN 12607), the Opatów MS (Oss.), and the Żagań MS are fully compliant, with regard to the arrangement of the articles, with the German texts in the Cracow MS (BJ 169), the Henryków MS (II F 8), the Baworowscy MS, and the Żagań MS; it also contains a selection of the *ortyle*.

All of the texts included in Group II have 24 divergences in common.[12] In the Działyńscy Codex IV / the Warsaw MS pair, in addition to those divergences, there is also a group of 12 individual features[13] as well as 8 divergences from the Gniezno MS which are consistent either with MS BN 12607 or MS II Q 4, one – in the Częstochowa / the Kielce MS pair.[14] A common feature of in the Baworowscy MS, the Opatów MS, and the Żagań MS is the presence of another 24 divergences from the Gniezno MS, apart from the 24 divergences already mentioned.[15] Furthermore, there is a relatively large group of variants that

---

11 No. 1, 60, 93, 175, 179, and 216.

12 No. *1*, 3, 10, 22, 45, 52, *60*, 79, 84, 88, 91, *93*, 102, *106*, 146, 166, 169, 170, 173, *175* (without Dział. IV), 195, *197*, 206, and *216*. The italicized cases also occur in some texts of the Sandomierz version that do not descend directly from MS Gn. See Section 4.3.

13 No. 5, 37 (also in 951b), 41, 71, 78, 83, 92, 113, 114, 119, 177, and 178. As large portions of the text of MS Warsz. have not survived, they could not be included in Records 1–165.

14 Conformity with MS BN 12607 and MS II Q 4 only: Nos. 46, 62, and 220. Conformity with MS BN 12607 only: No. 118. Conformity with MS II Q 4 only: Nos. 122, 150, and 188. Conformity with MS AJG/Kiel.: No. 28.

15 Nos. 15, 24, 29, 30, 33, 35, 38, 44, 65, 80, 81, 82, 83, 95, 107, 110, 130, 142, 158, 163, 165, 193, 204, and 217. Due to damage to the manuscript volume (missing folios), it is not possible to determine the consistency of MS Oss. with MS Gn. in Records 1–69, 72 and 145–152.

TABLE 11 Divergences from Gniezno MS (Gn.) in Baworowscy MS (BN 12607), Opatów MS (Oss.), and Żagań MS (II Q 4)

Divergences from MS Gn.	
common to MS BN 12607, MS Oss. and MS II Q 4	24 + 24
found only in MS II Q 4	23[a]
found only in MS Oss.	6[b]
found only in MS BN 12607	4[c]
found in both MS BN 12607 and MS Oss.	13[d]
found in MS BN 12607 and MS II Q 4	4[e]

a No. 2, 13, 40, 48, 58, 73, 75, 90, 109, 112, 122, 137, 141, 148, 150, 156, 180, 181, 188, 198, 199, 205, 213 and 214.
b No. 89, 94, 124, 127, 183 and 196.
c No. 6, 32, 118 and 152.
d No. 90, 96, 112, 132, 140, 153, 155, 156, 179, 180, 184, 198 and 199.
e No. 135, 145, 147, 220. The omission in the Opatów MS of a passage Nr. 220 that occurs in the Group II base is probably due to the copyist's individual decision which accidentally resulted in bringing his text in line with a matching passage in texts of Group I.

occur only in some of these three manuscripts. Their distribution is shown in Table 11.

As Table 11 indicates, the Opatów MS and the Baworowscy MS have a common source, as they contain a group of variants that are specific to them only and cannot be directly dependent on each other, as both display some individual features of their own. A larger percentage of divergences from the Gniezno MS in the Żagań manuscript than in the Baworowscy MS and the Opatów MS, as well as the presence of sets of individual features in MSS BN 12607 / Oss. and MS II Q 4 – which undoubtedly have the same source – indicate that they evolved independently of each other. One such individual divergences in the Żagań MS II Q 4 is of special significance, because it draws attention to the wording of Article 24. A closer analysis of this variant has enabled us to date the two groups. The data is shown in Table 12.

In the Gniezno MS, Article 24 is amplified to include a provision which allows the father to act as proxy for his son in cases of wounding. It contains two parts, one which mirrors a passage in the *Magdeburg Bench Law* and the Wawel manuscript (Item 2), and the other (Item 1) which comes from another source. All these regulations are present in the Baworowscy MS, although they are left out in the Żagań MS (Item 1). At the same time, the instrument of proxy (Item 2) reappears in Article 87 in the Baworowscy MS, the Opatów MS, and the

TABLE 12 Text displacements within Articles 24, 76, and 87

Item	Article in MS Gn. and Nos. in Appendix 2	Issue	MS Gn.	MS BN 12607	MS Oss.	MS II Q 4	MS BJ 169	MSR, MS BJ 168
1.	[24] No. 58	father acting as proxy for his son in cases of wounding (1)	+	+	NA	–	–	–
2.	[24] No. 59	father acting as proxy for his son in cases of wounding (2)	+	+	NA	+	–	+
3.	[24] No. 60	payment of servants' wages	+	+	NA	+	–	–
4.	[24] No. 61	complaints about food	+	+	NA	+	+	–
5.	[76] No. 172	complaints about food	–	+	+	–	–	–
6.	[76] No. 169 and 170	master's liability for his servant's debts	+	–	–	–	–	–
7.	[BJ 169: 76] No. 174	payment of servants' wages	–	+	+	+	+	+
8.	[87] No. 188	father acting as proxy for his son in cases of wounding (2)	–	+	+	+	–	–

Żagań MS (Item 8). The writer's intention was probably to bring together regulations concerning the same issue, since Article 87 deals also with the instrument of proxy.

Konrad of Sandomierz, the author of the Group I archetype, transferred the provision concerning servants' wages to Article 24, whose match is Article 76 in the Cracow manuscript (Item 3). In the Baworowscy MS, the Opatów MS, and the Żagań MS, this provision occurs both in Article 24 (Item 3) and at a point where it matches the order of the German text (Item 7).

In the Baworowscy MS and the Opatów MS, the provision for complaints about the price and quality of food from Article 24 is repeated in Article 76 (Item 5); Article 24 mirrors the German base (Item 4). The copyist's intention was probably to replace a longer passage on the master's liability for his servant's debts (Item 6) that had been introduced in the Gniezno MS following the model of the *Sachsenspiegel*.

As this analysis demonstrates, the Gniezno MS is the only text with no duplicated provisions. Comparing the passages in MSS BN 12607, Oss. and II Q 4 shows that they were redacted in different ways. Were we to assume that Group II texts predated those of Group I, we would have to conclude that its author/translator incorporated the provision concerning servants' payment twice, varying its wording on each occasion. This is too improbable to be acceptable.

TABLE 13 Provisions concerning servants' wages and complaints about the price and quality of food in Baworowscy MS (BN 12607)

Issue	MS BN 12607 Latin text	MS BN 12607 Latin text
Servants' wages	[24] *Si* autem famulus suam merdecem *super dominum suum obtinuerit coram iudicio, pro eo dominus nullam penam iudici demeretur,* sed *dominus* famulo eandem mercedem *die eodem solvere tenetur* indilate.	[76 numbering acc. to MS BJ 169] *Si* servus deservitum parcium *super suum dominum obtinuerit coram iudicio, pro eo dominus nullam iudici demeretur penam,* et *dominus* servo *solvere* hoc *tenetur die eodem.*
Complaints about the price and quality of food	[24] *Si alter alterum pro vino aut alio potu inculpare voluerit, evadet, sicud debitum in quo nullum dominum ostendere poterit aut protestare.*	[76 numbering acc. to MS BJ 169] *Eciam si conqueritur quis de alio pro cibariis preparatis et coatis, hic propius est obtinere iuramentis, quam ille ipsum evadere possit iuramentis.*

Furthermore, the repetition of a passage on complaints about the price and quality of food from Article 24 in Article 76[16] would hardly make any sense. Admittedly, Article 24 refers to the defendant clearing himself of the charge if the plaintiff proves their case, while Article 76 refers to the plaintiff's right to take precedence in presenting proof in such a case, but as a matter of fact, both provisions deal with the same issue.

The comparison indicates that Konrad of Sandomierz's text is earlier than the other texts. The author of the Group II archetype knew Konrad's translation, but he also picked up the German text to make another translation of Article 76.[17] And after deleting the regulation on the master's liability for his servant's debts, which did not feature in the German *Weichbild*, he put in its place a newly redacted regulation from Article 24 concerning complaints about the price and quality of food (see Table 13).

This is not the last of the puzzles related to the development of Group II. As we know, MSS BN 12607, Oss., and II Q 4 include supplementary material taken over from *ortyle* that are also part of the German-language texts of the Baworowscy MS and the Żagań MS. Does this mean that this amplification was already present in the Group II archetype? That is highly unlikely. After all, the authors of MS AJG/Kiel., MS Dział. IV/Warsz., and MS Flor. used an

16 Numbering according to MS Gn. numbering scheme.

17 According to MS BJ 169 numbering scheme.

unembellished base text. It was supplemented with the *ortyle* only later, as evidenced by the text of the *Weichbild* in MS BN 12607/Oss., MS II Q 4, and, on the authority of Emil Kałużniacki, the Sanok manuscript (see Section 3.20). And, if that line of thought were to be pursued, those additions would have had to be later deleted in MS AJG/Kiel., MS Dział. IV/Warsz., and MS Flor., a totally implausible conclusion.

What this comparative analysis shows is that the archetype of Group II was created after Konrad of Sandomierz, the author of Group I, completed his translation, and not later than 1368 (see Section 2.2). Originally, the text contained no *ortyle*. As to the questions asked in Chapter 1 – whether the supplementary material was introduced first in the German text or simultaneously in the German and Latin texts – there is no conclusive answer. It seems that the former alternative is more plausible. This would mean that the augmented German text was subsequently juxtaposed with the Latin text, a collation which produced a series of bilingual manuscripts. However, the fact that some manuscripts (the Opatów MS and the lost Sanok manuscript) carry only the Latin *Weichbild* may indicate that the demand for the bilingual text was not that great. The copyists would then supplement their received text with the *ortyle* from the Group II text, which reproduced the article sequence of the German-language manuscripts.

2.4 *Group III (Hybrid Compilations): MSS AJG, Kiel., Flor., 951b, and BN 3068*

The relations between similar texts of Group I and Group II in the Częstochowa MS (AJG) and the Kielce MS (Kiel.) are not too difficult to make out.[18] Their base text is a Group II manuscript which has 19 divergences from the Gniezno MS that are common to the AJG/Kiel. pair (see above),[19] as well as a number of other variants in common with the Baworowscy MS, the Opatów MS, and the Żagań MS.[20] Among them is a twice-copied provision concerning servants' wages, a reduplication which appears to mirror the arrangement of the text in Group II manuscripts. However, assigning the AJG/Kiel. MSS pair to a separate group of 'hybrid' manuscripts (Group III) is done not without good reason. Not only do both texts contain in Article 76 additions characteristic of Group I, taken over

18 Divergences from MS Gn. common to both texts – No. 14, 26, 53, 59, 131, 154, 171, 192 and 204; peculiar to MS Kiel. only – No. 50, 55 and 61.

19 No. 1, 3, 10, 22, 45, 52, 60, 79, 84, 88, 91, 93, 102, 106, 166, 175, 197, 206 and 216.

20 No. 110 and 175. Single case of conformity of the AJG / Kiel. with the Oss. consists in an omission and is probably accidental (No. 183). In four cases conformity was only found with the II Q 4 (nos. 58, 90, 122 and 141), in one with the BN 12607 (No. 89), in three with BN 12607 and II Q 4 (nos. 135, 151, 220), and in two with the BN 12607 and Oss. (nos. 156, 172).

from the *Sachsenspiegel*, but they also include Article 55 of the Gniezno MS, which is omitted in Group II texts. It seems that the copyist skipped Article 54 so as to synchronize his text with the numbering scheme of the Group I base text. The AJG/Kiel. MSS were thus created as a result of the copyist collating texts from both groups. Yet his redaction was by no means mechanical. His text displays a significant number of individual features – chiefly omissions – such as, for example, the omission in Article 24 of the requirement that a father must first be cleared of the charges against him before he can act as proxy for his son charged with the same offence.[21]

In the St Florian MS, in 110 records in Appendix 2 which cover Articles 50–109 there occur merely three divergences from the Gniezno MS, whereas in the other part, there are as many as 29. This goes to show that the *Weichbild* in the St Florian MS is a product of a virtually mechanical combination of two parts that descend from different groups of manuscripts and that the assignment of the St Florian MS to Group III (compilations) can be justified not only on the basis of its formal features, like the copying of the article on the *gerada* (Article 61 in MS Gn.) in two places corresponding to the location of this text in Group I and Group II. What can also be noted at this point is that the dissonance caused by the reduplication of this article prompted the copyist to skip Article 55 of the Gniezno MS. One more notable peculiarity of the St Florian MS is that its duplicate provisions on the *gerada* are not identical. This discrepancy offers further strong proof of the claim that the copyist used two texts, one of which was close to the Żagań MS, but not augmented with *ortyle*.

In the case of the Leipzig manuscript (MS 951b), the compilation process was the reverse of that of the St Florian MS. In Articles 1–62 in Appendix 2, only a few divergences from the Gniezno MS have been found, including those shared with the Marcin Zabowski's MS.[22] As both contain a number of individual features, any direct connection between these two texts must be ruled out.[23] At the same time, the presence of identical variants in both cannot be attributed to anything but a shared base. In the margins of the first folios of the Leipzig manuscript, there are glosses peculiar to the texts of Group II, but they are discontinued at Article 63. At that point, the copyist evidently decided that he would rather interweave the annotations with the main text. All of the 23 divergences from the text of the Gniezno MS Gn. in the Leipzig MS are identical with those in the *Weichbild* of the Żagań manuscript. However, the base used by the copyist of the Leipzig manuscript could not have been a

21 No. 59.
22 No. 65, 89, 90, 101, 104, 111, 112.
23 No. 74; No. 4, 98, 128 and 131.

close copy of the Żagań MS, as his text is at times closer to the *Statutes* than the Żagań MS.[24] Unfortunately, a conclusive identification of the source used by the author of the Leipzig MS seems impossible.

There are more than a few textual divergences from the Gniezno MS in the Tomasz of Bydgosz MS (BN 3068). The author of the latter, Tomasz of Bydgoszcz, evidently tried to make his text easy to use and annotate by prospective commentators. He divided the articles into smaller units and provided them with rubrics in red. He was, however, not consistent in that effort, and after several dozen articles, he abandoned his original purpose. In addition, he also introduced, in the margins, brief notes in black ink on the content of the adjacent passages. The Tomasz of Bydgosz MS is characterized by numerous divergences from the Gniezno MS. In several cases, these are individual divergences.[25] But not less numerous are variants consistent with characteristic features of the texts in Group II. That similarity, however, does not make MS BN 3068 just another Group II text, as on numerous occasions it follows the Gniezno manuscript, while Group II texts do not.[26] A notable discordance can be found, for example, in the article on escheat, which in fact has a completely different version in each group. In the Tomasz of Bydgosz MS, both versions of the provision are included in full.[27] The manuscript is dated to the early 16th century, but the *terminus a quo* should be moved to a time after 1506, as the text is clearly influenced by Jan Łaski's *Statutes*.[28] So, no doubt under the influence of the *Statutes*, the provision of Article 69 concerning the purchase of a stolen horse appears next to Article 38, which deals with this issue, but it then reappears as Article 69 – exactly as it does in the manuscripts of Group I and Group II. There are, however, several articles in MS BN 3068 whose wording is analogous to that in Group II manuscripts and not to the *Statutes*.[29] The copyist,

24 No. 193, 200, 213 and 217. Another instance of textual conformity can be found in No. 112 where a series of omissions is common to MS BOZ, MS 951b and the *Statutes*.

25 No. 11, 18, 19, 25, 39, 41, 76, 85, 87, 115, 123, 138, 143, 156, 176, 187, 191, 212 and 215. It is worth adding that occasionally a change of one word could alter the whole regulation. Article 6 provides for the option of appointing a deputy *sołtys* so that justice could be done to any thief caught in the act even if the *sołtys* was absent. In MS BN 3068 the word 'burghers' is replaced by 'councillors', with an additional remark on the margin, *Quis debet elegi in scultetum*.

26 No. 2, 35, 44, 45, 46, 58, 80, 81, 82, 83, 84, 90, 102, 147, 198 and 205. Unfortunately, the available data afford no clue which of the Group I texts was used by Tomasz of Bydgoszcz, the copyist of BN 3068.

27 No. 156.

28 See No. 12, 16 and 24; No. 64 was probably also taken from the *Statutes*.

29 No. 29 and 30.

TABLE 14 Two *ortyle* included in Articles 48 and 73 of the *Statutes* in selected German and Latin MSS

	Baworowscy MS (BN 12607) German	MS BN 12607 Latin	Żagań MS (II Q 4) German	MS II Q 4 Latin	Opatów MS (Oss.)	Łaski's *Statutes*	Tomasz of Bydgoszcz's MS (BN 3068)
Ortyl 1	reference to Article 74	Article 48	Article 48	Article 48	Article 48	Article 48	Article 15
Ortyl 2	Article 74	Article 73	Article 73	Article 73	Article 73	Article 73	Article 48 and 73

it seems, must have had at his disposal a text close to the Baworowscy MS.[30] After all, he refers to the German text in that bilingual manuscript when, in the final part of the addendum to Article 13, he introduces his own, improved translation consistent with the German text.[31] The use of a manuscript close to the Baworowscy MS is further evidenced by his handling of two *ortyle*.[32] The placement of the two *ortyle* in various manuscripts is presented in Table 14.

As noted in Chapter 1, Article 48 in the Baworowscy MS contains no German *ortyl*, but instead, refers the reader to Article 74. The reference is misleading because there are two separate regulations of the matter at hand, as seen by the wording of the Latin text in the same manuscript, the Latin texts of the Żagań MS and the *Statutes*, and in the German text of the Żagań MS. Why the author of the Baworowscy MS put in a reference to Article 74 in the German text of the *Weichbild* remains a mystery. In fact, he has a regulation that is very similar in two places, in Article 48 and 73, which gives the impression of making good on the reference in the German text. Moreover, in the German text in the Baworowscy MS and in the Latin text in Tomasz of Bydgoszcz's MS, the second *ortyl* is incorporated into Article 74 and not Article 73.[33] On the whole, the text in Tomasz of Bydgoszcz's MS is in some parts closer to the German text in the Baworowscy MS than to other manuscripts with *ortyle*. It is also worth noting that the copying twice of the regulation from *Ortyl 2* resulted in *Ortyl 1* being transposed form Article 48 (its proper place) to below Article 15. Further notable proof of direct filiation between MS BN 3068 and MS BN 12607

30 No. 6, 19 and 96. Individual alterations were made in MS BN 3068 in the numerous additions from Group II; see No. 142, 158, 165 and 172.

31 No. 38.

32 No. 163.

33 Numbering according to MS Gn. numbering scheme.

is afforded by a short passage with the explanation that a talent is equal to 20 shillings. It appears first as a gloss to Article 5 in the Baworowscy MS and is then incorporated into the main text of MS BN 3068 by Tomasz of Bydgoszcz.[34] In all, his edition of the *Weichbild* is carefully prepared and includes a number of useful supplements, like lists of *regulae iuris* and glossaries of Latin terms, one of which comes from the Działyńscy Codex I (see Section 4).

2.5 *Summary: The Division of the Latin* Weichbild *Texts on the Basis of Content*

The division of the Latin *Weichbild* texts into distinct groups is further corroborated by another series of comparative analyses of the content of texts collected in Appendix 2. The substance and shape of the provisions fall into patterns that correspond to the division into three groups distinguished in the previous subchapter 1. Moreover, a close textual study has revealed enough clues for *ad quem* dating of the two main groups of texts: Group I not later than 1359, with the Gniezno manuscript as a reference point; and Group II not later than 1368, with reference to the Petersburg MS. The latter does not quite fit the profile of Group II, but it is indebted to an earlier manuscript text which certainly represented that group.

Statistical analyses show that the texts of Group I conform to a large extent to the text of the Gniezno MS, the earliest manuscript in that group, while the texts of Group II are far more differentiated. The complex network of modifications in the texts of Group II are, after all, a record of the evolution of the *Weichbild*. On this basis, the history of the *Weichbild* can be reconstructed in the following stages: 1) the creation of the archetype of Group I; 2) the creation of the archetype of Group II (manuscripts whose content arrangement resembles the arrangement of the German-language Silesian-Małopolska compilation); 3) the augmentation of the German text with *ortyle* written in German; 4) the creation of bilingual Latin-German manuscripts with the German *ortyle* and their Latin translations; and 5) replacement of the bilingual texts with Latin-only texts augmented with *ortyle*.

The interaction of the texts among one another produced cross-breed compilations. In this scheme, such texts constitute the 'hybrid' Group III. The compilers' techniques varied a great deal. Some tried to combine the features of both main groups intelligently,[35] but others merely cobbled together bits and pieces of text from Group I and Group II.[36] An odd man out is the text in Tomasz of Bydgoszcz's MS, which is clearly dependent on the authorized

34 No. 19.
35 As in MS AJG/Kiel.
36 E.g. the St Florian MS, the Leipzig MS.

version of Łaski's *Statutes*, which means that it must have been compiled after the arrival of print.

3 Divergences from the German Base in the Latin Texts of the *Weichbild*

After establishing that the texts of the Latin *Weichbild* belong to or descend from two main groups, the question that can be asked is what led to the emergence of those groups of texts. To answer this, I have decided to compare the Latin texts with their German counterparts. The aim of this investigation is to assess the accuracy of the translation and to establish whether the differences between the two groups of Latin texts may have been the result of following different German base texts.

3.1 *Selection of Texts and Method of Comparison*

The copyists' decisions, which reflected either their own judgement or the influence of their masters, could not help but leave a mark on the final wording of the legal documents they copied or edited. Naturally, some of the divergences between texts result from error or negligence and were wholly unintentional. The combined operation of all the factors, both intentional and unintentional, produced multiple versions of a notionally single text, like the *Weichbild*. One well established method of ascertaining the ordering of such an assemblage of texts is to trace their lines of descent. In the case of the *Weichbild*, it has been possible to distinguish two groups of affiliated texts, a third group consisting of compilations of the two, and the *Commune incliti*, a definitive printed synthesis which was released with a seal of official authorization. The German-language texts are generally perceived as remote ancestors of the Latin *Weichbild* of the late Middle Ages. While acceptable as a broad generalization, this proposition is in need of a great deal of nuance and heightened scrutiny, not least with the tools of quantitative analysis. To that end, I have gathered in Appendix 3 a comprehensive collection of data that could be used to verify the degree of consistency of the German *Weichbild* of selected Latin texts representing Group I (descended from the Gniezno MS, dated 1359) and Group II, with the Baworowscy MS. This Baworowscy MS was selected as its base text because it contains the largest number of formal similarities with the German-language Silesian-Małopolska compilation of the *Weichbild*.[37] The

37 Of the Group II manuscripts, the Opatów MS has not survived in its entirety, while the Żagań MS counts as more distant from the Gniezno MS because of the greater number of its individual divergences. Furthermore, in the Żagań MS, Article 8 of the Latin *Weichbild*

third Latin text selected for this in-depth comparison is the *Weichbild* from the Działyńscy Codex IV. The latter has occupied a special position in the family of Latin texts of German and Magdeburg Law after Zygfryd Rymaszewski established that the *Sachsenspiegel* in the Działyńscy Codex IV is a second redaction of the *versio Sandomiriensis*. That fact – as well as the unique formal similarities of MS Dział. IV with the German-language Wawel MS – raises the question about the profile of the *Weichbild* in that codex. Here, my objective is to check whether there are any indications that would justify the repositioning of the *Weichbild* in the Działyńscy Codex IV in relation to its twin in the Warsaw MS. My reference for the divergence study is the earliest relevant German text of the *Weichbild* from the Cracow MS. Each of the divergences from the latter that are found in the Latin translation is set in a broader context. The aim is to trace its source and to make comparisons with other texts of the German *Weichbild* (except for the strongly modified and abridged text in the Żagań MS), *Magdeburg Legal Instructions for Wrocław*, and the *Magdeburg Bench Law*.

Thousands of samples – the product of comparative analyses of the Latin texts of the Gniezno MS, the Baworowscy MS, and the Działyńscy Codex IV with their German predecessors – are arranged in more than 200 records which showcase the divergences in the translation of specific provisions or clauses. Systematically trawling through those texts has revealed the presence of two types of divergences from the Cracow MS. The first such divergence is represented by a set of features that show a remarkable persistence in the process of manuscript transmission. The second such divergence consists of those aberrations from the Cracow MS that are peculiar to individual texts. Each of them – the persistent and the unique – will be discussed separately.

3.2 *Divergences from the German Base Texts That Are Common to All Latin Texts*

In 72 records[38] of Appendix 3 (approx. 34 per cent of all records; approx. 36 per cent, if the records registering material from the *ortyle* in the Baworowscy MS are excluded),[39] the register of divergences from the Cracow manuscript includes all Latin texts selected for analysis. This means that these variants must have been introduced at the beginning, by Konrad of Sandomierz, the

was omitted by mistake. In this phase of our analysis, we are not concerned with additions to the Baworowscy MS from the *ortyle*; they were discussed in Chapter 1.

38 No. 307, 308, 310, 313, 314, 315, 321, 323, 329, 330, 333, 334, 335, 336, 337, 339, 340, 344, 345, 346, 347, 348, 349, 351, 353, 354, 355, 357, 358, 359, 361, 366, 369, 370, 372, 373, 375, 378, 381, 382, 384, 385, 388, 390, 393, 396, 399, 401, 403, 405, 409, 410, 412, 415, 417, 420, 421, 423, 426, 431, 438, 441, 444, 454, 466, 487, 488, 491, 504, 505, 508, and 509.

39 See nos. 317, 319, 325, 328, 389, 422, 439, 446, 447, 476, 482, 485, and 502.

founding figure of Group I.[40] In most cases, they are amendments or additions which serve to make the text easier to understand. Demonstrative or personal pronouns were replaced with more specific nouns or phrases – for example, 'he' became 'scultetus' (the village headman) and 'he' became 'he that wounded another man'.[41] Moreover, in the Latin text, the translator takes care to use *ipse* for 'plaintiff' and *ille* for 'defendant' with rigorous consistency. He also ensures that he provides explanations whenever necessary. He certainly deserves a compliment for a job well done. Apart from being more direct in naming the law's cast of characters, the original translation does not skimp on other additions to clarify the abstruseness of a legal phrase or to draw the line when a provision leaves too much up for debate,[42] for instance, by making sure that verbal abuse qualifies as insult of a member of the jury.[43] In general, this approach leads to the amplification of the original text; elisions are very rare and affect words that perhaps should not have been omitted.[44]

Occasionally, when a word in the German text did not fit Polish realities, it was substituted in the earliest translation by a more appropriate term – for example, *keiseris straze* or 'Emperor's highway' became *strata regia* 'royal highway';[45] *pfenningen* became *pecunia* 'money'.[46] However, some substitutions impinged on the (legal) substance, as when 'debt cases' became 'court cases', which extended the scope of the regulation,[47] even though at another point in the text (provision on guarantee), Konrad of Sandomierz rendered the term 'property' as 'money'[48] and restricted the general provision on suing a person about to set off on a long journey to action of debt.[49] Another arguable substitution was the introduction of the terms *agnatus* or *cognatus* in place of a personal pronoun.[50] Article 41 became a regulation devoted not only

40 Admittedly, in some cases, changes can be noticed in the Latin texts but they were made already on the modification that is present in the original translation. No. 438 (addition in the BN 12607 and Dział. IV), no. 378 (omission of a passage in the BN 12607), nos. 330, 335, and 387 (amendments in the Gn.).

41 Cf. No. 308, 310, 315, 321, 323, 373, and 417.

42 No. 330, 333, 334, 336, 337, 346, 366, 369, 370, 372, 375, 377, 381, 382, 384, 385, 393, 403, 410, 412, 415, 421, 423, 441, 444, 504, and 505. For abridgements not affecting the sense of a regulation, see No. 344 and 493.

43 No. 336.

44 No. 466.

45 No. 353. Cf. also No. 399.

46 No. 307.

47 No. 357.

48 No. 441.

49 No. 335.

50 No. 359. Departures from the German text should be looked at in their context, i.e. the whole provision and its meaning. On some occasions the omission of a word or phrase need not result in a significant change of the legal meaning, e.g. a one-off use of the term

to hereditary rented property, but generally to any property received in any manner from a monastery or its owner.[51] In its references to compurgation, the *Weichbild* as a rule set down the conditions that had to be met by those participating in this procedure. When Konrad of Sandomierz came across an article in the German text that mentioned no such requirements, he supplied them himself.[52] In Articles 51–56, which set down the conditions and procedures for action of assault and wounding, he added some annotations of his own, for example, a reminder of the advantage gained by the party that is allowed to present their case first in the order of preceding (i.e. proof in the form of the judicial oath).[53] A clause that is introduced in the Latin texts of both groups specified what books could be made part of the *gerada* – while the German text spoke of religious books in general, the translator's addition in fact excluded them, with the exception of those that were used by women for prayer and worship.[54] By modifying the wording of the Jewish oath, the translator made it look like the formula of the purgatory oath.[55] However, in other cases, it is difficult to conjecture or to find clues as to why an alteration was introduced.[56]

In 17 instances out of the 72 mentioned above, the divergences from the Cracow manuscript have parallels in other German texts, namely, in 12 cases in the Wawel manuscript and elsewhere[57] and in four cases exclusively in the Wawel MS.[58] Divergences in numerous records[59] can be matched with provisions of the *Magdeburg Bench Law* in the wording known from the MS II Q 3 from the Wrocław University Library, printed by Paul Laband. Four out that number do not conform with the text known from the Wawel manuscript.[60] In one case, the divergence is matched exclusively in the German-language Henryków MS (II F 8), but it is a minor editorial elision, which is not that significant.[61] What all these examples show is that Konrad of Sandomierz, the author of the earliest Latin translation of the *Weichbild*, made use not only of a German text which was very close to the Cracow manuscript, but also of other

bona 'property' in the Latin text in place of *cins gut*, or 'rented property' in the German *Weichbild* (No. 372).

51 No. 375.

52 No. 390.

53 No. 396.

54 No. 426.

55 No. 508.

56 No. 488.

57 No. 314, 329, 347, 348, 354, 355, 358, 361, 388, 454, 487, and 509.

58 No. 314, 329, 487, and 509.

59 No. 313 (MSR only for Gn.), 340, 345, 347, 348, 349, 354, 355, 358, and 361.

60 No. 313 (MSR only for Gn.), 340, 345, and 349.

61 No. 351.

manuscripts that happened to be closer to certain other original sources of the *Weichbild*.

Whereas the divergences from the Cracow manuscript that we have discussed thus far usually did not impinge on the normative content of the original text – as their main purpose was to assist the reader's comprehension – about one-half of another raft of 17 divergences have a great practical importance.[62] The translator follows the Wawel MS in revising the provision of Article 24, which addresses the situation when father and son are charged with the same crime. He introduces the additional requirement that the father cannot act as proxy for his son unless he has cleared himself of the charge.[63] Another modification concerns the rules of succession in the case of inheriting from a grandfather by a grandson who was born to his daughter. The Latin text makes the grandson's claim dependent on his mother's having a share in the decedent's estate. This clause, which is absent from the Cracow manuscript, can be found in the Wawel and Henryków manuscripts.[64]

One of the claims made in this study (see Chapter 1) is that the Cracow manuscript is not the archetype of the German version of the Silesian-Małopolska compilation, which, regrettably, has not survived. The comparative analyses of variance in the extant German texts and the primary sources of the *Weichbild* give strength to the conjecture that such a base manuscript did exist and was a parent text of the Wawel MS. The differences between the two amounted to no more than a handful of unintentional omissions, probably caused by the copyist's skipping one of a pair of neighbouring phrases that began with the same word. This is suggested by the significant numerous instances of the Latin text's conformity with the Wawel MS in places which correspond to omissions in the Cracow MS.[65] However, at the same time, the provisions of the Wawel MS that contain words and phrases omitted in the Cracow MS have some individual features that not are absent from Konrad of Sandomierz's translation. It is the last of these findings which offers proof of the claim that Konrad of Sandomierz used a text that was not identical to the Wawel MS.

62 In two instances, the Latin text is closer to the Wawel MS than to the Cracow MS; neither divergence affects the legal regulation (No. 314 and 329). In most cases, the additional explanation or concretization did not modify or interfere with the regulation itself (No. 345, 347, 355, 358, 454 or 509). The elision or omission of a word or phrase would usually have a negative effect on the clarity of the text, but here, too, the content of the regulation was not affected (No. 491).

63 No. 340.

64 No. 388. For more additions, see No. 354 and 361.

65 That is probably the case in No. 348, 355, and 388.

Finally, barring a few exceptions, all the divergences that have no match in the Cracow MS are amplifications. They supplement the bare translation with practical explanations; some are substitutes of German terms whose function is to adapt the text to Polish realities. A close study of all types of divergences has produced new insights into the range of Konrad of Sandomierz's sources and techniques.

3.3 *Individual Divergences from the German Base in the Latin Texts*

Apart from divergences that are 'shared', that is, replicated in more than one manuscript, there are divergences which mark the individual character of each text, or, from the point of view of our comparative analysis, which reflect a lack of conformity between them. The number of individual divergences between the Gniezno and the Cracow manuscripts is 51 (45), which serves to express the distance between the two texts;[66] for MS BN 12607, it is also 51;[67] and for MS Dział. IV, it is 34.[68] The lower number of divergences in the Działyńscy Codex IV is primarily the result of its shorter length due to the omission of the several articles. These metrics offer some ground for a conjectural reconstruction of the archetype of Group II. We may presume that it was more consistent with its German base than the Latin text in the Baworowscy MS, as some of its divergences from the German texts do not occur in other manuscripts within this group.[69]

As in the case of the shared divergences, some of the individual differences can be accounted for by reference to a German text which is different from the Cracow MS. The metrics on which this argument rests are presented in Table 15. This comparative analysis does allow for matches indicating a level of conformity with more than one German text other than the Cracow MS. The number of such matches, or parallels, with one of the other German texts is shown in square brackets (the numbers of those records are highlighted in footnotes 1–12).

---

66 No. 302, 304, 309, 318, 327, 330, 335, 341, 343, 365, 368, 371, 374, 383, 385, 387, 394, 395, 406, 411, 437, 440, 442, 443, 448, 449, 451, 452, 453, 456, 458, 459, 462, 474, 477, 478, 479, 481, 483, 486, 490, 492, 493, 494, 495, 496, 497, 499, 500, 501, and 503. While the samples in No. 341, 385, 387, 459, 492, and 503 show that MS Gn. has a place of its own in the family of the German-language texts of the *Weichbild*, its first Latin translation by Konrad of Sandomierz is probably a direct descendant of the German base. Cf. the discussion in Section 4.3.

67 No. 303, 306, 311, 312, 316, 343, 362, 367, 378, 379, 380, 383, 391, 392, 406, 408, 409, 413, 414, 416, 419, 425, 429, 433, 434, 435, 438, 440, 442, 443, 445, 450, 452, 456, 458, 462, 465, 468, 470, 477, 480, 483, 484, 486, 489, 490, 493, 495, 496, 498, and 507.

68 No. 301, 305, 318, 324, 326, 338, 343, 350, 356, 363, 364, 367, 376, 388, 397, 398, 407, 425, 429, 430, 432, 438, 445, 450, 457, 462, 467, 471, 473, 475, 479, 498, 499, and 507.

69 E.g. No. 436.

TABLE 15 Conformity of the Latin texts in MS Gn., MS BN 12607, and MS Dział. IV with the German texts in the MSR, MS BJ 168, MS BN 12607 and MS BJ 170a as indicated by divergences that do not conform with MS BJ 169

	MS Gn.	MS BN 12607 Lat.	MS Dział. IV
Conformity with the MSR	5 (1)[a]	3 (1)[b]	4 (1)[c]
Conformity with MS BJ 168	4 (1)[d]	4 (1)[e]	7 (6)[f]
Conformity with MS BN 12607 Ger.	4 (3)[g]	5 (4)[h]	1 (1)[i]
Conformity with MS BJ 170a	6 (1)[j]	3 (0)[k]	3 (0)[l]

In the table notes records with evidence of parallels (conformity) between the Latin text and only one of the German texts in MSR, MS BJ 168, MS BN 12607 Ger., MS BJ 170a are highlighted.
a No. 313, *332*, 342, 363 and 364.
b No. *332*, 352 and 360.
c No. *332*, 363 and 364.
d No. *322*, 342, 455 and 510.
e No. 352, 360, *365* and 455.
f No. *322*, 352, *436*, *461*, *464*, *472* and *506*.
g No. *404*, *408*, *418* and 510.
h No. *322*, 400, *408*, *418* and *436*.
i No. *404*.
j No. 313, *331*, 342, 363, 364 and 455.
k No. 352, 360 and 455.
l No. 352, 363 and 364.

The most important indicator in our search for the conjectural German-language base text is the list of matches with only one German text other than the Cracow MS. The findings can be summarized as follows:

1) The Gniezno MS displays exclusive conformity with the *Magdeburg Bench Law* in 1 case, with the Wawel MS (BJ 168) in 1 case, with the Baworowscy MS (BN 12607) in 3 cases, and with MS BJ 170a in 1 case, which is probably of no significance as it concerns a contingent omission.
2) The Latin text in the Baworowscy MS exhibits exclusive conformity with the *Magdeburg Bench Law* (1 case), the Wawel MS (1 case), and with the German text in the Baworowscy MS (4 cases, excluding additions from the *ortyle* which are placed in parallel to the German and the Latin text).
3) The Działyńscy Codex IV displays exclusive conformity with the Wawel MS (6 cases) and in 1 configuration with the *Magdeburg Bench Law* and the Baworowscy MS, which is a case that is also evidenced in the Gniezno MS.

These results lead us to the conclusion that Konrad of Sandomierz, the author of the conjectural Group II archetype, and the author of the text in the Działyńscy

Codex IV relied on more than one German text for their additions and amendments. The results also demonstrate the extraordinary usefulness of the quantitative approach, as it can bring into sharp relief the differences between groups of manuscripts. In effect, quantitative analysis opens up a new perspective on textual variance (i.e. the formal features discussed in Section 1 and the substantive differences analysed in Section 2), as well as the scope and the role of the German-language texts in the process of manuscript transmission.

3.4 *Summary: Reliance on Different German Base Texts as a Factor in the Differentiation of the Latin Texts of the* Weichbild

The analysis of the data collected in Appendix 3 leads to the following conclusions: first, the divergences from the German base texts that are common to all Latin texts are, for the most part, additions which seek to specify or explain the original wording or construction. While some of these additions do not match the German text of the earliest Cracow manuscript (MS BJ 169), they seem to lock in with another German text, that of the Wawel manuscript (BJ 168). The introduction of amplifications of this kind no doubt signals the translator's concern for the clarity of the legal text, which, as we have noted earlier, was an individual trait of Konrad of Sandomierz, whose authorship of the texts of Group I can be treated as a certainty.

Second, while some characteristic divergences occur only in the texts of Group I, other divergences which exhibit a great deal of minor deviations are typical of Group II. In the case of divergences that appear only once, it is possible that they, too, have their origins in a lost German source.

The analysis shows that the emergence of two different groups of texts of the Latin *Weichbild* results from their authors' use of different (i.e. not identical) German base texts. We may now, having all these findings at hand, revisit the problem of the Latin *Weichbild* and ask whether there was just one Latin translation or whether there were two different translations.

4 Group I: *Versio Sandomiriensis*

4.1 *Complex Basis of the Original Latin Translation*

The foregoing comparative analysis of the Latin *Weichbild* in the Gniezno MS and the German text of the Cracow manuscript has brought to light a large number of divergences which are of no great importance for the filiations in the inner circle of the foundation manuscripts. Some of these changes are modifications that do not affect the meaning of the regulations which they augment for the purpose of clarification or contract by eliding a word or a phrase.[70] However, the majority of the divergences introduce substantive modifications, which, in a number of cases, have parallels in German texts other than the Cracow MS.[71] In addition to his base text, Konrad of Sandomierz studded his translation with words and phrases that have their matches in the German texts of the *Magdeburg Bench Law*, the Wawel MS, MS BJ 170a, and the Baworowscy MS (Table 15 in Section 3.3), and also from the *Magdeburg Legal Instructions for Wrocław* of 1261.[72]

Two of these German texts can be rejected: 1) it has been already mentioned that the convergence of the Gniezno MS and BJ 170a was probably accidental; and 2) if we focus our attention on parallel omissions, none is as significant as the absence of Articles 30 and 50 of the *Magdeburg Bench Law* from both the Sandomierz version and the German-language texts of the *Weichbild*. It is a clear indication that Konrad of Sandomierz had either no direct access to the *Magdeburg Bench Law*, or chose to not use it.

In my opinion, he may well have had at his disposal, in addition to his base text, close to the Cracow MS (which had features of German-language text in the Baworowscy MS), the *Magdeburg Legal Instructions for Wrocław* of 1261 and another German text (later lost) which combined some features of the *Magdeburg Bench Law* and the Wawel manuscript. The Wawel manuscript itself would be a descendant of that conjectured missing-link manuscript.

4.2 *Characteristic Features of the Sandomierz Version*

Konrad of Sandomierz was not only a translator, but also the author of another version of the text, probably longer than the one in the Cracow manuscript, aloof from all of the extant German texts. If the characteristic features of the *Weichbild* are put side-by-side with those features of the Gniezno MS that are important in connection with the Cracow manuscript, we can note the following:

1) additional provisions that come from the *Sachsenspiegel* (Articles 57, 76, and 77 of MS Gn.) and from the *Magdeburg Legal Instructions for Wroclaw* of 1261 (Article 55);[73]

---

70 No. 340, 383, 394, 395, 409, 411, 445, 452, 455, 456, 462, 474, 477, 479, 483, 486, 493, 494, 496, and 500.

71 One such exception is the clarification that the court in question is the Magdeburg Bench, whose president is called the *Burggraf* of Magdeburg; in MS BJ 169, this explanation is omitted (No. 455).

72 Article 72 of the *Magdeburg Legal Instructions for Wrocław* of 1261 was the parent text of Article 55 in the Gniezno MS, as we have shown in Section 1.

73 See Table 2.5.

2) changes in the order (sequence) of the provisions; some changes – like gathering the provisions on the *gerada, hergewet*, and general inheritance next to each other – seem to be dictated by simple common sense;[74]
3) some substantive features in the form of the absence of a passage that is present in the Cracow MS[75] – only a few such omissions occur in the German texts of the *Weichbild*, other than the Cracow MS;[76]
4) some substantive features in the form of additions of words and phrases that are absent in the Cracow MS;[77] some of them have their parallels in other German texts;[78] and
5) some substantive features in the form of an amendment of an existing regulation[79] or a legal term that is present in the Cracow MS.[80]

Of all the features listed above, by far the most numerous are additions which augment a given a regulation. Their purpose is obvious: they adapt the text for practical needs. Their function is merely explanatory, and in no way do they seek to modify the meaning of the legal text. The best proof of that intention is the introduction of the definitions of agnate and cognate[81] and the consistent use of these terms throughout the text. Occasionally, a German word is replaced by a descriptive phrase[82] or adapted to the Polish realities. Thus the term 'Burggraf' (*burgreve*) is translated as 'castellan', but with little consistency.[83] In

74 See Table 2.1.
75 No. 3 (304), 49 (332), 60 (341), 65 (343), 106 (387), 156 (437), 197 (481), and 205 (490).
76 No. 46 (331) [BJ 170a], 59 (340) [MSR], 81 (363) [MSR and BJ 170a], 82 (364) [MSR and BJ 170a], 405 [BN 12607], 220 (510) [BJ 168 and BJ 12607].
77 No. 1 (302), 22 (313), 28 (318), 33 (320), 52 (335), 58 (339), 62 (342), 82 (364), 83 (365), 91 (374), 93 (377), 102 (385), 119 (402), 120 (406), 141 (420), 166 (448), 169 (449), 195 (479) and 208 (495).
78 No. 22 (313) [MSR, BJ 170a], 35 (322) [BJ 168], 62 (342) [MSR, BJ 168, BJ 170a], 82 (364) [MSR, BJ 170a], 110 (391), 418 [BN 12607].
79 No. 10 (309), 45 (330), 83 (365), 175 (453), 216 (501).
80 No. 13, 16, 27, 110 (391), 185 (469).
81 No. 166 (448).
82 No. 499.
83 No. 13, 16, and 27. The word 'burgrave' is just co-opted into the Latin text in Articles 11 and 103; in Articles 82 and 98, it comes with an explanation that the term refers to the town of Magdeburg. The adoption of the term 'burgrave' in Poland is discussed by Inge Bily, "Die Rezeption des sächsisch-magdeburgischen Rechts in Osteuropa. Zum Analyseraster der Rechtstermini am Beispiel der Lexeme Burggraf und Lehen", in: *Kanzleisprache – ein mehrdimensionales Phänomen: Tagungsband für Prof. PhDr. Zdeněk Masařík, DrSc., zum 80. Geburtstag (Beiträge zur Sprachinselforschung)*, eds. Andrea Moshövel and Libuše Spáčilová (Wien, 2009), pp. 41–42. On the competences of burgraves in Magdeburg and Halle, especially their judicial functions, see Heiner Lück, "Das Gericht des Burggrafen von Magdeburg zu Halle an der Saale. Eine Skizze nach vorwiegend sächsichen Quellen", in: *Vertrauen in den Rechtsstaat. Beiträge zur deutschen Einheit im Recht. Festschrift für Walter Remmers*, eds. Jürgen Goydre, Dietrich Rauschning, Rainer Robra, Hans-Ludlig Schreiber, and Christian Wulff (Köln – Berlin – Bonn – München, 1995), pp. 687–701; Gerlinde

contemporary legal texts, the castellan was a royal office-holder with judicial powers over low-rank officials like the *sołtys* (village head, *scultetus*).[84] In the mid-14th century, when Konrad of Sandomierz was working on his translation of the *Weichbild*, the transformation of the local government in Małopolska into a system of smaller territorial units – each of them headed by a captain (*starosta, capitaneus*), whose deputy (*podstarosta, vicecapitaneus*), was also known as burgrave (*burgrabia*) – was in its early stages. It was accompanied by the strengthening of the institution of judicial districts centred on the castle burgrave.[85] The comeback of the term 'burgrave' in the 15th-century St Florian MS may indicate an intention to readapt the terminology for higher-level court authorities to fit the new circumstances. Likewise, the omissions in the text by Konrad of Sandomierz are not the result of negligence and carelessness – so common when copying texts in the same language – but are instead consistent with a deliberate design. One example of such a design may be the modification of the provision concerning escheat to guarantee greater rights to the monarch.[86] However, we must not assume that Konrad never made a mistake. For example, it is impossible to discern whether the change of the upper limit of the penalties imposed by the councillors from 36 to 30 shillings (*solidi*) was deliberate or was only a result of a mistake.[87]

Among the amendments modifying or extending the scope of a regulation, there is a description of the conditions to be met if a father were to replace his son in criminal proceedings.[88] There are also some changes concerning women's rights. Konrad of Sandomierz omits the requirement for the husband's consent with regard to a deathbed gift.[89] In clarifying the scope of the *gerada*, he extends the catalogue of items apportioned to women, even taking into account a wider catalogue of things which, after the wife's death, were supposed to serve the widower for daily use.[90] In two articles, he addresses the

---

Schlenker, "Das Magdeburger Burggrafenamt und Schultheißentum zu Halle/Salle", in: *Hanse, Städte, Bünde. Die sächischen Städte zwischen Elbe und Weser um 1500. Ausstellung Kulturhistorisches Museum Magdeburg 28. Mai bis 26. August 1996. Braunschweigisches Landesmuseum. Ausstellungszentrum Hinter Aegidien 17. September bis 1. Dezember 1996*, 1, ed. Matthias Puhle, (Magdeburger Museumsschriften) 4/1 (Magdeburg, 1996), pp. 129–130 and 132. See also Aleksander Zajda, *Staropolska terminologia prawnicza (do 1500 r.)* [Polish Legal Terminology (until 1500)] (Kraków, 1990), p. 134.

84 No. 208.

85 Karol Nabiałek, *Starostwo olsztyńskie od XIV do połowy XVII wieku* [Captainship of Olsztyn from the 14th until the Middle of the 17th Century] (Kraków, 2012), pp. 59–64.

86 No. 156.

87 No. 10.

88 No. 58 and 59.

89 No. 46.

90 No. 195.

problem of the axiological foundations of law and affirms the primacy of God's law and natural law.[91] As the regulation that restricted the monarch by imposing a mandatory waiting period of one year and one day prior to coming into inheritance under the escheat law are left out,[92] the regulations concerning servants are extended to include some sections from the *Sachsenspiegel* on the servant's liability for damage to his master's property and the principles of the master's liability for the acts of his servant.[93] A few more points may be added to this catalogue of the characteristic features of Konrad of Sandomierz's text from the discussion in Section 3.2 of the divergences from the Cracow MS common to the Gniezno MS, the Baworowscy MS, and the Działyńscy Codex IV.

4.3 *Divergences within the Texts of the* versio Sandomiriensis

The texts of the Sandomierz version are not uniform. Among its divergences from the Gniezno MS, there are some that are common not only to the manuscripts of Group II, but also Group I.[94] In all those cases, we can observe the remarkable consistency of the Działyńscy Codex I with the Gniezno MS. The divergences from the Gniezno MS in the *versio Sandomiriensis* are shown in the following list:

1) the omission of the clause declaring municipal by-laws invalid unless they conform to God's law (No. 1);
2) the omission of the clause that only free men are eligible for the office of the *sołtys* (*scultetus*) (No. 22);
3) consistent reinstatement of a phrase which was – seemingly accidentally – omitted in the Gniezno MS concerning the master's obligation to pay his servant's wages (No. 60);
4) the omission of the second part of the requirement that witnesses in property litigation must be (i) property owners (ii) whose right of possession is undisturbed (No. 93);
5) the addition to the provision concerning the disposal of property that gives the husband the right to alienate property acquired 'together with his wife' (No. 102);
6) the addition to the regulation concerning the inheritance rights of a grandson born to a female heir that transfers his right to inherit his grandfather's *hergewet* to the judge (No. 106);
7) the amendment reducing the number of oath-helpers from six to two in the action of debt (No. 175 and 216);

91 No. 1 and 91.
92 No. 156.
93 No. 169 and 170.
94 MSS F 143, Q II 157 (1), Q II 157 (2), BN 12600, BJ 4405, and Przem.

8) clarification of legal procedure: the judge may initiate summary proceedings without witnesses outside officially designated places in the action of debt (No 179); and
9) clarification of the rules of master-servant relations: if a master brings charges against his servant, the court cannot proceed without hearing the testimony of oath-helpers (No. 197).

Apart from an amendment which limits the scope of the regulation in Record 179, all of the modifications listed above can be found in texts of Group II.

Among the manuscripts of the *versio Sandomiriensis*, there is not a single pair whose texts would form a perfect match (i.e. 100 per cent consistency). Hence, there is a reason to expect that Mikołaj of Cieszyn, the copyist of the Gniezno MS, was an exception, and his text is fully consistent with his base, assuming that Mikołaj of Cieszyn used the autograph and not a copy. At any rate, it cannot be ruled out that the divergences listed above were originally consistent not only with the autograph by Konrad of Sandomierz, but also had parallels in the German texts. And, if we follow this line thought, we would expect the autograph to assign the *hergewet* to the judge in the case of the inheritance rights of a grandson born to a female heir (Record No. 106 in the Appendix 2). It would contain the full wording of Article 24 on servants' wages, including the missing word, without which this provision became almost incomprehensible (No. 60). Furthermore, in the original translation, there would be two short passages omitted in the Gniezno MS (Nos. 102 and 179). Probably, it would also contain the requirement that two and not six oath-helpers are sufficient to proceed in the action of debt, although the manuscripts are not wholly consistent on this point (Nos. 175 and 216). For what it is worth, this conjectural analysis certainly helps us to trace the bifurcation in the family tree of Group I. It also strengthens the claim that two variants of Konrad of Sandomierz's Latin translation were produced: one which reproduced the alterations (defects) characteristic of the Gniezno MS, and another one (now lost) which either had either only a few of those alterations or perhaps even none at all.

4.4 *Summary: Adaptation of the Magdeburg Law by Means of the Latin Translation*

The Latin translation of the *Weichbild* was an archetype of the Sandomierz version of the Silesian-Małopolska compilation. An examination of the extant sources suggests that Konrad did not produce a one-to-one translation. First, his base text could not have been solely the Cracow MS (BJ 169) or its copy, because the Latin text differs significantly from MS BJ 169. It has now been proven that those divergences match the text of other German-language versions of the *Weichbild*. Consequently, it can be surmised that Konrad of

Sandomierz used another manuscript for his translation, in addition to the Cracow MS, which shared the characteristic features of the *Magdeburg Bench Law* and the Wawel manuscript (MS BJ 168).

Konrad of Sandomierz's work was not a plain translation, but instead, an original Latin version of the Saxon-Magdeburg Law. Not only did he use more than a single base text, but he also supplemented the *Weichbild* with some regulations from the *Sachsenspiegel* and the *Legal Instructions for Wrocław* (1261). He expanded the received text with explanations and clarifications. He adapted the wording of the provisions to contemporary realities of the Kingdom of Poland in the 14th century, and he rearranged the order of the articles. It seems that all those alterations and editorial interventions had one purpose: to make the *Weichbild* as understandable and useful as possible for its users.

Konrad of Sandomierz's work must have been produced before 1359, the date of Mikołaj of Cieszyn's Gniezno manuscript, the earliest extant copy of the *versio Sandomiriensis*. It was that version that was continually modified in the process of transmission. The differences between subsequent copies accumulated, but they did not obliterate a family identity of texts like MSS Gn., Dział. I, Przem., Plesz., and BOZ (group A) and MSS F 143, Q II 157 (2)/BN 12600, Q II 157 (1), and BJ 4405 (group B).

This analysis is largely technical, but it also allows us to develop a better view of Konrad of Sandomierz's achievement, a combination of solid scholarship and pragmatism. The popularity of the Sandomierz version of the *Weichbild*, which soon eclipsed the German texts of the Silesian-Małopolska compilation, was no doubt related to a demand for a text in Latin, the language of the law in medieval Poland. If the success of the Sandomierz version was so assured, it begs the question: what were the reasons for the growth of another branch of the *Weichbild* tree from the Group II?

5 Group II: *Versio Cracoviensis*

5.1 *Conformity with the German Text*

The Latin *Weichbild*, included in Group II, is characterized, in opposition to the texts of the Sandomierz version, by formal features that are common to the German manuscripts (Section 1). Furthermore, according to statistical calculations, divergences in Group II texts from the Gn. MS vary between 33 per cent and 40 per cent. A comparison of the articles in the Baworowscy MS with the German texts provide further data which throws into relief the differences between both Groups I and II. The aggregate results are presented in Table 16.[95]

95 It does not take account of the additions from the *ortyle* in the Baworowscy MS.

TABLE 16 Divergences in the Latin translation in the Gniezno MS (Gn.) and the Baworowscy MS (BN 12607)

1.	Divergences from the German texts, common to MS Gn., MS BN 12607 and MS Dział. IV	72[a]
2.	Divergences from MS BJ 169 common to MS Gn., MS BN 12607 and MS Dział. IV, justified by conformity with other German texts	17[b]
3.	Divergences from the German texts, common to MS Gn. and MS BN 12607 absent from Dział. IV	19[c]
4.	Divergences from German texts in MS BN 12607 absent from MS Gn.	34[d]
5.	Conformity of MS BN 12607 with the German texts where MS Gn. displays a divergence	29[e]
6.	Conformity of MS BN 12607 exclusively with MS BJ 168 where MS Gn. displays a divergence from the German texts	1[f]
7.	Conformity of MS BN 12607 exclusively with the German text in MS BJ 12607 where MS Gn. displays a divergence from the German texts	1[g]
8.	Alteration of wording in MS BN 12607 which in MS Gn. is consistent with MS BJ 169 to a wording consistent with MS BJ 168/MSR	2[h]
9.	Alteration of wording in MS BN 12607 which in MS Gn. is consistent with MS BJ 169 to a wording consistent with MS BN 12607 Ger.	3[i]
10.	Alteration of wording in BN 12607 which in MS Gn. is consistent with MS BJ 168 to a wording consistent with MS BJ 169	1[j]
11.	Alteration of wording in BN 12607 which in MS Gn. is consistent with MS BJ 168 to a wording consistent with MS BN 12607 Ger.	1[k]
12.	Alteration of wording in BN 12607 which in MS Gn. is consistent with MS BJ 170a/MSR to a wording consistent with MS BJ 169/BN 12607 Ger.	4[l]

a Cf. Section 3.2.
b See *ibidem.*
c No. 383, 402, 406, 409, 440, 442, 443, 445, 452, 456, 458, 462, 477, 478, 486, 490, 493, 494, and 497.
d No. 303, 306, 311, 312, 316, 362, 367, 378, 379, 380, 391, 392, 413, 414, 416, 419, 425, 429, 433, 434, 435, 438, 450, 465, 468, 470, 480, 483, 484, 489, 495, 496, 500, and 507.
e No. 302, 304, 309, 318, 320, 330, 335, 339, 341, 368, 371, 375, 385, 394, 395, 411, 437, 448, 449, 451, 453, 459, 463, 474, 479, 492, 498, 499, and 501.
f No. 365.
g No. 503.
h No. 352 and 360.
i No. 400, 436 and 460.
j No. 510.
k No. 322.
l Nos. 331, 342, 363 and 364.

The divergences from the German texts that are common to the Gniezno MS, the Baworowscy MS, and the Działyńscy Codex IV (Items 1 and 2) have already been discussed in Section 3.2. There are as many as 72 of them. There is also a group of 19 divergences which are common exclusively to the Gniezno manuscript and the Baworowscy MS (Item 3; they are absent from the Działyńscy Codex IV). Notably, these alterations – usually phrases of no more than a few words – do not affect the meaning of the regulations.[96]

In almost 30 cases, the given manuscript remains consistent with the German texts, while the matching portions of the text in the Gn. MS display divergences (Item 5). Furthermore, in the Baworowscy MS, there is only one case of conformity with the Wawel MS (Item 6) and another such case with the German text in MS BN 12607 (Item 7). It should be borne in mind, however, that in six cases, a departure from the Gniezno MS does not necessarily signify a departure from Konrad of Sandomierz's autograph (for the discussion of that manuscript, see Section 4.3).[97] In 12 cases, the wording of the Gniezno MS that conformed with one group of German texts was altered to conform with other German texts (Items 8–12).

The conformity of the Baworowscy MS with the German texts concerns minor points[98] as well as issues of considerable importance. Let us take a brief look at a few of these issues. Similarly to the German texts, MS BN 12607 does not carry Konrad of Sandomierz's additions concerning the servant's liability for his master's lost property, the master's liability for a horse stolen from his servant,[99] the conditions attached to the instrument of proxy in criminal proceedings,[100] the requirement of compliance of laws enacted by the councillors with God's law,[101] or the affirmation that the right to inherit property

96 Only in three cases does the text of MS Gn. and MS BN 12607 – while deviating from the wording of the German texts – introduce a new quality. In No. 408, it is made clear that the disability claimed in connection with the appointment of a proxy could be either physical or mental. In No. 490, the removal of the clarification that the procedure required the presence of two jurymen might have led to uncertainty about their minimal number. In No. 495, the provision is extended: action against the *sołtys* could now be brought either before a *wójt* or before a castellan. However, in No. 402, the use of the narrower term 'to poison' instead of 'to kill' in the context of the whole provision does not change the regulation.

97 The autograph of Konrad of Sandomierz's translation could be consistent with the German text in 60 (341), 102 (385), 106 (387), 175 (453), 179 (459), and 216 (501).

98 No. 304, 335, 368, 394, 411, 462, 474, and 479.

99 No. 449.

100 No. 318.

101 No. 302.

from a relative is a natural right.[102] In the Baworowscy MS, as in the German texts, there is no definition of paternal and maternal relatives.[103] Moreover, the Group II text is consistent with the German text in its wording of the provisions concerning escheat[104] and the *gerada*;[105] it also includes the requirement, omitted in the Gniezno MS, concerning the husband's consent to his wife's *mortis causa* gift (made by her in expectation of impending death).[106] Nor does MS BN 12607 contain the errors of MS Gn., such as the incorrect figure for the penalty set for breaching the weights and measurements regulations (30 instead of 36 shillings).[107]

Many of them, however, are individual features which are peculiar to MS BN 12607/Oss.[108] Beside some minor alterations,[109] the Baworowscy MS contains a definition of public holidays[110] and a clarification of the requirement concerning the number of oath-swearers in cases of wounding.[111] The text is not free from errors, such as the introduction of the term *cognatus*, where the German text speaks of paternal relatives.[112]

Group II texts also include the provisions omitted by Konrad of Sandomierz. These are the final articles of the *Constitution of Courts*, appended to the Jewish oath. This is another piece of evidence that the translation was done by the author of this version.

5.2 *Divergences in the Wording of the Provisions and Vocabulary*

While Konrad of Sandomierz's translation was used in developing the text of Group II, some provisions are completely new, even though they are consistent with the German text. It includes also a number of articles whose regulations are consistent with the German base, both in the Sandomierz version and in Group II, but their wording is completely different. Table 17 presents representative examples of the latter from both versions.

In the first two examples, the translation of the German text is correct in both versions. The corresponding Latin texts are virtually identical except for a few details. The main difference is the use of a different term in the Latin

102 No. 374.
103 No. 448.
104 No. 437.
105 No. 483.
106 No. 331.
107 No. 309.
108 See Table 2.3.
109 No. 362, 378, 413, 416, 429, 434, 438, 470, 480, 483, 496, 499, 500, and 507.
110 No. 311.
111 No. 414.
112 No. 391.

TABLE 17 Notable divergences from the German base in the wording of some provisions in Gniezno MS (Gn.) and Baworowscy MS (BN 12607)

	MS BJ 169, MS BN 12607	MS Gn.	MS BN 12607
1. Control on terminology	[16 § 1] *Swaz so ein man gibit undir banne besitzit he damit iar und tac ane* rechte *widir sprache, daz ist he neher zcu behalden mit dem richtere und mit den sheppfen, den iz im iener untfuren muge.*	[16 § 1] *Quitquit masculus dat sub banno, si possidebit pacifice et quiete absque* arestacione *aliqua anno et die, hoc propius et melius optinere potest cum iudice et scabinis, quam ab ipso aliquis possit exbrigare.*	[16 § 1] *Quidquid masculus dat sub banno, si possidebit pacifice ac quiete absque* contradiccione *anno et die, hoc proprius ac melius obtimere potest cum iudice et scabinis, quam aliquis ab ipso possit exbrigare.*
2. Changes in the order of phrases	[33] *Wunden sich zwene undir ein andir,* der eine mit einem swerte, der andir mit einem mezzere, *ob di wunden kamfwertic sin, deme mit dem swerte get iz an di hant, deme mit dem mezzere get iz an den hals, wend daz mezzir ein duplich mort.*	[33] *Quod si se duo mutuo vulneraverint* unus cutello et alter gladio, *et si vulnera utriusque monomachalia fuerint, illi cum gladio solvit manum, illi cum cutello solvit collum, quia cutellus furtivam infert mortem.*	[35] *Quod si se duo mutuo vulneraverint* unus gladio, alter cultello, *et si vulnera utriusque monomachalia fuerint, illi cum gladio solvit manum, illi cum cultello solvit collum, quia cultellus furtivam infert mortem.*
3. New translation	[64] *Ob sich ein erbe virstirbit, daz sich nyman dar zcu zcuhit mit rechte* binnen iare und tage, *daz nimit di kunicliche gewalt.*	[66] *Quod si hereditas mortaliola* [*s*] *absque heredibus inventa seu reperta fuerit, regie cedet maiestati.*	[71] ~~*Quod*~~ *Si hereditas mortaliola* [*s*] ~~*absque*~~ sine *herede*~~*ibus*~~ *inventa* fuerit aut remanserit anno et die, ~~*seu reperta fuerit*~~ *regie cedet maiestati.*
4. New wording/new translation	[101] *Lage und daz man vrowen notet und heimsuche richtet der burcgreve und andirs niman, der shultheize nicht. Mac man di heimsuche*	[103] *Obsidia et quod femine stuprantur, et irruenciam domiciliorum, burgravius iudicat et nullus alter nec scultetus. Si irruencia domicilii probabiliter*	[107] ~~*Obsidia*~~ Insidias et stupra ~~*quod femine stuprantur*~~ *et* domorum *irruenciam,* ~~*domiciliorum*~~ *burgrabvius iudicat et nullus alter nec* eciam *scultetus. Si* domorum *irruencia* ~~*domicilii*~~

TABLE 17 Notable divergences from the German base (*cont.*)

	MS BJ 169, MS BN 12607	MS Gn.	MS BN 12607
	bewisen mit wunden und mit gewundetem gezcimmere, hat ein man des den richter und di shreiliute zcu gezcuge, iener ist im neher zcu antwurten mit eime campfe, wan he im entgen muge mit siner unshult.	*potest ostendi cum vulneribus et cum vulneratis edificiis, si super hoc iudicem et homines, qui clamorem audierunt, habere potuerit in testimonium, oportet desuper respondere cum duello, quam cum iuramento evadere possit.*	*probabiliter* ~~*potest*~~ *ostendi* potest *cum vulneribus* vel ~~*et cum*~~ edificio *vulnerato*~~*is*~~ ~~*edificiis*~~, *si super* ~~*hoc*~~ *iudicem et* clamatores ~~*homines qui clamorem audierunt habere potuerit*~~ *in testimonium* poterit habere, extunc ille propius sibi ~~*oportet de super respondere*~~ *cum duello* debet respondere, quam ille suo possit evadere~~, *quod cum*~~ *iuramento.* ~~*evadere possit.*~~

texts of Article 16: in the Gniezno MS, it is *arrestatio*, whereas the Baworowscy MS has *contradictio*, which is closer to the German base. As the term *arrestatio* constitutes a significant alteration of the German base, it could not have been anything other than deliberate. Article 33 in the Gniezno MS is almost consistent with the Cracow manuscript. The wording in the Baworowscy MS retains the word order of the German base in 'sword' and 'knife' (*swerte … mezzere* / *gladio … cultello*), as well as their direct juxtaposition, without the linking *et* (as in the Gniezno MS). All these details suggest the author of the Cracow version must have looked up the text of the Sandomierz version, checked it against the German base, and finally introduced alterations that he thought appropriate. However, in some provisions, the alterations go further than that. Such far-reaching interventions into the received text may have been due to the need to adapt a regulation to the German wording (Item 3) or to the fact that the provision could do with a better wording (Item 4). The provisions that have been much redacted include Articles 4, 5, 25, 26, 37, 38, 40, 48, 56, 65, 66, 75, 76, 83, 91, 94, 102, 103, 104, 106, 107, 108, and 109.[113] In fact, there is not a single article with identical wording in the Gniezno MS and the Baworowscy MS.

113 According to MS Gn. numbering scheme.

TABLE 18 Differences of vocabulary in selected Latin texts of the *Weichbild*

Article in MS Gn.	Gniezno MS	Baworowscy MS, Opatów MS, Żagań MS	Działyńscy Codex IV	*Statutes*
6	*legalitas*	*bannum*	*legalitas*	*legalitas seu bannum*
39	*suspendium*	*patibulum*	*patibulum*	*patibulum sive suspendium*
46	*apparatus*	*fundus*	*apparatus*	*fundus seu apparatus*
50, 61, 74, 96	*tutor*	*tutor*	*mundiburdius*	*tutor*
53	*advocatus*	*advocatus*	*prolocutor*	*advocatus*
79	*probus*	*fidedignus*[a]	*fidedignus*	*fidedignus*
101	*munera*	*munera*	*dona*	*munera*
102	*homines qui clamorem audierunt*	*clamatores*	*clamatores*	*clamatores*
103	*homines qui clamorem audierunt*	*clamatores*	*clamatores*	*homines qui clamorem audierunt*

a The terms *fidedignus*, 'trustworthy', and *probus*, 'honest' are rendered in Polish as *ludzie dobrzy*, 'good people'. Cf. Zajda, *Staropolska terminologia prawnicza (do 1500 r.)*, p. 121.

Apart from alterations of content and wording, the texts in both groups quite often do not use the same words and terms. The differences in vocabulary are shown in Table 18.

It is worth noting that in the Baworowscy MS, Article 5 refers to *legittime impedimentum*, where all other manuscripts have *legale impedimentum*; in Article 30, instead of *banca*, it has *scampna scabinalia* (as in a gloss of the Leipzig manuscript); in Article 32, *mercenarius* is replaced by *famulus*; in Article 56, we can find *scabini* instead of *iurati*; and in Article 96, *anni discrecionis* (as in the Opatów MS) is present in lieu of *anni pubertatis*. As Table 18 shows, the vocabulary used in the *Statutes* draws on both the Gniezno and the Baworowscy manuscripts. Meanwhile, in the Działyńscy Codex IV, we can find terms borrowed from both groups, as well as new constructs. Generally, such vocabulary substitutions did not count as modifications of the legal regulations.

5.3 *Circumstances of the Composition of the Cracow Version*

There can be no doubt that the Group II manuscripts constitute a different version of the Latin *Weichbild*. This is demonstrated by the distinct array of their formal features, namely, the list and arrangement of the articles, the contents of the provisions, the use of the German texts, and the additions from the Magdeburg *ortyle* in a number of manuscripts. Earlier, Konrad's *versio Sandomiriensis* has been identified as a good piece of work. Why then, it may be asked, would anybody go to the trouble of doing that work all over again and preparing another version of the Latin *Weichbild*? Perhaps, one might conjecture, the discrepancies between Konrad's text and the German *Weichbild* were noticed, and the dismay led to the commissioning of a new, more accurate translation. This must have taken place soon after Konrad completed his work, as the features characteristic of this new version appear for the first time in the St Petersburg MS (F 143) dated 1368, nine years earlier than the earliest extant text of the 1359 Sandomierz version.

Once this scenario is granted, another question must be asked, as well. Was this new version actually a new translation, or merely a revised redaction of the previous one? The author of the new version clearly made use of Konrad of Sandomierz's text, but he, too, consulted the earlier translation by Konrad of Opole while translating the *Sachsenspiegel*.[114] In other words, the use of an earlier text is not a strong enough argument to deny a new translation its 'newness' (even though, in a somewhat similar research project, the detection in Jacques Gohory's translation of Machiavelli's *Il Principe* of longer phrases identical to those in an earlier translation by Guillaume Cappel was thought to be sufficient to write off the former as a piece of plagiarism).[115]

Admittedly, the crux of the matter is that that we know neither the autograph of Konrad of Sandomierz's translation, nor the archetype of the new version. Additionally, the reconstruction of the features of the base texts that would have to be shared by the extant German manuscripts and Konrad of Sandomierz's translation and – conjecturally – the new version is anything but fragmentary. However, as the comparative analysis presented above indicates, the scope of the use of the German base texts was different in both the *versio Sandomiriensis* and the new version, which has relatively few phrases characteristic of the *Magdeburg Bench Law* and the Wawel MS. Hence, the new version had a different base text and cannot not be regarded as a revised copy of

114 Rymaszewski, *Łacińskie teksty Landrechtu Zwierciadła Saskiego w Polsce. Versio*, pp. 85–88.

115 Jean-Claude Zancarini, "*Uno Picolo Dono*: A Software Tool for Comparing the First Edition of Machiavelli's *The Prince* to Its Sixteenth Century French Translations", in: *The Radical Machiavelli. Politics, Philosophy and Language*, eds. Filippo Del Lucchese, Fabio Frosini, and Vittorio Morfino (Leiden – Boston, 2015), pp. 52–53, and esp. the samples in Table 2.3, p. 47.

Konrad of Sandomierz's translation.[116] Therefore, to summarize, the author of the new version:

1) gave it a formal coherence with the German text of the Silesian-Małopolska compilation, that is, he removed the additional provisions of *versio Sandomiriensis* and added the provisions of the *Constitution of Courts* that had been omitted by Konrad of Sandomierz, as well as Article 76;[117]
2) made some alterations in the text from the *versio Sandomiriensis* after checking another German base; and
3) re-edited numerous provisions by giving them a new wording which was different from that of the Sandomierz version; practically all the articles were given a new redaction.

What this summary makes clear is that the new version was not just a revised copy of Konrad of Sandomierz's translation, even if it depended on its predecessor to a significant extent.

The creation of the text used in the Częstochowa MS, the Kielce MS, the St Florian MS, the Działyńscy Codex IV, and the Warsaw MS did not mean that the translation was complete. The next stage was the supplementation of the Latin *Weichbild* with additions from the *ortyle*.[118] For those who contemplated the task of incorporating the *ortyle* into the *Weichbild*, the new version offered the obvious advantage of being consistent with the German text of the Silesian-Małopolska compilation. The evidence that the German *ortyle* were taken from a collection associated with Cracow and embedded into a German text dependent on the Cracow manuscript does exist (see Chapter 1). The well proven connection with Cracow also justifies the use of the term 'Cracow version' for the branch of the *Weichbild* which includes the Baworowscy MS, the

116 Otto Kade's classic definition of translation emphasizes the process of striving to render the original text. See: Mary Snell-Hornby *et al.* eds., *Handbuch Translation* (Tübingen, 1998), p. 37. However, if each version had a different base, the claim that Version B was merely a revised (improved) copy of the original translation must be rejected. After all, it is a commonplace of medieval translation studies that the creation of a translation was as often as not based on more than one any basic text. This observation is fully confirmed by the work done on the Latin translation of the *Weichbild*. See: Section 137 "Relationships between Text and Translation in Medieval Europe", in: *Translation. An International Encyclopedia of Translation Studies*, 2, eds. Harald Kittel, Armin P. Frank, Norbert Freiner, Theo Hermans, Werner Koller, José Lambert, Fritz Paul (Berlin – New York, 2007), p. 1298; cf. Theo Hermans, *What is (not) Translation?*, in: *The Routledge Handbook of Translation Studies*, eds. Carmen Millán and Francesca Bartina (London – New York, 2013), pp. 75–76.

117 According to the numbering scheme of the Cracow MS (BJ 169).

118 As is argued in Chapter 1, the inclusion of the *ortyle* in the Latin text could not have happened before they were incorporated into the German texts.

Opatów MS, the Żagań MS, and the lost Sanok manuscript, even though some of them contain the *ortyle*, while others do not. The authors of the manuscripts without the *ortyle*, as well as those who translated them and included them in the *Weichbild*, remain anonymous. Unfortunately, the clues that might enable us to trace them are missing.

5.4 *Summary: New Characteristics, a New Version*

The Cracow version must have been created prior to 1368, the date of the earliest manuscript (Petersburg MS F 143) with a text that displays the characteristic features of that version. Its author relied chiefly on the Sandomierz version, but allowed himself to be influenced by the text of the Cracow version.

The unknown author of the Cracow version also used Konrad of Sandomierz's Latin *Weichbild* as his base. Yet, in contrast to his predecessor, his concern was first and foremost with producing an accurate translation of what he thought was the authentic legal text. This assessment is based on the following facts. First, he translated and included in his work all those provisions of the German *Weichbild* that had been left out by Konrad of Sandomierz. Second, the wording of many provisions in his work differs markedly from that of Konrad. Third, he revised and pruned Konrad's text wherever it diverged from the German base, but, at the same time, introduced alterations of his own. Fourth, he drew on a greater range of German texts than did other authors working with the Sandomierz version.

The effort expended to bring the Latin *Weichbild* into conformity with its original German text and the freedom with which its anonymous author/translator introduces his own solutions at every level of text construction are the two key characteristics of the Cracow version. The latter stands in the way of treating the Cracow version as a revision, committed to a higher standard of accuracy and exactitude, of the old *versio Sandomiriensis*. The term 'Cracow version' is intended to mark its special position, determined by its affinities with the German-language Cracow manuscript (MS BJ 169) and its augmentation by an array of Magdeburg *ortyle* from a collection associated with Cracow.

The differences between the two versions named after Sandomierz and Cracow were hardly the result of cautious marginal tinkering, and the gap grew wider in the process of transmission. The Cracow version is probably older than its Latin form. It came into being when a conjectural German-language *Weichbild* was augmented with a set of *ortyle* in a manner which resembles the disposition of German texts (for a detailed argument, see Chapter 1). Later, manuscripts that stemmed from the Cracow version show a tendency to introduce daring editorial modifications (like changing the wording of provisions or excising whole articles). In this study, manuscript texts of the Cracow version that unequivocally represent that trend are grouped together under the label of 'the Wawel variant'.

6 The Wawel Variant of the Cracow Version

6.1 *Alterations within the Cracow Version*

The texts of the *Weichbild* in the Działyńscy Codex IV and the Warsaw MS are remarkably similar, even if this is not obvious from the columns of figures in our quantitative analyses. The reason for this is simple: the statistical count is distorted by the fact that a large portion of the Warsaw MS has been destroyed. Therefore, in effect, our analysis of the MS Warsz./MS Dział. IV pair has to depend on the latter, which – to complicate things further – includes a section entitled *In Colmensi* with a selection of provisions of the Chełmno Law (*Der Alte Kulm*). Nevertheless, the formal features of both texts leave hardly any doubt about their affiliation. They belong to the manuscripts of the Cracow version, a fact further borne out by statistical calculations based on the data in Appendix 2. This data indicates that the Działyńscy Codex IV, like other members of that group, departs significantly from Gniezno MS. What sets it apart from the Baworowscy MS (BN 12607), Opatów MS (Oss.) and Żagań MS (II Q 4) is that it does not include the *ortyle* – which needs to be taken into account in interpreting its lower number of divergences, *prima facie*, from the Gniezno MS than is the case with the other manuscripts. The divergences from the Gniezno MS in the Działyńscy Codex IV are principally of two kinds: individual alterations and omissions of whole provisions. Finally, the affiliation of MS Dział. IV/MS Warsz. with the Cracow version is confirmed by a comparison of the linguistic shape of more than a dozen provisions in the Działyńscy Codex IV and the Baworowscy MS; the wording is very similar in the two texts and significantly different from that of Gniezno MS.[119]

The comparative analysis of the data in Appendix 3 reveals that the author of the Działyńscy Codex IV made use of other manuscripts than the one containing the Cracow version. Therefore, for instance, his text has parallels with that of the Sandomierz version (the Gniezno MS). Although the Cracow version was his base text, he took over the whole of Article 37 from the *versio Sandomiriensis*. There is also other evidence to confirm that he had both

119 Articles 2, 4, 9, 25, 35, 39, 40, 70, 72, 75, 83, 92, 102, 105, 106, and 107. Cf. also the parallels between the Baworowscy MS and the Działyńscy Codex IV in Records 318, 331, 341, 352, 425, 442, 450, 499, 500, 504, 507, and 510.

versions at his disposal.[120] Furthermore, as already mentioned, the Działyńscy Codex IV omits the articles which are absent from the Wawel MS (BJ 168) and, what is more, spells out the reasons for such omissions, as does MS BJ 168. Moreover, we can find seven cases where the Latin text is consistent exclusively with the German-language Wawel manuscript (Table 15).[121] At least six of these cases are direct borrowings from the Wawel MS.[122] In the remaining three cases, the divergences from the Gniezno MS comply with the text of MS BJ 170a[123] or the Baworowscy MS – probably the result of the influence of the Wawel MS.[124] Thus, we may conclude that the author used both the Cracow and Sandomierz versions, and on top of that, consulted a text consistent with MS BJ 168.[125] He also introduced a number of individual changes which have no parallel in other Latin or German texts. Another feature of the Działyńscy Codex IV is its pronounced stylistic make-up due to the author's preference for shorter phrases and his concern for making the regulations as clear as possible.[126] He is in the habit of supplanting descriptive phrases with legal terms with medieval connotations. For example, he abbreviates *der uf den man clagit* ('the one against whom the complaint is brought') to a single word, *reus*, 'defendant',[127] and replaces the word *tutor* ('guardian') with *mundiburdius* (Articles 50, 61, 74, and 96),[128] *advocatus* with *prolocutor* in Article 53, and *munera* with *dona* in Article 101. Sometimes, however, he chooses a general term if it is more apt. For example, instead of translating *silbir* literally as *argentum*, 'silver', he opts for *pecunia* ('money').[129] His close attention to language does not render his translation fool-proof, as shown in the substitution

120 This is proven by Records 374 and 453, which indicate that the text in the Działyńscy Codex IV is a synthesis of the Gniezno MS and the Baworowscy MS, while Records 318, 360, 363, 364, and 460 are consistent with MS Gn. but at odds with the Baworowscy MS.

121 No. 322, 352, 436, 461, 472, and 506.

122 In one case, we can find a parallel between the Działyńscy Codex IV / the Gniezno MS and the Wawel MS (No. 322).

123 No. 331.

124 No. 404 and 408.

125 The only case of conformity with MS BJ 170a consists of the omission of a passage in Article 1 (No. 305); it is probably simply a copyist's error.

126 No. 301, 322, 431, 432, 471, 475, 479, 498, and 499. See also Nos. 318, 324, 356, and 438.

127 No. 429; cf. also No. 499.

128 For an analysis of the use of term *opiekun*, 'guardian', in Polish legal terminology, see: Aleksander Zajda, *Studia z historii polskiego słownictwa prawniczego i frazeologii* [Studies in the History of Polish Legal Terminology and Phraseology] (Kraków, 2001), pp. 46–51. He argues that the word *tutor* entered the Polish language in the 16th century and functioned alongside the accustomed *opiekun* and the now-obsolete *opiekadlnik* (also in the sense of 'fiduciary').

129 No. 469.

of *selbe sibende* with *cum septem testibus*,[130] a mistake which results in raising the number of oath-swearers from six to seven. Some changes also had practical consequences.

6.2 *Practical Effect of the Alterations in Działyńscy Codex IV*[131]

Further details were added to the regulations that concerned evidentiary proceedings, in both civil and criminal cases. The requirement specifying the number of oath-swearers in two provisions concerning debt payment was limited to two.[132] At the same, the requirement specifying the number of oath-helpers in disputes over land inheritance was reduced from six to two.[133] The trial of a person caught in the act would, under a new dispensation of the Działyńscy Codex IV, require the participation of six oath-helpers,[134] while in cases of rape, assault, burglary, murder, theft, or robbery, their number was reduced to was reduced to two (*mettertius*) in order to proceed more efficiently with these types of crime.[135] Similarly, should the plaintiff in the action of murder choose to forego his right to precedence in presenting evidence, the defendant could be allowed to clear himself of the charges by the oaths of two rather than six compurgators. It seems that the goal of these alterations was to speed up the litigation and to discipline the complainant.[136] The Działyńscy Codex IV also contains a definition of a duel[137] and an amplified formula of the Jewish oath, the latter modelled on the German text in the Wawel MS.[138] All of the modifications introduced by the author of MS Dział. IV are sensible and pragmatic.

In line with the tendency we have established in the Cracow version, the Działyńscy Codex IV also drops the term 'agnate' in favour of the more general term 'cognate' (i.e. a blood relative).[139] The omission of the reservation that the deceased's property may not be inherited by his children who were previously excluded from the inheritance means that they *are* included in the

130 No. 338.

131 See also, in connection with the profile of the Działyńscy Codex IV presented here in greater detail, Nos. 78, 84, 114, 119, and 188.

132 No. 175 and 177. The amendments made the provisions more specific, e.g. 'debt' was narrowed down to 'pecuniary debt' (No. 178), and the payment of debt should be made in 'money that is used in payments nowadays' (No. 181).

133 No. 92.

134 No. 118.

135 No. 113.

136 No. 83.

137 No. 71.

138 No. 509.

139 No. 79.

distribution of the estate.[140] Presumably, this would mean in practice that the disproportionally privileged heirs would have to give up some of their assets to their siblings now that the claims of those with no stake in the estate could be recognized.

The omission of the *sołtys* (*scultetus*) from the institutional authorities with jurisdiction over burghers was a concession to the Polish conditions (*sołtys* was and still is associated with villages).[141] *Sołtys'* subordination to the *wójt* (*advocatus*), and not to the castellan, also fits well with the state of things in Poland, where high courts of German law, headed by *wójt* (*advocatus supremi iudicii*), acted as appellate courts with jurisdiction over the *sołtys*, even though the captains (*starosta, capitaneus*) were occasionally allowed to take part in the proceedings.[142] On the other hand, the reason for omitting the passage about liability for breaking urban statutes (*wilkierze*) is unclear; perhaps the author thought that this could be inferred from the general wording of the provision.[143]

6.3 *Summary: The Wawel Variant*

As the discussion above shows, the author of the Działyńscy Codex IV was by no means a mere copyist. His work involved a considerable amount of research and editorial autonomy. His base was a Group II text, but he also made use of a Group I manuscript and had knowledge of the text of the Wawel MS (BJ 168). His manuscript has an extraordinary number of features that are unique. Its wide-ranging dependence on Group II, despite some modifications harking back to the Wawel MS and the omission from the *Sachsenspiegel* of several articles included in the *Weichbild*, as in MS BJ 168, provide good grounds for treating the Działyńscy Codex IV as an affiliate of the Cracow version rather than a new offshoot of the *Weichbild* tradition. However, to give due acknowledgement of its connections with the Wawel MS, the group containing the Działyńscy Codex IV and the Warsaw MS should be called the Wawel variant of the Cracow version. It also owes its individual character to, first, its author's determination and consistency in clearing up the overlaps between the *Weichbild* and the *Sachsenspiegel* and, second, to the clearheaded pragmatism of his numerous amendments, which range from substantive modifications of the law and judicial procedure to clarification of the language of legal provisions.

140 No. 41.

141 No. 202.

142 No. 208. See Ludwik Łysiak, "Sąd wyższy prawa niemieckiego w Bieczu" [The High Court of German Law in Biecz], *Czasopismo Prawno-Historyczne* 33/1 (1981), 7–10.

143 No. 5.

7 Conclusions: The Adaptation of the Saxon-Magdeburg Law and the Evolution of the Legal Text

The most important outcome of this comparative analysis is the establishment on the basis of compelling evidence that the Latin *Weichbild*, which was widely used in Poland from the 14th century onwards, can be sorted into two main types, descended from the Sandomierz version and the Cracow version, as well as a group of manuscripts in which elements of both types are combined. It has also been possible identify within the Cracow version a distinct sub-group, the Wawel variant, with a set of formal characteristics which can be traced to the German-language MS BJ 168, compiled for the High Court of German Law at the Royal Castle of Wawel.

The *versio Sandomiriensis* is a translation of a German text in which the wording of several provisions is closer to the *Constitution of Courts* and to another text antecedent to the Wawel MS than to the Cracow MS (BJ 169): the manuscript of the Cracow City Council. Konrad of Sandomierz also supplemented his translation with additions from the *Sachsenspiegel* and the *Magdeburg Legal Instructions for Wrocław* of 1261. The translation is quite faithful to the German text, although there are a considerable number of divergences. It was completed prior to 1359, that is, the year to which the Gniezno MS, the earliest extant manuscript with the Latin *Weichbild* of this version, can be dated back. For all we know, the Gniezno manuscript is not an exact copy of the lost archetype. Mikołaj of Cieszyn (or perhaps another copyist whose text Mikołaj of Cieszyn reproduced) made a few amendments which found their way verbatim into the Działyńscy Codex I, and then, to a varying extent, into some other manuscripts. These alterations have parallels in the German texts, which adds more weight to the argument that the evolution of the Latin text proceeded of its own accord.

The numerous divergences in the Silesia-Małopolska compilation from the German *Weichbild* may well have been the reason why – before 1368 – an anonymous author decided to produce another Latin translation. He made use of Konrad of Sandomierz's translation, but collated its text with his own German base. As a result, in this new translation, a number of articles received completely new wording and contents. Its author also decided to include the provisions of the *Constitution of Courts*, left out by Konrad of Sandomierz. They had little practical use, but thanks to their inclusion, the new translation was brought into alignment with the German texts of the Silesian-Małopolska compilation. A close comparison of Articles 24, 76, and 87 in the two versions indicates that Cracow version could not be dated earlier than the Sandomierz version. This leads us to the conclusion that the 'doublets' (unnecessary repetitions) in the manuscripts of the Cracow version resulted from an imperfect adaptation of the earlier text – or, that the author decided to make do with some clumsiness in order to achieve the greater goal of formal coherence with the German text of the Silesian-Małopolska compilation. However, what gave the Cracow version its distinctive character was not only a reconnection with its German sources, but also the augmentation of the *Weichbild* with a selection of the Magdeburg *ortyle*. Whoever thought of combining the *ortyle* with the Latin *Weichbild* must have found its Cracow version better suited for that union because of its formal coherence with the German *Weichbild*, which had been earlier supplemented with the *ortyle*. The reasons for naming the textual version that evolved away from the *versio Sandomiriensis* after Cracow could not be clearer: first, the German text with the *ortyle* descended from the Cracow MS; and second, the *ortyle* came from a collection that had been compiled in Cracow.

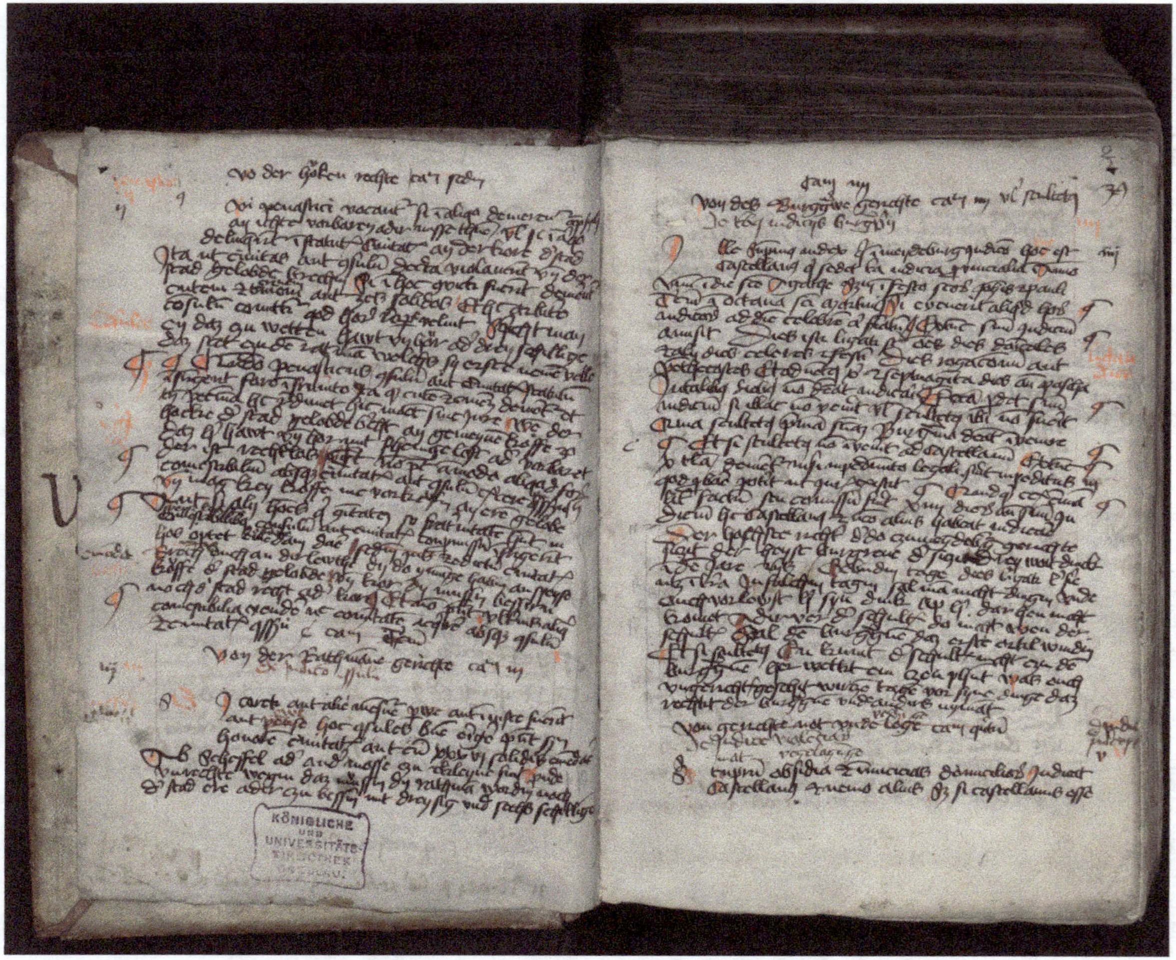

PHOTO 5 Żagań manuscript, Wrocław University Library, Shelfmark II Q 4, f. 2v–3r

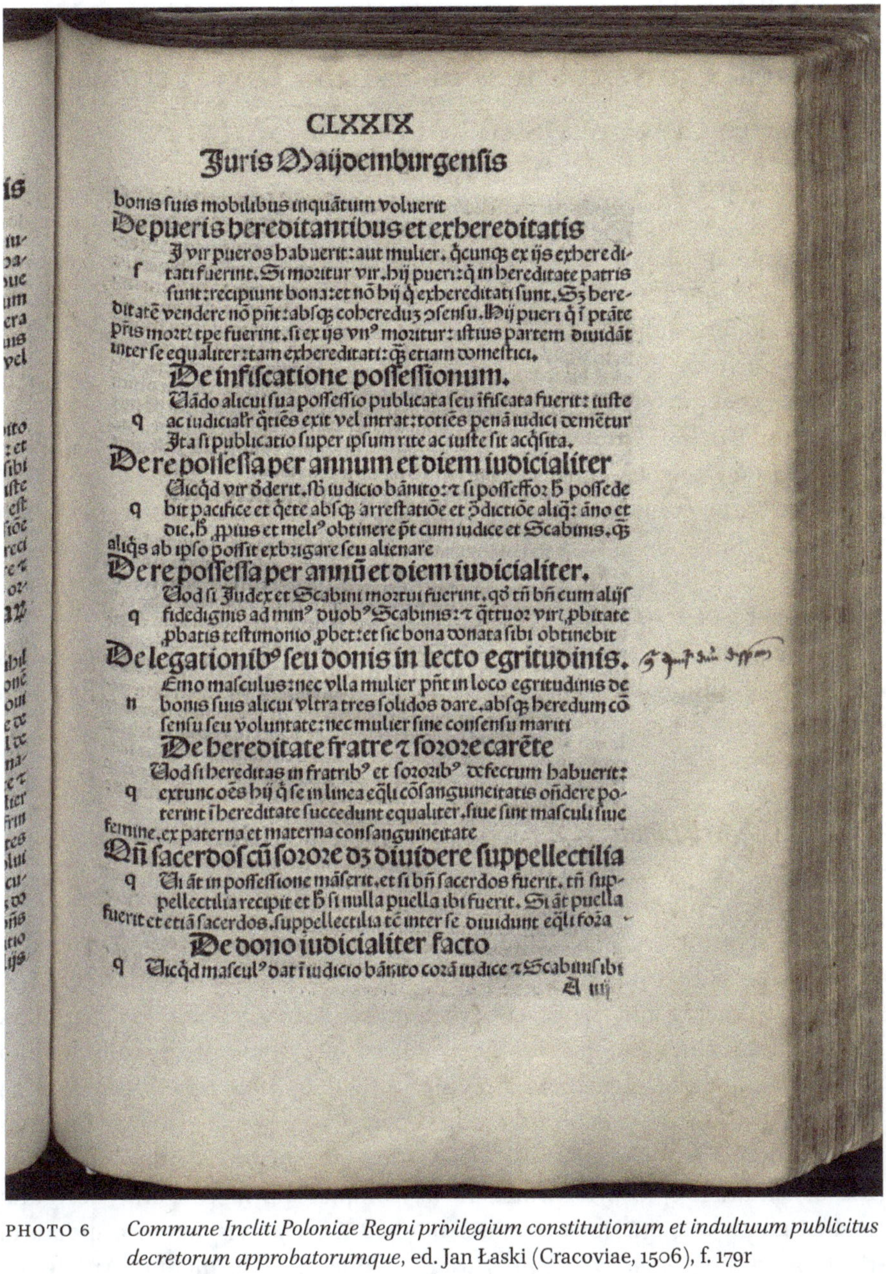

PHOTO 6 *Commune Incliti Poloniae Regni privilegium constitutionum et indultuum publicitus decretorum approbatorumque*, ed. Jan Łaski (Cracoviae, 1506), f. 179r

CHAPTER 3

Practical Consequences of Textual Divergences: From the Cracow MS to Jan Łaski's *Statutes*

The analysis in Chapter 2 has shown that the Silesian-Małopolska compilation of the Magdeburg *Weichbild* kept evolving during its circulation in Poland. All the evidence indicates that that the process originated with a conjectural German-language archetype which was markedly different from the vulgate *Weichbild* that circulated in Germany. The next stage came with the translation of the *Weichbild* into Latin. However, a close analysis of the Latin manuscripts has revealed that the divergences in the Latin texts form patterns that persisted throughout the *Weichbild*'s history. The only plausible explanation of this phenomenon is that initially there were two Latin translations of the *Weichbild* and that the Sandomierz version was a catalyst for the creation of yet another text, the Cracow version.

This chapter looks at the Magdeburg *Weichbild* in the final stage of its career – the authorized version published in Jan Łaski's *Stutues* in 1506 – which builds on both the Sandomierz version and the Cracow version.

1 The *Weichbild* in Jan Łaski's *Statutes*

1.1 *Formal Characteristics*

An analysis of the formal characteristics of the *Weichbild* in Jan Łaski's *Statutes* shows that it contains provisions that can be traced both to the *versio Sandomiriensis* and the Cracow version (see Tables 8 and 9 in Chapter 2). The former includes supplements introduced by Konrad of Sandomierz into Articles 24 and 76 as well as a provision originally transposed to Article 24 which, in the Cracow version, was additionally placed in a slot where it matches the German text.[1] Furthermore, Łaski's edition includes provisions from the *Constitution of Courts*, which in its complete form can only be found in the Cracow version. However, the sequence of the provisions corresponds to the order of the *versio Sandomiriensis*, including the placement of Articles 60 and 61 about the *gerada* and the *hergewet*. The *Statutes* also follows Konrad of

1 Article 86 of the *Statutes* or Article 76 according to the numbering scheme of the Cracow BJ 169.

Sandomierz's design by rearranging some contents for the sake of thematic consistency – for example, the provision about horse theft in Article 69 can also be found after Article 38, which is concerned with theft.

1.2 *Sources of the* Weichbild *in the* Statutes

An analysis of the data in Appendix 2 indicates that the *Weichbild* in the *Statutes* is indebted both to the *versio Sandomiriensis* and the Cracow version.

The text of the *Statutes* differs from the Gniezno MS in 68 records. In 12 cases, a new variant is introduced,[2] although it is usually a collation of available variants.[3] In effect, divergences from the Gniezno MS in the *Statutes* and other texts actually appear in 56 records. The *Commune incliti* shares the greatest number of similarities with the Żagań MS. Divergences between these two texts are exceptional; they occur in a few records only.[4] In the remaining 152 records, the *Statutes* text conforms to MS Gn. In as many as 132 cases, there are, however, individual divergences from the Gniezno MS in one manuscript or

TABLE 19 Characteristics of the *Weichbild* in Jan Łaski's *Statutes* as compared to the Gniezno MS (Gn.)

Characteristic feature	Number	Notes
Divergence from MS Gn.	7	individual variants
Divergence from MS Gn.	6	individual variation resulting from collation of different texts
Divergence from MS Gn.	55	matching other texts, especially Żagań MS (II Q 4)
Conformity to MS Gn.	20	variations from MS Gn. characteristic of the Cracow version
Conformity to MS Gn.	132	records indicating individual variants or variations characteristic for groups of other texts

2 No. 16, 35, 45, 75, 77, 81, 83, 111 139, 159, 160, 211, and 213. Conformity only with MS BN 3068 (No. 12 and 17), or only with MS BOZ and MS 951b (No. 112); it is not clear if they were added into the *Statutes* later, or whether they were part of it originally and adapted later into other texts. MS BN 3068, MS BOZ, and MS 951b come from the beginning of the 16th century.

3 No. 16, 35, 45, 81, 83, and 213.

4 No. 12, 17, 89, 90, and 112. Cf. note 2.

divergences that are peculiar to a group of manuscripts.[5] A remaining set of 20 records belongs to a different category. There, the text of the *Statutes* conforms to the Gniezno MS, although the records are characteristic of the Cracow version.[6] While the Cracow version of the *Weichbild* in *Statutes* comes from a text close to Żagań MS (though not identical to it), the *versio Sandomiriensis* depends in a similar way on the Żegota Pauli's MS or another manuscript like it. Only in the Żegota Pauli's MS, the *Statutes*, Pleszew MS, and Przemyśl MS do we find the qualification concerning household goods heritable by the deceased's widow – they include such goods 'in possession of her husband at the time of his death'.[7] It is certainly more probable that Łaski adopted that explanation from a manuscript associated with Cracow (i.e. the Żegota Pauli's MS) than from Przemyśl or from Pleszew.

The data from Appendix 2 can be complemented with a comprehensive comparison of the text of the *Statutes* with the matching passages in the manuscripts of the Sandomierz and the Cracow versions. Table 20 lists a number of cases which illustrate the adaptation of the latter by the author of the *Commune incliti*.

The wording of Article 16 is a blend of the Sandomierz and the Cracow versions, produced without any significant changes in meaning. Article 19 is similar compilation: the wording of the provision is practically identical in the Żegota Pauli's and the Baworowscy manuscripts. However, the text of Article 50 in the *Statues* is thoroughly revised. The addition of a passage from the Żegota Pauli MS's and the substitution of *agnatus* with *cognatus* show that at this point, the *Statutes* relies on the Sandomierz version (abridged). The text of Article 66, on the other hand, demonstrates exclusive reliance on the Cracow version.

The use by the *Statutes* of the texts of the two versions is presented in Table 21. The *versio Sandomiriensis* is represented here by the Gniezno MS and the Żegota Pauli's MS, while the Cracow version is represented by the Baworowscy MS and the Żagań MS.[8]

Table 21 indicates that 51 per cent of the provisions of the *Weichbild* in *Commune incliti* come exclusively from the Cracow version. If those articles whose text depends on both versions are counted, the dependence of Łaski's *Weichbild* on the Cracow version rises to 65 per cent. In sum, the dominant position of the Cracow version for Jan Łaski and his collaborators

5 For example MS BN 12607/Oss., MS AJG/Kiel., or the Wawel variant of MS Dział. IV/Warsz.

6 No. 1, 15, 22, 28, 52, 62, 65, 79, 88, 91, 93, 110, 130, 135, 166, 169, 170, 195, 197, and 220.

7 No. 64.

8 The *Weichbild* in the *Statutes* has many similarities with the text of the Żagań MS, but the latter also has many peculiarities of its own. For that reason, the comparison also includes another text of the Cracow version: the Baworowscy MS.

TABLE 20 Examples of the use and adaptation of provisions from the *versio Sandomiriensis* and the Cracow version in Łaski's *Statutes*

Article No. foll. MS Gn.	*versio Sandomiriensis* (Żegota Pauli's MS BJ 4405)	*versio Cracoviensis* (Żagań MS II Q 4)	Łaski's *Statutes*
[16] Part I	+ ***Quid masculus dat sub banno, si*** *possidebit pacifice* et quiete absque arrestacione *aliqua anno et die, hoc propius et melius optimere potest cum iudice et scabinis, quam* ab ipso aliquis possit exbrigare.	+ Quidquid vir dederit in iudicio sub bannito et si possessor hoc *possidebit pacifice* ***absque ullius*** contradicione *anno et die, hoc propius et melius* ***possessor*** *obtinere potest cum iudice et scabinis, quam* ***aliquis possidere*** seu alienare.	Significant amendation: NO Quicquit vir dederit sub iudicio bannito et si possessor hoc *possidebit pacifice* et quiete absque arrestacione et condictione *aliqua anno et die, hoc propius et melius obtimere potest cum iudice et scabinis, quam* aliquis ab ipso possit exbrigare seu alienare.
[19]	= *Quitquit masculus dat in iudicio banito coram iudice et scabinis, ibi recipiens dat unum solidum pro doni cognicione, quem recipiunt scabini.*	= *Quidquid masculus dat in iudicio bannito coram iudice [et] scabinis, ibi recipiens dat unum solidum pro doni cognicione, quem recipiunt scabini.*	Significant amendation: NO *Quitquid masculus dat in iudicio bannito coram iudice et scabinis, ibi recipiens dat unum solidum pro doni* ***recognicione,*** *quem recipiunt scabini* ***pro se.***
[50]	+ *Cum moritur vir, qui pueros habuerit, qui ad annos discrecionis nondum pervenerunt, proximus agnatus debet ipsorum esse tutor, usque ad annos pubertatis pervenerint.* ***Et si idem nondum adhuc annos pubertatis attingerit, adiutor suus esse debet proximus agnatus, usque ipse ad annos pervenerit discrecionis,*** *et racionem*	– *Cum moritur vir, qui pueros habuerit, qui ad annos discrecionis non dum pervenerunt, proximus* ***cognatus eorum*** *debet esse* ***eorum*** *tutor, quousque ad annos pervenerint* ***pubertatis. Et si idem nondum ad huc pubertatis annos attingerit, adiutor suus debet propior cognatus suus esse, quousque ad annos pervenerint discrecionis,*** *et racionem*	Significant amendation: YES *Cum moritur vir, qui pueros habuerit, qui ad annos discretionis nondum pervenerunt, proximus agnatus debet ipsorum esse tutor quousque ad annos pubertatis* ***et discretionis*** *pervenerint et racionem de anno ad annum de bonis pupillorum facere* ***debet vel*** *tenetur.*

TABLE 20 Examples of the use and adaptation of provisions (*cont.*)

Article No. foll. MS Gn.	*versio Sandomiriensis* (Żegota Pauli's MS BJ 4405)	*versio Cracoviensis* (Żagań MS II Q 4)	Łaski's *Statutes*
	de anno in annum de bonis pupillorum ***coram vero ipsorum tutore*** *facere tenetur.*	*de anno ad annum de bonis pupillorum* ***coram vero ipsorum tutore*** *facere tenetur* ***quidquid factus fuerit cum hiis bonis.***	
[66]	– *Quod si hereditas mortaliola [s] absque heredibus inventa seu reperta fuerit, regie cedet maiestati.*	+ *Quod hereditas obmortaliola,* ita quod nullus se trahat ad eadem infra annum et die, hoc pertinet ad regiam maiestatem.	Significant amendation: YES ***Si hereditas absque successoribus relinquitur,*** ita quod nullus se trahat ad eadem infra annum et die, hoc pertinet ad regiam maiestatem.

Words and phrases that are taken over verbatim by the *Statutes* are set in roman; words and phrases in bold indicate divergences. + indicates the presence in the *Statutes* of the text characteristic of that version; – indicates the absence in the *Statutes* of the text characteristic of either version; = indicates that the text of both versions may have been used.

TABLE 21 The origin of provisions and various significant amendations in Łaski's *Statutes*

Article		Characteristic features			Article		Characteristic features		
MS Gn.	*Statutes*	*v. Sand.*	*v. Crac.*	New	MS Gn.	*Statutes*	*v. Sand.*	*v. Crac.*	New
1	1	+	+	Yes	56	62	+	–	Yes
2	2	=	=	Yes	57	63	+	missing	Yes
3	3	–	+	Yes	58	64	=	+	Yes
4	4	+	–	Yes	59	65	+	–	Yes
5	5	+	–	Yes	60	66	–	+	Yes
6	6	+	+	Yes	61	67–68	–	+	Yes
7	7	+	+	Yes	62	69	–	+	Yes
8	8	+	–	No	63	70	–	+	Yes
9	9	+	+	Yes	64	71	–	+	No
10	10	–	+	Yes	65	72	–	+	Yes
11	11	=	=	Yes	66	73	–	+	Yes

TABLE 21 The origin of provisions and various significant amendations (*cont.*)

Article		Characteristic features			Article		Characteristic features		
MS Gn.	*Statutes*	*v. Sand.*	*v. Crac.*	New	MS Gn.	*Statutes*	*v. Sand.*	*v. Crac.*	New
12	12	=	=	Yes	67	74	–	+	No
13	13	=	+	No	68	75	–	+	No
14	14–15	+	+	Yes	69	45	+	–	Yes
15	16	+	–	Yes	70	76	+	–	Yes
16	17–18	+	+	No	71	77	–	+	Yes
17	19	–	+	No	72	78	–	+	Yes
18	20–21	–	+	Yes	73	79	–	+	Yes
19	22	=	=	No	74	80	–	+	No
20	23	+	–	Yes	75	81	+	–	Yes
21	24	+	–	Yes	76	82, 84	+	+	Yes
22	25	+	–	No	77	83	+	missing	Yes
23	26–27	+	+	Yes	78	85	–	+	Yes
24	28–30	–	+	No	–	86	missing	+	Yes
25	31	+	–	Yes	79	87	–	+	Yes
26	32	+	–	No	80	88	–	+	Yes
27	33	=	=	No	81	89	–	+	Yes
28	34	+	–	Yes	82	90	–	+	Yes
29	35	+	–	No	83	91	–	+	Yes
30	36	+	–	No	84	92	–	+	Yes
31	37	+	–	No	85	93	–	+	Yes
32	38	–	+	Yes	86	94	–	+	Yes
33	39	–	+	Yes	87	95–96	+	–	Yes
34	40	+	–	Yes	88	97	–	+	Yes
35	41	–	+	No	89	98	–	+	No
36	42	+	–	Yes	90	99	–	+	Yes
37	43	–	+	Yes	91	100	+	+	Yes
38	44	+	–	Yes	92	101	–	+	No
39	46	+	+	Yes	93	102	–	+	Yes
40	47	+	+	Yes	94	103	+	–	Yes
41	48	=	=	Yes	95	104–105	–	+	Yes
42	49	+	+	Yes	96	107–108	+	+	Yes
43	49	=	=	Yes	97	106	–	+	Yes
44	50	=	=	No	98	109	–	+	Yes
45	51	+	–	Yes	99	110	+	+	Yes
46	52	+	–	Yes	100	111	+	+	Yes
47	53	–	+	No	101	112	+	+	Yes
48	54	=	+	Yes	102	114	–	+	No
49	55	+	–	Yes	103	113	+	+	Yes
50	56	+	–	Yes	104	115	–	+	Yes
51	57	+	–	Yes	105	116	–	+	No

TABLE 21 The origin of provisions and various significant amendations (*cont.*)

Article		Characteristic features			Article		Characteristic features		
MS Gn.	*Statutes*	*v. Sand.*	*v. Crac.*	New	MS Gn.	*Statutes*	*v. Sand.*	*v. Crac.*	New
52	58	+	–	Yes	106	117	+	–	Yes
53	59	–	+	Yes	107	118	–	+	No
54	60	+	+	Yes	108	119	–	+	Yes
55	61	+	missing	Yes	109	119	–	+	Yes

+ indicates the presence in the *Statutes* of the text characteristic of that version; – indicates the absence in the *Statutes* of the text characteristic of either version; = indicates that the text of both versions may have been used. Yes – significant amendations in the text of the *Statutes*; No – lack of significant amendations in the text of the *Statutes*; U – addition characteristic of the Cracow version

is unquestionable. The share of the texts of the Sandomierz version and the Cracow version in Łaski's *Weichbild* is presented in Figure 3, below.

The text of approximately 80 per cent of the provisions in the *Statues* has been revised. The revised text:

- includes all the extensions of the Cracow version that result from the addition of the *ortyle* and some other supplementary materials;[9]
- retains passages from the *versio Sandomiriensis* that are missing from the Cracow version;[10]
- fills the gaps and cleans up the corruptions by collation with the German text;[11]
- conforms to the *versio Sandomiriensis* in the consistent use of the term *agnatus*[12] and retains the definition of agnatic and cognatic kinship from that version;[13]
- infrequently introduces its own solutions by fusing the two versions of the *Weichbild*;

9 The following contents are missing from the *Statutes*: the definition of a public holiday (No. 15); the mention of the beneficiary of the goods and chattels in the possession of the deceased husband (No. 65); the procedure of proving kinship (No. 130); a supplement saying that if a suit is brought against a servant it has to be backed by an oath (No. 197).

10 No. 1, 22, 28, 52, 62, 91, 93, 135, 169, 170, 195, and 220. Following the Żagań MS, there is an (exceptional) omission of an explanation of the negative consequences of a delay in lodging a complaint by a man who has been wounded (No. 33).

11 No. 3, 10, 60, 102, 175, 206, and 216.

12 No. 79, 88, 110, and 141.

13 No. 166.

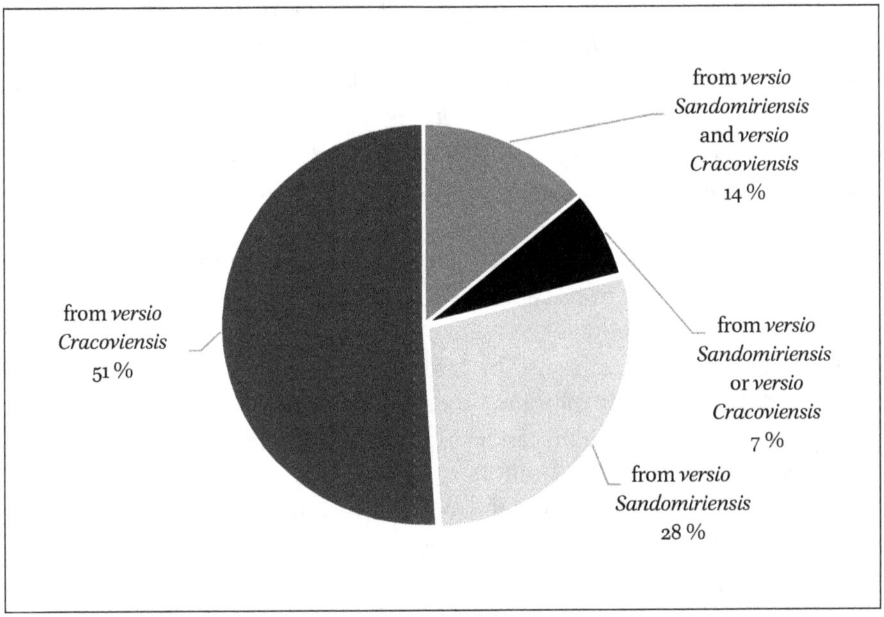

FIGURE 3 Share of the Sandomierz version and the Cracow version in the *Weichbild* of *Commune incliti*

- introduces amendations that take into account the Chełmno Law;[14] and
- introduces lexical corrections in the core text of the *Weichbild*[15] as well as in the passages taken over from the *ortyle*.[16]

1.3 *Summary: The* Statutes – *Culmination of the Medieval Evolution of a Legal Text*

The author of the *Weichbild* of the *Commune incliti* combined some characteristic elements of both versions of that key text that had been in use in Poland, namely, the supplements, occasional modifications of the basic texts, and careful lexical redaction. There is, however, almost no evidence that he consulted the original German text.[17]

14 No. 17, 18, 29, 139.

15 No. 77.

16 No. 163.

17 Similarly unfounded is the claim made by Stanisław Estreicher that Jan Łaski augmented his *Statutes* with excerpts from the Chełmno Law (Stanisław Estreicher, "Freimarkt and Frymark", *Czasopismo Prawnicze i Ekonomiczne* 25 (1929), 342). This problem is discussed by Zygfryd Rymaszewski in *Łacińskie teksty Landrechtu Zwierciadła Saskiego w Polsce. Versio Vratislaviensis, versio Sandomiriensis, Łaski* [Latin Texts of the Landrecht of

Those findings contrast with Zygfryd Rymaszewski's conclusions about the *Sachsenspiegel*. In collating the latter, Jan Łaski and his team of collaborators tended to reach out beyond the familiar sources and amend the text in a more decisive manner.[18] The *Sachsenspiegel* may well have been in need of more 'aggressive' editing than the *Weichbild*.[19] Originally a code of Saxon common law, although with notable input of regulations of a different kind,[20] it was subject to more intrusive adaptation for the needs of the burghers of the Kingdom of Poland than the *Ius municipale Magdeburgense*. The order in which the two appear in the *Statutes* (i.e. Book I: The *Weichbild* and Book II: The *Sachsenspiegel*) follows their customary sequence in the manuscripts of the Cracow version. It can also be interpreted that the editors regarded the *Weichbild*, albeit shorter than the other law book, as a source of higher rank. This plausibility of this claim can be tested by comparing the number of references in the *Weichbild* gloss of the *Statutes* to the provisions (legal acts) in other parts of the *Commune incliti* and the references pointing in the other direction. The *Weichbild* gloss contains only one reference to the *Sachsenspiegel* itself,[21] four to the Statutes of Kazimierz the Great,[22] five to the Statutes of Warta (1423),[23] one to the Parliament Statutes (*Konstytucje Sejmu*) of 1496,[24] one to

the Sachsenspiegel in Poland: Versio Vratislaviensis, versio Sandomiriensis, Łaski] (Łódź, 1975), p. 149.

18 Rymaszewski, *Łacińskie teksty Landrechtu Zwierciadła Saskiego w Polsce. Versio*, pp. 213–214.

19 *Ibid.*, p. 213.

20 For the latest monographic study of the *Sachsenspiegel*, see Heiner Lück, *Der Sachsenspiegel: Das berühmteste deutsche Rechtsbuch des Mittelalters* (Darmstadt, 2017). Cf. also Józef Matuszewski, *Artykuły słowiańskie Zwierciadła saskiego* [Slavic Articles of the *Sachsenspiegel*], *Czasopismo Prawno-Historyczne*, 1 (1948), 25–74. It includes the following statement: "The *Sachsenspiegel*, a monument of the German law, contains also important insights into Slavic legal customs. They are all the more precious as other sources from that period pass over a number of issues that are mentioned here" (*ibid.*, p. 70).

21 Reference to the provision about the dates of court sessions in Article 4.

22 Reference to the competences of a *kasztelan* in Article 5 dealing with the judicial procedure in cases of assault and house-breaking; in Article 12, reference to a provision concerning homicide in the *Statutes*; reference in Article 14 concerning the material situation of a widow; reference to a judge's appeal from Article 22 concerning a complaint against a judge who was accused of issuing an unjustified verdict (*nagana*).

23 Reference to the provision about price-fixing in Articles 3 and 1 (incorrect number of the folio referred to); reference from Article 11 concerning assault and house-breaking to a provision about the competences of the captain (*capitaneus, starosta*); reference to the article concerning the material situation of a widow from Article 14 on the same subject; reference to the provision concerning guardianship in Article 50.

24 Reference from Article 11 concerning assault and house-breaking to a provision about the competences of the captain (*capitaneus, starosta*). Cf. Wacław Uruszczak, Stanisław

Pope Gregory XI' s bull *Articuli reprobati* (a condemnation of some articles of the *Sachsenspiegel*, endorsed by King Alexander I Jagiellon),[25] one to Bishop Bodzanta's Statute of Tithes of 1369,[26] one to the Royal Privilege of Jedlnia and Cracow of 1433,[27] and one to the collection of judicial oath formulas authorized by King Alexander I.[28] The imbalance is hard to overlook. While the number of references to the *Sachsenspiegel* is kept at an absolute minimum, the reverse references are not that infrequent.[29] It seems the authors of the *Statutes* worked with the intention to connect the *Weichbild* with the key texts of Polish law; cross-referencing it with the *Sachsenspiegel* was of lesser importance to them. The relatively higher number of reverse links from the *Sachsenspiegel* to the *Weichbild* may suggest that the latter was regarded as the base text.

Prior to the publication of Łaski's *Statutes*, there were several attempts to normalize the Latin *Weichbild* within the framework of the Silesian-Małopolska compilation. They resulted in the creation of the Sandomierz version and the Cracow version, with its Wawel variant. All of them, despite some flaws and lexical errors, are products of highly competent authors. Łaski's team surely shared this assessment of the high standard of these translations, or if they had been of a different opinion, they would have started work on a new version of the *Weichbild*, let alone a new translation of that key source. Collated from the *versio Sandomiriensis* and the Cracow version, supplied with a refurbished gloss, and cleaned up linguistically, the text of Łaski's *Statutes* marked the ultimate high point of the evolution of the medieval *Weichbild* in the Kingdom of Poland. The impact of that process on contemporary legal practice will be discussed below. My analysis is divided into four parts, which correspond roughly with four main rubrics in collections of Magdeburg Law: 1) the urban community and its citizens; 2) crime and criminal procedure; 3) family and rules of inheritance; and 4) debtor and creditor. These are the topics of provisions that were continually emended and modified. A comprehensive review of the themes of the *Weichbild* can be found in the Introduction.

Grodziski and Irena Dwornicka, eds., *Volumina Constitutionum*, Vol. 1: 1493–1549, vol. 1. 1493–1526 (Warszawa, 1996), No. 13, p. 63.

25 Reference from Article 56, transposed into the *Weichbild* from the *Sachsenspiegel*.

26 Reference from Article 75 concerning the procedure to establish whether a man was free to provisions on tithes collected from knights and villeins.

27 Reference from the provision concerning a proxy in Article 93 to the royal Privilege of Jedlnia and Cracow (1433) is not clear.

28 Reference from the provision with the text of the Jewish oath (Article 108) to the formula of the Jewish oath.

29 Rymaszewski, *Łacińskie teksty Landrechtu Zwierciadła Saskiego w Polsce. Versio*, p. 169.

2 The Urban Community and Its Citizens

The differences with regard to the urban community and its citizens are, for the most part, almost imperceptible. Occasionally, however, the traditional formulas do give way to completely new arrangements, especially in what can be described as constitutional matters, namely, the administrative and judicial competences of the city authorities and the status of guests (aliens).

2.1 *The Town Council*

The first provision of the *Weichbild* deals with the city council and the jurors. The city council are to be elected every year, while the jurors are to serve for the remainder of their lives. The latter, however, was not an absolute rule.[30] The aldermen have the right to summon a meeting of the council whenever they wish, but they need to have the approval of the elders. The Żagań MS, Łaski's *Statutes*, and the Leipzig MS gloss emphasize the role of the elders as a guarantee of proper management of urban affairs. The gloss in the Żegota Pauli's MS mentions 'senior aldermen' in this context. We may therefore assume that in Poland, the term 'elders' meant retired senior aldermen, although other interpretations are also possible. This passage was amended in St Petersburg MS (F 143, dated 1368), in which the word 'elders' is replaced by 'wise men'.[31] In that manuscript, Article 1 is thoroughly revised, probably with an eye to Polish realities. A reflection of those realities is most likely the addition stipulating that the aldermen elect the mayor (*proconsul*) from among themselves.[32] This amendation must be seen in connection with another one in the St Petersburg MS and also in the Marcin Zabowski's MS (dated 1513), namely, the skipping of the clause about Emperor Otto I granting the city of Magdeburg a charter on the advice of the council of elders.[33]

Article 1 acknowledges the validity of the town council's legislation unless it contravenes God's law. This clause was introduced by Konrad of Sandomierz and provides additional proof of Zygfryd Rymaszewski's claim that Konrad

30 See Maciej Mikuła, *Prawodawstwo króla i sejmu dla małopolskich miast królewskich (1386–1572). Studium z dziejów rządów prawa w Polsce* [Royal and Parliamentary Legislation for the Royal Towns of Małopolska (1386–1572): A Study in the History of the Rule of Law in Poland] (Kraków, 2014), pp. 195–202, 205–208.

31 No. 7. See: Maria Bogucka, Henryk Samsonowicz, *Dzieje miast i mieszczaństwa w Polsce przedrozbiorowej* (Wrocław, 1986), pp. 478–484.

32 No. 8.

33 No. 4.

believed in the primacy of canon law and God's law over secular laws.[34] Normally, the latter must be obeyed, and the municipal authorities have the right to impose penal sanctions for their infringement.[35] Article 1 describes the competences of the town council to hear complaints concerning weights and measures, food, and, more broadly, trade, where the offence was punishable in skin and hair or merited a fine of three Slavic marks or 36 shillings. Identical penalties are stipulated in Article 3, which is concerned with the use of false measures and weights. In the manuscripts of the Sandomierz version, the worth of the fine is set at 3 shillings, an obvious scribal error which goes back to Konrad's omission of '6' in the figure 36.[36] The author of the *Statues* decided to follow the Cracow version with the correct figure and added an explanation that the penalty was intended to protect the interests of the poor.[37]

Both the Cracow version and Łaski's *Statutes* stress the role of the town council in defending the town's honour[38] and in the fair and unbiased administration of justice.[39] The high standards set for the aldermen were all too often belied by their conduct – hence the penalty of six *denarii* for those members of the council who failed to turn up at a session announced by bell ringing and five shilling if the summons was passed round by different means.[40] This differentiation of the penalty may reflect the distinction between routine and extraordinary sessions, with the latter announced by the ringing of bells. This issue was additionally regulated in the municipal by-laws (*wilkierze*).[41] All in all, it seems that ill-disciplined aldermen were not hard to come by.

2.2 *Judicial Competences of Other Municipal Bodies*

The *Weichbild* was a basic law code of various types of courts. They included the grand *Burggraf*'s court (*iudicium provincialium*), the grand *sołtys'/wójt's* court, ordinary courts (*iudicium bannitum*), temporary emergency courts, summary

34 No. 1. Cf. Rymaszewski, *Łacińskie teksty Landrechtu Zwierciadła Saskiego w Polsce. Versio*, p. 213.

35 No. 5.

36 No. 10.

37 No. 12, and similarly in MS BN 3068. MS BN 3068 mentions loss of honour as an additional penalty for the use of false measures and weights (No. 11).

38 No. 3.

39 No. 2.

40 Only in MS BN 12607 and MS BN 3068 is the fine for a sluggishness set at six *solidi* (shillings) (No. 6).

41 Maciej Mikuła, "O reformie prawa miejskiego w XVI wieku. Ciężkowicka uchwała o prawie prywatnym i administracji" [Reforms of Municipal Law in the 16th Century: A Statute concerning Private Law and Administration Adopted by the Municipality of Ciężkowice], *Krakowskie Studia z Historii Państwa i Prawa* 6/3 (2013), p. 229.

courts, and guest courts (*Gastgerichte*). What I am interested in is the terminology and certain differences between the *versio Sandomiriensis* and the Cracow version of the *Weichbild*.[42]

The competences of the *wójt* (*advocatus*), the *sołtys* (*scultetus*), and the *Burggraf* (*castellanus*) have been the subject of numerous in-depth studies which show that the meaning of these terms evolved when they came to be used in the medieval and 16th-century Kingdom of Poland. In the early 16th century, Johannes Cervus of Tuchola tried to reconnect the names of institutions and offices in the basic texts of the Saxon-Magdeburg Law with their counterparts in Polish towns. So, while the Grand Court of the *Burggraf* of Magdeburg was presided over by the *Burggraf* and the *Schultheiß* (*sołtys*),[43] similar courts in Cracow and Lviv' were headed by the major (*burmistrz, Burgermeister*), or an alderman officiating as his deputy, and the *wójt* (*Vogt, advocatus*).[44] 'Burggraf' is translated into Latin alternately as 'burgravius' and 'castellanus'.[45] The use of latter term in the 16th century could be an indication that the *kasztelan* (*castellanus*) exercised real influence in municipal courts of royal towns and cities.[46] Otherwise, the *Burggraf* or the *kasztelan* makes an

42 The section on the functioning of urban courts is one where we find a great deal of modifications introduced by the writers of individual manuscripts. Even if not all of them can be accounted for by the need to adjust the regulations of the Magdeburg Law, the general impression is inescapable. The accumulation of changes in that portion of text reflects the process of adaptation of the text of the law to local conditions, e.g. revised dates of court sessions. Cf. No. 14 (MS F 143, MS AJG and MS Kiel.), No. 15 (MS BN 12607 and MS II Q 4) and No. 21 (MS F 143).

43 So in MS Q II 157 (1) in Środa Śląska [Neumarkt in Silesia], No. 201. See also: Wieland Carls, "Zur Verbreitung des Halle-Neumarkter Rechts in Schlesien", in: *Halle im Licht und Schatten Magdeburgs. Eine Rechtsmetropole im Mittelalter*, eds. Heiner Lück, (Forschungen zur hallischen Stadtgeschichte) 19 (Halle/Saale, 2012), pp. 191–201; Zbigniew Zdrójkowski, "Stan badań nad problematyką prawa średzkiego. Studium na 750-lecie pouczenia miasta Halle dla Środy Śląskiej (1235–1985)" [Stan badań nad problematyką prawa średzkiego. Studium na 750-lecie pouczenia miasta Halle dla Środy Śląskiej (1235–1985)] *Czasopismo Prawno-Historyczne* 37/2 (1985), 75–86; Zbigniew Zdrójkowski, "Geneza prawa średzkiego i jego rola dziejowa (1223–1511)", *Acta Universitatis Wratislaviensis. Historia* 70 (1990), 53–67; Krystyna Kamińska, "Prawo średzkie jako instrument polityki osadniczej i gospodarczej w Polsce od XIII do początku XVI wieku", in: *Historia integra. Księga pamiątkowa ofiarowana prof. Stanisławowi Salmonowiczowi w siedemdziesięciolecie urodzin* [Historia integra: A Festschrift in Honour of Professor Stanisław Salmonowicz on His 70th Birthday], eds. Danuta Janicka, Ryszard Łaszewski (Toruń, 2001), pp. 146–160.

44 Władysław Bojarski and Zbigniew Naworski, *Jan Jelonek Cereus z Tucholi i jego twórczość prawnicza. Ustrój sądów i prawo procesowe*, [Johannes Cervus of Tuchola and His Legal Works: The Constitution of Courts and Procedural Law] (Toruń, 1993), p. 14.

45 No. 13 and 202.

46 Cf. another irregular situations: Witold Maisel, "Sąd miejski prawa polskiego w Kaliszu w XVI wieku" [Sąd miejski prawa polskiego w Kaliszu w XVI wieku], *Czasopismo Prawno-Historyczne* 23/2 (1971), 129–39.

appearance in provisions concerning public order crimes like rape, assault, and house-breaking[47] and in regulations concerning summary courts hearing cases of *causae maiores* crimes originally assigned (i.e. in the town charter) to the jurisdiction of the town founder.[48]

In one further case, the terms used about the administration of justice are highly significant. The *Weichbild* contains two articles taken over from the *Constitution of Courts* that deal with the trial of a *sołtys* (*der shultheize*) and the *wójt* (*der vogite*), accused of abuse in the administration of justice.[49] For some reason, the author of the Żagań MS replaced the word 'wójt' with 'Burggraf'; the *Statutes* uses both words at this point, which looks like a compromise solution.[50] The legal glossary in Tomasz of Bydgoszcz's MS translates the term *Burgrabius supremus* as '*nawẏssẏ sandzÿa grodszkÿ wẏssego prawa*' [supreme municipal justice of higher law].

One of the provisions enumerates the requirements that are to be met by the *sołtys* (*scultetus*). Konrad of Sandomierz and Jan Łaski, who follows the *versio Sandomiriensis*, adopt the regulation from the *Magdeburg Bench Law* (*Das Magdeburg Schöffenrecht*), adding to it the characteristic 'free' ('*liber esse debet*').[51] It is worth noting that throughout that period, there was a keen interest in cataloguing personal qualities that a person holding public office should possess. We find such lists in both municipal *wilkierze* and royal legislation.[52]

The principles of the functioning of the *sołtys*' and the *Burggraf*'s court, as well as the composition of the jury (11 aldermen and the *sołtys*), are laid down in the *Constitution of Courts*, appended to the *Weichbild* after the Jewish oath (Article 120 in the *Statutes*). Whereas not all of the Latin texts include the provisions of that supplement, the *Statutes* follows the Cracow version and adopts all of them.

47 No. 16. Crimes listed in Article 5 belong to the so-called four articles that are the prerogative of the *captain*, as defined by the 1423 Statute of Warta. That explains the appearance at Article 5 in the *Statutes* of a reference to f. XIV which features the relevant provision from the Statute of Warta. See Karol Koranyi, "W sprawie genezy czterech artykułów starościńskich" [The Origin of the Four Articles That Are the Prerogative of the Captain], *Sprawozdania Towarzystwa Naukowego we Lwowie* 11/1 (1931), 19–22.

48 No. 27 and 28. For exemplification, see No. 28.

49 In the Gniezno MS, these provisions can be found in Articles 100 and 101.

50 No. 213. The use of the word 'sołtys' instead of 'wójt' in Article 100 (No. 206) is a scribal error committed by Konrad of Sandomierz.

51 No. 22. To establish his freeman's status, the burgher needed the oaths of six compurgators. In Marcin Zabowski's MS (No. 167), Article 75, which contains this provision, is for some reason corrupt. Cf. also individual emendations in Article 100 of the passage on sanctions faced by a *sołtys* found guilty of a breach of duty (No. 207, 208, 209, and 210).

52 Mikuła, *Prawodawstwo króla i sejmu*, pp. 220–226.

2.3 *Burghers and Guests*

The *Weichbild* is rather sparing in its treatment of burghers' duties and rights. More information on this subject can be found in Magdeburg judgments (*ortyle*) excerpted and incorporated into the Cracow version and the *Statutes*. Although the relevant passage is mainly concerned with heritable property (which is discussed below, in Section 5.2), it also mentions an oath taken in connection with the payment of municipal (property) tax.[53] The *Weichbild* treats the subject of guests/aliens (*hospes*) from the point of view of their obligations. This problem will be discussed at length in Section 5.3. In the Żagań MS and the *Statutes*, the definition of a guest is expanded with a formula borrowed from an *ortyl*. To qualify as guest, a person must be at least 11 miles away from home or, according to the *Statutes*, at least 12 miles away from home.[54] The amended figure in the *Statutes* corresponds exactly with the distance included in a similar definition in the *Magdeburg's Instructions to Chełmno* (Kulm).

2.4 *Summary: Modifications for Practical Use*

The modifications of the *Weichbild* text discussed here can be divided into four groups: 1) changes of terminology; 2) amendations and amplifications that took into account local legal practice; 3) legal definitions; and 4) supplementary doctrinal clarifications. The first of these categories is exemplified by the appearance of the words *wójt* (*advocatus*) and *burgrabia* (*burgrabius*) in the provision concerning judicial magistrates, which reflected the customary names of offices in the justice system of Polish towns. The amendations and amplifications in the provisions concerning jurors (as in the St Petersburg MS F 143) introduced, *inter alia*, the rule, common in Polish towns, that the mayor (*proconsul*) was elected by the acting aldermen. Legal definitions like that of a guest (*hospis*) in the Cracow version and in the *Statutes* were intended to eliminate and simplify possible controversies. Finally, the introduction in the Sandomierz version of the stipulation that municipal statutes must conform to God's law should come as no surprise; arguably, it enhanced the authority of the council as legislators. In short, the modifications of the *Weichbild* were clearly aimed at enhancing its use value and attractiveness (which implies that it was perceived primarily as a legal text for practical use).

53 No. 142 and 198.

54 No. 29.

3 Crime and Criminal Procedure

The catalogue of criminal acts in the *Weichbild* is not very long. It includes murder (with poisoning), wounding, rape, overt assault in the street, house-breaking, theft, and insult. The comparative analyses undertaken in the course of this study indicate that the model descriptions of criminal acts remain relatively intact along the lines of manuscript transmission.[55] Generally, in the *Weichbild*, problems of crime and punishment are never treated separately from questions of criminal procedure.[56] The code is made up of provisions whose large number makes the emergence of textual variants during the copy process practically inevitable. The majority of the alterations pertain to particular places in the text and are open to correction or a thorough revision – as happened to the *Weichbild* in Łaski's *Statutes*. However, in the history of the *Weichbild*, there are also two more complex and more tenacious sets of alterations which have given rise to two distinct versions of the original text: *versio Sandomiriensis* and *versio Cracoviensis*. They are different by virtue of the alterations which affect key problem areas featured in a code of criminal law. What follows is a comparative survey of their impact and evolutionary momentum, culminating in the text of Jan Łaski's *Statutes* rather than a systematic presentation of the *Weichbild* model of criminal law.

3.1 *'Who Started It?'*

According to the *Weichbild*, criminal liability and the severity of punishment depend on the circumstances of each act. Moreover, the regulations themselves allow room for the choice of trial depending on the conduct of the parties. The admission of the 'who started it?' question is just one example of how a plaintiff with a strong case could be thwarted. The Sandomierz and the Cracow versions (followed by text of the *Statutes*) of Article 37 differ in the delineation of the procedure when a suit is brought by both parties who participated in an affray. According to the *versio Sandomiriensis*, if one of the

55 For exceptions, see No. 119 – in the Działyńscy Codex IV, where 'poisoning' is replaced by 'killing'; No. 125 – in the Petersburg MS, the omission of a phrase naming the places where the breach of the peace took place; No. 161 – in MS Q II 157 (2) and in MS BN 12600 'poisoning' transferred from the main text to the rubric (2); No. 214 – only in the Żagań MS was the clause 'whoever commits house-breaking' broadened into 'whoever commits violence'.

56 Cf. Maciej Mikuła, "Czynniki ograniczające prawo retraktu w średniowiecznej Polsce" [Factors Limiting *ius retractus* in Medieval Poland], in: *Studia z dziejów państwa i prawa* [Studies in the History of the State and the Law], 9/1, ed. Jacek S. Matuszewski (Lublin – Łódź, 2006), p. 109; and Jana Pacyna, *Mittelalterliche Judenrechte. Norm und Anwendung im Magdeburger Rechtskreis* (*1250–1400*) (Halle/Saale, 2015), p. 18.

participants died of wounds, his agnate may sue the other party for murder. The defendant can then rebut the charge by claiming that he did not start the fight and clear himself by the oaths of six compurgators (*metseptimus*). Alternately, if the agnate of the deceased were to demand an ordeal, the defendant would have no choice but to take up the challenge. Were he to lose the duel, he would also lose his life. While the general rules are common to all versions, the Cracow version and the *Statutes* supplement them with some specific regulations. Only the *Statutes* upgrades the ordeal by combat as a decisive means of proof by allowing the agnate of the deceased to resort to it in addition to the summoning of the oath-helpers.[57] The *Statutes* also follows the Cracow version in insisting that for the defendant, the lost duel is tantamount to a death sentence.[58] The provision concerning the time allowed to the defendant for mustering his oath-helpers is modified, too. Out of three fortnightly sessions, he has to choose one. The Sandomierz version merely stipulates that the compurgation should take place in the course of six weeks.[59] Only the *Statutes* reinstates the provision that the defendant needs the oaths of six men to acquit himself of the charge of having begun the fray. In the Sandomierz and the Cracow versions, this mode of trial is mentioned several times, and the *Statutes* reproduces all such mentions from both versions.[60] Thanks to its numerous explanations and supplements, the provisions of the *Statutes* seem to be clearer and more precise.

3.2 *Aiding and Abetting*

Article 12 of the *versio Sandomiriensis* stipulates that the number of the individuals accused in a case of wounding must not exceed the number of wounds.[61] If the plaintiff lays charges against a larger number of people, those who are above that limit can clear themselves by the oaths of six compurgators. In the Cracow version and the *Statues*, this provision is given a different interpretation. The eventuality that a larger number of persons than the number of inflicted wounds may be liable is not ruled out. The supernumerary defendants that are charged with aiding and abetting the crime of murder or of injury meriting a duel (*vulnus duellaris*), with the latter called 'fatal wounds' in the glossary of the Magdeburg Law terms in the Tomasz of Bydgoszcz's MS. Those defendants could acquit himself of the charge by their own oaths. But if the charge was backed by testimonial evidence, two compurgators were still

57 No. 80.

58 No. 82.

59 No 83.

60 No. 81 and 83. Only in the Działyńscy Codex IV was this time limitation reduced to two oath-helpers (*mettertius*).

61 No. 35.

needed. These additional clauses can only be found in the Baworowscy MS and the Żagań MS (i.e. the bilingual manuscripts of the Cracow version).

3.3 *Court Procedure*

Magdeburg Law envisages not only the institution of the attorney,[62] but also allows in certain circumstances the father to act on behalf of his son. The regulations concerning the latter eventuality are copied *verbatim* and even duplicated in the manuscripts. One such duplication occurs in the *Statutes*. The clause which requires the father who wants to represent his son to clear himself first from the charge brought against him and his son is included, following the Sandomierz version, in Article 24 and also, following the Cracow version, in Article 86 (in the numbering scheme of the *Statutes*).[63]

The amount of time that passed between the commission of a crime and the formal accusation was of considerable importance (i.e. the right to precedence in presenting evidence).[64] In particular, according to Article 10, the plaintiff's putting off of court action to the following day gave the accused the right to produce six oath-helpers to clear himself of the charge. The text of that provision in the *Statutes*, following the Żagań MS, omits the justification of this rule.[65] Likewise, the *Statutes* follows the Żagań MS in expanding Article 33 concerning counter-charges. In the latter case, the *Statutes* mirrors the matching German text of the Żagań MS dealing with case of combatants brought before the court after being caught in the act (*in facto manifesto*) of duelling.[66]

Both the Cracow version and the *Statutes* insist that neither the plaintiff nor the defendant is in charge of the legal proceedings, asserting that it is the judge who plays that role. It is worth noting that this supplementary clause is included in the provision allowing the latter to deal summarily (outside the court calendar and the officially designated places) with a case of recovery of debt where no oath-taking was required.[67] The *Statutes*, following the addition in the German and Latin text of the Żagań MS, also reaffirms the obvious rule that both the judge (i.e. *Burgraf/kasztelan/wójt/sołtys*) and the jurors are involved in the decision-making.[68] If the jurors could not make up their

62 Cf. amendations in MS Q II 157 (1), MS Q II 157 (2), MS BN 12600, MS Dział. IV, and MS II Q 4 concerning the criteria that have to be met by an attorney representing a party in the trial (No. 120).

63 No. 58 and 188. Cf. also No. 59 and 187.

64 For various individual variants see No. 31, 32, 34, 67, 68, 70, 127, and 189.

65 No. 33.

66 No. 75.

67 No. 180. Cf. MS BN 3068 where the instrument of summary procedure without witnesses can be applied in actions other than recovery of debt (No. 179).

68 No. 150 (430).

mind, they had the right to postpone the decision until – at the latest – the second session in a row. This supplementary clarification was borrowed from an *ortyl*.[69]

3.4 *Proof*

The *Weichbild* admits the following types of proof: oath, collective oath compurgation, the ordeal (*duellum*), and inquest (inspection).[70] That list may be extended to include hearings, since the code allowed a challenge of witness testimony (*pro falso*).[71] Moreover, Article 53 provides for the dispatching of three persons to the injured person to find out about his condition and report back to the court.[72] The outcome, not only in a criminal court, depended on the right to precedence in presenting evidence to the attention of the court. That condition needed no further deliberation when the perpetrator was caught in the act and the evidence was at hand.[73] In other circumstances, the right to precedence in presenting evidence was established according to precise rules, which are discussed in the Introduction (cf. a synopsis of the contents of *Ius municipale Magdeburgense*) and in Section 3.1.

While the largest number of amendments deals with the administration of the oath and the compurgators, most of the modifications are peculiar to individual manuscripts. In the *Statutes*, the modifications concern Article 37 (as indicated earlier in Section 3.1), that is, the time limit of the compurgation in cases of fatal wounding in an affray. Moreover, the *Statutes* follows the Cracow version in replacing the six-week time limit with a clause allowing the defendant to choose one of successive two-week periods in which the oath is to take place.[74] This is further modified by a rule granting the judge the right to adjourn the proceedings if the time limit expired on a public holiday (one of

69 No. 193.

70 Article 65. Cf. No. 154 with variants in the Częstochowa MS and the Kielce MS.

71 No. 108.

72 A minor modification of that rule appears in the Działyńscy Codex I and MS BN 3068, where a clause that the statement before the court is to be made by one of the 'inspectors' is omitted (No. 121).

73 Minor modifications occur in No. 74, 114, 115, 116, 117, 118, 120, and 176. Cf. the discussion in Section 5.1.

74 No. 83. In the early modern period in the towns of Royal Prussia, the time limit for the administration of the oath (*iuramentum*) was usually one week. See Piotr Kitowski, "Przysięga dowodowa w polskim prawie miejskim i ziemskim w XVII–XVIII wieku" [The Evidentiary Oath in Polish Municipal Law and Polish Land Law in the 17th–18th Century], in: *Nil nisi veritas. Księga dedykowana Profesorowi Jackowi Matuszewskiemu* [Nil nisi veritas: A Festschrift in Honour of Professor Jacek Matuszewski], eds. Marcin Głuszak and Dorota Wiśniewska-Jóźwiak (Łódź, 2016), p. 326.

the *dies feriatos*).[75] Additionally, the rigidity of the formal procedure was softened by an amendment allowing a stutterer to go through the formulae of the oath for a second time. An important amendment of the *Weichbild* text in the *Statutes*, inspired by the example of the Cracow version, concerns the possibility of retracting the promise of swearing an oath.[76] However, this clause must be read in the context of the original provision of Article 97, that is, if anybody binds himself by promise to swear an oath before the court in an action for insult, robbery, assault, or bloodshed, he cannot absolve himself from that obligation unless he has the permission of the court. This amendment treats in a similar manner the situation when it is the plaintiff's intention to absolve the defendant from his promise. The failure to obtain the judge's permission and to swear the oath as promised is punished by a mulct (a fine for a judge) of no more than eight shillings, which is be imposed for each instance of noncompliance separately. The Jewish oath, too, is subject to various amendments in the individual manuscripts. The changes concern the details of the ceremony, the oath-swearer's dress and gestures,[77] and the wording of the oath itself.[78] In fixing its own formula of the *iuramentum Judaeorum*, the authors of the *Statutes* drew on the texts of the Cracow and the Sandomierz versions.

In the manuscripts, numerous amendments were introduced regarding the number of compurgators, which varies from two to six. Many of the changes appear to be dictated by common sense, as in the case of the Działyńscy Codex IV, reducing their number from six to two in bringing in the charges of rape, assault, house-breaking, murder, theft, or robbery when the perpetrator was caught in the act.[79] A clear delimitation of the number of persons required to participate in a given procedure is a characteristic feature of the *Statutes*, which, in this respect, follows the text of the Żagań MS and the German base. Therefore, for example, the charge of insult of a court official could not be

---

75 No. 158.

76 No. 200.

77 No. 219, amended in MS Q II 157 (2) and MS BN 12600.

78 No. 220.

79 No. 113. Additions that are fully appropriate include the requirement that the owner of stolen goods is to prove ownership by swearing an oath in MS BN 3068 (No. 87), or that the seven compurgators are to deliver proof (swear an oath *tacto sacramento*) of no consanguinity (consanguinity was also a legal hindrance in judicial ordeals) in the Baworowscy MS, the Opatów MS, and the Żagań MS (No. 130). Cf. also No. 92. On the other hand, there are amendments that cannot be called improvements, like the one in MS Q II 157 (1), No. 56 (an obvious scribal error) or the omission of the number of compurgators in MS Q II 157 (1), No. 190. Sometimes, however, the missing number at one point in the text does not matter, for it is mentioned in other provisions that are appropriate, as in No. 215.

admitted unless backed by the judge and 'two' jurymen.[80] The details of the judicial combat carefully regulated in Article 56 on the basis of the provisions of the *Sachsenspiegel* were also subject to modifications in individual manuscripts. Thus, according to the Żagań MS and to the *Statutes*, not only the judge but also the court usher had the right to warn the members of the audience that interference in the ordeal was a capital offence.[81]

3.5 Recompensa, Emenda, Pena

In the Latin *Weichbild*, punishment is referred to by several different words. The term *pena* seems to refer consistently to a mulct. *Recompensa* is translated in the Latin-Polish glossary of the legal terms of Magdeburg Law in Tomasz of Bydgoszcz's MS as 'zapłata głowna' (lit. the price of a man's head; wergild).[82] 'Emenda' (amends) is translated in this manuscript as 'pokup', or damages. In accordance with the German text, *manum* means '[the cutting off of] the hand', and *collum* (neck) means decapitation. In the latter case, checking the German text dispels any doubts that the word may refer to poll tax. The penalties in all their aspects are subject to considerable modifications in the manuscripts. Most of those amendments were ultimately passed over by the authors of the *Statutes*.[83] The clauses that echo the provisions of the Chełmno Law concerning the payment of wergild (up to twelve weeks), mulct (up to six weeks), and compensation (up to 14 days after mulct) are an exception.[84] The same is true for the clause, taken over from an *ortyl* in the Cracow version, setting down

80 No. 205. In the Częstochowa MS and the Kielce MS, the requirement of proof delivered by oath-helpers is omitted in the action concerning insult of a member of the jury (No. 192).

81 No. 134. A number of amendments are peculiar to the Żagań MS, e.g. the omission of the requirement to swear an oath before the judicial combat by both parties (No. 137). For other changes concerning the duel, see No. 78, 128, 129, 131, 132, 133, 135, 136, 138, 139, 140, and 153.

82 In the modern Polish translation of the Old Chełmno Law (*Der alte Kulm*) both *weregelt* and *recompensa* are rendered as 'główszczyzna' or 'zapłata głowna' (lit. the price of a man's head), PS II.31/37. Cf. Aleksander Zajda, *Staropolska terminologia prawnicza (do 1500 r.)* [Polish Legal Terminology (until 1500)] (Kraków, 1990), p. 193.

83 E.g. reduction of the mulct for the *kasztelan* by half (No. 20, in connection with No. 19, and also No. 25); fixing the amount of compensation to a man beaten with sticks over the head and the back at 30 shillings and a mulct of eight shillings (No. 155); damages of 30 shillings for jurors insulted in court (No. 191). Clauses omitted in various manuscripts and nonetheless do appear in the Gniezno MS and the *Statutes*; see No. 55, 138, 194, 203, 204, and 209. Conversely, for variants concerning extrajudicial agreement peculiar to individual manuscripts that are not taken over by the *Statutes*, see No. 55, 56, 57, and 69. Cf. also a variant that occurs only in MS Q II 157 (1) concerning *res iudicata* that is not included in the *Statutes* (No. 157).

84 No. 17, and in MS BN 3068 additionally No. 18.

the pledge guaranteeing the appearance in court of a defendant accused of murder. If the accused were to flee, his responsible surety would have to pay the judge the 14 pounds wergild and a mulct of eight shillings.[85] The *Statutes* does not include, however, a clause added in the Żagań MS which stipulates a mulct of 9 shillings for wounding. It is equally unclear why the *Statutes* leaves out a clause which states that a recompense amounting to half of the wergild is be paid to the plaintiff by a *sołtys* who failed to issue a judgement in a case of wounding, even though the perpetrator had been brought before the court.[86] The *Statutes* follows the Cracow version in confirming that theft during daytime is to be punished in skin and hair if the perpetrator has a good reputation and the value of the stolen goods does not exceed three shillings. The manuscripts of the *versio Sandomiriensis* use at this point the phrase 'less than three shillings'. The difference could not have been more trifling, yet it illustrates the subtlety of the changes introduced by individual copyists.[87]

3.6 *Summary: Concern for Clarity*

The modifications in the area of criminal law seemed to have had three main purposes. The first of such purpose was to eliminate ambiguity and uncertainty. Thus, for example, the *Weichbild* is not clear about whether in a case of serious crime the party that was given precedence in the order of the trial had the right to choose a judicial duel (wager by battle) or the accusatory oath. The *Statutes* cleared up this difficulty. Clarification often went hand-in-hand with ensuring the inner coherence of the *Weichbild* regulations. For example, the *wójt* (*Vogt*) or *sołtys* (*Schultheiss*) had the right to adjourn a court session until the following day after a holiday, but apparently had no right to do likewise in the case of oath-taking trials. The *Statutes* did away with this ambiguity, too, by introducing a uniform rule. Whereas some modifications were simply regulatory (e.g. the introduction of precise time limits for the payment of court fines), the third purpose, or perhaps tendency, is to soften the edges of some rules, such as lowering the maximum number of oath-swearers or making adjustments for people who stammer.

---

85 No. 24. Cf. also the regulation – found only in MS BN 3068 – concerning the retraction of a promise to swear an evidential oath (No. 212).

86 No. 211.

87 No. 84. Cf. also No. 86, where a substantial passage concerns the seizure of the property of a man accused of wounding and killing towards the payment of compensation (wergild) and mulct in MS Q II 157 (2) and MS BN 12600. Cf. also No. 194.

4 The Family and Family Property

4.1 Agnatus *and* Cognatus

Amendments concerning marriage, inheritance, and guardianship law can be found in several *Weichbild* texts. A modification of considerable significance concerns the terms *agnatus* and *cognatus*. The *Statutes* took over the definition of this pair of words from the *versio Sandomiriensis* and applied it with great consistency.[88] The Cracow version does not appear to be aware of this supplementary clarification and makes no distinction between a cognate and a relative. That could lead to some confusion. Thus, Article 50 in the Gniezno MS states that guardianship falls to the nearest agnate of the children. However, in a number of manuscripts, we can find at this point the term *cognatus*, and the Opatów MS. features both terms. In the Działyńscy Codex I, the text uses the term *cognatus*, but the copyist inserted a superscript *a* over the *co*. The latter two examples indicate that at least some copyists were not sure of which term to use. In this context, it is worth noting that the legal glossary attached to Tomasz of Bydgoszcz's MS provides not only Polish equivalents of Latin terms, but also brief definitions – in this case, *Agnati dicuntur successores post patrem* and *Cognatus successor post matrem*.[89]

4.2 *Guardianship*

According to Article 50, guardianship is a legal obligation that falls to the nearest male relative of a fatherless child, and if that agnate were to be underage, it would fall to his nearest male relative. The *Statutes* employs the term *agnatus*, citing the first part of this provision, but omits the second part which refers to the situation when the primary guardian (*adiutor, tutor*) is a minor and thus incapable of exercising the custody.[90] The guardian's duties included the accounting of his administration of the ward's property in annual reports. If a deputy guardian was appointed, for example, when the primary guardian was still a minor, he was obliged to present his account accompanied by the latter (*coram vero tutor*), and according to the Baworowscy MS and the Opatów MS, also in the presence of aldermen or jurymen. This provision is missing from the *Statutes*, which, as we have noted, passes over the problem of deputy guardianship.[91] The question of accounting is raised again in Article 74, where a distinction is made between children up to the age of 12 (*in pupillari aetate*) and adolescents. The latter had the right to choose his guardian (*curator*), who,

88 No. 166.
89 MS BN 3068, f. 224r and 224v.
90 No. 111.
91 No. 112.

when appointed, was obliged to render account of his administration of his ward's property to the minor and the child's mother.[92] In this description of the rights of the adolescent, the *Statutes* follows an *ortyl* incorporated into the Cracow version. Even when placed under the care of a guardian, the minor from the age of 12 had certain legal rights – for example, the right to dispose of property, although in the case of heritable property, he could not act without the heirs' consent.[93] The mature minor is not exempt from adult systems of legal responsibility and prosecution. This regulation has to be read in conjunction with Article 96, which states that until the appointment of a guardian (*verus tutor*), the minor up to the statutory age of puberty was exempt from prosecution. Article 50 of the *Statutes* refers to a provision in the Statutes of Kazimierz the Great which forbids both the alienation of the ward's property and litigation against a minor *in pupillari aetate*. The prohibition of the sale of the ward's property (unless it is necessary to finance the minor's needs and the guardian has obtained the permission of the judge) also features in the additional Article 140 in Paweł Szczerbic's *Ius Municipale* (1581).

4.3 *The Dower*

The Magdeburg Law restricted the legal capacity of the widow or widower to inherit property from a deceased spouse. The only way the right of succession of the surviving spouse could be guaranteed was by a will *inter vivos*. These dispositions usually concerned the widow's jointure and the dower (*wiano, dotalitium*).[94] This was the main change in comparison with in the *Sachsenspiegel*, in which the principal instrument was the 'morning gift' (*Morgengabe*). The modifications of the text in the *Weichbild* refer to the rights of the widow to administer the property that belonged to her deceased husband or a minor child.[95] The modifications clarify the rules under which she was able to hold on to assets that were bestowed upon her during her husband's lifetime. Most important in this respect is Article 14, which lays down the general rule that a widow does not succeed to her husband's estate apart from the portion she was given as her dower (*pro dotalitio aut vite provisione*).[96] That

92 No. 164.

93 No. 165.

94 In contrast to the Magdeburg Law, the Chełmno Law affirms the principle of joint ownership for married couples which entails considerable differences in their rights of survivorship. The problem is dealt with in MS Dział. IV, which contains a supplement *In Colmense* appended to the articles of the *Weichbild* (cf. Chapter 4).

95 Cf. No. 162.

96 The translation of *Morgengabe* as *dotalitium* shows how the term was understood in medieval Poland. See Margret Obladen, *Magdeburger Recht auf der Burg zu Krakau: Die güterrechtliche Absicherung der Ehefrau in der Spruchpraxis des Krakauer Oberhofs* (Berlin, 2005), Chapter 3 on the dower, and especially the conclusions, p. 130; Nataliia

estate, as per Article 14, is to revert to the heirs of her husband upon her death. If the husband did not assign a dower, the widow had the right to remain in the family home and claim support from their children. She forfeited those rights upon remarriage. If her dower were to be disputed, a widow could validate her claim by summoning seven oath-helpers.[97] Both men and women were eligible for this wager of law. This provision was heavily criticized by Bartłomiej Groicki, who cited numerous examples of its abuse by widows. However, its efficacy was weakened by municipal legislation (*wilkierze*).[98] Further clarifications of the widow's interest were introduced by the *ortyle*; these amendations became part of the Cracow version and then incorporated into the *Statutes*.[99] They regulated the issue of dower assets that were encumbered by debt. If the dower assignment was in the form of cash, the payment of the debts due from the deceased husbands came first; if, however, the dower was assigned in heritable property, the order was reversed. The assumption was that a husband was free to establish a dower in real estate which he could freely alienate (i.e. 'acquired property' as opposed to 'inherited property'), as well as in chattels.

4.4 *The Compulsory Portion* (Mußteil), Gerada, *and* Hergewet

The problem of the elements of a deceased person's estate is addressed in the *Weichbild* in four separate articles, which reflect the polyphonic structure of the compilation. Article 26 was originally part of the *Magdeburg Bench Law* (*Magdeburger Schöffenrecht*, Art. 46); Articles 60 and 61 came from *Magdeburg's Legal Instructions for Wrocław* (*Rechtsmitteilungen Magdeburgs*

Ivanusa, *Frauen im Sächsisch-Magdeburgischen Recht. Die Rechtspraxis in kleinpolnischen Städten im 16. Jahrhundert* (Studien zur Ostmitteleuropaforschung) 38 (Marburg, 2017), pp. 137–138, and 143–149. The modern translation of the Old Chełmno Law (*Der Alte Kulm*) uses the word 'podarek poranny' (literally 'Morgengabe') (PS III.39–41, pp. 110–111). Paweł Szczerbic in his translation of the *Weichbild* uses the word 'wiano' (dower) (*SzIM, Article* XXII, pp. 107–118). On the Polish equivalent of the term *Morgengabe* as wiano (dower) in the Polish translation of the Magdeburg ortyle, see Inge Bily, "Der Rechtsterminus *Morgengabe* im deutsch-polnischen Sprachvergleich (untersucht auf der Grundlage eines frühneuhochdeutschen und eines altpolnischen Textes der *Magdeburger Urteile*)", in: *Deutsch-slawische Kontakte – Geschichte und Kultur. Festschrift für Mária Papsonová*, eds. Michaela Kováčová, Jörg Meier, and Ingrid Puchalová, (Acta facultatis philosophicae Universitatis Šafarikinae) 12 (Kosice, 2011), pp. 115–125.

97 The number of compurgators is omitted in MS BN 3068 (No. 39).

98 Bartłomiej Groicki, *Tytuły prawa majdeburskiego* [Titles of the Magdeburg Law], ed. Karol Koranyi, *Biblioteka Dawnych Polskich Pisarzy-Prawników* [Library of Ancient Polish Jurists] 3 (Warszawa, 1954), pp. 48–49. See also Mikuła, "O reformie prawa miejskiego w XVI wieku", pp. 238–239.

99 No. 44.

für Breslau) of 1261 (Articles 62 and 63); and Article 94 came from *Magdeburg's Legal Instructions for Wrocław* of 1295 (§ 18).[100]

According to the *Weichbild*, the deceased's property was divided into the *gerada* (Ger. *Gerade*, Lat. *suppellectilia*), which fell to the closest female relative; the *hergewet*, inherited by the male successors; and the general inheritance (*dziedzictwo*). The *gerada* excluded a special category of food (*pulmentaria*), called *rzeczy strawne* in Szczerbic's translation (the latter mirrors the German term *Mußteil*). The manuscripts differ chiefly by the scope of the inventories of items of the *gerada* (usually clothes and kitchen utensils), but in no case is there any alteration of the inheritance rule itself.[101] While some lists are more detailed, some do not include items that are mentioned elsewhere (presumably to avoid repetition).[102] Amendments in the scope of the inherited property are introduced, following the example of the Cracow version (or the Żegota Pauli's MS), by way of a supplement which stipulates the division of the *gerada* into two equal shares between heirs if one of them was a clergyman.[103] This rule remained intact until the introduction of a major reform which paved the way for it to be altered by *wilkierze* (municipal by-laws) approved by the king or the town's feudal landlord.[104]

---

100 A counterpart of Article 26 discussed here is not included in the vulgate, nor can it be found in Jaskier's or Szczerbic's editions of the *Weichbild*. This article contains a broad list of items that should be treated general inheritance (*dziedzictwo*).

101 Cf. Piotr Suski, "Spory wokół gerady i hergewetu w polskim miejskim prawie spadkowym w XVI w". [Debates about *gerada* and *hergewet* in Polish Urban Inheritance Law in the 16th Century], in: *Prawo blisko człowieka. Z dziejów prawa rodzinnego i spadkowego* [The Law and the Ordinary People: From the History of Family and Inheritance Law], ed. Maciej Mikuła (Kraków, 2008), pp. 168–169; Urszula Sowina, "Trousseau according to the *Ius municipale Magdeburgense* by Paweł Szczerbic and the position of a woman in the craftsman family at the beginning of the early modern time", *Kwartalnik Historii Kultury Materialnej* 68/4 (2020), pp. 494–506.

102 No. 42 and 195. It is not clear why the item 'objects permanently attached to the property' is excluded from the *gerada* list in the Petersburg MS (No. 66).

103 No. 49. With regard to clergymen who opted out of the land law jurisdiction, the *Statutes* has taken over the supplementary regulation of the Sandomierz version (cf. No. 148). More precise definitions of the person eligible for the *gerada* can be found in the Przemyśl MS (the *gerada* falls to the agnate and cognate female relative) and in MS BN 3068 (sister-in-law), while other texts refer to a cognate female relative or simply a female relative (which, however, depends on the meaning of the term *cognata* (No. 143). See Maciej Mikuła, "Modyfikacje łacińskich tekstów Weichbildu magdeburskiego a ewolucja prawa w średniowiecznych miastach polskich. Uwagi wstępne" [Modifications of Latin Texts of the Magdeburg *Weichbild* and the Evolution of Law in Medieval Polish Towns: An Introduction], in: *Acta Iuridico-Historica Pilsnensia*, 2012–2013 (published 2014; ed. Vilém Knoll), p. 147.

104 Maciej Mikuła, "Die Könige und das Reformationsverfahren des Rechts in den polnischen Städten vom 14. bis zum 16. Jahrhundert", *Beiträge zur Rechtsgeschichte Österreichs* 2/2

Amendments concerning the compulsory portion are on the whole left out of the *Statutes*;[105] those that are included merely clarify a given provision. Therefore, for example, Article 60, following the Żagań MS, expressly bars a female relative from that portion, although it should be clear from the context.[106] Another point worth noting is that Article 26 refers to the compulsory portion of the widow (and not a female relative of the deceased), while Article 60 lists items that fall to the widower.

As the Saxon *hergewet*, with its focus on armour and war horses, was hardly relevant for the burghers, it became an obvious target of the urban law reform, which gave more scope for *wilkierze* approved by the king or the town's landlord. The supplementary amendation, taken over from the German base – which stipulates that a grandson born to a female heir is not entitled to inherit his grandfather's armour (it is to be handed over to the judge)[107] – is missing from just a few manuscripts.[108] This regulation was introduced to deal with a case in which the line of succession to the *herewet* is first broken as the deceased person has no sons and then appears to be restored when his daughter gives birth to a male child. The law made to resolve this problem affirmed the validity of the general rule that the *herewet* cannot fall to and be transmitted by a female heir.

4.5 *Rules of Succession*

When it comes to the devolution of a deceased person's real property, the *Weichbild* distinguishes between heritable freehold, heritable leasehold, and property acquired during marriage. These categories are essential in determining the property's alienability.[109] All transfers of property acquired during marriage (although some manuscripts of the *versio Sandomiriensis* do not contain that clause)[110] are excluded from the claims of heirs.[111] According to the *Weichbild*, property can be acquired through purchase, gift, or pledge.[112] The law protects the owner of both acquired and inherited property;[113] it also

(2013), p. 504; and Mikuła, *Prawodawstwo króla i sejmu*, pp. 280–286, which includes a bibliographical list of earlier studies.

105 No. 63 and 65.

106 No. 144.

107 No. 106.

108 The Gniezno MS, the Działyńscy Codex I, the Przemyśl MS, and Marcin Zabowski's MS.

109 No. 62 and 103.

110 Especially in the Leipzig MS and the Tomasz of Bydgoszcz's MS, No. 104.

111 No. 102.

112 No. 89.

113 No. 50 and 199. For an exception from the rule of quiet possession, see the St Florian MS, No. 100.

upholds the principle of acquired rights, namely, that a donor cannot give away the same item of property twice.[114]

The assets of inherited and acquired property which did not count as *gerada*, the compulsory portion, or *hergewet* constituted the general inheritance (*dziedzictwo*). Konrad of Sandomierz refers to the acquisition of their inheritance by the heirs at law as a natural right, as does the *Statutes*.[115] To prove his title to succession in court, the heir has to present a number of landowning oath-helpers. In most manuscripts, their number is set at six, except for the Działyńscy Codex IV, where it is reduced to two.[116] The right of succession is not affected by the decedent's misconduct or negligence. A supplementary amendment, taken over from an *ortyl*, reaffirms this principle with regard to assets whose true value was concealed by the decedent to evade taxation. The heir cannot be stripped of his estate unless he relinquishes his rights to it by an express waiver before the court or an assembly of aldermen (acting in their official capacity). In that case, the aldermen are responsible for managing or disposing of the released assets to benefit the urban community.[117] This provision complements another one from an *ortyl* attached to Article 58 of the *Statutes* (following the Cracow version), which says that whoever conceals his assets to evade taxation and then admits that they belong to him is guilty of perjury and, in effect, loses his burgher's rights.[118]

As a rule, the general inheritance falls to the deceased's children. Article 25, however, stipulates that upon the wife's death, if the couple has no children, the surviving widower has a claim on the property acquired during marriage prior to her relatives, provided he was her equal in honourable status:[119]

> Si moritur femina absque herede, ita quod nullum heredem a suo marito pepererit, ipsa heredat sua successoria, seu sua prospera fortuna acquisita super suum proximum naturalem successorem, sive sit masculus sive femina, qui sibi sit paris condicionis. Idem facit vir illi, qui sibi paris fuerit condicionis.

This passage reproduces the German text of *Magdeburg's Instructions for Wrocław* of 1261, the *Magdeburg Bench Law*, the Wawel MS, and BJ 170a; however, the latter sentence is missing from the Cracow MS.[120] The omission can

---

114 No. 100.
115 No 90 and 91.
116 No. 92, 93, and 94 (the divergence in the Opatów MS is probably due to scribal error).
117 No. 198.
118 No. 142.
119 No. 62.
120 Appendix 3, No. 341.

be interpreted as an additional condition: to acquire the estate, the widower has to have no lesser status than the other claimants (i.e. the relatives of his deceased wife). This condition does not appear in the Latin manuscripts of the Cracow version, but, following the *versio Sandomiriensis*, it resurfaces in the *Statutes*.

Another important modification is introduced by an *ortyl* attached to Article 73.[121] According to the *Statutes*, if the children who had inherited the main estate (*dziedzictwo*) after their father's death died before their mother, it would fall to her. After her death, the estate would then fall to her closest relatives, regardless of whether they were agnates or cognates. The *ortyl* also states that the *dziedzictwo* (general inheritance) cannot be alienated without express approval of the heirs. This condition does not apply to moveables or to property acquired during marriage.

In accordance with the general rules of inheritance under the Magdeburg Law, the preferential order of succession and distribution includes descendants, ascendants (parents), brothers and sisters, and extended family.[122] In the most distant class (the extended family), the *Statutes*, following the Żagań MS, gives no preference to male or female heirs and treats the matrilineal and the patrilineal lines equally.[123] The *Statutes* also addresses certain more complex or puzzling cases by drawing on the judicial wisdom of the *ortyle*. One such issue arises when the estate is distributed among (some of) the children before the death of their father. The general rule in Article 14 says that the children who have already received their share are excluded from the distribution of the property left at the time of their father's death.[124] Only if one of the children (implicitly, without offspring) died after their father's death, would his estate be distributed among the rest regardless of whether they were excluded.[125] The

121 No. 163.

122 Cf. Ludwig Meuten, *Die Erbfolgeordnung des Sachsenspiegels und des Magdeburger Rechts. Ein Beitrag zur Geschichte des sächsich-magdeburgischen Rechts* (Frankfurt am Main, 2000), pp. 150, 197, 208 and 225; and Piotr Kitowski, *Sukcesja spadkowa w mniejszych miastach województwa pomorskiego w II połowie XVII i XVIII wieku. Studium prawno-historyczne* [Inheritance Succession in Small Towns of the Voivodship of Pomerania in the Late 17th–18th Century: A Study in Legal History] (Warszawa, 2015), pp. 50–51. For more individual variants in passages referring to inheritance law, see No. 98, 99 and 105.

123 No. 48.

124 A notable variant in No. 41: the appearance in the Latin text of the term *exhereditatus*. It can, of course, mean 'disinherited', but in the context of the whole passage, it almost certainly refers to heirs that have already received their portion of the patrimony. (*Słownik łaciny średniowiecznej* [A Dictionary of Medieval Latin], 3, compiled by Marian Plezia and Julia Mruk (Wrocław – Warszawa – Kraków, 1969), col. 1396).

125 For variants, see No. 43.

ortyl attached to Article 48 regulates the question of succession in the situation when a son dies before his father by making it dependent on whether he has already taken his share. However, the problem becomes more complicated if the prematurely deceased son has children. In that case, if he was not excluded, the estate was distributed equally between the grandchildren and their uncles. If, however, the deceased son was excluded, his children would get equal distributive shares in the portion that fell to their father,[126] and, in all probability, be worse off for the exclusion. In either case, the children of a daughter do not inherit from their grandfather if there are other living heirs descended from his sons. The latter restriction does not apply when the devolved estate was owned by their grandmother.

The texts of the Cracow version, the *Statutes*, and the Przemyśl manuscript contain an aphoristic instruction on how to ensure the equal division of the inheritance: *senior dividit et iunior eligit* ('the elder brother carves up, the younger brother picks out').[127] Another addition relating to the division of the inheritance – namely, that each of the co-heirs has the right to demand and receive his separate share of the estate – can be found in the *Statutes* and in the Cracow version.[128]

4.6 *Deathbed Gifts*

A thread that runs through all of the texts of *Weichild* is the rule declaring all deathbed dispositions of property (*donatio in lecto egritudinis*) whose value exceeds three shillings invalid unless it is approved by the heirs. The Sandomierz version, however, omits a clause prohibiting wives to makes deathbed gifts without their husbands' permission. On this point, the *Statutes* follows the Cracow version, which sticks to the German base.[129] In late editions of *Weichbild* – Mikołaj Jaskier's and Paweł Szczerbic's translations – the wording of this provision does not differ from the Cracow version with its explicit regulation concerning the validity of a married woman's deathbed gifts of property.[130] For Szczerbic, it is the natural consequence of the traditional law of coverture, that is, by marriage, a woman comes under the protection and guardianship of her husband,[131] does not have a separate legal existence, and cannot dispose of property without her husband's consent. Originally, the

126 No. 107.

127 No. 146.

128 No. 147.

129 No. 46. The provision is expanded in MS Q II 157 (1), No. 47.

130 *JIM*, Article LXV and *SzIM*, Article LXV.2.

131 *SzIM*, Article LXV.1 This explanatory passage carries an annotation by Paweł Szczerbic, who notes that it can be found exclusively in the German-language sources.

Magdeburg Law had little to say about the modalities of testamentary disposition: it just recognized the deathbed gift under the formula 'in the anticipation of death' (*donatio post obitum*).[132] It was not until the 14th century that Poland's towns began to work on the clarification of this concept. In Cracow, the first regulations concerning testamentary disposition date back to 1342. It became the subject of a string of urban statutes (*wilkierze*), issued until the late 16th century.[133] Clearly, in this field the *Weichbild* could hardly satisfy the needs and expectations of burghers wishing to dispose of their property within an unambiguous legal framework.

4.7 *Escheat*

The *Weichbild* addresses the problem of escheat (*ius caducum*) in just one article. The Sandomierz version states laconically that the property of the intestate is to be forfeited to the king. In Łaski's *Statutes*, which on this point follows the Cracow version and its German base, this regulation is expanded upon. The editorial modification does not affect the substance of the provision; it merely sets a time frame – a year and a day – for the prospective heirs to come forward with their claims. The phrase 'a year and a day' (*annus et dies*) is also to be found in the gloss of the Żegota Pauli's MS and the Leipzig MS. The Przemyśl MS goes even further by stipulating that the one year and a day limitation is to be suspended once the forfeiture is challenged. An identical clause appears in the gloss of the Działyńscy Codex I. The limitation clause also features in the print editions of the vulgate; in Paweł Szczerbic's text, the time span is even extended to one year and six weeks.[134] It is worth noting that other provisions of the *Weichbild* explain that the *annus et dies* period was exactly a year and six weeks.[135] Moreover, Article 80 of Book III of the *Sachsenspiegel*,

132 Friedrich Ebel, "Das spreke wy vor eyn recht ... Versuch über das Recht der Magdeburger Schoppen", in: Friedrich Ebel, *Unseren fruntlichen grus zuvor: Deutsches Recht des Mittelalters in mittel- und osteuropäischen Raum. Kleine Schriften*, eds. Andreas Fijal, Hans-Jörg Leuchte and Hans-Jochen Schiewer (Köln [u.a.], 2004), pp. 477–478. Cf. Adrian Schmidt-Recla, *Kalte oder warme Hand? Verfügungen von Todes wegen in mittelalterlichen Referenzrechtsquelle*, Forschungen zur deutschen Rechtsgeschichte, 29 (Köln, 2011), pp. 84–88, 421, 426.

133 Maciej Mikuła, "Statuty prawa spadkowego w miastach polskich prawa magdeburskiego (do końca XVI wieku)" [Inheritance Statutes in Polish Towns under Magdeburg Law (until the End of the 16th Century)], *Z Dziejów Prawa* 7 (15) (2014), 33–63. Cf. also Krystyna Bukowska-Gorgoni, "Das sächsisch-magdeburgische Recht und die vermogensrechtlichen Verhaltnisse in den polnischen Stadten der Renaissance", in: *Studien zur Geschichte des sächsich-magdeburgischen Rechts in Deutschland und Polen*, eds. Dietmar Willoweit and Winfried Schich, Rechtshistorische Reihe 10 (Frankfurt am Main, 1980), p. 37.

134 *SzIM*, Article LIX.1.

135 Cf. Stephan Dusil, *Jahr und Tag* in: *Handwörterbuch zur Deutschen Rechtsgeschichte*, 2nd ed., 2 (Berlin, 2011), col. 1348–1350.

which Mikołaj Jaskier referenced, has more rules concerning the treatment of an intestate estate of a peasant with his own farm. Land in excess of 30 *łans* (*Hufe*) is to escheat to the crown; medium sized farms of between 30 and 3 *łans* are to revert to the local feudal lord; and smaller farms are to be taken over by the *sołtys* (*scultetus*). The same regulations can be found in Jaskier's *Weichbild* gloss with a direct reference to the aforementioned Article 80 of the *Sachsenspiegel*.[136] This regulation had no practical significance in so far as in 16th-century Poland, land was either owned by the landlords or by the crown, and thus there was no room for crossover succession arrangements. Royal towns were the only place where the *Weichbild* escheat rule held water. Yet, as the research of Zygfryd Rymaszewski shows, the realization of escheats by the royal chancery in a town as prosperous as Gdańsk was extremely difficult.[137]

4.8 *Liability for the Decedent's Debts*

As mentioned earlier in the discussion of the Polish dower (*wiano*), the payment of debts is given priority over other obligations if the dower has been assigned in cash. A fairly long addition in the *Statutes*, following the Cracow version, lays down the rule that debts left by the heirs' father are to be paid from the decedent's estate,[138] that is, if there are not enough assets in the estate to cover all the liabilities, the heirs are under no obligation to make up the difference. If the heirs refuse to settle the debts, the estate can be seized and sold to pay off the creditors. In MS BN 3068, the text was altered. There, the *debitum* seems to mean more than a sum of money due by an express contract; it is rather a claim or obligation whose recognition the claimant has to enforce on the heir through court action. Like most manuscripts, the *Statutes* says that the requisite compurgation procedure can go ahead with just three witnesses – a notable change from the Gniezno manuscript, where it was seven.[139]

4.9 *Summary: Pressing Needs, Numerous Alterations*

The alterations and amplifications discussed above had three main functions. First, they offered a clarification of practical difficulties of interpretation. For example, if the dower, which provided the widow with a means of support

---

136 *JIM*, Article LIX glo., col. 46; and *SzIM*, Article LIX.6 glo.

137 Zygfryd Rymaszewski, "Kłopoty Gdańska z kadukami królewskimi" [Gdańsk's Problems with Royal Escheats], in: *Historia integra. Studia z historii państwa i prawa, dziejów kultury, religii i oświaty epoki nowożytnej. Księga pamiątkowa ofiarowana Prof. Stanisławowi Salmonowiczowi w siedemdziesięciolecie urodzin* [Historia integra: A Festschrift in Honour of Professor Stanisław Salmonowicz on His 70th Birthday], eds. Danuta Janicka and Ryszard Łaszewski (Toruń, 2001).

138 No. 217.

139 No. 216.

upon the death of her husband, was in the form of cash, the payment of the debts due from the deceased husbands came first. Second, some regulations were made more flexible. Thus, for example, until the time of full majority, the heir could neither sell or dispose of his property, nor could he appear in court. Yet, this rule was relaxed in the Cracow version, and later by Łaski's *Statutes*, to allow some qualified legal rights to minors from the age of 12. Third, some modifications in the laws of succession tended to rebalance them in favour of natural heirs (the close family) as against the claims of collateral heirs. Changes in the law of escheat also gave more scope for the family interest. All these alterations of the text of the *Weichbild* or additions to it from the Magdeburg *ortyle* amounted to little more than modest modifications of the traditional legal code; the carriers of more fundamental revisions were the *wilkierze*, municipal laws introduced by or on behalf of the town owners.

5 Debtor and Creditor

5.1 *Debt Claim and Recovery*

In addition to monetary debt, the *Weichbild* distinguishes various types of debt in kind (e.g. food or horses). Sometimes it makes use of no other term than *debitum* as an equivalent of German 'Schuld'. Yet the purpose of the substitution of 'money' (*pecunia*) for *debitum* in Article 86 concerned with inheritance debts (following the Żagań MS)[140] is not clear.[141]

The *Statutes* follows the example of the manuscripts of the Cracow version in introducing a separate article on complaints about the provision of food and drinks. It sets down the rule that the party that claims to be the owner of the products has the burden of proof.[142] This formula is restated later in another article.[143]

In his analysis of the *Statutes*, Stanisław Estreicher notes that the additional provision about the liability of a buyer of a stolen horse was borrowed from the Chełmno Law. He argues that the recognition of a horse sale transacted in an inn (with a feast – *litkup*) is characteristic of Polish law, whereas German law insists that a disputed transaction must be decided by the court.[144] This argu-

140 No. 185. A more precise formulation in Article 92 that 'debt' means a monetary debt appears in the Działyńscy Codex I and the Warsaw MS (No. 178).

141 In connection with the use of terms 'debt' / 'money', it may be noted that Article 76 declares 'debts or money' in incurred by gambling unenforceable. The word 'debts' is omitted in MS Q II 157 (1), the Przemyśl MS and the Marcin Zabowski's MS (No. 168).

142 No. 61.

143 No. 172.

144 Cf. Introduction, Note 17.

ment cannot be accepted without a minor correction. The additional provision is by no means new; it is an article which was already part of the *Weichbild*, as indicated earlier (1.2).[145] Estreicher is right when he notes the adoption by the *Weichbild* of the testimony of witnesses of the transaction (*litkupnicy*, or *iudices mericipotum*) as evidence of a purchase in good faith. However, the claim that it constitutes an abandonment of the general principle of alienation by municipal tribunals lacks precision and needs to be checked against actual practice. Originally, under Magdeburg Law, the type of alienation with which the courts (*Auflassung*) were preoccupied were property transfers.[146] Gradually, the conveyances became more complex because of the multiplication of rights and encumbrances. At the same time, alienations of movables were a rarity in municipal records. It would be unrealistic to see in this proportion a reflection of what things are like in the real world, where trade in movables is at all times incomparably greater than transfers of immovables. In the case at hand, we may assume that, for example, in Zgorzelec (Görlitz) in the early 14th century the sale of a horse was a fairly simple business transaction unaffected by legal formalities in front of the bench jury. This is not to deny that the scope of cognition of the urban authorities was evolving and enlarging, yet it could also involve the recognition of *litkup*, a custom mentioned in the rulings of the High Court of German Law at Wawel in Cracow as early as 1457.[147]

In our discussion of the criminal procedure, we have noted the change in the minimum number of compurgators. A similar process seems to have been taking place in actions for the recovery of debt. The Gniezno MS and its close affiliate, the Działyńscy Codex I, require the presence of six oath-takers to establish proof, while all the other manuscripts follow the German base in finding the testimony of two fully sufficient.[148] The *Statutes* adopted a formula that is more favourable for the defendant, carefully editing out annotations

---

145 No. 160. For individual variations in the procedure for establishing the horse's owner, see No. 183 and 184.

146 Rudolph Sohm, "Zur Geschichte der Auflassung", in: *Festgabe zum Doctor-Jubiläum des Herrn Geheimen Justizrathes Professors Dr. Heinrich Thöl* (Strassburg, 1879), pp. 112–118; Herbert Zander, *Das Rote Buch der Stadt Gorlitz 1305–1416* (Leipzig, 1929), p. 27; and Werner Ogris, "Auflassung", in: *Handwörterbuch zur deutschen Rechtsgeschichte*, 1st ed., 1 (1971), col. 341–342.

147 *Decreta I*, No. 88.

Najstarsza zgorzelecka księga miejska 1305–1416 (1423). Edycja i komentarz [The Earliest Book of Municipal Court Records of Zgorzelec (Görlitz) 1305–1416 (1423): A Critical Edition and Commentary], 1, eds. Krzysztof Fokt, Christian Speer, Maciej Mikuła, Fontes Iuris Polonici 5 (Kraków, 2017), No. 112, 557.

148 No. 175 and 216.

from other manuscripts that specify the number of oath-takers.[149] At another point it, made into law the broad definition of debt repayment from the Żagań MS, namely, that the debt can be paid in such *denarii* (i.e. coins, or simply money) that are used in the court that hears the case (i.e. that are in circulation in that area).[150]

In addition to obligations arising from contracts, the *Weichbild* addresses the issue of obligations in tort. Article 77 sets down the liability for damage to property deposited for safe-keeping or pledged as collateral.[151] To obtain release from liability, the keeper must prove that the damage occurred through no fault of his own. If he succeeds and the collateral was an animal that died, the creditor shall lose his pledge. This provision was taken over from *Sachsenspiegel* by Konrad of Sandomierz before being incorporated into the *Statutes*.[152] Therefore, in this case, too, the *Statutes* does not come up with a formula that is new or original.

The security for debt is the subject of Article 64 of the *Weichbild*. Its provisions were passed on to the *Statutes* via the Cracow version without any notable alteration. Yet a most pertinent extension from the Gniezno MS that all heirs, not just his children, did not succeed to the security for debt of their deceased father was available to the authors of the *Statutes*.[153] Whether they chose to ignore it or just missed it is a question of some interest, albeit probably unresolvable.

5.2 *The Guest as Debtor and Creditor*

The early texts of the *Weichbild* provide for common-sense exceptions from general rules if one of the litigants is an alien. The problem of defining who may qualify as alien/guest (*hospes*) is discussed above in Section 2.3. The definition is dictated by practical considerations. As he has to go back home to collect the money he owes in debt, the alien should be given an extension of the payment deadline. Two additions in the Cracow version and the *Statutes* also deal with the question of pledges that guarantee the payment of a debt. The

149 No. 96, 152, 177, and 186. For alterations in the provision concerning the suspension of legal proceedings against a person setting off on a long journey (business, pilgrimage), see No. 52, 53, and 54. For adjustments within the provisions concerning the enforcement of debt payment in the Tomasz of Bydgoszcz's MS, see No. 176; and a revision of the regulations concerning pledge and wergild in MS Q II 157 (2) and the Mikołaj of Smogorzewo's MS, see No. 194.

150 No. 181.

151 No. 173.

152 The problem of damage caused by animals is addressed in an addition in the Przemyśl MS, see No. 218.

153 No. 151.

court should accept a guest (i.e. a person) as security for debt.[154] Another rule or recommendation, which also derives from the *ortyle*, says that objects must not accepted as pledge. If, however, this type of arrangement between parties (when one of them was a guest) did take place, general rules apply, except where the contract makes an exemption.[155]

5.3 *The Servant as Debtor and Creditor*

Following the text of the Sandomierz version, the *Statutes* reaffirms the general principle that the master cannot be held responsible for his servant's goods, as the latter was free to dispose of them as he chose.[156] There was, however, one exception to this rule: the master was liable to his servant in a situation when the latter's horse was stolen.[157] As the Częstochowa MS and the Kielce MS explain, the liability extends to all assets that are essential for the servant's livelihood as it is the master's duty to maintain his servant.[158] At the same time, the law solemnly declares that all transactions (especially bets) made a by servant which involve the loss, damage, or sale of his master's property are invalid. Those additions come from the *Sachsenspiegel*, but they can also be found in other texts, such as the Chełmno Law. Thus, Konrad of Sandomierz's decision to include them in his *Weichbild* compilation was no innovation. Nonetheless, the author of *Statutes* chose drop the procedural formula (found in some texts of both the Sandomierz and the Cracow version) which made the master's suit against his servant dependent solely on the testimony of oath-helpers. This is understandable, as by that time the courts were accustomed to relying on other forms of obtaining proof (i.e. by examining documents).[159]

5.4 *Summary: Liability Made More Precise*

Changes and augmentations concerning liability for debt were aimed first of all at increasing the precision of individual provisions. The *Statutes*, for example, explicitly stated what money was to be used to pay the debt. Some rules were amended to make them more coherent: for example, the exemption of children from the pledges of their deceased father was to apply to relatives, as well. Clarifications and additional regulations were introduced into provisions concerning liability for damage to leased property or to property pledged as collateral. Finally, the *Statutes* opened up other forms of obtaining proof,

154 No. 30.
155 No. 38.
156 No. 169.
157 No. 170.
158 No. 171.
159 No. 197. Cf. also No. 196.

which were more appropriate in the changing times, in cases of debt as an alternative to the traditional oath-swearing. These changes show that adaptation for practical use was a major factor in the evolution of the *Weichbild*.

6 Conclusions

A textual comparison of the earliest extant German *Weichbild* with the *Weichbild* in Łaski's *Statutes* shows the effect of the evolution of the *Ius Municipale Magdeburgense* over more than two hundred years. The material covered in this analysis includes Latin translations of numerous German texts in the Sandomierz and Cracow versions, provisions carried over from the *ortyle* and the *Sachsenspiegel*, adaptations (during the translation phase) of the Saxon-Magdeburg Law to the requirements of its Polish users, and other alterations (both in substance and in form). The authors of the *Statutes* had at their disposal at least two Latin texts of both versions, but, we may assume, they did not see all of the *Weichbild* manuscripts that were produced over that period. Their product – the *Statutes* – is a thoughtful and carefully executed synthesis of the Sandomierz and Cracow versions and can unreservedly be described as a legal text that is both complete and authoritative.

The *Statutes*' redaction of the *Weichbild* did not bring substantial changes to the texts widely used in legal practice. Nor was the incorporation of *ortyle* – judgments of the Magdeburg Bench – from the Cracow version into the new, authorized book of laws in any way dramatic. After all, they had been a legitimate source of law before. A series of alterations, discussed in detail in Section 1.1, are hardly far-reaching enough to justify the opinion that the publication of the *Weichbild* in the *Statutes* constituted a reform of Poland's urban law. However, the impact of the printing of the *Statutes* cannot be overestimated. Lawyers and courts all over Poland received a uniform text of the law, more comprehensive and reliable than any of its versions handed down in Latin manuscripts, furnished with a vast network of references to Polish land law and the *Sachsenspiegel*.

We know of no manuscript of Saxon-Magdeburg Law with the *Weichbild* as its sole source. Consequently, the study of the textual evolution of the *Weichbild* cannot ignore other sources of that law, especially the *Sachsenspiegel* and the Magdeburg *ortyle*, which make up each of the extant texts in varying degrees. In other words, in practice, the modification of the text of the *Weichbild* in any individual manuscript depends on the positioning of its companion texts. This is not much of a problem in a manuscript where the *Weichbild* pruned some articles from the *Sachsenspiegel*, but the latter is part of it, all written in a single hand. Then there is the Żegota Pauli's MS without the *Sachsenspiegel*, an arrangement which makes the additional provisions and alterations in its *Weichbild* so much more important for the legal practice. Of even greater importance are the *ortyle*, which, in the Cracow version, became part of the text of the *Weichbild*, and which were ultimately blended into the *Statutes* in a manner which preserved none of their distinctive origin. Yet the fact that so many legal formulas from the *ortyle* were adopted by the *Statutes*, the official code of law, proves their worth and significance. What should also be borne in mind is the fact that – notwithstanding the amendations and the collation of the Sandomierz and Cracow versions – the text in the *Statutes* does not constitute a new translation or version of the *Weichbild*. It is the most comprehensive revised version of the Silesian-Małopolska compilation of the *Weichbild*. Although it became the authorized version, it was by no means the last one to be made and circulated. The replacement of the old manuscripts by a uniform text in print took years. In the meantime, new manuscripts of the *Weichbild* were produced, including copies of the extant Gniezno MS (MS BOZ) and *Commune incliti* (MS BN 3068). The continued use of the manuscripts may have been caused by the inadequate number of the printed copies of the *Statutes*, as well as the persistence of old habits and the difficulty of accepting the formula that the text of the *Statutes* was sacrosanct. Tomasz of Bydgoszcz, the copyist of MS BN 3068, certainly represents the old mind-set. His work is not a verbatim copy of the *Statutes*, but a compilation, thick with alterations of all kinds.

The changes in text of the *Weichbild* in diverse manuscripts and in the *Commune incliti*, which brought to an end the medieval history of that legal text, indicate that its evolution was driven by its functional uses. These functions can be identified as follows: 1) concern for the realities of Polish towns which resulted in the introduction of Polish terminology; 2) concern for precision shown in the introduction of legal definitions; 3) elimination of ambiguity and uncertainty; 4) the need for legal practitioners to have a legal text that would take into account the clarifications of the Magdeburg judgments (*ortyle*); and 5) the need to adapt the legal formulas of the *Weichbild* to the realities of urban life in late medieval Poland. While the evolution of the *Weichbild* was marked by piecemeal adaptation rather radical breaks, the common denominator of the all changes was adapting the text of the Magdeburg Law for judicial practice in a new environment. Its wide practical use is attested by numerous hand-written notes in the margins of all copies of the *Weichbild*, in the medieval manuscripts, and in the incunabula of the *Commune incliti*. Those annotations are discussed in the following chapter.

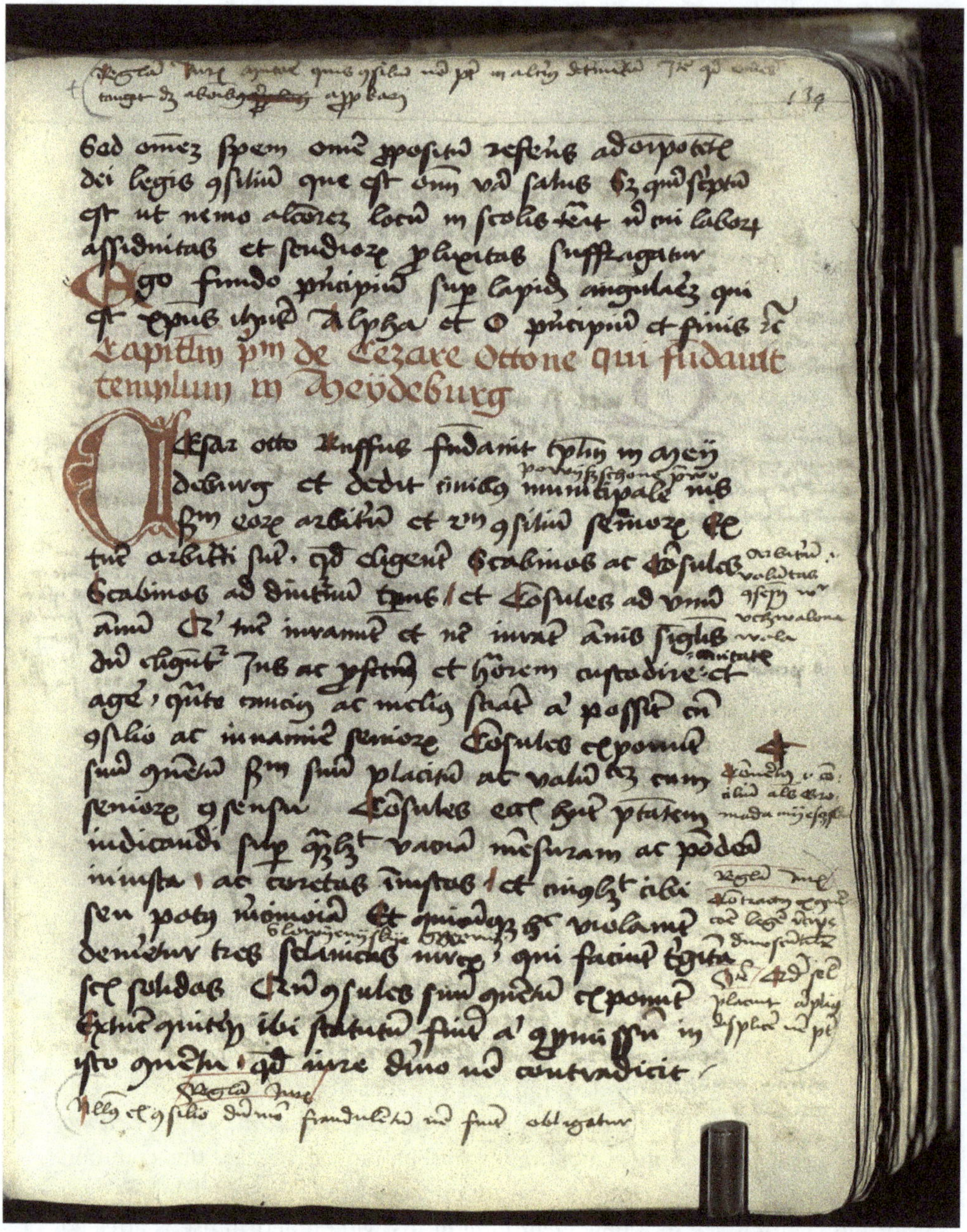

PHOTO 7 Działyńscy Codex I, The Kórnik Library of the Polish Academy of Sciences, Shelfmark 801, f. 139v

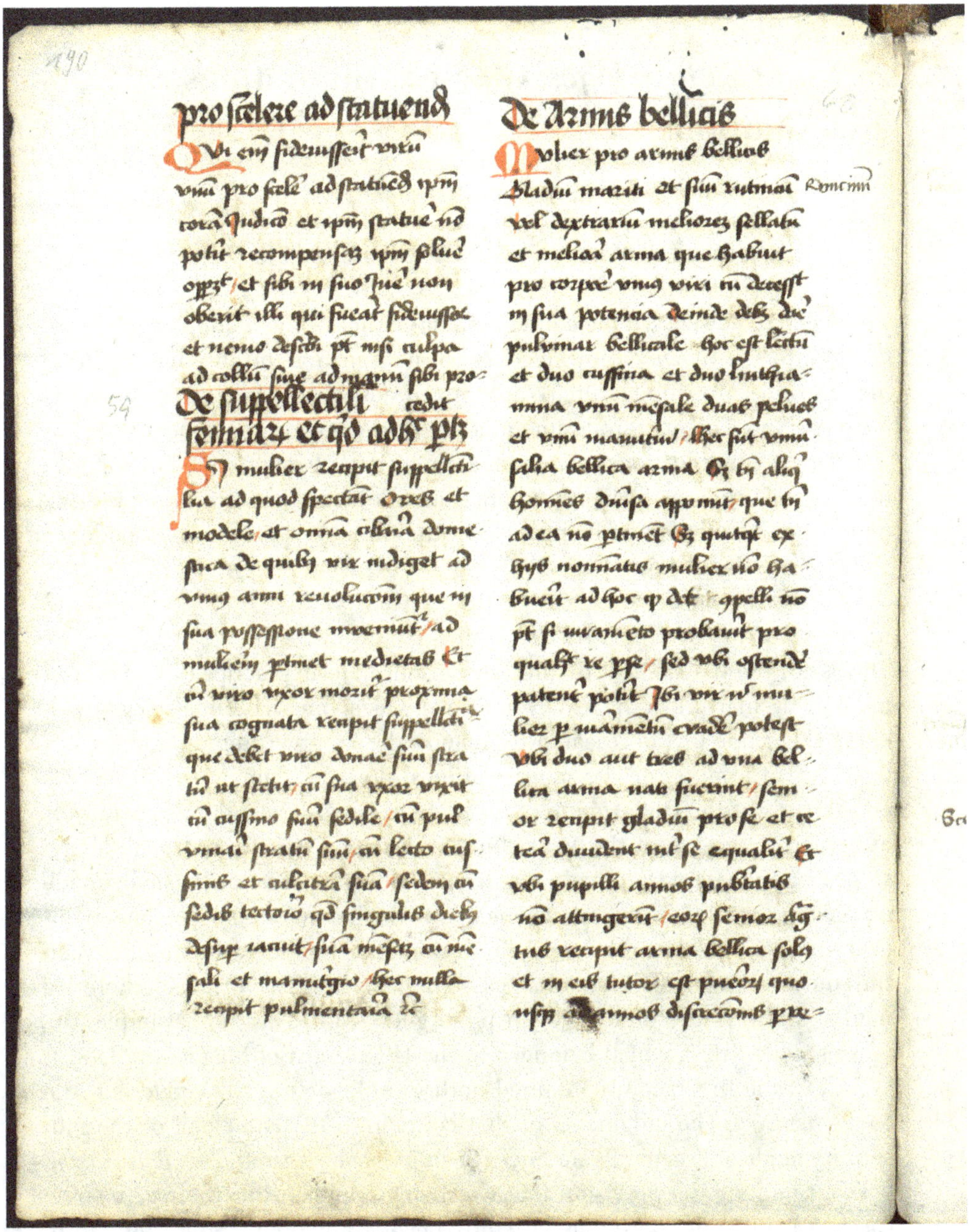

PHOTO 8 Żegota Pauli's manuscript, Jagiellonian Library in Cracow, Shelfmark 4405, f. 100v

CHAPTER 4

Habent sua fata leges: Glosses, Annotations, and Additions

1 Evidence of the Use of the *Weichbild* in Legal Practice

In Chapter 3, I discussed the content and functions of the modifications introduced into the *Weichbild* in the course of its transmission through medieval manuscripts until the landmark authorized edition in Jan Łaski's *Commune incliti* in 1506. The numerous amendments of the received text, be it clarifications or the modifications of individual provisions, were intended to enhance its practical usefulness. This argument finds additional justification in the evidence that *Weichbild* was being used in the municipal courts. This evidence will be discussed below.

1.1 *Evidence of Legal Practice*

The use of the *Weichbild* and other regulations in legal practice can be proved not only by analyses of the text evolution and legal practice, but also by broadening the scope of the research to include the hand-written annotations of the users of legal texts. The sources of legal practice, namely, urban records and records of the High Courts of Magdeburg Law in Poland, offer countless examples of the use of the Magdeburg *Weichbild*, even if a thorough analysis of its application is difficult. The records of legal procedures usually made no precise mention of the provisions upon which the courts of the late medieval Kingdom of Poland based their judgments. Therefore, the link between the court's ruling in any individual case and its legal basis (of which there are many) is always the product of inspired guesswork. Thus, for example, the Wawel MS (BJ 168), which belonged to the High Court of Magdeburg Law at Wawel Castle in Cracow, contained both the Magdeburg *Weichbild* and the *Sachsenspiegel*. The judgments of that court from the latter half of the 15th century made only general references to *ius Mageburgense* and *ius Teutonicum*, without naming the provision that was being applied. Nonetheless, in some cases, it is possible to establish the link beyond any doubt. So a ruling from 1460 ordered the administration of a purgatory oath within the following six weeks in accordance with German law (*iuxta formam iuris Teutonici*), which corresponds with Article 37 of the *Weichbild* (cf. Appendix 4).[1] Article 84 of

1 Decreta I No. 287 from 22 January 1460. Cf. Appendix 2 No. 83.

the *Weichbild* says that the debtor's property is to be confiscated if he fails to comply with a third order to pay his debt. Exactly this provision was echoed in one of the High Court judgments with the general formula *iuris Teutonici iuxta formam*.[2] Similarly, it is a *Weichbild* provision that requires a purgatory oath of six oath-swearers (*metseptimus*) in a case of debt clearance, and exactly that requirement can be found in a judgment, issued by the High Court at Wawel Castle from 1462, which referred to *iuris Teutonici iuxta formam*.[3] These are not isolated cases, although it cannot be taken for granted that access to written law was as easy in small towns (little different from bigger villages) as it was in Cracow or towns in their own right. At any rate, the relationship between municipal court judgments and the legal basis of those rulings is a subject worthy of a separate study. Here, I am going to look at another category of evidence which offers material proof of the use of the *Weichbild*: the hand-written annotations on the extant copies of the *Ius municpale Magdeburgense*.

1.2 *Types of Paratext in the Latin Texts*

Marginal annotations to *Ius municipale* offer significant insights into the organization of the text itself, as well as the circumstances of its evolution. Their content is amazingly diverse, ranging from references within the *Weichbild* through notes, hints, Polish equivalents of Latin terms, indices, and digests, to legal maxims and rules juxtaposed for the sake of comparison. Nevertheless, not all manuscripts are overgrown with the barnacles of notes and commentaries. There are basically no annotations in the Częstochowa MS, the Przemyśl MS, Mikołaj of Smogorzewo's MS, Q II 157 (2), the Działyńscy Codex IV, the Warsaw MS, the Opatów MS, or the Żagań MS. There is a relatively small number of annotations in the St Florian MS (Flor.), Marcin Zabowski's MS (BOZ), and the Kielce MS (Kiel.); and a significant number in MS Q II 157 (1), the St Petersburg MS (F 143), and the Baworowscy (BN 12607).[4] A great deal of interesting annotations can be found in the Działyńscy Codex I (Dział. I), Żegota Pauli's MS (BJ 4405), the Leipzig MS (951b), and Tomasz of Bydgoszcz's BN 3068, although not all them are of a later date than the main text. In BN 3068, at least two hands can be distinguished, whereby one of them (A) looks identical to the hand of the main text. Additionally, in the Działyński Codex I (Dział. I), the hand of numerous marginal annotations resembles that of the

---

2 Decreta I No. 341 from 19 July 1460.

3 Decreta I No. 498 from 20 December 1462.

4 BN 12607 with some German glosses in a hand different the main text, apart from the Latin ones, e.g. in Articles 60 and 61, the clarification of what belongs to the *gerada* and the *hergewet*, respectively.

main text. In the opening section of that manuscript (up to Article 20), the scripture is small and fine (the glossator uses a distinctive writing instrument and ink), and the annotations to the remaining articles look very much like the hand of the main text, except for one notable difference. Whereas all of the main text is written in a small hand, the letters of the glosses get steadily larger. The uncertainty can eventually be cleared by a close comparison of the two texts. Despite their resemblance, they are the product of two hands.[5] The same is true of the Żegota Pauli's MS (BJ 4405): the glossator is certainly not the author of the main text. The annotations in copies of Jan Łaski's *Statutes* need to be dealt with separately. Types of glosses added to the texts of the *Weichbild* are shown in the Table 22.

TABLE 22 Types of glosses added to the texts of the *Weichbild*

Type of gloss	Gn.	F 143	Q II 157 (1)	Dział. I	BJ 4405	BOZ	Kiel.	Flor.	Warsz.	BN 12607	915b	BN 3068
Amendation	+	–	–	+	–	–	–	–	–	–	–	–
Reference	–	+	–	–	–	–	–	+	–	+	–	–
Index/digest	–	–	+	+	–	+	+	–	–	+	–	+
Borrowing from the Cracow version	–	–	–	+	+	–	–	–	–	–	+	–
Other supplement	–	–	–	+	–	–	–	–	–	+	–	+
Chełmno Law	–	–	–	–	–	–	–	–	–	–	–	–
Polish terms	–	–	–	+	–	–	–	–	–	–	+	+
Regulae iuris	–	–	–	+	–	–	–	–	–	–	–	+

5 Whenever omissions in the base text are corrected by the original scribe, they are introduced as a flagged interlinear gloss in superscript. Other supplements, e.g. *regulae iuris* or longer passages added by the commentator, neither appear in the form of interlinear glosses, nor are they marked in any way. Only at one point does the scribe insert a manicule to indicate that the *regulae* copied in the upper margin refer to Article 40, further down the page, and not to the adjacent Article 39.

2 Amendations and Additions

2.1 *Amendations of Errors in the Sandomierz Version*

The later glossator added only a few annotations and amendations to the Gniezno manuscript. As a comparison with other texts of the *versio Sandomiriensis* shows, they appear beside four articles. The gloss to Article 48 invests the court with the right to make a decision about the *hergewet* when a nephew claims the right to inherit after his maternal grandfather.[6] In Article 100, the gloss corrects an evident error: the mulcts imposed on a *sołtys* (Ger. *Schultheiß* / Lat. *scultetus*) were to be collected not by him, but by the *wójt* (Ger. *Vogt* / Lat. *advocatus*) who ruled on such cases.[7] The gloss to Article 105 sets the number of compurgators in claims regarding debt payment at two rather than six;[8] however, that amendation is missing at Article 79. A brief gloss to Article 67 makes its provision clear.[9] Amendations to Articles 48, 79, 100, and 105 can also be found in the glosses of the Działyńscy Codex I.[10]

Additionally, a reader of the Żegota Pauli's MS introduced some linguistic corrections into the text. For example, when in Article 52 he spotted an error, evidently made by the copyist of the base text, he put a frame around the superfluous conjunction *per* (which might be regarded as a less intrusive way of signalling a mistake).[11] He also filled in the missing words in the date of the second session of the *Burggraf*'s courts (instead of St John's and St Paul's Day St John's in the original manuscript),[12] and the same amendation as that added by a reader in Gn. is introduced in Article 100. Corrections of textual errors can also be found in the Leipzig MS, but, as noted earlier, they were introduced by the copyist of the main text.[13]

---

6 Cf. Appendix 2, No. 106.

7 Cf. *ibidem*, No. 206.

8 Cf. Chapter 2. Section 4.3.

9 [67] *Quod si vir, qui pueros habuerit, occisus fuerit, tres aut plures, et si vir unus iudicialiter pro eo inpulsatus fuerit ...*

10 The gloss also fills in other missing fragments of Article 14: *si moritur vir, hii pueri, qui in hereditate patris sunt, recipiunt bona et non hii, qui exhereditati sunt* (No. 41); Article 24: *ita si sibi dominus consentire voluerit. Si autem dominus iuraverit tacto sacramento* (No. 60); Article 29: *coram iudice et scabinis*; Article 53: *unus interrogetur ad dicendum, quid ab eo audierint*; Article 56: *ipsum solus vidi, hoc est in persona propria*. Minor amendations can also be found in Article 24, 25 and 53.

11 [52] ... *quod per tutorem ipsum querulari opportet*, per *prolocutorem per sententiam petat ...*

12 No. 14.

13 Article 24: *si moritur vir, hii pueri, qui in hereditate patris sunt, recipiunt bona et non hii, qui exhereditati sunt* (No. 41). Minor amendations can also be found in Article 1, 4, 5, 13, 14, 30, 34 and 40.

2.2 *Cross-references and Registers*

Cross-references to other articles are rare. There are four of them in the Baworowscy MS, and they refer to matching provisions of the *Weichbild*.[14] In the St Petersburg MS, as we have noted in Chapter 1, Section 3.2, they probably refer to the *Sachsenspiegel*. Among the rather careless entries made by Commentator B in the Baworowcy MS, there are only two cross-references.[15] One is attached to Article 50, which deals with guardianship, and refers to Articles 80, 72, and 73 (indicating that the point at issue is the age of the ward). The Działyńscy Codex I has an identical note: *de etate pupili iste lxxx c. Item in provinciali lxxii et lxxiii*. It would seem that MS Dział. I indicates precisely the corresponding provisions of both the *Weichbild* and the *Sachsenspiegel* (*Ius provinciale*). Yet the first cross-reference in the Działyńscy Codex I and Tomasz of Bydgoszcz's MS are really a shot in the dark, as Article LXXX of the *Weichbild* does not deal with guardianship at all. The second cross-reference in Tomasz of Bydgoszcz's MS, at Article 70, is concerned with the definition of mulct and points to *Sachsenspiegel*.

Tomasz of Bydgoszcz's MS contains a large number of indices in the form of marginal glosses.[16] In the bilingual Żagań MS, the original indices (*regesta*) are German; the Latin supplements are a later addition. In the first part of MS Q II 157 (1), some digests are written in the same hand as the main text, while some are in a different hand. The rest of the text is left un-glossed. The main text of the *Weichbild* in the Baworowscy MS has no original indices. Those that do appear in some articles were introduced by a commentator at a later date. His is also a comment (heading) next to Article 27 *Sequntur capitula de vulneribus per totum*. This is absolutely pertinent because the following dozen or so articles deal with crimes of assault and wounding. The indices usually form a cluster of at the beginning of an article (they also feature in the general index prefixed to the main text and written in a different hand). Occasionally, however, an article is prefixed with a laconic indication of content or even a single-word 'heading'.[17] Some articles, which the commentator deemed for some

14 In the *ortyl* attached to Article 7, concerned with lien, the reference to f. XVII of Book I (i.e. to the *Weichbild*) should in fact point to f. XVII verso (or in the foliation as we have it now 43v) where there is Article 59 on the subject of lien. Further cross-references appear at Article 22 on f. XXV to Article 90 (insulting a member of the jury); at Article 25 on f. XI to Article 43 and other articles dealing with donations and inheritance; and at Article 86 on o f. XXVIII to Article 105 (proof of a debt claim).

15 These are two short notes in Polish concerning judicial procedure.

16 At Articles 2, 4, 5, 6, 7, 9, 12, 20, 23, 24, 25, 26, 38, 39, 46, 47, 49, 51, 56, 57, 61, 65, 69, 73, 74, 75, 81, 87, 91, and 100 (numbers according to Gniezno MS).

17 For example, Article 13 is prefixed with a laconic and pertinent heading '*obligatio*'; the first word of Article 17, '*Nemo*', is copied as a marginal gloss alongside the main text; a gloss on

reason to be more important than others, are signposted with a manicule.[18] A smaller number of auxiliary indices can be found in the St Florian MS,[19] the Działyńscy Codex I,[20] Marcin Zabowski's MS,[21] and the Kielce MS.[22]

2.3 *Borrowings from the Cracow Version*

The manuscripts of the Cracow version have no glosses that would indicate later collation with the Sandomierz version. When such annotations do make their appearance, it is at the stage of copying and preparing 'hybrid' manuscripts, like the St Florian MS, the Częstochowa MS, and the Kielce MS. Two manuscripts of the *versio Sandomiriensis* – the Żegota Pauli's MS and the Działyńscy Codex I – were collated at a later stage. The case of the Leipzig MS is more complex: in the first part (up to Article 40), the scribe copied the glosses alongside the main text, but then he changed his mind, and in the second part of the manuscript, he incorporated them in the text itself (cf. Chapter 2, Section 3.4).[23] They include both minor, although often significant, annotations, as well longer passages from the *ortyle*. A list is presented in Table 23.

The use of the Cracow version in later collations was somewhat erratic. The commentator of the *Weichbild* from the Działyńscy Codex I made use of the main text, but left out the supplementary material (*ortyle*). The author of the Leipzig MS used the Cracow version most extensively. A significant number of those borrowings overlap with Łaski's *Commune incliti*, but the two texts are not quite identical. A comparison of the provisions of one portion of the *Weichbild* in the Leipzig MS with its counterparts in the *Statutes* and the manuscripts of the Cracow version reveals a telling similarity between the Leipzig MS and the Żagań MS. Meanwhile, a comparison of the annotations added to the Żegota Pauli's MS shows that they are similar to the apparatus of the

the upper margin above the text of Article 16 contains its initial phrase '*Quidquid masculus*'; Article 14 is signposted with '*Si aliqui pueri fuerint exhereditati*'; similarly, the upper margin gloss above Article 20 repeats the initial phrase of the latter '*Quicunque aliquem*'.

18 At Article 43 (requirements to be met by compurgators), 65 (inflicting of grievous bodily harm by assault with batons and sticks), 76 (non-enforcement of gaming debts), 81 (*flagrans delictum*), 82 (the *Burggraf*'s court), and 86 (debt recovery after the debtor's death).

19 At the article concerning the Jewish oath, the headline annotation *De iuramentum iudeorum* is written along the edge in the left margin.

20 In the Działyńscy Codex I, the initial lines of Article 100 are copied into a gloss in the upper margin of the page.

21 At Article 10.

22 At Articles 14, 25, 29, 39, 48, and 61.

23 The commentator acted similarly in the case of the *Sachsenspiegel*, where he incorporated the gloss into the main text of the articles at the beginning of this law book.

TABLE 23 Borrowings from the Cracow version in Działyńscy Codex I (Dział. I), Żegota Pauli's MS (BJ 4405) and Leipzig MS (951b)

No. as in MS Gn. and Appendix II	MS Dział. I	MS BJ 4405	MS 951b
[1] No. 2	–	–	*Et hoc non dimittendo, non ratione amoris, molestie, ire vel munerum, sicut eos iuvet Deus et sancti eius.* **as in MS II Q 4 and the *Statutes***
[1] No. 3	*et honorem* civitatis *custodire*	–	–
[3] No. 10	–	–	*triginta* sex *solidis*
[10] No. 32	–	–	metseptimus *suis vicinis* **as in MS BN 12607 but missing in the *Statutes***
[12] No. 35	–	–	*vel quivis sua sola manu pro adiutorio ratione homicidii vel vulneris duellaris, vel mettertius ad hoc si pro eo cum testibus fuerit impulsatus.* **as in the *Statutes***
[13] No. 38	–	–	*Nullus hospes ab alio advena, et contra, indiget pignus recipere pro debito recognito. Si autem ipsum receperit, extunc acquirere et prosequi prout alter vir iuridice oportebit, nisi aliter fuisset inter eos ordinatum verbotenus in contractu.* **as in MS BN 12607, MS II Q 4, and the *Statutes***
[14] No. 44	–	–	*Sed deservitum parcium et rationabile debite debeant solvi de bonis mortui viri pro dotalitio, et hoc si mulier fuerit dotata pecuniis in paratis. Si autem dotata fuerit in hereditate, propria tunc suum dotalitium pro aliis debitis iure valeat optinere. Etiam quivis vir habens mansionem infra municipale, ille sue conthorali dare potest pro dotalicio suam propriam hereditatem, quam in posse habeat alienandi, et etiam in aliis bonis mobilibus in quantum voluerit.* **as in MS BN 12607, MS II Q 4, and the *Statutes***

TABLE 23 Borrowings from the Cracow version (*cont.*)

No. as in MS Gn. and Appendix II	MS Dział. I	MS BJ 4405	MS 951b
[17] No. 46	*nec mulier sine consensu viri*	*nec mulier sine consensu viri*	*nec mulier sine consensu viri*
[18] No. 48	–	–	*sive sit masculi sive femine, ex paterna et materna consanguineitate* **as in MS II Q 4 and the *Statutes***
[18] No. 49	*inter se dividunt* equaliter. **as in MS II Q 4**	–	*inter se dividunt* equali forma. **as in the *Statutes***
[33] No. 75	–	–	*Ad hoc si ambo in recenti accione cum clamore ad iudicium fuerint deducti.* **as in MS II Q 4 and the *Statutes***
[42] No. 95	–	*In nullus causis precio conventi seu empti possunt esse testes, quia iure possunt eici.* **as in MS BN 12607, MS Oss., and MS II Q 4**	–
[61] No. 146	*ita tamen, quod senior dividit et iunior eligit*	–	**[in the main text]**
[63] No. 150	*In omni loco iuris est, ut iudex et iudicet cum sentenciis* scabinorum.	–	**[in the main text]**
[66] No. 156	*ita quod nulla se trahet ad hanc infra annum et diem ... nisi legale inpedimentum ipse propedierit.* **as in MS Przem.**	*inventa seu reperta* anno et die *fuerit* **as in MS AJG, MS Kiel., MS BN 12607, and MS Oss.**	**[in the main text] as in MS II Q 4 and the *Statutes***
[76] No. 173	*Eciam si conqueritur quis de alio de cibariis preparatis et coctis, hic propius [s] est obtinere iuramento, quam ille ipsum evadere possit iuramento.*	–	**[in the main text]**

TABLE 23 Borrowings from the Cracow version (*cont.*)

No. as in MS Gn. and Appendix II	MS Dział. I	MS BJ 4405	MS 951b
[95] No. 198	–	*Consules si iuramentum unius viri receperint, quod secundum iustam sententiam civitatis et statuta consuetudinem exactionem dedisset, et si tunc post mortem illius iurantis plura bona sub ipsius possessione fuerint inuenta, quam exactionata fuisset, illa bona consules non habent recipere, sed ipsius defuncti heredes, nisi aliquis heredum denegata eadem bona coram iudicio vel sedenti consilio recipere abrenunciasset, extunc ipsa bona consulibus pro utilitate civitatis permanent quemadmodum arbitratur seu per arbitrum dimissum est.* **as in MS BN 12607 and MS Oss.**	**[in the main text] as in MS II Q 4 but missing in the *Statutes***
[97] No. 200	–	*Actor etiam reum pro iuramentis promissis causa Dei vel petitionis hominum mittere voluerit absolutum, extunc iudici etiam competit ad hoc dare suam voluntatem, et si suum consensum noluerit adhibere, tunc actorem iuramenta accipere oportebit vel iudici demeretur in pena octo solidorum, et non plus pro causis singulis.* **as in MS BN 12607 and MS Oss.**	**[in the main text] as in the *Statutes***

Baworowscy MS and the Opatów MS; it is not clear, however, why the glossator of MS BJ 4405 selected certain items rather than others.[24]

2.4 *Additions Made by the Author/Compiler of the Text*

In the text of the manuscripts, we often find additions made by their authors/compilers. A significant number of these additions can be found in the gloss to the text of the Działyńscy Codex I. These additions typically consist of a word or two, such as, for example, the oath-swearing requirement being extended to the jurors (apart from the judge).[25] In some cases, the additions are longer, but they do not alter the nature of the regulation, as in Article 105 where the added phrase postulates that the compurgators' rights must not be questioned. This elementary guarantee is repeated in connection with other provisions. Article 2, which deals with the manner in which the town council's decisions concerning trade are to be made public, is expanded with the formula that the announcement should made all over town (in its four corners) as soon as they have been passed.[26]

Article 14 in the Żegota Pauli's MS is supplemented with the regulation that the dower is excluded from the widow's inheritance, and an extension of Article 45 reaffirms the admissibility of handing over to the wife the goods and chattels bought with money acquired from the sale of heritable property (but the handing over could be done only in court). Moreover, in the upper margin above Articles 1 and 2, there is a partially legible brief note about elder aldermen (*consules veteres*, see Chapter 3, Section 2.1.).[27] Article 100, which deals with the *sołtys*' mulct, is supplemented with a clause obliging a former judge to sojourn in the town where he used to officiate for 50 days after quitting his seat. This requirement was guarantee the efficacy of hearing any complaints

24 See Maciej Mikuła, "*Weichbild* magdeburski w rękopisie Biblioteki Jagiellońskiej nr 4405" [The Magdeburg *Weichbild* in MS BJ 4405], in: *Nil nisi veritas. Księga dedykowana Profesorowi Jackowi Matuszewskiemu* [*Nil nisi veritas.* A Festschrift Dedicated to Professor Jacek Matuszewski], eds. Marcin Głuszak and Dorota Wiśniewska-Jóźwiak (Łódź, 2016), pp. 151–157.

25 Article 51 and 53.

26 *Edicto publico item quatuor anugulos civitatis, si eo arbitro quod civitas ipsa cum senioribus statuit de consensu sue conventis.*

27 *Consul a consulendo vel a iudicando, nam et hoc consules veteres vocantur … ad [h]uc remanet illud rogat bonum consulitis et bonum iudicialis.*

brought against him.[28] As can be seen from this overview, the range and purpose of the additions varied a great deal.[29]

2.5 *A Comparison of the Provisions of the* Weichbild *with the Chełmno Law in the Działyńscy Codex* IV

The reasons why the author of the Działyńscy Codex IV decided to include in it additional information about the regulations of the Chełmno Law are unknown. In fact, these regulations are not copied *verbatim*, but made available in the form of summaries and digests. Comparisons with the Chełmno Law are attached to 16 articles in the first part of the text. They are concerned with four points: 1) property relations between spouses; 2) payment of debts; 3) the status of guests (aliens); and 4) procedural issues in criminal cases. Let us consider a few examples.

In Article 14, the author points out that under Chełmno Law, the spouses hold their property jointly,[30] and the concept of general inheritance (Chapter 3, Section 4.4) also includes movable goods.[31] Whereas under Magdeburg Law, the proof of property ownership required the participation of respectable compurgators, namely, property owners who live in the same judicial circuit (Article art. 42), this procedure under Chełmno Law was based first of all on the depositions of jurors or aldermen. Only if one of them died, could his testimony be substituted by that of two property owners.[32] Debt recovery could not pursued without the participation of jurors, aldermen, an arbiter (in cases of out-of-court settlement), or witnesses of the transaction (Pol. *litkupnicy*, Lat. *iudices mericipotum*).[33] The latter are also mentioned in Article 38, when the defendant needs to prove that a horse, allegedly stolen, was acquired by him lawfully. Łaski, too, thought it important to retain in his work this extra clause,

28 *Quilibet iudex post resignacionem sui officii debet pausare L diebus in eodem loco, ubi tempore officium reposuit, offerens se responsorum omnibus de se querulantibus publiceque sua quevis negocia et non latenter disponere.*

29 It may be noted that a gloss to Article 5 in the Baworowscy MS (BN 12607) contains an explanation that one *talent* (pound) equals 20 *szelągi* (shillings). Cf. also Note No. 19 in Appendix 2).

30 Article 14: *In Colmensi. Dividit uxor cum viro bona per medium, si bona directe ad virum spectant, et e converso.*

31 Article 26: *In Colmensi. Quicumque mobilia bona ab alto et basso pro bonis hereditariis computantum.*

32 Article 42: *In Colmensi. Cum scabinis vel consulibus. Si autem mortui fuerint et unus illorum manserit, tunc loco illorum cuiuslibet modum duobus possesionatis, quibus fides adhiberi debet, super proprio probari potest.*

33 Article 43: *In Colmensi. Cum consulibus, scabinis, arbitris et iudicibus mercipotariis solummodo debitorum probari potest, non aliis hominibus.*

which allows a party accused of acquiring a stolen horse to call in witnesses of the transaction (*litkup*, festive repast) and thus rebut the charge.[34] At two points the Działyńscy Codex IV mentions the legal status of guests. The author of the Działyńscy Codex IV writes that to prove their status they need the oath of two compurgators, whereas the *Weichbild* defines a guest as one whose home is a certain distance away from town, but does not indicate the manner in which this fact is to be established.[35] In cases of assault where both assailants have inflicted the wounds, the author of the Działyńscy Codex IV says that the party faced with charges in an unfamiliar language should appoint a proxy, whereas according to the *Weichbild*, the defendant need not respond to the accusation.[36] In such cases, the Chełmno Law gave the right to precedence in presenting evidence to the party that was first to bring their complaint before the judge or the jurors; according to the *Weichbild*, that right could be claimed when the complaint was lodged before four jurors, and not the judge in his home.[37] For the *Weichbild*, the testimony of the arbiters concerning an out-of-court settlement had the same weight as conclusive proof, and the settlement was to be regarded as *res iudicata*; the regulations of the Chełmno Law were analogous.[38] The Magdeburg Law set the penalty for a *sołtys* found guilty of violence and house-breaking at 8 shillings; in the Chełmno Law, the corresponding mulct was only half of that sum, as was the penalty for wounding.[39]

The extensive references to the Chełmno law gave rise to conjectures that the Działyńscy Codex IV originated in Wielkopolska or Mazovia, in the vicinity of towns incorporated under that law. However, there is nothing that rules out the other possibility, that is, that the codex was produced in a place nowhere near the Chełmno Law jurisdictions.[40] We need only to consider the case of the Żegota Pauli's MS. Its Cracow provenance is beyond doubt, and yet it contains more than a dozen provisions of the Chełmno Law, different from the ones included in the Działyńscy Codex IV (*nota bene*, Wadowice, a town near

---

34 Appendix 2, No. 160.

35 Article 9: *Secundum Colmensem mettertius*. Cf. Appendix 2, No. 29.

36 Article 28: *In Colmensi. Potest per procuratorem sive mundiburdium*. Cf. Appendix 2, No. 68. This requirement is missing in the Old Kulm, cf. PS III.4.

37 Article 31: *In Colmensi. Qui prius ad iudicium venerit, vel ad scabinos, ille apud Colmensem principium actionis obtinebit*. Cf. PS III.17 concerning the priority to be given to a complaint presented to the jurors.

38 Article 23: *In Colmensi. Arbitri, quecumque recogo[ve]r[u]nt, licet extra iudicium sit concordia facta, vadit in rem iudicatam*.

39 Article 5: *Pena sculteti in Colmensi quatuor solidi alias XVI quadrantes* (cf. PS II.25). Article 22: *In Colmensi. Consuli et scabino ferto cuilibet et quod fertones, tot sculteto quatuor solidi*.

40 Cf. Chapter 1, Section 3.10.

Cracow, was founded according to the Chełmno Law; it was an exception in Małopolska).[41] Moreover, what must not be forgotten in the discussion about the provenance of MS Dział. IV is the fact that the text of its *Weichbild* was collated with the manuscript of the High Court of German Law in Cracow. While that filiation points to a Cracow trail in the history of that codex, it is in itself not sufficient to prove or rule out any of the above scenarios.

3 Polish Equivalents of Latin Legal Terms

The purpose of including lists of Polish equivalents of Latin terms alongside the text of the law was no doubt practical.[42] There are two manuscripts which are furnished with more than a fair share of such lists.[43] The reasons why certain terms rather than others were selected are not clear. It is, however, possible to identify the source used by the glossators, which is a pair of bilingual glossaries, of different length, in the Działyńscy Codex I.[44] One of them found its way into the St Florian MS, the Przemyśl MS, Jan Wincenty Bandtkie's collection, and Tomasz of Bydgoszcz's MS. So far, due acknowledgement has been made of the texts in MS Dział. I, MS Flor., and J.W. Bandtkie's collection.[45] An

41 Stanisław Kuraś, ed., *Zbiór dokumentów małopolskich* [Collection of Lesser-Poland Documents], 3 (Warszawa, 1969), No. 429 (dated 1430).

42 Friedrich Ebel, *Über die Legaldefinitionen. Rechtshistorische Studie zur Entwicklung der Gesetzgebungstechnik in Deutschland, insbesondere über die Verhältnis von Rechtsetzung und Rechtsdarstellung*, (Schriften zur Rechtsgeschichte) 6 (Berlin, 1974), p. 42.

43 In the Opatów MS (Oss.), the *Weichbild* is glossed with three bilingual terms: *satisdatio gwarra* (Article 32), *rana śmiertelna* [fatal wound] (Article 34), and *defensorem zachoczcza vel warmana* (Article 40). In the Leipzig MS, Article 21 is glossed with a short note: *inducias vulgariter rokÿ*. The introduction of short explanations in the vernacular was common in Latin Europe. Cf. "Section 136. Translations and the Role of the Vernacular Languages in Medieval Europe", in: *Translation. An International Encyclopedia of Translation Studies*, 2, eds. Harald Kittel, Armin P. Frank, Norbert Freiner, Theo Hermans, Werner Koller, José Lambert, Fritz Paul (Berlin – New York, 2007), p. 1289; Agnieszka Bartoszewicz, *Piśmienność mieszczańska w późnośredniowiecznej Polsce* [Urban Literacy in Late Medieval Poland] (Warszawa, 2012), pp. 278–279 and Ebel, *Über die Legaldefinitionen*, p. 40.

44 *Secuntur vocabula juris Meydeburgensis* (f. 117–122v); *Vocabula juris provincialis et feodalis* (f. 129r).

45 Joachim Lelewel, "Słownik 87 wyrazów. Vocabula iuris Magdeburgensis koło roku 1455 spisany" [A Glossary of 87 Words – Vocabula iuris Magdeburgensis Written Down c.1455], in: *Polska wieków średnich* [Medieval Poland], 2nd ed. (Poznań, 1951), pp. 232–235; Wacław A. Maciejowski, *Historia prawodawstw słowiańskich* [History of Slavic Legislatures], 6 (Warszawa, 1858), pp. 409 and 411–412; Zygmunt Celichowski, *Słowniczek łacińsko-polski wyrazów prawa magdeburskiego z wieku XV* [A Latin-Polish Glossary of

extended version of these glossaries can be found in Jan Cervus Tucholczyk's *Farrago actionum*, and especially in *Farraginis actionis*,[46] which may be treated as another indication of their usefulness and of a demand which continued well into the 16th century.

The glossators of the *Weichbild* in Działyńscy Codex I (Dział. I) and Tomasz of Bydgoszcz's MS (BN 3068) certainly made use of them, as shown by the lists in Table 24. The lexicographic comparison in Table 24 reveals, quite surprisingly,

---

Magdeburg Law Terms from the 15th Century] (Poznań, 1875); Aleksander Brückner, "Średniowieczne słownictwo prawne" [Medieval Legal Vocabulary], *Prace Filologiczne* 5 (1895), 35–37; Bolesław Ulanowski, "Opisy rękopisów" [Descriptions of Manuscripts], in: *Archiwum Komisji Prawniczej*, 2 (Kraków, 1921), pp. XII–XIV; Janusz Sondel, *Słownik łacińsko-polski dla prawników i historyków* [A Latin-Polish Dictionary for Lawyers and Historians] (Warszawa, 1997), pp. XXV–XXVI; Janusz Sondel, "Ze studiów nad rolą i miejscem łaciny prawniczej w kulturze europejskiej" [Studies on the Role and Position of Legal Latin in European Culture], *Krakowskie Studia z Historii Państwa i Prawa* 7/1 (2014), 88; Anna Łosowska, *Kolekcja Liber legum i jej miejsce w kulturze umysłowej późnośredniowiecznego Przemyśla* [The Liber legum MS and Its Place in the Intellectual Culture of Late-Medieval Przemyśl] (Warszawa – Przemyśl, 2007), pp. 250–251; Maciej Mikuła, "Niezbędnik średniowiecznego praktyka prawa miejskiego: łacińsko-polski słownik terminów prawnych w rękopisie Biblioteki Narodowej w Warszawie, sygn. 3068 III" [A Necessary Equipment of Municipal Lawyer: Latin-Polish Legal Dictionary in MSS National Library in Warsaw Sign. 3068 III], in: *Semper fidelis. Prace dedykowane pamięci Profesora Janusza Sondla legendzie krakowskiego fakultetu prawniczego* [*Semper fidelis.* Works in Honour of Professor Janusz Sondel], eds. Dorota Malec, Łukasz Marzec, Tomasz Palmirski (Kraków, 2017), pp. 273–278.

46 Johannes Cervus Tucholiensis, *Farrago actionum juris Magdeburgensis* (Cracoviae, 1535), f. 101v–110r; Johannes Cervus Tucholiensis, *Farraginis Actionum Iuris Civilis et provincialis, Saxonici, Municipalisq[ue] Maydeburgensis Libri septem…*, Book VI (*Liber sextus*) (Cracoviae, 1546), f. 249–330v. See Maria Karplukówna, *Słownik Jana Cervusa z Tucholi* [*Johannes Cervus of Tuchola's Glossary*] (Wrocław, 1973); Marian Plezia, "Wstęp" [Introduction], *Słownik łacińsko-polski* [The Latin-Polish Dictionary], 1 (Warszawa, 1959), pp. XII–XIII; Maria R. Mayenowa, *Walka o język w życiu i literaturze staropolskiej* [The Struggle for Language in Polish Life and Literature (until the 18th Century)] (Warszawa, 1955), p. 50, No. 3 (Catalogue of Old Polish Dictionaries); Elżbieta Kędelska, *Łacińsko-polskie słowniki drukowane pierwszej połowy XVI wieku i ich stosunek do źródeł czeskich* [Latin-Polish Printed Dictionaries of the Early 16th Century and Czech Sources] (Wrocław, 1986), p. 88ff.; Władysław Bojarski, *Jan Jelonek Cervus z Tucholi. Z dziejów prawa rzymskiego w Polsce. Prawo prywatne materialne* [Johannes Cervus of Tuchola: A Chapter in the History of Roman Law in Poland. Substantive Private Law] (Toruń, 1989), pp. 45–46; Sondel, *Słownik łacińsko-polski*, p. XXVI; Janusz Sondel, *Z rozważań o łacińsko-polskiej terminologii i leksykografii prawniczej* [Reflections on Latin-Polish Legal Terminology and Lexicography], in: *Parlament, prawo, ludzie. Studia ofiarowane Profesorowi Juliuszowi Bardachowi* [Parliament, the Law and the People: A Festschrift in Honour of Professor Juliusz Bardach], eds. Katarzyna Iwanicka, Maria Skowronek, and Kazimierz Stembrowicz (Warszawa, 1996), p. 272; and Sondel, *Ze studiów nad rolą i miejscem łaciny*, p. 88.

that the explanations in MS BN 3068 do not come from the *Vocabula* in that manuscript, but from the *Vocabula iuris Meydeburgensis* known to us from MS Dział. I.

TABLE 24 A list of Latin legal terms and their Polish equivalents including extracts from bilingual glossaries of the Magdeburg Law in Działyńscy Codex I (Dział. I) and the Tomasz of Bydgoszcz's MS (BN 3068)

Gloss text		**Vocabulary text**	
MS Dział. I	**MS BN 3068**	**MS Dział. I**	**MS BN 3068**
communitas *gmÿn mÿesczsky* [1] [2]	–	communitas *mÿesczskÿ gmÿn*	communitas *gmÿn*
arbitrum voluntas consensus vulgariter *uchwalona wola* [1]	arbitrium vel voluntas consensus *uchwala wolna,* alias dicitur *wyelkyerz wsiithkych* [1]	arbitrum vel voluntas consensus alias *uchwalona wola* alias dicitur *wilkerz wsthÿstkych*	arbitrum vel voluntas
conventus vel consilium alias *gromada mÿesczka* [1]	conventus vel consilium vulgariter *gromada mieszczka* [1]	conventus vel consilium vulgariter *gromada mÿesczska*	–
{municipale ius} *powÿszschone prawo* [1]	municipale ius vulgariter *powÿêszone prawo* [1]	municipale ius *powÿsszone prawo*	municipale ius *zawyessone prawo*
{Sclavicas marcas} *slowÿenÿskÿe grzywny* [1]	Sclavonica marca vulgariter *Szlowaczka grzÿwna* [1]	Slavica marcis *Slovienska grzÿwna*	–
solidus hic videlicet Xii alenses … *szelag* [1]	solidus hic valorem XII allenseli [1]		–
agere *conacz* [2]	agere vulgariter *konacz* [3]	agere *konacz*	–
{decreta} *ustawÿ* [2]	decreta vel statuta vulgariter *ustawÿ* [2]	decreta vel statuta vulgariter *ustawÿ*	–
emenda *pokup* emendare *pokupÿcz* [2]	emenda vulgariter *pokup* [2]	emenda *pokup*	emenda *pokup*
feriatus dies debet dies dominicus eclesie dies *naroczÿty dzen* [4]	feriatus dies est vulgariter deicus dies vel celebris et solemnis dies vulgariter *naroczÿsztÿ dzÿen* [4]	celebris dies vel solemnis alias *naroczithy dzyen*; feriatus dies vel dominicus dies; in feriato die vel tempore *w nÿedziela abo naroczÿtÿ dzen abo czas*	dies feriati *uroczÿszte szwyatha*
{legale impedimentum} *sprawiedliwa przekarza* vel *nagabanÿe* [4]	legale impedimentum vulgariter *sprawyedlywa przekarza* vel *nagabanye* [4]	legale impedimentum *sprawyedlywa przekarza* vel *przegabanÿe*	legale impedimentum *przegabane prawa*

TABLE 24 A list of Latin legal terms and their Polish equivalents (*cont.*)

Gloss text		Vocabulary text	
MS Dział. I	MS BN 3068	MS Dział. I	MS BN 3068
–	sentencia vulgariter *orthel* [4]	–	sentencia *orthýl*
talentum *rubl* et fat xxti ex argenti pury in sua summa inhabet loco [3]	talentum vulgariter *rubl* et facit xx grossos argenti puri in sua summa [4]	talentum *rubl* et facit xx grossos argenti puri in sua summa	talentum *rubl* et facit xxti solidos denariorum
{irruenciam domiciliorum} *uderzenÿe na dom* [5]	irruencia domiciliorum vulgariter *uderzenÿe na dom* [5]	irruencia domiciliorum *uderzenÿe na dom*	–
{stuprum} *s. odlyeganie dzewstina* [5]	–	stuprum *odleeganÿe dziew.*	stuprum defloracio
{obsidia} *zasadzenÿa* [5]	obsidium vulgariter *zaszadzenye na drodze* [5]	obsidium *zasadzenÿe na drodze*	obsidium vel *zaszayadzyenye na drodze*
{castellani pena et recompensa} *glowna zaplata* [5]	recompensa vulgariter *glow[na] zaplata* [5]	recompensa *glowna zaplata*	recompensa *glowna zaplata*
–	temeraria violencia vulgariter *szmÿalem gwałtem* [12]	–	–
–	obligare vulgariter *szastawÿ* [14]	obligat vel inpignorat *zastawya* vel *zawÿedze*	–
–	consanguineitatis vulgariter *pokolenya krewnego* [19]	consanguineitas *pokolenÿe krewne*	–
–	linea vulgariter *kresza* [19]	linea *kresa*	–
–	creditor *gÿszczercz albo dowyerzcza* [22]	creditor – *gÿzczecz* vel *dowÿerzcza*	–
–	fiscat vel pignorat vulgariter *ma bÿcz rzÿadzana* [?] [22]	fiscata vel iuradicata *zastawÿona* fiscatio vel oblicacio est *zastawa*	fiscatio eciam vel oblicacio
–	impulsaverit vel querulaverit vulgariter *pozalowałbÿ* [22]	impulsaverit vel querulaverit *poszalowałbÿ*	–
–	sua possessio vulgariter *gyego wladza* albo *gyego gymÿenye* [22]	sua posessio – *gego wladza* albo *gÿmÿenye*	–
–	de limina sanctorum vulgariter *poszwÿaczÿ* [23]	–	–

TABLE 24 A list of Latin legal terms and their Polish equivalents (*cont.*)

Gloss text		Vocabulary text	
MS Dział. I	MS BN 3068	MS Dział. I	MS BN 3068
–	paris condicionis et heredes legittimi natus secundum formam Sancte Ecclesie vulgariter *czẏsthego loza polozonẏ* [29]	paris condicionis vel heredes legittimi natus secundum formam Sancte Ecclesie alias *cistego losza narodzonẏ*	–
–	pulmentaria vulgariter *jarzẏnẏ* [29]	pulmentaria vel legumina vulgariter *ẏarzẏnẏ*	–
–	proprium dicitur hereditas sicut domus area fundus, predium et omnes agri ortus vineca humulentus vulgariter *chmẏe[l]nẏk* [30]	proprium dicitur hereditas sicut domus area fundus, predium et omnes agri ortus vinca et humulentus alias *chmyelnyk*	–
–	vasa distillatoria *szadẏ spusczadlne* [30]	vasa distillatoria *sadẏ spusczadlne* –	vasa distillatoria *pẏwne albo vẏnne* alias *beczkẏ*
–	pro imbecillitate corporis vulgariter *dla mgloszczẏ czyeleszneẏ* [31]	–	–
–	monomachaliter et duellatorie vulgariter *szmertelnye* [41]	monomachia vel duellariter *smẏertelnẏe*	duellum vel mortalitas...; monomachaliter *szmyerthelnẏe*
–	nepos dicitur *wnuk* alias *dzẏad* [53]	nepos *wnuk*	nepos *wnuk*
–	federa pacis et firmata pacem vulgariter *sczywierdzonẏ mẏr* [58]	federa pacis et firmata pacem vulgariter *sczywyrdzonẏ mẏr*	–
–	linea vestimentum vulgariter *parczẏane dzyenye* [61]	linea vestimentum *parczane odzenẏe*	–
–	hereditas obmortua vulgariter *dzẏedzẏna odumarla albo puscza przes dzyedzẏcza* [71]	hereditas obmortua *dzedzina odumarla* vel *pusczina przez dzyedzicza*	–
–	refricacio vel innovacio vulgariter *wsznowyenye* [72]	refricacio vel invocacio vulgariter *wznowyenye*	refricare vel innovare
{mare aquilonis} *za morze na polnoczẏ* [69]	ultra mare *za morze na pulnoczẏ* [74]	ultra mare ... *za morze na polnoczẏ*	

TABLE 24 A list of Latin legal terms and their Polish equivalents (*cont.*)

Gloss text		Vocabulary text	
MS Dział. I	MS BN 3068	MS Dział. I	MS BN 3068
–	vel sub tutorem *vulgariter na zachoczcza albo splaczcza* [74]	tutor vel proloqutor … vel eciam *zachodzcza* vel *splaczcza*	–
–	proscriptus vulgariter *wẏszwẏeczon* [77]	–	proscriptus *wẏrugowanẏ albo wẏszwyeczonẏ*
–	illiber alias obnoxious vulgariter *nyewolnik* alias vulgariter *szuusz* [80]	illiber vel obnoxious vulgariter *szruusz* alias *nẏewolnẏk*	illiber vel obnoxious *nyewolnyk*
–	alloquitur vel arrestaverit vulgariter *narzeklby zasthaw* [89]	alloquitur vel arrestaverit alias *narzeklbẏ zasthaw*	–
–	hereditavit vel dimisit vulgariter *oddzẏełẏl od szyebye* [93]	–	–

Extracts from the text of articles in the Działyńscy Codex I at which the commentator introduced the Polish term without copying it into the gloss are reproduced in curly brackets {}.

4 *Regulae iuris*[47]

The *Regulae iuris*, which formed an appendix to Boniface VIII's *Liber sextus*, became widely known in Poland thanks to a popular commentary to the papal code written by Joannes Andreae.[48] At the end of 15th century, *regulae iuris*

47 The problem of the presence of *regulae iuris* in the *Weichbild* is the subject of detailed analyses in this author's article 'Was Canon Law in Use in Municipal Courts in Late-Medieval Poland? Regulae iuris in Libro sexto in Manuscripts of Municipal Law' (in print). This subchapter is an altered version of that publication.

48 Wacław Uruszczak, "Krakowski komentarz reguł prawa z początku XVI wieku (*Lectura super titulo de regulis iuris Libro Sexto*)" [A Cracow Commentary on the *regulae iuris* from the Early 16th Century (*Lectura super titulo de regulis iuris Libro Sexto*)], *Czasopismo Prawno-Historyczne* 25/2 (1973), 70, Note 5; Wacław Uruszczak, *Regulae Iuris* w kulturze prawnej dawnej Polski [*Regulae iuris* in the Legal Culture of Poland until the 18th Century], *Krakowskie Studia Prawnicze* 22 (1989), 79–108. Both articles are reprinted in: Wacław Uruszczak, *Opera historico-iuridica selecta. Prawo kanoniczne – nauka prawa – prawo*

were even made the subject of a special lecture course at the Faculty of Law at the University of Cracow.[49] The *regulae iuris*, or maxims or secondary rules formulated on the basis of existing regulations, were usually employed in legal argument to express in a terse and impressive way certain fundamental principles of law and justice. Collections of *regulae iuris* of various provenance can be found in the St Petersburg MS (f. 141v–142) and the Działyńscy Codex I.[50] In MS Dział. I (f. 239–246) and MS BJ 4405 (f. 5v–9v), they provide the guidelines for the division into groups and the formation of digests of the provisions of the Magdeburg Law.

Some *regulae* appear as glosses to the *Weichbild* in the Działyńscy Codex I and Tomasz of Bydgoszcz's MS. Of the 88 *regulae* in the appendix to Boniface VIII's *Liber Sextus*, 24 were taken over by the author of MS Dział. I. He also picked up two more from other sources,[51] one from the *Digesta* and one from a treatise *Versus de sancto Laurento* by Marbodius, Bishop of Rennes.[52] As not all of them appear in MS BN 3068, a much later work, it can be assumed that the collection in the latter manuscript is secondary. The possible filiation

---

wyznaniowe [Opera historico-iuridica selecta: Canon Law – Legal Scholarship – Law on Religion], eds. Maciej Mikuła *et al.* (Kraków, 2017). See also the classic monograph by Peter Stein, *Regulae iuris. From Juristic Rules to Legal Maxims* (Edinburgh, 1966). Numerous studies of *regulae iuris* focus mainly on Classical Antiquity and stress the didactic and pragmatic functions of such maxims; see the collection of studies *Regulae iuris. Ipotesi di lavoro tra storia e teoria del dirito* (Napoli, 2016). There are also studies of the impact of legal rules and maxims in contemporary public discourse, e.g. Agnieszka Kacprzak, Jerzy Krzynówek, and Witold Wołodkiewicz, *Regulae iuris: łacińskie inskrypcje na kolumnach Sądu Najwyższego Rzeczypospolitej Polskiej* [*Regulae iuris*: Latin Inscriptions on the Columns of the Supreme Court of the Republic of Poland], ed. Witold Wołodkiewicz (Warszawa, 2001).

49 Wacław Uruszczak, "Wydział Prawa Uniwersytetu Jagiellońskiego i jego profesorowie w latach 1364-1780" [Faculty of Law of the Jagiellonian University and Its Professors in 1364–1780], in: Krzysztof Ożóg, Krzysztof Fokt, Maciej Mikuła, Maciej Zdanek, Dagmara Wójcik-Zega, and Katarzyna Kuras, *Profesorowie Wydziału Prawa Uniwersytetu Jagiellońskiego, 1: 1364–1780* [Professors of the Faculty of Law of the Jagiellonian University, 1: 1364–1780], ed. Wacław Uruszczak (Kraków, 2015), pp. XI–XII; Maciej Zdanek, "Jakub z Szadka h. Wieniawa (zm. 28 X 1487)" [Jakub of Szadek (Clan Wieniawa) (d. 28 October 1487)], in: Ożóg *et al.*, *Profesorowie Wydziału Prawa*, pp. 106–107.

50 This is a short, random collection of *regulae* (f. 129v).

51 They are given a summary treatment by Johannes Andreae in his *Questiones mercuriales super regulae iuris*, where he discusses – in addition to the *regulae* from *Liber sextus* – the *regulae* from the *Digesta* (this observation is based on the Venetian edition of the *Questiones* (Venetiae, 1490)).

52 Jean Jacques Bourassé, eds., *Venerabilis Holdeberti primo Cenomanensis episcopi deinde Turonensis archiepiscopo opera omnia, tam edita, quam inedita accesserunt Marboni Redonensis episcopi, ipsius Hildeberti supparis opuscula* (Paris, 1854), PL 171:1608.

between the two manuscripts is indicated by fairly conclusive evidence that Tomasz of Bydgoszcz, the author of MS BN 3068, made use not only of the *Weichbild* from MS Dział. I, but also its Latin-Polish legal glossary. It should be noted though that the *regulae* added to the *Weichbild* do not come from the collections from the St Petersburg MS, the Działyńscy Codex I, or the Żegota Pauli's MS.

TABLE 25 *Regulae iuris* in the *Weichbild* of Działyńscy Codex I (Dział. I) and Tomasz of Bydgoszcz's MS (BN 3068)

No.	*Regulae iuris*	MS Dział. I	MS BN 3068
1.	*Actus legitimi conditionem non recipiunt neque diem* (50)	[27], [34], [79]	[31], [38], [88]
2.	*Ad facinus duplex non sufficit ultio simplex* (Marbordius of Rennes)	[22]	[25]
3.	*Contra eum qui legem dicere potuit apertius est interpretatio facienda* (57)	[22]	[24][a]
4.	*Contractus ex conventione legem accipere diagnoscuntur* (85)	[1]	–
5.	*Cum sunt partium iura reo pocius est faciendum quam actori* (11)[b]	[28]	[32]
6.	*Factum legitimum retrotrahi non debet, licet casus postea eveniat a quo non potuit inchoari* (73)	[34]	[38], [88]
7.	*In pari delicto et causa potior est conditio possidentis* (65)	[96]	–
8.	*In poenis benignior est interpretatio facienda* (49)	[96]	–
9.	*Infamibus porte non pateant dignitarum* (87)	[58]	[63]
10.	*Inputari ei non debet per quem non stat, si non faciet quod per eum fuerat faciendum* (41)	[24]	[28]
11.	*Innanis est ex actio, quam excusat inopia debitoris* [D.4.3.6]	[20]	[22]
12.	*Ius naturale ante omnia obtinet privatum*	[40]	[45]
13.	*Mutare quis consilium non potest in alterius detrimentum* (33) [D.50.17.75]	[1]	[1]
14.	*Nemo potest plus iuris conferre, quam sibi competere dignoscatur* (79) [D.50.17.54]	[22]	[25]

a It should be in Article 25 according to the numbering scheme of MS BN 3068.
b In *Liber sextus*: *Quum sunt partium iura obscura reo fovendum est potius quam actori.*

TABLE 25 *Regulae iuris* in the *Weichbild* of Działyńscy Codex I (*cont.*)

No.	*Regulae iuris*	MS Dział. I	MS BN 3068
15.	*Non confirmatur tractu temporis, quoad de iure ab inicio non subsistit* (18)	[40]	[45]
16.	*Non debet aliquis alterius odio praegravari* (22)	[96]	–
17.	*Non est sine culpa, qui rei quae ad se non pertinet, se immiscet* (19)	[99]	–
18.	*Non praestat impedimentum, quod de iure non sortitur effectum*	[21]	–
19.	*Nullus ex consilio dummodo fraudulentum non fuerit, obligatur* (62)	[1]	[2][c]
20.	*Pluralis locutio duorum numero est contenta* (40)	[79]	[86]
21.	*Possessor male fidei ullo tempore non prescribit* (2)	[40]	[45]
22.	*Pro possessore habetur, qui dolo desivit possidere* (36) [cf. D.50.17.128]	[40]	[45]
23.	*Quod omnes tangit debet ab omnibus approbari* (29)[d]	[1]	[1]
24.	*Quod semel placuit amplius disciplire non potest* (21)	[1]	[1]
25.	*Scienti et non facienti non est iniuria neque dolus* (27)[e]	[28]	[32]
26.	*Semel malus semper presumitur esse malus* (8)	[39]	[44]
27.	*Successorum naturam sequi congruit principalis* (42)[f]	[40]	[45]

c It should be in Article 1.

d Wacław Uruszczak, "Reguła Quod omnes tangit debet ab omnibus approbari dawnego prawa kanonicznego i jej znaczenie" [The Maxim Quod omnes tangit debet ab omnibus approbari in the Old Xanon Law ant its Meaning], in: *Servabo legem Tuam in toto corde meo. Księga pamiątkowa dedykowana Księdzu Profesorowi Józefowi Krzywdzie CM, Dyrektorowi Instytutu Prawa Kanonicznego UPJPII z okazji 70. rocznicy urodzin* [*Servabo legem Tuam in toto corde meo*. A Festschrift in Honour of Professor Józef Krzywda CM, Manager of the Canon Law Institute of Pontifical University of John Paul II, on His 70th Birthday], eds. Arkadiusz Zakręta CM, Andrzej Sosnowski CR (Kraków, 2013), pp. 545–559. The article is reprinted in: Wacław Uruszczak, *Opera historico-iuridica selecta*. On legislative assemblies, see Krystyna Kamińska, "Communitas civium w miastach polskich rządzących się prawem magdeburskim", *Acta Universitatis Nicolai Copernici. Prawo* 30 (1990), 25–37; Maciej Mikuła, *Prawodawstwo króla i sejmu dla małopolskich miast królewskich (1386–1572). Studium z dziejów rządów prawa w Polsce* [Royal and Parliamentary Legislation for the Royal Towns of Małopolska (1386–1572): A Study in the History of the Rule of Law in Poland] (Kraków, 2014), pp. 208–215.

e In *Liber Sextus*: *Scienti et consentienti non fit iniuria neque dolus.*

f In *Liber Sextus*: *Accessorium naturam sequi congruit principalis.*

In round brackets the number of the *regula* in the standard version of *Regularum iuris* appended to Boniface VIII's *Liber sextus*.

Table 25 is an expanded version of a table of *regulae iuris* in my article "Was Canon Law in Use in Municipal Courts in Late-Medieval Poland?"

On the whole, the *regulae* were adopted by the authors of the manuscripts to reinforce provisions concerning urban legislation, private law, and procedural and criminal law. Let us turn to a few examples of their application.[53] The maxim *Quod omnes tangit* (No. 23 above) is applied to urban by-laws, which, since they concern all, have to be approved by all. Once passed, they must not be changed, nor can those who approved them say that they are not bound them (No. 4 and No. 24). The law must not be altered to serve a malicious intent of doing harm to any particular person (No. 13). Statutes that are adopted fraudulently are invalid (No. 19). The maxim *Nullus ex consilio dummodo fraudulentum non fuerit, obligatur* appears next to a stipulative statement, characteristic of Konrad of Sandomierz's translation, that urban statutes are binding as long as they conform to God's law. It is doubtlessly a good match.

A number of maxims were added to Article 40, which is concerned with disputed inheritance. According to the Magdeburg Law, if somebody can prove he has held a disputed property in peaceable possession for a year and a day, the court should rule in his favour. This provision is complemented with a pair of maxims – one stating that only a possessor in bad faith cannot benefit from the limitation (prescription) period (No. 21), and the other insisting that an unlawful acquisition will not be made legal by the passage of time (No. 15). Furthermore, the unlawful deprivation of possession was not effective (No. 22). The maxim *Ius naturale ante omnia obtinet privatum* (No. 12) complements that part of the provision which insists that *cum inpossibile sit aliquem de naturali porcione defraudari*.[54] Of the three maxims at Article 79, only one is directly relevant to its interpretation: *Pluralis locucio duorum numero est contenta* – any plural reference includes two (No. 20). Article 79 deals with proof in action for the recovery of debt in which the plaintiff was expected to produce witnesses, the (minimum) number of which is not specified: *Si vir conqueritur super alterum pro suo debito cum testibus, hoc bene potest optinere cum viris fidedignis*. In this case, the *regula* provides the necessary clarification – two are enough. What the other two maxims (Nos. 1 and 6) add to the meaning of Article 79 is hard to make out.

The offence of insulting a member of the jury is addressed in Article 22. Here, too, of the three *regulae*, two (Nos. 3 and 14) are only loosely connected with the subject, even if they are not quite irrelevant. However, the remaining one – *Ad facinus duplex non sufficit ultio simplex* (i.e. for double crime, a single penalty is not enough) – is crucial for sentencing a defendant charged with

53 For an in-depth analysis, see *ibidem*.

54 Cf. Appendix 2, No. 91.

a qualified offence (contempt of the authority represented by the juryman). Article 39 is concerned with the punishment of theft. In general, the penalties for theft depend on the value of stolen goods. For stealing goods worth less than three shillings, the culprit faced punishment in skin and hair (branding); stealing anything worth more than that that amount was punishable by death (hanging).[55] In this context, the maxim *Semel malus semper presumitur esse malus* (i.e. who does wrong once is presumed to be a wrongdoer always) reads like an instruction on how to treat repeat offenders.

In general, from the cases discussed above, we get a sense of an intelligent mind who set himself the task of matching the universal and rather abstract *regulae iuris* with the detailed, narrowly focused regulations of the *Weichbild*, even if occasionally the connection between the two is not obvious. These commentators most likely gained their legal expertise at an ecclesiastical court and/or had an academic background. Certainly, their idea of expanding the gloss represents a new trend in the legal culture of late-medieval Poland.[56] The author of MS BN 12607 was also familiar with the *regulae* and decided to add one to Article 6 in his text: *Summa iuris actus legit cum condicione non recipiunt neque diem*, a slightly altered version of Rule No. 1 from Table 25.

5 Glosses in Printed Copies of Jan Łaski's *Statutes*: Persistence of the *Weichbild*'s Medieval Conventions

5.1 *Copies with Few or No Annotations*

A number of copies of Łaski's *Statutes* examined in the course of this project do not contain a glossed *Weichbild* (or, in some cases, a glossed *Sachsenspiegel*). The gloss is missing in printed copies of the *Statutes* retained in the Jagiellonian Library,[57] the National Library in Warsaw,[58] the University of Wrocław Library,[59] the National Museum in Cracow,[60] and the Ossoliński National Institute.[61] In the copy held by the University of Warsaw Library,

55 Cf. Appendix 2, No. 84, 85 and 86.

56 Uruszczak, "*Regulae Iuris* w kulturze", p. 79.

57 Shelfmark St. Dr. Cim. 8008, a copy dated 1638, according to S. Wieczorkowski's catalogue; according to another provenance note, it belonged to Collegium Maioris of the University of Cracow. It is heavily annotated (especially the *Summa legum* by Raymundus Parthenopaeus), but it does not comprise the source texts German law. St. Dr. Cim. 8009: *Summa legum* only; St. Dr. Cim. 51 one folium (print).

58 Stare druki (Early Printed Books): Shelfmarks No. 88, 211, 335, 350 and 735.

59 University of Wrocław Library, Shelfmark St. Dr. 401097.

60 National Museum in Cracow, Shelfmark MNK VIII–XVI.134.

61 Ossoliński National Institute, Shelfmark XVI.F.4654.

the *Weichbild* has no gloss, but the articles of the *Sachsenspiegel* have been given numbers following the scheme in Mikołaj Jaskier's edition and complemented with a gloss of six short commentaries in the same hand.[62] One marginal gloss (*De proprietate*) appears in the *Sachsenspiegel* in one of the copies held in the Ossoliński National Institute,[63] and two brief glosses are in one of the copies in the National Library.[64] In the codex which used to belong to Antoni Zygmunt Helcel, the *Weichbild* is signposted with a few manicules at the articles on guardianship and deposit. More signs of this kind can be found in the *Sachsenspiegel*, and there is a longer gloss at the provision concerning the election of jurors according to the Lübeck Law. More annotations, some of them Polish (e.g. the direction *czÿtaÿ to* 'read this') appear next to the text of *Summa legum* by Raymundus Parthenopaeus. The glosses in that copy of the *Statutes* are in at least two hands.[65] The codex which is now retained by the Juliusz Słowacki Public Library at Tarnów contains two annotations. One is attached to the article on the *hergewet* in the *Weichbild*; the other, added to the *Sachsenspiegel*, is unrelated to the *Weichbild*. The former is a mere heading providing information on the subject of the article. The latter is a reader's comment on the imprecise preface to the article (the rubric says that it is *De armis bellicis, ad quem devoluntur per successionem. Item de tutore puerorum*, whereas it deals as well with the *gerada*).[66] The copy retained in The Princes Czartoryski Library in Cracow had had a number of blank pages that were filled with excerpts from the land law and a list of Poland's senatorial offices.[67] Its *Weichbild* contains a number of glosses which are no more than headings and a pair of cross-references between Articles 79 and 105, which deal with the payment of debts of a deceased relative. Moreover, someone has written on one of the blank pages a Magdeburg *ortyl* addressed to the Cracow City Council entitled *Questiones de Cracovia in Meydburg pro iure misse questio prima*.

5.2 *The* Weichbild*'s Adaptation to Polish Realities (Jagiellonian Library, St. Dr. Cim. 8002–8003)*

Probably soon after its publication, the commentator of this copy of the *Statutes* (Jagiellonian Library, St. Dr. Cim. 8002–8003) supplemented the text

62 Shelfmark BUW Sd.612.523. Annotations: Book I, art. 6, 14, 25, 64; Book II, art. 44 i 62.

63 Shelfmark XVI.F.4320, f. 202v.

64 Shelfmark SD XVI.F.337, Article 38: *Quis potest esse testis* (f. 181v), and also an entry on f. 182. The annotations to articles of the *Sachsenspiegel* – f. 200 (the Polish gloss), 225, 232, and 242.

65 Jagiellonian Library St. Dr. Cim. 8470.

66 Juliusz Słowacki Public Library at Tarnów, Shelfmark SD 173.

67 Princes Czartoryski Library in Cracow, Shelfmark 30 III Cim.

with a number of annotations so that its Polish readers would find it easier to use. His glosses provide detailed information about the content of individual articles. Therefore, for instance, a marginal gloss to Article 1 about aldermen and jurors describes the competences of the aldermen, including the right to convene an assembly of burghers (*consulum est facere conventum sive gromode vulgariter*),[68] and mentions the penalties for aldermen who fail to turn up. One of the practical problems faced by the glossator was the adaptation of the offices mentioned in the *Weichbild* to Polish realities. In his comment on Article 5, which mentions the courts of the *Castellan*, the *Burggraf*, and the *Schultheiß* (*sołtys*, *scultetus*), he explains that those terms refer to the owner of the domain, the *wójt* (*advocatus*), and *podwójci* (*vice-advocatus*), respectively; he also adds a cross-reference to the *Constitution of Courts* [*Rechtsbuch von der Gerichtsverfassung*] on f. 196. Consequently, the gloss to Article 6, which sets the time for the three annual rounds of the court called by the *Schultheiß/sołtys*, explains that the regulation refers to the *wójt*'s court. A brief note next to Article 9 provides information about its content (*ius hospitum*). In Article 19 (in the *Statutes* numbering) on deathbed gifts and in Articles 56 and 67 on the duties of guardians, the commentator merely underlined the key phrases in the text of the provisions.[69]

5.3 *References and Digests (Partly Post-1535) (Jagiellonian Library, St. Dr. Cim. 8004–8005)*

The most profusely annotated *Weichbild* is part of a copy of the *Statutes* owned in 1584 by the Cracow captain (*podstarości*, *vice-capitaneus*) Józef Kowalowski.[70] Another characteristic of this book is the complete lack of annotations in the texts of the land law, a notable contrast to the heavily glossed *Weichbild*, *Sachsenspiegel*, and Master Raymundus' *Summa legum*. The commentaries are the work of various hands, although most of the annotations to the *Weichbild* and the *Summa legum*, as well as the gloss of the *Sachsenspiegel*, is definitely in one hand (Commentator A). The same glossator also marked

68 The Polish term *gromada* (here: assembly) is used in the same place in the text by the commentator of the Działyńscy Codex I.

69 Similar annotations can be found in two articles of the *Sachsenspiegel*, f. 199v and f. 214v.

70 Józef Kowalowski held a number of offices, including the deputy *starost* of Biecz, deputy *starost* of Cracow, and deputy judge of the Cracow land court. See Irena Kaniewska, "Kowalowski Józef", in: *Polski Słownik Biograficzny* [Dictionary of Polish Biography], 14 (Wrocław, 1968–1969), p. 532. The following provenance entry dated 1656 names Marcin Olbrychtowic as owner of this book. See Marian Malicki, Ewa Zwinogrodzka, eds., Marian Malicki, Małgorzata Gołuszka, Wanda Ptak-Korbiel, Zofia Wawrykiewicz, Ewa Zwinogrodzka, coop., *Katalog poloników XVI wieku Biblioteki Jagiellońskiej* [Catalogue of *Polonica* from 16th Century in Jagiellonian Library], 1: A–Ł (Kraków, 1992), p. 426.

articles concerned with usucaption and disinheritance in the digest to the *Summa legum*, whereas the annotations to digests of source texts of municipal law are in two other hands. Entries in hand A are concentrated around the articles at the beginning of *Weichbild*, and there are few of them elsewhere. In some cases, Commentator A tries to draw a general conclusion from a rather specific regulation.[71] Two articles are glossed with cautionary notes that the regulations contained in them were condemned by Pope Gregory XI in his *Articuli reprobati*;[72] some articles are cross-referenced or supplemented with references to Master Raymundus' *Summa legum*.[73] Most often, however, the annotations merely highlighted the most important points of an article,[74] either by underlining the key phrases in the main text or copying them in the margin.[75] The annotations in hand B are intended to help the reader find his way through pages crammed tight with print: they are merely headline glosses with information about the subject of the adjacent passage (e.g. *testes, qui non possunt fieri* next to the Article 'De vulnerante aliquem' [Art. 38 in the *Statutes* numbering]).

The text of a reference at Article 2, *Spe. Sax. Juri municip[al]ii Art. 44 et 19*, makes it possible to date the commentary in hand A. The reference itself is misleading (probably a scribal error), for the relevant Articles 44 and 19 the concerning measures and weights were to be found in the *Weichbild* rather than the *Sachsenspiegel*. The commentator seems to have noticed this, but what makes this slip all the more puzzling is the fact that the numbers fit the

71 For example, *Probus homo propior evadere* (Article 8 'Accusatus de conflicto', f. CLXXVIII); *Cause sine mora iudicandi hospiti* (Article 9 'De iudicio', f. CLXXVIII); *Prescriptio possessionis Annus et dies* (Article 17 'De re possessa', f. CLXXIX); *Equalis divisio fratribus cum sororibus* (Article 20 'De hereditate', f. CLXXIX); and *Tres solidi sex grossos valent* (Article 46 'De fure diei et noctis', f. CLXXXII verso).

72 The note about Gregory XI's *Articuli reprobati*: *Articulus iste est reprobatus Sp. Sax Art. LII lib primo* is inscribed next to Article 15 'De pueris', f. CLXXIX) and his *Reprobatus Articulus Spe Sax lib I Ar. LII* next to Article 19 'De legationibus', f. CLXXIX).

73 *Spe. Sax. Juri municipii Art. 44 et 19* (Article 2 'De penesticis', f. CLXXVII recto); *Rajmundus fol. 23, Exhereditatio Spec Sax lib I Ar. 17 At. 14*.

74 For example, *Divisio scabinorum cum consulibus eligendi*; *Rota iuramentum scabinorum*; *Pena 36 solidi*; *Consulum potestas iudicandi*; *Inobediens cum nemine neglexerit penam deme[retur]* (Article 1 'De electione', f. CLCCVI verso and CLXXVII recto); *Penestici dicuntur*; *De venditore*; *Pena eorum si modum excesserit* (Article 2 'De penesticis', f. CLXXVII recto); *Testimonium vulnerorum*; *Evictio*; *Solidorum computacio*; *In defectu evictori*; *Recompensa in emenda iudici* (Article 7 'De iudicio', f. CLXXVII verso and CLXXVIII); *Contumatio actori racione vulnerum* (Article 10 'De pernocrato vulnere'); *Probatio possessionis* (Article 18 'De re possessa', f. CLXXIX).

75 'Prologus in ius Maydemburgense', i.e. ten copied extracts (f. CLXXVI recto i verso); *Pro vulnere manum, pro homicidio collum* (Article 7 'De iudicio', f. CLXXVII verso).

Weichbild in Mikołaj Jaskier's *Ius Municipale* of 1535 (Article 19 on f. 19r and 19v and Article 44 on f. 38v and ff.).

5.4 *A Glossary of Legal Terms (Post-1531) (National Library in Warsaw, Shelfmark SD 57)*

Apart from four annotations with digests of the provisions of Articles 9 (status of guests), 13 (lien), 14 (legal status of widows), and 20 (payment of debt), the copy of the *Statutes* held in the National Library contains a Latin-Polish glossary of the legal terms of Magdeburg Law. It is divided into two parts, written on two folia – one added to the digest of *Ius municipale Magdeburgense* and *Speculum Saxonum*, and the other to the Lübeck Law. The list of entries is fully compatible with *Vocabula Iuris Maydemburgensis* from Johannes Cervus Tucholiensis' *Farrago actionum civilium*, published in 1531.[76]

5.5 *German, Latin, and Polish Glosses (Partly Post-1559; Jagiellonian Library, St. Dr. Cim. 8006–8007)*

In another copy of the *Statutes* in the Jagiellonian Library, the annotations to the *Sachsenspiegel* are more than twice as numerous (33) as those added to the *Weichbild* (15). Only a handful of glosses can be found in the margins of the Lübeck Law and *Lehnrecht*, and there are very few of them on the pages of Master Raymundus' *Summa legum* (f. XIII). Although they are in various hands, a great majority of the annotations can be attributed to just two hands. The German glosses are in hand A. They accompany the *Sachsenspiegel* and the Lübeck Law; their author, not unlike the Latin glossator, is convinced of the importance of a 'bemerkig' (i.e. note, observation). The Latin glosses are in hand B. They can be found in the *Weichbild* and other key texts of German law in Łaski's collection. Their sole function is usually to draw attention to a given provision and its importance (that signalling function seems to exhaust the meaning of the glossator's favourite words, *nota* and *notandum*). Only two entries are of interest. One, at Article 2, introduces a Polish equivalent of 'revenditor' in '*Penesticus id est revenditor, przekopien*' (f. CLXXVII), and the other, at Article 57, 'De iudicio apprehensi', refers the reader to what the *Sachsenspiegel* has to say about *manifestum factum* (i.e. a situation when the offender is caught red-handed [*super libro 2 folio CCXX*]). Meanwhile, a reference placed next to the provision 'De facto manifesto' in the *Sachsenspiegel* (f. CCXX verso) points back to the *Weichbild*, namely, *Res manifesta vide supra primo libro folio CLXXXIIII*. Commentator B has made only a few annotations to the Lübeck

76 Johannes Cervus Tucholiensis, *Farrago actionum civilium Iuris Maydeburgensis* (Cracoviae, 1531), f. 50v–59r. The user of the copy held in the Kórnik Library (Shelfmark Cim.o.24) expanded the vocabulary list by adding 17 more entries (edition 1535, 110r).

Law, including this one, about the election of aldermen, *Notandum. Quod duo ex uno artifico non eliguntur ad consulatum* (f. CCXLIIII verso). He does not say much, yet his selection of themes to be marked as noteworthy seems to indicate a growing interest in institutional norms and legal order.

For annotations of more substantial length, we must go to the volume's originally blank pages and three other places in the *Sachsenspiegel*, two at the beginning of the *Landrecht*[77] and one in the *Lehnrecht*.[78] They were inscribed in the second half of the 16th century, after 1559, as they include extracts from Bartłomiej Groicki's *Porządek sądów i spraw miejskich prawa majdeburskiego w Koronie Polskiej* [The Constitution of Courts and Urban Matters According to Magdeburg Law in the Kingdom of Poland], published that year. A long note on blank pages 287r[79] and 287v. is a farrago of themes ranging from inheritance debts, the abolition of the law banning the surviving spouse (in the absence of children) from becoming heir to the deceased's estate,[80] the definition of

77 1) Sequitur de Jure Provinciali. Privinciale Jus. Które liud się jednego Króletwa albo krainy miendzi zsobą trzymacz postanowili, jako jest prawo ziemskie Polskie stanowi riczerskiemu dane, jako też jest prawo ziemskie saskie, które zowam Speculum Saxonum (f. CXCVIII). ["The land law is that which the people of a Kingdom or a land have decided to hold on to in common: Polish land law has been given to the nobility, and there is also Saxon land law, also known as *Speculum Saxonum*".]. 2) *Jus Saxonum Provinciale Prawo Ziemskie Saskie Które zowyą Speculum Saxonum* (f. CXCVIII verso).

78 Feudale ius quia. Ius Feudale alias miejskie zakupne prawo, które łacinnicy zowią feudale do rycerskiemu człowiekowi za wojenną służbę bywa dane jakie imienie czasem do żywota, czasem też do potomków tegoż pokolenia, tym sposobem, aby w łączność tego imienia została przy pierwszym własnym panie, a użytkowanie tylko jest przy tym, któremi jest dany, aby stamtąd czynił jaką posługę krolie swego albo jakiemu państwo albo panu onego imienia. (f. CCXLV verso). ["*Ius feudale*, or urban acquired rights, which the clerks call *feudale* because it is held with a fee granted to a knight for his military service; its tenure either expires with the tenant's death or is inherited by his offspring in such a way that the ownership continues to be attached to the original overlord, while possession and use is passed on jointly with the obligation to perform knight-service to the king, the state, and the owner of the fee".] This *glossa* is similar to the fragments in Bartłomiej Groicki and Paweł Szczerbic's works: Bartłomiej Groicki, *Porządek sądów i spraw miejskich prawa majdeburskiego w Koronie Polskiej* [The Constitution of Courts and Urban Matters According to Magdeburg Law in the Kingdom of Poland], (Biblioteka Dawnych Polskich Pisarzy-Prawników) 1, ed. Karol Koranyi (Warszawa, 1953), p. 5; *SzIM* Article 1 No. 17.

79 There, of course, with another hand, a provenance note – Michał, Kazimierz i Prochna Czepielowscy, 22 I 1650. There, too, a provenance note, in a different hand to be sure, dated 22 January 1659, naming Michał, Kazimierz, and Prochna Czepielowscy as owners of this book.

80 Dziedziców kiedy nie masz, mąsz zonam po sobie spa[dek] biorą, mimo skarb królewski. ["If there are no heirs, the estate falls to the surviving spouse, save the exchequer's portion".]

wergild,[81] the definition of *szeląg* (*shilling*),[82] a diagram showing the branches of the law (copied from Groicki's *Constitution*),[83] and a description of the principles of law and justice (*praecepta iuris*), also copied from Groicki's treatise.[84]

The main conclusion from the analysis of a number of the surviving copies Łaski's *Statutes* (1506) is that the key texts of the Saxon-Magdeburg Law continued to be read and used after 1535, that is, after the publication of a new, revised edition of those texts by Mikołaj Jaskier. The users of the *Statutes* continued to annotate them in the vein of medieval glossators. The new additions came primarily from the works of Johannes Cervus of Tuchola and Bartłomiej Groicki, while Jaskier's edition of the *Weichbild* became the new standard text of that old source. Interestingly, in some of the copies of the *Statues*, the annotations are inscribed exclusively in the margins of the key texts of municipal law and Master Raymundus' *Summa legum*. In other copies, the gloss is concentrated exclusively around key texts of land law or on the initial leaves of a manuscript.[85] This distribution of the supplementary material is undoubtedly

81 Wergeld co jest. Cały wergeld czyni dwadzieścia złotych reńskich w monecie, które przegodzą ku wadzę dwój, jest to złotych polskich na monetę. (f. 287). ["What is wergild. The whole wergild amounts to twenty Rhinish złotys in coins, or the equivalent of its weight, twice as many Polish złotys for coin".]

82 Solidus co jest. Szelągów trzydzieści wodlia rachunku czynią groszy 20. Szelągów sześćdziesiąt czynią groszy sterdzieści. Wina burgrabska szelągów ośm czynią groszy pięć. Szeląg wina wójtowska. (f. 287) ["What is a solidus. Thirty shillings are made up of 20 groszy. Sixty shillings are made up of 40 groszy. The Burgraf's fine of eight shillings equals five groszy. The wójt's fine is one shilling".]

83 Ius est aequm et iniqui cognitio. Summa wszytkich praw wedle rozdziału wyżej opisanego w porządku prawnym. ["The summa of all laws according to the chapter described above in the order of the law".] [chart: division of law into God, natural and human, with further division of human law into spiritual and secular, dividing into earthly, war, purchasing and urban] (Groicki, *Porządek*, p. 7).

84 Iuris descriptio. Prawo tedy jest nauka, która widzie ku wszelkiej poczciwości, a odwodzi od każdej nieprawości, aby przez taką naukę i skutek jej zuchwalstwo ludzi hamowane było, a między dobremi niewinność w bezpieczeństwie trwała. Summa praw wszytkich. Tej nauki ta summa jest, aby każdy poczciwie żył, bliźniego nie obrażał, każdemu co jest jego dał. Albo prawo tak się inszym sposobem opisuje: jest postanowienie sprawiedliwości od zwierzchniego pana, na poddanie swoje, ku chwale Bożej, ku poczciwemu życiu, a zachowaniu pokoju pospolitego. ["The law is therefore a knowledge which leads to all kinds of respectability and dissuades from every dishonesty so that by that science and its effects people's presumption was tempered and innocence could safely flourish among the good. The summa of all laws. The sum of all this knowledge [allows] everybody to live honestly, to avoid offending his neighbor and to give everyone else his due. Or, there is a different way of describing what law is: it is a command of justice from the overlord, given to those who submit, for the greater glory of God, to achieve an honest life and for the keeping of the peace".] (Groicki, *Porządek*, p. 2).

85 Biblioteka Narodowa, stare druki Shelfmark No. 88, 211, 335, 350 and 735.

connected with the functioning and the uses of Łaski's book. Mikołaj Jaskier's *Ius Municipale* were published almost 30 years after the *Statutes*, a sufficiently length time for the text of the latter to be widely adopted, and yet the old texts were not thrown out (cf. Chapter 3, Section 6.). Jaskier's new edition gained ground fast, and its impact can be felt in the treatises on municipal law written by Johannes Cervus of Tuchola and Jan Kirstein Cerasinus.[86] The reception of Jaskier's updated version in the circles of legal practitioners was greatly accelerated after 1559, that is, the publication of its Polish translation by Bartłomiej Groicki.

King Zygmunt I wanted Jaskier's work to become the sole official book of the Saxon-Magdeburg Law, but, as might be expected, old habits were not to be stamped out overnight.[87] Lawyers continued to make glosses in the margins of their copies of the *Statutes* after 1539 – and even after 1559. The provisions of urban law from Łaski's *Commune incliti* were read and commented on long after the publication of Jaskier's *Ius Municipalis* in 1535.[88]

6 Conclusions

Habent sua fata leges – this paraphrase of a well-known maxim is in no way an inadequate description of the history of the Latin texts of the *Weichbild*. Copyists and users not only made alterations in its main text, but also supplemented it with a variety of subsidiary annotations, marks, and glosses, both

---

86 Karol Koranyi, "Johannes Cervus Tucholiensis i jego dzieła (z dziejów praw obcych i literatury prawniczej w Polsce)" [Johannes Cervus Tucholiensis and His Work (Chapters from the History of Foreign Laws and Legal Literature in Poland)], *Przewodnik Historyczno-Prawny* 1 (1930), pp. 22 and 28; Bojarski, *Jan Jelonek Cervus z Tucholi*, p. 64; Lesław Pauli, *Jan Kirstein Cerasinus (1507–1561). Krakowski prawnik doby Odrodzenia. Studium z dziejów praw obcych i literatury prawniczej w Polsce* [Jan Kirstein Cerasinus (1507–1561): A Cracow Jurist of the Renaissance. A Study in the History of Foreign Laws and Legal Literature in Poland] (Kraków, 1961), pp. 6–7; Lesław Pauli, "Die polnische Literatur des Magdeburger Rechts im 16. Jahrhundert", in: *Studien zur Geschichte des sächsich-magdeburgischen Rechts in Deutschland und Polen*, eds. Dietmar Willoweit and Winfried Schich, Rechtshistorische Reihe 10 (Frankfurt am Main, 1980), pp. 150–157.

87 Cf. "Law Books During the Transition from Late-Medieval to Early-Modern Legal Scholarship", in: *The Formation and Transmission of Western Legal Culture. 150 Books that Made the Law in the Age of Printing*, Serge Dauchy, Georges Martyn, Anthony Musson, Heikki Pihlajamäki, Alain Wijffels, eds., coop. Naoko Seriu (Studies in the History of Law and Justice) 7, series eds. Georges Martyn, Mortimer Sellers (New York – Berlin – Heidelberg, 2016), p. 17.

88 Whether the inclusion of a glossed *Weichbild* and a glossed *Sachsenspiegel* was intended as a compensation for the exclusion of the *ortyle* is a point that still needs to be examined.

marginal and interlinear. They had different functions, yet the reasons for their presence were always pragmatic. Their authors used them to amend mistakes in the main text, set up cross-references within the text, and compile indices and digests. The sign of the pointing hand, or manicule, drew attention to regulations that were deemed more important than others. Various kinds of notes sought to help the reader gain a better understanding of the text. A careful analysis of the glosses in the Silesian-Małopolska compilation has shown that amendations and annotations were most common in the manuscripts of *versio Sandomiriensis*. These texts were also dotted with excerpts from the *versio Cracoviensis*, which superseded an earlier translation by Konrad of Sandomierz (the Działyńscy Codex I) and by pulling in numerous annexes, mostly *ortyle*, or judgments of the courts of Magdeburg Law. This was the formula of the Żegota Pauli's MS. Another type of supplement was a bilingual vocabulary list. To compile such a list, the scribes usually drew on a source like the glossary in MS Dział. I. This was replicated in the *Weichbild* of that manuscript and in Tomasz of Bydgoszcz's MS. The authors of those manuscripts also brought in *regulae iuris*, drawn from Boniface VIII's *Liber Sextus*, to balance the detailed and narrowly focused provisions of the Magdeburg Law with more general legal maxims. There are also manuscripts which have no glosses at all; we can only guess as to the reasons why they remained in that condition.

The Działyńscy Codex I and Tomasz of Bydgoszcz's MS (BN 3068) have a full range of supplements. In MS BN 3068, the *regulae iuris* appear both in the main text (in red ink) and in the margin. The latter are written in script which may well belong to a different hand. It is clear that they are written with a different type of utensil than the main text. A comparative analysis of the Polish terms and *regulae iuris* in both texts indicates that Tomasz of Bydgoszcz must have used the Działyńscy Codex I. This therefore makes it his third source, alongside Łaski's *Statutes* and a text close to the Baworowscy MS. The argument that Tomasz of Bydgoszcz relied on MS Dział. I is based on the following observations. The list of *regulae iuris* in the gloss of the Działyńscy Codex I is longer than the one in MS BN 3068. Tomasz copied the list, but left some maxims out. He also added to his manuscript a list of Latin legal terms with their Polish equivalents. The Polish terms come from the glossary *Vocabula iuris Meydeburgensis* in MS Dział. I, but the number of Polish words in BN 3068 is greater than in Tomasz's source. It looks as if after copying the words from the Działyńscy Codex I glossary, he decided to add some more himself. On one occasion, however, he took a word not from the *Vocabula* glossary, but directly from the Działyńscy Codex I gloss. The former lists the word *przegabanÿe*, whereas the gloss of MS Dział. I and MS BN 3068 have *nagabanÿe*.

The presence of regulations of the Chełmno Law in the Działyńscy Codex IV have been interpreted as an indication that the provenance of that manuscript must be connected with towns of Northern Poland, that is, the area where the Chełmno Law was common. However, manuscripts of Chełmno Law were also available in Cracow, and given the collation of the text of the Działyńscy Codex IV with the Wawel MS, the Cracow provenance of Dział. IV can no longer be ruled out.

In a number of cases, the collation of manuscripts led to the creation of miscellaneous codices like the Częstochowa MS, the Kielce MS, and the Leipzig MS. The *Weichbild* in Łaski's *Statutes* belongs to the category of complex compilations. Its main text had two parents, the Sandomierz version and the Cracow version; later, it grew, and shed, all kinds of annotations and supplements – rubrics, notes, indexes, digests, and vocabulary lists of legal terms. The identification of these annotations' and supplements' sources made it possible to conclude that glosses continued to be produced after 1535, and to a lesser extent even after 1559. In all, copies of Łaski's *Statutes* remained in use in urban legal practice even after the loss of its official status after the publication of a thoroughly new edition of the *Weichbild* and other sources of Magdeburg Law by Mikołaj Jaskier in 1535.

This analysis of the annotations and commentaries found in the margins of the *Weichbild* demonstrates that its use in legal practice was absolutely common. The text of the *Weichbild* was regularly analysed and annotated. Its readers compared their copies, marked out divergences, and inserted explanations, Polish equivalents, and excerpts from other normative acts. All that work could have no other aim than to help other members of the legal community to use their prime law book.

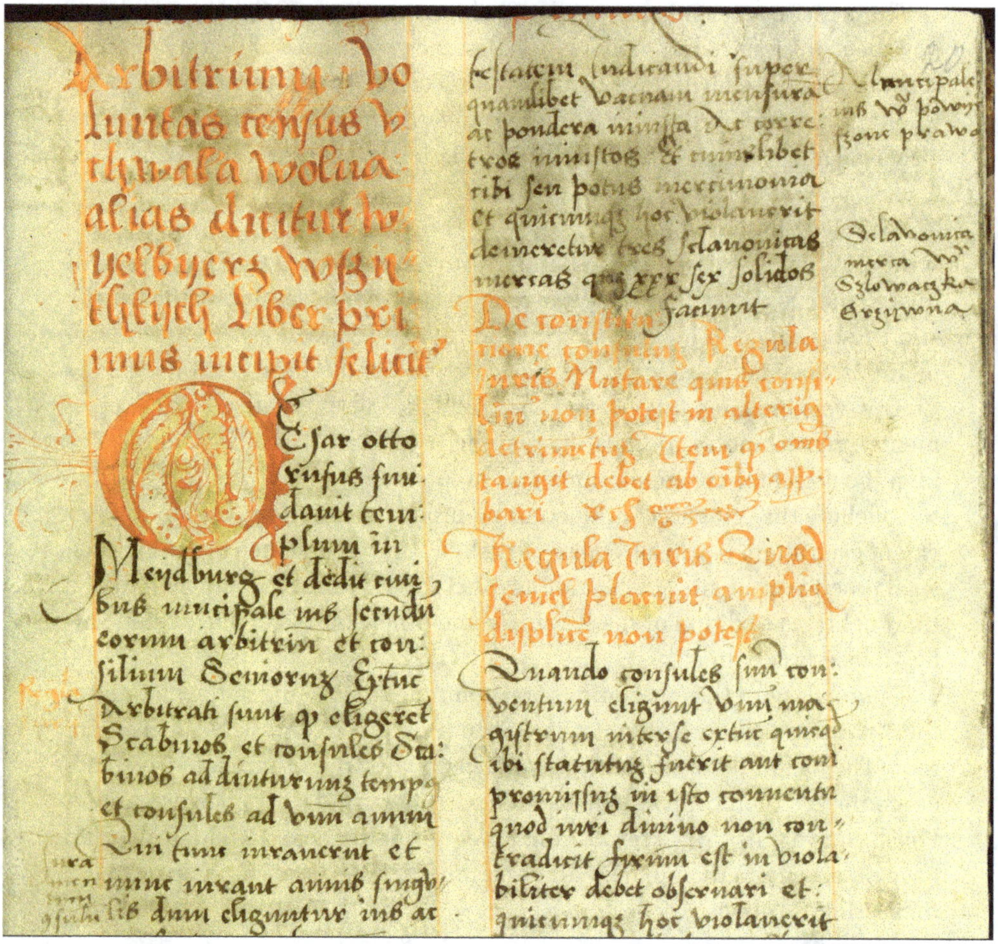

PHOTO 9 Tomasz of Bydgoszcz's manuscript, The National Library in Warsaw, Shelfmark 3068 III, f. 20r

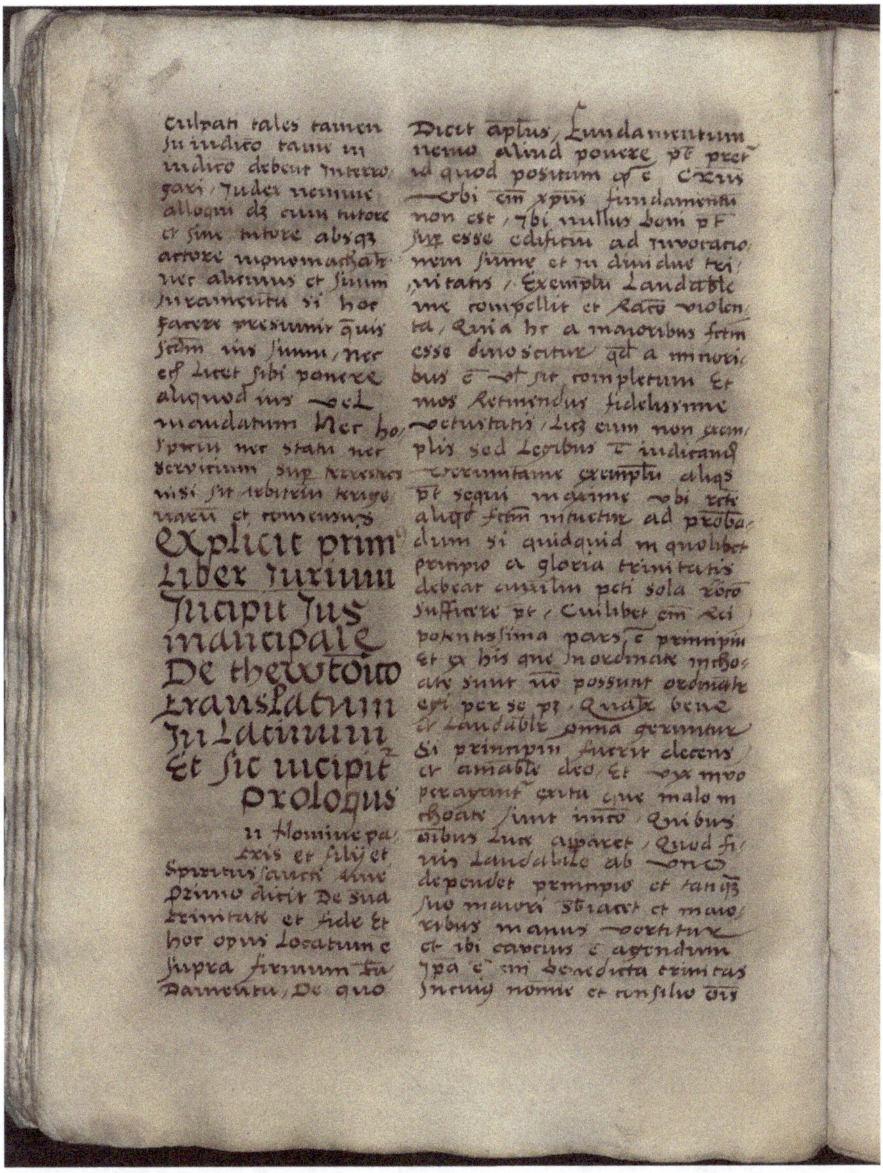

PHOTO 10 Marcin Zabowski's manuscript, The National Library in Warsaw, Shelfmark BOZ 90, f. 45v

Conclusions

The aim of this study of the history of the Magdeburg *Weichbild* in the medieval Kingdom of Poland was a thorough examination of the following issues:

1) The Introduction set the stage of the debate by focusing on the key issues of the functioning of the *Weichbild* in legal practice and the expanding range of its regulations. An examination of the sources at the point of its origin in Chapter 1 established the distinctly urban bias of the 'Polish' *Weichbild.*
2) Chapter 1 focuses on the extant Latin texts of the *Weichbild.* They outnumber by far the corresponding German texts, which indicates that the former were in much greater demand in the Kingdom of Poland.
3) Chapter 2 analyses at length the dynamics of the Latin text and its mutations. It also tries to establish the characteristic features of the Latin texts and classify them.
4) Chapter 2 notes the special role of Cracow in the history of municipal law in the Kingdom of Poland, too.
5) Chapter 3 argues that the evolution of the *Weichbild* in the Kingdom of Poland was the product of a process of adaptation of the Magdeburg Law to the needs of its users.
6) Chapter 4 shows that it is possible to detect lines and stages of historical development in a seemingly irregular proliferation of the *Weichbild*'s texts and variations. The process began with a few German texts, which spawned a large number of Latin offshoots; it came to an end with an authorized print version, Jan Łaski's *Commune incliti.*
7) The use of the *Weichbild* in legal practice is documented by a vast number of entries in municipal court records and annotations in the margins of manuscripts and printed copies of *Commune incliti.*
8) The evolution of the *Weichbild* is closely connected with manuscript copying during which the text could be modified at any point. This phenomenon was inseparable from medieval legal culture. After the invention of print, it became possible to equip all users with a uniform text and thus safeguard the law's integrity and reliability. However, the transition to the new system took time.

1 The Significance *Weichbild* among Other Sources of the Saxon-Magdeburg Law

Thus far, there have been several attempts to assess the importance of the *Weichbild*. After analysing the manuscripts of the Silesian-Małopolska compilation, Emil Kałużniacki came to the conclusion that *Ius municipale Magdeburgense* had acquired far greater importance than the *Speculum Saxonum*, which played only a secondary role.[1] Stanisław Kutrzeba found the *Weichbild* to be the most important legal act of Magdeburg Law. An unmistakable clue about the relative rank of the two legal codes is offered by the contemporary practice of giving the Magdeburg *Weichbild* pride of place in collections of urban law (e.g. in MSS of the Cracow version). It is no accident, either, that the Magdeburg judgments were, as a rule, attached to the *Weichbild* and not to the *Sachsenspiegel*. The *Weichbild*'s priority was preserved by Jan Łaski, who included it in Book One of his magisterial *Commune incliti*. Moreover, apart from volumes that comprise both law codes, there are a number of manuscripts which contain the *Weichbild*, but not the *Sachsenspiegel*. Clearly, in deciding to copy the *Weichbild*, and, secondly, the Magdeburg judgments, the medieval writers must have been guided by contemporary priorities.

Post-war historiography, however, became dominated by the view that in the field of judicial law, the *Weichbild* practically mirrored the provisions of the *Sachsenspiegel*, and its sole original feature was a handful of rules concerning the *Constitution of Courts*.[2] Such assessments were reinforced by the belief in the supreme authority of the *Sachsenspiegel*.[3] This claim was no doubt based on the opinions of 16th-century legal scholars. Thus, Mikołaj Jaskier in his gloss to Article 1 of *Ius municipale* writes that the *Weichbild* is founded on Saxon Law supplemented by the Magdeburg urban by-laws (Pol. *wilkierze*,

1 Emil Kałużniacki, "Die polnische Recension der Magdeburger Urtheile und die einschlägigen deutschen, lateinischen und czechischen Sammlungen", *Sitzungsberichte der phil.-hist. Classe der Kaierischer Akademie der Wissenschaften* 111 (1886), pp. 119–120, Note 5.

2 Witol Maisel, *Poznańskie prawo karne do końca XVI w* [Poznań Criminal Law until the 16th Century] (Poznań, 1963), p. 304; Zygfryd Rymaszewski, *Łacińskie teksty Landrechtu Zwierciadła Saskiego w Polsce. Versio Vratislaviensis, versio Sandomiriensis, Łaski* [Latin Texts of the Landrecht of the Sachsenspiegel in Poland: Versio Vratislaviensis, versio Sandomiriensis, Łaski] (Łódź, 1975), pp. 152–153; Zygfryd Rymaszewski, "Forum commune a forum liberum", *Studia z Dziejów Państwa i Prawa Polskiego* 2 (1995), 87; Krystyna Kamińska, *Lokacje miast na prawie magdeburskim na ziemiach polskich do 1370 r. Studium historyczno-prawne* [Incorporation of Towns under Magdeburg Law in Poland until 1370: A Study in the History of Law] (Toruń, 1990), p. 61.

3 Rymaszewski, *Łacińskie teksty Landrechtu Zwierciadła Saskiego w Polsce*, p. 6.

Ger. *Willküren*),[4] and Paweł Szczerbic offers the following explanation in his book (1581):

> Magdeburg urban law, called *Weichbild* by the Germans and *Ius municipale* by the Poles, is in fact the *wilkierz* of the town of Magdeburg, taken over from the *Speculum Saxonum*; it does not have all the things that can be found in *Speculum Saxonum*; it is shorter and easier to read. But there is nearly everything in the books of *Speculum Saxonum* which I have presented in Polish in alphabetical order.[5]

We must not forget, however, that these statements refer to the vulgate *Weichbild*, which differs from the Silesian-Małopolska compilation. The authors of the latter did not take over the provisions of the *Sachsenspiegel* directly (as was the case with the vulgate), but drew on the *Magdeburg's Legal Instruction for Wrocław* from 1261 and 1295, the *Magdeburg Bench Law* (*Das Magdeburger Schöffenrecht*), and to some extent on the *Constitution of Courts* (*Rechtsbuch von der Gerichtsverfassung*). That the case law of Magdeburg lay judges relied on the *Sachsenspiegel* was known to Konrad of Sandomierz and the author of the Wawel variant of the Cracow version of *Weichbild*, who removed or rearranged identical provisions that appeared in both the *Weichbild* and the *Sachsenspiegel*. Moreover, it is worth noting Paweł Szczerbic's admission that the legal text of the *Sachsenspiegel* had been remade before being incorporated into the *Weichbild*. In other words, the *Weichbild* is a collection of legal norms promulgated by the Magdeburg aldermen who looked to the Saxon Law for guidance, but who *adjusted* what they found there to the circumstances and realities of urban life.

For the editor of the modern edition of Paweł Szczerbic's treatise, Grzegorz M. Kowalski, the vulgate *Weichbild* and Szczerbic's *Sachsenspiegel* fit together well, as though they were parts of a whole.[6] This conciliatory appraisal seems correct not only with regard to the 16th century, but also to the era before the arrival of print, when the two law codes were as a matter of course copied

---

4 Maisel, *Poznańskie prawo karne*, p. 9.

5 *SzIM*, p. 5.

6 Grzegorz M. Kowalski, "*Speculum Saxonum* w przekładzie Pawła Szczerbica (Lwów 1581)" [*Speculum Saxonum* in Paweł Szczerbic's Translation (Lwów 1581)], in: Paweł Szczerbic, *Speculum Saxonum, albo prawo saskie i majdeburskie, porządkiem obiecadła z łacińskich i niemieckich egzemplarzów zebrane. A na polski język z pilnością i wiernie przełożone* [*Speculum Saxonum* or Saxon and Magdeburg Law, in Alphabetical Order, Collected from Latin and German Copies. A New and Meticulously Accurate Translation into Polish], 1, ed. Grzegorz M. Kowalski (Kraków, 2017), p. XIV.

into the same manuscript. The fact of their co-existence may justify the use of the term 'Saxon-Magdeburg Law' for the late Middle Ages, although their joint functioning in medieval legal practice requires further study.

2 The Demand for Latin Texts

Municipal authorities, magistrates' and Magdeburg Law courts, and monasteries were all interested in having the copies of the text of the Saxon-Magdeburg Law. The demand for the Magdeburg *Weichbild* existed not only in the biggest cities (like Cracow), but also in medium-sized towns, like Przemyśl, and even in small towns (like Słupca in Wielkopolska or Pleszew). In addition to numerous copies of the *Sachsenspiegel* in German and Latin, a significant number of collections of Magdeburg *ortyle* in German, Latin, and Polish was in use. The latter category may be extended to various compilations and municipal collections, like the *Poznań Book of the Magdeburg and Meissen Law*. Finally, a catalogue of medieval legal texts would be incomplete without mentioning the collections in use in Silesia and the towns of Pomerania that adopted the Chełmno Law (Kulmer Recht).

A characteristic feature of the Saxon-Magdeburg Law used in Poland after the reunification of the country in the early 14th century and in the Kingdom of the Jagiellons was the preference for the Latin text.[7] While the

7 Danuta Janicka, "Zur Topographie der Städte des Magdeburger Rechts in Polen: das Beispiel Kulm und Thorn", in: *Grundlagen für ein neues Europa. Das Magdeburger und Lübecker Recht in Spätmittelalter und Früher Neuzeit*, eds. Heiner Lück, Matthias Puhle, and Andreas Ranft, (Quellen und Forschungen zur Geschichte Sachsen-Anhalts) 6 (Köln – Weimar – Wien, 2009), p. 79, and Aleksander Zajda, "Deutsche Einflüße in der altpolnischen juristischen Terminologie", in: *Rechts- und Sprachtransfer in Mittel- und Osteuropa. Sachsenspiegel und Magdeburger Recht. Internationale und interdisziplinäre Konferenz in Leipzig vom 31. Oktober bis 2. November 2003*, eds Ernst Eichler, Heiner Lück, and Wieland Carls, (Ivs Saxonico-Maidebvrgense in Oriente) 1 (Berlin, 2009), p. 293. See also: Agnieszka Bartoszewicz, *Piśmienność mieszczańska w późnośredniowiecznej Polsce* [Burgher Writing in Late Medieval Poland] (Warszawa, 2012), esp. p. 277; Agnieszka Bartoszewicz, "Urban Literacy in Small Polish Towns and the Process of 'Modernisation' in the Latter Middle Ages", in: *Writing and the Administration of Medieval Towns: Medieval Urban Literacy I*, eds. Marco Mostert and Anna Adamska (Turnhout, 2014), pp. 159–164. Cf. also an account of the use of German in the Cracow Chancellery in the 14th Century in Anna Adamska, "Away with the Germans and Their Language?", in: *Uses of the Written Words in Medieval Towns. Medieval Urban Literacy II*, eds. Marco Mostert and Anna Adamska (Brepols: 2014), pp. 72, 74 and 84 (Here also, a comprehensive bibliography, including the follow-up to Bożena Wyrozumska's monograph *Kancelaria miasta Krakowa w średniowieczu* [Chancellery of the City of Cracow in the Middle Ages], Kraków 1995).

basic collections, like the *Posener Buch des Magdeburger und Meissner Rechts*, the *Magdeburg-Breslauer systematische Schöffenrecht* and the *Alter Kulm* (Old Chełmno Law), were in German, the texts of the Saxon-Magdenburg law employed in legal practice under the last Piasts and the Jagiellons were Latin translations. Their history starts with the translation of the *Sachsenspiegel* by Master Konrad at the end of the 13th century. It was followed by another translation by Konrad of Sandomierz in the first half of the 14th century. The latter, after a series of amendments, was soon refitted for a revised edition. Both Konrad of Sandomierz's Latin Magdeburg *Weichbild* and a second Latin translation of *Weichbild* known as the Cracow version were subsequently collated with the German text of the Wawel MS; the Cracow version was supplemented with an assortment of *ortyle*, too. *Nota bene*, the collections of *ortyle* were translated into Latin at least twice. The shorter version is based on the German text of MS BJ 170b, while the longer version contains a collection of *ortyle* similar to that in MS BJ 399 and the Pilzno collection. Translations into Polish also appeared, both more ample (*ortyle*) and shorter, with extracts from the *Weichbild* and the *Sachsenspiegel*.[8]

Rather than focusing on the systematization of the German text, the early compilers set their minds on translation. An indication of the great demand for the Latin text is the fact that the number of extant copies of the *Weichbild* in Latin vastly exceeds the number of the copies of the Silesian-Małopolska compilation in German.[9]

3 Versions and Variants of an Archetype Compilation

The first Latin translation of the *Weichbild* was made by Konrad of Sandomierz. On the basis of textual modifications concerning the number of compurgators as well as some minor omissions, it is possible to distinguish within the Sandomierz version a group of manuscripts that overlap with the Gniezno MS. The remaining manuscripts follow the original translation. While in some of them (Q II 157 (1), Q II 157 (2), and BN 12600), the influence of the Cracow version cannot be ruled out, only in the case of the St Petersburg MS (F 143) is that influence quite obvious. On the whole, the differences between the manuscripts of the *versio Sandomiriensis* are relatively small and justify

8 Józef Reczek and Wacław Twardzik, *Najstarsze staropolskie tłumaczenie ortyli magdeburskich* [*The Earliest Polish Translation of the Magdeburg ortyle*], 1–3 (Warszawa 1970); it includes a survey of the earlier editions.

9 Rymaszewski, *Łacińskie teksty Landrechtu Zwierciadła Saskiego w Polsce. Versio*, p. 5.

introducing further subdivisions (variants). The virtues of the *Weichbild* are perhaps best exemplified by the Przemyśl MS. Although the manuscript itself has an ecclesiastical provenance (the Chapter of the Przemyśl Cathedral), its redactors followed Konrad's translation and simultaneously adapted it to the local conditions.

The significance of the work done by Konrad of Sandomierz is hard to overestimate. He not only translated the *Weichbild* from the German, but also introduced a number of modifications into the text and supplemented it with some provisions from the *Sachsenspiegel*. He collated with great care the manuscripts for his translation job: he doubtless relied on more than a single text that happened to be at hand. It is also certain that his version of the *Weichbild* must have been completed before 1359.

The need to adjust the structure and the content of Konrad's Latin translation of the German texts of the *Weichbild* was most probably the reason why an anonymous writer started work on a new version some time before 1368. After all, even a glance at the *versio Sandomiriensis* showed that it differed considerably from the German *Weichbild* in the Silesian-Małopolska compilation (e.g. with regard to the scope of the articles, their sequence, and the wording of individual clauses). The author of the new version did not intend merely to verify and rearrange Konrad's text. He still relied on it in a broad sense, although he also reached out to other German texts, added his own translations of some passages, and altered the wording of many existing ones. Whereas some of the characteristic features of the *versio Sandomiriensis* were ironed out, the new version was no less distinct thanks to its own modifications of the German prototype. It must have been produced before 1368, because that is the date of St Petersburg MS (F 143), which is based on the Sandomierz version, although it exhibits traces of the Cracow version, as well. Originally, the new version did not include the text of judgments (*ortyle*), as shown by the Częstochowa MS, the Kielce MS, and the St Florian MS. The *ortyle* were added later; their appearance marks the textual evolution of both the Cracow and the Sandomierz versions. The amplification of the Cracow version by the inclusion of the assorted judgments greatly enhanced the normative value of the *Weichbild*. This was all the more important because the official *Commune incliti* did not include any other selection of *ortyle* apart from those that had already become part of the Cracow version. The complex history of the Polish *ius municipale* is further attested by the glosses produced by its users. Those annotations suggest that there had been some connection between the Działyńscy Codex I and the Tomasz of Bydgoszcz's MS (BN 3068). Moreover, the weight of all the notes, cross-references, short indices (*regesta*), glossaries of Polish legal terms, collections of *regulae iuris* intended as an aid in legal argument, and comparisons with similar provisions of the Chełmno Law indicates that the practitioners of that law were well versed in a variety of legal texts.

The text published by Jan Łaski was neither a new nor a more radically updated version of the *Weichbild*. He compiled the Sandomierz and the Cracow versions, but not in a mechanical way, as did the author of the St Florian MS (1453), who copied them in succession as Part I and Part II. In the *Statutes*, the two were carefully collated, and a number of articles redrawn. The final text was complete – it included the supplementary material from both versions and, at the same time, managed to preserve a character of its own. Occasionally, it carried over the text from both versions, especially to illuminate equivalent legal terms. Thus, the *Weichbild* of the *Statutes* may well represent the final stage of the evolution of a medieval legal text, whereas the Wawel variant, whose author excluded the provisions of the *Sachsenspiegel*, represents its narrowest realization.

A comparison of the Polish adaptations of the *Sachsenspiegel* and the *Weichbild* suggests that the scope of editorial interventions was much smaller in the case of the Magdeburg Law. This may result from the fact that the *Weichbild* was originally a collection of legal rules for towns. Its dependence on the provisions of the *Speculum Saxonum* was limited, even though the starting point (e.g. the formula of the court proceedings) was shared by both.[10] Consequently, the *Sachsenspiegel*, in so far as it was an embodiment of Saxon common law, was bound to undergo a more extensive adaptation when transplanted to an alien setting. It cannot be ruled out, however, that at least some points that represent the legacy of the *Sachsenspiegel* in the *Statutes* had made their way into the Polish tradition much earlier and were simply carried over by Łaski from a Polish source. Emil Kałużniacki, who conducted a study of the Sanok MS before it went missing, claimed that it was that very source from which the compiler of the *Commune incliti* took his basic texts of both the *Sachsenspiegel* and the *Weichbild*. Kałużniacki's description seems to indicate that the text of the Sanok MS, or at least its *Weichbild*, belongs to the Cracow version with the *ortyle* supplement. That group also includes the Baworowscy MS (BN 12607), the Opatów MS (Oss.), and the Żagań MS (II Q 4). It is possible that further

10 Clausdieter Schott, "Magdeburger Recht und Sachsenspiegel – Stadtrecht und Landrecht", in: *Das Burger Landrecht und sein rechtshistorisches Umfeld. Zur Geschichte der Landrechte und ihrer Symbolik im Mittelalter von Rügen bis Niederösterreich*, eds. Dieter Pötschke, Gerhard Lingelbach, Bernd Feicke, and Ulrich-Dieter Oppitz (collab.) (Berlin, 2014), p. 150. He claims – on the basis of a gloss to the vulgate *Weichbild* – that it had the role of *lex specialis* in regard of the *Sachsenspiegel* (*ibid.*, p. 152).

studies of the reception of the *Sachsenspiegel*, especially with regard to the bilingual manuscript BN 12607, would shed some light on this problem.

The *Weichbild* which was in use in Poland in the Middle Ages is referred to in this study as 'the Silesian-Małopolska compilation'. This is an umbrella term which encompasses both the German texts of the *Weichbild*, also known as the compilation bearing the name of Konrad of Opole, and various Latin texts, descended from German sources. The reasons for proposing the former designation are as follows: 1) Konrad of Opole was just a copyist of the German compilation and not its author; 2) the relevant German text can be traced back to Silesia – we are fairly certain of the Silesian provenance of Henryków MS (II F 8) which appears to be slightly closer to the original *Weichbild* than the Cracow MS (BN 169) signed by Konrad of Opole; and 3) the territorial scope of its early application as well as the territory where they were subjected to considerable transformations (i.e. a string of translations and the emergence of the Cracow version) was Małopolska (later also Wielkopolska). Even the *Weichbild* of the Działyńscy Codex IV (Dział. IV), with its references to Chełmno Law, originated almost certainly in Cracow, where its author had access not only to the German-language Wawel MS (its use is corroborated by the text of MS Dział. IV), but also to collections of the Chełmno Law.[11]

The subdivisions of the Latin texts of the *Weichbild* in the Silesian-Małopolska compilation are shown in Figure 4.

4 Cracow – Home of the Urban Law Reform

The significance of Cracow as the centre where the urban law was made and from which it spread across Southern Poland can be analysed on several levels. Most importantly, Cracow's incorporation charter was taken up as a model by newly founded towns all over Małopolska. This created a long-lasting bond, as the affiliated towns kept coming back to the Cracow Council for permission to copy the parent city's new laws, which had their source in the aldermen's *wilkierze* or royal privileges. The provincial guilds, keen to imitate the new regulations of Cracow counterparts, behaved in the same way.[12] New collections of Magdeburg *ortyle*, a significant number of which were handed

11 Excerpts representing that branch of the German town law can be found in Żegota Pauli's MS (BJ 4405), among others.

12 Maciej Mikuła, *Prawodawstwo króla i sejmu dla małopolskich miast królewskich (1386–1572). Studium z dziejów rządów prawa w Polsce* [Royal and Parliamentary Legislation for the Royal Towns of Małopolska (1386–1572): A Study in the History of the Rule of Law in Poland] (Kraków, 2014), pp. 278 and 280–282.

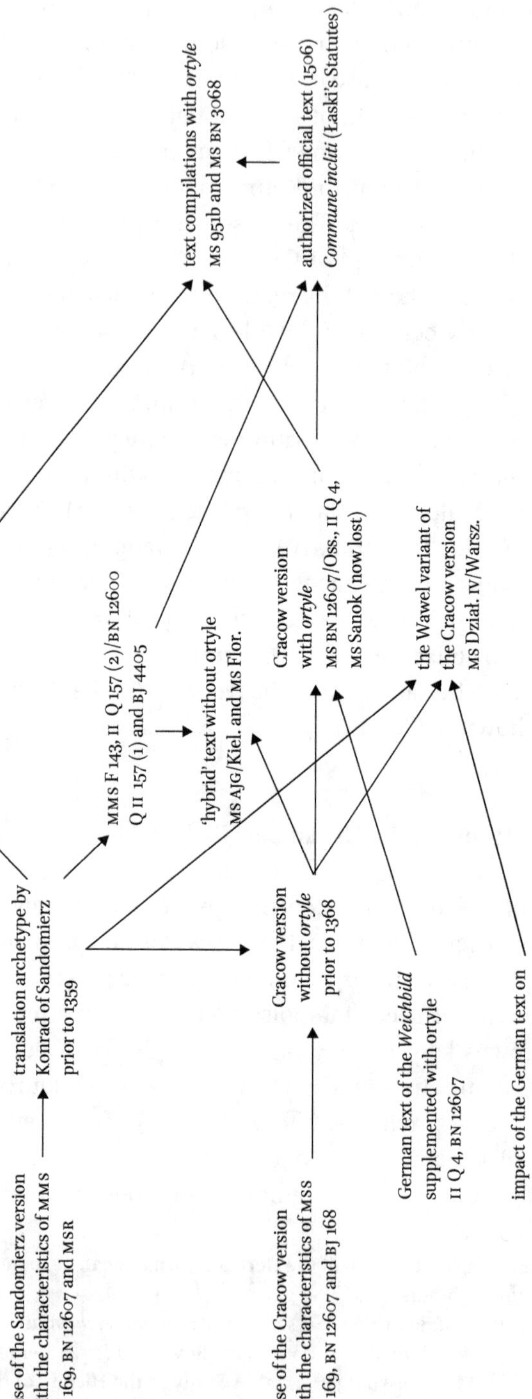

FIGURE 4 Evolution of the Latin texts of the Weichbild in the Silesian-Małopolska compilation. A slash separates manuscripts that form close pairs even though they are not directly related

down in response to queries of the Cracow City Council, were produced in Cracow, and their translation from German into Latin was financed from the municipal treasury.[13] They were widely circulated in Poland and abroad. One of them was quarried for the German-language version of the *Weichbild* that descended from the Cracow City Council MS. This supplementary material was later translated into Latin (not to be confused with the Latin translations of *ortyle*) and incorporated into a separate Cracow version of the *Weichbild*, a Latin text of relatively early date named after its place of origin. The case law of the High Court of German Law at the Royal Castle of Wawel had a major role in the diffusion and the processes of adaptation of the Saxon-Magdeburg Law. The Court's judgments were based on written law, which meant that whenever the provisions of the Saxon-Magdeburg Law had been superseded or supplemented by the *wilkierze* or royal legislation, the judges took into consideration those revisions. Therefore, for instance, the Court upheld the privilege given to Cracow that its citizens may not be summoned to appear before any tribunal except the Cracow municipal court.[14] Thus, it can be argued that Cracow functioned as an example to other towns, both in the implementation of new ideas and in the consolidation of written law through the case law of the High Court of German Law.[15] It was also a centre where lawyers would consult and make use of the Latin or the German *Weichbild*, as a larger number of available manuscripts allowed them to supplement and modify the interpretation of texts that were considered basic.

5 Adaptation of the Saxon-Magdeburg Law in Poland

A careful reading of the manuscripts of the Saxon-Magdeburg Law leads to the conclusion that the adaptation of the rules of the Magdeburg Law in the Kingdom of Poland was complex and selective.[16] As Zygfryd Rymaszewski

13 Edward Potkowski, *Książka rękopiśmienna w kulturze Polski średniowiecznej* [The Hand-written Book in the Culture of Medieval Poland] (Warszawa, 1984), p. 176.

14 *Decreta* II 833 from 23 July 1501 and *Decreta* II 1044 from [29 January] 1509.

15 The functioning of the High Court of German Law in Cracow is discussed in Lidwik Łysiak, *Ius supremum Maydeburgese castri Cracoviensis 1356–1794. Organisation, Tätigkeit und Stellung des Krakauer Oberhofs in der Rechtsprechung Altpolens* (Frankfurt am Main, 1990).

16 Rolf Lieberwirth describes these developments using the concept of the assimilation of the law; he argues that an important element of that process was the textual evolution of the *Sachsenspiegel* and the *Weichbild*. See: Rolf Lieberwirth, "Einführung oder Rezeption? Mittelalterlich deutsches Recht in slawischen Herrschaftsgebieten. Das Beispiel: Polen", in: *Rechts- und Sprachtransfer in Mittel- und Osteuropa. Sachsenspiegel und Magdeburger*

noted in his study of the *Sachsenspiegel*, translation was one of the key elements of that process.[17] This was also true of the *Weichbild*.[18]

Indeed, the first stage of the adaptation process involved choosing those parts of text that were deemed appropriate for translation. For example, in the Sandomierz version, some provisions from the treatise about the system of courts were left out. Such omissions were not a bad thing, as the articles in question had no relevance to the situation of Polish cities. Although the complete translation of the new Cracow version did include those articles, they were not copied in many other related manuscripts (the copyists usually left off after the provision of the Jewish oath, a decision demonstrating their belief that the remaining portion of the law book was of little use in Poland).

The next stage in the adaptation process involved the modification of the original text in the course of the translation. Passages that were found to be

---

Recht. Internationale und interdisziplinäre Konferenz in Leipzig vom 31. Oktober bis 2. November 2003, eds. Ernst Eichler and Heiner Lück, (Ivs Saxonico-Maidebvrgense in Oriente) 1 (Berlin, 2008), p. 178. The importance of the adaptation of the law to local requirements is also discussed in Elisabeth Nowak, *Die Verbreitung und Anwendung des Sachsenspiegels nach der überlieferten Handschriften*, Dissertation zur Erlangung der Doktorwürde der Philosophischen Fakultät der Universität Hamburg (Hamburg, 1965) [typescript], p. 326; Inge Bily, "Neb wykpildske prawo – to gest miestczke prawo", in: *Městské právo ve střední Evropě. Sborník příspěvků z mezinárodní právnické konference Práva městská Království českého*, 19–21 září 2011, Praha [Urban Law in Central Europe: Proceedings of the International Conference on Law and History: Urban laws of the Kingdom of Bohemia, 19–21 September 2011, Prague], eds. Karel Malý and Jiři Šouša jr. (Praha, 2013), p. 357. For Wieland Carls, the processes of adaptation of legal language are closely linked to the process of reception. He argues, on the basis of a fairly narrow chunk of evidence, that the Saxon-Magdeburg Law went through the process of adaptation virtually unscathed: "Soweit das auf Grund der noch schmalen Textbasis schon möglich ist, kann man davon ausgehen, dass das sächsisch-magdeburgische Recht den Prozess der Adaptation nahezu verlustfrei vollzogen hat, indem die rechtlichen Termini und Institute in der Zielsprache erkennen lassen, dass es sich um ein bereits etabliertes und gelebtes Rechtssystem handelt. Anpassungen an sich ändernde Rechtsvorstellungen sind dem Wesen des Magdeburger Rechts ohnehin immanent und haben den Rezeptionsprozess stets befördert". Wieland Carls, "*Hy hebit sich an magdburgisch recht*: Wege eines europäischen Rechts und seiner Erforschung", *Denkströme: Journal der Sächsischen Akademie der Wissenschaften zu Leipzig* 5 (2010), 153.

17 Rymaszewski, *Łacińskie teksty Landrechtu Zwierciadła Saskiego w Polsce. Versio*, p. 210. Modern theory of legal translation accords adaptation an indispensable role in the process of translation, cf. Anne Wagner, King Kui Sin and Le Cheng, "Cultural Transfer and Conceptualization in Legal Discourse", in: *The Ashgate Handbook of Legal Translation* (Ashgate, 2014), p. 39.

18 In her discussion of the Chełmno Law, Danuta Janicka observes that its characteristic profile is the effect of the adaptation of the Magdeburg Law to local conditions. See Janicka, "Zur Topographie der Städte", p. 78; and Danuta Janicka, "Die Rezeption des *Sachsenspiegels* und des Magdeburger Rechts am Beispiel von Thorn im Kulmer Land", in *Rechts- und Sprachtransfer*, pp. 61–74.

inappropriate for the conditions in Poland were amended and supplemented with additional material, whose chief purpose was to clarify and expand existing provisions. Most, although by no means all, of the textual variants in the *Weichbild* manuscripts made their appearance during the translation phase and evolved further within each of the main manuscript branches.

The third stage of the reception of the Latin text involved its adaptation to the needs of its recipients through amendations, omissions, and additions while the manuscript was being copied. The redactors of the new copies tried to adapt them to local conditions, such as, for example, in the Przemyśl MS and the Q II 157 (1) of the *versio Sandomiriensis*, or to modify them to express a reformist view of the judicial procedure, as in the Cracow version (the Działyńscy Codex IV and Warsaw MS). The process of textual differentiation was driven both by modifications and omissions of the received text. A pair of manuscripts, Q II 157 (1) and BN 12600, are rather special in this respect: both of them have a significant number of omissions, but practically no supplementary material, nor any modifications of the copied text. In a case like that, the omission may well have been caused by scribal error. Changes affecting the substance of text paved the way for individual interpretations (to be differentiated from 'private' interpretations)[19] implemented in legal practice. Moreover, the fact of their implementation was used in turn to justify their authority. These changes did have consequences for the shape of the law. At the same time, there is no evidence that the redactors of any new copy of the amended *Weichbild* or the *Sachsenspiegel* ever sought the approval of the authorities of the city by which it had been commissioned, unless we take a general approbation of the city charter and privileges as an expression of such an approval (that would have been too far-fetched).[20] A notable exception to this practice, namely, an explicit adoption of a new, amended version of the law, was Jan Łaski's *Commune incliti*, which, by virtue of that formal declaration, became the sole official text of the Saxon-Magdeburg Law in the Kingdom of Poland.

Finally, the fourth stage of the reception of the Latin text consisted of its selective implementation. The proof that such selective practices actually took place must, however, be sought in a different category of sources. It needs also the acknowledgment of the fact that municipal law could be changed not only by new legislation from the king, the Sejm, and municipal by-laws (*wilkierze*, or Ger. *Willkür*), or by statutes set down by the town owners, but also due to inexplicit alteration of the text of the law, a practice generally tolerated in contemporary legal culture. Evolution and adaptation are a pair of terms that together

19 Heiner Lück, "Rechtsbücher als 'private' Rechtsaufzeichnungen?", *Zeitschrift für Neuere Rechtsgeschichte* 131 (2014), 432.

20 Mikuła, *Prawodawstwo króla i sejmu*, pp. 66–71 and 43–145.

aptly describe the nature of the reception of the German law in Polish towns. Whereas the term 'transfer', preferred in German literature, refers primarily to the diffusion of ideas and practices (not just from the field of law, but from the domain of culture in general, through the medium of language,[21] which

---

21 For Friedrich Ebel, the concept of transfer has a broader scope than reception; it involves the import of a range of solutions which may lead to the displacement of those that were in force previously (Friedrich Ebel, "Rechtsentstehung und Rechtstransfer im Spiegel der Überlieferung (Magdeburger und Lübecker Recht)", in: *Grundlagen für ein neues Europa*, p. 38; Friedrich Ebel and Renate Schelling, "Die Bedeutung deutschen Stadtrechts im Norden und Osten des mittelalterlichen Europa. Lübisches und Magdeburger Recht als Gegenstand von Kulturtransfer und Träger der Moderne", in: *Die Stadt im Europäischen Nordosten. Kulturbeziehungen von der Ausbreitung des Lübischen Rechts bis zur Aufklärung. Beiträge anläßlich des II. Internationalen Symposiums zur deutschen Kultur im europäischen Nordosten der Stiftung zur Förderung deutscher Kultur (Aue-Stiftung) Helsinki in Zusammenarbeit mit dem Stadtarchiv Tallinn, dem Estnischen Kunstmuseum, der Ostsee-Akademie Lübeck-Travemünde und dem Deutschen Kulturinstitut Tallinn vom 10. bis 13. September 1998 in Tallinn, Estland*, eds. Robert Schweitzer, Waltraud Bastman-Bühner, and Jörg Hackmann (collab.), (Aue-Säätiön julkaisuja / Skrifter utgivna Aue-Stiftelsen / Veröffentlichungen der Aue-Stiftung) 12 (Helsinki – Lübeck, 2001), esp. pp. 38–39). According to Heiner Lück, the concept of transfer is associated with the perspective of the 'sender', while the term reception tends to prioritize the point of view of the recipient (Heiner Lück, "Rechtstransfer und Rechtsverwandtschaft. Zum Einfluss des Magdeburger Stadtrechts im Königreich Böhmen", in: *Městské právo ve střední Evropě, Sborník příspěvků z mezinárodní právnické konference Práva městská Království českého*, 19–21 září 2011, Praha [Urban Law in Central Europe: Proceedings of the International Conference on Law and History: Urban Laws of the Kingdom of Bohemia, 19–21 September 2011, Prague], eds. Karel Malý and Jiři Šouša jr. (Praha, 2013) p. 299). Cf. also Heiner Lück, "Die Rezeption des Sachsenspiegels und des Magdeburger Rechts in Ostmitteleuropa", in: *Eike von Repgow, Sachsenspiegel, Die Dresdner Bilderhandschrift Mscr. Dresd. M 32. Aufsätze und Untersuchungen*, (Codices selecti) 107 (Graz, 2011), pp. 151–159; Heiner Lück, "Aspects of the Transfer of the Saxon-Magdeburg Law to Central and Eastern Europe", *Rechtsgeschichte – Legal History* 22 (2014), 79–89; and Wieland Carls, "Das sächsisch-magdeburgische Recht – Sprach- und Rechtstransfer in Mittel- und Osteuropa. Versuch einer Bestandsaufnahme am Beispiel der heutigen Slowakei", in: *Deutsche Sprache in der Slowakei. Festschrift für Ilpo Tapani Piirainen zum 65. Geburtstag. Internationale Fachtagung, Piešťany, den 13–15 Juni 2007*, eds. Peter Ďurčo, Ružena Kozmová, and Daniela Drinková (Trnava – Bratislava, 2009), pp. 257–265. The concept of transfer is often used in studies of linguistic history; see Irena Szczepankowska, "Rola łaciny w kształtowaniu terminologii prawa polskiego w okresie od XVI do XVIII wieku. Problemy transferu pojęć i nazw" [The Role of Latin in the Development of Polish Legal Terminology in the 16th–18th Century: Problems of the Transfer of Concepts and Names], in: *Język w urzędach i w sądach* [Language in Offices and Courts], ed. Maria Lizisowa (Kraków, 2006), pp. 75–89; Marija Lazar, "Transfer des Rechts und Transfer der Rechtssprache. Sächsisch-magdeburgisches Recht und seine Verbreitung im Ostmitteleuropa nach den Hussitenkriegen", in: *Persönlichkeiten in der tschechischen Sprach- und Kulturgeschichte. Beiträge zum 8. Bohemicum Dresdense: Tomáš Garrigue Masarik (1850–1937) 07.11.2014 und 9. Bohemicum Dresdense: Jan Hus (~1370–1415) – Erbe und Bedeutung 30.10.2015*, eds. Holger Kuße and Hana Kosourová, (Specimina Philologiae Slavicae) 191 (Leipzig, 2016),

is borne out by the legal advice issued by Magdeburg for numerous towns in Central and Eastern Europe), 'adaptation' serves as a specifying and explicative complement to the broadly based concept of reception.[22] The use of the term 'adaptation' makes it easier to differentiate between levels and forms of reception, whether material (the adaptation of legal institutions) or formal (the adoption of legal terminology and points of legislative procedure), in response to local needs. The role of the latter is hard to overestimate, as the choice of German law (broadly speaking) for the purpose of incorporation or refoundation of towns was driven by the demand for new solutions and the attractiveness of a legal code brought by the migrants who became more numerous from the 13th century onwards. The new code was adopted without constraint,[23] and yet the choice was no doubt necessary and appropriate. Nevertheless, it should be noted that from the start, the imported law was combined with other sources of municipal law, among them customary law, whose influence remained as strong as ever. Given the complexity of the sources of law in use in Polish towns incorporated according to the Magdeburg Law, that law may well be referred to as – following the suggestion of Bartłomiej Groicki – Polish urban law.[24]

---

pp. 177–202. In the context of importing constitutional solutions, the concept of adaptation is used by Ebel and Schelling, "Die Bedeutung deutschen Stadtrechts", pp. 40–42. At this point it may be worth mentioning the phrase 'legal transplant' whose meaning is defined by Allan Watson as "the moving of a rule or a system of law from one country to another, or from one people to another – [processes that] have been common since the earliest recorded history" (Allan Watson, *Legal transplants. An Approach to Comparative Law*, 2nd ed. (Athens – London, 1974), p. 21).

22 For an explanation of the ideas of reception in the context of the French humanities see Juliusz Bardach, "Pojęcie recepcji i jej zakres w dziejach państwa i prawa" [The Concept of Reception and Its Scope in the History of State and Law] in: *Ars historica. Prace z dziejów powszechnych i Polski ofiarowane G. Labudzie* [Ars historica: Studies in World History and the History of Poland. A Festschrift in Honour of Professor Gerard Labuda] (Poznań, 1976), pp. 91–99; Juliusz Bardach, "Recepcja w historii państwa i prawa" [Reception in the History of State and Law], *Czasopismo Prawno-Historyczne* 29/1 (1977), 1–62; Juliusz Bardach, "Recepcja w dziejach: harmonia i dysharmonia w spotkaniu kultur" [Reception in History: Harmony and Disharmony] in: *Pamiętnik XII Powszechnego Zjazdu Historyków Polskich, Katowice 17–20 września 1979* [Proceedings of the 12th General Congress of Polish Historians, Katowice, September 17–20, 1979], 1 (Katowice, 1979), pp. 101–111. See also Maciej Mikuła, "Wpływ 'Summa utriusque iuris' mistrza Rajmunda na regulację dziedziczenia testamentowego w Statucie litewskim I z 1529 roku" [The Impact of Master Raymund's *Summa utriusque iuris* on Testamentary Inheritance in the Lithuanian Statute of 1529], *Czasopismo Prawno-Historyczne* 60/2 (2008), 58ff (it includes an outline of the conventions regulating the use of the term 'reception' in Polish historiography).

23 Lieberwirth, "Einführung oder Rezeption?", p. 174.

24 Bartłomiej Groicki, *Porządek sądów i spraw miejskich prawa majdeburskiego w Koronie Polskiej* [The Order of Judges and Urban Courts of the Magdeburg Law in the Kingdom

6 Practical Consequences of the Evolution of the *Weichbild*

The scope of modifications introduced into the provisions of the *Weichbild* in the course of its transmission was extraordinarily broad. Virtually all areas of life were affected, from urban governance, the administration of justice, and criminal law, down to the order of succession, the passing on of property, and the network of obligations. Some of the alterations in the rules are symptomatic of both the local needs and a general trend of historical change. These modifications include provisions concerning the functioning and the competences of the town council. Its authority was certainly strengthened by Konrad of Sandomierz's introduction of a phrase proclaiming that the laws enacted by the urban commune be compliant with God's law. The explanations and augmentations of the law concerning the status and definition of guests (aliens) reflect the growing importance of mobility and trade. Even the relatively minor alterations related to the wording of individual provisions express the tendency for greater clarity and precision in the language of the law.

A similar trend seems to have been at work in criminal law, namely, the rules of order in presenting proof, the understanding of aiding and complicity, and the guidelines for oath-swearing. The legal ritual of compurgation was cleared of ambiguities and cumbersome formalism (as in the tendency to reduce the mandatory number of oath-swearers). The pressure of everyday realities and the striving for coherence seem to have prompted a string of modifications concerning damages, court fines, and wergild. A sizable part of these modifications were in fact additions to the received text carried over from the Magdeburg *ortyle*.

A conspicuous expansion of the old rules took place in the sphere of family and inheritance law. Again, the source of the supplementary material was

of Poland], repr. in Biblioteka Dawnych Polskich Pisarzy-Prawników, 1, ed. Karol Koranyi (Warszawa, 1953), p. 24. According to Krystyna Bukowska: "the burgher-lawyers strive with great determination to free themselves from the shackles of German law and create their own [national] legal culture"; Krystyna Bukowska, "Jeszcze w sprawie rozwoju miejskiego prawa prywatnego w Polsce" [More on the Development of Urban Private Law in Poland], *Czasopismo Prawno-Historyczne* 22/1 (1970), 224. See also Krystyna Bukowska, *Orzecznictwo krakowskich sądów wyższych w sporach o nieruchomości miejskie (XVI–XVIII w.). Studium z historii prawa rzymskiego w Polsce* [The Caselaw of Cracow High Courts Concerning Disputes over Real Property in Towns (16th–18th Century): *A Study in the History of Roman Law in Poland*] (Warszawa, 1967), p. 107; and Grzegorz M. Kowalski, *Bartłomiej Groicki – prawnik polskiego Odrodzenia. Wystawa w 400-setną rocznicę śmierci. Biblioteka Jagiellońska 5–29 kwietnia 2005* [Bartłomiej Groicki – A Jurist of the Polish Enlightenment: Special Exhibition 400th Anniversary of His Death, Jagiellonian Library, 5–12 April 2005] (Kraków, 2005), p. 15).

often the case law of the courts of the Magdeburg Law (*ortyle*). In general, the changes in the regulations concerning the dower, heritable property, and succession tended to give better protection to the interests of the family in-group, in particular the widow, against claims based on the proximity of blood principle. However, the anachronistic distinction of the deceased's estate into *gerada*, hergewet, and the core estate remained intact until a series of Cracow statutes (*wilkierze*) enacted with royal assent came to be adapted by other towns in the Kingdom of Poland. The provision concerning *ius caducum* was subject to a number of modifications which put some limits on the right of the monarch to take over the property of the intestate.

In the provisions concerning the law of obligations, the alterations and additions dealt primarily with debt and the manner in which it was to be proven, especially with regard to guests and servants.

The modifications in this fairly comprehensive collection of texts of the *Weichbild* used in the Kingdom of Poland can be classified as follows: 1) changes in terminology; 2) explanations of legal terms; 3) elimination of ambiguities; 4) alterations and additions that took into account local legal practice; 5) supplementary regulations carried over from other sources of the Saxon-Magdeburg Law; 6) alterations to ensure the coherence of the regulations within the legal code; 7) replacement of outdated clauses by formulations better adapted to contemporary realities, which were also easier to apply; and 8) alterations, usually omissions, caused by scribal error.

The changes in the *Weichbild* were not intended to produce a new law code, nor did they result in the emergence of a law that resigned its Saxon-Magdeburg identity. The innovations were grafted onto the old stem sparingly through legislative acts issued by the monarch, the Sejm, town owners, and town councils. For the most part, the modifications of the *Weichbild* were driven by practical considerations, that is, adapting its provisions and their wording to the needs of its users in the towns of the late medieval Kingdom of Poland.

7 Annotations by the *Weichbild* Users

This study, focused on the normative text of a historic law code, is part of the ongoing research into the medieval legal sources, while, at the same time, it is concerned with the judicial practice of the High Court of Magdeburg Law in Cracow. The latter is analysed here for essentially one reason: namely, to back up my contention that the modifications of the *Weichbild* were to a significant extent adaptations to the demand created by its use. This study, it should be made clear, does offer a full picture of the functioning of written law in Polish towns in the late Middle Ages. That could be the subject of a separate study, based on preliminary studies of normative acts of the Saxon-Magdeburg Law and other legal sources. Here, the problem of the practical use of the *Weichbild* is examined from different angle, namely, what the annotations tell us about the user's approach to the text.

Most of the copies of the *Weichbild* are annotated. Virtually all of the annotations can be described as practical, even if they are not of the same type. A great number of them are corrections, that is, missing words or passages interpolated by a reader who noticed the omission after checking another manuscript. Such comparisons could result in quite substantial annotations; for example, some manuscripts with the Sandomierz version are patched up with passages from the Cracow version. The users also tried to help one another to navigate the text by putting in indices and cross-references. In the margins we can also find Polish equivalents of Latin words used in the text. Less common are legal maxims inscribed next to individual provisions, most likely inserted with the intention to help subsequent users construct a legal argument.

Printed copies of Jan Łaski's *Commue incliti* (1506) were similarly annotated with cross-references, commentaries, and indices. Some annotations were made after 1535, the year when a new edition of the Magdeburg *Weichbild*, by Mikołaj Jaskier, was published. This fact shows that the *Commue incliti* continued to be used alongside a revised text with a royal imprimatur.

8 The Road to a Single, Authoritative Law Text

According to Wacław Uruszczak, Alexander I Jagiellon's royal assent covered not only those parts of *Commune incliti* that were concerned with Polish land law, but also included the part of Jan Łaski's statute book which dealt with urban law.[25] However, the claim that the royal authorization of the first printed code of law entailed a ban on the use of earlier texts is open to serious doubt.[26]

25 Wacław Uruszczak, "*Commune incliti Poloniae Regni privilegium constitutionum et indultuum*: O tytule i mocy prawnej Statutu Łaskiego z 1506 roku" [The Title and Legal Authority of Łaski's *Statutes* of 1506] in: *Prace poświęcone pamięci Adama Uruszczaka* [Festschrift in Honour of the Late Adam Uruszczak], eds. Jan Halberda, Michał Hosowicz, and Anna Karabowicz, (Prace Instytutu Prawa Własności Intelektualnej UJ) 96 (Zakamycze, 2006), pp. 121–123 and 127–131. It has been generally held that codes of urban law did have the status of official documents vested. For a dissenting voice cf. Józef Matuszewski, "*Proles illegittima* w polskim prawie ziemskim" [*Proles illegitima* in Polish Land Law], *Czasopismo Prawno-Historyczne* 18/2 (1966), p. 89, Note 85).

26 See Matuszewski, "Proles illegittima", p. 89, and Rymaszewski, *Łacińskie teksty Landrechtu Zwierciadła Saskiego w Polsce. Versio*, pp. 145–146.

Even if the privilege of exclusivity had been intended for *Commune incliti*, the facts on the ground showed that the introduction in 1506 of a uniform official law code did not put an end to the production of manuscripts with versions of the Magdeburg *Weichbild* that differed from Łaski's text. That is, for example, the case of MS BOZ (1513). Moreover, there is sufficient evidence to suggest that the author (copyist) of MS BN 3068 took the authorized text of the *Weichbild* and introduced numerous modifications, including some that altered the wording of the legal provisions. The transition from the medieval paradigm, in which the legal text was believed to be valid because it was used in practice, to the modern paradigm, in which the availability of a uniform printed copy made control of the text used in legal practice possible, took time.[27] In the 16th century, the pressure for the codification (i.e. establishment of uniformity) of the law became very strong, with regard to both land law and urban law. The course of reform and codification of both branches of the law was on the whole quite similar, including spectacular setbacks. The failed attempt to promulgate the statues *Correctura Iurium* in 1534 in one field (land law) was matched by the failure in 1523 of Maciej Śliwnicki's reform of the municipal law (although it did come into effect in the lands of the bishopric of Łowicz), although each project was rejected for different reasons.[28]

27 Cf.: "in spite of the strongly increased use of printed law books by legal professionals from the mid-sixteenth century onwards, manuscripts continued to co-exist and play an important part in the dissemination of legal texts and literature. Moreover, in spite of the importance of records, written and printed material, the common law profession retained a significant oral culture in the formal and informal handling of its legal business and interests". "Law Books During the Transition from Late-Medieval to Early-Modern Legal Scholarship", in: *The Formation and Transmission of Western Legal Culture. 150 Books that Made the Law in the Age of Printing*, Serge Dauchy, Georges Martyn, Anthony Musson, Heikki Pihlajamäki, Alain Wijffels, eds., coop. Naoko Seriu (Studies in the History of Law and Justice) 7, series eds. Georges Martyn, Mortimer Sellers (New York – Berlin – Heidelberg, 2016), p. 18.

28 Wacław Uruszczak, *Próba kodyfikacji prawa polskiego w pierwszej połowie XVI wieku. Korektura praw z 1532 r.* [An Attempt to Codify Polish Law in the First Half of the 16th Century: Correctura Iurium of 1532] (Warszawa, 1979), pp. 55–56. Krystyna Bukowska-Gorgoni, "Das sächsisch-magdeburgische Recht und die vermogensrechtlichen Verhaltnisse in den polnischen Stadten der Renaissance", in: *Studien zur Geschichte des sächsich-magdeburgischen Rechts in Deutschland und Polen*, eds. Dietmar Willoweit and Winfried Schich, (Rechtshistorische Reihe) 10 (Frankfurt am Main, 1980), p. 130; Jarosław Reszczyński, "*Sigismundina* Macieja Śliwnickiego. Uwagi o genezie dzieła, technice wprowadzania norm i interesie państwa jako ratio legis" [Maciej Śliwnicki's *Sigismundina*: Some Remarks about the Origin of the Treatise, Methods of Promulgating Norms and the Raison d'état as *ratio legis*], in: *Honeste vivere. Księga pamiątkowa ku czci Profesora Władysława Bojarskiego* [Honeste vivere: Festschrift in Honour of the Late Professor Władysław Bojarski], eds. Ewa Gajda and Andrzej Sokala (Toruń, 2001), p. 550;

While the failure of attempts to codify the land law resulted in the emergence of private codes of law, the early setbacks did not thwart the reform in the sphere of urban law – or more precisely, the law used in towns incorporated under the Magdeburg Law – based on new glossed editions of the *Weichbild* and the *Sachsenspiegel*.[29] They were published by Mikołaj Jaskier in 1535 and authorized by King Zygmunt I the Old for court use as the sole official text of the law. Mikołaj Jaskier's printed text retained its exclusive status even after the publication in 1581 of a Polish edition of the two codes of law. Paweł Szczerbic's translation did not follow Jaskier's Latin version – it was more like a compilation of that text and a variety of other legal sources.[30] Yet even after 1535, the earlier versions continued to be used, as shown by the glosses on the pages of several copies of *Commune incliti*. Those annotations can be dated back with great certainty to a time after the publication of Jaskier's *Ius municipalis et*

Jarosław Reszczyński, *Sądownictwo i proces w kodyfikacji Macieja Śliwnickiego z 1523 roku: o wpływach prawa rzymskiego i praw obcych na myśl prawną polskiego Odrodzenia* [The Justiciary and the Trial in Maciej Śliwnicki's Draft Code of 1523: The Influence of Roman Law and Foreign Laws on the Legal Thought of the Polish Renaissance] (Kraków, 2008), esp. p. 30, 33–35 and 50.

29 The role of the legal books in the legal practice cf. "Preface", in: *The Formation and Transmission of Western Legal Culture. 150 Books that Made the Law in the Age of Printing*, Serge Dauchy, Georges Martyn, Anthony Musson, Heikki Pihlajamäki, Alain Wijffels, eds., coop. Naoko Seriu (Studies in the History of Law and Justice) 7, series eds. Georges Martyn, Mortimer Sellers (New York – Berlin – Heidelberg, 2016), p. 5. The introduction of glosses onto the pages of the *Sachsenspiegel* and the Magdeburg *Weichbild* was a multidimensional expansion (with regard to norms, ideas, cultural interaction) of the original text. This is demonstrated by the analysis of the characteristics of an exemplary gloss added to the text of the *Sachsenspiegel* Johann von Buch. See Bernd Kannowski, *Die Umgestaltung des Sachsenspiegelrechts durch die Buch'sche Glosse*, (Monumenta Germaniae Historica, Schriften) 56 (Hannover, 2007). In his edition of the *Weichbild* Mikołaj Jaskier relied heavily on the gloss written by Burchard von Mangefeld (See Krystyna Bukowska, "O wpływach obcych w dawnym prawie miast polskich" [Foreign Influences on Early Urban Law of Polish Towns], *Czasopismo Prawno-Historyczne* 17/1 (1965), 263; Bukowska-Gorgoni, "Das sächsisch-magdeburgische Recht", p. 131; and Lesław Pauli, "Die polnische Literatur des Magdeburger Rechts im 16. Jahrhundert", in: *Studien zur Geschichte des sächsich-magdeburgischen Rechts*, pp. 151–152). For an analysis of the 'French' glosses in Jaskier's treatises and the way they clash with the case law of the High Court of German Law at Wawel and the Commissary Court of the Six Towns, see Bukowska, *Orzecznictwo*.

30 In the case of the *Sachsenspiegel*, it is an alphabetical list of legal issues based on both the *Sachsenspiegel* and the *Weichbild*. While preparing his edition of the Magdeburg *Weichbild*, Paweł Szczerbic collated its Latin and German versions. In his book, those passages that could be found only in the German sources and those that appeared only in the Latin texts are marked appropriately. Even a brief comparison of Szczerbic's text with the edition of the vulgate *Weichbild* prepared by Alexander von Daniels and Franz von Gruben leaves no doubt about the solid quality of his accomplishment.

provincialis. We may thus treat that new translation not just as an attempt to produce a revised edition, free of the errors of the earlier texts, but as a harbinger of Renaissance reforms, codification of the law, and a new age of legal uniformity and certainty.[31] This aspect of the transition has already been noted by a number of eminent historians of Polish law, such as Adam Vetulani,[32] Krystyna Bukowska,[33] and Jarosław Reszczyński.[34]

The process of transition from the law transmitted by hand-written manuscripts to uniform, printed law was a lengthy one, but it was, in fact, irreversible. Another milestone on this road from manuscript to print was Bartłomiej Groicki's collections and treatises of municipal law in Polish. His books, as it soon turned out, proved to be more useful than the Latin manuals of Jan Cerasinus Kirstein and Jan Cervus Tucholczyk. The process of change was also actively supported by Poland's kings. One notable example was Kazimierz IV Jagiellon's recognition in 1476 of the Chełmno Law (from the collection of laws entitled *Der alte Kulm*) as the sole legal text valid in Royal Prussia. It was also used in Ducal Prussia. For much of the 16th century, it was still evolving and continued to be reformed.[35] When it eventually went into print in Toruń in

31 Cf. Wacław Uruszczak, "Europejskie kodeksy prawa doby renesansu" [European Legal Codices of the Renaissance], *Czasopismo Prawno-Historyczne* 40/1 (1988), 885–900.

32 Adam Vetulani, "W sprawie prawa chłopskiego w Polsce feudalnej" [Concerning Peasant Law in Feudal Poland], *Państwo i Prawo* 10 (1956), 624–5. Meanwhile Rymaszewski remains sceptical of the interpretation others find so compelling. He argues that: "a large number of manuscripts with the same content as can be found in Łaski would surely indicate that the laws he collected and published had been in general use before; therefore it makes little sense to talk about a shift towards unification" (Rymaszewski, *Łacińskie teksty Landrechtu Zwierciadła Saskiego. Versio*, p. 150). This cannot be right. After all, the arrival of printing made it possible not only to set up a canon of the sources of urban law but also to produce a large number of identical copies of the legal text. Rymaszewski's stance must come as a surprise, especially as we know he has good eye for differences between various versions of the *Sachsenspiegel* and even between manuscripts of the same version (*ibid.*, pp. 137, 210 and 214–215). The diversity is even more conspicuous in the case of the *Weichbild* manuscripts – I have not seen two identical ones.

33 Bukowska, *Orzecznictwo*, pp. 7–8. For a critical view of the matter, cf. Rymaszewski, *Łacińskie teksty Landrechtu Zwierciadła Saskiego w Polsce. Jaskier*, p. 6, Note 10. Bukowska claims that the publishing of glossed editions of the *Sachsenspiegel* and the *Weichbild* reflected the demand for a legal text that would be more suited for legal practice than Master Raymund's *Summa utriusque iuris* appended to the *Commune inciliti* (Bukowska, *Orzecznictwo*, pp. 105–106).

34 Reszczyński, *Sądownictwo i proces*, pp. 30 and 50.

35 Danuta Janicka, *Prawo karne w trzech rewizjach prawa chełmińskiego z XVI wieku* [Criminal Law in Three Revisions of the Chełmno Law in the 16th Century] (Toruń, 1992), esp. pp. 130 and 135.

1568, the text was extensively glossed.[36] Unfortunately, not a single copy of the first printed edition survived the confiscations ordered by the Duke of Prussia. He had them destroyed because he feared the judges would continue to credit the glosses with the same authority as the main text. That would have been contrary to King Kazimierz's original intention and would have greatly hindered the duke's plans of unification of the Chełmno Law. The Toruń incident no doubt signalled the advent of a new era. If legal culture is to regarded as a complex of individual and collective attitudes towards the law, the arrival of print, a new medium which changes its transmission and availability, the legal culture is bound to change as well – gradually, but inexorably.

36 Zbigniew Zdrójkowski, "Wstęp historyczny" [A Historical Introduction], in: *Prawo starochełmińskie* [*Der alte Kulm Law Code*] 1584 (1394), eds. Witold Maisel and Zbigniew Zdrójkowski, trans. Andrzej Bzdęga and Anna Gaca, (Teksty Pomników Prawa Chełmińskiego w Przekładach Polskich) 2 (Toruń, 1985), p. 8.

APPENDIX 1

Concordance Table of Articles

In the table below Roman numerals reproduce the numbering schemes of the original texts. Items in the Statutes column are also identified by their leaf numbers (f.). In the MS BJ 170a column the apostrophe reproduces the numbering of the Digest B (the manuscript contains two digests of the articles of the *Weichbild*); missing leaves are marked 'lost'. Articles from the *Constitution of Courts* added to the *Weichbild* after the Jewish oath (set against a dark gray background) are shaded in light grey. The numbers in Henryków MS (II F 8) differs from the numbering scheme proposed by Paul Laband in *Magdeburger Rechtsquellen* (p. 48). In Leipzig MS (951b) Article 128 contains a provision concerning jurymen who became aware of a litigant committing perjury; it has no equivalent in the German texts. In Żagań MS (II Q 4) continuous numbering is affixed to the Latin and the German text, although occasionally an article is missing in one of them (they are Articles 9, 72, 73, 78 and 79 following the Gniezno MS numbering scheme).

TABLE 26 Concordance table of articles, part 1

Gn.	1261Wr.	MSR	1295Wr.	RGV	BJ 169
[1]	[1–4]	[1]	–	–	[1]
[2] II	[5]	[2], [29]	–	–	[2]
[3] III	[6]	[3]	–	–	[3]
[4] IV	[7, 8 § 1]	[4 § 1]	–	–	[4]
[5] V	[8 § 2, 19]	[4 § 2]	–	–	[5]
[6] VI	[9–10]	[5 § 1–2]	–	–	[6]
[7] VII	[11]	[6 § 1]	–	–	[7]
[8] VIII	[27]	[6 § 2]	–	–	[8]
[9] IX	[12]	[5 § 3]	–	–	[9]
[10] X	[13]	[7 § 1]	–	–	[10]
[11] XI	–	[33]	–	–	[11]
[12] XII	[21]	[7 § 2]	–	–	[12]
[13] XIII	–	[35]	–	–	[13]
[14] XIV	[14, 28, 15, 29]	[16]	–	–	[14]
[15] XV	[30]	[17 § 1]	–	–	[15]
[16] XVI	[16–7]	[17 § 2–3]	–	–	[16]
[17] XVII	[18]	[18]	–	–	[17]
[18] XVIII	[20, 22]	[19–20]	–	–	[18]
[19] XIX	[23]	[21 § 1]	–	–	[19]
[20] XX	[24–5]	[22 § 2]	–	–	[20]
[21] XXI	[31, 26]	[23, 21 § 2]	–	–	[21]
[22] XXII	[32–3]	[24]	–	–	[22]
[23] XXIII	[34–8]	[25–6]	–	–	[23]
[24] XXIV	[73, 75]	[27–8]	–	–	[24]
[25] XXV	–	[45]	–	–	[25]
[26] XXVI	–	[46]	–	–	[26]
[27] XXVII	[53]	[15 § 1]	–	–	[27]
[28] XXVIII	[54]	[15 § 2]	–	–	[28]
[29] XXIX	–	[44]	–	–	[29]
[30] XXX	–	[9]	–	–	[30]
[31] XXXI	–	[8]	–	–	[31]
[32] XXXII	–	[51]	–	–	[32]
[33] XXXIII	–	[10]	–	–	[33]
[34] XXXIV	–	[11]	–	–	[34]
[35] XXXV	–	[12]	–	–	[35]
[36] XXXVI	–	[13]	–	–	[36]
[37] XXXVII	–	[14]	–	–	[37]
[38] XXXVIII	–	[31]	–	–	[38]
[39] XXXIX	–	[32]	–	–	[39]
[40] XL	–	[49]	–	–	[40]
[41] XLI	–	[41]	–	–	[41]
[42] XLII	–	[42]	–	–	[42]
[43] XLIII	–	[43]	–	–	[43]
[44] XLIV	–	[39]	–	–	[44]
[45] XLV	–	[36]	–	–	[45]

II F 8	BJ 170a	BJ 168	BJ 12607 Ger.	II Q 4 Ger.
[1]	I	[1] I	[1]	[1] I
[2]	III–IIII	[2] II	[2–3]	[2] II
[3]	II	[3] III	–	[3] III
[4]	XI	[4] IIII	[4]	[4] IIII
[5]	XII	[5] V	[5]	[5] V
[6]	XIII	[6] VI	[6]	[6] VI
[7]	XIIII	[7] VII	[7–8]	[7] VII
[8]	XV	[8] VIII	[9]	[9] VIII
[9]	XVI	[9] IX	[10–11]	[8] IX
[10]	XVII	[10] X	[12]	[10] X
[11]	XVIII	[11] XI	[13]	[11] XI
[12]	XXI'	[12] XII	[14]	[12] XII
[13]	XXXIIII	[13] XIII	[15–16]	[13] XIII
[14]	LIIII	[14] XIIII	[17–18]	[14] XIIII
[15]	XIX part 1	[15] XV	[19]	[15] XV
[16]	XIX part 2, XXI	[16] XVI	[20]	[16] XVI
[17]	V	[17] XVII	[21]	[17] XVII
[18]	VI–VII	[18–9] XVIII–IX	[22–3]	[18–9] XVIII–XIX
[19]	XXII'	[20] XX	[24]	[20] XX
[20]	XXXIII	[21] XXI	[25]	[21] XXI
[21]	VIII	[22–3] XXII–III	[26–7]	[22–3] XXII–III
[22]	XX	[24] XXIIII	[28]	[24] XXIIII
[23]	XXII–III	[25–6] XXV–VI	[29–30]	[25–6] XXV–VI
[24]	XXXV–VI	[27–9] XXVII–IX	[31]	[27] XXVII
[25]	XLVIII	[30] XXX	[32]	[28] XXVIII
[26]	XLIX	[31] XXXI	[33]	[29] XXIX
[27]	XXIII'	[32] XXXII	[34]	[30] XXX
[28]	XLVII	[33] XXXIII	[35]	[31] XXXI
[29]	XLVI	[34] XXXIIII	[36]	[32] XXXII
[30]	XXV	[36] XXXVI	[38]	[33] XXXIII
[31]	XXIIII	[35] XXXV	[37]	[34] XXXIIII
[32]	LVII	[37] XXXVII	[39]	[35] XXXV
[33]	XXVI	[38] XXXVIII	[40]	[36] XXXVI
[34]	XXVII	[39] XXXIX	[41]	[37] XXXVII
[35]	XXVIII	[40] XL	[42]	[38] XXXVIII
[36]	XXIX	[41] XLI	[43]	[39] XXXIX
[37]	XXX	[42] XLII	[44]	[40] XL
[38]	IX	[43] XLIII	[45]	[41] XLI
[39]	X	[44] XLIIII	[46]	[42] XLII
[40]	LIII	[45] XLV	[47]	[43] XLIII
[41]	XLIII	[46] XLVI	[48]	[44] XLIIII
[42]	XLIIII	[47] XLVII	[49]	[45] XLV
[43]	XLV	[48] XLVIII	[50]	[46] XLVI
[44]	XLI	[49] XLIX	[51]	[47] XLVII
[45]	XXXVII	[50] L	[52]	[48] XLVIII

TABLE 26 Concordance table of articles, part 1 (*cont.*)

Gn.	1261Wr.	MSR	1295Wr.	RGV	BJ 169
[46] XLVI	–	[37–8]	–	–	[46]
[47] XLVII	–	–	–	–	[47]
[48] XLVIII	–	–	–	–	[48]
[49] XLIX	–	–	–	–	[49]
[50] L	–	[48]	–	–	[50]
[51] LI	–	[52 § 1]	–	–	[51]
[52] LII	–	–	–	–	[52]
[53] LIII	[72 excerpt]	–	–	–	[53]
[54] LIV	–	–	–	–	[54]
[55] LV	–	–	–	–	–
[56] LVI	[64–68]	–	–	–	[56]
[57] LVII	–	–	–	–	–
[58] LVIII	[69]	–	–	–	[57]
[59] LIX	[70–1]	–	–	–	[58]
[60] LX	[58] <c>	[47]	–	–	[55]
[61] LXI	[55–61]	–	–	–	[59]
[62] LXII	[62]	–	–	–	[60]
[63] LXIII	[63]	–	–	–	[61]
[64] LXIV	[52]	–	–	–	[62]
[65] LXV	[39]	–	–	–	[63]
[66] LXVI	[41]	–	–	–	[64]
[67] LXVII	[42]	–	–	–	[65]
[68] LXVIII	[43]	–	–	–	[66]
[69] LXIX	[44 § 1]	–	–	–	[67]
[70] LXX	[44 § 2, 45]	–	–	–	[68]
[71] LXXI	[46]	–	–	–	[69]
[72] LXXII	[47]	–	–	–	[70]
[73] LXXIII	[48]	–	–	–	[71]
[74] LXXIV	[49]	–	–	–	[72]
[75] LXXV	[50]	–	–	–	[73]
[76 part 1,3] LXXVI	–	–	–	–	–
[76 part 2] LXXVI	[51]	–	–	–	[74]
[77] LXXVII	–	–	–	–	–
[78] LXXVIII	–	[34]	–	–	[75]
–	[75]	–	–	–	[76]
[79] LXXIX	[76]	–	–	–	[77]
[80] LXXX	[77]	–	–	–	[78]
[81] LXXXI	–	[52 § 1]	–	–	[79]
[82] LXXXII	–	–	[1–2]	–	[80]
[83] LXXXIII	–	–	[3–4]	–	[81]
[84] LXXXIIII	–	–	[5]	–	[82]
[85] LXXXV	–	–	[6–7]	–	[83]
[86] LXXXVI	–	–	[8]	–	[84]
[87] LXXXVII	–	–	[9–10]	–	[85]
[88] LXXXVIII	–	–	[11]	–	[86]

II F 8	BJ 170a	BJ 168	BJ 12607 Ger.	II Q 4 Ger.
[46]	XXXVIII–XL	[51] LI	[53]	[49] XLIX
[47]	LVI, XXIIII'	[51] LII	[54]	[50] L
[48]	XXV'	[53] LIII	[55]	[51] LI
[49]	XXVI'	[53] LIIII, CIII	[56]	[52] LII
[50]	LII	[54] LV	[57]	[53] LIII
[51]	II', XXVII'	[55] LVI	[58]	[54] LIIII
[52]	I'	[57] LVIII part 2	[61]	[57] LVII
[53]	–	[56] LVII	[59]	[55] LV
[54]	III'	[57] LVIII part 1	[60]	[56] LVI
–	–	–	–	–
[56]	–	–	[63]	[59] LIX
–	–	–	–	–
[57]	XXVIII'	–	[64]	[60] LX
[58]	–	–	[65]	[61] LXI
[55]	LI	[59] LIX	[62]	[58] LVIII
[59]	–	–	[66]	[62] LXII
[60]	–	–	[67]	[63] LXIII
[61]	–	–	[68]	[64] LXIIII
[62]	XXVIIII'	[61] LXI	[69]	[65] LXV
[63]	XXX'	[62] LXII	[70]	[66] LXVI
[64]	XXXI'	[63] LXIII	[71]	[67] LXVII
[65]	XXXII'	[64] LXIIII	[72]	[68] LXVIII
[66]	XXXIII'	[65] LXV	[73]	[69] LXIX
[67]	–	[66] LXVI	[74]	[70] LXX
[68]	XXXIIII'	–	[75]	[71] LXXI
[69]	XXXV'	[67] LXVII	[76]	[72] LXXII
[70]	XXXVII'	[68] LXVIII	[77]	[73] LXXIII
[71]	XXXVIII'	[69] LXIX	[78]	[74] LXXIIII
[72]	XXXVI'	[70] LXX	[79]	[75] LXXV
[73]	–	[71] LXXI	[80]	[76] LXXVI
–	–	–	–	–
[74]	XXXIX'	[72] LXXII	[81]	[77] LXXVII
–	–	–	–	–
[75]	XXXI	[73] LXXIII	[82]	[78] LXXVIII
[76]	XL' § 1	[74] LXXIIII	[83]	[79] LXXIX
[77]	–	[75] LXXV	[84]	[80] LXXX
[78]	XL' § 2	[76] LXXVI	[85]	[81] LXXXI
[79]	LVIII § 1	–	[86]	[82] LXXXII
[80]	VI'	[77] LXXVII	[87]	[83] LXXXIII
[81]	VII'	[78] LXXVIII	[88]	[84] LXXXIIII
[82]	VIII'	[79] LXXIX	[89]	[85] LXXXV
[83]	IX'	[80] LXXX	[90]	[86] LXXXVI
[84]	X'	[81] LXXXI	[91]	[87] LXXXVII
[85]	XI'	[82] LXXXII	[92]	[88] LXXXVIII
[86]	XII'	[83] LXXXIII	[93]	[89] LXXXIX

TABLE 26 Concordance table of articles, part 1 (*cont.*)

Gn.	1261Wr.	MSR	1295Wr.	RGV	BJ 169
[89] LXXXIX	–	–	[12]	–	[87]
[90] LXXXX	–	–	[13]	–	[88]
[91] XCI	–	–	[14–5]	–	[89]
[92] XCII	–	–	[16]	–	[90]
[93] XCIII	–	–	[17]	–	[91]
[94] XCIIII	–	–	[18]	–	[92]
[95] XCV	–	–	[19]	–	"
[96] XCVI	–	–	[21–2]	–	[94–5]
[97] XCVII	–	–	[20]	–	[93]
[98] XCVIII	–	–	[23]	–	[96]
[99] XCIX	–	–	–	[16 § 3]	[97]
[100] C	–	–	–	[17]	[98]
[101] CI	–	–	–	[18]	[99]
[102] CII	–	[33]	–	–	[101]
[103] CIII	[40]	–	–	–	[100]
[104] CIIII	[45 § 2]	–	–	–	[102]
[105] CV	[76 § 2]	[40]	–	–	[103]
[106] CVI	[74]	–	–	–	[104]
[107] CVII	–	[52 § 2–3]	–	–	[105]
[108–9]	–	–	–	–	[106]
[110]	–	–	–	[6]	[107 part 1]
[111]				[7, 8, 9 § 1]	[107 part 2, 108, 109 part 1]
[112]	–	–	–	[9 § 2, 3]	[109 part 2]
[113]	–	–	–	[10]	[110]
[114]	–	–	–	[11]	[111]
[115]	–	–	–	[12]	[112]
[116]	–	–	–	[13 § 1, 2]	"
[117]	–	–	–	[13 § 3]	"
–	–	–	–	[13 § 4]	"
–	–	–	–	[14 § 1]	"
–	–	–	–	[14 § 2]	"
–	–	–	–	[15 § 1]	"
–	–	–	–	[15 § 2]	"

II F 8	BJ 170a	BJ 168	BJ 12607 Ger.	II Q 4 Ger.
[87]	XIII'	[84] LXXXIIII	[94]	[90] XC
[88]	XIIII'	[85] LXXXV	[95]	[91] XCI
[89]	XV'	[86] LXXXVI, CVII	[96]	[92] XCII
[92]	XVI'	[87] LXXXVII	[97]	[93] XCIII
[92]	XVI'!	[88] LXXXVIII	[98]	[94] XCIIII
[92]	No number	[89] LXXXIX	[99]	[95] XCV
"	–	[90] XC	"	"
[94–5]	XVIII'–XIX'	[92–3] XCII–III	[101–2]	[97–98] XCVII–VIII
[93]	XVII'	[91] XCI	[100]	[96] XCVI
[96]	XX'	[94] XCIIII	[103]	[99] XCIX
[97]	–	[95] XCV	[104]	[100] C
[98]	–	[96] XCVI	[105]	[101] CI
[99]	–	[97] XCVII	[106]	[102] CII
[101]	–	[99] XCIX	[108]	[104] CIIII
[100]	XLI'	[98] XCVIII	[107]	[103] CIII
[102]	–	[100] C	[109]	[105] CV
[103]	XLII	[101] CI	[110]	[106] CVI
[104]	–	[102] CII	[111]	[107] CVII
[105]	LVIII § 2	[103] CIII	[112]	[108] CVIII
[106–7]	IIII'	[112] CXII	[113]	–
[108]	Provisions in another part of MS	Provisions in another part of MS	[114 part 1]	[110 part 1] CX part 1
[109–13]	"	"	[114 part 2, 115–6]	[110 part II, 111–2] CX part 2, CXI–CXII
[114]	"	"	[117]	[113] CXIII
[115]	"	"	[118]	[114] CXIIII
[116]	"	"	[119]	[115] CXV
[117]	"	"	[120]	[116] CXVI
[118]	"	"	[121–2]	[117–8] CXVII–VIII
[119]	"	"	[123 part 1]	[119 part 1] CXIX part 1
[120 part 1]	"	"	[123 part 2]	[119 part 2] CXIX part 2
[120 part 2]	"	"	[124]	[120] CXX
[121]	"	"	[125]	[121] CXXI
[122]	"	"	[126]	[122] CXXII
[123]	"	"	[127]	[123] CXXIII

TABLE 27 Concordance table of articles, part 2

Gn.	F 143	Q II 157 (1)	BN 12600	Q II 157 (2)	Dział. I
[1]	[1]	[1]	[1]	[1]	[1]
[2] II	[2]	[2]	[2]	[2]	[2] II
[3] III	[3]	[3]	[3]	[3]	[3] III
[4] IV	[4]	[4]	[4]	[4]	[4] IV
[5] V	[5]	[5]	[5]	[5]	[5] V
[6] VI	[6]	[6]	[6]	[6]	[6] VI
[7] VII	[7]	[7]	[7]	[7]	[7, 7a] VII
[8] VIII	[8]	[8]	[8]	[8]	[8] VIII
[9] IX	[9]	[9]	[9]	[9]	[9] IX
[10] X	[10]	[10]	[10]	[10]	[10] X
[11] XI	[11]	[11]	[11]	[11]	[11] XI
[12] XII	[12]	[12]	[12]	[12]	[12] XII
[13] XIII	[13]	[13]	[13]	[13]	[13] XIII
[14] XIV	[14]	[14]	[14]	[14]	[14] XIV
[15] XV	[15]	[15]	[15]	[15]	[15] XV
[16] XVI	[16]	[16]	[16]	[16]	[16] XVI
[17] XVII	[17]	[17]	[17]	[17]	[17] XVII
[18] XVIII	[18–9]	[18]	[18]	[18]	[18] XVIII
[19] XIX	[20]	[19]	[19]	[19]	[19] XIX
[20] XX	[21]	[20]	[20]	[20]	[20] XX
[21] XXI	[22]	[21]	[22]	[22]	[21] XXI
[22] XXII	[23]	[22]	[21]	[21]	[22] XXII
[23] XXIII	[24]	[23]	[23]	[23]	[23] XXIII
[24] XXIV	[25–6]	[24–6]	[24]	[24]	[24] XXIV
[25] XXV	[27]	[27]	[25]	[25]	[25] XXV
[26] XXVI	[28]	[28]	[26]	[26]	[26] XXVI
[27] XXVII	[29]	[29]	[27]	[27]	[27] XXVII
[28] XXVIII	[30]	[30]	[28]	[28]	[28] XXVIII
[29] XXIX	[31]	[31]	[29]	[29]	[29] XXIX
[30] XXX	[32]	[32]	[30]	[30]	[30] XXX
[31] XXXI	–	[33]	[31]	[31]	[31] XXXI
[32] XXXII	[33]	[34]	[32]	[32]	[32] XXXII
[33] XXXIII	[34]	[35]	[33]	[33]	[33] XXXIII
[34] XXXIV	[35]	[36]	[34]	[34]	[34] XXXIV
[35] XXXV	[36]	[37]	[35]	[35]	[35] XXXV
[36] XXXVI	[37]	[38]	[36]	[36]	[36] XXXVI
[37] XXXVII	[38]	[39]	[37]	[37]	[37] XXXVII
[38] XXXVIII	[39]	[40]	[38]	[38]	[38] XXXVIII
[39] XXXIX	[40]	[41]	[39]	[39]	[39] XXXIX
[40] XL	[41]	[42]	[40]	[40]	[40] XL
[41] XLI	[42]	[43]	[41]	[41]	[41] XLI
[42] XLII	[43–4]	[44]	[42]	[42]	[42] XLII
[43] XLIII	[45]	[45]	[43]	[43]	[43] XLIII
[44] XLIV	[46]	[46]	[44]	[44]	[44] XLIV
[45] XLV	[47]	[47]	[45]	[45]	[45] XLV

BJ 4405	Przem.	Plesz.	BOZ	AJG	Kiel.
[1]	[1]	[1]	[1] I	[1]	[1]
[2]	[2] II	[2]	[2] II	[2]	[2]
[3]	[3] III	[3]	[3] III	[3]	[3]
[4]	[4] IV	[4]	[4] IV	[4]	[4]
[5]	[5] V	[5]	[5] V	[5]	[5]
[6]	[6] VI	[6]	[6] VI	[6]	[6]
[7]	[7] VIII	[7]	[7] VII	[7]	[7]
[8]	[8] X	[8]	[8] VIII	[9]	[9]
[9]	[9] XI	[9]	[9] IX	[8]	[8]
[10]	[10] XIV	[10]	[10] X	[10]	[10]
[11]	[11] XV	[11]	[11] XI	[11]	[11]
[12]	[12] XVI	[12]	[12] XII	[12]	[12]
[13]	[13] XVII	[13]	–	[13]	[13]
[14]	[14] XVIII	[14]	[13] XIIII	[14]	[14]
[15]	[15] XIX	[15]	[14] XV	[15]	[15]
[16]	[16] XX	[16]	[15] XVI	[16]	[16]
[17]	[17] XXI	[17]	[16] XVII	[17]	[17]
[18]	[18] XXII	[18]	[17] XVIII	[18–9]	[18–9]
[19]	[19] XXIII	[19]	[18] XIX	[20]	[20]
[20]	[20] XXIV	[20]	[19] XX	[21]	[21]
[21]	[21] XXV	[21]	[20] XXI	[22]	[22]
[22]	[22] XXVI	[22]	[21] XXII	[23]	[23]
[23]	[23] XXVII	[23]	[22] XXIII	[24–5]	[24–5]
[24]	[24–6] XXVIII	[24]	[23–4] XXIIII	[26]	[26]
[25]	[27] XXIX	[25]	[25]	[27]	[27]
[26]	[28] XXX	[26]	[26] XXVI	[28]	[28]
[27]	[29] XXXI	[27]	[27] XXVII	[29]	[29]
[28]	[30] XXXII	[28]	[28] XXVIII	[30]	[30]
[29]	[31] XXXIII	[29]	[29] XXXIX	[31]	[31]
[30]	[32] XXXIV	[30]	[30] XXX	[32]	[32]
[31]	[33] XXXV	[31]	[31] XXXI	[33]	[33]
[32]	[34] XXXVI	[32]	[32] XXXII	[34]	[34]
[33]	[35] XXXVII	[33]	[33] XXXIII	[35]	[35]
[34]	[36] XXXVIII	[34]	[34] XXXIIII	[36]	"
[35]	[37] XXXIX	[35]	[35] XXXV	[37]	[36]
[36]	[38] XL	[36]	[36] XXXVI	[38 § 1, 39]	[37 § 1, 38]
[37]	[39] XLI	[37]	[37] XXXVII	[40, 38 § 2]	[39, 37 § 2]
–	[40] XLII	[38	[38] XXXVIII	[41]	[40]
[38]	[41] XLIII	[39]	[39] XXXIX	[42]	[41]
[39]	[42] XLIV	[40]	[40] XL	[43]	[42]
[40]	[43] XLV	[41]	[41] XLI	[44]	[43]
[41]	[44] XLVI	[42]	[42] XLII	[45]	[44]
[42]	[45] XLVII	[43]	[43] XLIII	[46]	[45]
[43]	[46] XLVII	[44]	[44] XLIIII	[47]	[46]
[44]	[47] XLVIII	[45]	[45] XLV	[48]	[47]

TABLE 27 Concordance table of articles, part 2 (*cont.*)

Gn.	F 143	Q II 157 (1)	BN 12600	Q II 157 (2)	Dział. I
[46] XLVI	[48]	[48]	[46]	[46]	[46] XLVI
[47] XLVII	[49]	[49]	[47]	[47]	[47] XLVII
[48] XLVIII	–	[50]	[48]	[48]	[48] XLVIII
[49] XLIX	[50]	[51]	[49]	[49]	[49] XLIX
[50] L	[51]	[52]	[50]	[50]	[50] L
[51] LI	[52–3]	[53]	[51]	[51]	[51] LI
[52] LII	[54]	[54]	[52]	[52]	[52] LII
[53] LIII	[55]	[55]	[53]	[53]	[53] LIII
[54] LIV	[56]	[56]	[54]	[54]	[54] LIV
[55] LV	–	[57]	[55]	[55]	[55] LV
[56] LVI	[57]	[58 § 1–5]	[56]	[56] missing folio	[56] LVI
[57] LVII	[58–9]	[59–60] LIX–LX	[57]	[57]	[57] LVII
[58] LVIII	[60]	[61] LXI	[58]	[58]	[58] LVIII
[59] LIX	"	[62–3] LXII–III	[59]	[59]	[59] LIX
[60] LX	[61–2]	[64] LXIIII	[60]	[60]	[60] LX
[61] LXI	[63–5]	[65–6] LXV	[61]	[61]	[61] LXI
[62] LXII	[66]	[67–8]	[62]	[62]	[62] LXII
[63] LXIII	[67]	[69]	[63]	[63]	[63] LXIII
[64] LXIV	[68]	[70]	[64]	[64]	[64] LXIV
[65] LXV	[69]	[71]	[65]	[65]	[65] LXV
[66] LXVI	[70]	[72]	[66]	[66]	[66] LXVI
[67] LXVII	[71]	[73]	[67]	[67]	[67] LXVII
[68] LXVIII	[72]	–	[68]	[68]	[68] LXVIII
[69] LXIX	[73]	[74]	[69]	[69]	[69] LXIX
[70] LXX	[74–5]	[75–6]	[70]	[70]	[70] LXX
[71] LXXI	–	[77]	[71]	[71]	[71] LXXI
[72] LXXII	[76]	[78]	[72]	[72]	[72] LXXII
[73] LXXIII	[77]	[79]	[73]	[73]	[73] LXXIII
[74] LXXIV	[80]	[80]	[74]	[74]	[74] LXXIV
[75] LXXV	[81]	[81]	[75]	[75]	[75] LXXV
[76 part 1,3] LXXVI	[82]	[82]	[76]	[76]	[77 part 1, 3] LXXVI
[76 part 2] LXXVI	[78]	[102]	"	"	[77 part 2]
[77] LXXVII	[83]	[83]	[77]	[77]	[76] LXXVII
[78] LXXVIII	[79]	[84]	[78]	[78]	[78] LXXVIII
–	–	–	–	–	–
[79] LXXIX	[84]	[85]	[79]	[79]	[79] LXXIX
[80] LXXX	[85]	[86]	[80]	[80]	[80] LXXX
[81] LXXXI	[86]	[87]	[81]	[81]	[81] LXXXI
[82] LXXXII	[87]	[88]	[82]	[82]	[82] LXXXII
[83] LXXXIII	[88]	[89]	[83]	[83]	[83] LXXXIII
[84] LXXXIIII	[89]	[90]	[84]	[84]	[84] LXXXIIII

BJ 4405	Przem.	Plesz.	BOZ	AJG	Kiel.
[45]	[48] XLIX	[46]	[46] XLVI	[49]	[48]
[46]	[49] L	[47]	[47] XLVII	[50]	[49]
[47]	[50] LI	[48]	[48] XLVIII	[51]	[50]
[48]	[55] LV	[49]	[49] XLIX	[52]	[51]
[49]	[51] LII	[50]	[50] L	[53]	[52]
[50]	[52–3] LIII	[51]	[51] LI	[54]	[53]
[51]	[54] LIV	[52]	[52] LII	[57]	[56]
[52]	[56] LVI	[53]	[53] LIII	[55]	[54]
[53]	[57] LVII	[54]	[54] LIIII	–	–
[54]	[58] LVIII	[55]	[55] LV	[56]	[55]
[55]	[59] LIX	–	[56] LVI	[59]	[58]
[56]	[60] LX	–	[57] LXII	–	–
[57]	[61] LXI	–	[58] LXIII	[60]	[59]
[58]	[62] LXII	–	[59] LXIIII	[61]	[60]
[59]	[63] LXIII	–	[60] LXV	[58]	[57]
[60]	[64] LXIV	–	[61] LXI	[62]	[61]
[61]	[65] LXV	–	[62] LXII	[63]	[62]
[62]	[66] LXVI	–	[63] LXIIII	[64]	[63]
[63]	[67] LXVII	–	[64] LXIIII	[65]	[64]
[64]	[68] LXVIII	–	[65] LXV	[66]	[65]
[65]	[69] LXIX	–	[66] XCI	[67]	[66]
[66]	[70] LXX	–	[67] LXVII	[68]	[67]
[67]	[71] LXXI	–	[68] LXVIII	[69]	[68]
[68]	[72] LXXII	–	[69] LXIX	[70]	[69]
[69]	[73] LXXIII	–	[70] LXX	[71]	[70]
[70]	[74] LXXIV	–	[71] LXXI	[72]	[71]
[71]	[75] LXXV	–	[72] LXXII	[73]	[72]
[72]	[76] LXXVI	–	[73] LXXIII	[74]	[73]
[73]	[77] LXXVII	–	[74] LXXIIII	[75]	[74]
[74]	[78] LXXVIII	–	[75] LXXV	[76]	[75]
[75 part 1,3]	[79–80 part 1] LXXIX–X	–	[76] LXXIIII	[77 part 1, 3]	[76 part 1, 3]
[75 part 2]	[80 part 2] LXXX	–	"	[77 part 2, 78]	[76 part 2, 77]
[76]	[81–2] LXXXI–II	–	[77] LXXVII	[77 § 4]	[76 § 4]
[77]	[83] LXXXIII	–	[78] LXXVIII	[79]	[78]
–	–	–	–	[80]	[79]
[78]	[84] LXXXIIII	–	[79] LXXIX	[81]	[80]
[79]	[85] LXXXV	–	[80] LXXX	[82]	[81]
[80]	[86] LXXXVI	–	[81] LXXXI	[83]	[82]
[81]	[87] LXXXVII	–	[82] LXXXII	[84]	[83]
[82]	[88] LXXXVIII	–	[83] LXXXIII	"	"
[83]	[89] LXXXIX	–	[84] LXXXIIII	[85]	[84]

TABLE 27 Concordance table of articles, part 2 (*cont.*)

Gn.	F 143	Q II 157 (1)	BN 12600	Q II 157 (2)	Dział. I
[85] LXXXV	[90]	[91]	[85]	[85]	[85] LXXXV
[86] LXXXVI	[91]	[92]	[87]	[86]	[86] LXXXVI
[87] LXXXVII	[92]	[93]	[88]	[87]	[87] LXXXVII
[88] LXXXVIII	[93]	[94]	[89]	[88]	[88] LXXXVIII
[89] LXXXIX	[94]	[95]	[90]	[89]	[89] LXXXIX
[90] LXXXX	[95]	[96]	[91]	[90]	[90] LXXXX
[91] XCI	[96]	[97]	[91]	[91]	[91] LXXXXI
[92] XCII	[97]	[98]	[92]	[92]	[92] LXXXXII
[93] XCIII	[98]	[99]	[93]	[93]	[93] LXXXXIII
[94] XCIIII	–	[100]	[94]	[94]	[94] LXXXXIIII
[95] XCV	–	[103]	[95]	[95]	[95] LXXXXV
[96] XCVI	[100–1]	[104–5]	[97]	[97]	[96] LXXXXVI
[97] XCVII	[99]	[101]	[96]	[96]	[97] LXXXXVII
[98] XCVIII	–	[106]	[98]	[98]	[98] LXXXXVIII
[99] XCIX	[102]	[107]	[99]	[99]	[99] LXXXXIX
[100] C	[103]	[108]	[100]	[100]	[100] C
[101] CI	[104]	[109]	[101]	[101]	[101] XI
[102] CII	[106]	[110]	[103]	[103]	[102] CII
[103] CIII	[105]	[111]	[102]	[102]	[103] CIII
[104] CIIII	[107]	[112]	[104]	[104]	[104] CIIII
[105] CV	[108]	[113]	[105]	[105]	[105] CV
[106] CVI	[109]	[114]	[106]	[106]	[106] CVI
[107] CVII	[110]	[115]	[107]	[107]	[107] CVII
[108–9]	[111–2]	[116–7]	[108–9]	[108–9]	[108–9] CVIII
[110]	–	[118]	–	[110]	[110]
[111]	–	[119–20]	[110]	[111–4]	[111]
[112]	–	[121]	[111]	[115]	[112]
[113]	–	–	[112]	–	[113]
[114]	–	–	–	–	[114]
[115]	–	–	[113]	–	[115]
[116]	–	–	–	–	[116]
[117]	–	–	–	–	[117]
–	–	–	–	–	–
–	–	–	–	–	–
–	–	–	–	–	–
–	–	–	–	–	–
–	–	–	–	–	

BJ 4405	Przem.	Plesz.	BOZ	AJG	Kiel.
[84]	[90] LXXXX	–	[85] LXXXV	[86]	[85]
[85]	[91] LXXXXI	–	[86] LXXXVI	[87]	[86]
[86]	[92] LXXXXII	–	[87] LXXXVII	[88]	[87]
[87]	[93] LXXXXIII	–	[88] LXXXVIII	[89]	[88]
[88]	[94] LXXXXIIII	–	[89] LXXXIX	[90]	[89]
[89]	[95] LXXXXV	–	[90] XC	[91]	[90]
[90]	[96] LXXXXVI	–	[91] XCI	[92]	[91]
[91]	[97] LXXXXVII	–	[92] XCII	[93]	[92]
[92]	[98] LXXXXVIII	–	[93] XCIII	[94]	[93]
[93]	[99] LXXXXIX	–	[94] XCIIII	"	"
[94]	[100] LXXXXX	–	–	"	"
[96]	[101] C	–	[96] XCVII	[96–7]	[95–6]
[95]	[102] CI	–	[95] XCV	[95]	[94]
[97]	[103] CII	–	[97] XCVIII	[98]	[97]
[98]	[104] CIII	–	[98] XCIX	[99]	[98]
[99]	[105–6] CIIII–V	–	[99] C	[100–1]	[99–100]
[100]	[107] CVI	–	[100] CI	[102]	[101]
[101]	[108] CVII	–	[102] CIII	[103]	[102]
[102]	[109] CVIII	–	[101] CIII	[104]	[103]
[103]	[110] CIX	–	[103] CIIII	[105]	[104]
[104]	[111] CX	–	–	[106]	[105]
[105]	[112] CXI	–	[104] CV	[107]	[106]
[106]	[113] CXII	–	[105] CVII	[108]	[107]
[107–8]	[114] CXIII	–	[106–7] CVIII	[109]	[108]
[109]	–	–	[108]	[110 part 1]	[109 part 1]
–	–		[109–111]	[110 part 2, 111–2]	[109 part 2, 110–1]
–	–	–	[112]	[113]	[112]
–	–	–	–	[114]	[113]
–	–	–	–	[115]	[114]
–	–	–	[113]	[116]	[115]
–	–	–	[114]	[117–8]	[116–7]
–	–	–	[115]	[119 part 1]	[118 part 1]
–	–	–	–	[119 part 2]	[118 part 2]
–	–	–	–	[120]	[119]
–	–	–	–	[121]	[120]
–	–	–	–	[122]	[121]
–	–	–	–	[123]	[122]

TABLE 28 Concordance table of articles, part 3

Gn.	Flor.	Dział. IV	Warsz.	BN 12607
[1]	[1] I	[1]	[1] missing folio	[1]
[2] II	[2]	[2] II	[2] missing folio	[2]
[3] III	[3] II	[3] III	[3] missing folio	[3]
[4] IV	[4] III	[4] IV	[4] missing folio	[4]
[5] V	[5] IV	[5] V	[5] missing folio	[5]
[6] VI	[6] V	[6] VI	[6] missing folio	[6]
[7] VII	[7] VI	[7] VII	[7] missing folio	[7–8]
[8] VIII	[8] VII	[8]VIII	[8] missing folio	[9]
[9] IX	[9] VIII	[9] IX	[9] missing folio	[10–11]
[10] X	[10] IX	[10] X	[10] missing folio	[12]
[11] XI	[11] X	[11] XI	[11] missing folio	[13]
[12] XII	[12] XI	[12] XII	[12] missing folio	[14]
[13] XIII	[13]	[13] XIII	[13] missing folio	[15–6]
[14] XIV	[14]	[14] XIV	[14] missing folio	[17–8]
[15] XV	[15]	[15] XV	[15] missing folio	[19]
[16] XVI	[16]	[16] XVI	[16] missing folio	[20]
[17] XVII	[17]	[17] XVII	[17] missing folio	[21]
[18] XVIII	[18–9]	[18] XIX	[18] missing folio	[22–3]
[19] XIX	[20]	[19] XX	[19] missing folio	[24]
[20] XX	[21]	[20] XXI	[20] missing folio	[25]
[21] XXI	[22–3]	[21 § 1–2] XXII–III	[21] missing folio	[26–7]
[22] XXII	[24]	[22] XXIIII	[22] missing folio	[28]
[23] XXIII	[25–6]	[23–4] XXV–VI	[23] missing folio	[29–30]
[24] XXIV	[27]	[25] XXVII	[24] missing folio	[31]
[25] XXV	[28]	[26] XXVIII	[25] missing folio	[32]
[26] XXVI	[29]	[27] XXIX	[26] missing folio	[33]
[27] XXVII	[30]	[28] XXX	[27] missing folio	[34]
[28] XXVIII	[31]	[29] XXXI	[28] missing folio	[35]
[29] XXIX	[32]	[30] XXXII	[29] missing folio	[36]
[30] XXX	[34]	[32] XXXIII	[30] missing folio	[38]
[31] XXXI	[33]	[31] XXXII	[31] missing folio	[37]
[32] XXXII	[35]	[33] XXXV	[32] missing folio	[39]
[33] XXXIII	[36]	[34] XXXVI	[33] missing folio	[40]
[34] XXXIV	[37]	[35] XXXVII	[34] missing folio	[41]
[35] XXXV	[38]	[36] XXXVIII	[35] missing folio	[42]
[36] XXXVI	[39]	[37] XXXIX	[36] missing folio	[43]
[37] XXXVII	[40]	[38] XL	[37] missing folio	[44]
[38] XXXVIII	[41]	[39] XLI	[38] missing folio	[45]
[39] XXXIX	[42]	[40] XLII	[39] missing folio	[46]
[40] XL	[43]	[41] XLIII	[40] missing folio	[47]
[41] XLI	[44]	[42] XLIIII	[41] missing folio	[48]
[42] XLII	[45]	[43] XLV	[42] missing folio	[49]
[43] XLIII	"	[44] XLVII	[43] missing folio	[50]
[44] XLIV	[46]	[45] XLVI	[44] missing folio	[51]
[45] XLV	[47]	[46] XLVII	[45] missing folio	[52]

Oss.	II Q 4	951b	BN 3068	*Statute*
[1] missing folio	[1] I	[1]	[1 § 1–4]	[1] f. 176v–177
[2] missing folio	[2] II	[2 § 1–3]	[2 § 1–2] II	[2] f. 177
[3] missing folio	[3] III	[3]	[3 § 1–3] III	[3] f. 177
[4] missing folio	[4] IIII	[4 § 1–2]	[4 § 1–3] IV	[4] f. 177–177v
[5] missing folio	[5] V	[5 § 1–3]	[5] V	[5] f. 177v
[6] missing folio	[6] VI	[6 § 1–3]	[6] VI	[6] f. 177v
[7] missing folio	[7] VII	[7 § 1–2]	[7] VII	[7] f. 177v–178
[8] missing folio	[9] VIII	[8]	[9] VIII	[8] f. 178
[9] missing folio	[8] IX	[9 § 1–3]	[10 § 1–2]	[9] f. 178
[10] missing folio	[10] X	[10]	[11] X	[10] f. 178
[11] missing folio	[11] XI	[11 § 1–2]	[12] XI	[11] f. 178–178v
[12] missing folio	[12] XII	[12]	[13] XII	[12] f. 178v
[13] missing folio	[13] XIII	[13]	[14] XIII	[13] f. 178v
[14] missing folio	[14] XIIII	[14 § 1–5]	[15] XIV	[14–5] f. 178v–179
[15] missing folio	[15] XV	[15]	[16] XV	[16] f. 179
[16] missing folio	[16] XVI	[16 § 1–2]	[17] XVI	[17–8] f. 179
[17] missing folio	[17] XVII	[17]	[18] XVII	[19] f. 179
[18] missing folio	[18–9] XVIII–XIX	[18 § 1–2]	[19–20] XVIII–XIX	[20–1] f. 179
[19] missing folio	[20] XX	[19]	[21] XX	[22] f. 179–f. 179v
[20] missing folio	[21] XXI	[20 § 1–4]	[22] XXI	[23] f. 179v
[21] missing folio	[22–3] XXII–III	[21]	[23–4] XXII–III	[24] f. 179v
[22] missing folio	[24] XXIIII	[22]	[8] VII, [25] XXIIII	[25] f. 179v
[23] missing folio	[25–6] XXV–VI	[23 § 1–4]	[26–7 § 1–2] XXV–VI	[26–7] f. 179v–180
[24] missing folio	[27] XXVII	[24 § 1–5]	[28 § 1,2] XXVII	[28–30] f. 180
[25] missing folio	[28] XXVIII	[25 § 1–3]	[29 § 1,2] XXVIII	[31] f. 180–180v
[26] missing folio	[29] XXIX	[26 § 1,2]	[30] XXIX	[32] f.180v
[27] missing folio	[30] XXXIII	[27]	[31] XXX	[33] f. 180v
[28] missing folio	[31] XXIX	[28]	[32 § 2] XXXI	[34] f. 180v
[29] missing folio	[32] XXXII	[29]	[33] XXXII	[35] f. 181
[31] LI	[33] XXXIII	[30]	[34] XXXIII	[36] f. 181
[30] missing folio	[34] XXXIIII	[31]	[35] XXXIIII	[37] f. 181
[32–3] LII–LIII	[35] XXXV	[32 § 1,2]	[36] XXXV	[38] f. 181–181v
[34] LIIII	[36] XXXVI	[33]	[37] XXXVI	[39] f. 181v
[35] LV	[37] XXXVII	[34]	[38] XXXVII	[40] f. 181v
[36] LVI	[38] XXXVIII	[35 § 1,2]	[39] XXXVIII	[41] f. 181v–182
[37] LVII	[39] XXXIX	[36 § 1,2]	[40] XXXIX	[42] f. 182
[38] LVIII	[40] XL	[37 § 1,2]	[41] XL	[43] f. 182
[39] LIX	[41] XLI	[38]	[42] XLI	[44] f. 182
[40] LX	[42] XLII	[39 § 1–3]	[44] XLII	[46] f. 182v
[41] LXI	[43] XLIII	[40]	[45] XLIII	[47] f. 182v
[42] LXII	[44] XLIIII	[41]	[46] XLIIII	[48] f. 182v–183
[43] LXIII	[45] XLV	[42 § 1,2]	[47] XLV	[49] f. 183
[44] LXIV	[46] XLVI	[43]	[48] XLVI	"
[45] LXV	[47] XLVII	[44]	[49] XLVII	[50] f. 183
[46] LXVI	[48] XLVIII	[45]	[50] XLVIII	[51] f. 183

TABLE 28 Concordance table of articles, part 3 (*cont.*)

Gn.	Flor.	Dział. IV	Warsz.	BN 12607
[46] XLVI	[48]	[47] XLVIII	[46] missing folio	[53]
[47] XLVII	[49]	[48] LIX	[47] missing folio	[54]
[48] XLVIII	[50]	[49] L	[48] missing folio	[55]
[49] XLIX	[51]	[50] LI	[49] missing folio	[56]
[50] L	[52]	[51] LII	[50] missing folio	[57]
[51] LI	[53–4]	[52] LIII	[51] missing folio	[58]
[52] LII	[56]	[55] LVI	[52] missing folio	[61]
[53] LIII	[55]	[53] LIIII	[53] missing folio	[59]
[54] LIV	[57]	[54] LV	[54] missing folio	[60]
[55] LV	–	–	[55] missing folio	–
[56] LVI	[59]	–	[56] missing folio	[63]
[57] LVII	[60]	–	[57] missing folio	–
[58] LVIII	[61]	[57] LVIII–LIX	[58] missing folio	[64]
[59] LIX	[62]	[58] LX	[59] missing folio	[65]
[60] LX	[58, 63]	[56] LVII	[60] missing folio	[62]
[61] LXI	[64]	[59] LXI	[61] missing folio	[66]
[62] LXII	[65]	[60] LXII	[62] missing folio	[67]
[63] LXIII	[66]	[61] LXIII	[63] missing folio	[68]
[64] LXIV	[67]	[62] LXIIII	[64] missing folio	[69]
[65] LXV	[68]	[63] LXV	[65] missing folio	[70]
[66] LXVI	[69]	[64] LXVI	[66] missing folio	[71]
[67] LXVII	[70]	[65] LXVII	[67] missing folio	[72]
[68] LXVIII	[71]	[66] LXVIII	[68] missing folio	[73]
[69] LXIX	[72]	[67] LXIX	[69] missing folio	[74]
[70] LXX	[73]	[68] LXX	[70] missing folio	[75]
[71] LXXI	[74]	[69] LXXI	[71] missing folio	[76]
[72] LXXII	[75]	[70] LXXII	[72] missing folio	[77]
[73] LXXIII	[76]	[71] LXXIII	[73] missing folio	[78]
[74] LXXIV	[77]	[72] LXXIIII	[74] missing folio	[79]
[75] LXXV	[78]	[73] LXXV	[75] LXXV	[80]
[76 part 1,3] LXXVI	[79 part 1,3]	–	–	–
[76 part 2] LXXVI	[79 part 2]	[74] LXXVI	[76] LXXVI	[81]
[77] LXXVII	[80]	–	–	–
[78] LXXVIII	[81]	[75] LXXVII	[77] LXXVII	[82]
–	–	[76] LXXVIII	[78] LXXVIII	[83]
[79] LXXIX	[82]	[77] LXXIX	[79] LXXIX	[84]
[80] LXXX	[83]	[78] LXXX	[80] LXXX	[85]
[81] LXXXI	[84]	–	–	[86]

Oss.	II Q 4	951b	BN 3068	*Statute*
[47–8] LXVII, LXVI	[49] XLIX	[46 § 1–5]	[51–52 § 1] XLIX–L	[52] f. 183v
[49] LXVII	[50] L	[47 § 1–4]	[52 § 2]	[53] f. 183v
[50] LXVIII	[51] LI	[48]	[53] LI	[54] f. 183v–184
[51] LXIX	[52] LII	[49 § 1–2]	[54] LII	[55] f. 184
[52] LXX	[53] LIII	[50]	[55] LIII	[56] f. 184
[53–6] LXXI–IV	[54] LIIII	[51 § 1–3]	[56] LIIII	[57] f. 184–184v
[60] LXXVIII	[57] LVII	[52]	[57] LV	[58] f. 184v
[57–8] LXXV–VI	[55] LV	[53]	[58] LVI	[59] f. 184v–185
[59] LXXVII	[56] LVI	[54]	[59] LVII	[60] f. 185
–	–	[55]	[60] LVIII	[61] f. 185–185v
[62–3] LXXX–I	[59] LIX	[56 popart 96 kon.]	[61 § 1–2] LIX	[62] f. 185v–186v
–	–	[97, 61]	[62] LX	[63] f. 186v
[64–5] LXXXII–III	[60] LX	[62]	[63] LXI	[64] f. 187
[66–7] LXXXIV–V	[61] LXI	[63]	[64] LX	[65] f. 187
[61] LXXIX	[58] LVIII	[64 § 1–2]	[65] LXI	[66] f. 187
[66] LXXXVI fragment	[62] LXII	[65 § 1–5]	[66] LXI, [32 § 1] XXXI	[67–8] f. 187–188
[69] missing folio	[63] LXIII	[66]	[67] LXII	[69] f. 188
[70] missing folio	[64] LXIIII	[67]	[68] LXIII	[70] f. 188
[71] missing folio	[65] LXV	[68]	[69] LXIIII	[71] f. 188
[73] XCII	[66] LXVI	[69 § 1–2]	[70] LXV	[72] f. 188
[72] XCIII	[67] LXVII	[70]	[71] LXVI	[73] f. 188
[74] XCIIII	[68] LXVIII	[71]	[72] LXVII	[74] f. 188v
[75] XCV	[69] LXIX	[72–4]	[73] LXVIII	[75] f. 188v
[76] XCVI	[70] LXX	[75]	[74] LXIX [43] XLI	[45] f. 182v
[77] XCVII	[71] LXXI	[76]	[75] LXX	[76] f. 188v
[78] XCVIII	[72] LXXII	[77]	[76] LXXI	[77] f. 188v
[79] XCIX	[73] LXXIII	[78]	[77] LXXII	[78] f. 188v
[80] C	[74] LXXIIII	[79]	[78] LXXIII	[79] f. 188v–189
[81] CI	[75] LXXV	[80]	[79] LXXIIII	[80] f. 189
[82] CII	[76] LXXVI	[81 § 1,2]	[80] LXXV	[81] f. 189
–	–	[82]	[81] LXXVI	[82] f. 189–189v
[83] CIII	[77] LXXVII	[84 § 1,2]	[83] LXXVIII	[84] f. 189v
–	–	[83]	[82] LXXVII	[83] f. 189v
[84] CIIII	[78] LXXVIII	[85]	[84] LXXIX	[85] f. 189v
[85] CV	[79] LXXIX	[86]	[85] LXXX	[86] f. 189–190
[86] CVI	[80] LXXX	[87]	[86] LXXXI	[87] f. 190
[87] CVII	[81] LXXXI	[88]	[87] LXXXII	[88] f. 190
[88] CVIII	[82] LXXXII	[89]	[88] LXXXIII	[89] f. 190

TABLE 28 Concordance table of articles, part 3 (*cont.*)

Gn.	Flor.	Dział. IV	Warsz.	BN 12607
[82] LXXXII	[85]	[79] LXXXI	[81] LXXXI	[87]
[83] LXXXIII	[86]	[80] LXXXIII	[82] LXXXII	[88]
[84] LXXXIIII	[87]	[81] LXXXIV	[83] LXXXIII	[89]
[85] LXXXV	[88]	[82] LXXXVI	[84] LXXXIIII	[90]
[86] LXXXVI	[89]	[83] LXXXVI	[85] LXXXVI	[91]
[87] LXXXVII	[90]	[84] LXXXVII	[86] LXXXVII	[92]
[88] LXXXVIII	[91]	[85] LXXXVIII	[87] LXXXVIII	[93]
[89] LXXXIX	[92]	[86] LXXXIX	[88] LXXXIX	[94]
[90] LXXXX	[93]	[87] XC	[89] LXXXX	[95]
[91] XCI	[94]	[88] XCI	[90] XCI	[96]
[92] XCII	[95]	[89] XCII	[91] XCII	[97]
[93] XCIII	[96]	[90] XCIII	[92] XCIII	[98]
[94] XCIIII	[97]	[91] XCIIII	[93] XCIIII	[99]
[95] XCV	[98]	"	"	"
[96] XCVI	[99]	[93–4] XCVI–VII	[95–6] XCVI–VIII	[101–2]
[97] XCVII	[100]	[92] XCV	[94] XCV	[100]
[98] XCVIII	[101]	[95] XCVIII	[97] XCVIII	[103]
[99] XCIX	[102]	[96] XCIX	[98] XCVIIII	[104]
[100] C	[103]	[97] C	[99] C	[105]
[101] CI	[104]	[98] CI	[100] CI	[106]
[102] CII	[105]	[99, 99a] CII–CIII	[102] CIII	[108]
[103] CIII	[106]	[100] CIII	[101] XII	[107]
[104] CIIII	[107]	[101] CIIII	[103] CIIII	[109]
[105] CV	[108]	[102] CV	[104] CV	[100]
[106] CVI	[109]	[103] CVI	[105] CVI	[111]
[107] CVII	[110]	[104] CVII	[106] CVII	[112]
[108–9]	[111–12]	[105] CVIII	[107] CVIII	[113]
[110]	[113]	[106 part 1] CIX part 1	[108 part 1] CIX part 1	[114 part 1]
[111]	[114 part 1]	[106 part 2, 107–8] CIX part 2, CX–I	[108 part 2, 109–10] CIX part II, CX	[114 part 2, 115–6]
[112]	[114 part 2]	[109] CXII	[111]	[117]
[113]	[115]	[110] CXIIII	[112]	[118]
[114]	[116]	[111] CXV	[113]	[119]
[115]	[117]	[112]	[114]	[120]

Oss.	II Q 4	951b	BN 3068	*Statute*
[89] CIX	[83] LXXXIII	[90 § 1–2]	–	[90] f. 190
[90] CX	[84] LXXXIIII	[91 § 1–2]	–	[91] f. 190–190v
[91] CXI	[85] LXXXV	[92]	–	[92] f. 190v
[92–3] CXII–III	[86] LXXXVI	[93]	[89] LXXXV	[93] f. 190v
[94] CXIII	[87] LXXXVII	[94]	[90] LXXXVI	[94] f. 190v–191
[95] CXIIII	[88] LXXXVIII	[95]	[91] LXXXVII	[95–6] f. 191
[96] CXIIII	[89] LXXXIX	[96 popart]	[92] LXXXVIII	[97] f. 191
[97] CXV	[90] XC	[57]	[93] LXXXIX	[98] f. 191–191v
[98] CXVI	[91] XCI	[58]	[94] XC	[99] f. 191v
[99–100] CXVII–VIII	[92] XCII	[59]	[95] XCI	[100] f. 191v
[101] CXXX	[93] XCIII	[60]	[96] XCII	[101] f. 191v
[102] CXXI	[94] XCIIII	[98]	[97] XCIII	[102] f. 191
[103] CXXII	[95] XCV	[99]	[98 § 1] XCIIII	[103] f. 191v–192
"	"	[100–1]	[98 § 2]	[104–5] f. 192
[106–7] CXXIIII–V	[97–8] XCVII–VIII	[103 § 1,2]	[100–1] XCVI–VII	[107–8] f. 192
[104–5] CXXII–III	[96] XCVI	[102]	[99] XCV	[106] f. 192
[108] CXXVI	[99] XCIX	[104]	[102] XCVIII	[109] f. 192–192v
[109–10] CXXVII–VIII	[100] C	[105]	[103] XCIX	[110] f. 192v
[101–113] CXXIX–XI	[101] CI	[106 § 1–5]	[104] C	[111] f. 192v–193
[114] CXXXII	[102] CII	[107]	[105] CI	[112] f. 193
[116] CXXXIIII	[104] CIIII	[109]	[107] CIII	[114] f. 193
[117] CXXXIII	[103] CIII	[108]	[106] CII	[113] f. 193–193v
[118] CXXXV	[105] CV	[110]	[108] CIV	[115] f. 193v
[119] CXXXVI	[106] CVI	[111]	[109] CV	[116] f. 193v
[120] CXXXVII	[107] CVII	[112]	[110] CVI	[117] f. 193v
[121] CXXXVIII	[108] CVIII	[113]	[111] CVII	[118] f. 193v
[122] CXXXIX	[109] CIX	[114–5]	[112] CVIII	[119] f. 193v–194
[123 part 1] CXXXX part 1	[110 part 1] CX part 1	[116]	[113–4] CIX	[120 part 1] f. 194–194v
[123 part 2. 124–5] CXXXX part 2, CXXXXI–CXLII	[110 part 2, 111–2] CX part 2. CXI–CXII	[117–20]	[115–18] CIX–CX	[120 part 2, 121–2] f. 194–195
[126–7] CXLIII–IIII	[113] CXIII	[121]	[119] CXI	[123] f. 195
[128–9] CXLV–VI	[114] CXIIII	[122]	[120] CXII	[124] f. 195–195v
[130] CXLVII	[115] CXV	[123]	[121] CXIII	[125] f. 195v–196
[131] CXLVIII	[116] CXVI	[124]	[122–3] CXIIII	[126] f. 196

TABLE 28 Concordance table of articles, part 3 (*cont.*)

Gn.	Flor.	Dział. IV	Warsz.	BN 12607
[116]	[118]	[113–4]	[115–6]	[121–2]
[117]	[119]	[115 part 1]	[117 part 1]	[123 part 1]
–	–	[115 part 2]	[117 part 2]	[123 part 2]
–	–	[116]	[118]	[124]
–	–	[117]	[119]	[125]
–	–	[118]	[120]	[126]
–	–	[119]	[121]	[127]

Oss.	II Q 4	951b	BN 3068	*Statute*
[132–3] CXLIX–CL	[117–8] CXVII–VIII	[125–6]	[124–5] CXV–VI	[127–8] f. 196–196v
[134 part 1] CLI part 1	[119 part 1] CXIX part 1	[127 cz. 1]	[126] CXVII	[129 part I] f. 196v
[134 part 2] CLI part 2	[119 part 2] CXIX part 2	[127 cz. 2]	–	[129 part II] f. 196v
[135] CLII	[120] CXX	[129 !]	–	[130] f. 196v
[136] CLIII	[121] CXXI	[130 !]	–	[131] f. 197
[137] CLIIII	[122] CXXII	–	–	[132] f. 197
[138] CLV	[123] CXXIII	–	–	[133] f. 197

APPENDIX 2

Divergences in the Latin Texts of the *Weichbild*

The differences between the texts analyzed in this study can be categorized as follows:

1) modification of a provision (e.g. *metseptimus* replaced by *mettertius*);
2) amendations intended to clarify the meaning of the text ([*consules*] *honorem civitatis custodire*);
3) amendations that can be confusing (e.g. *Vir si vulneratus ~~aut trucidatus~~ fuerit* – the phrase removed from the text and inserted into the heading of the article);
4) additions reaffirming an existing regulation (e.g. *aliquis subtraxerit* – the phrase *aut subtracto fuerit* is added);
5) omission of tautologies or unnecessary words and phrases (e.g. *actor et ~~ille, hoc est superquem conqueritur~~, ~~respondens est sive~~ reus, possunt habere colloquia*);
6) linguistic amendations – introduction of synonymous words and phrases (e.g. *probare oportet* replaced by *iurare oportet*);
7) amendations of grammar and spelling (e.g. *sententiis* replaced by *sentenciis*);
8) changes in the sequence of words and short phrases (e.g. *tria talenta demeretur* replaced by *demeretur tria talenta*).

For the sake of clarity only the first three categories are indicated in the Concordance Table (it can be assumed that the remaining ones are of no consequence for any practical use of the texts).

The entries contain: 1) number of the article in the Latin text of MS Gn.; 2) a list of manuscripts that include a given feature; 3) notes and explanations concerning the corresponding German text, and cross-references to other legal texts.

1

1. [1] Qum consules suum conventum exponunt, extunc quitquit ibi statutum fuerit aut conpromissum in isto conventu, *quod iuri divino non contradicit*, firmum et inviolabiliter debet observari [Gn.]

2a. in: Gn., Dział. I, BJ 4405, Plesz., BOZ, 951b, BN 3068, *Statutes*

2b. missing: F 143, Q II 157 (1), Q II 157 (2), BN 12600, Przem., AJG, Kiel., Flor., Dział. IV, BN 12607, II Q 4

2c. missing folio: Oss., Warsz.

3a. F 143 Art. 1 Article 1 radically amended, the underlined words missing

3b. see No. 302

2

1. [1] Et hoc non dimittendo ratione amoris, molestie, ire vel munerum, sicut eos iuvet Deus et sancti eius. [*Statutes*]
2a. in: II Q 4, *Statutes*
2b. missing: Gn. and other Latin texts except 2a
2c. missing folio: Oss., Warsz.
3a. as a gloss in 951b; cf. NS I.4
3b. see. No. 303

3

1. [1] [Consules et scabini] Dum eliguntur ius ac profectum et honorem
1a. custodire [Gn. and other Latin texts except 1b, 1c]
1b. *civitatis* custodire [AJG, Kiel., Flor., Dział. IV, BN 12607, II Q 4, BN 3068, *Statutes*]
1c. *et fructum civitatis* conservare [F 143]
2. missing folio: Oss., Warsz.
3a. included in a gloss in Dział. I
3b. see No. 304

4

1. [1] Cesar Otto Rufus fundavit templum in Meydeburc et dedit civibus municipale ius secundum eorum arbitrium *et secundum consilium seniorum* [Gn.]
2a. in: Gn. and other Latin texts except 2b
2b. missing: F 143, BOZ
2c. missing folio: Oss., Warsz.
3. cf. No. 7

5

1. [1] Et quicunque violaverit, hoc consules habent agere [Gn.]
2a. in: Gn. and other Latin texts except 2b
2b. missing: Dział. IV
2c. missing folio: Oss., Warsz.
3. see No. 305

6

1. [1] Et quicumque ad conventum venire neglexerit, cum signum datur per campanam, demeretur sex denarios. Sin autem sibi conventus sibi pronunciatus fuerint, demeretur *quinque/sex* solidos. [Gn.]

2a. *sex*: BN 12607, BN 3068

2b. *quinque*: Gn. and other Latin texts except 2a

2c. missing folio: Oss., Warsz.

3. see No. 306

7

1a. [1] Consules exponunt suum conventum secundum suum placitum ac voluntatem cum seniorum consensus. [Gn.]

2b. [Consules] exponunt legale suum iudicium, quando volunt, cum consilio sapienciorum. [F 143]

2a. derivation only in F 143

2b. missing folio: Oss., Warsz.

3. cf. No. 4

8

1. [1] Consules inter se eligunt proconsulem [F 143]

2a. in: F 143

2b. missing: Gn. and other Latin texts except 2a

2c. missing folio: Oss., Warsz.

3. –

9

1. [1] Si mensure alique aut pense nimis parve sint aut iniuste, hoc consules bene repetant secundum decreta civitatis, aut recipiant melioracionem in emenda triginta sex solidorum. [F 143]

2a. in: F 143

2b. missing: Gn. and other Latin texts except 2a

2c. missing folio: Oss., Warsz.

3. F 143 repeats here a regulation of Art. 3 but a punishment is in inconsistent with the version of Sandomierz, and consistent with the Cracow version

10

1. [3] Si metrete aut alie mensure parve seu iniuste fuerint et iniuste pense, quod consules bene agere possunt secundum honorem civitatis aut cum *triginta* solidis emendare [Gn.]
2a. triginta: Gn. and other Latin texts except 2b
2b. XXXVI: AJG, Kiel., Flor., Dział. IV, BN 12607, II Q 4, BN 3068, *Statutes*
2c. missing folio: Oss., Warsz.
3a. 951b in gloss *sex* written by a commentator
3b. see No. 309

11

1. [3] Si que res mercionales falsificantur, sive ulnas duas vel libras habuerint, ille honore privatur et satis consulibus facere compellitur. Si quis parvulus convictus fuerit, ille honore privatur et satisfacere consulibus compellitur, et iudici solvet penam [e]ius. [BN 3068]
2a. in: BN 3068
2b. missing: Gn. and other Latin texts except 2a
2b. missing folio: Oss., Warsz.
3. concerning forgery and the use of false weights and measures, see in NS, MS D I.14–15, MS P I.14

12

1. [3] Ius enim consulum est civitati sic providere, quod singule emptiones, et in iure mechanici, et pauper populus, valeant sufficere ac sustinere, quod ipsi non efficiantur periuri. [*Statutes*]
2a. in: BN 3068, *Statutes*
2b. missing: Gn. and other Latin texts except 2a
2c. missing folio: Oss., Warsz.
3. slight linguistic divergences between BN 3068 and *Statutes*

13

1. [4] [courts of] *castellanus* [Gn.] / *burgrabius* [Flor.]
2a. *castellanus*: Gn. and other Latin texts except 2b i 2c
2b. *burgrabius*: Flor.

2c. *both*: II Q 4
2d. missing folio: Oss., Warsz.
3. each German texts burgrabius (burgraf)

14

1a. [4] Secundum [iudicium magnum] in festo sanctorum *Johannis et Pauli*. [Gn.]
1b. Secundum [iudicium] in festo sanctorum *Petri et Pauli*. [AJG]
2a. Gn. and other Latin texts except 2b–2c: *Johannis et Pauli*
2b. AJG, Kiel.: *Petri et Pauli*
2c. F 143: a free space to suplement
2d. missing folio: Oss., Warsz.
3. BJ 4405: *Joannis*; *Pauli*: addendum in gloss

15

1. [4] Dies ligati sunt omnes dies dominicales et festi dies: dies rogacionum aut Penthecostes et adventus Christi et septuaginta dies ante Pascha, in talibus quibus diebus non debent iudicari. [BN 12607]
2a. in: BN 12607, II Q 4
2b. missing: Gn. and other Latin texts except 2a
2c. missing folio: Oss., Warsz.
3a. gloss in BN 3068 and Dział. I: Polish translation of *dies celebres* (*naroczẏsztẏ dzẏen*)
3b. only in the German text in II Q 4: *In sulchin tagin sal man nicht dingin*
3c. in: NTO No. 158 and in the Latin collection of Magdeburg *ortyle* in BJ 4405 No. 148, f. 45r

16

1. [5] [courts of] *castellanus* [Gn.] / *burgrabius* [Flor.]
2a. *castellanus*: Gn and other Latin texts except 2b and 2c
2b. *burgrabius*: Flor.
2c. *both*: *Statutes*, BN 3068
2d. missing folio: Oss., Warsz.
3. each German texts burgrabius (burgraf)

17

1. [5] Pena ad sex ebdomadas solvi debet, emenda post penam ad XIIII dies. *Recompensa debet solvi ad XII ebdomadas.* [*Statutes*]
2a. complete wording in the *Statutes*
2b. no underlined fragment: BN 3068
2c. missing: Gn. and other Latin texts except 2a and 2b
2d. missing folio: Oss., Warsz.
3a. cf. PS II.31 and PS II.37
4b. cf. No. 18

18

1. [5] Si autem vir emendam ante pena acquisierit, exsolvi debet ad sex ebdomadas et pena post hoc ad XIIII dies. Recompensa debet solvi ad XII ebdomadas ad domum illius, cui debitum tenetur, ante solis occasum, aut in propria domo, si ibi domum non habuerit.
2a. in: BN 3068
2b. missing: Gn. and other Latin texts except 2a
2c. missing folio: Oss., Warsz.
3. cf. No. 17

19

1. [5] Talentum autem signat XX solidos.
2a. in: BN 3068
2b. missing: Gn. and other Latin texts except 2a
2c. missing folio: Oss., Warsz.
3a. BN 12607 in gloss: Talentum XX solidorum
3b. cf. PS II.37

20

1a. [5] Pena castellani *tria talenta* ... [Gn.]
1b. Pena castellani *30 solidi* ... [F 143]
2a. *tria talenta*: Gn. and other Latin texts except 2b

2b. *30 solidi*: F 143
2c. missing folio: Oss., Warsz.
3. 30 solidi does not equal 3 talenta

21

1. [5] Et statim iudicium sculteti disponit a proximo ad duas septimanas. [Gn.]
2a. in: Gn. and other Latin texts except 2b
2b. missing: F 143
2c. missing folio: Oss., Warsz.
3. –

22

1. [6] [scultetus] *Insuper liber esse debet* et legittime natus de terra. [Gn.]
2a. the underlined words: Gn., Q II 157 (1), Q II 157 (2), BN 12600, Dział. I, BJ 4405, Przem., BOZ, 951b, BN 3068, *Statutes*
2b. missing: F 143 AJG, Kiel., Flor., Dział. IV, BJ 12607, II Q 4
2c. missing folio: Oss., Warsz.
3a. see No. 313
3b. in MS BN 12607 the copyist appended to the article the maxim: *Summa iuris actus legit cum condicione non recipiunt neque diem* of *Liber sextus*

23

1. [6] Iudicium sculteti nemo potest hominum indicere, nisi scultetus solus vel preco, *nec suus famulus* … [Gn.]
2a. the underlined words: Gn. and other Latin texts except 2b
2b. missing: F 143
2c. missing folio: Oss., Warsz.
3. –

24

1a. [7] Si quis eciam fideiusserit aliquot iudicio pro aliquo adiutorio praesentare ex parte homicidii et eundem non representat, extunc fideiussorem dare oportet querulatori unam recompensam, videlicet *XVIII talenta*, et iudici suam penam octo solidos. *Si autem sentencia fuerit pro uno vulnere duellari, protunc fideiussor det unam mediam reconpensam querulanti, scilicet novem talenta, et iudici suam penam octo solidos*, istorum nummorum, qui in eodem iudicio sunt currenti communiter et dativi. [BN 12607, II Q 4]

1b. Sed si quis per fideiussoriam obligat aliquem pro adiutorio ex parte homicidii statuere et eundem non representat, extunc fideiussor tenetur actori seu querulanti dare plenam recompensam, hoc est *XIIII talenta*, et iudici emendam VIII solidorum, istorum nummorum, qui in eodem iudicio et districtu sunt currenti communiter et dantur. [BN 3068, *Statutes*]

2a. missing the whole text: Gn. and other Latin texts except 2a

2b. *XVIII talenta*: Latin and German text: BN 12607, II Q 4

2c. *XIIII talenta*: BN 3068, *Statutes*

2d. *Si autem sententiam fuerit pro uno vulnere duellari, pro tunc fideiussor det unam mediam reconpensam querulanti scilicet novem talenta, et iudici suam penam octo solidos*: Latin and German text: BN 12607 and II Q 4

2e. slight linguistic divergences between BN 3068 and *Statutes*

2f. missing folio: Oss., Warsz.

3a. compliance of German texts in BN 12607 and II Q 4

3b. in: NTO No. 62 and in the Latin collection of Magdeburg *ortyle* BJ 4405 No. 151, f. 45v; cf. MFr. II.2.8 (P. Laband, *Magdeburger Rechtsquellen*, s. 98)

3c. see No. 317

25

1. [7] Talentum quis facit XX solidos denariorum.

2a. in: BN 3068

2b. missing: Gn. and other Latin texts except 2a

2c. missing folio: Oss., Warsz.

3. cf. (PS II.37)

26

1. [9] *Castellanus* et scultetus bene possunt omni die iudicare pro debito, pro quo absque testimonio agitur, nisi si civis agat contra hospitem vel hospes contra civem pro debito *cum/absque* testimonio [Gn./F 143]

2a. *cum*: Gn. and other Latin texts except 2b

2b. *absque*: F 143, AJG

2c. missing folio: Oss., Warsz.

3. –

27

1. [9] [courts of] *castellanus* [Gn.] / *burgrabius* [Flor.]

2a. *castellanus*: Gn and other Latin texts except 2b

2b. *burgrabius*: Flor.

2c. missing folio: Oss., Warsz.

3. each German texts burgrabius (burgraf)

28

1. [9] Nec sculteto, nec castellano tenetur scabinus nec civis aliquem sentenciam extra veros dies iudiciales diffinire, nisi sit factum manifestum, *ut vulnera mortalia* aut homicidia, *vel furta seu alia criminalia*. [Gn.]

2a. the complete text in: Gn., Q II 157 (1), Q II 157 (2), BN 12600, Dział. I, BJ 4405, Przem., Plesz., BOZ, 951b, BN 3068, *Statutes*

2b. the words in italics missing in: Flor., BN 12607, II Q 4

2c. the underlined words missing in: F 143, AJG, Kiel., Dział. IV

2d. missing folio: Oss., Warsz.

3. see No. 317

29

1. [9] Ille debet esse hospes qui ultra *undecem*/*XII* miliaria extra iudiciuum suum domicilium habet. [BN 12607/*Statutes*]

2a. *undecem*: BN 12607, II Q 4, BN 3068

2b. *XII*: *Statutes*

2c. the complete phrase missing: Gn. and other Latin texts except 2a, 2b

2d. missing folio: Oss., Warsz.

3a. compliance of the German texts in BN 12607 and II Q 4

3b. cf. *undecem*: NTO No. 160; in the Latin collection of Magdeburg *ortyle* in BJ 4405 No. 151, f. 45r; in MFr. II.2.8 (P. Laband, *Magdeburger Rechtsquellen*, s. 98); in the collecion of Magdeburg *ortyle* in BN 12607

3c. cf. *XII*: § 7 of *Magdeburg's Legal Instructions for Chełmno* (Laband p. 141)

3d. see No. 319

30

1a. [9] Hospites, si hospiti vel alteri, qui in iudicio non habuerit possessionem, racione debiti per manum fuerit presentatus, hunc iudex illi servare debet tam diu, quousque se de debito expurget iuridice vel persolvet. [BN 12607]

1b. Et si aliquis alienigena datur per manum in modum pignori, iudex tenetur eum dare ad observandum tamdiu, quousque se debito expurget iuridice aut illud persolvat. [*Statutes*]

2a. slight linguistic divergences between BN 12607, II Q 4, BN 3068

2b. partly another linguistic redaction in the *Statutes*

2c. missing: Gn. and other Latin texts except 2a, 2b

2d. missing folio: Oss., Warsz.

3a. slight linguistic divergences between German texts in BN 12607 and II Q 4

3b. cf. NTO No. 160 and the Latin collection of Magdeburg *ortyle* in BJ 4405 No. 151, f. 45v

3c. see No. 319

31

1. [10] Quodsi *vir/victor* vulneratus fuerit

2a. *vir*: Gn. and other Latin texts except 2a

2b. *victor*: Q II 157 (2), BN 12600

2c. missing folio: Oss., Warsz.

3. –

32

1. [10] Quodsi vir vulneratus fuerit et ea die iudicium non fuerit, quesierit et sua querimonia pernoctaverit et, qui inculpatur, tunc conparuerit, evadit eum

2a. *metseptimus* [Gn., Q II 157 (1), Q II 157 (2), BN 12600, Dział. I, BJ 4405, Przem., Plesz., BOZ, II Q 4, 951b, BN 3068, *Statutes*]

2b. *metseptimus suis vicinis* [Kiel., BN 12607]

2c. *septem suis vicinis* [AJG, Flor., Dział. IV]

2d. *sola manu* [F 143]

2e. missing folio: Oss., Warsz.

3. in gloss in 951b: 2b

33

1. [10] evadit eum … *quam ille super eum possit protestare.* [Gn.]
2a. the underlined words: Gn. and other Latin texts except 2a
2b. missing: BN 12607, II Q 4, *Statutes*
2c. missing folio: Oss., Warsz.
3. the underlined words missing in the German texts, see No. 320

34

1. [11] Si aliquis irruit super alterius domicilium tempore nocturno aut diurno, temeraria violencia, nulla procedente querimonia, et si in manuali facto deprehensus fuerit cum clamore, et si clamorem cum auditoribus metseptimus *suorum vicinorum* [Gn.]
2a. the underlined words: Gn. and other Latin texts except 2b
2b. missing: F 143
2c. missing folio: Oss., Warsz.
3. –

35

1a. [12] Sin autem plures iudicialiter infestaverit, quam vulnera habuerit, alii omnes evadent suo *iure quivis metseptimus.* [Gn. and other Latin texts except 1b and 1c]
1b. Si autem plures iudicialiter infestaverit, quam vulnera habuerit, alii omnes evadent suo *iuramento, qui ius* [s] *sua sola manu pro eo, quoadiutorio racione homicidii vel vulneris duellaris, vel mettertus ad hoc, si pro eo cum testibus fuerit impulsatus.* [BN 12607, II Q 4]
1c. Si autem plures iudicialiter infestaverit, quam vulnera habuerit, alii omnes evadent suo iure quilibet metseptimus, *vel quivis sua sola manu pro adiutorio ratione homicidii vel vulneris duellaris, vel mettertius ad hoc, si pro eo cum testibus fuerit impulsatus.* [*Statutes*]
2. missing folio: Oss., Warsz.
3a. in gloss in 951b
3b. see No. 322

36

1. [12] Sin autem hii homines conparuerint, duellum in ipsis acquirere potest. [Gn.]
2a. in: Gn. and other Latin texts except 2b
2b. missing: F 143
2c. missing folio: Oss., Warsz.
3. –

37

1. [13] Obligat aliquis mercimonia aut alia bona *mobilia* ex parte iudicii, et ille pronunciet tribus iudiciis, ut est iuris, et quarto iudicio super eo dominium receperit ac appropriatum sibi fuerit, et congnoscencie dominii dederit coram iudice et scabinis. [Gn.]
2a. in: Gn. and other Latin texts except 2b, 2c
2b. missing: Dział. IV, 951b
2c. missing Article: BOZ
2d. missing folio: Oss., Warsz.
3. see No. 324

38

1a. [13] Nullus etiam hospes ab alio advena, et e contra, indiget pignus recipere pro debito recognito. Si autem ipsum receperit, extunc ipsum acquirere et prosequi prout alter vir iuridice oportebit, *nisi aliter fuisset inter eos ordinatum verbotenus in contractu.* [*Statutes*]
1b. Etiam non debet aliquis hospes nec aliena unus ab alio aliquod pignus actipere pro debito quem fatetur, sed si hoc pignus reciperit, hec debet iure obtinere et acquirere in iudicio, sicut alii homines, *exceptis si hoc pignus recipit cum prolocucione et excepcione.* [BN 3068]
2a. compliance: BN 12607, II Q 4, *Statutes*
2b. another redaction: BN 3068
2c. the complete phrase missing: Gn. with other Latin texts except 2a, 2b
2d. missing Article: BOZ
2e. missing folio: Oss., Warsz.
3a. compliance of the German texts in BN 12607 i II Q 4
3b. the text in BN 3068 by Art. 9

3c. in gloss in 951b

3d. cf. NTO No. 159 and the Latin collection of Magdeburg *ortyle* in BJ 4405 No. 151, f. 45r; cf. pledge for a guest in § 8 of *Magdeburg's Legal Instructions for Chełmno* (Laband p. 141); cf. collection of Magdeburg *ortyle* in BN 12607

3e. see No. 325

39

1a. [14] Et si *pueri vellent* dotalicium infringere, servare potest testimonio virorum ac mulierum *metseptima* [Gn.]

1b. Et si *mulieri vellent* dotalicium infringere, servare potest testimonio virorum ac mulierum *metseptima* [Plesz.]

1c. Et si *pueri vellent* dotalicium infringere, servare potest testimonio virorum ac mulierum [BN 3068]

2a. compliance: Gn. and other Latin texts except 1b and 1c

2d. missing folio: Oss., Warsz.

3. –

40

1a. [14] Si vir oves habuerit, *quas mulier recipiet* ad suppellectile [Gn.]

1b. Si vir oves habuerit ad suppellectilia recipient [II Q 4]

2. missing: II Q 4

2c. missing folio: Oss., Warsz.

3. –

41

1. [14] si moritur vir, hii pueri, qui in hereditate patris sunt, recipiunt bona, *et non hii, qui exhereditati sunt* [Gn.]

2a. the underlined words missing: Dział. IV

2b. the complete phrase missing: Dział. I, BOZ, 951b (suplement in gloss)

2c. BN 3068: a longer portion of the Article is missing, undoubtedly due to copyist's error

2d. in: Gn. and other Latin texts except 2a–2c

2e. missing folio: Oss., Warsz.

3. see No. 326

42

1. [14] Si vir oves habuerit, quas mulier recipiet ad suppellectile. [Gn.]
2a. in: Gn. and other Latin texts except 2b
2b. missing: Q II 157 (1)
2c. missing folio: Oss., Warsz.
3. –

43

1. [14] Hii pueri, qui in potestate patris *mortis* tempore *fuerunt, si ex hiis unus* moritur, istius partem dividunt inter se equaliter, tam exhereditati quam domestici. [Gn.]
2a. in: Gn. and other Latin texts except 2b
2b. the underlined words missing: Q II 157 (2)
2c. missing folio: Oss., Warsz.
3. –

44

1. [14] Sed deservitum precium et rationabile debitum debeant solvi de bonis mortui viri pre dotalitio, et hoc si mulier fuerit dotata pecuniis in paratis. Si autem dotata fuerit in hereditate propria, tunc suum dotalitium pre aliis debitis iure valeat obtinere.
Etiam quivis vir habens mansionem infra ius municipale, ille sue contorali dare potest pro dotalitio suam propriam hereditatem, quam in posse habeat alienandi, et etiam in aliis bonis suis mobilibus in quantum voluerit. [*Statutes*]
2a. in: BN 12607, II Q 4, *Statutes*
2b. missing: Gn. and other Latin texts except 2a
2c. missing folio: Oss., Warsz.
3a. compliance of German texts in BN 12607 and II Q 4
3b. the first part can be found in MFr. II.2.7, the second part in H. Wasserschleben's edition of the *Magdeburger Urteile* (p. 84; Dresden MS); both in: *Poznańska księga prawa magdeburskiego* IV.150,151, in the Latin translation of the Magdeburg *ortyle* in MS BJ 4405 and in a collection of German *ortyle* from Pilzno
3c. in gloss in 951b
3d. see No. 328

45

1. [16] Quitquit masculus dat sub banno, si possidebit pacifice et quiete

1a. absque *arestacione* aliqua anno et die [Gn., Q II 157 (1), Q II 157 (2), BN 12600, Dział. I, BN 4405, Przem., Plesz., BOZ, 951b, BN 3068]

1b. absque *contradicione* aliqua anno et die [F 143, AJG, Kiel., Flor., Dział. IV, BN 12607, II Q 4]

1c. absque *arrestacione et condictione* aliqua anno et die [*Statutes*]

2. missing folio: Oss., Warsz.

3. see No. 330

46

1. [17] Nemo masculus, nec ulla mulier possunt in lecto egritudinis de suis bonis alicui ultra tres solidos dare absque heredum consensu seu voluntate, *nec mulier sine consensu sui viri.* [Flor.]

2a. the underlined words: Flor., Dział. IV, BN 12607, II Q 4, *Statutes*

2b. missing: Gn., F 143, Q II 157 (1), Q II 157 (2), BN 12600, Dział. I, BJ 4405, Przem., Plesz., BOZ, AJG, Kiel., 951b, BN 3068

2c. missing folio: Oss., Warsz.

3a. in gloss in Dział. I, BJ 4405 and 951b

3b. see No. 331

47

1. [17] Aliquis potest sua bona dare in infirmitate positus, nisi tali racione, videlicet quando aliquis esset in aliqua manifesta, tunc sellabitur [*?*] sibi equus et induat se arma bellica vel vestes suas meliores, et si posset equm asscendere de lapide, qui esset altus ad unam ulnam, vel de aliquo et tunc equitaret ad iudicium et sedens in equo potest, quidquid vult, ita [*?*] quod simul posset ad similem lapidem descendere de equo.

2a. in: Q II 157 (1)

2b. missing: Gn. and other Latin texts except 2a

2c. missing folio: Oss., Warsz.

3. –

48

1. [18] extunc omnes hii, qui se linea equali consanguinitatis ostendere poterint, in hereditate succedunt equaliter, *sive sit masculi sive femine, ex paterna et materna consanguneitate*. [*Statutes*]
2a. the underlined words: II Q 4, *Statutes*
2b. missing: Gn. and other Latin texts except 2a
2c. missing folio: Oss., Warsz.
3a. in gloss in 951b
3b. in the German text only in II Q 4: iz man adir vap von vatir adir von mutir halbin.

49

1. [18] Si autem puella et sacerdos fueri[n]t, tunc supellectilia inter se dividunt. [Gn.]
1a. ... *equaliter*. [F 143, BJ 4405, II Q 4]
1b. ... *equali forma*. [*Statutes*]
2a. missing: Gn. and other Latin texts except 1a, 1b
2b. missing folio: Oss., Warsz.
3a. in gloss: 951b (as *Statutes*) and Dział. I (as II Q 4)
3b. see No. 332

50

1. [19] Quitquit masculus dat in iudicio bannito coram iudice et scabinis, ibi recipiens dat unum solidum pro doni cognicione, *quod* recipiunt scabini, *quod possidebat quiete*. [Kiel.]
2a. the underlined words: Kiel.
2b. missing: Gn. and other Latin texts except 2a
2c. missing folio: Oss., Warsz.
3. –

51

1. [20] Quociens tunc mandatum debitor adimplere neglexerit, tociens penam suam iudex in eo acquisivit, *nisi iure se excusaverit*. [Przem.]
2a. the underlined words: Przem.

2b. missing: Gn. and other Latin texts except 2a
2c. missing folio: Oss., Warsz.
3. –

52

1. [21] Si aliquis ad limina sanctorum aut ad nundinas extra provinciam aut extra *limites et* terminos ire voluerit [*Statutes*]
2a. the underlined words: *Statutes*
2b. missing: Gn. and other Latin texts except 2a
2c. missing folio: Oss., Warsz.
3. see No. 335

53

1a. [21] Et si uni *debitum* adiudicatum fuerit, [F 143]
1b. Et si uni *testis* adiudicatum fuerit, [AJG]
1c. Et si uni *testimonium* adiudicatum fuerit, [Gn.]
inducias trinas duas ebdomadas optinebit, quodcumque elegerit aut iudicio proximo.
2a. *debitum*: F 143
2b. *testis*: AJG, Kiel.
2c. *testimonium*: Gn. and other Latin texts except 2a, 2b
2d. missing folio: Oss., Warsz.
3. –

54

1. [21] Et si uni *testimonium* adiudicatum fuerit, inducias trinas *duas* ebdomadas optinebit, quodcumque elegerit aut iudicio proximo. [Flor.]
2a. the underlined words: Gn. and other Latin texts except 2b
2b. missing: Flor.
2c. missing folio: Oss., Warsz.
3. –

55

1. [23] Sin autem contingeret, quod alter eam infringeret, hunc tamen emendare cum reconpensa oportet, pro vulnere novem talenta, *pro homicidio decem et octo tale[n]ta* [Gn.]
2a. the underlined words: Gn. and other Latin texts except 2b
2b. missing: Kiel.
2c. missing folio: Oss., Warsz.
3. –

56

1. [23] Sed ubicunque concordia ordinata fuerit extra iudicium, hoc facilius potest probare vir cum *sex* testibus solus septimus [Gn.]
2a. *sex*: Gn. and other Latin texts except 2b, 2c
2b. *tribus*: Q II 157 (1)
2c. *septem*: Dział. IV
2d. missing folio: Oss., Warsz.
3. see No. 338

57

1. [23] Ubi concordia et vera fremitus diuturna coram iudicio confirmata fuerit, si ipsam violat adversa pars, et si vincetur, ut ius dictaverit, *cum* iudice et scabinis, pro vulnere manum, pro homicidio collum. [Gn.]
2a. *cum*: Gn. and other Latin texts except 2b
2b. *coram*: F 143
2c. missing folio: Oss., Warsz.
3. –

58

1. [24] Similiter et vir potest filium suum, quem in potestate habet, tribus vicibus eximere, ubi aut ad collum aut ad manum pertransit. Quarta vero vice ipsum solum propria in persona respondere oportebit, et primum in suo iure non impediet, si filius prius bene respondisset. [Gn.]

2a. in: Gn. and other Latin texts except 2b
2b. missing: AJG, Kiel., II Q 4, *Statutes*
2c. missing folio: Oss., Warsz.
3. see No. 339

59

1. [24] Sin autem pater cum filio simul in eodem crimine coram iudicio inpulsati fuerint, extunc pater filium eximere non potest, nisi prius se ab eodem crimine expurgabit. [Gn.]
2a. in: Gn. and other Latin texts except 2b
2b. missing: AJG, Kiel.
2c. missing folio: Oss., Warsz.
3. see No. 340

60

1. [24] Famulus potest mercedem suam, quam promeruit, quinque solidos probare tacto sacramento *mettercius, ita tamen, si dominus voluerit consentire. Si autem dominus velit probare tacto sacramento* mettercius, quod sibi solvit [*Statutes*]
2a. the underlined words: F 143, Q II 157 (1), Q II 157 (2), BN 12600, BJ 4405, Przem., BOZ, AJG [partly], Kiel. [partly], Flor., Dział. IV, BN 12607, II Q 4, BN 3068, *Statutes*
2b. missing: Gn., Dział. I, Plesz., 951b
2c. missing folio: Oss., Warsz.
3a. in gloss in Dział. I
3b. see No. 341

61

1. [24] Si alter alterum pro vino aut alio potu inculpare voluerit, evadet ut aliud debitum, in quo nullum *dominium/dampnum* ostendere poterit aut protestare. [Gn.]
2a. *dampnum*: Kiel., Przem.
2b. *dominium*: Gn., F 143, Q II 157 (1), Q II 157 (2), BN 12600, Dział. I, BJ 4405, Plesz., BOZ, AJG, Flor., Dział. IV, BN 12607, II Q 4, 951b, *Statutes*
2c. *both*: BN 3068
2d. missing folio: Oss., Warsz.
3. –

62

1. [25] Si moritur femina absque herede, ita quod nullum heredem a suo marito pepererit, ipsa heredat sua successoria, seu sua prospera fortuna acquisita super suum proximum naturalem successorem, sive sit masculus sive femina, qui sibi sit paris condicionis. *Idem facit vir* illi, qui sibi paris fuerit condictionis. [Gn.]

2a. the words in italic: Gn., F 143, Q II 157 (1), BN 12600, Dział. I, BJ 4405, Plesz., BOZ, AJG, Kiel., Flor., 951b, BN 3068, *Statutes*

2b. the words in italic missing: Przem., Dział. IV, BN 12607, II Q 4,

2c. only the underlined words: Q II 157 (2)

2d. missing folio: Oss., Warsz.n

3. see No. 342

63

1. [25] Insuper omne aurum et argentum non informatum [*s*], et omnis siligo et carnes cum cervisia et vino, et panis, que vel quod aut quantum post trecesunum permansit, vel permanserunt, totum cedit heredibus viri et non mulieribus, exceptis pulmentariis, de quibus mulier *mediam* recipit partem [Gn.]

2a. *mediam*: Gn. and other Latin texts except 2a, 2b

2b. in Dział. I missing *mediam*, written in gloss

2c. *mediam* missing: F 143

2d. missing folio: Oss., Warsz.

3. Przem. again in Art. 100

64

1. [26] Ubi pulmentaria dantur et omnis expensa domestica, que in potestate viri est *tempore mortis*, et omnes vacue cuppe, pulvinaria recipit mariti uxor, et non sua cognata proxima. [*Statutes*]

2a. the underlined words: BJ 4405, Przem., Plesz., BN 3068, *Statutes*

2b. missing: Gn., F 143, Q II 157 (1), Q II 157 (2), BN 12600, Dział. I, BOZ, AJG, Kiel., Flor., Dział. IV, BN 12607, II Q 4, 951b

2c. missing folio: Oss., Warsz.

3. –

65

1. [26] a text see No. 65
1a. ... recipit mariti uxor, *non sua congnata proxima*. [Gn. and other Latin texts except 1b–1e]
1b. ... recipit mariti uxor, *non sua agnata proxima*. [BOZ, 951b]
1c. ... recipit mariti uxor, *non cognata proxima ipsius mariti*. [II Q 4]
1d. ... recipit mariti uxor, et cognata *proxima*. [F 143]
1e. ... recipit mariti uxor, *non cognata sua*. [BN 12607]
2. missing folio: Oss., Warsz.
3. see No. 343

66

1. [26] *Omne proprium, quod locando possessum est* ... spectant ad hereditatem. [Gn.]
2a. the underlined words: Gn. and other Latin texts except 2b
2b. missing: F 143
2c. missing folio: Oss., Warsz.
3. –

67

1. [27] conqueratur iudici *et scabinis*, et ostendat sua vulnera [Gn.]
2a. the underlined words: Gn. and other Latin texts except 2b
2b. missing: BOZ
2c. missing folio: Oss., Warsz.
3. –

68

1. [28] alterum non oportet sibi respondere, si placet, nisi conqueratur in eo ydiomate [Gn.]
2a. in: Gn. and other Latin texts except 2b
2b. missing: Q II 157 (1)
2c. missing folio: Oss., Warsz.
3. –

69

1. [29] [after a compromise] iste sibi suus adversarius respondere non tenebitur *coram iudicio* [Gn.]
2a. in: Gn. and other Latin texts except 2b, 2c
2b. missing the underlined text: Plesz., BN 3068
2c. missing the sentence: Q II 157 (2), BN 126000
2d. missing folio: Oss., Warsz.
3. –

70

1. [30] Quodsi se duo mutuo vulneraverint *equaliter* [Gn.]
2b. the underlined words: Gn. and other Latin texts except 2a
2a. missing: Przem
2c. missing folio: Warsz.
3. –

71

1. [31] Duellum quamvis dicitur duorum bellum, hic tantum accipitur pro illo, qui obtinet principium agendi. [Dział. IV]
2. in: Dział. IV
2b. missing: Gn. and other Latin texts except 2a
2c. missing folio: Warsz.
3. see No. 350

72

1. [31] Et si se duo mutuo vulneraverint equaliter et querulantur equaliter, quicunque ex eis in alterum duellum acquisierit, tunc eius
1a. adversarius *manum* demeretur [Gn. and other Latin texts except 1b]
1b. adversarius *colum* demeretur [Q II 157 (2)]
2a. missing Article: F 143
2b. missing folio: Oss., Warsz.
3. –

73

1. [32] Etiam ullo precio conventi in aliquibus causis non valent contestari, qui eiici iure possunt. [*Statutes*]
2a. in: II Q 4, *Statutes* – both compliance with German text II Q 4
2b. missing: Gn. and other Latin texts except 2a
2c. missing folio: Warsz.
3a. cf. No. 95 – the same regulation in BN 12607, Oss., II Q 4 in Art. 42
3b. in gloss in 951b
3c. the German text only in II Q 4: Ouch mogen keyne gewette lawte geczengin yn keyner sache, wen man mag sy vorferfin mit rechte.

74

1. [32] Ille, qui ipsum captivum in manifesto facto detinuit,
1a. facilius eum vincere potest cum testimonio, *quam ipse captivus cum testimonio* evadere possit. [Gn. and other Latin texts except 1b]
1b. facilius eum vincere potest cum testimonio, *eum* evadere possit. [951b]
2. missing folio: Warsz.
3. –

75

1. [33] et hoc si ambo in recenti actione cum clamore ad iudicium fuerint deducti. [*Statutes*]
2a. in: II Q 4, *Statutes* – both compliance with German text II Q 4
2b. missing: Gn. and other Latin texts except 2a
2c. missing folio: Warsz.
3a. in gloss in 951b
3b. the German text only in II Q 4: Ap si beide in den hantaffte tat gerufte vor gerichte brocht werden.

76

1. [34] Si autem vulnus monomachale fuerit, tunc continnuo sibi iudex formari debet pro facto manifesto. [Gn. and other Latin texts except 2]
2. BN 3068: the complete text in Art. 12 and as a gloss in Art. 35
3. –

77

1a. [34] Si autem vulnus monomachale fuerit, tunc continnuo sibi iudex *formari* debet pro facto manifesto. [Gn. and other Latin texts except 1b]
1b. Si autem vulnus monomachale fuerit, tunc in continenti sibi iudex *iudicium facere* debet pro facto manifesto. [*Statutes*]
2. missing folio: Warsz.
3. the *Statutes* includes language corrections

78

1. [35] Sin autem ad diem duellum dilatum fuerit, et si alter pugilem convenerit super alterum, et si ille protestare poterit, quod pugil sit *mercennarius*, extunc iure sibi a duello cedere potest. [Gn.]
2a. *mercennarius*: Gn. and other Latin texts except 2a
2b. missing: Dział. IV
2c. missing folio: Warsz.
3. see No. 356

79

1. [37] Si se duo mutuo vulneraverint et ambo coram iudicio conparent et querulose proponant, et querimonia usque ad iudicium dilata fuerit, qui primo querulatus fuerit, moriatur ab hiis vulneribus, mortuus ad iudicium portetur, et alter vulneratus eciam conparuerit, et unus, de mortui,
1a. *agnatus* loquatur [Gn., F 143, Q II 157 (1), Q II 157 (2), BN 12600, Dział. I, BJ 4405, Przem., Plesz., BOZ, Flor., 951b, *Statutes*]
1b. *cognatus* loquatur [AJG, Kiel., Dział. IV, BN 12607, Oss., II Q 4, BN 3068]
2. missing folio: Warsz.
3. see No. 359

80

1. [37] a text see No. 79
1a. loquatur super vulneratum cum testimonio [Gn., F 143, Q II 157 (1), Q II 157 (2), BN 12600, Dział. I, BJ 4405, Przem., Plesz., BOZ, AJG, Kiel., Dział. IV, 951b, BN 3068]

1b. loquatur super vulneratum cum testimonio *sive duello* [Flor., BN 12607, Oss., II Q 4, *Statutes*]
2. missing folio: Warsz.
3. see No. 362

81

1. [37] Si hoc, ut iuris est, protestaverit, propius est evadere
1a. quam ille super eum poterit protestare. [Gn., F 143, Q II 157 (1), Q II 157 (2), BN 12600, Dział. I, BJ 4405, Przem., Plesz., BOZ, AJG, Kiel., Dział. IV, 951b, BN 3068]
1b. *metseptimo*, quam ille super eum protestari possit. [Flor., BN 12607, Oss.]
1c. *homicidium metseptimus*, quam vincere possit. [II Q 4]
1d. quam ille super eum protestari possit *homicidium metseptimus*, alias quam protestari et vinci possit. [*Statutes*]
2. missing folio: Warsz.
3a. text in the *Statutes*: compilation of Gn. and II Q 4
3b. see No. 363

82

1a. [37] *quia ambo coram iudicio querimoniam inceperunt. Sed* suum testimonium sic debet procede, quod inicium contecionis illius fuerit, et non suum.... *Sin autem ille ipsum monomachaliter alloquitur, extunc ipsum pro suo collo pugnare oportebitur.* [Gn.]
1b. *Si autem ille ipsum duellare fuerit alloqutus, extunc ipsum pro suo collo respondere oportet. Si autem evaserit cum testimonio, tunc* suum testimonium sit procedere debet, quod inicium contecionis illius fuerit et non suum. [Flor.]
1c. *Et si evadet, tunc* suum testimonium debet sic procedere, quod inicium contecionis illius fuerunt et non suum. [BN 12607, Oss.]
1d. *Si autem aliquis agnatus ipsius mortui duellarie salutaverit ipsum, tunc pro collo suo respondere opotet. Si autem evadere voluerit cum testibus, extunc* testimonium sic debet procedere, quod initium contencionis illius mortui fuisset et non suum. [II Q 4, *Statutes*]
2a. compliance of Gn. with F 143, Q II 157 (1), Q II 157 (2), BN 12600, Dział. I, BJ 4405, Przem., Plesz., BOZ, AJG, Kiel., Dział. IV, 951b, BN 3068
2b. slight linguistic divergences between II Q 4 and *Statutes*
2c. missing folio: Warsz.
3. see No. 364

83

1a. [37] Et si suus testes incontinenti habere non poterit, terminum *sex ebdomadis acquirit, tunc facilius potest evadere homicidium* ***metseptimus***, *quam ille cum testimonio ipsum vincere possit.* [Gn., F 143, Q II 157 (1), Q II 157 (2), BN 12600, Dział. I, BJ 4405, Przem., Plesz., BOZ, AJG, Kiel., Dział. IV, 951b, BN 3068]

1b. *potest evadere homicidium* ***mettercius*** [Dział. IV]

1c. Et si quis incontinenti habere non poterit, terminum *trium quindenarum acquirit, ex hiis sibi eligat unam quindecinam quamcumque voluerit.* [Flor., II Q 4]

1d. Et si suos testes incontinenti habere non potuerit terminum ad sex ebdomadas *acquirit, hiis sibi eligat unam quindecinam quicumque voluerit.* [Oss., BN 12607]

1e. Et si suos testes incontinenti habere non poterit, inducias et terminum trium quindenarum *acquiret, ex iis sibi eligat unam quindenam, quamcunque voluerit, in qua facilius possunt evadere homicidium metseptimus, quam ille cum testimonio ipsum vincere possit.* [*Statutes*]

2a. in MS Flor. and MS II Q 4 a substantive divergence from MS Gn.; but also found in the German texts of MS BJ 168, MS BN 12607 Ger. and MS II Q 4 Ger.

2b. text in *Statutes* is a compilation of Gn. and II Q 4

2c. missing folio: Warsz.

3. see No. 365

84

1. [39] Si fur clara luce diei deprehensus fuerit, qui bone fame sit, et

1a. furtum *minus quam tres* solidos [Gn., F 143, Q II 157 (1), Q II 157 (2), BN 12600, Dział. I, BJ 4405, Przem., Plesz., BOZ, 951b, BN 3068]

1b. furtum *tres solidos* [Dział. IV]

1c. furtum *non plus quam tres* solidos [AJG, Kiel., Flor., BN 12607, II Q 4, Oss., *Statutes*]

2. missing folio: Warsz.

3a. in gloss in Dział. I: *Solidus hic valet tres grossos*

3b. see No. 367

85

1. [39] minus quam tres solidos valeat, *cutem cum crine demerentur. Sed si furtum ultra tres solidos*, reus est suspendio. [Gn.]

2a. the underlined words: Gn. and other Latin texts except 2b

2b. missing: BN 3068

2c. missing folio: Warsz.

3. –

86

1. [39] Si autem fur tempestate noctis deprehensus fuerit cum *sex* denariis, reus est suspendio. [Gn.]

2a. in: Gn. and other Latin texts except 2b, 2c

2b. in F 143: *VII*

2c. missing: Q II 157 (2), BN 126000

2d. missing folio: Warsz.

3. –

87

1. [39] Sed vel quitquid suarum rerum, qui sibi subtractum vel captum fuerint, ad hoc se trahere debet tacto sacramento, ut iuris est.

2a. in: BN 3068

2b. missing: Gn. and other Latin texts except 2a

2c. missing folio: Warsz.

3. –

88

1. [40] Conqueritur vir super alterum pro bonis, quod vera sua hereditas sit, et quod ille teneat cum iniuria, et sua vera sit succession a patre suo,

1a. vel ab alio *suo angnato*, aut a suo predecessore [Gn., F 143, BJ 4405, Przem., Plesz., BOZ, 951b, *Statutes*]

1b. vel ab alio *suo cognato*, aut a suo predecessore [Q II 157 (1), BN 12600, Dział. I, BJ 3068]

1c. vel a *suo alio amico*, aut predecessore [AJG, Kiel., Dział. IV, BN 12607, Oss., II Q 4]

1d. predecessore [Q II 157 (2)]

1e. decessore [Flor.]

2. missing folio: Warsz.

3a. in Dział. I written by a commentator 'amico'

3b. see No. 368

89

1a. [40] actor conservat suam legalem proprietatem, in bonis eisdem, quia quivis homo conservat suam innatam hereditatem, *sive naturalem porcionem, facilius quam alter emptam hereditatem, aut obligatam hereditatem, aut datam proprietatem, aut predium censuale* [Gn., Dział. I, BN 4405, Przem., AJG, Kiel., Flor., Dział. IV, BN 12607, II Q 4, BN 3068]
1b. missing: *facilius quam alter emptam hereditatem* [BOZ, 951b]
1c. missing: *obligatam hereditatem* [Q II 157 (2), BN 12600]
1d. missing: *datam proprietatem* [Q II 157 (2), BN 12600, Oss., *Statutes*]
1e. missing: *predium censuale* [Q II 157 (1)]
2. missing folio: Warsz.
3. –

90

1a. [40] quivis homo conservat suam innatam hereditatem, *sive naturalem porcionem* [Gn., F 143, Q II 157 (1), Q II 157 (2), BN 12600, Dział. I, BJ 4405, Przem., Plesz., Dział. IV, BN 3068]
1b. quis homo suam innatam hereditatem, *seu porcionem* [AJG, Kiel., Flor, II Q 4]
2a. the underlined words missing: BN 12607, Oss., *Statutes*
2b. a longer portion of the text is missing: BOZ, 951b
2c. missing folio: Warsz.
3. see No. 374

91

1. [40] actor conservat suam legalem proprietatem … cum impossibile sit aliquem de naturali porcione defraudari. [Gn.]
2a. in: Gn., Q II 157 (1), Q II 157 (2), BN 12600, Dział. I, BJ 4405, Przem., Plesz., BOZ, 951b, BN 3068, *Statutes*
2b. missing: F 143, AJG, Kiel., Flor., Dział. IV, BN 12607, Oss., II Q 4
2c. missing folio: Warsz.
3. see No. 374

92

1. [41] Si homo habuerit hereditaria censualia et bona a quodam monasterio, aut alio domino, et si dominus aut abbas sibi non fatetur, aut conventus, hic vir potest *metseptimus* protestare [Gn.]
2a. *metseptimus*: Gn. and other Latin texts except 2a
2b. *mettertius*: Dział. IV
2c. missing folio: Warsz.
3. see No. 376n

93

1. [42] Si debet vir producere testimonium super proprium alterius metseptimus, aut mettercius, hoc facere oportet cum possessis hominibus, *qui in suo iure argui non possunt* [Gn.]
2a. the underlined words: Gn., Dział. I, Przem., BOZ, 951b, BN 3068, *Statutes*
2b. missing: F 143, Q II 157 (1), Q II 157 (2), BN 12600, BJ 4405, Plesz., AJG, Kiel., Flor., Dział. IV, BN 12607, Oss., II Q 4
2c. missing folio: Warsz.
3. see No. 377

94

1. [42] a text see No. 93
1a. metseptimus aut mettercius [Gn. and other Latin texts except 1b]
1b. metseptimus aut octavus [Oss.]
2. missing folio: Warsz.
3. –

95

1a. [42] In nullis causis precio conventi seu empti valeant *protestare, quia* iure possunt *eici*. [BN 12607, Oss., II Q 4]
1b. In nullis eciam causis precio conventi seu empti valeant *contestari, qui eici* iure possunt. [*Statutes*]
1c. Oss.: *eici* replaced by *vinci*
2a. missing: Gn. and other Latin texts except 1a, 1b
2b. missing folio: Warsz.

3a. cf. No. 73 – the text in II Q 4 and in *Statute* in Art. 32
3b. in gloss in BJ 4405: In nullis causis precio conventi seu empti, possunt esse testes, quia iure possunt eici.
3c. see No. 379

96

1. [43] Si aliquis debet persoluta debita protestari vel probare pro debito, hoc facere debet talibus cum hominibus, qui in suo iure argui non possunt *mettercius*. [Oss.]
2a. *mettercius*: BN 12607, Oss., BN 3068
2b. missing: Gn. and other Latin texts except 2b
2c. missing Article: *Statutes*
2d. missing folio: Warsz.
3. see No. 380

97

1. [44] Si vir ducit viduam que unum filium aut plures pueros habuerit et ipse nulla bona habuerit nec ipsa, **et vir unum filium habuerit cum sua prima uxore**, et si fortuna arridente per suos labores bona habuerint et proprietatem sive hereditatem emerint, aut super bona mobilia sive mercimonia posuerint, et inposterum vir moritur et uxor, extunc filius viri propior est recipere hereditatem, quam *pueri femine*, aut pueri sororis *sue, vel eciam nepotes seu nepte* ex filia sua. [Gn.]
2a. the underlined words in: Gn. and other Latin texts except 2b
2b. missing: Q II 157 (1)
2c. missing folio: Warsz.
3. –

98

1. [44] a text see No. 97
1a. **et vir unum filium habuerit cum sua prima uxore** [Gn.]
2a. in: Gn. and other Latin texts except 2b
2b. missing: BOZ
2c. missing folio: Warsz.
3. –

99

1. [45] Si vir aliquis dederit pueris suis aliqua bona sua, et sue uxori, in iudicio bannito circa vitam suam, et bone racionis, et si sibi pueri paris condicionis fuerint, *et si desuper vera pax firmata fuerit* [Gn.]
2a. the underlined words: Gn. and other Latin texts except 2b, 2c
2b. missing: Flor.
2c. missing folio: Warsz.
3. –

100

1. [45] et inposterum aliteri in eisdem bonis aliquit dederit *aut heres fuerit, aut* ille, cui prima donacio sit data, bene contradicere potest de iure. [Gn.]
2a. the underlined words: Gn. and other Latin texts except 2b
2b. missing: F 143, Q II 157 (2)
2c. missing folio: Warsz.
3. –

101

1. [46] Si vir mercimonia aut bona mobilia habuerit, quod cum bonis emerit eisdem
1a. successoriis paterna successione [Gn. and other Latin texts except 1b]
1b. sunt censariis paterna successione [BOZ, 951b]
2. missing folio: Warsz.
3. –

102

1. [46] Sin autem vir habuerit bona mobilia aut mercimonia, que sibi propriis laboribus aut prospera fortuna accreverunt
1a. que potest dare [Gn., Q II 157 (1), Dział. I, Przem., Plesz., BOZ, 951b, BN 3068]
1b. *cum sua uxore*, potest dare [F 143, Q II 157 (2), BN 12600, BJ 4405, AJG, Kiel., Flor., Dział. IV, BN 12607, Oss., II Q 4, *Statutes*]
2. missing folio: Warsz.
3. see No. 385

103

1a. [46] Sin autem *vir habuerit bona mobilia aut* hereditaria *censualia* bona fuerint, [Plesz.]
1b. Sin autem hereditaria *censualia* bona fuerint, [Gn.]
extunc sue uxori dare non potest absque heredum consensu, vel absque domini proprietatis consensu, in cuius bonis sunt.
2a. *censualia*: Gn. and other Latin texts except 2c
2b. the words in italics: Plesz.
2c. missing both: Dział. IV
2d. missing folio: Warsz.
3. see No. 386

104

1. [46] de iure liberti in emendis sine [*s*] obnoxii et in successionibus in bonis naturalibus. [BOZ]
2a. in: 951b i BOZ
2b. missing: Gn. and other Latin texts except 2a
2c. missing folio: Warsz.
3. this fragment is mistakenly included in the text of the provision the title of the next article, in the wording close to Gn.

105

1. [47] Quando obnoxius moritur, extunc *suo domino aut* suo advocato oportet dare denarios obnoxietarum [*s*] et meliorem equm, quem habet [Gn.]
2a. the underlined words: Gn. and other Latin texts except 2b
2b. missing: Przem.
2c. missing folio: Warsz.
3. –

106

1. [48] Si moritur vir absque herede et nepotem ex filia habuerit, que exheredata fuerit circa suam vitam, idem nepos maiori iure recipit bona avi materni,

quam iudicium, qui sibi est paris condicionis. *Iudicium recipit sua arma bellica.* [Dział. IV]

2a. the underlined words: Q II 157 (1), Q II 157 (2), BN 12600, BJ 4405, Plesz., AJG, Kiel., Flor., Dział. IV, BN 12607, Oss., II Q 4, BN 3068, *Statutes*

2b. missing: Gn., Dział. I, Przem., BOZ

2c. missing Article: F 143

2d. missing folio: Warsz.

3a. written by commentators: Gn. and Dział. I

3b. see No. 387

107

1a. [48] Si etiam filius duxerit uxorem tempore vite sui patris, et premoriatur patri indivisus a sua hereditate, extunc ipsius filii hereditatem sui avi recipiunt, equaliter cum suis patruis, et non filii filiarum. Si autem filium a se diviserit, protunc filii filiorum in bonis sui avi equalem recipiunt portionem. Sed in hereditatibus avie recipiendis filie filiorum et filiarum iuridice sunt equales. [*Statutes*]

1b. Si autem filius uxorem duxerit vincule patre. Si moritur filius absque divisione patris in hereditate, tunc pueri eiusdem filii hereditatem patris: partem patris recipiunt sed non pueri filie seu ancille. Sin autem filium a se diviserit cum hereditate, tunc cum sui pueri recipient partem equalem in hereditate ave, sed in hereditate ave equalem divisionem, tam filiorum pueri, quam filiarum. [BN 3068]

2a. in: BN 12607, Oss., II Q 4, *Statutes*

2b. another linguistic redaction BN 3068, in Art. 15

2c. missing: Gn., Q II 157 (1), Q II 157 (2), BN 12600, Dział. I, BJ 4405, Przem., BOZ, AJG, Kiel., Flor., Dział. IV, 951b

2d. missing Article: F 143

2e. missing folio: Warsz.

3a. cf. NTO No. 164 and in Latin collection of Magdeburg *ortyle* in BJ 4405 No. 153, f. 45v–46r; cf. also MFr. I.7.13. (P. Laband, *Magdeburger Rechtsquellen*, p. 98)

3b. the German text in II Q 4; in BN 12607 Ger. only a free space and a return to f. XXI (current f. 47v), where another German fragment about inheritance, see No. 163 and No. 389

108

1. [49] cum *malefactore* ad iudicium deductum fuerit [Gn.]
2a. *malefactore*: Gn. and other Latin texts except 2a
2b. *malediccione*: Q II 157 (1)
2c. *viro:* Dział. IV
2d. missing folio: Warsz.
3. –

109

1. [49] hoc oportet, quod faciat mettercius cum talibus hominibus
1a. qui in suo iure argui non possunt. [Gn. and other Latin texts except 1b]
1b. iudicio astantibus ac fidedignis. [II Q 4]
2. missing folio: Warsz.
3. –

110

1. [50] Cum moritur vir, qui pueros habuerit, qui ad annos discrecionis non dum pervenerunt, proximus *agnatus* / *cognatus* debet ipsorum esse tutor
2a. *agnatus*: Gn., F 143, Q II 157 (1), Dział. I, BJ 4405, Przem., Plesz., BOZ, Dział. IV, 951b, BN 3068, *Statutes*
2b. *cognatus*: Q II 157 (2), BN 12600, AJG, Kiel., Flor., BN 12607, Oss., II Q 4
2c. missing folio: Warsz.
3a. a commentator changed *agnatus* into *cognatus* in Dział. I
3b. see No. 391

111

1. [50] *Et si idem non dum ad huc annos pubertatis* attingerit, adiutor suus esse debet *proximus agnatus suus*, eousque ipse ad annos pervenerit discrecionis [Gn.]
2a. in: Gn., F 143, Q II 157 (1), Q II 157 (2), BN 12600, Dział. I, BJ 4405, Plesz., Dział. IV, AJG, Kiel., Flor., BN 12607, Oss., II Q 4, BN 3068
2b. the complete phrase missing: *Statutes*

2c. the italic text missing: Przem.
2d. the underlined words missing: BOZ, 951b
2e. missing folio: Warsz.
3. –

112

1. [50] [tutor] racionem anno ad annum de bonis pupillorum
1a. coram vero ipsorum tutore facere tenetur. [Gn., F 143, Q II 157 (1), Q II 157 (2), BN 12600, Dział. I, BJ 4405, Przem., Plesz., AJG, Kiel., Flor., Dział. IV, BN 3068]
1b. coram vero ipsorum tutore vel coram consulibus aut scabinis. [BN 12607, Oss.]
1c. quidquid factum fuerit cum hiis bonis. [II Q 4]
2a. missing: BOZ, 951b, *Statutes*
2b. missing folio: Warsz.
3. see No. 392

113

1. [51] Et si factum manifestum cum viro ad iudicium deductum fuerit, stuprum et obsidium, et irruenciam domicilii, homicidium, furtum, spolium, probat homo protestando *metseptimus*. [Gn.]
2a. *metseptimus*: Gn. and other Latin texts except 2b
2b. *mettertius*: Dział. IV
2c. missing folio: Warsz.
3. see No. 397

114

1. [51] [oath] "Domine iudex, ego conqueror Deo et vobis, quod hic homo iste venit intra municipalia, et in me pacem violavit, et me stupravit corpore et rebus et honore muliebri, de quo sufficiens habeo testimonium per eos, qui meum clamorem audierunt, et ostendere volo factum, ut de iure teneo aut debeo, *et requiro in sentencia diffinitiva, quomodo ipsum vincere debeam*, ut michi proficiat in iure meo".
2a. the underlined words: Gn. and other Latin texts except 2b
2b. missing: Dział. IV
2c. missing folio: Warsz.
3. see No. 398

115

1. [51] Item factum manifestum eciam est ibi, ubi unum cum gladio aut cultello aut alia *sica* in manu deprehenderit [Gn.]
2a. in: Gn. and other Latin texts (also another weapon) except 2b
2b. BN 3068: *litiosa* (res furtivae)
2c. missing folio: Warsz.
3. –

116

1. [51] Et factum manifestum dicitur quam quis scientur claves ad furta gesserit, aut ea in sua defensione tenuerit, nec sin tam parva [*s*], quod ad [*?*] cellarii reponi sive ipsius scitu valeant. [F 143]
2a. in: F 143
2b. missing: Gn. and other Latin texts except 2a
2c. missing folio: Warsz.
3. –

117

1. [51] Tunc diffinitur iure, quod possit ipsum possibilius vincere cum hiis, qui suum clamorem audierunt, quam evadere possit. [Gn.]
2a. in: Gn. and other Latin texts except 2b
2b. missing: F 143
2c. missing folio: Warsz.
3. –

118

1. [52] Et sicut ipsum in manifesto facto deduxit ad iudicium, sic in sentencia requirit, quomodo ipsum vincere debeat, ut sibi proficuum sit in suo iure.
1a. *Et sic diffinitur cum clamore metseptimus eum vincere debet.* [BN 12607]
1b. *Tunc diffinitur metseptimus.* [Dział. IV]
2a. missing: Gn. and other Latin texts except 1a and 1b
2b. missing folio: Warsz.
3. see No. 400

119

1. [53] [accusation] Tunc hic conqueritur super virum ·N· et super ·N·, quod ipsi venerunt intra municipale, et in eo pacem infregerunt, et ipsum vulneraverunt aut suum affinem *proximum trucidaverunt*, si homicidium fuerit, et ipsum spoliaverunt corpore et rebus, et pro eo iudicium petit. [Gn.]
2a. *proximum trucidaverunt* [Gn. and other Latin texts except 2b, 2c]
2b. *occiderunt* [Dział. IV]
2c. *trucidaverunt* [BJ 4405]
2d. missing folio: Warsz.
3. see No. 402

120

1. [53] Si vulneratus vir ad iudicium cum clamore deductus fuerit *in facto manifesto, et si ita* inbecillis aut *debilis fuerit*, quod per tutorem ipsum querulari oportet et prolocutorem per sentenciam petat [Gn.]
2a. in: Gn. and other Latin texts except 2b, 2c
2b. missing the cursive text: Q II 157 (1)
2c. the underlined words missing: Q II 157 (2), BN 12600, Dział. IV, II Q 4
2d. missing folio: Warsz.
3. see No. 406

121

1. [53] [two persons sent to the victim] *Tunc unus interrogetur* ad dicendum, quid ab eo audierint. [Gn.]
2c. the underlined text: Gn. and other Latin texts except 2b, 2c
2b. missing: Przem.
2c. a longer portion of the text is missing: Dział. I, BOZ, BN 3068
2d. missing folio: Warsz.
3. in gloss in Dział. I

122

1a. [53] [victim] si iam profecerit, cum sibi diffinitur, quod sic, et eciam secundus et tercius *interrogetur. Extunc sibi diffinitur, quod profecerit. Extunc* querelam incipiat [Gn., Q II 157 (1), Q II 157 (2), BN 12600, Dział. I, BJ 4405, Przem., Plesz., BOZ, Flor., BN 12607, Oss., 951b, BN 3068, *Statutes*]

1b. si iam profecerit, cum sibi diffinitur, quod profecerit secundus et tertius, deinde querelam incipiat [II Q 4, AJG, Kiel.]

1c. sic interrogetur secundus et tertius, deinde querela incipiat [Dział. IV]

1d. si iam profecerit, deinde querelam incipiat: [F 143]

2. missing folio: Warsz.

3. see No. 407

123

1. [53] [asking for an attorney] diffinitur, quod non. Extunc sibi petat correccionem. Cum obtinuerit coreccionem [Gn.]

2a. in: Gn. and other Latin texts except 2b

2b. missing: BN 3068

2c. missing folio: Warsz.

3. –

124

1. [56] Qui monomachaliter suum equalem salutare seu alloqui voluerit, hunc iudicem petere oportebit, ut se intromittere possit de uno suo pacis violatore, quem videat in presenti. Cum hoc sibi per sentenciam diffinitum fuerit, tunc eciam in sentencia requirat, per quem modum se de ipso intromittere debeat, ut sibi in suo iure proficere possit. Tunc sibi de iure diffinitur, curialiter *per oram vestimenti.* [Gn.]

2a. the underlined words: Gn. and other Latin texts except 2b

2b. missing: Oss.

2c. missing Article: Plesz., Dział. IV

2d. missing folio: Q II 157 (2), Warsz.

3. –

125

1. [56] Et cum se de ipso intromittat, pronunciet sibi causam, pro qua se de ipso intromiserit, quod statim facere potest, si vult, aut pro eo habere colloquium.

Tunc ipsum inculpare oportebit, quod pacem in eo infregerit *aut in strata regia, aut in villa*, qualiter infregerit, eodem modo queruletur super eum. [Gn.]

2a. the underlined words: Gn. and other Latin texts except 2b

2b. missing: F 143

2c. missing Article: Plesz., Dział. IV

2d. missing folio: Q II 157 (2), Warsz.

3. –

126

1. [56] *Si sub banno regio fuerit.* Extunc ille petat satisdacionem, *quam sibi facere debet.* [Gn.]

2a. the underlined words: Gn. and other Latin texts except 2b

2b. missing: F 143

2c. missing Article: Plesz., Dział. IV

2d. missing folio: Q II 157 (2), Warsz.

3. –

127

1a. [56] *Tamen* vir potest suam querimoniam meliorare ante satisdacionem [Gn.]

2a. *Tamen*: Gn. and other Latin texts except 2b, 2c

2b. *Pauper*: [Oss.]

2c. a longer portion of the text is missing: F 143

2c. missing Article: Plesz., Dział. IV

2d. missing folio: Q II 157 (2), Warsz.

3. –

128

1. [56] quod ipsum spoliaverit bonis suis et de ipsis sibi tanta receperit, quod bene duellum meretur. Hec tria criminalia facta omnia simul conqueratur [Gn.]

2a. in: Gn. and other Latin texts except 2b

2b. missing: BOZ

2c. missing Article: Plesz., Dział. IV

2d. missing folio: Q II 157 (2), Warsz.

3. –

129

1a. [56] Hec tria criminalia facta omnia simul conqueratur, de quoqumque horum trium *de uno obliviscitur aut tacuerit,* extunc suum *duellum* amisit. [Gn. and other Latin texts except 1b]

1b. Hec tria criminalia facta omnia simul conqueratur, de quoqumque horum trium *obtinuerit,* ex tunc suum ammisit. [Flor.]

2c. missing Article: Plesz., Dział. IV

2d. missing folio: Q II 157 (2), Warsz.

3. –

130

1a. [56] A duello eciam potest accipere suos affines, si uterque suus affinis et ita consanguineitatis linea coniuncti fuerint, quod simul pungnare non poterint. [Gn., and other Latin texts except 1b]

1b. A duello eciam excipere potest vir suos affines, si uterque suus affinis *fuerit, hoc probare debet metseptimus tacto sacramento* et ita sanguineitatis linea coniuncti fuerint, quod simul pungnare non poterint. [BN 12607, Oss., II Q 4]

2a. slight linguistic divergences in II Q 4

2b. missing Article: Plesz., Dział. IV

2c. missing folio: Q II 157 (2), Warsz.

3. see No. 414

131

1. [56] Quivis vir potest se a duello excusare *illi viro, qui sibi paris condicionis non fuerit.* Ille autem, qui nobilioris nature fuerit, *ille preesse non potest* [*illi*], *qui deterioris nature fuerit,* si ipsum alloquetur. [Gn.]

2a. the underlined words and the cursive text: Gn. and other Latin texts except 2b, 2c

2b. the underlined words missing: BOZ, AJG, Kiel.

2c. missing the cursive text: Przem.

2d. missing Article: Plesz., Dział. IV

2e. missing folio: Q II 157 (2), Warsz.

3. –

132

1. [56] iudex eciam debet habere clippeum *et gladium* [Gn.]
2a. the underlined words: Gn. and other Latin texts except 2b
2b. missing: BN 12607, Oss.
2c. missing Article: Plesz., Dział. IV
2d. missing folio: Q II 157 (2), Warsz.
3. –

133

1. [56] [court duel] unum clipeum rotundum in *sinistra* manu [*Statutes*]
2a. *sinistra*: II Q 4, *Statutes*
2b. missing: Gn. and other Latin texts except 2a
2c. missing Article: Plesz., Dział. IV
2d. missing folio: Q II 157 (2), Warsz.
3. –

134

1. [56] Etiam iudex, *vel preco communis*, debet indicere pacem circa collum, quod nemo eos inpediat circa duellum. [*Statutes*]
2a. the underlined words: II Q 4, *Statutes*
2b. missing: Gn. and other Latin texts except 2a
2c. missing Article: Plesz., Dział. IV
2d. missing folio: Q II 157 (2), Warsz.
3. –

135

1a. [56] Cuilibet ipsorum iudex unum virum *habeat, qui flangam ferat, qui ipsos in nichilo nullo inpedire debent, nisi si unus ceciderit, quod* flangam interponat, aut si vulneratus fuerit. *Aut si* flangam desiderat, hoc idem facere, nisi voluntas iudicis fuerit, non potest. [Gn. and other Latin texts except 1b, 1c]
1b. Cuilibet ipsorum iudex unum virum dare debet, *qui flangam ferat. Qui ipsos in nichilo impedire debet, nisi si unus cecidit, quod* flangam desiderat. Quod idem facere nisi voluntas iudicis fuerit non potest. [BN 12607, II Q 4, AJG, Kiel.]

1c. Cuilibet ipsorum iudex unum virum dare debet, qui falangam desiderat. Quod ille facere nisi voluntas iudicis fuerit non potest. [Oss.]
2a. missing Article: Plesz., Dział. IV
2b. missing folio: Q II 157 (2), Warsz.
3. see No. 416

136

1a. [56] *Finalia ferramenta de vaginis gladiorum deponere debent*, nisi a iudice licenciam habuerint. [Gn. and other Latin texts except 1b]
1b. *Vinculos [?] fereos debent affringere*, nisi ex iudicis licencia possunt optinui. [Przem.]
2a. missing Article: Plesz., Dział. IV
2b. missing folio: Q II 157 (2), Warsz.
3. –

137

1. [56] [before duel] Ambo ornati debent ire ante iudicem, *et ambo iurare debent*: unus, scilicet actor, quod causa sit vera, pro qua super ipsum querelam fecerit, et respondens, quot sit innocens. [Gn.]
2a. the underlined words: Gn. and other Latin texts except 2b, 2c
2b. missing: Przem.
2c. the complete phrase missing: II Q 4
2d. missing Article: Plesz., Dział. IV
2e. missing folio: Q II 157 (2), Warsz.
3. –

138

1. [56] Si vincetur ille, super quem conqueritur, tunc iudicetur sentencia capitali. Sin autem vicerit, dimittetur cum pena et *emenda*. [Gn.]
2c. *emenda*: Gn. and other Latin texts except 2b
2b. missing: BN 3068
2c. missing Article: Plesz., Dział. IV
2d. missing folio: Q II 157 (2), Warsz.
3. –

139

1a. [56] Et iudex sibi iudicare debet, sicut *per duellum adversarius suus* convictus. [*Statutes*]
1b. Et iudex sibi iudicare debet, sicut *fuisset duello* convictus. [Gn. and other Latin texts]
2a. missing Article: Plesz., Dział. IV
2b. missing folio: Q II 157 (2), Warsz.
3. cf. PS II.75, p. 56

140

1. [56] Si autem alter **agnatus** mortui quiscumque fuerit loco ipsius ad duellum se exhibuerit, hic extinguet omne testimonium, quia tunc ipsum absque *duello* vincere non potest, *nisi fuerit prescriptus*, ut superius est expressum. [BN 12607]
2a. the underlined text in: BN 12607, Oss.
2b. missing: Gn. and other Latin texts except 2a
2c. in II Q 4 *duello* replaced by *testimonio*
2d. missing Article: Plesz., Dział. IV
2e. missing folio: Q II 157 (2), Warsz.
3. see No. 419

141

1. [56] text in No. 140
2a. **agnatus**: Gn., Q II 157 (1), BJ 4405, Przem., BOZ, Flor., BN 12607, Oss., 951b, BN 3068, *Statutes*
2b. **cognatus**: F 143, BN 12600, Dział. I, AJG, Kiel., II Q 4
2c. missing Article: Plesz., Dział. IV
2d. missing folio: Q II 157 (2), Warsz.
3. see No. 420

142

1a. [58] Et si tempore vite unius plura bona fuerint, quam quod suo iuramento exactionaliter alias solvendo exactionem comprobasset, et si fatetur eadem bona esse sua, tunc periurius existit, perdidit omne ius suum civile et caret iure, propter

quod infamis dicitur. Et quidcunque periurus debeat protestari, hoc coram iudicio oportet fieri, ita quod sibi causa nominatur propter quam sit periurus. Et si fateatur, vel bona sub ipso valeant promptari, alias cognosci vel inveniri, pro quibus patenter iuravit, extunc periurus est et convictus carensque iure et perdens suum ius civile. [*Statutes*]

1b. Et si eciam circa vitam unus vir plura bona invenerint, quam sub iuramento adidiam [*s*] dederit secundum arbitrium civitatis, ille homo est periurus, sic homo debet fieri et perdit omne ius suum, si bona illa fatetur, quod sua sint, et si homo vincertur, quod periurius sit, hoc quod debet fieri coram iudicio bannito et si factum et actum, queritur, quare periurus factus sit et si fatetur, possunt bona dicta sub potestate inveniri, pro quibus iuramentum prestitit ac inquit, qui possunt protestari, tunc ius suum perdit et honorem et hominem [*s*]. [BN 3068]

2a. in: BN 12607, Oss., II Q 4; slight linguistic divergences in the *Statutes*

2b. another linguistic redaction: BN 3068

2c. missing: Gn. and other Latin texts except 2a, 2b

2d. missing Article: Plesz., Dział. IV

2e. missing folio: Q II 157 (2), Warsz.

3a. German text in II Q 4 shorter than in BN 12607

3b. cf. NTO p. 151 and a Latin collection of Magdeburg *ortyle* in BJ 4405 No. 140, 141, f. 43r–v

3c. see No. 422

143

1. [60] Et cum viro uxor moritur,

1a. proxima sua *congnata* recipit suppellectilia. [Gn. and other Latin texts except 1b, 1c]

1b. uxor *propria* sua *agnata seu neptis* recipit supellectilia. [BN 3068]

1c. proxima sua *agnata vel* cognata recipit suppellectilia. [Przem.]

2a. missing Article: Plesz.

2b. missing folio: Warsz.

3. –

144

1. [60] *Hec eadem cognata* nulla recipit pulmentaria. [*Statutes*]

2a. the underlined words: II Q 4, *Statutes*

2b. missing: Gn. and other Latin texts except 2a

2c. missing Article: Plesz.
2d. missing folio: Warsz.
3. –

145

1. [61] Et ubi pupilli annos pubertatis nondum attigerint, et
1a. *eorum senior agnatus* recipit arma bellica solus [Gn. and other Latin texts except 1b, 1c]
1b. *eorum senior cognatus* recipit arma bellica solus [Q II 157 (2), II Q 4]
1c. *eorum senior* recipit arma bellica solus [BN 12600, AJG, Kiel.]
2a. missing Article: Plesz.
2b. missing folio: Warsz. i Oss.
3. see No. 424

146

1. [61] ita, quod senior dividet [a heritage] et iunior eliget. [*Statutes*]
2a. in: Przem., Dział. IV, BN 12607, II Q 4, 951b, *Statutes*
2b. missing: Gn. and other Latin texts except 2a
2c. missing Article: Plesz.
2d. missing folio: Warsz. i Oss.
3a. in gloss in Dział. I
3b. see No. 425

147

1. [61] Ubi etiam duo vel plures unam simul habuerint hereditatem, ibi unus alium ad divisionem iure valeat coartare. [*Statutes*]
2a. in: BN 12607, II Q 4, 951b, *Statutes*
2b. missing: Gn. and other Latin texts except 2a
2c. missing Article: Plesz.
2d. missing folio: Warsz. i Oss.
3. –

148

1a. [61] Sin autem vir, qui dum annos pubertatis inplevit, religionem intraverit, *hic se a iure terrestri ac feodali alienavit*, et sua feoda vacant, *quia scutum bellicum resignavit*. [Gn. and other Latin texts except 1b–1d]

1b. Si autem vir, qui annos pubertatis inplevit, religionem intraverit, *hic se a iure terrestri ac pheodali alienavit*, et sua pheoda vacant, *si hoc possit protestari metseptimus cum hiis, qui eum* [?] *incli vita viderunt*. [F 143]

1c. Si autem vir, qui dum annos pubertatis implevit religionem, et sua feoda vacant, *quia bellicum resignavit*. [Q II 157 (2)]

1d. Qui alienavit et sua feoda vacant, *quia scutum bellicum resignavit* alienavit. [II Q 4]

2a. missing Article: Plesz.

2b. missing folio: Warsz. i Oss.

3. –

149

1. [62] Ambo actor et ille, hoc est super quem conqueritur, respondens est sive reus, possunt habere colloquia pro qualibet causa

1a. *tribus* vicibus, eousque ipsos preco revocet. [Gn. and other Latin texts except 1b]

1b. *tam diu et tot* vicibus, quousque eos preco revocet. [F 143]

2a. missing Article: Plesz.

2b. missing folio: Warsz. i Oss.

3. –

150

1. [63] In omni loco iuris est, iudex iudicet cum sententiis *scabinorum*. [Dział. IV]

2a. *scabinorum*: Dział. IV, II Q 4, 951b, *Statutes*

2b. the underlined word missing: Gn. and other Latin texts except 2a and 2c

2c. the complete phrase missing: F 143

2d. missing Article: Plesz.

2e. missing folio: Warsz. i Oss.

3a. underlined word missing also in the German text in BN 12607

3b. in gloss in Dział. I

3c. see No. 430

151

1. [64] Si homo et ubi vir pro pecunia aut debito fuerit et moritur vir, sui pueri *aut sui heredes* non tenentur pro eo solvere. [Gn.]
2a. the underlined words: Gn. and other Latin texts except 2b, 2c
2b. missing: F 143, AJG, Kiel., Dział. IV, BN 12607, II Q 4, 951b, *Statutes*
2c. missing Article: Plesz.
2d. missing folio: Warsz. i Oss.
3. see No. 432

152

1. [64] Si vir pro pecunia fideiussor fuerit, fideiussorem pecuniam solvere oportet solum, aut probare *mettercius*, quod pecunia sit integraliter persoluta. [BN 12607]
2a. *mettertius*: BN 12607
2b. missing: Gn. and other Latin texts except 2a
2c. missing Article: Plesz.
2d. missing folio: Warsz. i Oss.
3. see No. 433

153

1. [65] Si vir cum fustibus aut baculis percussus fuerit … ipse est duellum proprius super eos aquirere, quam ipse eum evadere possit suo iure, *id est vincere eum cum testibus, quam ipse cum testibus evadere possit.* [BN 12607]
2a. the underlined words: BN 12607, Oss.
2b. missing: Gn. and other Latin texts except 2a
2c. missing Article: Plesz.
2d. missing folio: Warsz. i Oss.
3. see No. 434

154

1. [65] Sin autem super caput et brachia percussus fuerit, quod alter ostendere non possit, illi homines melius ostendere possunt, quam ipse super eos probare possit suo iure. [Gn.]
2a. in: Gn. and other Latin texts except 2b

2b. missing: AJG, Kiel.
2c. missing Article: Plesz.
2d. missing folio: Warsz.
3. –

155

1. [65] Sin autem fatentur, quivis amittit emendam
1a. et iudex acquirit suam penam. [Gn. and other Latin texts except 1b, 1c]
1b. XXX solidos, et iudex aquirit suam penam ·VIII· solidos. [BN 12607]
1c. XXX solidos. [Oss.]
2a. missing Article: Plesz.
2b. missing folio: Warsz.
3. see No. 435, 436

156

1a. [66] Quod si hereditas mortaliola [s] absque heredibus inventa seu reperta fuerit, regie cedet maiestati. [Gn. and other Latin texts except 1b–d]
1b. Si *mortariola* hereditas absque heredibus inventa fuerit *aut remanserit anno et die,* regi cedet maiestati. [AJG, Kiel., BN 12607, Oss.]
1c. Si hereditas absque *successoribus relinquitur, ita quod nullus se trahat ad eandem infra annum et die, hoc pertinet ad Regiam Maiestatem.* [Dział. IV, II Q 4, 951b, *Statutes*]
1d. Si hereditas mortaliola absque heredibus inventa seu reperta fuerit, **ita quod nullus se ad hanc** *trahet infra annum et diem nisi legale impedimentum inpedierit.* [Przem.]
2a. in BN 3068 two Articles: 1/ in compliance with Gn., 2/ in compliance with *Statutes*
2b. missing Article: Plesz.
2c. missing folio: Warsz.
3a. in gloss in BJ 4405, close to Przem.
3b. see No. 437

157

1. [67] Quod si vir, qui pueros habuerit, occisus fuerit, tres aut plures, et si vir unus iudicialiter pro ⟨eo⟩ inpulsatus fuerit et evaserit, ut ius dictaverit, et si sibi super

eam querimoniam vera satisdacio facta fuerit, non tenetur, nec debet *ab aliis pueris* inposterum pro eodem homicidio infestari. [Gn.]

2a. the underlined text: Gn. and other Latin texts except 2b

2b. missing: Q II 157 (1)

2c. missing Article: Plesz.

2d. missing folio: Warsz.

3. –

158

1a. [68] Si etiam iuramenta promissa venerint super diem ligatum et feriatum, hec iudex protrahere potest super alium diem iudicialem, qui venerit extra dies ligatos. Etiamsi vir balbutiens vel alter, seu testis aliquis fuerit impeditus, ita quod imperfecte suum dixerit iuramentum, ille se ipsum emendare valeat, quotiens impeditur et manebit de huiusmodi melioratione sine damno. [*Statutes*]

1b. Si homini iuramenta pervenerint ad dies feriatos, iudex bene potest postponere ad secundum et tertium diem iuramenta. Si eciam homo, qui non est facundus ad loquendum aut si testes imperiti fuerint, quod iuramentum bene loqui non potest, tunc potest bene se reiterare quantum voluerit et si nichil nocebit. [BN 3068]

2a. in: BN 12607, Oss., II Q 4, 951b, *Statutes*

2b. another linguistic redaction in BN 3068

2c. missing: Gn. and other Latin texts except 2a, 2b

2d. missing Article: Q II 157 (1), Plesz.

2e. missing folio: Warsz.

3a. the whole German text in BN 12607, the short version in II Q 4

3b. cf. NTO No. 158, 167 and in Latin collection of Magdeburg *ortyle* in BJ 4405 No. 148, 156 f. 45r, 46r; cf. MFr. I.16.2. (P. Laband, *Magdeburger Rechtsquellen*, p. 98)

3c. see No. 439

159

1a. [69] Et *si sibi defectus fuerit et neminem pro se habuerit respondentem, utpote venditorem habere poterit, ut se coram iudicio iactitavit, et tunc* fideiussorie *faciat* cautionem iudi⟨ci⟩ pro pena et pro expensis [Gn. and other Latin texts except 1b]

1b. Et *tunc ibi qui se revocat ad venditorem*, fideiussoriam cautionem *faciat* iudici pro pena et pro expensis [*Statutes*]

2a. missing Article: Plesz.
2b. missing folio: Warsz.
3. –

160

1. [69] Sin autem dixerit, quod equm in foro communi aut libero emerit, extunc suam pecuniam, quam pro eodem equo dedit, integraliter ammittit, et illi
1a. suum equm reddere oportet, et nullam penam pro eo ammittit. [Gn. and other Latin texts except 1b]
1b. non habuerit hospitem, qui mercipotum benedixit. [*Statutes*]
2a. missing Article: Plesz.
2b. missing folio: Warsz.
3a. the same regulation in Art. 85, except in Q II 157 (2) and BN 12600
3b. see No. 183

161

1a. [71] De *viro* qui *vulneratus aut percussus* fuerit et querulare noluerit. // Vir si vulneratus *aut trucidatus* [Gn. and other Latin texts except 1b]
1b. De *eo* qui *trucidatus* fuerit et querulare noluerit. // Vir si vulneratus [Q II 157 (2)]
2a. in Q II 157 (2) and BN 12600 a part of the Art. was moved to the title of the Art.
2b. missing Article: F 143, Plesz.
2c. missing folio: Warsz.
3. –

162

1. [73] Et mater cum hiis bonis nichil facere potest, absque heredum consensu ac voluntate. [Gn.]
2a. in: Gn. and other Latin texts except 2b
2b. missing: Q II 157 (2), BN 12600
2c. missing Article: Plesz.
2d. missing folio: Warsz.
3. –

163

1a. [73] I. **Si vero omnes** ***pueri*****, patre mortuo, moriuntur, extunc bona sua heredant super suam matrem**, et postea, si mater decesserit ab hac luce, *tunc eadem omnia bona heredant* ***super mulieris*** *proximiores heredes, sive sint masculi, sive femine, ex paterna et materna consanguineitate.* II. *Etiam mulier non potest talem hereditatem vendere nec donare, sed cum rebus mobilibus potest facere quicquid vult. Sed cum hereditate quicunque facere non potest absque consensu heredum.* [*Statutes*]

1b. **I. Si autem moriuntur pueri omnes post mortem patris, tunc heredant sua bona super matrem.** Si moritur mater, tunc bona *statim spectant ad agnatos sive cognatos mulieris, quicumque fuerint paris condicionis.* II. *Etsi mulier non potest talem hereditatem dare nec vendere, sed cum rebus mobilibus potest facere, quid vult. Sed cum hereditate quicquam non potest facere absque consensu heredum.* [BN 3068 in Art. 74]

1c. I. Si moritur mulier post hoc, tunc hereditas *spectat ad heredes mulieris, qui sunt sibi paris condicionis, sive sunt de patre sive de matre.* II. *Vir sive mulier eciam non potest iure eciam cum talis hereditate quaequam facere absque heredum con*[*sen*]*su, que spectat post mortem ipsius. Sed tamen cum rebus mobilibus et immobilibus potest facere quid voluerit absque consensu heredum.* [BN 3068 in Art. 48]

2a. general compliance: BN 12607, Oss., II Q 4, 951b, *Statutes*

2b. only in Oss.: si *pater* decesserit ab hac luce

2c. only in the *Statutes*: sed cum rebus mobilibus potest facere quicquid vult

2d. BN 3068 in Art. 74: 1st part specific regulation, 2nd part in accordance with the *Statutes*

2e. BN 3068 in Art. 48: specific regulation in comparison with *Statutes*

2f. missing: Gn. and other Latin texts except 2a–2c

2g. missing Article: Plesz.

2h. missing folio: Warsz.

3a. the German text of Article 74 in MS BN 12607 corresponds with the Latin text of Article 74 in MS BN 3068 (2b)

3b. linguistic divergences between German texts in II Q 4 and BN 12607

3c. cf. NTO No. 152 and in Latin collection of Magdeburg *ortyle* in BJ 4405 No. 142, f. 3v–44r; cf. MFr. I.7.1. (P. Laband, *Magdeburger Rechtsquellen*, p. 98)

3d. see No. 446

164

1. [74] Quando puer est duodecim annorum, tunc potest eligere pro sua voluntate quem voluerit pro tutore. Et qui suus fuerit tutor, matri racionem facere *habet et adolescenti*, quit cum bonis factum fuerit. [Gn.]
2a. *habet et adolescenti:* Gn. and other Latin texts except 2b
2b. *tenetur:* BOZ
2c. missing Article: Plesz.
2d. missing folio: Warsz.
3. –

165

1a. [74] Cum etiam puer fuerit duodecim annorum, is mundiburdius alias sui potens est factus, et potest in eo iudicium perpetrari et etiam bona sua a se sine tutore alienare. Sed innatam hereditatem et proprium debet dare cum consensu heredum. Etiam iste puer de iure ad responsionem valeat coartari seu compelli. [*Statutes*]
1b. Eciam quando duodecim annorum et antiqu[us], nunc potest sua bona absque tutore vendere cui vult, excepta hereditate sive domorum [*s*], hoc debet dare cum consensu heredum, qui [*s*] ad hoc spectant, qui eciam pueris opportet ostendere coram iudicio iure. [BN 3068]
2a. in: BN 12607, Oss., II Q 4, 951b, *Statutes*
2b. another linguistic redaction: BN 3068
2c. missing: Gn. and other Latin texts except 2a, 2b
2d. missing Article: Plesz.
2e. missing folio: Warsz.
3a. the German text in MS II Q 4 is shorter than the one in MS BN 12607
3b. cf. NTO No. 143 and in Latin collection of Magdeburg *ortyle* in BJ 4405 Nr. 153, f. 44r; cf. MFr. I.9.1. (P. Laband, *Magdeburger Rechtsquellen*, p. 98)
3c. see No. 447

166

1. [75] Et hoc scire debet quilibet legens, ubi scribitur agnatus, designat ex parte patris et ex parte gladii. Et ubi scribitur cognatus, ex parte matris desingnatur. [Gn.]

2a. in: Gn., F 143, BN 12600, Q II 157 (2), Dział. I, BJ 4405, Przem., BOZ, Flor., 951b, BN 3068, *Statutes*
2b. missing: Q II 157 (1), AJG, Kiel., Dział. IV, Warsz., BN 12607, Oss., II Q 4
2c. missing Article: Plesz.
3a. in MS F 143 this regulation was transposed to Article 73
3b. see No. 448

167

1. [75] Libertatem suam vir probare potest
1a. cum *tribus congnatis et tribus agnatis* [Gn. and other Latin texts except 1b, 1c]
1b. cum *agnatis* [BOZ]
1c. cum *tribus cognatis* [Q II 157 (2), BN 12600, Oss.]
2. missing Article: Plesz.
3. –

168

1. [76] Si eciam aliquis conqueritur super aliquem pro debito aut *pecunia* ludo seu taxillis aquisita, pro eo sibi non habet respondere. [Gn.]
2a. *debito aut pecunia*: Gn. and other Latin texts except 2b, 2c
2b. missing the underlined text: Przem.
2c. missing the cursive text: Q II 157 (1)
2d. missing the sentence: BOZ
2e. missing Article: Plesz.
3. in 951b, Q II 157 (1) and in the *Statutes* this regulation was moved into another Art., in F 143 as a separate Art.

169

1. [76] Si servus bona domini sui perluserit taxilis, aut obligat aut vendit, dominus bene potest arestare denuo iure, ut se ad ea bona trahat, ut iuris sit. Sin autem propria bona sua deluserit, aut quocunque modo a se alienaverit sua voluntate, dominus super ea nichil alloqui potest, quia servus solvere tenetur, et sic domino pro bonis servi non est licitum respondere. [Gn.]
2a. in: Gn. and other Latin texts except 2b

2b. missing: Dział. IV, Warsz., BN 12607, Oss., II Q 4
2c. missing Article: Plesz.
3a. cf. SSp III 6 § 1–2 and PS III.80
3b. see No. 449

170

1. [76] Sin autem servo suus equs, vel alia bona sua furtive, aut spoliando recepta fuerint absque culpa, sin in domini servicio, hoc oportet dominum solvere servo, et pro eo oportet dominum respondere, si super eo queruletur. [Gn.]
2a. in: Gn. and other Latin texts except 2b
2b. missing: Q II 157 (2), Dział. IV, Warsz., BN 12607, Oss., II Q 4
2c. missing Article: Plesz.
3a. cf. SSp III 6 § 3 and PS III.80
4b. see No. 449

171

1. [76] text see Nr. 170, supplement: ter de bonis, que alicui data fuit ad servandum. [AJG]
2a. in: AJG, Kiel.
2b. missing: Gn. and other Latin texts except 2a
2c. missing Article: Plesz.
3. –

172

1a. [76] Si aliquis etiam conqueritur super alium pro cibariis preparatis, hic propior est obtinere iuramento, quam ille ipsum evadere possit suo iuramento. [*Statutes*]
1b. Si conqueritur hospes super hospitem pro expensis suis comestibilibus, tunc hospes suas melius potest obtinere sub iuramento tacto sacramento, quam ille possit evadere. [BN 3068]
2a. in: F 143, AJG, Kiel., Dział. IV, Warsz., BN 12607, Oss., 951b, *Statutes*
2b. amendment: BN 3068
2c. missing: Gn. and other Latin texts except 2a, 2b
2d. missing Article: Plesz.

3a. in MS F 143 this regulation was transposed to a separate article
3b. in MS Dział. I in a gloss at Article 79
3c. see No. 450

173

1. [77] De bonis, que alicui danda sunt ad servandum in deposito. // Quicumque alteri bona sua dederit ad servandum, aut in deposito posuerit, si sibi subtracta fuerint, aut spoliatus eis fuerit, aut conbusta, vel si mortuum fuerit, si equs vel pecora fuerint, non debet aliquot dampnum pro eo sustinere, si presumpserit iurare, quod absque sua culpa amissum fuerit. Sed quid viro concessum aut obligatum fuerit, hoc in destructum reddere tenetur, aut solvere secundum suum valorem. Sin autem moritur equs aut pecus infra obligacionem absque illius culpa, cui obligatum fuerat, si hoc probaverit, et si iuramentum pro eo prestare presumpserit, quod sine sua culpa decessit, non solvit, sed suam reconpensam amittit, in qua sibi fuerat obligatum. [Gn.]
2a. in: Gn. and other Latin texts except 2b
2b. missing Article: Dział. IV, Warsz., BN 12607, Oss., II Q 4
3. see SSp. III 6 § 3–5

174

1. [missing Article in Gn., in the *Statutes* Art. 86] Si servus deservitum precium super suum dominum obiurgaverit coram iudicio, pro eo dominus ullam iudici demeretur penam et dominus servo hoc tenetur eodem die solvere. [*Statutes*]
2a. in: AJG, Kiel., Dział. IV, Warsz., BN 12607, Oss., II Q 4, 951b, BN 3068, *Statutes*
2b. missing Article: Gn. and other Latin texts except 2a
3a. a similar regulation can be found in Article 24 in all Latin texts, but in the German text only in this place
3b. see No. 451

175

1. [79] Sin autem respondens dixerit se debitum persolvisse, extunc inpedit sibi suum testimonium. Hoc bene probare potest cum probis viris *metseptimus* tacto sacramento. [Gn.]

2a. *metseptimus*: Gn., Dział. I, Dział IV
2b. *mettertius*: Q II 157 (1), Q II 157 (2), BJ 4405, Przem., BOZ, AJG, Kiel., Flor., Warsz., BN 12607, Oss., II Q 4, 951b, BN 3068, *Statutes*
2c. *both*: BN 12600
2d. the regulation missing: F 143
2e. missing Article: Plesz.
3a. the gloss in MS Dział. I has tercius
3b. see No. 453

176

1a. [81] ubi unum cum gladio aut cultello aut alia sica in manu deprehenderit, cum quo pacem infregit, aut si in fuga facti captivatus fuerit et captivus ad iudicium deductus fuerit cum clamore. Hunc actor met septimus vincere debet circa ius pacis, si factum manifestum cum reo ad iudicium deductum fuerit. [Gn. and other Latin texts except 1b]
1b. Ubi apud virum potest cum scitu, si tunc ultra aliquid suum debitum superfuerit cum scitu, illi reddere debet, cuius fuit hereditas, debet, si deficit, agat ulterius. [BN 3068]
2. missing Article: Dział. IV, Plesz.
3. text in 1b also in Art. 84

177

1. [82] et si duxerit, quod persolverit, hoc probabit hominibus fidedignis *mettercius* [Dział. IV]
2a. *mettertius*: Dział. IV, Warsz.
2b. missing: Gn. and other Latin texts except 2a, 2b
2c. missing Article: Plesz., BN 3068
3. see No. 457

178

1. [82] In iudicio burgrabii vir bene potest pro debito *pecuniali* querulari super actorem [Dział. IV]
2a. *pecuniali*: Dział. IV, Warsz.

2b. missing: Gn. and other Latin texts except 2a
2c. missing Article: Plesz., BN 3068
3. see No. 458

179

1. [83] Iudex debet iudicium exercere, et eo temptare cottidie in vero iudicii loco, nisi sit, quod vir conqueritur *pro debito* absque testibus voluerit [F143]
2a. *pro debito*: F 143, Q II 157 (1), Q II 157 (2), BN 12600, BJ 4405, Przem., Dział. IV, Warsz., BN 12607, Oss.
2b. missing: Gn. and other Latin texts except 2a
2c. missing Article: Plesz., BN 3068
3. see No. 459

180

1a. [83] Iudex eciam tenetur iudicium comportare, et non actor neque reus. [BN 12607, Oss.]
1b. Iudex etiam iudicium *coordinare debet, quando iudicare debet*, et non actor nec reus. [II Q 4, 951b, *Statutes*]
2a. missing: Gn. and other Latin texts except 1a, 1b
2a. missing Article: Plesz., BN 3068
3. see No. 460

181

1. [83] Reconpensam et emendam et penam iudicis solvere debent ad diem, ut fuerit diffinitum,
1a. ut tunc pagamentum consuetum fuerit [Gn. and other Latin texts except 2b–2c]
1b. cum denariis, prout extunc valent in pagamento [Dział. IV]
1c. cum talibus denariis, prout tunc in eodem iudicio sunt transeuntes et daturi [II Q 4, 951b, *Statutes*]
2a. the complete phrase missing: F 143, Przem.
2b. missing Article: Plesz., BN 3068
3. see No. 461

182

1. [83] reconpensam et emendam actori et penam iudici. [Gn.]
2a. in: Gn. and other Latin texts except 2b
2b. missing: F 143, Q II 157 (2), BN 12600
2c. missing Article: Plesz., BN 3068
3. –

183

1. [85] Sin autem equus [fuerit], quem vir alloquitur, quod sibi subtractus sit, aut eo spoliatus sit, ad hoc se trahere debet, *cum suo dextro pede calcare debet* equo super suum pedem anteriorem, et sinistra manu equm capere *per dextram aurem* [Gn.]
2a. the underlined words: Gn. and other Latin texts except 2b, 2c
2b. the underlined words missing: in Oss.
2c. the words in italics missing: Q II 157 (2), BN 12600
2d. missing Article: Plesz.
3. –

184

1. [85] Et tunc ille ad suum se trahat venditorem *et ipsum iurare oportet super sanctos, quod trahat se cum equo ad verum venditorem*, ibi eum sequi oportet [Gn.]
2a. the underlined words: Gn. and other Latin texts except 2b
2b. missing: AJG, Kiel., BN 12607, Oss.
2c. missing Article: Plesz.
3. see No. 166

185

1. [86] Si vir conqueritur super virum pro *debito* [Gn.]
2a. *debito*: Gn. and other Latin texts except 2b
2b. *pecunia*: II Q 4, *Statutes*
2c. missing Article: Plesz.
3. see No. 469

186

1. [86] hoc oportet iuramento probare *metseptimus* tacto sacramento. [Gn.]
2a. *metseptimus*: Gn. and other Latin texts except 2b
2b. missing: Q II 157 (1)
2c. missing Article: Plesz.
3. see No. 190

187

1. [87] Unus vir potest filium suum eximere unica manu, qui est in pane suo non uxoratus, tacto sacramento, quod filius suus reus non sit. *Hoc potest facere in eodem iudicio aut per sex ebdomadas querimonia facta aliternorum* [s]. [BN 3068]
2a. the underlined words: BN 3068
2b. missing: Gn. and other Latin texts except 2a, 2c
2c. the complete phrase missing: F 143, Q II 157 (1)
2d. missing Article: Plesz.
3. cf. 58 and 59

188

1. [87] Si autem pater et filius ambo pro uno facto fuerint impulsati, extunc patrem oportet se primo de facto veridice expurgare. [*Statutes*]
2a. in: Dział. IV, Warsz., II Q 4, 951b, BN 3068, *Statutes*
2b. the same linguistic redaction: Dział. IV, Warsz.
2c. the same linguistic redaction: II Q 4, 951b, *Statutes*
2d. another redaction: BN 3068
2e. missing: Gn. and other Latin texts except 2a–2d
2e. missing Article: Plesz.
3. see No. 472

189

1. [87] Si hoc, ut iuris est, metseptimus protestabitur cum probis hominibus, qui hoc viderunt et audierunt, vel qui presentes fuerunt, primam querelam acquirit. *Sed si sua querela pernoctabitur, hoc facere non potest.* [F 143]
2a. the underlined words: F 143

2b. missing: Gn. and other Latin texts except 2a
2c. missing Article: Plesz.
3. –

190

1. [88] Si femina deprehensa fuerit in facto manifesto in homicidio aut vulneribus duello dingnis, ac ipsam propius est vincere *metseptimus* cum hominibus fidedingnis, quam innocens fieri possit. [Gn.]
2a. *metseptimus*: Gn. and other Latin texts except 2b
2b. missing: Q II 157 (1)
2c. missing Article: Plesz.
3. see No. 186

191

1. [90] Si vir scabinum in scampno indecenter in iudicio bannito increpaverit, si hoc probaverit *per suos consodales*, qui audiverunt, illum oportet dare emendam
1a. *scabino* et iudici *suam* penam. [Gn. and other Latin texts except 1b]
1b. *scabinis XXX solidos*. [BN 3068]
2. missing Article: Plesz.
3. –

192

1. [90] text see No. 192
2a. *per suos consodales* in: Gn. and other Latin texts except 2b
2b. missing: AJG, Kiel.
2c. missing Article: Plesz.
3. –

193

1a. [90] Scabini si non fuerint in una sententia unanimes, vel eam ignorantes, extunc eandem ad secundum et tertium iudicium valebunt differre, et tunc eam inferre debent, vel eam mittere ferre illuc quo competit si nequant invenire et non diutius prolongare. [*Statutes*]

1b. ignorant quousque ad iudicium tercium, tunc sentenciam debent invenitur, longius non tardare. [BN 3068]

2a. compliance: BN 12607, Oss., II Q 4

2b. slight linguistic divergences: 951b, close to *Statutes*

2c. broader linguistic divergences: *Statutes*

2d. another version: BN 3068

2e. missing: Gn. and other Latin texts except 2a–2d

2f. missing Article: Plesz.

3a. compliance of the German and the Latin texts (2a) in II Q 4; missing the German text in BN 12607

3b. cf. NTO No. 165 and in Latin collection of Magdeburg *ortyle* in BJ 4405 Nr. 154, f. 46r; cf. PS II.8

3c. see No. 476

194

1. [91] [querulatus] Et si non conparet iudicio eodem, tunc debet describi *et reconpensa super suam hereditatem iudicatur, et iudici sua pena. Et eciam nullus alcius cogi potest caucionem facere fideiussoriam, quam se sua extendit reconpensa, nisi sit pro debito, quod maius sit.* [Gn.]

2a. the underlined words: Gn. and other Latin texts except 2b

2b. missing: Q II 157 (2), BN 12600

2c. missing Article: Plesz.

3. –

195

1. [94] Et quando vir moritur, tunc uxori oves presentari debent ad sup[e]llectilia, ubicunque ierint. *Anete, colcidre, vela, tecture curruum, olle picte eciam ad supellectilia pertinent.* [Gn.]

2a. the underlined words: Gn. and other Latin texts except 2b

2a. missing: Dział. IV, Warsz., BN 12607, Oss., II Q 4

2c. missing Article: F 143, Plesz.

3. see No. 479

196

1. [95] Nemo potest nec pro homicidio, nec pro vulneribus, nec pro aliquo *debito* suum probare incolatum. [Gn.]
2a. *debito*: Gn. and other Latin texts except 2b
2b. missing: Oss.
2c. missing Article: F 143, Plesz., BOZ
3a. the regulation in Dział. I also as a gloss in Art. 97
3b. see No. 480

197

1. [95] pro aliquo debito suo *iuramento* probare incolatum. [AJG]
2a. *iuramento*: Q II 157 (1), Q II 157 (2), BN 12600, BJ 4405, Przem., AJG, Kiel., Dział. IV, Warsz., BN 12607, Oss., II Q 4, 951b, *Statute*
2b. missing: Gn. and other Latin texts except 2a
2c. missing Article: F 143, Plesz., BOZ
3. see No. 481

198

1. [95] Consules si iuramentum unius viri recipient, quod iuste secundum civitatis statuta et consuetudinem exactionem dedisset, tandem vero post mortem illius iurantis plura bona sub ipsius possessione fuerint inventa, quam peractionata fuissent, illa bona consules non habent recipere, sed ipsius defuncti heredes nisi aliquis heredum eadem denegata bona coram iudicio vel sedenti consilio recipere abrenunciasset, et tunc ipsa bona consulibus pro utilitate civitatis permanent quemadmodum arbitratur *et laudum civitatis disponit.* [*Statutes*]
2a. the phrase: BN 12607, Oss., II Q 4, 951b, *Statutes*
2b. the underlined words: *Statutes*
2c. linguistic compliance: BN 12607, Oss.
2d. linguistic compliance: II Q 4, 951b
2e. linguistic divergences: *Statutes*
2f. missing: Gn. and other Latin texts except 2a
2g. missing Article: F 143, Plesz., BOZ
3a. in gloss in BJ 4405 – text 2c

3b. missing the German text in BN 12607, a small part in II Q 4
3c. cf. NTO No. 149 and in Latin collection of Magdeburg *ortyle* in BJ 4405 Nr. 139, f. 43r; cf. MFr. I.1.16. (P. Laband, *Magdeburger Rechtsquellen*, p. 98)
3d. see No. 482

199

1. [96] Et si vir super alterum conqueritur, quod sibi abedificaverit aliquit de suis bonis aut de hereditate, hoc ille possibilius optinet, qui habet in possessione unica manu, nisi ipsum cum testimonio allocutus fuerit. Extunc possessor cum testibus servat, si vult *mettercius.* [BN 12607]
2a. the text in italic: BN 12607, Oss.
2b. the underlined words: Gn. and other Latin texts except 2a, 2c
2c. missing: Q II 157 (2), BN 12600, II Q 4
2d. missing Article: Plesz.
3. see No. 484

200

1. [97] Actor etiam si reum pro iuramentis premissis causa Dei vel petitionis hominum proborum mittere absolutum voluerit, extunc iudici etiam competit ad hoc dare suam voluntatem. Et si suum consensum noluerit adhibere, tunc actorem iuramenta recipere oportebit, vel iudici demeretur in pena octo solidorum, et non plus pro causis singulis specialiter. [*Statutes*]
2a. in: BN 12607, Oss., II Q 4, 951b, BN 3068, *Statutes*
2b. liguistic compliance: BN 12607, Oss.
2c. liguistic compliance: 951b, *Statutes*
2d. slight linguistic derivation II Q 4 towards 2b and 2c
2e. slight linguistic derivation BN 3068 towards 2d
2f. missing: Gn. and other Latin texts except 2a
2g. missing Article: Plesz.
3a. in gloss in BJ 4405
3b. the German text in BN 12607 in the compliance with 2b, the shorter version of the German text in II Q 4
3c. cf. NTO No. 166 and in Latin collection of Magdeburg *ortyle* in BJ 4405 Nr. 155, f. 46r; cf. PS II.42
3d. see No. 485

201

1. [98] Eousque cives *Meydeburgenses* veram accionem seu responsivam tenuerint [Gn.]
2a. *Magdeburgenses*: Gn. and other Latin texts except 2b
2b. in *Novo Foro aut in Meÿdeburc*: Q II 157 (1)
2c. missing Article: F 143, Plesz.
3. –

202

1. [98] et se coram suo domino pontifice ac *burgravio ac sculteto* ad iusticiam se [s] exhibuerint [Gn.]
2a. *burgravio ac sculteto*: Gn. and other Latin texts except 2b
2b. *burgravio*: Dział. IV, Warsz.
2c. missing Article: F 143, Plesz.
3. –

203

1. [99] Si contingerit in iudicio castellani, tunc tria talenta demerentur, et in iudicio *sculteti* octo solidi [Gn.]
2c. *sculteti*: Gn. and other Latin texts except 2b, 2c
2b. missing: Przem.
2c. the complete phrase missing: Q II 157 (2), BN 12600
2d. missing Article: Plesz.
3. see No. 488

204

1a. [99] acquirit *emendam et iudex acquirit suam* penam ... ubi homo *suam emendam acquirit, ibi optinet iudex* suam penam. [Gn. and other Latin texts except 1b, 2a and 2b]
1b. acquirit penam ... ubi homo suam penam acquisivit. [AJG, Kiel.]
2a. missing the underlined text: BN 12607, Oss., II Q 4, 951b
2b. missing the second part of the text: Q II 157 (2), BN 12600

2c. missing Article: Plesz.

3. see No. 489

205

1. [99] Si hoc contra iusticiam fecerit, et si paciens ipsum protestaverit cum iudice et *duobus* scabinis [Dział. IV]

2a. *duobus*: Dział. IV, Warsz., II Q 4, 951b, *Statutes*

2b. missing: Gn. and other Latin texts except 2a

2c. missing Article: Plesz.

3. see No. 490

206

1. [100] Si hoc non ostenderit [inculpatus scultetus] et non nominaverit, et hoc per iusticiam facere denegaverit se excusare de sua iniuria, quam exercuit, et se ad iusticiam exhibere [debet], extunc condempnatur advocato in decem talentis idem *advocatus* ⟨scultetus⟩ et illi suum debitum, de quo denegavit, facere iusticiam, et medio quo illa [s] non solvit solus, aut se iure excusaverit iudicio proximo, tunc nullus iudex esse potest, nisi se ex hac culpa eximerit, secundum ut est premissum. Sin autem pro facto criminali pro quo iudicium facere recusavit, sicut pro vulneribus, aut homicidio, aut furto, aut spolio, aut ecclesie violenta, aut incendium, aut hiis similia, que crimina capitalia tanguntur. [Gn.]

2a. *scultetus*: F 143, Q II 157 (1), BOZ, AJG, Kiel., Dział. IV, Warsz., BN 12607, Oss., II Q 4, 951b, BN 3068, *Statutes*

2b. *advocatus*: Gn., BJ 4405, Przem., BOZ, Flor.

2c. a longer portion of the text is missing: Q II 157 (2) and BN 12600, see No. 207

2d. missing Article: Plesz.

3a. in Gn., Dział. I and BJ 4405 correction *scultetus* written by a commentator

3b. see No. 492

207

1. [100] the text see No. 206

2a. the complete phrase: Gn. and other Latin texts except 2b

2b. missing: Q II 157 (2), BN 12600

2c. missing Article: Plesz.

3. –

208

1. [100] Si pro eo coram *castellano aut* advocato inpulsatus fuerit cum testibus [Gn.]
2a. *castellano aut*: Gn. and other Latin texts except 2b
2b. missing: Dział. IV, Warsz.
2c. missing Article: Plesz.
3. see No. 495

209

1. [100] media reconpensa facit novem talenta. [Gn.]
2a. in: Gn. and other Latin texts except 2b
2b. missing: Q II 157 (2), BN 12600
2c. missing Article: Plesz.
3. –

210

1. [100] Sin autem vir cedere voluerit a testimonio et ipsum inculpare pro suo scitu, de quo unica manu evadere potest. [Gn.]
2a. in: Gn. and other Latin texts except 2b
2b. missing: BOZ
2c. missing Article: Plesz.
3. –

211

1. [100] Sin autem [s] unus vir pro debito in captivitatem publicam presentatus fuerit ad tenendum iure, si ipsum amiserit aut si evaserit absque sua culpa aut negli[g]encia pro crimine, quod transit ad collum, pro eo solvet [scultetus] integram reconpensam. *Sin autem pro manu, tunc mediam solvit reconpensam.* [Gn.]
2a. the underlined words: Gn. and other Latin texts except 2b
2b. missing: *Statutes*
2c. missing Article: Plesz.
3. –

212

1. [100] Ubi eciam vir promiserit iuramentum coram iudicio pro enormibus verbis aut depilacione, aut verberibus, aut effusione sanguinis, de quo solitus dimitti non potest, nisi voluntas fuerit iudicis et consensus. [BN 3068]

2a. in: BN 3068

2b. missing: Gn. and other Latin texts except 2a

2c. missing Article: Plesz.

3. –

213

1. [101] scultetus iudex esse debet super *advocatum seu super burgrabium* [*Statutes*]

2a. *advocatum*: Gn. and other Latin texts except 2b, 2c

2b. *burgrabium*: II Q 4

2c. *both*: 951b, *Statutes*

2d. missing Article: Plesz.

3. –

214

1a. [102] Si aliquis *irruenciam domicilii* fecerit [Gn. and other Latin texts except 1b]

1b. Si aliquis fecerit *violenciam* [II Q 4]

2. missing Article: Plesz.

3. –

215

1. [103] et homines, qui clamorem audierunt, habere potuerit in testimonium *metseptimus* [BN 3068]

2a. *metseptimus*: BN 3068

2b. missing: Gn. and other Latin texts except 2a

2c. missing Article: Plesz.

3. Art. 103 in AJG is a synthesis of Gn. Art. 102 and Gn. Art. 103

216

1. [105] Sin autem dixerit, quod
1a. ipsum persolverit, hoc iurabit *metseptimus*. [Gn.]
1b. hoc debitum solus persolverit, hoc *mettertius* iurabit heres. [*Statutes*]
2a. *metseptimus*: Gn., Dział. I, Q II 157 (2), BN 12600, Flor.
2b. *mettertius*: F 143, Q II 157 (1), BJ 4405, Przem., AJG, Kiel., Dział. IV, Warsz., BN 12607, Oss., II Q 4, 951b, BN 3068, *Statutes*
2c. missing Article: Plesz., BOZ
3a. mettertius in gloss: Gn. and Dział. I
3b. see No. 501

217

1a. [105] Si vero debitum sui patris recognoscit, hoc solvere debet, in quantum recepta hereditas se extendit. Et si solvere noluerit vel heres hoc consentire recusat, tunc sibi hereditas sua vel proprium potest iudicio possideri pro isto debito et acquiri, aliter ille non potest constringi ad vendendam hereditatem et proprium suum. [*Statutes*]
1b. Si autem milles querulatur pro debito patris sui super heredem, ille debet persolvere, ita ut hereditas valeat. Si autem non vult persolvere debitum et quod sibi heredes consentire nolunt, tunc potest sibi hereditas appropriari et cum iudicio protestari querelam, eciam extorquere pro debito, aliter non potest agravare hereditatem. [BN 3068]
2a. in: MS BN 12607, Oss., II Q 4, 951b, BN 3068, *Statutes*
2b. compliance: Oss., II Q 4
2c. compliance: 951b, *Statutes* (slight linguistic derivation towards 2b)
2d. a slightly different redaction in MS BN 12607
2e. another regulation: BN 3068, in Art. 107
2f. missing; MS Gn. complies with other Latin texts except 2a–2e
2g. missing Article: Plesz., BOZ
3a. a shorter German version in II Q 4; this part of the German text missing in BN 12607
3b. cf NTO Nr. 154 and in Latin collection of Magdeburg *ortyle* in BJ 4405 Nr. 144, f. 44r
3c. see No. 502

218

1. [106] Qui canem servat oculte mordentem vel feram indomitam aut avem vel ursum aut symeam, qualecumque damnum faciunt, solvere tenere. Et si eas dampno proprietrato alienaverit, per hoc non est innocens, si mettercus poterint protestare et probare, quod eas detinuerit, quousque dampnum facientem. Si homo eradit [*s*] canem vel feram vel ursum, cum sibi nocere voluerit, manere debet sine satisfaccione, si hoc tacto sacramento probare presumpserit, quod se defendendo hoc fecerit. Qui feras bestias extra gaya banita servare voluerit, debet ea servare sub custodia. [Przem.]
2a. in: Przem.
2b. missing: and other Latin texts except 2a
3. cf. NS, ms D I.21, ms P I.23; cf. SSp. II.40, III.49

219

1. [108] [Jewish oath] Ipse debet verti contra solem seorsum, stare nudipes debet super sedem unam, indutus clamide esse debet et pilleum Iudaicum habere debet super caput. [Gn.]
2a. in: Gn. and other Latin texts except 2b
2b. missing: Q II 157 (2), BN 12600
2c. missing Article: Plesz.
3. –

220

1. [109] [Jewish oath] Nunc omnes dicite: amen. [Dział. IV]
2a. in: AJG, Kiel., Dział. IV, Warsz., BN 12607, II Q 4, 951b
2b. missing: Gn. and other Latin texts except except 2a
2c. missing Article: Plesz.
3a. in gloss in BJ 4405
3b. see No. 510

APPENDIX 3

Agreement of the Latin Texts in Gniezno MS (Gn.), Baworowscy MS (BN 12607) and Działyńscy Codex IV (Dział. IV) with the Corresponding German Texts

The entries in this appendix contain: 1) variants of the Latin texts in MS Gn., MS BN 12607 and MS Dział. IV; 2) variants in the German texts of the *Weichbild* (MS BJ 169, MS II F 8, MS BJ 168, MS BJ 170a and MS BN 12607); and wherever relevant also 1261Wr., MSR and 1295Wr.; 3) cross references to Appendix 2. The manuscript (shelfmark) listed first is the source of the quotation.

All quotations of the *Magdeburg Bench Law* (MSR) are taken from Paul Laband's edition; and of 1261Wr. and 1295Wr. from Wilhelm Ebel's edition. In quotations from German manuscripts the spelling of vowels was adapted to their phonetic value, i.e. v → *u*, w → *u*,[1] y → *i*, ji (ÿ) → *ii*. Expanded abbreviations are not marked; words added to clarify meaning within the quotation are enclosed in square brackets; curly brackets {} enclose repetitions. The features of the spelling of German manuscripts (example of the word in MS BJ 169) have been preserved.

301

1a. [1] Extunc arbitrati sunt, quod eligerent scabinos *ac consules. Scabinos* ad diuturnum tempus et consules ad unum annum. [Gn., BN 12607]

1b. Extunc arbitrati sunt, quod eligerent scabinos ad diuturnum temporis et consules ad unum annum. [Dział. IV]

2. Da wurden si zcu rate, daz si kuren sheppfen *und ratman. Di sheppen* zcu langir zcit, di ratman zcu einem iare. [BJ 169, II F 8, BJ 168, BJ 170a, BN 12607]

3. –

1 For example *Lwte* → *liute*.

302

1. [1] quod iuri divino non contradicit [Gn.]
2. –
3. see No. 1

303

1. [1] Et hoc non dimittendo ratione amoris, molestie, ire vel munerum sicut eos iuvet Deus et sancti eius. [BN 12607]
2. –
3. see No. 2

304

1a. [1] Ius ac prefectum et honorem custodire [Gn.]
1b. Ius ac prefectum et honorem custodire *civitatis* [BN 12607, Dział. IV]
2. der *stat* recht und ere und vrumen zcu bewarne [BJ 169, II F 8, BJ 168, BJ 170a, BN 12607]
3. see No. 3

305

1a. [1] Et quicunque violaverit, hoc consules habent agere. [Gn., BN 12607]
1b. missing Dział. IV
2a. Swer so daz brichit, daz sullen di ratman vorderen. [BJ 169, II F 8, BJ 168, BN 12607]
2b. missing 170a
3. see No. 5

306

1a. [1] Sin autem sibi conventus sibi pronunciatus fuerint, demeretur *quinque* solidos. [Gn., Dział. IV]
1b. Sin autem sibi conventus sibi pronunciatus fuerint, demeretur *sex* solidos. [BN 12607]

2. Wirt abir im daz burdink gekundet, he wettet *vumf* shillinge. [BJ 169, II F 8, BJ 168, BJ 170a, BN 12607]
3. see No. 6

307

1. [2] et cum *pecunia* redimet [Gn., BN 12607, Dział. IV]
2. mit *pfenningen* loset [BJ 169, II F 8, BJ 168, BJ 170a, BN 12607]
3. –

308

1. [3] consules [Gn., BN 12607, Dział. IV]
2. sie [BJ 169, II F 8, BJ 168, BJ 170a, BN 12607]
3. –

309

1a. [3] cum triginta solidis emendare. [Gn.]
1a. cum triginta *sex* solidis emendare. [BN 12607, Dział. IV]
2. mit *sechs und* drizic shillingen. [BJ 169, II F 8, BJ 168, BJ 170a, BN 12607]
3. see No. 10

310

1. [4] scultetus [Gn., BN 12607, Dział. IV]
2. he [BJ 169, II F 8, BJ 168, BJ 170a, BN 12607]
3. –

311

1. [4] Dies ligati sunt omnes dies diucales et festivi dies: dies rogacionum ante Penthecostes et adventus Christi et septuaginta dies ante Pascha, in quibus diebus non debent iudicari. [BN 12607]
2. –
3. see No. 15

312

1a. [5] Quando castellanus surgit et iudicavit, tunc iudicium *suum expiravit. Et statim iudicium* sculteti disponit a proximo ad duas septimanas. [Gn., Dział. IV]

1b. Quando castellanus surgit et iudicavit, tunc iudicium sculteti disponit a proximo die ad duas septimanas. [BN 12607]

2. Swenne der burcgreve ufstet und gedingit hat, so *ist sin gedinge uz, und leget alzcuhant* des shultheizen dinc uz von dem nesten tage ubir vircen nacht. [BJ 169, II F 8, BJ 168, BJ 170a, BN 12607]

3. –

313

1a. [6] Scultetus etiam debet habere legalitatem a domino terre et cum eo debet esse feodatus et verum suum feodum esse debet. *Insuper liber esse debet* et legittime natus de terra. [Gn.]

1b. Scultetus etiam debet habere legalitatem a domino terre et cum debet esse feodatus et verum suum feodum esse debet et legittime natus de terra. [BN 12607, Dział. IV]

2a. Die schultheize sal haben die gewalt van des landes herren; her sal ouch damite belênt wesen vnde sal sin rechte lên wesen vnde echt geboren vnde van deme lande. [1261Wr.]

2b. Der schultheise sal belent sin vnd is sal sin recht legen sin; her sal ouch den ban haben von dem heren des landes; *her sal ouch vri wesen* vnde echt geboren vnde van dem lande, da das gerichte binnen ligget. [MSR]

2c. Der shultheize sal ouch den ban haben von dem herren des landes. [BJ 169, II F 8, BN 12607]

2d. Der schultheise sal ouch habin den ban, das ist di gewalt von des landes. [BJ 168]

2e. Der schultheize sal belenet wesen, und diz sal sin recht len sin, her sal ouch vri wesen und geborn von dem lande, do daz gerichte binnen lit. [BJ 170a]

3. see No. 22

314

1. [6] Unum in Epiphania Domini aut die sequenti. [Gn., BN 12607, Dział. IV]

2a. Einez ist dem zwelflen tage. [BJ 169, II F 8, BJ 170a, BN 12607]

2b. Eyn dinc des neesten tagis noch dem czwelstin tage czu winachtin. [BJ 168]

3. –

315

1. [7] et si ceperit hunc, qui ipsum vulneravit [Gn., BN 12607, Dział. IV]
2. und vet he den man [BJ 169, II F 8, BJ 168, BJ 170a, BN 12607]
3. –

316

1a. [7] acquirit homo duellum pro *uno* vulnere, *et si victor fuerit, victus* a victo[re] pro vulnere manum, pro homicidio collum. [Gn.]
1b. acquirit homo duellum pro *uno* vulnere, *et si victor fuerit, victus* ammittit pro vulnere manum, pro homicidio collum. [Dział. IV]
1c. acquirit homo duellum pro vulnere [BN 12607]
2. gewinnit ein man einen campf um *eine* wunde, *und vichtit he sige, iz get ieneme* an di hant, umme totslac an den hals. [BJ 169, II F 8, BJ 168, BJ 170a, BN 12607]
3. –

317

1. [7] Si quis eciam fideiusserit aliquot iudicio pro aliquo adiutorio praesentare ex parte homicidii et eundem non representat, extunc fideiussorem dare oportet querulatori unam recompensam, videlicet XVIII talenta, et iudici suam penam octo solidos. Si autem sentencia fuerit pro uno vulnere duellari, pro tunc fideiossor det unam mediam reconpensam querulanti, scilicet novem talenta, et iudici suam penam octo solidos, istorum nummorum, qui in eodem iudicio sunt currenti communiter et dativi. [BN 12607]
2. Burget auch ein man den andern umme wolleist einis totslagis unde brenget her in nicht vo̊r, so sal der burge dame [*s*] clåger ein vol wergelt gaben, das sint achczen phunt, unde dame [*s*] richter sein gewette acht schillinge. Ist is abir umme eine kampfer wunde, zo gebit der burge dame [*s*] clager ein halp wergelt nuen phunt und dame [*s*] richter sein gewette acht schillinge, sulchir warunge und phenninge, als in dame [*s*] gerichte deme gånge und gebe seit. [BN 12607]
3. see No. 24

318

1a. [9] nisi sit factum manifestum, *ut vulnera mortalia* aut homicidia, *vel furta seu alia criminalia.* [Gn.]

1b. nisi sit factum manifestum, ut *vulnera mortalia vel furtum seu alia criminalia.* [Dział. IV]

1c. nisi sit factum manifestum. [BN 12607]

2. iz en si in einer hanthaften tat. [BJ 169, II F 8, BJ 168, BJ 170a, BN 12607]

3. see No. 28

319

1. [9] Ille dicitur esse hospes, qui ultra XI miliaria extra iudicium habuerit mansionem. Hospes, si hospiti vel alteri, qui in iudicio non habuerit possessionem, racione debiti per manum fuerit presentatus, hunc iudex illi servare debet tam diu, quousque se de debito expurget iuridice vel persolvet. [BN 12607]

2. Eyn gast heyset der, der do ferrer wenne eylff meylen hawsin dame [*s*] gerichte gesessen ist und wirt eyn gast eyme gaste adir eyme andern der do yn dame [*s*] gerichte keyne eygen wonunge hat, umme schult geentwort, so sal der richter den man behaldin lossen bys so lange, das her der schult gerecht werde adir beczale. [BN 12607]

3. see No. 29, 30

320

1a. [10] et, *qui inculpatur,* tunc conparuerit, evadit eum metseptimus, *quam ille super eum possit protestare.* [Gn., Dział. IV]

1b. the underlined words missing BN 12607

2. und iener denne vorkumit, he entget im selbe sibende. [BJ 169, II F 8, BJ 168, BJ 170a, BN 12607]

3. see No. 33

321

1. [11] *malefactor* collum demeretur. [Gn., BN 12607, Dział. IV]

2. *iz* get ieneme an den hals. [BJ 169, II F 8, BJ 168, BJ 170a, BN 12607]

3. –

322

1a. [12] Sin autem plures iudicialiter infestaverit, qua[m] vulnera habuerit, alii omnes evadent suo iure, quivis met septimus. [Gn., Dział. IV]

1b. Si autem plures iudicialiter infestaverit, quam vulnera habuerit, alii omnes evadunt suo *iuramento, qui ius* [s] *sua sola manu pro eo, quoadiutorio racione homicidii vel vulneris duellaris, vel mettercius ad hoc, si pro eo cum testibus fuerit inpulsatus.* [BN 12607]

2a. Hat he abir me[r] liute beclagit, den der wunden sin, *und wurde als manic man virvestit als der wunden sin*[*t*], di anderen entgen im mit irme rechte menlich selbe sibende. [BJ 169, II F 8, BJ 170a]

2b. Hat he aber me[r] lute beclagit, wen der vundin [*s*] sein, di an andern enken im mit irme rechte menlich selb sebinde. [BJ 168]

2c. Hat her abir mer lewte beclagit, denne der wunden synt, dy andern entgen im mit irme rechte *mit seynis einis hant adir salp dritte ab her mit geczewgen wirt becla*[*g*]*it manlich salpdritte.* [BN 12607]

3. see No. 35

323

1. [13] *possidens* propius est suum pingnus servare [Gn., BN 12607, Dział. IV]

2. *dirre erste* ist neher sinen wetteshatz zcu behalden [BJ 169, II F 8, BJ 168, BJ 170a, BN 12607]

3. –

324

1a. [13] Obligat aliquis mercimonia aut alia bona *mobilia* [Gn., BN 12607]

1b. *mobilia* missing Dział. IV

2. Virserzit ein man koufshatz odir ander *varnde* habe [BJ 169, II F 8, BJ 168, BJ 170a, BN 12607]

3. see No. 37

325

1. [13] Nullus etiam hospes ab alio advena et contra indiget pignus recipere pro debito recognito. Si autem receperit, extunc ipsum acquirere et prosequi prout

alter vir iuridice oportebit, nisi alter fuisset inter eos ordinatum verbotenus in contractu. [BN 12607]

2. Auch endarff keyn wirt noch gast iir eynir von dame [*s*] andern phant namen vorbekrante schult. Adir niimt her das phant, so sal her das phant noch rechte erwerbin und irvolgen in gerichte als eyn ander man, is en sey das her das phant neme mit vorwortin und mit undir scheide. [BN 12607]

3. see No. 38

326

1a. [14] bona et non hii, qui exhereditati sunt [Gn., BN 12607]

1b. missing Dział IV

2. daz gut, di uz geradit sin nicht [BJ 169, II F 8, BJ 168, BJ 170a, BN 12607]

3. see No. 41

327

1a. [14] et si pueri vellent *mulieri* dotalitium infringere, servare potest [Dział. IV, BN 12607]

1b. *mulieri* missing Gn.

2. welde man *der vrowen* ir morgengabe brechen [BJ 169, II F 8, BJ 168, BJ 170a, BN 12607]

3. –

328

1. [14] Deservitum parcium rationabile debitum debent solvi de bonis mortui viri pro dotalitio ad hoc, si mulier fuerit dotata pecuniis in paratis. Si autem dotata fuerit in hereditate vel proprio, tunc suum dotalicium pro aliis debitis iure valeat obtinere. Etiam quivis vir habens mansionem infra municipale, ille sue conthorale [*s*] dare potest pro dotalicio suam ipsam hereditatem, quam in posse habet alienandi. Et etiam in aliis suis mobilibus in quantum voluerit. [BN 12607]

2. Vordinet lon und redeliche schult sal man von eynes todes manne gute czu vorne gelden vor morgengobe, ab dii vrawe do an dame [*s*] gereiichen gute begobit ist. Ist abir ir morgengobe an standin eygin adir erbe gegabin, so sal dii vrawe dy dor an beheldin czu vor mit rechte. Ouch mak yczlich man der bynnen weiikbylde besessen und wonhaftyg yst seyme weibe an seyme standin eygin ader erbe, des

her gewalt hot czu vorgabin und ouch an anderem seyme gute und varende habe czu morgengobe gabin, was her will. [BN 12607]

3. see No. 44

329

1. [15] Quando alicui sua possessio publicata fuerit *iuste ac iudicialiter* [Gn., BN 12607, Dział. IV]

2a. Swo einem manne sine gewere gevronit wirt [BJ 169, II F 8, BJ 170a, BN 12607]

2b. Swo einem manne sine gewere gevronit wirt *mit rechtin urteilin in gehegetim dinge binnen wichbilde* [BJ 168]

3. –

330

1. [16] si possidebit *pacifice et quiete absque* contradicione aliqua anno et die, hoc *propius et melius* optinere potest [BN 12607, Dział. IV]

1b. si possidebit *pacifice et quiete absque* arestacione aliqua anno et die, hoc *propius et melius* optinere potest [Gn.]

2. besitzit he damit iar und tac *ane rechte widir sprache*, daz ist he *neher* zcu behalden [BJ 169, II F 8, BJ 168, BJ 170a, BN 12607]

3. see No. 45

331

1a. [17] nec mulier sine viri consensu. [BN 12607, Dział. IV]

1b. missing Gn.

2a. noch daz wip ane des mannes gelop. [BJ 169, II F 8, BJ 168, BN 12607]

2b. missing BJ 170a

3. see No. 46

332

1a. [18] Si autem puella et sacerdos fueri[n]t, tunc supellectilia inter se dividunt. [Gn., Dział. IV, BN 12607]

1b. Si autem puella et sacerdos fuerint, tunc supellectilia inter se dividunt *equaliter*. [II Q 4]

2a. Jst dar ein iuncvrowe vnde ein paphe, die teilen die rade vnder sich. [1261Wr., MSR]

2b. Ist da abir ein iuncvrowe unde ein pfaffe, si teilen die rade *geliche* under sich. [BJ 169, II F 8, BJ 168, BJ 170a, BN 12607]

3. see No. 49

333

1a. [20] et si *tempore statuto* debitor non solverit [Gn., BN 12607]

1b. et si *ad tempores vel tempore statuto* debitor non solverit [Dział. IV]

2. En gildit her nicht [BJ 169, II F 8, BJ 168, BJ 170a, BN 12607]

3. –

334

1. [20] debitum *creditori* et pena *iudici* [Gn., BN 12607, Dział. IV]

2. di shult vnd daz gewette [BJ 169, II F 8, BJ 168, BJ 170a, BN 12607]

3. –

335

1a. [21] Si aliquis ad limina sanctorum aut ad nundinas extra provinciam *aut extra terminos* ire voluerit, et si aliquis ipsum *pro debito* impedire voluerit [Gn.]

1b. Si aliquis ad limina sanctorum aut ad nundinas extra provinciam ire voluerit, et si aliquis ipsum *pro debito* impedire voluerit [BN 12607, Dział. IV]

2. Ist daz ein man betvart odir ⟨sines koufes⟩ koufvart varen wil buzen landes, wil den [n]iman hinderen [BJ 169, II F 8, BJ 168, BJ 170a, BN 12607]

3. see No. 52

336

1. [22] Quicumque scabinum in scampno iudiciali improperaverit *aut turpibus verbis obruerit* [Gn., BN 12607, Dział. IV]

2. Swer so einen scheppfen shildit uf der banc [BJ 169, II F 8, BJ 168, BJ 170a, BN 12607]
3. –

337

1. [23] tunc protestatur *cum hominibus fidedignis, qui iudicio affuerunt.* [Gn., BN 12607, Dział. IV]
2. so tut he iz nur *den dinc liuten.* [BJ 169, II F 8, BJ 168, BJ 170a, BN 12607]
3. –

338

1a. [23] cum sex testibus solus septimus [Gn., BN 12607]
1b. *cum septem testibus* [Dział. IV]
2. mit sechs mannen selbe siben [BJ 169, II F 8, BJ 168, BJ 170a, BN 12607]
3. see No. 56

339

1. [24] Simili et vir potest filium suum, quem in potestate habet, tribus vicibus eximere, ubi aut ad collum aut ad manum pertransit. Quarta vero vice ipsum solum propria in persona respondere oportebit, et primum in suo iure non impediet, si filius prius bene respondisset. … Si autem famulus suam merdecem super suum dominum optinuerit coram iudicio, pro eo dominus iudici nullam penam demeretur, sed dominus famulo eandem mercedem eadem die solvere tenetur indilate. [Gn., BN 12607, Dział. IV]
2. missing in the German texts
3. see nr 58

340

1a. [24] Sin autem pater cum filio simul in eodem crimine *coram iudicio* inpulsati fuerint, ex tunc pater filium eximere non potest, nisi prius se ab eodem crimine expurgabit. [Gn., Dział. IV]

1b. Si autem pater cum filio simul in eodem crimine inculpati fuerint, extunc pater filium eximere non potest, nisi prius se de eodem crimine expurgabit. [BN 12607]

2a. Ist aber beide vatir vnd son beclaget, so en mac her den sun nicht uszihen, her en habe sich selber aller erst us genommen des vngerichtes. [MSR]

2b. Ist abir beide vatir und son beclagit *czu male*, umme ein ungerichte, des mus sich der vatir allir irst unschuldigin. [BJ 168]

2c. missing: BJ 169, II F 8, BJ 170a, BN 12607

3. see No. 59

341

1a. [24] Famulus potest mercedem suam, quam promeruerit, quinque solidos probare tacto sacramento mettercius, quod sibi persolvit, tunc propiis est evadere, quam famulus optinere. [Gn.]

1b. Famulus potest mercedem suam, quam promeruit, quinque solidos tacto sacramento *probare*, ita si ut sibi dominus consentire noluerit. *Si autem dominus iuravit tacto sacramento* met tercius, quod sibi persolvit, tunc propius est evadere, quam famulus prorestare. [BN 12607, Dział. IV]

2. Ein man mac sin virdinit lon *behalden* uffen heiligen vumf shillinge. *Wil abir der herre daz volbrengen* selbe dritte uffen heiligen, daz he im virgoldin habe, he ist neher im zcu engene, dan iener zu behaldene. [BJ 169, II F 8, BJ 168, BJ 170a, BN 12607]

3. see No. 60

342

1a. [25] Idem facit vir illi, qui sibi paris fuerit condicionis. [Gn.]

1b. missing: BN 12607, Dział. IV

2a. Dasselbe tut der man synen, der im ebinburtic ist. [MSR, BJ 168, BJ 170a]

2b. missing: BJ 169, II F 8, BN 12607

3. see No. 62

343

1a. [26] pulmentario [*s*] recipit mariti uxor, et non sua cognata proxima. [Gn., BN 12607, Dzisł. IV]

1b. pulmentario [*s*] recipit mariti uxor, non sua cognata proxima *ipsius mariti.* [II Q 4]
2. Di musteile nimit *des mannis* wip und nicht ir neste spinne. [BJ 169, II F 8, BJ 168, BJ 170a, BN 12607]
3. see No. 65

344

1. [27] et ipse acquirit querimoniam primam. [Gn., BN 12607, Dział. IV]
2. he gewinnet ienem di erste clage *mit rechte.* [BJ 169, II F 8, BJ 168, BJ 170a, BN 12607]
3. –

345

1. [28] quod sibi innatum est *per ius municipale.* [Gn., BN 12607, Dział. IV]
2a. di in angeborn ist. [BJ 169, II F 8, BJ 168, BJ 170a, BN 12607]
2b. diu ime angeboren ist, *nach wichbildes rechte.* [1261Wr., MSR]
3. –

346

1. [29] de voluntate iudicis *et consensu* [Gn., BN 12607, Dział. IV]
2. mit des richteris willen [BJ 169, II F 8, BJ 168, BJ 170a, BN 12607]
3. –

347

1. [29] nec ultra causam peragendam [Gn., BN 12607, Dział. IV]
2a. vnd nicht me di clage czu vorderene [MSR, BJ 168, BJ 170a]
2b. missing: BJ 169, II F 8, BN 12607
3. –

348

1. [30] alter veniat ad quatuor bancos et conqueratur cum clamore scabinis [Gn., BN 12607, Dział. IV]
2a. den sheppfen [BJ 169, BJ 170a]
2b. *den andir ge in di vire bencke vnd chlage mit gerufte* den sheppfen [MSR, II F 8, BJ 168, BN 12607]
3. –

349

1. [30] si testes super hoc habuerit *a scabinis aut astantibus iudicio* [Gn., BN 12607, Dział. IV]
2a. ob he des gezuc hat [BJ 169, II F 8, BJ 168, BN 12607]
2b. ob he des geczuc hat, *an den scheppen oder an den dingeluten.* [MSR, BJ 170a]
3. –

350

1. [31] Duellum quorumvis dicitur duorum bellum, hic tamen accipitur pro illo, qui obtinet principium agendi. [Dział. IV]
2. –
3. see No. 71

351

1. [32] qui ipsum vulneravit in facto *retenti* [Gn., BN 12607, Dział. IV]
2a. der in gewundit hat in der *hanthaften vrisshen* tat [BJ 169, BN 12607]
2b. der in gewundet hat in der *frischen* tat [II F 8]
2c. der … gewundet hat in einer *hanthaften* tat [MSR, BJ 168, BJ 170a]
3. –

352

1a. [32] qui sic queruletur *cum prolocutore* [Gn.]
1b. ille sic queruletur [BN 12607, Dział. IV]
2a. der sal alsus clagen *mit vorsprechen* [BJ 169, II F 8, BN 12607]

2b. di clage alsus gen [MSR, BJ 168, BJ 170a]

3. –

353

1. [32] ipse venit intra municipalia *vel in strata regia* [Gn., BN 12607, Dział. IV]

2. he ist kumen binnen wichbilde *odir in des keiseris straze* [BJ 169, II F 8, BJ 168, BJ 170a, BN 12607]

3. –

354

1. [32] *illi solvet collum, si est homicidium*, vel ad manum, *si vulnus est monomochale* [Gn., BJ 12607, Dział. IV]

2a. iz get ienem an di hant [BJ 169, II F 8, BN 12607]

2b. is get im an di hant, *ab di wunde kampwirdic ist, vmme den totslaq an den hals.* [MSR, BJ 168, BJ 170a]

3. –

355

1a. [34] Et si vulneratus fuerit *et vulnus* monomochale non fuerit [Gn., Dział. IV]

1b. Et si vulneratus fuerit [BN 12607]

2a. Wirt ein man gewunde nicht campfwertic ist [BJ 169]

2b. Wirt ein man gewundet vnde *die wunde* nicht kampfwertic ist [MSR, II F 8, BJ 168, BJ 170a, BN 12607]

3. –

356

1a. [35] et si ille protestare poterit, quod pugil sit *mercennarius*, extunc iure sibi a duello cedere potest. [Gn., BN 12607]

1b. *mercennarius* missing Dział. IV

2. und mac iener das beczugen, daz der cempfe *ein merce man*, si he weigert im campfes mit rechte. [BJ 169, II F 8, BJ 168, BJ 170a, BN 12607]

3. –

357

1. [36] et si fideiussores posuerit pro *causa* eadem [Gn., BN 12607, Dział. IV]
2. und wirt he virburgit umme di *shult* [BJ 169, II F 8, BJ 168, BJ 170a, BN 12607]
3. –

358

1. [37] mortuus ad iudicium portetur [Gn., BN 12607, Dział. IV]
2a. tot *vor gerichte* bracht zcu dinge [BJ 169, II F 8, BN 12607]
2b. tot vorbracht czu dem gedinge [MSR, BJ 168, BJ 170a]
3. –

359

1a. [37] agnatus [Gn.]
1b. cognatus [BN 12607, Dział. IV]
2. –
3. see No. 79

360

1a. [37] quod ipse suum affinem occiderit [Gn., Dział. IV]
1b. quod ipse suum *proximum* affinem occiderit [BN 12607]
2a. daz he sinen geteilinc gemordit habe [BJ 169, II F 8, BN 12607]
2b. das he sinen *neestin* getelinc geslagen habe [MSR, BJ 168, BJ 170a]
3. –

361

1. [37] Extunc ille petat satisdacionem de iure [Gn., BN 12607, Dział. IV]
2a. So bite iener einer gewere czu rechte [MSR, BJ 168, BJ 170a]
2b. missing: BJ 169, II F 8, BN 12607
3. –

362

1a. [37] cum testimonio *sive duello* [BN 12607]
1b. sive duello missing Gn., Dział. IV
2. mit gezuge [BJ 169, II F 8, BJ 168, BJ 170a, BN 12607]
3. see No. 80

363

1a. [37] *et ostendat suam innocenciam cum suo testimonio evadendo homicidium. Si hoc, ut iuris est, protestaverit*, propius est evadere [Gn., Dział. IV]
1b. hoc tum propius est evadere *metseptimo* [BN 12607]
2a. entgen des totslages *selbe sibende* [BJ 169, II F 8, BJ 168, BN 12607]
2b. *vnd brenge sine vnschult mit sime geczuge czu engende des totslages. Geczuget her is als recht ist*, her ist iz neher im czu engene [MSR, BJ 170a]
3. see No. 81

364

1a. [37] *quia ambo coram iudicio querimoniam inceperunt*. Sed suum testimonium sit debet procedere [Gn., Dział. IV]
1b. *Et si evadet*, tunc suum testimonium ita debet sic procedere [BN 12607]
2a. Entget he abir mit gezuge, so sal sin gezuc alsus gen [BJ 169, II F 8, BN 168, BN 12607]
2b. *wande si bede der chlage vor gerichte begunt haben*. Sin geczuc sal aber also gen [MSR, BJ 170a]
3. see No. 82

365

1a. [37] tunc facilius potest evadere homicidium *metseptimus*, quam ille cum testimonio ipsum vincere possit. [Gn.]
1b. [ex] hiis sibi eligat unam quindenam quamcumque voluerit. [BN 12607]
1b. tunc facilius potest evadere *mettercius* homicidium, quam ille cum testimo vincere possit. [Dział. IV]

2a. darundir mac her kisin vircen nacht swelche her wil. [BJ 168]
2b. missing: BJ 169, II F 8, BJ 170a, BN 12607
3. see No. 83

366

1. [38] quod stabilis non fuerit, ita quod a loco discedere tempore se offerente noluerit, et videre apparens sit cecus, et eciam a iusta arestacione. [Gn., BN 12607, Dzial. IV]
2. daz iz nicht stetit en si noch starblint vnd unrechtes anevanges. [BJ 169, II F 8, BJ 168, BJ 170a, BN 12607]
3. –

367

1a. [39] furtum *minus quam tres* solidos valeat [Gn.]
1b. furto et *non plus quam tres* solidos valeat [BN 12607]
1c. furtum *tres* solidos valeat [Dział. IV]
2. di dube *nimme den drier* shillinge wert ist [BJ 169, II F 8, BJ 168, BJ 170a, BN 12607]
3. see No. 84

368

1a. [40] ab alio suo *angnato* [Gn.]
1b. ab alio suo *amico* [BN 12607, Dział. IV]
2a. von einen anderen sinem *vrunde* [BJ 169, II F 8, BN 12607]
2b. the linguistic divergences in BJ 168 i BJ 170a
3. see No. 88

369

1. [40] bona possederit *pacifice et quiete,* anno et die [Gn., BN 12607, Dział. IV]
2. habe di gewere an dem gute iar und tac [BJ 169, II F 8, BJ 168, BJ 170a, BN 12607]
3. –

370

1. [40] et est iuste *ac rite* [Gn., BN 12607, Dział. IV]
2. und si sin recht [BJ 169, II F 8, BJ 168, BJ 170a, BN 12607]
3. –

371

1a. [40] cum *defendente seu* defensore [Gn.]
1b. cum defensore [BN 12607, Dział. IV]
2. mit dem geweren [BJ 169, II F 8, BJ 168, BJ 170a, BN 12607]
3. –

372

1a. [40] conservat sua *bona* [Gn.]
1b. conservabit sua *bona* [BN 12607, Dział. IV]
2. und beheldit ... sin *cins gut* dar an [BJ 169, II F 8, BJ 168, BJ 170a, BN 12607]
3. –

373

1. [40] actor [Gn., BN 12607, Dział. IV]
2. iener [BJ 169, II F 8, BJ 168, BJ 170a, BN 12607]
3. –

374

1a. [40] homo conservat suam innatam hereditatem, *sive naturalem porcionem ... cum impossibile sit aliquem de naturali porcione defraudari.* [Gn.]
1b. homo conservat suam innatam hereditatem [BN 12607]
1c. homo conservat suam innatam hereditatem, *seu porcionem naturalem* [Dział. IV]
2. beheldit sin erbe eigen [BJ 169, II F 8, BJ 168, BJ 170a, BN 12607]
3. see No. 90, 91

375

1a. [41] Si homo habuerit hereditaria censualia *et bona* a quodam monasterio, *aut alio domino*, et si dominus *aut abbas* sibi non fatetur [Gn.]

1b. Si homo habuerit hereditaria censualia *et bona* a quodam monasterio, et si dominus *aut abbas* sibi non fatetur [BN 12607, Dział. IV]

2. Hat ein man erbe cins gut von einem Gotis hus und bekennit is im der herre nicht [BJ 169, II F 8, BJ 168, BJ 170a, BN 12607]

3. –

376

1a. [41] vir potest *metseptimus* protestare [Gn., BN 12607]

1b. vir *mettertius* protestari [Dział. IV]

2. der man muz iz behalden selbe sibende [BJ 169, II F 8, BJ 168, BJ 170a, BN 12607]

3. see No. 92

377

1a. [42] cum possessis hominibus, *qui in* suo iure argui non possunt, *et qui iudicio astare solent, et domicilia habentibus in iudicio supradicto*. [Gn.]

1b. cum posessis hominibus, *qui iudicio astare solent et domicilia habentes et in iudicio predicto*. [BN 12607, Dział. IV]

2. mit besezzenen liuten, *di da dinc pflichtit sin in dem gericht*. [BJ 169, II F 8, BJ 168, BJ 170a, BN 12607]

3. see No. 93

378

1a. [42] possessi homines *domicilia habentes*, si hoc *in iudicio non viderunt*, nec in iudicio *fuerit confirmatum*. [Gn., Dział. IV]

1b. possessi homines *domicilia habentes*, si hoc *in iudicio non fuerit confirmatum*. [BN 12607]

2a. besezzen liute sin, ob iz vor gerichte nicht geshen ist. [BJ 169, II F 8, BJ 168, BN 12607]

2b. besessen sin, *di do ding pflichtic sin in dem gerichte*, ab iz vor gerichte nicht geschen ist. [BJ 170a]

3. –

379

1. [42] In nullis causis precio conventi seu empti valeant protestare, quia iure possunt eici. [BN 12607]

2. –

3. see No. 95

380

1a. [43] cum talibus hominibus, qui in suo iure argui non possunt. [Gn., Dział. IV]

1b. cum talibus hominibus, qui in suo iure argui non possunt *mettercius*. [BN 12607]

2. mit so getanen liuten, di undirworfen sin an irme rechte. [BJ 169, II F 8, BJ 168, BJ 170a, BN 12607]

3. see No. 96

381

1. [44] Si vir ducit viduam que *unum filium aut plures* pueros habuerit [Gn., BN 12607, Dział. IV]

2. Nimit ein man eine witwen, di kindir hat [BJ 169, II F 8, BJ 168, BJ 170a, BN 12607]

3. –

382

1. [44] *et si fortuna arridente per suos labores* bona habuerint et proprietatem *sive hereditatem* emerint [Gn., BN 12607, Dział. IV]

2. *vnd irerbeiten* [s] *si gut* und legen iz an eigen [BJ 169, II F 8, BJ 168, BJ 170a, BN 12607]

3. –

383

1a. [44] proxima congnata uxoris recipit suppellectilia *de iure*. [Gn., BN 12607]
1b. proxima congnata uxoris recipit suppellectilia. [Dział. IV]
2a. Der vrowen neste spinne nimit abir di rade. [BJ 169, II F 8, BJ 168, BN 12607]
2b. missing BN 170a
3. –

384

1. [45] in iudicio bannito circa vitam suam, *et bone racionis* [Gn., BN 12607, Dział. IV]
2. in gehegetem dinge bi sinem libe [BJ 169, II F 8, BJ 168, BJ 170a, BN 12607]
3. –

385

1a. [46] propriis laboribus *aut prospera fortuna* accreverunt [Gn.]
1b. propriis laboribus *aut prospera fortuna* accreverunt *cum sua uxore* [BN 12607, Dział. IV]
2. irerbeitit [s] hat *mit sinem wibe* [BJ 169, II F 8, BJ 168, BJ 170a, BN 12607]
3. see No. 102

386

1a. [46] Sin autem hereditaria *censualia* bona fuerint [Gn., BN 12607]
1b. Si hereditaria bona fuerint [Dział. IV]
2. Ist iz abir erbe *cins* gut [BJ 169, II F 8, BJ 168, BJ 170a, BN 12607]
3. see No. 103

387

1a. [48] Iudicium recipit sua arma bellica. [Dział. IV, BN 12607]
1b. missing Gn.
2. Daz gerichte nimit abir sin herwete. [BJ 169, II F 8, BJ 168, BJ 170a, BN 12607]
3. see No. 106

388

1. [48] Si moritur vir absque herede et nepotem ex filia habuerit, *que exheredata fuerit circa suam vitam* [Gn., BN 12607, Dział. IV]
2a. Stirbit ein man ane erben und hat he einer tochtir sun [BJ 169, BJ 170a, BN 12607]
2b. Stirbet ein man ane erben und hat er eine tochtir *ufgeradet bey seinem leibe, die ienen* son hat [II F 8, BJ 168]
3. –

389

1. [48] Si eciam filius ducerit [*s*] uxorem tempore vite sui patris et per moriatur patri indivisus sua hereditate, extunc ipsius filii hereditatem avi recipiunt et non filii filiarum. Si autem pater filium a se divisit, protunc filii filiorum et filiarum in bonis sui avi equalem recipiunt porcionem. Sed in hereditaribus sue avie filii filiorum et aliarum iuridice sunt equales. [BN 12607]
2. Nympt [u]och der sey veip bey des vatris lebin und stirbit er, wenne seyn vatir unvorbeteilet von seyne erbe, so nemen des selbin sonis kinder irs aldirs watirs erbe glich eren wetirn, unde nicht der tochter kinder hat. Adir der elder vatir seyn son sich geteilet, so synt des sonis kinder unde der tochtir kinder gleiche des elder vatir erbe czu nemen. Mer czu der aldir mutir erbe synt eris sonis kinder gleich an erbe czu nemen. [II Q 4]
3. see No. 107

390

1. [49] quod faciat met tertius *cum talibus hominibus, qui in suo iure argui non possunt.* [Gn., BN 12607, Dział. IV]
2. daz muz he tun selbe dritte [BJ 169, II F 8, BJ 168, BJ 170a, BN 12607]
3. see No. 109

391

1a. [50] proximus agnatus [Gn., Dział. IV]
1b. proximus cognatus [BN 12607]
2. neste ebinburtic swert [BJ 169, II F 8, BJ 168, BJ 170a, BN 12607]
3. see No. 110

392

1. [50] racionem anno ad annum de bonis pupillorum coram vero ipsorum tutore facere tenetur *vel coram consulibus aut scabinis.* [BN 12607]
2. –
3. see No. 112

393

1. [51] Et si factum manifestum cum viro *ad iudicium* deductum fuerit [Gn., BN 12607, Dział. IV]
2. ob di hanthafte tat mit dem manne vorbracht wirt. [BJ 169, II F 8, BJ 168, BJ 170a, BN 12607]
3. –

394

1a. [51] et me stupravit corpore et rebus [Gn.]
1b. et me stupravit *et spoliavit me* corpore et rebus [BN 12607, Dział. IV]
2. und hat mich genot zogit *und hat mich geroubit* an lyb und an gute [BJ 169, II F 8, BJ 168, BJ 170a, BN 12607]
3. –

395

1a. [51] ille possit evadere, cum ad iudicium sit deductus. [Gn.]
1b. ipse possit evadere cum *in facto manifesto* ad iudicium sit deductus. [BN 12607, Dział. IV]
2. he vor gerichte *in der hanthaften tat* mir gerufte bracht ist. [BJ 169, II F 8, BJ 168, BJ 170a, BN 12607]
3. –

396

1. [51] Tunc diffinitur iure, quod possit ipsum possibilius vincere cum his, qui suum clamorem audierunt, quam evadere possit. [Gn., BN 12607, Dział. IV]

2. –
3. –

397

1a. [51] probat homo protestando *metseptimus*. [Gn., BN 12607]
1b. probat homo *mettercius* protestando. [Dział. IV]
2. gezugit ein man *selbe sibende*. [BJ 169, II F 8, BJ 168, BJ 170a, BN 12607]
3. see No. 113

398

1a. [51] et requiro in sentencia diffinitiva, quod ipsum vincere debeam [Gn., BN 12607]
1b. missing Dział. IV
2. und vrage in einen urteile zcu virsuchen, wi ich in des vorwinden sulle [BJ 169, II F 8, BJ 168, BJ 170a, BN 12607]
3. see No. 114

399

1. [52] vobis, nostro domino, *regi aut* duci [Gn., BN 12607, Dział. IV]
2. unsern heren dem herczogen [BJ 169, II F 8, BJ 168, BJ 170a, BN 12607]
3. –

400

1a. [52] Et sic diffinitur *cum clamore* metseptimus *eum vincere debet*. [BN 12607]
1b. tunc diffinitur metseptimus. [Dział. IV]
1c. the complete phrase missing in Gn.
2a. So findit man ym *mit gerufte* salpsebinde. [BN 12607]
2b. the complete phrase missing in BJ 169, II F 8, BJ 168, BJ 170a
3. see No. 118

401

1. [53] Si vulneratus vir ad iudicium cum clamore deductus fuerit *in facto manifesto* [Gn., BN 12607, Dział. IV]
2a. Wirt ein gewundet man vor gerichte bracht mit gerufte [BJ 169]
2b. Wird ein gew[u]ndit man vor gerichte bracht mit gerufte *in einir handhaftin tat* [BJ 168, II F 8, BN 12607]
2c. missing Article: BJ 170a
3. –

402

1a. [53] aut suum affinem *proximum trucidaverunt* [Gn., BN 12607]
1b. aut suum affinem *occiderunt* [Dział. IV]
2a. odir sinen *nesten geteilinc gemordit* [BJ 169, II F 8, BJ 170a, BN 12607]
2b. missing Article: BJ 170a
3. see No. 119

403

1a. [53] Domine iudex, *si me huic vulnerato,* dedistis *pro advocato* [Gn., BN 12607]
1b. Domine iudex, *si me huic vulnerato* dedistis *prolocutorem* [Dział. IV]
2a. Herre her richter, habit ir mich nu zcu einen vorsprechen gegeben [BJ 169, II F 8, BJ 168, BN 12607]
2b. missing Article: BJ 170a
3. –

404

1a. [53] aut sustinere, cum suam causam propter iuris exigenciam teneo. [Gn., Dział. IV]
1b. *quas iure tenere debeam* aut sustinere cum suam causam propter iuris exigenciam teneo. [BN 12607]
2a. *di ich durch recht haben sulle* wand ich sin wort spreche durch rechtes willen. [BJ 169, BJ 168, II F 8]
2b. wan sin wort spreche durch rechtes willen. [BN 12607]
2c. missing Article: BJ 170a
3. –

405

1. [53] *tunc unus interrogetur ad dicendum*, quid ab eo audierint. [Gn., BN 12607, Dział. IV]
2a. *da si gesworen haben*, waz si gehort haben von im. [BJ 169, II F 8, BJ 168]
2b. *das si sigen*, waz ze gehort haben von im. [BN 12607]
2c. missing Article: BJ 170a
3. –

406

1a. [53] et si ita *inbecillis aut* debilis fuerit [Gn., BN 12607]
1b. et si ita debilis fuerit [Dział. IV]
2a. und also uncreftic ist [BJ 169, II F 8, BJ 168, BN 12607]
2b. missing Article: BJ 170a
3. see No. 120

407

1a. [53] si iam profeterit, cum sibi diffinitur quod sic, et eciam secundus et tertius interrogetur. Extunc sibi diffinitur, quod profecerit. Extunc querelam incipiat [Gn., BN 12607]
1b. quod sic interrogetur secundus et tertius, deinde querela incipiat [Dział. IV]
2a. ob he mit im volkumen si, so vindit man im zcu rechte, he si, also sal he vragen den anderen und umme den dritten, so vindit man im, he si volkumen, so sal he der clage beginnen [BJ 169, II F 8, BJ 168, BN 12607]
2b. missing Article: BJ 170a
3. see No. 122

408

1a. [54] Et requiro [Gn., BN 12607]
1b. Et requiro *in sentencia* [Dział. IV]
2a. und vrege *in einem urteile zcu versuchene* [BJ 169, II F 8, BJ 168, BJ 170a]
2b. und vrege [BN 12607]
3. –

409

1a. [54] Idem iudicium fiat *pro spolio et super raptorem*. [Gn., BN 12607]
1b. Idem iudicium fiat *cum spoliatore*. [Dział. IV]
2. Dese selbe clage get *uf den rouber*. [BJ 169, II F 8, BJ 168, BJ 170a, BN 12607]
3. –

410

1a. [56] de quoqumque horum trium de uno *obliviscitur aut* tacuerit [Gn., BN 12607]
1b. missing Article: Dział. IV
2a. swelchir der drier einez he vorswigit [BJ 169, II F 8, BN 12607]
2b. missing Article: BJ 168, BJ 170a
3. –

411

1a. [56] tunc loquatur ulterius: Tunc ipsum solum, hoc est in persona propria, *ipsum solus vidi, hoc est in persona propria* [Gn.]
1b. tunc loquatur ulterius: Tunc ipsum solum hoc in persona propria [BN 12607]
1c. missing Article: Dział. IV
2a. So spreche er vorbaz, do sach ich selbe in selben [BJ 169, II F 8, BN 12607]
2b. missing Article: BJ 168, BJ 170a
3. –

412

1a. [56] Tamen vir potest suam querimoniam meliorare, ante satisdacionem, *si voluerit*. [Gn., BN 12607]
1b. missing Article: Dział. IV
2a. doch muz der man seine clage wol bezzeren vor der were [BJ 169, II F 8, BN 12607]
2b. missing Article: BJ 168, BJ 170a
3. –

413

1a. [56] Facta satisdacione ille exhibeat suam innocenciam, hoc est iuramentum, *quod ipsum iurare oportet, et iuramentum monomachale* [Gn.]

1b. Facta satisdacione ille suam exhibeat innocenciam, hoc est iuramentum monomochale [BN 12607]

1c. missing Article: Dział. IV

2a. swenne die gewere gethan ist, so butut ienir man seine unschult, daz ist ein eit, *den muz he sweren, und einen campf eit* [BJ 169, II F 8, BN 12607]

2b. missing Article: BJ 168, BJ 170a

3. –

414

1a. [56] si uterque suus affinis [Gn.]

1b. si uterque suus affinis *fuerit, hoc probare debet metseptimus tacto sacramento* [BN 12607]

1c. missing Article: Dział. IV

2a. ob si beide sine moge sin [BJ 169, II F 8, BN 12607]

2b. missing Article: BJ 168, BJ 170a

3. see No. 130

415

1a. [56] Eciam *iudex* debet iudicare pacem circa collum [Gn., BN 12607]

1b. missing Article: Dział. IV

2a. Ouch sal man den warne fride gebieten bi dem halse [BJ 169, II F 8, BN 12607]

2b. missing Article: BJ 168, BJ 170a

3. –

416

1a. [56] quod *flangam interponat, aut si vulneratus fuerit aut si* flangam desiderat [Gn.]

1b. quod flangam desiderat [BN 12607]

1c. missing Article: Dział. IV

2a. daz *he den bowin undirstoze, odir ob hr gewunt wirt,* odir des bovines gert [BJ 169, II F 8, BN 12607]

2b. missing Article: BJ 168, BJ 170a

3. see No. 135

417

1a. [56] Ambo ornati debent ire ante iudicem, et *ambo* iurare debent: unus, *scilicet actor*, quod causa sit vera, pro qua super ipsum querelam fecerit, *et respondens*, quot sit innocens [Gn., BN 12607]

1b. missing Article: Dział. IV

2a. Si sullen beide gegerbit gan vor den richter un[de] sullen sweren, *der eine*: daz sine shult war, si do he in umme beclagit habe, *unde der ander*, daz he unshuldic si [BJ 169, II F 8, BN 12607]

2b. missing Article: BJ 168, BJ 170a

3. –

418

1a. [56] Si alter diu tardaverit, *iudex* debet ipsum per preconem mittere vocare [Gn., BN 12607]

1b. missing Article: Dział. IV

2a. ob der andir zcu lange sumit [*s*], der sal in lazen vor heishen den vrone boten [BJ 169]

2b. ab der andir zu lange sewmit, der *richter* sal en lossin vor heischen den frone botin [II F 8, BN 12607]

2c. missing Article: BJ 168, BJ 170a

3. –

419

1a. [56] hic extinguet omne testimonium, quia tunc ipsum absque duello vincere non potest [Gn.]

1b. hic extinguet omne testimonium, quia tunc ipsum absque duello vincere non potest, *nisi fuerit prescriptus* [BN 12607]

1c. missing Article: Dział. IV

2a. der vorlegit allen geczuc, wan so enmac he in ane campf nicht vorwinden [BJ 169, II F 8, BN 12607]
2b. missing Article: BJ 168, BJ 170a
3. see No. 140

420

1a. [56] alter agnatus [Gn., BN 12607]
1b. missing Article: Dział. IV
2a. einer [BJ 169, II F 8, BN 12607]
2b. missing Article: BJ 168, BJ 170a
3. see No. 141

421

1a. [58] Qui vitam aut manum *pecunia* redimerit [Gn., BN 12607]
1b. Qui vitam aut manum redimerit [Dział. IV]
2a. Swer lip odir hant ledigit [BJ 169, II F 8, BJ 170a, BN 12607]
2b. missing Article: BJ 168
3. –

422

1. [58] Si tempore unius viri plura bona fuerint adinventa, quam quod suo iuramento exactionaliter comprobasset, et si fatetur eadem bona esse sua, tunc periurus existitit et perdit ius suum civile et caret iure, propter quod dicitur infamis. Et quicumque periurus debeat protestari, hoc coram iudicio fieri oportet, quod causa sibi nominator, propter quam sit periuris, et si fateatur vel si bona sub ipso valeant permostrari, pro quibus patenter iuravit, extunc periurius est convictus omni iure carens, et suum perdit ius civile. [BN 12607]
2. Wirt auch beii eynis mannis labin undir iim meer gutis gefunden, wenne her beii seyme eyde vorschossit hat, und bekennet des gutis, das ys seyn seii, so ist der man meiineiidig und hat sein burmal vorlor[e]n, und sal recht loz seyn, das ist anruchtig. Und wiil man eyn meiineiidig bereden, das muß man vor gerichte thun, als das man ym dy sache benenne, dor umme her meiineiidigt seii wurden bekennet, her iis adir mak man das gut undir iim bewem beweiisen, do vor her

har wyssintlich gesworn, so ist her meiineiidig und recht loz wurden, und hat seyn burmal vorloren. [BN 12607]

3. see No. 142

423

1. [59] Qui etiam fideiusserit unum virum unum pro scelere ad statuendum *ipsum coram iudicio* [Gn., BN 12607, Dział. IV]
2. Swer ouch borgit einen man umbe ungerichte vor zcu brengen [BJ 169, II F 8, BJ 168, BJ 170a, BN 12607]
3. –

424

1a. [61] *eorum senior agnatus* recipit arma bellica [Gn., Dział. IV, BN 12607]
1b. *eorum senior cognatus* recipit arma bellica [II Q 4]
2a. *ir eldiste ebenbortic swert* mog nimit daz herwete [BJ 169, II F 8, BN 12607]
2b. missing Article: BJ 168 and BJ 170a
3. see No. 145

425

1a. [61] Ita quod senior dividit et iunior eligit. [BN 12607, Dział. IV]
1b. missing: Gn.
2. missing: BJ 169, II F 8, BJ 168, BJ 170a, BN 12607
3. see No. 146

426

1. [61] psalteria et omnes libri, *in quibus mulieres legere consueverunt*, qui ad Dei cultum pertinent [Gn., BN 12607, Dział. IV]
2a. salter und alle buchir, di zcu gotis dinste gehoren [BJ 169, II F 8, BN 12607]
2b. missing Article: BJ 168, BJ 170a
3. –

427

1. [61] Sin autem vir, qui dum annos pubertatis inplevit, *religionem intraverit* [Gn., BN 12607, Dział. IV]
2a. Begibit sich abir ein man, die zcu sinen iaren kumen ist [BJ 169, II F 8, BN 12607]
2b. missing Article: BJ 168, BJ 170a
3. –

428

1a. [61] hic se a iure terrestri ac feodali alienavit [Gn., Dział. IV, BN 12607]
1b. alienavit [II Q 4]
2a. der hat sich von lantrechte und von lenrechte getteilit [BJ 169, II F 8, BN 12607]
2b. missing Article: BJ 168, BJ 170a
3. see No. 148

429

1a. [62] ambo actor et *ille, hoc est super quem conqueritur, respondens est sive reus* [Gn.]
1b. ambo actor et *reus seu respondens* [BN 12607]
1c. actor et reus [Dział. IV]
2a. Beide, der clegere und der, uf den man clagit [BJ 169, II F 8, BN 12607]
2b. missing Article: BJ 168, BJ 170a
3. –

430

1a. [63] cum sentenciis. [Gn., BN 12607]
1b. cum sentenciis *scabinorum.* [Dział. IV]
2a. mit urteile [BJ 169, II F 8, BN 12607]
2b. mit dem *scheppin* orteile [II Q 4]
2c. missing Article: BJ 168, BJ 170a
3. see No. 150

431

1. [64] pecunia [Gn., BN 12607, Dział. IV]
2. gut [BJ 169, II F 8, BJ 168, BJ 170a, BN 12607]
3. –

432

1a. [64] Si *homo et ubi* vir pro *pecunia aut* debito ⟨fi[deiussor]⟩ fuerit et moritur vir, sui pueri *aut sui heredes* non tenentur pro eo solvere. [Gn.]

1b. Si vir pro debito fideiussor fuerit et idem vir moritur, sui pueri non tenentur pro eo solvere. [BN 12607]

1c. Ibi vir fuerit fideiussor et moritur, pueri sui pro eo [solvere] non tenentur. [Dział. IV]

2. Swo ein man burge wirt und stirbit he sine kint, endurfen vor si nicht gelden. [BJ 169, II F 8, BJ 168, BJ 170a, BN 12607]

3. see No. 151

433

1. [64] probare *mettercius* [BN 12607]
2. volbrengen *salp dritte* [BN 12607]
3. see No. 152

434

1. [65] id est vincere eum cum testibus, quam ipse cum testibus evadere possit [BN 12607]
2. –
3. see No. 153

435

1. [65] emendam *XXX solidos*. [BN 12607]
2. –
3. see No. 155

436

1. [65] iudex aquirit suam penam ·*VIII*· *solidos*. [BN 12607]
2. der richter gewinnet sein gewette ·*VIII*· *schillinge*. [BN 12607]
3. see No. 155

437

1a. [66] Quod si hereditas mortaliola [*s*] absque heredibus inventa *seu reperta* fuerit, regie cedet maiestati. [Gn.]
1b. Si hereditas mortaliola sine herede inventa fuerit *aut remanserit anno et die*, regie cedet maiestati. [BN 12607]
1c. Si hereditas obmoriatur, ita quod nullus se trahat ad hanc *infra a*[*n*]*num et diem*, hoc [*s*] nu[n]quam cedit regie maiestati. [Dział. IV]
2. Ob sich ein erbe virstirbit, daz sich nyman dar zcu zcuhit mit rechte binnen *iare und tage*, daz nimit di kunincliche gewalt. [BJ 169, II F 8, BJ 168, BJ 170a, BN 12607]
3. see No. 156

438

1a. [68] *sine pena* potest super ponere [Gn.]
1b. *sine pena bene* potest super ponere [BN 12607]
1c. *debet iurare hic bene* super ponere potest [Dział. IV]
2. he muz wol uf legen [BJ 169, II F 8, BJ 168, BJ 170a, BN 12607]
3. –

439

1. [68] Si eciam iuramenta promissa venerint super diem ligatum, hec iudex protrahere potest super alium diem iudicialem, qui venerit extra dies ligatos. Et si eciam vir balbuciens vel alter seu testis ipsius fuerit impeditus, ita quod inperfecte suum dixerit iuramento, ille seipsum emendare valeat, quociens impeditur et manebit de huiusmodi sive dampno. [BN 12607]
2. Komen auch eiide gelob de off eynen gebunden tag, dii mak der richter wol vorsp[re]chenden [*?*] off eynen andern ding tag, der awsen den gebundin tagin kommit. Wirt auch eyn stavmme[l]der man adir eyn andir man adir seyn

geczewg gehyndirt, daß her den eiit nicht recht noch spricht, so mak her sich wol irhoben, wii dicke her an dame [*s*] eyde gehyndert wirt und sal is bleyben ane schaden. [BN 12607]

3. see No. 158

440

1a. [69] venditor [Gn., BN 12607]
1b. tutor [Dział. IV]
2. geweren [BJ 169, II F 8, BJ 168, BJ 170a, BN 12607]
3. –

441

1. [69] pecunia [Gn., BN 12607, Dział. IV]
2. silber [BJ 169, II F 8, BJ 168, BJ 170a, BN 12607]
3. –

442

1a. [69] adversarius suus [Gn., BN 12607]
1b. ille [Dział. IV]
2. umme [BJ 169, II F 8, BJ 168, BJ 170a, BN 12607]
3. –

443

1a. [69] non autem sequi ipsum debet ultra Mare Aquilonis. Et si sibi defectus fuerit *et neminem pro se habuerit respondentem, utpote venditorem habere poterit,* ut se coram iudicio iactitavit [Gn.]

1b. non autem ipsum sequi debet ultra Mare Aquilonis. Sed si sibi defectus fuerit, *et neminem pro se respondentem habuerit, utpote* iudicio *venditorem habere* non *poterit,* ut se coram iudicio iac[ti]tavit [BN 12607]

1c. non autem ipsum sequi debet ultra Mare Aquilonis. Et si defectum habuerit, *ita quod sibi tutorem habere poterit,* ut se coram iudicio iactitavit [Dział. IV]

2. wan ubir di gewaldigen se nicht, unde wirt un des bruch, und en mac he des keinen weren habin, als he sich vir mezzen hat [BJ 169, II F 8, BJ 168, BJ 170a, BN 12607]

3. –

444

1a. [70] etsi *per bonum pacis* medio tempore concordatum fuerit [Gn.]

1b. etsi medio tempore concordatum *per bonum pacis* fuerit [BN 12607, Dział. IV]

2a. und wirt iz in binnen des geebinit [BJ 169, II F 8, BJ 170a, BN 12607]

2b. missing Article: BN 168

3. –

445

1a. [73] absque heredum consensu *ac voluntate*. [Gn., BN 12607]

1b. absque heredum consensu [Dział. IV]

2. ane ir erben gelop. [BJ 169, II F 8, BJ 168, BJ 170a, BN 12607]

3. –

446

1. [73] Si autem omnes pueri, patre mortuo, moriuntur, extunc bona sua heredant super suam matrem. Et si post hoc mater decesserit ab hac luce, protunc eadem omnia bona heredant super suos proximiores heredes, sive sint masculi, sive femine, ex paterna vel materna consanguineitate. Etiam mater cum talibus innatis mobilibus bonis facere et dimittere potest sine suorum heredum consensu, sed cum heredibus stantibus et propriis nichil facere potest sine consensu et voluntate propinquorum heredum suorum. [BN 12607]

2. Sterbin abir dii kindir alle noch des vatirs tode, so erbit ir gut off dii muttir. Stirbit dornach dii muttir, zo erbet ze das gut alzo fort off eren nesten erbin, dii ir abiburtig synt, ys sey von fatir adir von mutir, man adir weiip. Auch mak dy mutir mit sulchem angestorbenem an varnder habe von und lassen ane erbin varnde, adir an gestorbenem, stande erbe und eiigen mak se ane erer nesten erben lawbe und wybben nicht vorgabin. [BN 12607]

3. see No. 163

447

1. [74] Cum eciam puer fuerit XII annorum, extunc mundiburdius est {est} factus, et potest in eo iudicio perpetrare et eciam sua bona a se sue tutore alienare. Sed innatum hereditatem et proprium debet dare cum consensu heredum, eciam iste puer ad responsionem de iure valeat coartari. [BN 12607]
2. Auch wen eyn kint czwelf yar alt ist, so ist is mundig unde man mag obir is richtin auch so mak is seyn gut czu vormunden und an vormunden vorgaben. Sundir an der starben standen eiigen und erbe sal is mit erbin lawbe gabin, doch mak man denne das kiint czu entwor twingen mit rechte. [BN 12607]
3. see No. 165

448

1. [75] et hoc scire debet quilibet legens, ubi scribitur agnatus, designat ex parte patris et ex parte gladii. Et ubi scribitur cognatus, ex parte matris desingnatur. [Gn.]
2. –
3. see No. 166

449

1. [76] Si servus bona domini sui perluserit taxilis, aut obligat aut vendit, dominus bene potest arestare denuo iure, ut se ad ea bona trahat, ut iuris sit. Sin autem propria bona sua deluserit, aut quocunque modo a se alienaverit sua voluntate, dominus super ea nichil alloqui potest, quia servus solvere tenetur, et sic domino pro bonis servi non est licitum respondere. … Sin autem servo suus equs, vel alia bona sua furtive, aut spoliando recepta fuerint absque culpa servi in domini servicio, hoc oportet dominum solvere servo, et pro eo oportet dominum respondere, si super eo queruletur. [Gn.]
2. –
3. see No. 169, 170

450

1a. [76] Si quis eciam conqueritur super aliquem pro cibariis preparatis, hic propius est obtinere hoc iuramento, quam ille ipsum evadere possit suo iuramento. [Dział. IV, BN 12607]

1b. missing: Gn.

2. –

3. see No. 172

451

1a. [in BJ 169 Art. 76] Si servus deservitum parcium super suum dominum obtinuerit coram iudicio, pro eo dominus nullam iudici demeretur penam, et dominus servo solvere hoc tenetur die eodem. [BN 12607, Dział. IV]

1b. missing Article: Gn.

2. Beheldit ein knecht sin vordimit lon uf sinen herren vor gerichte, da en ist der herre dem richter kein gewette umme shuldic, unde der herre sal im gelden binnen dem tage. [BJ 169, II F 8, BJ 168, BJ 170a, BN 12607]

3. see No. 174

452

1a. [79] pro suo *debito* cum testibus [Gn., BN 12607]

1b. pro suo *debito* cum testibus *coram iudicio* [Dział. IV]

2a. umme *gelt vor gerichte* mit gezuge [BJ 169, II F 8, BJ 168, BN 12607]

2b. missing Article: BJ 170a

3. –

453

1a. [79] cum *probis viris metseptimus* tacto sacramento. [Gn.]

1b. cum *viris fidedignis mettercius* tacto sacramento. [BN 12607]

1c. cum *viris fidedignis metseptimus* tacto sacramento. [Dział. IV]

2a. daz muz he volbrengen *selbedritte* uffen heiligen mit *erhaften liuten*. [BJ 169, II F 8, BJ 168, BN 12607]

2b. missing Article: BJ 170a

3. see No. 175

454

1a. [80] Satisdacione facta suam querimoniam meliorare non potest. [Gn., BN 12607]
1b. nec querelam meliorare. [Dział. IV]
2a. und man ouch dar ubir di da ge nicht mer gebessin en mac. [BJ 168]
2b. missing: BJ 169, II F 8, BJ 170a, BN 12607
3. –

455

1a. [82] In iudicio burgravii Meydeburgensis [Gn., BN 12607]
1b. In iudicio burgravii [Dział. IV]
2a. In des borchgreuen dinge zů Meideburch [1295Wr., BJ 168, II F 8, BJ 170a]
2b. In des burgreven dinge [BJ 169, BN 12607]
3. –

456

1a. [82] sex ebdomadas [Gn., BN 12607]
1b. per tres quindecinas [Dział. IV]
2. dri virzcen nacht [BJ 169, II F 8, BJ 168, BJ 170a, BN 12607]
3. –

457

1. [82] *metIIIus* [Dział. IV]
2. –
3. see No. 177

458

1a. [82] pro debito *peccuniali* [Dział. IV]
1b. *peccuniali* missing: Gn., BN 12607
2. mac ein man wol umme gelt clagen [BJ 169, II F 8, BJ 168, BJ 170a, BN 12607]
3. see No. 178

459

1a. [83] quod vir absque testibus conqueri voluerit [Gn.]
1b. quod vir conqueri *pro debito* absque testibus voluerit [BN 12607]
1c. conqueri *pro debito* absque testibus voluerit [Dział. IV]
2. daz ein man *umme gelt* clagen wil ane gezcuc [BJ 169, II F 8, BJ 168, BJ 170a, BN 12607]
3. see No. 179

460

1. [83] Iudex eciam iudicium tenetur compartare, et non actor neque reus. [BN 12607]
2a. Der richter ist phlictig noch scheppin czu senden und nicht der clage noch entworten. [BN 12607]
2b. Ouch sal der richter czusamnen kegen beneman richter sal, nicht der clager ader der beclageter man. [II Q 4]
3. see No. 180

461

1a. [83] ut fuerit diffinitum [Gn., BN 12607]
1b. ut fuerit diffinitum *cum denariis* [Dział. IV]
2a. als denne genge und gebe ist [BJ 169, II F 8, BJ 170a]
2b. *mit sulchin pfeiningin* als denne genge und {genge und} gebe sin [BJ 168]
2c. als *yn* denne *laude gelt* genge und gebe ist [BN 12607]
2d. missing in II Q 4
3. see No. 181

462

1a. [84] tribus diebus et *tribus* noctibus. [Gn., Dział. IV]
1b. tribus diebus ac noctibus. [BN 12607]
2. dri tage unde nacht [BJ 169, II F 8, BJ 168, BJ 170a, BN 12607]
3. –

463

1. [84] missing in Latin texts
2a. immer ubir virzcen nacht zcu dem virden dinge [BJ 169, BJ 168, BJ 170a]
2b. missing in II F 8, BN 12607
3. –

464

1a. [84] cum scitu. [Gn., BN 12607]
1b. cum scitu *hominum proborum*. [Dział. IV]
2a. mit wizzenshaft. [BJ 169, II F 8, BJ 170a, BN 12607]
2b. mit wissenschaft *vromir lute*. [BJ 168]
3. –

465

1a. [85] quod sibi subtractum *aut raptum* fuerit. [Gn., Dział. IV]
1b. quod sibi subtractum fuerit. [BN 12607]
2. daz iz im abe gestolen odir geroubit. [BJ 169, II F 8, BJ 168, BJ 170a, BN 12607]
3. –

466

1. [85] et ad hoc se trahere debet. [Gn., BN 12607, Dział. IV]
2. da sal her sich *mit rechte* alsus zcu zcihen. [BJ 169, II F 8, BJ 168, BJ 170a, BN 12607]
3. –

467

1a. [85] et iurabit equo *tacto sacramento* super caput [Gn.]
1b. et iurabit equo super capud *tacto sacramento* [BN 12607]
1c. et iurabit equo super capud [Dział. IV]
2. und sal *uf den heiligen* dem pferde ubir dem houbite sweren [BJ 169, II F 8, BJ 168, BJ 170a, BN 12607]
3. –

468

1a. [85] Et tunc ille ad suum se trahat venditorem *et ipsum iurare oportet si sanctos, quod trahat se cum equo ad verum venditorem* [Gn., Dział. IV]

1b. Ex tunc ille se ad suum venditorem trahit, ibi eum sequi oportet, nisi trans Mare Acquilonis. *Arestatur* [s] *oportet iurare, quod se trahit ad verum suum venditorem.* [BN 12607]

2. so zcut sich iener an sinen geweren *unde muz sweren uffen heiligen, daz he daz pfert zcihe zcu rechtir zcucht* [BJ 169, II F 8, BJ 168, BJ 170a, BN 12607]

3. –

469

1a. [85] argentum [Gn., BN 12607]

1b. pecunia [Dział. IV]

2. silbir [BJ 169, II F 8, BJ 168, BJ 170a, BN 12607]

3. see No. 185

470

1. [86] post mortuam manum hoc statim facere potest. [BN 12607]

2. –

3. –

471

1a. [86] *vel in eo non sit obligatus* aut quod persolverit [Gn., BN 12607]

1b. aut ille persolverit [Dział. IV]

2. *he si is unshuldit* odir he habe iz im vergoldin [BJ 169, II F 8, BJ 168, BJ 170a, BN 12607]

3. –

472

1a. [87] Si autem noxa una tam super patrem quam filium fuerit querulata simul, extunc patrem semper primo oportet eximere de tali noxa. [Dział. IV]

1b. in Gn. in Art. 24
1c. missing: BN 12607
2a. Wirt abir beide vatir und son beclagit um ein ungerichte, so mus sich der vatir allir irst unschuldigin des ungerichtis. [BJ 168]
2b. missing: BJ 169, II F 8, BJ 170a, BN 12607
3. see No. 188

473

1a. [88] aut aliquid inposterum contrarium pati. [Gn., BN 12607]
1b. aut aliquid *pro eo* pati. [Dział. IV]
2. den si di keine not vorbaz me dar umme liden sulle. [BJ 169, II F 8, BJ 168, BJ 170a, BN 12607]
3. –

474

1a. [89] Et quitquit superfluum fuerit *aut supermanserit* [Gn.]
1b. extunc quicquid superfluum fuerit [Dział. IV, BN 12607]
2. Und waz da boven denne blibit [BJ 169, II F 8, BJ 168, BJ 170a, BN 12607]
3. –

475

1a. [90] Si vir *scabinum in scampno* indecenter in iudicio bannito increpaverit [Gn., BN 12607]
1b. Si vir indecenter in iudicio bannito increpaverit [Dział. IV]
2a. Ob *ein scheppfe in gehegetem dinge* uf der banc missehandilt wurde [BJ 169, BN 12607]
2b. Ap ein *scheppfe in gehegeteme dinge* uf der banc mit vnbillichen worten van einem manne missehandelet worde [1295Wr., II F 8, BJ 168, BJ 170a]
3. –

476

1. [90] Scabini si in una sententia non fuerint unanimes vel eam ignotantes, extunc eandem ad secundam [*s*] vel ad terciam [*s*] proximum iudicium valeant dilatare,

extunc eam inferre debent vel mittere eam ferre illuc, quo conpetit, si nequeant invenire, et non diucius prolongare. [BN 12607]

2. Wisse dye scheppen eynis ortils nicht adir synt das nicht eyn, so mogin daz ortil vorschibin in daz andir adir in daz dritte ding, denne sulle sy daz ortil sprechin adir se dy von sich gehort legen, ap sy daz nicht wunde kunen, und lengir sullen sy nicht beytin. [II Q 4]

3. see No. 193

477

1a. [91] et ipse accomodaverit circa suam hereditatem [Gn., BN 12607]

1b. et ipse se *ad ius* accomodaverit circa suam hereditatem [Dział. IV]

2. und der man sich borgit bi sinem erbe *zcu rechte* [BJ 169, II F 8, BJ 168, BJ 170a, BN 12607]

3. –

478

1a. [91] caucionem facere fideiussoriam [Gn.]

1b. caucionem *iure* fideiussorie facere [BN 12607]

1c. cogi potest alicuius [?] fideiussores ponere [Dział. IV]

2. *mit rechte* hoher getwingen burgen zcu setzcen [BJ 169, II F 8, BJ 168, BJ 170a, BN 12607]

3. –

479

1a. [94] Et quando vir moritur, tunc uxori oves presentari debent ad sup[e]llectilia, ubicunque ierint. Anete, colcidre, vela, tecture curruum, olle picte eciam ad supellectilia pertinent. [Gn.]

1b. Et quando vir moritur, tunc uxori debent dari et suppellectilia, oves et *de iure* inserere, ubi ierint. [BN 12607]

1c. Si quando vir moritur, tunc uxori nunc oves dari debent ad supellectile ubi, ierint. [Dział. IV]

2. Unde swenne der man stirbit, so sal man der vrowen *zcu rechte* di shof zcu der rade in brengen, swo si gan. [BJ 169, II F 8, BJ 168, BJ 170a, BN 12607]

3. see No. 195

480

1a. [95] nec pro vulneribus, nec pro aliquo debito [Gn., Dział. IV]
1b. missing: BN 12607
2a. umme wunde odir umme di keine shult [BJ 169, II F 8, BJ 168, BN 12607]
2b. missing Article: BJ 170a
3. see No. 196

481

1a. [95] suum probare incolatum. [Gn.]
1b. suum *iuramento* probare incolatum. [BN 12607, Dział. IV]
2a. di kein ellende *gesweren*. [BJ 169, II F 8, BJ 168, BN 12607]
2b. missing Article: BJ 170a
3. see No. 197

482

1. [95] Consules si iuramentum unius viri recipient, quod secundum intram sentenciam civitatis et statuta consuetudinem exactionem dedisset et si tunc post mortem illius iurantis plura bona sub ipsius possessione fuerint inventa, quam perexactionata fuissent, illa bona consules non habent recipere, sed ipsius defuncti heredes, nisi aliquis heredum denegata eadem bona coram iudicio vel sedenti consilio recipere abrenunciasset, extunc ipsa bona consulibus pro utilitate civitatis permanerent quemadmodum arbitratur. [BN 12607]
2. Nemen dy ratman einis mannis eiit, daz her seyn gut nach der gewonet und wilkor der stat vorschult habe, wirt denne noch seynen tode me gutis gefundin. [II Q 4]
3. see No. 198

483

1a. [96] quod sibi abedificaverit aliquit de suis *bonis aut de* hereditate [Gn., BN 12607]
1b. quod sibi aliquid abedificaverit de sua hereditate [Dział. IV]
2. daz he im sines erbis icht ab gebuwet habe [BJ 169, II F 8, BJ 168, BJ 170a, BN 12607]
3. –

484

1a. [96] Extunc possessor cum testibus servat, si voluerit. [Gn., Dział. IV]
1b. Extunc possessor cum testibus servat, si vult *mettercius*. [BN 12607]
2a. der iz in der gewere hat mit gezuge behalden, ob he wil. [BJ 169, II F 8, BJ 168, BJ 170a, BN 12607]
2b. slight linguistic divergences between BJ 169 and BJ 168, BJ 170a
3. see No. 199

485

1. [97] Actor eciam si reum pro iuramentis promissis causa Dei vel peticionis horum dimittere voluerit absolutum, extunc iudici eciam competit ad hoc dare suam voluntatem. Et si suum consensum noluerit adhibere, tunc actorem iuramenta accipere opotebit vel iudici demeretur in pena octo solidorum, et nec plus pro causis singulis specialiter et quibusvis etc. [BN 12607]
2. Und wiil auch {auch} eyn clager eyde durch Got adir durch der lewte båte wyllen vorlossen, zo fugit dame [*s*] richter wol, das her seynen wyllen dar czu gaben. Wil her seynen willen dor czu nicht gabin, so muß der clager dy eyde namen adir her wirt dame [*s*] richter wette haft acht schillinge und nicht mer. [BN 12607]
3. see No. 200

486

1a. [98] tunc nemo eos extra civitatem in alio iure occupare, *seu contra eos agere*, in iudicio alieno. [Gn., BN 12607]
1b. tunc nemo eos extra civitatem in alio iure occupare potest in iudicio aliquo. [Dział. IV]
2. so en mac man si buzen der stat zcu rechte nicht brengen in ein andir gerichte. [BJ 169, II F 8, BJ 168, BJ 170a, BN 12607]
3. –

487

1. [99] cum iniuriis, talibus inpedimentis [Gn., BN 12607, Dział. IV]
2a. *und vride dar ubir geworcht wirt*, zcu unrechte mit so getanen dingen [BJ 169, II F 8, BN 12607]

2b. the underlined words missing in BJ 168
3. missing Article: BJ 170a

488

1. [99] Si contingerit in iudicio *castellani* [Gn., BN 12607, Dział. IV]
2a. Geshit iz in einem *vogit* dinge [BJ 169, II F 8, BJ 168, BN 12607]
2b. missing Article: BJ 170a
3. see No. 203

489

1a. [99] extunc suam acquirit *emendam et iudex acquirit suam* penam. [Gn., Dział. IV]
1b. extunc suam aquirit penam. [BJ 12607]
2a. so gewinnit *he im sin buze abe und dem richten* sin gewette. [BJ 169, II F 8, BJ 168, BN 12607]
2b. missing Article: BJ 170a
3. see No. 204

490

1a. [99] si hoc contra iusticiam fecerit, et si paciens ipsum protestaverit cum iudice et scabinis [Gn., BN 12607]
1b. si hoc contra iusticiam fecerit, et si paciens poterit protestari cum iudice et *duobus* scabinis [Dział. IV]
2a. Tut ein man daz mit unrechte und verzcugit in iener des mit dem richtere und *mit zweien* sheppfen [BJ 169, II F 8, BJ 168, BN 12607]
2b. missing Article: BJ 170a
3. see No. 205

491

1. [100] Nunc attendatur [Gn., BN 12607, Dział. IV]
2a. Nu vornemit *und horit* [BJ 169, II F 8, BJ 168, BN 12607]
2b. missing Article: BJ 170a
3. –

492

1a. [100] extunc condempnatur advocato in decem talentis idem *advocatus* ⟨sculte- tus⟩ [Gn.]
1b. extunc condempnatur advocato in decem talentis idem scultetus [BN 12607]
1c. extunc idem *scultetus* est advocato in decem talentis condempnatus [Dział. IV]
2a. so irteilit man zcu hant dem vogite uf den *shultheizen* zcen pfunt [BJ 169, II F 8, BJ 168, BN 12607]
2b. missing Article: BJ 170a
3. see No. 206

493

1a. [100] quam exercuit, et se ad iusticiam exhibere. [Gn., BN 12607]
1b. quam exercuit, et se ad iudicium *iure* exhibere. [Dział. IV]
2. und dem vogite *rechtes* zcu helfene [BJ 169, II F 8, BJ 168, BJ 170a, BN 12607]
3. –

494

1a. [100] aut hiis similia, que crimina *capitalia* tanguntur [Gn. 100]
1b. aut hiis similia, que criminalia facta tanguntur. [BN 12607]
1c. aut hiis similia, que noxalia facta tanguntur. [Dział. IV]
2a. odir sogetanis dingis icht, daz an ungerichte triffit [BJ 169, II F 8, BJ 168, BN 12607]
2b. missing Article: BJ 170a
3. –

495

1a. [100] si pro eo coram *castellano aut* advocato inpulsatus fuerit [Gn., BJ 12607]
1b. si pro eo coram advocato inpulsatus fuerit [Dział. IV]
2a. wirt he vor dem vogite darum me beclagit mit gezcuge [BJ 169, II F 8, BJ 168, BN 12607]
2b. missing Article: BJ 170a
3. see No. 208

496

1a. [101] qui sibi iudicare debet simili modo, ut advocatus super scultetum iudicare debuit. Eodem modo *scultetus iudicet advocatum.* [Gn., BN 12607]
1b. sibi debet iudicare simili modo, ut advocatus super scultetum debuerit. Eodem modo *advocatus iudicet scultetum.* [Dział. IV]
2a. der sal im richten zcu glichir wis ubir den vogit, als *der vogit ubir den shultheizen solde.* [BJ 169, II F 8, BJ 168, BN 12607]
2b. missing Article: BJ 170a
3. –

497

1a. [102] homines, qui suum clamorem audierunt habuerit [Gn.]
1b. clamatores [BN 12607, Dział. IV]
2a. shreiman [BJ 169, II F 8, BJ 168, BN 12607]
2b. missing Article: BJ 170a
3. –

498

1a. [103] et quod femine stuprantur [Gn.]
1b. stupra [BN 12607, Dział. IV]
2. und daz man vrowen notet [BJ 169, II F 8, BJ 168, BJ 170a, BN 12607]
3. –

499

1a. [103] homines, qui suum clamorem audierunt habuerit [Gn.]
1b. clamatores [BN 12607, Dział. IV]
2. shreiman [BJ 169, II F 8, BJ 168, BJ 170a, BN 12607]
3. –

500

1a. [103] oportet desuper respondere cum duello, quam cum iuramento evadere possit. [Gn.]

1b. extunc ille [actor] *propius* cum duello debet respondere, quam [reus] suo possit evadere iuramento. [Dział. IV, BN 12607]

2. iener ist im *neher* zcu antwurten mit eine campfe, wan he im entgen muge mit siner unshult. [BJ 169, II F 8, BJ 168, BJ 170a, BN 12607]

3. –

501

1a. [105] Sin autem dixerit, quod ipsum persolverit, hoc iurabit *metseptimus.* ⟨tertius⟩ [Gn.]

1b. Si autem dixerit, quod hoc debitum solus persolverit, hoc mettercius iurabit heres. [BN 12607, Dział. IV]

2a. Sprichit he abir, he habe im selbe vorgoldin, daz swerit he *selbe dritte.* [BJ 169, II F 8, BJ 168, BN 12607]

2b. the phrase missing in BJ 170a

3. see No. 216

502

1. [105] Si de debito sui patris recognoscat hoc solvere debet, in quantum recepta hereditas se extendit, et si solvere noluerit vel heredes hoc consentire recusant, tunc sibi hereditas sua vel proprium potest iudicio possideri pro isto debito et acquiri, aliter ille constringi non potest suam hereditatem et proprium. [BN 12607]

2a. Bekenen adir so muß he geldin, vil adir nicht geldin, so mag {mag} seyn erbe besiczen mit gerichte, andirs mag eyn man nicht twingen seyn erbe czu vorken sin. [II Q 4]

2b. missing in BN 12607 Ger.

3. see No. 217

503

1a. [106] *et noxam sive* dampnum fecerit [Gn.]
1b. si hoc damnum fecerit [Dział. IV, BN 12607]
2. abir wol schaden thut [BN 12607]
3. –

504

1a. [107] Sin autem edificium *iudicialiter* fiscatum fuerit [Gn.]
1b. Si autem *iudicialiter* edificia fuerint abiudicata [BN 12607, Dział. IV]
2. Wirt abir *einem manne* sin gebu[de] vorteilit [BJ 169, II F 8, BJ 168, BJ 170a, BN 12607]
3. –

505

1a. [107] Si aliquis spoliaverit cives suos, qui proprium aut feodum *aut hereditatem* intra municipale habeat [Gn.]
1b. Si quis spoliaverit suos civitatum homines, qui proprium aut feodum *vel hereditatem* habuerit intra municipale jus [BN 12607]
1c. Si quis spoliaverit suos civitatenses, qui proprium aut feodum *vel hereditatem* habuerint intra municipalia [Dział. IV]
2. Roubit ein man sine stetere, der eigen und len binnen wichbilde hat [BJ 169, II F 8, BJ 168, BJ 170a, BN 12607]
3. –

506

1a. [109] gramina et flores, *quod prius non fuerat.* [Dział. IV]
1b. underlined words missing: Gn., BN 12607
2a. blumen und gras, *des do vor nicht enwas* [BJ 168]
2b. underlined words missing: BJ 169, II F 8, BJ 168, BJ 170a
3. –

507

1. [109] Et si reus sis, quod tu pereas in tua anima tua et in tuo corpore et in tuis rebus. [BN 12607, Dział. IV]
1b. missing in the same place: Gn.
2. –
3. –

508

1. [109] quod Iudeus iurare *sive evadere* debet Christianum [Gn., BN 12607, Dział. IV]
2. ein Iude gerichten sal dem Cristen [BJ 169, II F 8, BJ 168, BJ 170a, BN 12607]
3. –

509

1. [109] quod te deleat *Adonay et sua* deitatis potencia [Gn. 109, BN 12607, Dział. IV]
2a. daz dich geweldige gotheit [BJ 169, II F 8, BJ 170a, BN 12607]
2b. daz dich *velle Adonai und sine* geweldige gotheit [BJ 168]
3. –

510

1a. [109] Nunc omnes dicite: Amen. [BN 12607, Dział. IV]
1b. missing: Gn.
2a. Sprecht alle Amen. [BJ 169, II F 8, BJ 170a]
2b. missing: BJ 168, BN 12607
3. see No. 220

APPENDIX 4

Weichbild's Edition of Gniezno MS

The format used in this edition follows Adam Wolff's Guidelines for editors of historical sources. Marked abbreviations are resolved silently, without enclosing the expansion in brackets; brackets signal that the abbreviation sign is missing. The vertical bar | marks the beginning of a new column on a page, curly brackets {} enclose repetitions, and a pair of quill bars ⊦ ⊣ wrap around phrases that were struck out by the scribe. Throughout the manuscript the obviously incorrect form *propius* is used instead of *propior*; this error has been left uncorrected. No attempt has been made to correct his habitual misspelling of *protestari* as protestare, or to adjust the wrong gender of some nouns and adjectives. The double *vv* in words like *vunera* have been distinguished as *vu* for ease of reading. The original numbering scheme (in Roman numerals) of the articles in the manuscript does not cover the Jewish oath (Article 108 and 109) or the *Constitution of Courts* (Articles 110–117). As in other manuscripts these two elements are combined, they have been given consecutive numbers for ease of reference. This critical edition ends with a text which is not a part of the Weichbild, *Conclusio libri*, appended to the latter by the copyist Mikołaj of Cieszyn.

Gniezno MS

f. 82 | ⟨[a]- Insuper ius municipale cum huius racione -[a]⟩

Hic[b] incipitur ius municipale de Theutonico translatum in Latinum per Conradum notarium quondam Sandomiriensem ac civem civitatis supradicte.

Incipitur prologus.

In nomine Patris et Filii et Spiritus Sancti. Amen. Primo dicit de summa Trinitate et fide, et hoc opus locatum est supra firmum fundamentum, de quo dicit Apostolus: Fundamentum aliud nemo ponere potest, preter id, quod positum est, quod est Christus. Ubi enim Christus fundamentum non est, ibi nullius boni operis potest superesse edificium ad invocacionem summe et individue Trinitatis. Exemplum laudabile me conpellit et racio violenta, quia | hoc a maioribus factum esse dinoscitur, quod a minoribus sit conpletum. Et mos retinendus est fidelissime vetustatis, licet enim non exemplis, sed legibus est iudicandum, verumptamen exemplum potest aliquis sequi maxime, ubi recte factum aliquod intuetur. Ad probandum, siquidem quod in quolibet

principio a gloria Trinitatis debeat auxilium peti, sola racio sufficere potest, cuiuslibet enim rei potissima pars est principium, et ex hiis, que inordinate inchoata sunt, non potest ordinabiliter agi. Quod per se patet, qualiter et bene et laudabiliter omnia
geruntur, si principium fuerit decens et amabile Deo, et vix ·I·^{us} [c] | est, ut bono peragan- f. 82^{v}
tur exitu, que malo inchoata sunt inicio. Quibus omnibus luce clarius apparet, quod finis laudabilis a bono dependet principio et tamquam suo maiori subiacet et maioribus maius vertitur et ibi caucius est agendum. Ipsa[d] est enim benedicta Trinitas, in cuius nomine et consilio omnis actus progreditur. Sic enim ad omnipotentis Dei auxilium debemus oculos erigere, ut non in armis sciencie vel eloquencie iaculis confidere valeamus, sed omnem spem, omne propositum erigamus ad providenciam Trinitatis, ipsa enim laborantibus aurem aperit et inclinat: Apprehendite etenim disciplinam | et sapienciam, nequando irascatur dominus et pereatis de via iusta [Ps 2,12]. Nos sermo propheticus exhortat, felix exhortacio, dulce consilium; qui enim apprehendit sapienciam, Christum, ut verum, fateor, apprehendit. Ipse enim est sapiencia, iusticia, veritas, fortitudo, sancitas. Et qui ingnorat sapienciam et Scripturas, Christum ingnorare scripture testimonio perhibetur. Cristus [*s*] etenim Dei virtus est sapiencia, ignorancia autem Scripturarum ingnominia est Christi ⌈iuxta apostolicum[e]⌉. Apprehendit siquidem sapienciam, qui insipienciam procul pellit, egressus enim unius alterius operatur
ingressum. Cum renunciatur inprobitati, nanciscitur virtus. Qui enim | sapienciam f. 83
non apprehendit, inproperabitur ei a Domino, et ideo sacerdocio non fungetur et in tenebris ignorancie latitans, mentis oculis excecatus iusticiam invenire non poterit. Sine qua, etsi ceterarum virtutum in ipso fulgeant radii, pro nihilo reputantur, ipsa est enim, que inter ceteras virtutes perfectissima dicitur, que iura omnibus distribuit et ex causa iusticia appellatur, ut legitur in auctoritatibus, ut omnes obediant iudicio. Hec est enim illa virtus laudabilis, que diffinicioni nobili diffinitur. Iusticia ergo est constans et perpetua voluntas, ius suum cuique tribuens, que concupiscencie conatus sua virtute conprimit ac de [*s*] | desiderat refrenare, ut in prohemio decretalium. Cum igitur subiectum libri presentis nullum sit aliud ponere preter ius et iusticiam, felix liber cui tam nobile famulatur subiectum, felix, inter cuius verba liber iste tamquam mirre fasciculus poterit commorari. Merito igitur, qui opus tantum agreditur, ut librum signatum septem ⟨sigillis[f]⟩ apperiat, summe Trinitatis auxilium expetet et inploret. Ego siquidem inter ceteros ⟨lectores[f]⟩ minimum me reputans et ignorancie mee tenebras non ignorans, excusare me deberem, cum propheta dicente: ·A,·a,·a· Domine Deus, ecce
nescio loqui, qui puer ego sum [Jr 1,6], quoniam altus est puteus sapiencie, et non | est f. 83^{v}
cum quo hauriam, quemadmodum mulier Chananea, cum de Dei omnipotentis, qui aquam vivam distribuit et largitur, confisus misericordia opus presens aggredior spem gerens firmissimam, quod de fonte graciarum suarum ad siccitatem meam rivulum derivando, de pane sue consolacionis, ne in via deficiam, buccelam michi porrigat. Ne igitur prolixitas, que frequenter parit fastidium, sermonem protrahat in inmensum, sed attendens, quam omne artificium per exercicium recipit incrementum, non in

armis sciencie vel eloquencie iaculis confisus, sed omnem | spem, omnem propositum referens ad omnipotentis Dei legis consilio, Qui est omnium vera salus. Sed quoniam scriptum est, ut nemo alciorem locum in scolis teneat, nisi cui laborum assiduitas et studiorum prolixitas suffragatur, ego fundo principium super lapidem angularem, qui est Christus Ihesus, Alpha et Omega, principium et finis.

Hic finitur prologus.

[a–a] in the top margin by a different hand; [b] decorated initial *H*, three lines in height; [c] decorated with floral patterns; [d] letter *I* two lines in height; [e] crossed out by the author of the base text, in the right margin; [f] in the right margin, an insertion sign +, written by the author of the base text

[1] Incipitur de Cesare Ottone, qui fundavit templum in Meydeburc.

f. 84 ·I· Cesar[a] Otto Rufus | fundavit templum in Meydeburc et dedit civibus municipale ius secundum eorum arbitrium et secundum consilium seniorum. Extunc arbitrati sunt, quod eligerent scabinos ac consules, scabinos ad diuturnum tempus et consules ad unum annum, qui tunc iuraverunt et nunc iurant annis singulis, dum eliguntur, ius ac profectum et honorem custodire et agere, quanto caucius ac melius sciant aut possunt, cum consilio ac iuvamine seniorum. Consules exponunt suum conventum secundum suum placitum ac voluntatem cum seniorum consensu. Consules eciam habent potestatem iudicandi | super quamlibet vacuam mensuram ac pondera iniusta, ac coretos iniustos et cuiuslibet cibi seu potus mercimonia. Et quicumque hoc violaverit, demeretur tres Sclavicas marcas, qui [s] faciunt triginta sex solidos. Qum consules suum conventum exponunt, extunc quitquit ibi statutum fuerit aut conpromissum in isto conventu, quod iuri divino non contradicit, firmum et inviolabiliter debet observari. Et quicumque violaverit, hoc consules habent agere. Et quicumque ad conventum venire neglexerit, cum signum datur per campanam, demeretur sex denarios. Sin autem con-
f. 84v ventus | sibi pronunciatus fuerit, demeretur quinque solidos.

[a] decorated initial *C*, six lines in height, drawing a head.

[2] De iure penesticorum et conmestibilia vendencium.

·II· Qui penestici vocantur, si in aliquo demerentur vel si in aliquo delinquerint in statutis civitatis, ita ut civitatis aut consulum decreta violaverint, si in hoc convicti fuerint, demerentur cutem cum crinibus aut tres solidos. Et hoc arbitrio consulum committitur, quod horum recipere velint. Quando penesticus consulum aut civitatis statutum infringerit foro infrunito, ita quod cutem cum crine demeretur et cum pecunia[a] redimet, hic manet sine iure et non potest ammodo aliquem in fo|rum conmestibile absque civitatis aut consulum consensu exercere. Et si alii homines, qui communitatem seu fraternitatem habent in conmestibilibus, consulum seu civitatis conpromissum, seu hos oportet emendam dare secundum ius et edictum civitatis, et non possunt ulterius aliqua conmestibilia vendere, nec communitatem habere seu acquirere absque consensu consulum et civitatis.

[a] *i* erased in *pe*[*cu*]*nia*, which can suggest *pena*; in another MSS *pecunia*.

[3] De iniustis mensuris et iniustis pensis ac ponderibus.

·III· Si metrete aut alie mensure parve seu iniuste fuerint et iniuste pense, quod consules bene agere possunt secundum honorem civitatis aut cum | triginta solidis f. 85
emendare.

[4] De tribus iudiciis provincialibus advocati provincie.

·IIII· Ille[a] supremus iudex, qui in Meideburc iudicio presidet, hoc est castellanus, qui sedet tria iudicia provi[n]cialia in anno: unum iudicium in die sancte Agathe, secundum in die sanctorum Johannis et Pauli, tercium in octava beati Martini. Si ceciderit aut evenerit aliquod horum iudiciorum ad diem celebrem aut feriatum, extunc amisit suum iudicium. Et si scultetus aut solus castellanus ad iudicium non venerit, quia scultetus castellano primam sentenciam debet invenire, et si scultetus non venerit ad castellanum, | extunc[b] decem talenta demeretur, nisi legale inpedimentum, ⊦nisi legale inpedimentum [c]⊣ quod probare potuerit, ut ius dictaverit. Quitquit criminalis cause factum seu conmissum[d] fuerit quatuordecim diebus ante suum iudicium, ⊦comiserit sine [c]⊣ hoc castellanus debet iudicare et nemo ⊦s [c]⊣ alius.

[a] *I* seven lines in height; [b] *e* elaborated with flourishes; [c] crossed out by the author of the base text; [d] the last stroke of the second *m* and the following letters illegible.

[5] De iudicio burgravii.

·V· Stuprum et obsidia et irruenciam domiciliorum iudicat castellanus et nullus alter. Sed si castellanus presens esse non poterit, extunc cives eligunt unum iudicem loco castellani, pro excessu manifesto. Castellani pena et reconpensa, quod acquisitum

fuerit in iudicio | bannito, debet solvi per sex ebdomadas. Pena castellani tria talenta, f. 85v
pena sculteti octo solidi. Quando castellanus surgit et iudicavit, tunc iudicium suum expiravit et statim iudicium sculteti disponit a proximo ad duas ⊦[a]⊣ septimanas.

[a] an illegible word crossed out and erased by the author of the base text.

[6] De iure sculteti in tribus iudiciis.

·vi· Scultetus eciam habet tria iudicia legalia in anno, unum in Epiphania Domini aut die sequenti, secundum tercia feria post conductum Pasche, tercium feria tercia post festum Trinitatis. Post hec disponit sua iudicia continue ad duas ebdomadas. Si dies iudicialis evenerit ad | diem celebrem, bene potest ultra diem unam aut duos post diem celebrem iudicium suum disponere. Iudicium sculteti nemo potest hominum indicere, nisi scultetus solus vel preco, nec suus famulus. Quodsi scultetus in domo non fuerit et si criminale nephas exortum fuerit, cives statuant unum iudicem pro crimine manifesto. Scultetus eciam debet habere legalitatem a domino terre et cum eo debet esse feodatus et verum suum feodum esse debet. Insuper liber esse debet et legittime natus de terra.

[7] De clamore in vulneribus et in monomachalibus vulneribus.

f. 86 ·vii· Quodsi homo vulneratus fuerit, si clamorem | proclamaverit et si ceperit hunc, qui ipsum vulneravit, et eum ad iudicium usque deduxerit, et si tunc ipsum cum hiis, qui suum clamorem audierunt, protestare poterit metseptimus, propius est eum vincere, quam ille possit eum evadere. Pro vulnere manum, pro homicidio collum. Si vulnus profunditatem unguis et longitudinem membri habuerit, acquirit homo duellum pro uno vulnere, et si victor fuerit, victus a victo[re][a] pro vulnere manum, pro homicidio collum.

[a] extension *victo[re]* uncertain.

[8] De conflictu, qui fit in die aut tempestate noctis.

·viii· Si continget criminale nephas aut confl|ictus nocte vel die et si probus homo pro eo accusetur, propius est evadere metseptimus, quam ille possit super eum protestare, quia in isto loco conflictus per neminem visus.

[9] De diffinicionibus sentenciarum et quit sit iuris de debitis.

·IX· Nec sculteto, nec castellano tenetur scabinus nec civis aliquem sentenciam extra veros dies iudiciales diffinire, nisi sit factum manifestum, ut vulnera mortalia aut homicidia, vel furta seu alia criminalia. Castellanus et sultetus bene possunt omni die iudicare pro debito, pro quo absque testimonio agitur, nisi si civis agat | contra hospitem et hospes super civem pro debito cum testimonio, de quo alter alteri fassus est, quod bene potest iudicari sine mora. Et si uni adiudicatur debitum, habet solvere sequenti die, quod tenetur. Sed hospitem oportet iuramento probare, quod sit alienigena et ita remote domicilium habeat, quod una die ad iudicium venire non possit. f. 86v

[10] De querimonia, que pernoctaverit pro vulneribus.

·X· Quodsi vir vulneratus fuerit et ea die iudicium non fuerit, quesierit et sua querimonia pernoctaverit et, qui inculpatur, tunc conparuerit, evadit eum met|septimus, quam ille super eum possit protestare. Sed si tribus iudiciis non conparet, quarto iudicio describetur, ita tamen, si iusto modo citatus et super eum conquestus fuerit.

[11] De stupro et insidiis et irruenciis domicilii et iure burgravii.

·XI· Stuprum et obsidium et irruenciam domicilii burgravius ⟨iudicat [a]⟩ nec alter ullus. Si aliquis irruit super alterius domicilium tempore nocturno aut diurno, temeraria violencia, nulla procedente querimonia, et si in manuali facto deprehensus fuerit cum clamore, et si clamorem cum auditoribus metseptimus suorum vicinorum | hoc ostendendo probare poterit secundum iuris exigenciam, malefactor collum demeretur. Sin autem manifestum factum non fuerit, extunc propius est evadere metseptimus, quam aliquo testimonio vinci possit. f. 87

[a] annotation in the margin, probably by a different hand using a pen with a different nib.

[12] De homine, qui multis vulneribus fuerit vulneratus.

·XII· Quicumque[a] vulneratus fuerit, si clamorem proclamaverit et ad iudicium pervenerit, de quocumque querulatur, qui presens fuerit, et si habuerit hos, qui suum clamorem audierunt, et quot vulnera habuerit, tot homines potest inculpare. Sin autem hii homines conparuerint, | duellum in ipsis acquirere potest. Sin autem plures iudicialiter infestaverit, qua[m] vulnera habuerit, alii omnes evadent suo iure, quivis metseptimus.

[a] *Q* elaborated with a flourish.

[13] De obligacione pignorum.

·XIII· Obligat aliquis mercimonia aut alia bona mobilia pro debito ex parte iudicii, et ille pronunciet tribus iudiciis, ut est iuris, et quarto iudicio super eo dominium receperit ac appropriatum sibi fuerit, et congnoscencie dominii dederit coram iudice et scabinis. Et si iste inposterum ad repetendum sua bona pervenerit, possidens propius
f. 87v est suum pingnus servare cum scabinis ac iudice, qua[m] ille, | qui caret possessione.

[14] De iure feminarum et si pars puerorum eradicati fuerint. [*ss*]

·XIV· Si aliquis ducit uxorem et si vir de hac luce discedit, uxor nichil habet in suis bonis, nisi sibi dederit pro dotalicio aut vite provisione pro sua vita in iudicio bannito. Nulla mulier potest vite provisionem, nec dotalicium hereditarie observare. Et cum de hac luce discedit, ad heredes revertitur sui mariti. Quodsi sibi maritus mulieri nichil in suis bonis dederit, in possessione bonorum sui mariti debet permanere, et pueri sibi necessaria ministrabunt, | eousque in viduitate et si sine marito permanere voluerit. Si vir oves habuerit, quas mulier recipiet ad suppellectile. Et si pueri vellent dotalicium infringere, servare potest testimonio virorum ac mulierum metseptima, qui tunc presentes fuerunt. Si vir pueros habuerit, aut mulier, quicunque ex hiis exhereditati sunt, si moritur vir, hii pueri, qui in hereditate patris sunt, recipiunt bona et non hii, qui exhereditati sunt, sed hereditatem vendere non possunt absque choheredum con-
f. 88 sensu. Hii pueri, qui in potestate patris mortis tempore fuerunt, si ex hiis unus | moritur, istius partem dividunt inter se equaliter, tam exhereditati, quam domestici.

[15] De publicacione seu fiscacione possessione [s].

·XV· Quando alicui sua possessio publicata fuerit iuste ac iudicialiter, quociens exit vel intrat, tocies penam iudici demeretur, ita si publicacio super ipsum rite ac iuste sit acquisita.

[16] De pacis firmitate et de dono infra annum possesso.

·XVI· Quitquit masculus dat sub banno, si possidebit pacifice et quiete absque arestacione aliqua anno et die, hoc propius et melius optinere potest cum iudice et | scabinis, quam ab ipso aliquis possit exbrigare. Quodsi iudex et scabini mortui sunt, quod tamen bene cum aliis fidedignis ad minus duobus scabinis et quatuor viris probitate probatis testimonio [probet], et sic bona sibi donata optinebit.

[17] De dono in infirmitate donato.

·XVII· Nemo masculus, ⊢nec[a]⊣ nec ulla mulier possunt in lecto egritudinis de suis bonis alicui ultra tres solidos dare absque heredum consensu seu voluntate.

[a] word partly erased.

[18] De hereditate, ubi nec fratres nec sorores reperiuntur.

·XVIII· Quodsi[a] hereditas in fratribus et sorori | bus defectum habuerit, extunc omnes f. 88v
hii, qui se linea equali consanguinitatis ostendere poterint, in hereditate succedunt equaliter. Qui autem in possessione est, si bene sacerdos est aut manserit, tamen suppellectilia recipit, quodsi nulla puella fuerit. Si autem puella et sacerdos fueri[n]t, tunc supellectilia inter se dividunt.

[a] *Q* elaborated with a flourish.

[19] De firmacione pacis donacioni pro hereditate.

·XIX· Quitquit masculus dat in iudicio bannito coram iudice et scabinis, ibi recipiens dat unum solidum pro doni congnicione, quem recipiunt scabini.

[20] De debito per iuris extorsionem | acquisito et de iudicio, ubi conqueritur et fatetur.

·XX· Quicumque aliquem coram iudicio pro debito inpulsaverit, si debitum coacto iure consecutus fuerit, oportet eadem die solvere et iudex in eo suam penam acquisivit. Sin autem querimonia facta fuerit super aliquem pro debito, de quo fatetur, solvere

tenetur infra duas ebdomadas, et si tempore statuto debitor non solverit, extunc iudex in eo suam penam acquisivit. Extunc solvere mandat ad octo dies, deinde ad tres dies, extunc die sequenti. Quociens tunc mandatum debitor adimplere neglex | erit, tociens f. 89
penam suam in eo iudex acquisivit. Si penam iudici et debitum creditori solvere contempserit, extunc fiscatur sua possessio. Per hoc conpellitur, quod debitum creditori et pena iudici persolvatur. Si autem possessione caruerit, extunc banno conpellitur, extunc bene potest conprehendi, ubi visus fuerit pro debito et pro pena. Et quicunque ipsum ultra hoc tenuerit aut penam iudici demeretur.

[21] De inpedimento ad limina sanctorum extra provinciam aut ad nundinas.

·XXI· Si aliquis ad limina sanctorum aut ad nundinas extra provinciam | aut extra terminos ire voluerit, et si aliquis ipsum pro debito impedire voluerit, hoc fieri non debet, oportet ius suum coram suo iudice recipere. Et si uni testimonium adiudicatum fuerit, inducias trinas duas ebdomadas optinebit, quodcumque elegerit aut iudicio proximo.

[22] De pena illius, qui scabinum illicitis verbis in sede iudiciali obruit.

·XXII· Quicumque scabinum in scampno iudiciali inproperaverit aut turpibus verbis obruerit, scabinus lucratur suam emendam triginta solidos, et iudex suam penam
f. 89v acquirit. ⟨non [a]⟩ Obruitur[b] autem scabinus[c], | postquam sua sentencia diffinita sit et consensus aliorum scabinorum preterierit, extunc omnes emendas acquirunt et iudex penas, et quot emende fuerint, totidem et pene iudici acquiruntur.

[a] flush with the penultimate line in the right margin, penned with a different hand; [b] beneath the word [*ob*]*ruitur* an outline of a head and a hand; [c] the word *scabinus* is marked off with a manicule with an elongated index finger.

[23] De concordia et rancore, que coram iudicio concordata fuerit aut absque iudicio.

·XXIII· Quando concordia inter discordantes coram iudicio ordinata fuerit, diuturnus fremitus, homo protestare potest cum iudice et scabinis. Quodsi scabini mortui fuerint, tunc protestatur cum hominibus fidedignis, qui iudicio affuerunt. Quitquit scabini protestantur, hoc iudex cum ipsis debet protestare, simul et confirma|re. Sed[a] ubicunque concordia ordinata fuerit extra iudicium, hoc facilius potest probare vir cum sex testibus solus septimus, qui interfuerunt et viderunt concordiam esse factam. Ubi concordia et vera fremitus diuturna coram iudicio confirmata fuerit, si ipsam violat adversa pars, et si vincetur, ut ius dictaverit, cum iudice et scabinis, pro vulnere manum, pro homicidio collum. Sin autem contingeret, quod alter eam infringeret, hunc tamen emendare cum reconpensa oportet, pro vulnere novem talenta, pro homicidio decem et octo tale[n]ta, nisi se possit excusare secundum iuris edictum.

[a] *S* elaborated à la plume.

[24] | De filio excipere coram iudicio et mercede de servito iudicialiter optinere. f. 90

·XXIIII· Et vir quivis filium suum ter potest eximere, quem habet in potestate, coram iudicio pro quolibet crimine capitali tacto sacramento metseptimus secundum ius municipale. Similiter et vir potest filium suum, quem in potestate habet, tribus vicibus eximere, ubi aut ad collum aut ad manum pertransit. Quarta vero vice ipsum solum propria in persona respondere oportebit, et primum[a] in suo iure non impediet, si filius prius bene respondisset. Sin autem pater cum filio simul in eodem crimine coram iudicio inpulsati fuerint, ex|tunc pater filium eximere non potest, nisi prius se ab eodem crimine expurgabit. Famulus potest mercedem suam, quam promeruerit, quinque solidos probare tacto sacramento mettercius, quod sibi persolvit, tunc propius est evadere, quam famulus optinere. Si autem famulus suam merdecem super suum dominum optinuerit coram iudicio, pro eo dominus iudici nullam penam demeretur, sed dominus famulo eandem mercedem eadem die solvere tenetur indilate. Si alter alterum pro vino aut alio potu inculpare voluerit, evadet ut aliud debitum, in quo nullum dominium ostendere po | terit aut protestare[b]. f. 90v

[a] reading uncertain, following W. Maisel's edition of the Magdeburg Law of Pleszew, p. 74; [b] final *e* elaborated with an outline trefoil.

[25] De hereditate, quod datur viro vel femine coram iudicio, aut dono.

·XXV· Donum, quod viro vel mulieri datum fuerit in iudicio bannito, in eo mulier cum sua parte sive dono pro suo arbitrio facere potest absque omni contradiccione quitquit placet. Idem potest vir cum parte sui doni, quitquit deliberaverit modo simili, quam ipse suscepit. Si moritur femina absque herede, ita quod nullum heredem a suo marito pepererit, ipsa heredat sua successoria, seu sua prospera fortuna acquisita super suum proximum naturalem successorem, sive sit masculus sive femina, qui | sibi sit paris condicionis. Idem facit vir illi, qui sibi paris fuerit condicionis. Insuper omne aurum et argentum non informatum [*s*][a], et omnis siligo et carnes cum cervisia et vino, et panis, que vel quod aut quantum post trecesunum permansit, vel permanserunt, totum cedit heredibus viri et non mulieris, exceptis pulmentariis, de quibus mulier mediam recipit partem et heredes viri reliquam mediam tollunt partem.

[a] the double negative in effect cancels the point of the regulation, cf. Article 26.

[26] De hiis, qui pertinent ad hereditatem.

·XXVI· Ista[a] sunt, que ad hereditatem spectant: omne aurum et argentum informatum,
f. 91 omnia vasa argentea, et tela, que non incisa aut formata ad mu | liebria vestimenta, non [*s*][b] et sartagines, que a loco non moventur, et dolea, et vasa distillatoria, et omnia caldaria, excepto caldari, in quo liquesit cera, quod spectat ad suppellectile. Omne proprium, quod locando possessum est, et omnia arma et omnes gladii, et eciam omnes olle eree ac morsee, et cinguli, bracciles, et annuli viri, hec predicta spectant ad hereditatem. Mense et lavatoria, omnes ciste planis cooperimentis, et sedilia spectant ad hereditatem, pelves cupree, et ciste pharine, et ciste pl[ene][c] annonarum, et porci, qui in curiis sive in domibus nutriuntur, eciam spectant ad hereditatem. Et omnes por|ci inpinguati spectant ad pulmentaria. Ubi pulmentaria dantur et omnis expensa domestica, que in potestate viri est, et omnes vacue cuppe, pulmentario [*s*] recipit mariti uxor, et non sua congnata proxima.

[a] *I* six lines in height, elaborated with a trefoil trailing downwards; [b] the double negative cancels the point of the regulation; [c] reading uncertain.

[27] De viro, qui alterum vulnerat vitam suam defendendo et eciam solus fuerit vulneratus.

·XXVII· [Si] vulnerat quis alterum vitam suam defendendo supra viam publicam, quod ille ipsum percutit aut vulnerat, et si clamore proclamaverit, et invasor conparet violenter, seu proterve, et conqueritur iudici, et hic non potest, nec audet, pro inbeci-
f. 91v llitate sui corporis conparere, tunc | et inposterum ea die conpareat et conqueratur iudici et scabinis, et ostendat sua vulnera, et protestetur per hos, qui suum clamorem audierunt, quod inicium contencionis sui adversarii fuerit et non suum, et quod ipse se defenderit in defensione vite sue, et ipse acquirit querimoniam primam. Sed si pernoctabit, extunc hoc fieri non potest.

[28] De duobus, qui de stirpe Sclavica se mutuo vulnerant intra ius municipale.

·XXVIII· Quodsi duo se vulnarant [*s*] mutuo in iure municipali, qui ambo processerunt de stirpe Sclavica et tamen Sclavi non sunt, | conpareat unus et conqueratur in Sclavonico ydiomate, alterum non oportet sibi respondere, si placet, nisi conqueratur in eo ydiomate, quod sibi innatum est per ius municipale.

[29] De causa, de qua promittitur coram iudicio termimari [s].

·XXIX· Quod si duorum virorum querimonie dilate fuerint in iudicio bannito coram iudice, de voluntate iudicis et consensu, et parcium arbitrium utrorumque [*s*], quod inter ipsos concordia extra iudicium debeat terminari, nec ultra causam peragendam, et se arbitri ad hoc electi de causa intromittant concordandi, absque iudicio et querimoniam | non repetendo cum consensu iudicis. Et si alter ex eis suam querimoniam f. 92
inposterum vellet renovare pro hac causa coram iudicio, iste sibi suus adversarius respondere non tenebitur coram iudicio, si protestare potuerit cum iudice et scabinis, quod causa absque iudicio debeat terminari.

[30] De duobus, qui se mutuo vulnerant equaliter.

·XXX· Quodsi se duo mutuo vulneraverint equaliter, ex hiis unus vadat ad iudicem in domum suam, et querimoniam faciat, alter veniat ad quatuor bancos et conqueratur cum clamore scabinis et iudicio astantibus, et vulnera ostendat, et mittat pro iudi|ce et conqueratur, ipse primam querimoniam optinebit, si testes super hoc habuerit a scabinis aut astantibus iudicio, quod inter quatuor bancos querimoniam fecerit.

[31] De duobus, qui se mutuo vulneraverunt equaliter et querulantur equaliter.

·XXXI· Et si se duo mutuo vulneraverint equaliter et querulantur equaliter, quicunque ex eis in alterum duellum acquisierit, tunc eius adversarius manum demeretur. Ita tamen, si vulnus monomachale fuerit. Et si alter ex eis, antequam duellum acquisitum fuerit, moritur, adversarius collum demeretur.

f. 92v [32] De viro, qui alterum vulnerat, | et si ad iudicium in facto manifesto deductus fuerit.

·XXXII· Si aliquis detinet hunc, qui ipsum vulneravit in facto recenti et ipsum cum clamore ad iudicium deducit, qui sic queruletur cum prolocutore: "Domine iudex, ego cum querela propono super istum virum, quod ipse venit intra municipia vel in strata regia, et in me pacem violavit, et me spoliavit in meo corpore et in bonis meis, et me vulneravit, dum pacem in me confregit. Tunc vidi ego ipsum in persona propria et proclamavi eum cum clamore, et ipsum captivum hoc ad iudicium deduxi, et volo eum vincere per eos, qui clamorem meum audie|runt, et cum meo testimonio vero, ut ius michi diffinierit. Et in sentencia requiro, quomodo hoc probare debeam, ita ut michi proficiat in iure meo". Extunc satisdacionem adversarius rectam petat pro hac querimonia, et dicat se de facto innocentem. Ille, qui ipsum captivum in manifesto facto detinuit, facilius eum vincere potest cum testimonio, quam ipse captivus cum testimonio evadere possit. Si, ut iuris est, probaverit testimonio, illi solvet collum, si est homicidium, vel ad manum, si vulnus est monomochale, cum ad iudicium ipsum cum
f. 93 manifesto facto perduxerit. Pro[a] teste potest | quivis vir alteri astare, qui in suo iure non possit argui, excepto patre et fratre, et filio et mercennario.

[a] elaborated with a floral flourish.

[33] De duobus, qui se mutuo vulneraverint: unus cutello et alter gladio.

·XXXIII· Quod si se duo mutuo vulneraverint: unus cutello et alter gladio, et si vulnera utriusque monomachalia fuerint, illi cum gladio solvit manum, illi cum cutello solvit collum, quia cutellus furtivam infert mortem.

[34] De vulneribus, que pernoctaverint, et de quibus eodem die fit querimonia.

·XXXIIII· Eciam si alter alterum vulnerat et causa sua pernoctaverit sibi debet indici in iudicium proxi|mum. Et si vir vulneratus fuerit et vulnus monomachale non fuerit, et si comparuerit et conquestus fuerit, sibi indici debet ad iudicium proximum. Si autem vulnus monomachale fuerit, tunc continnuo sibi iudex formari debet pro facto manifesto.

[35] De duobus, qui se vulnerantur et ambo coram iudicio conquirent.

·XXXV· Si duo vulnerantur et ambo coram iudicio conparent et querimonias proponunt, qui primam precellentem querimoniam protestare poterit, aput suum adversarium duellum atquirit, si ipsum iusto modo salutaverit, et si vulnus monomachale fuerit. Sin autem ad | diem duellum dilatum fuerit, et si alter pugilem convenerit super f. 93v
alterum, et si ille protestare poterit, quod pugil sit mercennarius, extunc iure sibi a duello cedere potest.

[36] De viro, qui alterum vulnerat et ipsis pax indicta fuerit.

·XXXVI· Si vulnerat vir alterum, et si caucionem fideiussorie fecerit usque ad iudicium, et si iudex ipsis pacem indixerit, et si ipsum postea occiderit, et si fideiussores posuerit pro causa eadem, ipse tamen propius est evadere metseptimus de homicidio, quam ipsum aliquis protestare possit. Sin autem coram iudicio conparuerit, et si | in iudicio bannito manu pax promissa fuerit coram iudice et scabinis pro primo vulnere, et si ipsum postea occiderit, hoc melius potest super eum protestare, quam ipse evadere possit.

[37] De duobus, qui se mutuo vulneraverint et ambo querulaverint, et querimonia usque ad iudicium disposita fuerit.

·XXXVII· Si se duo mutuo vulneraverint et ambo coram iudicio conparent et querulose proponant, et querimonia usque ad iudicium dilata fuerit, qui primo querulatus fuerit, moriatur ab hiis vulneribus, mortuus ad iudicium portetur, et alter vulneratus eciam conparuerit, et unus, de mortui, agnatus loquatur | super vulneratum cum tes- f. 94
timonio, quod ipse suum affinem occiderit, et pro eo petat iudicium. Extunc ille petat satisdacionem de iure et ostendat suam innocenciam cum suo testimonio evadendo homicidium. Si hoc, ut iuris est, protestaverit, propius est evadere, quam ille super eum poterit protestare, quia ambo coram iudicio querimoniam inceperunt. Sed suum testimonium sic debet procedere, quod inicium contencionis illius fuerit, et non suum. Et si suos testes incontinenti habere non poterit, terminum sex ebdomadas acquirit, tunc facilius potest evadere | homicidium metseptimus, quam ille cum testimonio ipsum vincere possit. Sin autem ille ipsum monomachaliter alloquitur, extunc ipsum pro suo collo pugnare oportebit.

[38] De equo, quit in eo, cum venditur, promitti teneri debeat.

·XXXVIII· Si mas equm vendiderit, promittere debet in eo equo, quod stabilis non fuerit, ita quod a loco discedere tempore se offerente noluerit, et videre apparens [quod non][a] sit cecus, et eciam [quod est liber][a] a iusta arestacione.

[a] the extension following the suggestion of W. Maisel (*Prawo magdeburskie miasta Pleszewa*, p. 77).

[39] De fure, qui in die ·III· solidos aut in nocte ·VI· denarios, aut plus, subtraxerit.

·XXXIX· Si fur clara luce diei deprehensus fuerit, qui bone fame sit, et furtum minus
f. 94v quam tres | solidos valeat, cutem cum crine demeretur. Sed si furtum ultra tres solidos
valeat, reus est patibulo. De hiis denariis ·III· solidi medium fertonem debent ponderare. Sin autem fur tempestate noctis deprehensus fuerit ⊦n[a]⊣ cum sex denariis, reus est suspendio.

[a] crossed out by the author of the base text.

[40] De viro, qui super alium querimoniam fecerit pro bonis, que sibi dicit esse innata.

·XL· Conqueritur vir super alterum pro bonis, quod vera sua hereditas sit, et quod ille teneat cum iniuria, et sua vera sit successio a patre suo, vel ab alio suo angnato, aut a suo predecessore, et si ille conparet | super quem querela proposita fuerit, et dicit se habere bonorum defensorem, et bona possiderit pacifice et quiete, anno ⟨et[a]⟩ die, contradiccione qualibet non obstante et est ⟨iuste[b]⟩ ac rite meum predium censuale, ipsum oportet suum defensorem nominare, et ad dies statuere, si possit, et cum defendente seu defensore conservat sua bona in eo, si defensus fuerit, ut iuris est, a defensore. Sin autem sibi defectus fuerit in defensore, actor conservat suam legalem proprietatem, in bonis eisdem, quia quivis homo conservat suam innatam hereditatem, sive naturalem
f. 95 porcionem, fa | cilius quam alter emptam hereditatem, aut obligatam hereditatem, aut
datam proprietatem, aut predium censuale, cum inpossibile sit aliquem de naturali porcione defraudari.

[a] interlinear superscript; [b] in the right margin, an insertion sign +, written by the author of the base text.

[41] De hereditariis censualibus bonis a claustro aut alio domino.

·XLI· Si homo habuerit hereditaria censualia et bona a quodam monasterio, aut alio domino, et si dominus aut abbas sibi non fatetur, aut conventus, hic vir potest metseptimus protestare suorum choheredum, qui [*s*] quilibet iurabit singulariter, quot iustum ac successorium suum sit predium censuale. Et si dominus seu abbas hiis septem de ip[*s*]orum bonis | denegaverit aut fateri noluerit, extunc quivis ipsorum metseptimus suorum coheredum bona sua optinebit.

[42] De testimonio pro persolutis debitis aut proprio metseptimus[a].

·XLII· Si debet vir producere testimonium super proprium alterius metseptimus, aut mettercius, hoc facere oportet cum possessis hominibus, qui in suo iure argui non possunt, et qui iudicio astare solent, et domicilia habentibus in iudicio supradicto. Sin autem debet vir persoluta debita protestare super proprietatem alterius, hoc iterum esse debent possessi homines domicilia habentes, si hoc in iudicio non viderunt, | nec f. 95v
in iudicio fuerit confirmatum.

[a] at the end of the line in which the text of the article begins.

[43] De testimionio pro debito persoluto.

·XLIII· Si aliquis debet persoluta debita probare, protestando pro debito, hoc facere debet cum talibus hominibus, qui in suo iure argui non possunt.

[44] De viro habenti [*s*] filium, et [qui] viduam ducit habentem pueros.

·XLIIII· Si vir ducit viduam, que unum filium aut plures pueros[a] habuerit et ipse nulla bona habuerit nec ipsa, et vir unum filium habuerit cum sua prima uxore, et si fortuna arridente per suos labores bona habuerint et proprietatem sive hereditatem emerint, aut super bona mobilia sive mercimonia | posuerint, et inposterum vir moritur et uxor, extunc filius viri propior est recipere hereditatem, quam pueri femine, aut pueri sororis sue, vel eciam nepotes seu nepte ex filia sua. Ita tamen, si filius patri sit paris condicionis. Proxima congnata uxoris recipit suppellectilia de iure.

[a] in MS *plueros*.

[45] De viro, qui bona sua in iudicio bannito uxori sue aut pueris suis dederit.

·XLV· Si vir aliquis dederit pueris suis aliqua bona sua, et sue uxori, in iudicio bannito circa vitam suam, et bone racionis, et si sibi pueri paris condicionis fuerint, et si
f. 96 desuper vera pax | firmata fuerit, et inposterum alteri in eisdem bonis aliquit dederit aut heres fuerit, aut ille, cui prima donacio sit data, bene contradicere potest de iure. Ita tamen, si testimonium desuper iudicis habuerit et scabinorum, quod sibi primum donum donatum sit absque contradiccione illius, qui ad hoc successor fuerit infra annum et diem. Extunc contradicere non potest, si illi desuper testes habuerint.

[46] De hereditariis censualibus bonis et edificiis super censualia bona donacione uxore coram iudicio.

·XLVI· Si vir sue uxori[a] sua edificia dederit, que super bona censualia edificata fuerint, coram domino | proprietatis, et coram suis vicinis, tempore vite sue, et inducit eam in possessionem, et si discedit ab hac luce sine prole, si heres suus super bona eadem loqui debeat ⊦voluerit[b]⊣ post mortem viri, nichil in eis poterit optinere, si mulier protestaverit[c], quod sibi datum fuerit. Sin autem apparatus et edificia viri proprium fuerit, extunc heres mulieri infringere potest, nisi donacio in iudicio bannito fuerit confirmata. Quia nullus suum proprium dare potest, nisi in iudicio bannito, vel coram iudice et scabinis, nisi suus heres contradicat. Sin autem hereditaria censualia bona fuerint,
f. 96v extunc | sue uxori dare non potest absque heredum consensu, vel absque domini proprietatis consensu, in cuius bonis sunt. Si vir mercimonia aut bona mobilia habuerit, quod cum bonis emerit eisdem successoriis paterna successione, hoc sue uxori dare non potest, nisi in iudicio bannito coram iudice et scabinis. Sin autem vir habuerit bona mobilia aut mercimonia, que sibi propriis laboribus aut prospera fortuna accreverunt, que [*s*][d] potest dare in valitudine vite sue cuicunque placet, cuiuslibet sine contradiccione.

[a] scribal correction of *e* to *a*; [b] *voluerit* dots under word (crossed out); [b] *verit* in the margin; [d] Maisel in his edition of the *Magdeburg Law of Pleszew* (p. 78, Note r) amends to *illa*.

[47] De iure liberto [*s*] in emendis sive [*s*] obnoxii et in successori|bus in bonis naturalibus et in iniuriis.

·XLVII· Ubi alicuius monasterii obnoxius suam penam demeretur, hoc sunt triginta solidi, obnoxius bene potest bona sua resingnare et iterum suscipere et dare cui placet,

contradiccione qualibet non obstante, quod [*s*] propriis laboribus acquisivit. Ubi obnoxius suo domino suum censum subtraxerit, pro eo tria talenta demeretur. Quitquit obnoxius criminalis cause commiserit, pro eo queret iudicium nisi domini advocati. Quando obnoxius moritur, extunc suo domino aut suo advocato oportet dare denarios obnoxie | tarum [*s*] et meliorem equm, quem habet. Idem oportet facere sacerdotem f. 97
suo archipresbitero, dum moritur, tunc sibi oportet dare suum meliorem equm.

[48] De viro, qui absque herede moritur et nepotem ex filia habuerit.

·XLVIII· Si moritur vir absque herede et nepotem ex filia habuerit, que exheredata fuerit circa suam vitam, idem nepos maiori iure recipit bona avi materni, quam iudicium, qui ⸠sit⸡ sibi est paris condicionis ⟨sed iudicium recipit arma bellica [a]⟩.

[a] insertion sign +, in the right margin in a different hand, probably in the 15th century; cf. Article 100.

[49] De abtestacione manus pro falso aut vulneribus.

·XLIX· Si unus alteri manum suam abtestare voluerit pro falso, hoc oportet, quod faciat mettercius | cum talibus hominibus, qui in suo iure argui non possunt. Si autem facere debet pro vulnere in facto manifesto, oportet quod hoc faciat metseptimus, per iusticiam pacis, ita tamen, si manifestum factum cum malefactore ad iudicium deductum fuerit.

[50] De viro, qui moritur et pueros habuerit, qui ad annos pubertatis non dum pervenerunt[a].

·L· Cum moritur vir, qui pueros habuerit, qui ad annos discrecionis non dum pervenerunt, proximus agnatus debet ipsorum esse tutor, eousque ad annos pubertatis pervenerint. Et si idem nondum ad huc[b] annos pubertatis | attingerit, adiutor suus esse f. 97v
debet proximus agnatus suus, eousque ipse ad annos pervenerit discrecionis, et racionem anno ad annum de bonis pupillorum coram vero ipsorum tutore facere tenetur.

[a] *nerunt* below the right margin; [b] below a floral motif sketched with a different pen than the one used by the scribe of the base text.

[51] De qualibet querimonia et testimonio, quod ad iudicium pervenerit.

·LI· Omnis querimonia et testimonia, que cum criminosis violenciis cum clamore ad iudicium, in facto manifesto deprehense et deducte fuerint, virum metseptimum [s] protestare oportet circa ius pacis, exceptis vulneribus, que monomachalia non fuerint. Manifestum | factum ibi esse dicitur, ubi vir captivatur cum furtu aut spolio, deprehensus ducitur ad iudicium cum clamore. Insuper eciam manifestum factum ibi esse dicitur, ubi viro cutellus aut gladius, aut alia sica in sua manu deprehensa fuerit, cum qua pacem infregit, aut si in fuga facti deprehensus fuerit, et captivus ad iudicium cum clamore ductus fuerit. Hunc actor metseptimus vincere debet circa ius pacis. Et si factum manifestum cum viro ad iudicium deductum fuerit, stuprum et obsidium, et irruen-
f. 98 ciam domicilii, homicidium, furtum, spo | lium, probat homo protestando metseptimus. Si vir de istis conqueritur, extunc sua querimonia sic debet procedere: "Domine iudex, ego conqueror Deo et vobis, quod hic homo iste venit intra municipalia, et in me pacem violavit, et me stupravit corpore et rebus et honore muliebri, de quo sufficiens habeo testimonium per eos, qui meum clamorem audierunt, et ostendere volo factum, ut de iure teneo aut debeo, et requiro in sentencia diffinitiva, quomodo ipsum vincere debeam, ut michi proficiat in iure meo". Extunc ille petit [s] satisdacionem, | si vult, quam sibi facere oportet, et dicat se de facto esse innocentem. Tunc tutor mulieris interroget in sentencia diffinitiva, si mulier violenciam melius protestare poterit cum hiis, qui clamorem suum audierunt, quam ille possit evadere, cum ad iudicium sit deductus. Tunc diffinitur iure, quod possit ipsum possibilius vincere cum hiis, qui suum clamorem audierunt, quam evadere possit. Et si hoc protestabitur, ut iuris est, adversarius collum demeretur. Idem vero iudicium super irruenciam domicilii iudicatur.

[52] [a]De obsidiis et spolio[a]

f. 98v ·LII· Hic stat Cunradus et conqueri[b] | tur super Heinricum Deo et vobis, nostro domino, regi aut duci, aut vobis, domine iudex ac toti universitati civitatis, divitibus ac pauperibus, quod ipse inter municipale venerit ad locum talem, ubi Cunradus pac[ific]e et quiete perfrui debuerat et sibi obsidium fecit in strata regia, et in regia {et in regia} pace, et in eo munici[pali] pacem infregit ac ipsum v[u]lneravit ac destruxit et spoliavit in corpore et rebus, et in eo talem strepitum perfecit, quem bene probare potest, cum ipse in eo pacem violavit et strepitum in eo commisit, tunc propria in persona vidit ipsum in perso|na propria et ipsum clamore proclamavit. Si hoc fatetur diligit, sin autem negabit, ipse eum vincere intendit per hos, qui suum clamorem audierunt ac suo testimonio. Et sicut ipsum in manifesto facto deduxit ad iudicium, sic in sentencia requirit, quomodo ipsum vincere debeat, ut sibi proficuum sit in suo iure.

[a] the rubric is not marked off; the title opens with an initial capital letter, which elsewhere marks the beginning of an article; [b] below a sketch of a floral flourish.

[53] De uno, qui vulneratus fuerit et ad iudicium in manifesto facto deductus fuerit.

·LIII· Si vulneratus vir ad iudicium cum clamore deductus fuerit in facto manifesto, et si ita inbecillis aut debilis fuerit, quod per tutorem ipsum querulari oportet et prolocutorem per senten | ciam petat, extunc tali modo sua procedat querimonia: "Domine f. 99
iudex, si me huic vulnerato dedistis pro advocato, extunc in sententia requiro, si per iusticiam insidias per aliquem pati debeam, quam iure terreri [s][a] debeam aut sustinere, cum suam causam propter iuris exigenciam teneo". Extunc sibi diffinitur, quod non. Extunc sibi petat correccionem. Cum obtinuerit coreccionem, tunc petat colloquium pro consilio, et cum colloquium habuerit, tunc requirat, qualiter suam querelam inchoare debeat, et hoc per sentenciam diffinitivam, ut sibi proficiat | in suo iure. Ex⟨tunc[b]⟩ diffinitur cum clamore. Tunc interrogetur sentencialiter, si requiri debeat de ore ad os, a quo suam habeat lesionem. Tunc sibi diffinitur, quod debeat. Extunc emittuntur duo scabini et cum ipsis preco, aut duo viri, qui iudicio astare consueverunt, qui ab ipso solo audiant, a quo sua receperit vel habuerit dampna, aut quis in eo pacis federa confregerit. Extunc requiritur sentencialiter, si requirere debeant circa iuramentum prestitum ac ius civitatis, quid ab eo audierint. Tunc unus interrogetur ad dicendum, quid ab eo audierint. | Audita responsiva, tunc in sentencia requiratur, f. 99v
si iam profecerit, cum sibi diffinitur, quod sic, et eciam secundus et tercius interrogetur. Extunc sibi diffinitur, quod profecerit. Extunc querelam incipiat: "Domine iudex, placeat attente audire". Tunc hic conqueritur super virum ·N· et super ·N·, quod ipsi venerunt intra municipale, et in eo pacem infregerunt, et ipsum vulneraverunt aut suum affinem proximum trucidaverunt, si homicidium fuerit, et ipsum spoliaverunt corpore et rebus, et pro eo iudicium petit. Extunc illi ter vocantur, quando | vocati per clamorem ter fuerint, tunc conqueratur ulterius et nominet malefactores, ut prius querulatum fuerit. Idem faciat tercia vice. Extunc inducie indicantur per noctem. Si tunc non conparent, describentur. Sin autem conparent, duellum in eis acquiri potest.

[a] in the Magdeburg Law of Pleszew: *tueri*; [b] interlinear superscript.

[54] De fure vel raptore obtestare in facto manifesto.

·LIIII· Quando vir furem aut spoliatorem protestare voluerit, qui cum manifesto facto ad iudicium cum clamore deductus fuerit, qui conqueratur sic: "Domine iudex, conqueror Deo et vobis super meum furem, quem cum apparenti furtu | captivavi et liga- f. 100
tum ad iudicium usque perduxi, quod venit intra meos quatuor angulos et subtraxit michi mea bona, super quo bonum habeo testimonium cum hiis, qui meum clamorem audierunt, et ipsum vincere volo iure meo ac meo testimonio, ut his hic michi ius dictaverit. Et requiro, quomodo ipsum vincere debeam, ut michi proficiat in iure meo". Tunc sibi diffinitur metseptimus, si furtum presens fuerit. Idem iudicium fiat pro spolio et super raptorem.

[55] De eo, qui alterius prolocutor fuerit in iudicio.

·LV· Ubi vir alterius verbum loqui debet, ad quod | sentenciis scabinorum vel iure conpellitur in facto manifesto, dicat sic: "Domine iudex me dedistis illi homini prolocutorem, extunc requiro in sentencia, si ab aliquot pro eo inimicitias aut timorem habere debeam, quod verbum suum pro iuris loquar exigenciam, quantum melius possum ac valeo". Quando sibi hoc diffinitum fuerit, tunc sibi diffiniat correccionem, quod si ipsum in aliquo neglexerit, quod se corrigere poterit mecum aut per me aut alterum
f. 100v advocatum. Cum sibi hoc diffinitum fuerit, petit colloquium, si vult, et re | quirat in sentencia, quando querelam inchoare debeat, ut sibi proficiat in suo iure. Cum sibi hoc diffinitum fuerit, tunc in sentencia interroget, si lesus interrogari debeat, quis in eo pacem infrigerit, si ita fuerit debilis, quot suum malefactorem nominare non possit. Cum igitur hoc diffinitum fuerit et ipsum iudex aut duo scabini aut duo viri, qui iudicio astare solent, viderint, requirat in sentencia, si ipsi causa iusticie dicere debeant circa iuramentum ipsorum et ius civitatis, quod notorium ipsis de hoc facto sit. Cum hoc | sibi diffinitur ab uno ad secundum et tercium, extunc requirat in sentencia, si iam profecerit. Cum sibi hoc diffinitum fuerit et pacis violator citatus per clamorem fuerit, ut iuris est, tunc dicat sic: "Domine iudex, placeat audire verbum suum". Tunc conqueritur vobis super hunc ·N·, quod ipsum in strata libera infestavit ac intra municipalia in eo pacem infregit, ac ipsum vulneravit et violenciam in eo peregit, quam probando ostendere potest, et ipsum depredavit corpore et rebus, et tantum recepit sibi,
f. 101 quod non minus valeat, nisi bene duellum mereatur. Et | super eo a vobis iustum petit iudicium. Extunc pacis violator proclamatur[a] primo et secundo et tertio, per nomen suum, ·N·, et iterum suam querimoniam renovet in hunc modum: "Vobis conqueritur super virum ·N·, quod ipse venit intra municipale in strata regia, in eo Dei pacem infringendo", et ipsum rebus et corpore sanitatis depredavit ac ipsum vulneravit et in eo strepitum fecit, quam apparenter potest demonstrare, et pro eo petit iudicium, et sic tercia vice faciat. Tunc ostendet vulnus et interroget in sentencia diffinitiva, si suum pacis violatorem in aliquo loco invene|rit, si ipsum licite arestare possit ex parte iudicii. Cum igitur diffinitum fuerit, tunc petat pacem, qui [*s*] sibi indici debet.

[a] *proclamator*: superscript *u* over *o*.

[56] De monomachali incitacione et iure duelli et testimonio monomachali.

·LVI· Qui monomachaliter suum equalem salutare seu alloqui voluerit, hunc iudicem petere oportebit, ut se intromittere possit de uno ⟨suo[a]⟩ pacis violatore, quem videat in presenti. Cum hoc sibi per sentenciam diffinitum fuerit, tunc eciam in sentencia requirat, per quem modum se de ipso intromittere debeat, ut sibi in suo iure proficere

k. 101v possit. Tunc sibi de iure diffinitur, curialiter per oram vestimenti. Et cum se de ipso intromittat, pronunciet sibi causam, pro qua se de ipso intromiserit, quod statim facere potest, si vult, aut pro eo habere colloquium. Tunc ipsum inculpare oportebit, quod pacem in eo infregerit aut in strata regia, aut in villa, qualiter infregerit, eodem modo queruletur super eum. Tunc ipsum iterum inculpet, quod ipsum depredaverit et eam vim in eo fecerit, quam bene probare poterit. Tunc vulnus aut cicatricem demonstret, si vulnus sanatum | fuerit. Tunc ulterius conqueratur, quod ipsum spoliaverit bonis suis et de ipsis sibi tanta receperit, quod bene duellum meretur. Hec tria criminalia facta omnia simul conqueratur, de quocumque horum trium de uno obliviscitur aut tacuerit, extunc suum duellum amisit. Tunc loquuntur ulterius: tunc ipsum solum, hoc est in persona propria, ipsum solus vidi, hoc est in persona propria, et ipsum clamore proclamavi. Si fateri voluerit, quod diligo, et si non fatebitur,
ipsum omni iure vincere volo, ut michi vulgus iudicaverit, | aut scabini, si sub banno f. 102
regio fuerit. Extunc ille petat satisdacionem, quam sibi facere debet. Tamen vir potest suam querimoniam meliorare ante satisdacionem, si voluerit. Facta satisdacione ille exhibeat suam innocenciam, hoc est iuramentum, quod ipsum iurare oportet, et iuramentum monomachale, si ipsum iure incitaverit et si ibi fuerit, hoc est perficere si potuerit pre inbecillitate sui corporis. Quivis vir potest se a duello excusare illi viro, qui sibi paris condicionis non fuerit. Ille autem, qui nobilioris nature fuerit, ille | preesse non potest [illi], qui deterioris nature fuerit, si ipsum alloquetur. A duello eciam cedere potest, qui post meridiem allocutus fuerit, nisi ante meridiem esset inchoatum, iudex eciam debet habere clippeum et gladium illi, super quem allocutum fuerit. A duello eciam potest accipere suos affines, si uterque suus affinis et ita consanguineitatis linea coniuncti fuerint, quod simul pungnare non poterint. Iudex eciam duos nuncios dare debet cuilibet hiis, qui pungnare debent, qui videant, ut habeant attinencia secundum
veram | consuetudinem. Coreum et linea indumentum [s] induere possunt, quantum f. 102v
placet. Caput et pedes antea nudi sint, in manibus cirotecas habeant, unum gladium nudum in manu et alio cinctus, aut duobus {et alio cinctus, aut duobus}, hoc arbitrio eorum committitur, et unum clippeum rotundum in manu, ubi non aliud quam lignum aut oreum sit, preter manu tectorium, quot potest esse ferreum, unam tunicam absque manicis super preparamenta. Eciam iudex debet indicere pacem circa collum, quod nemo eos inpediat circa duellum. Cuilibet ipsorum iudex unum virum | habeat, qui flangam ferat, qui ipsos in nichilo[b] impedire debet[c], nisi si unus ceciderit, quod flangam interponat, aut si vulneratus fuerit. Aut si flangam desiderat, hoc idem facere, nisi voluntas iudicis fuerit, non potest. Postquam circulo pax indicta fuerit, ambo debent circulum affectare, quem ipsis iudex licenciare debet. Finalia ferrimenta de vaginis gladiorum deponere debent, nisi a iudice licenciam habuerint. Ambo ornati debent ire ante iudicem, et ambo iurare debent: unus, scilicet actor, quod causa sit vera, pro qua
super ipsum querelam | fecerit, et respondens, quot sit innocens. Sic ipsis Deus adiu- f. 103
vet ad suum duellum. Sol eciam dividi ipsis debet recte, quando primo conveniunt.

Si vincetur ille, super quem conqueritur, tunc iudicetur sentencia capitali. Sin autem vicerit, dimittetur cum pena et emenda. Actor primo circulum intrabit. Si alter diu tardaverit, iudex debet ipsum per preconem vocare in illa domo, ubi se preperaverit, et duos scabinos cum ipso mittere debet. Sic citare[d] debent primo et secundo et tercio, et si ad terciam citacionem non venerit, tunc queru|lator surgat et se ad duellum exhibeat. Et statim percuciet duos ictus et semel fingat contra ventum, cum eo ipse suum adversarium devicit tali causa sive querela, pro qua ipsum fuerat allocutus. Et iudex sibi iudicare debet, sicut fuisset duello convictus, sic mortuus debet convi[n]ci, si in furtu aut rapina, aut in tali crimine occisus fuerit. Sin autem mortuus cum septem testibus protestari poterit, extunc ad duellum se non indiget exhibere contra ipsum.
f. 103v Sin autem alter agnatus mortui, quiscunque fuerit, loco ipsius per duellum | se exhibuerit, hic extinguet omne testimonium, quia tunc ipsum absque duello vincere non potest, ut superius est expressum. Sic[e] vincetur eciam et ille, qui ad duellum captivatus aut salutatus fuerit, aut promittit aut fideiussorie caucionem fecerit conparere et non conparuerit ad iustam responsivam.

[a] *suo* in the margin, probably due to the scribe's inattention; [b] in the manuscript: *michilo* (incorrect); [c] in the manuscript: *debent* (incorrect); [d] in the manuscript: *citati* (incorrect); [e] in the manuscript: *sin* (incorrect).

[57] De ⟨eo[a]⟩, qui alium ad iudicium aut mortuum vel vulneratum perduxerit, et ipsum pacis violatorem devincere voluerit.

·LVII· Quicunque occisum seu vulneratum virum captivum ad iudicium duxerit et ipsum pacis violatorem {pacis} accusaverit, per duellum | vel absque duello si non probaverit secundum iuris exigenciam ipse aut super ipsum, idem iudicium iudicari debeat, quod super illum procedere debuerat, ac si iudicio convictus fuisset, et hoc per iusticiam pacis. Si vulneratus vir hunc alloquitur, qui ipsum vulneravit, per duellum et si pro debilitate corporis duellum perficere non possit, et si tutorem ⟨non[b]⟩ habuerit, qui pro ipso pungnare velit, inducie sibi ordinari debent, quousque suum duellum perficere possit.

[a] in the interlinear space; [b] insertion in the interline, probably by the author of the base text.

[58] De viro, qui vitam aut manum pecunia redimerit.

f. 104 ·LVIII· Qui vitam aut manum pecunia re | dimerit, quod iure demeruerit, hic iure suo privetur.

[59] De fideiussoria caucione pro viro ad statuendum coram iudicio pro aliquo scelere.

·LIX· Qui eciam fideiusserit unum virum pro scelere ad statuendum ipsum coram iudicio, et ipsum statuere non potuerit, reconpensam ipsum solvere oportet, et sibi in suo iure non oberit illi, qui fuerat fideiussor, et nemo describi debet, nisi culpa ad collum sive ad manum sibi procedit.

[60] De suppellectili feminarum et quit ad hoc pertineat.

·LX· Si mulier recipit suppellectilia, ad quod spectant oves, ad quod | et modele [*s*] et omnia cibaria domestica, de quibus vir indiget ad unius anni revolucionem, que in sua possessione inveniuntur, ad mulierem pertinet medietas. Et cum viro uxor moritur, proxima sua congnata recipit suppellectilia, que debet donare viro suum stratum, ut stetit, cum uxor sua vixit, cum kossino, et suum sedile cum pulvinare, suum stratum cum lecto, kossinis et colcidra, suam sedem cum sedis tectorio, quod singulis diebus de super iacuit, suam mensam cum mensali et manuterio. Hec nulla recipit pulmentaria.

[61] De armis bellicis et suppel k. 104v lectili feminarum et sacerdotum iure ac monachorum.

·LXI· Mulier pro armis bellicis gladium mariti et suum runcinum vel dextrarium meliorem sellatum et meliora arma, que habuit pro corpore unius viri, cum decessit in sua potencia, deinde dare debet pulvinar bellicale, hoc est lectum et duo kossina, et duo lintheamina, et unum mensale, et duas pelves, unum manuterium. Hec sunt universalia bellica arma. Sed tamen aliqui homines diversa apponunt, que tamen ad ea non pertinent, sed quitquit ex hiis nomina|tis mulier non habuerit, ⟨ad [a]⟩ hoc, quod det, conpelli non potest, si iuramento probaverit pro qualibet re per se. Si vir ostendere patenter poterit, ibi vir nec mulier per iuramentum evadere potest. Ubi duo aut tres ad una bellica arma nati fuerint, senior recipit gladium pro se et cetera divident inter se equaliter. Et ubi pupilli annos pubertatis nondum attigerint, et eorum senior agnatus recipit arma bellica solus, et in eis tutor est puerorum quousque ad annos discrecionis pervenerint, extunc ipsis reddere tenetur et in super omnia ipsorum k. 105 bona, nisi racionem fecerit eis, quo ea ad eorum profectum converterit, aut per spolium aut per apparens infortunium et absque sua voluntate amiserit. Ipse eciam {eciam} est vidue tutor, quousque maritum ducet, si paris condicionis sibi fuerit. Post arma bellica mulier vite provisionem recipere potest et alia omnia, que ad suppelectilia pertinent, hoc sunt omnes oves et auce, ciste cum elevatis tecturis, omnia strata pulvinaria, kossina, linteamina mensalia, pelves, manuteria, lucibula, kandelabra, semen linii et linum, et omnia muliebria vestimenta, annuli et brachialia et crinalia, | psalteria et omnes libri, in quibus mulieres legere consueverunt, qui ad Dei cultum pertinent, sedilia ac scrinia, tapecia, dorsalia, vela tectoria, balneamina et omnia pepla, et alia ornamenta capitis muliebria, hoc est, quod ad femine spectat supellectile. Et ad hoc diversa sunt clenodia ⸠sui[b]⸡, que ad suppellectilia pertinent, singulariter ea non nomino, sicut sunt seticule, pectenes, forpices, specula. Sed tela non incisa, nec aurum, nec argentum non textum non pertinet ad feminas. Et quitquit extra prenominata in rebus inventum fuerit, pertinet ad k. 105ᵛ heredes. Si aliquit ex hiis obligatum fuerit circa vitam viri, qui mortuus est, exemet, si vult, ad quem de iure pertinet. Sacerdos dividet cum fratre, sed non qui monachus est. Si[c] puer in annis pubertatis religionem intraverit, bene potest exire, si vult, intra annos et ius observat feodale et terrestre. Sin autem vir, qui dum annos[d] pubertatis inplevit, religionem intraverit, hic se a iure terrestri ac feodali alienavit, et sua feoda vacant, quia scutum bellicum resignavit. Quod hoc possit protestari per hos, cum quibus similem vitam visus est suscepisse.

[a] written on the erasure, not by the author of the base text; [b] dots under word (crossed out); [c] in the manuscript: *Sic* (incorrectly); [d] in the manuscript: *annnos.*

[62] De diffinicionibus sente[n]ciarum. |

·LXII· De qua sentencia prius requiritur, hec prior diffiniri debet. Ambo actor et ille, hoc est super quem conqueritur, respondens est sive reus, possunt habere colloquia pro qualibet causa tribus vicibus, eousque ipsos preco revocet.

[63] De iudicio iudicum et locucione viri.

·LXIII· In omni loco iuris est, ut iudex iudicet cum sentenciis. Aperte vir non loquatur iudicio, postquam prolocutorem habuerit, nisi si iudex eum requisierit, si in verbo consenciat sui advocati, bene dicere potest, sic autem non sit, aut desuper petere colloquium.

[64] De fideiussoria pro bonis.

f. 106 ·LXIIII· Si homo et ubi vir pro pecunia | aut debito ⟨fideiussor [a]⟩ fuerit et moritur vir, sui pueri aut sui heredes non tenentur pro eo solvere. Si vir pro pecunia fideiussor fuerit, fideiussorem pecuniam solvere oportet solum, aut probare, quod pecunia sit integraliter persoluta.

[a] interlinear superscript, not by the author of the base text.

[65] De viro, qui fustibus aut baculis percussus fuerit, ita quod verbera inflata fuerint.

·LXV· Si vir cum fustibus aut baculis percussus fuerit supra dorsum aut supra ventrem, et verbera fusca aut flavea fuerint et inflata, si desuper pro teste iudicem habere poterit et homines, qui hoc viderunt et audierunt, ipse est duellum propius super eos acquirere, quam ipsi | eum evadere possent suo iure. Sin autem super caput et brachia percussus fuerit, quod alter ostendere non possit, illi homines melius ostendere possunt, quam ipse super eos probare possit suo iure. Sin autem fatentur, quivis amittit emendam et iudex acquirit suam penam. Sin autem verbera mortalia fuerint, respondere tenentur cum duello, qui pro eo iudicialiter inpulsati fuerint. Sin autem mortales [*s*] non fuerint, respondebit unus cum duello et alii respondebunt absque duello, quia ipsi evadunt cum suo iuramento.

[66] De hereditate, que mortuo domino permanet sine successore.

| ·LXVI· Quod si hereditas mortaliola [*s*] absque heredibus inventa seu reperta fuerit, f. 106v
regie cedet maiestati

[67] De viro, qui occisus fuerit et pueros tres aut plures habuerit.

·LXVII· Quod si vir, qui pueros habuerit, occisus fuerit, tres aut plures, et si vir unus iudicialiter pro ⟨eo[a]⟩ inpulsatus fuerit et evaserit, ut ius dictaverit, et si sibi super eam querimoniam vera satisdacio facta fuerit, non tenetur, nec debet ab aliis pueris inposterum pro eodem homicidio infestari.

[a] interlinear superscript, not by the author of the base text.

[68] De viro, qui alteri coram iudicio iurare debuerit.

·LXVIII· Si vir alteri iuraverit coram iudicio digne | et sine pena, potest superponere et deponere absque licencia, quod per hoc non amittit.

[69] De arestacione equorum.

·LXIX· Si aliquis arestat equm et dicit, quod sibi aliquis subtraxerit aut subtractus fuerit aut eo sit spoliatus, ad hoc se trahere debet, ut iuris est, extunc ille bene ad suum venditorem se trahere potest et venditorem nominare debet, super quem se traxerit, et iurare tenetur tacto sacramento, quod ad verum se trahat venditorem. Quocunque sibi nominaverit, ibi ipsum sequi oportet, non autem sequi ipsum debet ultra Mare Aquilonis. Et si sibi defectus fuerit et neminem pro se habuerit respondentem, utpote
f. 107 | venditorem habere poterit, ut se coram iudicio iactitavit, et tunc sibi fideiussorie faciat caucionem iudi⟨ci[a]⟩ pro pena et pro expensis, quas adversarius suus expendit, et diem nominare, quando ibidem debeat pervenire. Sin autem dixerit, quod equm in foro communi aut libero emerit, extunc suam pecuniam, quam pro eodem equo dedit, integraliter ammittit, et illi suum equm reddere oportet, et nullam penam pro eo ammittit.

[a] interlinear superscript by the author of the base text.

[70] De pena iudicis et hereditate[a].

·LXX· Quando iudex suam extorquet suam[b] penam, ulterius nec aliquam super hanc penam potest extorquere. Et si vir bona iudicialiter alloquitur, ut iuris | est, vel hereditatem, pro eo non indiget iudici dare quicquam, cum ipse sibi ad iusticiam iuvare teneatur. Et si homo suam querelam tenere promiserit, etsi per bonum pacis medio tempore concordatum fuerit, pro eo non plus ammittat, quam iudex acquirit suam penam.

[a] followed by a punctuation mark, three dots, another sign and one dot; [b] traces of a word having been erased.

[71] De viro, qui vulneratus aut percussus fuerit et querulare noluerit.

·LXXI· Vir, si vulneratus aut trucidatus fuerit et conqueri noluerit, iudex ipsum conpellere nec ad aliquam[a] potest querimoniam ultra suam voluntatem.

[a] originally *aliquem*, amended later to *aliquam* by a different hand.

[72] De bonis illius, qui ad mortem condempnatur aut qui est descriptus.

·LXXII· Et si vir descriptus fuerit et ad penam | mortis iudicatus fuerit, sua bona[a] nullus recipere habet, quam sui veri heredes. f. 107v

[a] originally *bonas*, with *s* erased probably by the author of the base text.

[73] De viro, qui pueros habeat et moritur, et bona habuerit nulli donata.

·LXXIII· Quando vir moritur, qui habeat[a] pueros et si bona donata nulli habuerit, sibi succedunt pueri, si equalis sibi nature fuerunt. Et si ex hiis pueris unus decesserit, mater sibi in sua parte succedit. Et mater cum hiis bonis nichil facere potest absque heredum consensu ac voluntate.

[a] in MS *hebeat*.

[74] De etate puerorum, quando tutores eligere possunt.

·LXXIV· Quando puer est duodecim annorum, | tunc potest eligere pro sua voluntate quem voluerit pro tutore. Et qui suus fuerit tutor, matri [[a]] ⊦facere[b]⊣ racionem facere habet et adolescenti, quit cum bonis factum fuerit.

[a] erasure; [b] crossed out by the author of the base text.

[75] De viro, quomodo suam libertatem possit probare.

·LXXV· Si alloquitur vir aliquem, quod suus sit illiber, [a-]si potest suam libertatem[-a] si potest suam libertatem protestare, propius est evadere, quam ille ipsum vincere possit. Libertatem suam vir probare potest cum tribus congnatis et tribus agnatis, sic metseptimus esse debet, sive sint viri sive femine. Et hoc scire debet ⟨nota[b]⟩ quilibet legens, ubi scribitur agnatus, designat ex parte patris et ex parte gladii. | Et ubi scribitur congnatus, ex parte matris desingnatur. f. 108

[a–a] words partly erased; [b] in the right margin by the author of the base text.

[76] De pecunia ludo aut taxillis acquisita.

·LXXVI· Si servus bona domini sui perluserit taxillis, aut obligat aut vendit, dominus bene potest arestare denuo iure, ut se ad ea bona trahat, ut iuris sit. Sin autem propria bona sua deluserit, aut quocunque modo a se alienaverit sua voluntate, dominus super ea nichil alloqui potest, quia servus solvere tenetur, et sic domino pro bonis servi non est licitum respondere. Si eciam aliquis conqueritur super aliquem pro debito aut pecunia ludo seu taxillis acquisita, pro eo sibi non habet respondere. Sin autem | servo suus equs, vel alia bona sua furtive, aut spoliando recepta fuerint absque culpa servi in domini servicio, hoc oportet dominum solvere servo, et pro eo oportet dominum respondere, si super eo queruletur.

[77] De bonis, que alicui danda sunt ad servandum in deposito.

·LXXVII· Quicumque alteri bona sua dederit ad servandum, aut in deposito posuerit, si sibi subtracta fuerint, aut spoliatus eis fuerit, aut conbusta, vel si mortuum fuerit, si equs vel pecora fuerint, non debet aliquot dampnum pro eo sustinere, si presumpserit
f. 108v iurare, quod absque sua culpa amissum fuerit. Sed quid viro concessum aut | obligatum fuerit, hoc in destructum reddere tenetur, aut solvere secundum suum valorem. Sin autem moritur equs aut pecus infra obligacionem absque illius culpa, cui obligatum fuerat, si hoc probaverit, et si iuramentum pro eo prestare presumpserit, quod sine sua culpa decessit, non solvit, sed suam reconpensam amittit, in qua sibi fuerat obligatum.

[78] De eo, qui se a descripcione iuramento expurgavit.

·LXXVIII· Qui se extraxerit a descripcione et solutus, diiudicatus fuerit, iudex tamen in eo suam optinet penam. Et si sibi iudex fateri noluerit, ipse eum | bene deponere [potest] per unum, qui eodem interfuit iudicio, quia nec captivus iudicio conparuit, nec proclamatus. Sin autem iudex ipsum inposterum obiurare voluerit, ipsum in nullo ulterius obiurare potest, quam ad suam penam, si super eo testes habuerit, quod se extra descripcionem abiuravit.

[79] De viro, super quem querulatum fuerit pro debito.

·LXXIX· Si vir conqueritur super alterum pro suo debito cum testibus, hoc bene potest obtinere cum viris fidedignis, qui in suo iure non possunt reprobari. Ita tamen, si
f. 109 ille dicit se esse innocentem. Sin autem respondens | dixerit se debitum persolvisse,

extunc inpedit sibi suum testimonium. Hoc bene probare potest cum probis viris metseptimus tacto sacramento.

[80] De querela, que facta fuerit super aliquo et ipse pecierit satisdacionem.

·LXXX· Si super virum conquestum fuerit et satisdacionem pecierit, alter eam sibi negare non potest, quin eam sibi faciat, si ipsum per sentenciam ad hoc co[m]pulerit. Sin autem satisdacionem fecerit sibi, ad suum ius non nocet, nec ille plus lucra[tur] cum satisdacione, qui eam petit, nisi quod ipsum nullus amicorum suorum inpedire a modo potest pro hac causa. Satisdacione facta | suam querimoniam meliorare non potest.

[81] De facto manifesto, quod ad iudicium fuerit.

·LXXXI· Omnis querela, que ad iudicium[a] pro capitali crimine in facto manifesto deducta fuerit, debet conqueri cum clamore propter factum manifestum, quod ostendi debet. Manifestum factum ibi est, ubi vir cum furto aut preda captivus ad iudicium deductus fuerit cum clamore. Item factum manifestum eciam est ibi, ubi unum cum gladio aut cultello aut alia sica in manu deprehenderit, cum quo pacem infregit, aut si in fuga facti captivatus fuerit et capti | vus ad iudicium deductus fuerit cum clamore. f. 109v
Hunc actor metseptimus vincere debet circa ius pacis, si factum manifestum cum reo ad iudicium deductum fuerit.

[a] in MS *iuducium*.

[82] De iudicio burgravii.

·LXXXII· In[a] iudicio burgravii Meydeburgensis potest vir pro debito bene querulare super actorem, aut oporte[t] ab uno iudicio burgravii ad aliud iudicium suam sequi querelam, ita quod semper suo adversario denunciet. Si autem super virum querimonia cum testimonio facta fuerit in eodem iudicio pro debito, et si dicit, quod persolverit, hoc probabit per homines fidedignos, quam ille ip|sum vincere possit, quod facere potest incontinenti, si vult, aut per sex ebdomadas [[b]] in iudicio sculteti. Sin autem vir iuramentum unica manu prestare debet, quod [*s*] in eodem iudicio facere oportet.

[a] letter *I* in *In* 5.5 lines in height; [b] erasure, c. 18 words in length.

[83] De iudicio iudicis.

·LXXXIII· Iudex[a] debet iudicium exercere, et id temptare cottidie in vero iudicii loco, nisi sit, quod vir absque testibus conqueri voluerit, quod statim iudicare potest sine mora. Reconpensam et emendam et penam iudicis solvere debent ad diem, ut fuerit diffinitum, ut tunc pagamentum consuetum fuerit, reconpensam et emendam actori et penam iu | dici. f. 110

[a] letter *I* in *In* 8 lines in height.

[84] De fiscacione seu publicacione bonorum.

·LXXXIV·[a] Si viro sua bona publicata seu fiscata fuerint iure, in eo ille possideat, qui hoc in fiscacionem deduxit cum fiscacione tribus diebus et tribus noctibus. Insuper in eo debet conmedere et bibere cum fiscacione, similiter et dormire. Deinde debet coram iudicio pronunciare tribus vicibus semper ad duas ebdomadas, ad quartum iudicium iudex sibi pacem desuper formare debet, et sibi debet appropriare, et sentenciis scabinorum vendere. Extunc vendere potest cum scitu. Si tunc aliquit ultra suum debitum superfuerit, eo cum scitu | illi reddere debet, cuius fuit hereditas. Sed si deficit, agat ulterius.

[a] exceptionally, the number of the article is in the inner margin.

[85] De bonorum arrestacione, similiter et equorum.

·LXXXV· Si vir [alloquitur] aliqua bona, pannos vel quitquit suarum rerum fuerit, quod sibi subtractum aut raptum fuerit, ad hoc se unica manu trahere debet et iurare debet tacto sacramento, quod tunc suum fuit et nunc suum sit, cum sibi subtractum seu raptum fuerit. Sin autem equus [fuerit], quem vir alloquitur, quod sibi subtractus sit, aut ⌈a [a]⌉ eo spoliatus sit, ad hoc se trahere debet, cum suo dextro pede calcare debet equo
f. 110v super suum pedem anteriorem, et | sinistra manu equm capere per dextram aurem, et petere debet reliquias et prolocutorem. Et iurabit equo tacto sacramento super caput, quod tunc suus fuerit et nunc suus sit, cum sibi subtractus aut eo depredatus fuerit. Et tunc ille ad suum se trahat venditorem et ipsum iurare oportet super sanctos, quod trahat se cum equo ad verum venditorem, ibi eum sequi oportet, nisi trans Mare Acquilonis. Sin autem dicit, quod equm emerit in foro libero et venditorem habere non possit, tunc equm amittit et argentum pro eo datum, et non amittit aliquam penam.

[a] crossed out by the author of the base text.

[86] Si vir conqueritur post | debitum a manu mortua.

·LXXXVI· Si vir conqueritur super virum pro debito a manu mortua, et ipsum infestare voluerit secundum edictum iuris, hoc facere potest unica manu tacto sacramento, si ille consenserit. Sin autem dixerit hic, super quem querimonia prolata fuerit, quod de debito nesciat vel in eo non sit obligatus, aut quod persolverit, hoc oportet iuramento probare metseptimus tacto sacramento.

[87] De viro, qui probabiliter aut scienter contra alium ad iusticiam se exhibuerit.

·LXXXVII· Si vir cum scitu contra alium ad iusticiam se exhibuerit, et alter noluerit aut spre | verit, et vulneret illum non querulando absque iure, et ille, qui vulneratus sit, inveniat defensionem et vulneret illum mutuo, et hic, qui primo vulneravit suum adversarium, primo ad iudicium veniat et conqueratur, alter, in quo pax sit violata, eciam postea veniat circa lucem diei et dicat, quod inicium illius fuerit et non suum. Si hoc, ut iuris fuerit, metseptimus protestabitur cum probis hominibus, qui viderunt et audierunt, qui presentes fuerunt, acquirit primam querelam. Unus vir potest filium suum eximere unica manu, qui est in pane suo non uxoratus, tacto sacramento, quod filius suus reus non sit. f. 111

[88] De mulieribus, que | in manifesto facto detente fuerint.

·LXXXVIII· Si femina deprehensa fuerit in facto manifesto in homicidio aut vulneribus duello dingnis, ac ipsam propius est vincere metseptimus cum hominibus fidedingnis, quam innocens fieri possit. Extunc ipsam iudicium pati oportet. Si autem vir querulatur super feminam pro homicidio aut vulneribus, quod eadem die factum fuerit aut visum, et si femine [s] fideiussorie caucionem fecerit supra ius, de quo femina propius est evadere cum hominibus fidedingnis metseptima, quam ultra aliquam vim in ea agere | possit. Si autem femina inculpatur pro querimoniis pernoctatis, eo propius est evadere femina unica manu tacto sacramento, quam aliquis eam vincere possit, aut aliquit inposterum contrarium pati. f. 111v

[89] De viro, qui habeat duplices pueros.

·LXXXIX· Si vir duplices pueros habuerit et primos antea eradicavit exponendo, et si postea secundis pueris aliquit dederit in suis bonis, et moriatur idem vir, hoc secundi pueri ante tollunt. Et quitquit superfluum fuerit aut supermanserit, hoc equaliter inter se dividunt, cum omnes equales sibi fuerint in natura. |

[90] De inproperacione scabinorum.

·XC· Si vir scabinum in scampno indecenter in iudicio bannito increpaverit, si hoc probaverit per suos consodales, qui audiverunt, illum oportet dare emendam scabino et iudici suam penam.

[91] De homicidio aut vulneribus.

·XCI· Si super virum querimonia facta pro homicidio fuerit aut pro vulneribus, et ipse accomodaverit circa suam hereditatem ad conparandum, et si profugus factus fuerit, quod non conparet, tunc debet vocari cum clamore, ut iuris est. Et si non conparet iudicio eodem, tunc debet describi et reconpensa super suam hereditatem iudicatur,
f. 112 et iudici sua pena. | Et eciam nullus alcius cogi potest caucionem facere fideiussoriam, quam se sua extendit reconpensa, nisi sit pro debito, quod maius sit.

[92] De contencione, que facta fuerit in die aut tempore noctis.

·XCII· Si casu contencio oritur clara die, si probus ⟨VII[a]⟩ vir in eo accusetur, qui ibi visus non fuerit, de quo propius est evadere metseptimus cum hominibus fidedingnis, qui presentes fuerunt, quam in eo duellum acquirere possit. Si autem super virum ydoneum circa noctis tempestatem pro homicidio aut vulneribus duello dingnis allocutum fuerit, quod noctis tempore factum sit, de quo propius evadet met|septimus cum hominibus probitate probatis, circa quos tunc fuit, cum hoc factum perpetratum est, cum sit de facto innocens.

[a] insertion sign + in margin, written in the inner margin.

[93] De peticione prolocutorum.

·XCIII· Quem vir pro advocato rogaverit, hunc suam causam tenere oportet iure, nisi se excusaverit cum pena.

[94] De supellectili feminarum.

·XCIIII· Et quando vir moritur, tunc uxori oves presentari debent ad sup[e]llectilia, ubicunque ierint. Anete, colcidre, vela, tecture curruum, olle picte eciam ad supellectilia pertinent.

[95] De iuramento incolatus.

·XCV· Nemo potest nec pro homicidio, nec pro vulneribus, nec pro aliquo [a] | debito suum probare incolatum. f. 112v

[a] below an outline floral flourish.

[96] De tutoribus pupillorum.

·XCVI· Quando pupilli suum verum tutorem habere [a] non poterint, eousque nullus ipsos ad aliquem [*s*] iudicialem responsivam deducere potest, nisi prius ad annos pubertatis pervenerint. Et si vir super alterum conqueritur, quod sibi abedificaverit [*s*] aliquit de suis bonis aut de hereditate, hoc ille possibilius optinet, qui habet in possessione unica manu, nisi ipsum cum testimonio allocutus fuerit. Extunc possessor cum testibus servat, si voluerit.

[a] an outline of a manuscule, the finger points to *habere*.

[97] De iuramento pro enormibus verbis coram iudicio. |

·XCVII· Ubi eciam vir iuramentum promiserit coram iudicio pro enormibus verbis aut depilacione, aut verberibus, aut effusione sanguinis, de quo solutus dimitti non potest, nisi voluntas fuerit iudicis et consensus.

[98] De civibus Meydeburgensibus.

·XCVIII· Eousque cives Meydeburgenses veram accionem seu responsivam tenuerint et se coram suo domino pontifice ac burgravio ac sculteto ad iusticiam se [*s*] exhibuerint circa civitatis ius, tunc nemo eos extra civitatem in alio iure occupare, seu contra eos agere in iudicio alieno [potest].

[99] De inpedimento coram iudicio.

·XCIX· Nullus alterum inpe | dire debet coram iudicio, postquam iudicium bannitum f. 113
fuerit cum iniuriis, talibus inpedimentis, que ipsum inpedire possint in sua querela, sicut clamore aut turpiloquiis, aut ceteris insolenciis. Si hoc contra iusticiam fecerit, et si paciens ipsum protestaverit cum iudice et scabinis, extunc suam acquirit emendam

et iudex acquirit suam penam. Si contingerit in iudicio castellani, tunc tria talenta demerentur, et in iudicio sculteti octo solidi. Et ubi homo suam emendam acquirit, ibi optinet iudex suam penam.

[100] De sculteto, si aliquem inpedierit in sua querela[a].

·c· Nunc[b] atten|datur super eo, si scultetus aliquem inpedierit in sua querela et sibi iusticiam non fecerit, et hoc sibi iniuste recusat. Si pro eo coram castellano aut advocato inpulsatus fuerit cum testibus, extunc cum testibus ipsum evadere oportet. Cum qualicunque testimonio super iudicem querulatum fuerit, tali ipsum iudicem testimonio evadere oportebit, sive sint scabini aut alii astantes iudicio. Sin autem hoc coram iudicio bannito actum fuerit, tunc melius vinci potest testibus iure, quam ipse testibus
f. 113v evadere possit. Sin autem vir cedere voluerit a testimonio et | ipsum inculpare pro suo scitu, de quo unica manu evadere potest. Quando querimonia super ipsum coram advocato fuerit pro hac causa, pro eo respondere tenetur sine mora, ita quod ibi sit iudicium bannitum, quia ipsum oportet ibi esse presentem, nisi legale inpedimentum ipsum occupaverit. Quod inpedimentum statim probare oportet. Si hoc non ostenderit et non nominaverit, et hoc per iusticiam facere denegaverit se excusare de sua iniuria, quam exercuit, et se ad iusticiam exhibere [debet], extunc condempnatur advocato in [c]decem talentis [c]idem | advocatus ⟨scultetus [d]⟩ et illi suum debitum, de quo denegavit, facere iusticiam, et medio quo illa [*s*] non solvit solus, aut se iure excusaverit iudicio proximo, tunc nullus iudex esse potest, nisi se ex hac culpa eximerit, secundum ut est premissum. Sin autem pro facto criminali, pro quo iudicium facere recusavit, sicut pro vulneribus aut homicidio, aut furto, aut spolio, aut ecclesie violent[i]a, aut incendium [*s*], aut hiis similia [*s*], que crimina capitalia tanguntur, idem iudicium super eum, quod super illum ire debuerit, pro eo nec reconpensam, nec aliquit facere potest, si in
f. 114 hiis vincitur, ut iuris est. Sin [c] autem [e] | Sin autem [*s*] unus vir pro debito in captivitatem publicam presentatus fuerit ad tenendum iure, si ipsum amiserit aut si evaserit absque sua culpa aut negli[g]encia pro crimine, quod transit ad collum, pro eo solvet integram reconpensam. Sin autem pro manu, tunc mediam solvit reconpensam et hoc ipsum iuramento probare oportet tacto sacramento, si sibi parcere noluerit, quod ipsum absque omni sua culpa amiserit. Integra reconpensa ⟨·nota·⟩[f] facit decem et octo talenta, media reconpensa facit novem talenta.

[a] the rubric extends over three lines; it shares the last two of them with the text of the article; [b] *N* decorated with a floral flourish; [c] below an outline of a floral flourish; [d] superscript over advocatus written in a hand identical with the annotation to Article XLVIII; [e] in the lower section of margin wrapped up in floral flourishes *quartus quintus*; in the lower right corner of the page crossed-out unus; [f] in the margin.

[101] Iudi[a-]cium super advocato[-a].

·CI· Nunc de advocato atten|datur, si non iuste iudicaverit, cum sibi querulatur, et hoc propter amorem aut munera, aut ob aliquam causam dimittit, vel si solus noxam fecerit iniustam, quod de iure facere non debuit, postquam ad iudicem electus sit ius confortare et iniurias suffocare. Si querela super ipsum in suo iudicio facta fuerit, tunc scultetus iudex esse debet super advocatum et per hoc cogitur cum sentenciis, quod ante ipsum oportet respondere, ut inposteri[u]s patebit. Petat advocatum surgere per sentenciam, quod super ipsum habeat querulare et per sentenciam | petat, ut alium f. 114v
iudicem ponat loco suo, quod ipsum facere oportet. Et tunc locet scultetum, qui sibi iudicare debet simili modo, ut advocatus super scultetum iudicare debuit. Eodem modo scultetus iudicet advocatum. Idcirco advocatus iudicium bannitum habere absque sculteto non potest, quia coram eo iure se debet exhibere, si super ipsum aliquis voluerit querulare. Si hoc contra iusticiam anno et die recusaverit, tunc domino terre iudicium vacat, quod habuit, et regi bannum, si prosecutus fuerit cum veris sentenciis.

a–a in the second line, in the text of the article itself.

[102] De irruencia domiciliorum. |

·CII· Si aliquis irruenciam domicilii fecerit nocte aut die, et si ille eum detinuerit in facto manifesto, et ipsum captivum cum clamore ad iudicium perduxerit, si super eo homines, qui suum clamorem audierunt, habuerit metseptimus suorum vicinorum, factum ostendere possit, ut iuris sit, illi ad collum transit. Sin autem manifestum factum ostendi non potest, extunc ille propius est evadere metseptimus, quam per eum vinci possit.

[103] De obsidiis et quod femine stuprantur.

CIII Obsidia et quod femine stuprantur, et irruenciam domiciliorum burgravius iudicat | et nullus alter nec scultetus. Si irruencia domicilii probabiliter potest ostendi cum f. 115
vulneribus et cum vulneratis edificiis, si super hoc iudicem et homines, qui clamorem audierunt, habere potuerit in testimonium, oportet desuper respondere cum duello, quam cum iuramento evadere possit.

[104] De promissione querele tenenda.

·CIIII· Et si vir querelam suam tenere promiserit, et si tempore medio concordia facta fuerit, extunc pro eo non plus amittit, nisi iudici dat suam penam.

[105] De debitis ex parte patris.

·CV· Si vir conquerulatur super alterum pro de|bito, quod sibi a patre suo teneatur, ipse debet super eo certificari, ut iuris est. Sin autem iurare voluerit, quod pater suus debitum persolverit, hoc ipsum facere oportet metseptimum post manum mortuam. Sin autem dixerit, quod ipsum persolverit, hoc iurabit ⊦metseptimus[a]⊣. ⟨tercius [b]⟩

[a] *septimus* crossed out and with dots underneath, by a different hand in the margin; [b] *tercius* probably as alternative to *septimus*, by a different hand in the margin.

[106] De pecudibus, que noxam inferunt.

·CVI· Si aliquis habuerit equm vel canem aut aliud pecus quidcunque, quod loquela careat, et noxam sive dampnum fecerit, sin autem dicit suum non esse dampno perpetrato, sibi in suo iure non nocebit.

[107] De eo, qui spoliat civitates aut suos concives.

f. 115v | ·CVII· Si aliquis spoliaverit cives suos, qui proprium aut feodum aut hereditatem intra municipale habeat et si hic non prehabita querela [a] faciat ante dominum terre vel ad suum iudicem, illi sua edificia abiudicare supra curiam suam et secari, et illa edificia erunt communia et omnibus publicantur hominibus. Sin autem edificium iudicialiter fiscatum fuerit, ita quod ibi puella aut femina stuprata fuerit intra illud edificium, debet resecari et abinde[b] nullas duci.

[a] in the margin a minute outline of a floral motif; [b] *e* on the erasure.

[108] De iuramento Iudeorum.

Hoc est illud iudicium et illud iuramentum, cum quo aut per | quod Iudeus iurare sive evadere debet Christianum[a], quot scriptum est in iure inperatorum. Ipse debet

verti contra solem seorsum, stare nudipes debet super sedem unam, indutus clamide esse debet et pilleum Iudaicum habere debet super caput. Si lapsus ter fuerit, totiden fertonem ammittit. Et si quarto manet in causa reus, tunc dicit ille, qui sibi predicit iuramentum[b]: "Ego te moneo, ·N·, Iudee, per has tres litteras et per hanc legem, quam Dominus dedit Moysi in tabula lapidea in monte Sinai, quod liber iste aut hoc rodale verum ac iustum sit, super quem aut tu, Iudee, iurare[c] debes huic viro | Christiano[d], ·N·, f. 116
pro tali culpa sive pro qua te huc ad iudicium deduxerit". Extunc sic iurare debet, et sic sibi predicetur, ut sequitur [e].

[a] *Xpianum*; [b] an outline of a bearded face; [c] below a floral motif; [d] *Xpiano*; [e] two floral motifs.

[109] Sic iurabit [a].

Quod tu in hac causa reus non sis, qua te hic idem vir Christianus[b] inculpet, quod te Deus adiuvet. Idem Deus, qui celum et terram creavit, aerem et rorem, montes cum vallibus, frondes, flores ac gramina. Et si sis reus, quod terra te absorbeat, que Dathan et Abyron absorbuit, et si reus fueris, quod te venenum ac gutta ac lepra invadat, que precibus Elyzey Naaman Syrum dimisit et Yezi d [*s*] invasit. Et si [c] reus fueris, quod te | ignis conburet celestis et caducus invadat morbus, et sanguinis invadat fluxus. Et si reus fueris, quod tu pereas in tua anima et in tuo corpore et in tuis rebus. Et si reus es, quod ad sinum Abrahe nunquam perveneris et tibi accidet, ut uxori Loth, que transmutata fuit in effigiem salis, dum Sodoma pereiit et Gomorra. Et si reus es, quod ad sinum Abrahe nunquam pervenies [*s*], et eciam ad resurreccionem nunquam pervenies, ubi Christiani[d] et Iudei et gentiles ante Creatorem omnium rerum resurgent. Et si reus fueris, quod te lex deleat, quam Dominus [c] | dedit Moysi in monte Synai, quam f. 116v
Deus solus suo scripsit digito supra lapideam tabulam, et te confundat omnis scriptura, que scripta est in quinque libris Moysi. Et si tuum iuramentum non iustum nec mundum fuerit, quod te deleat Adonay et sua deitatis potencia. ⊦Amen[e]⊣[f]

Explicit liber iuris municipalis domini Nicolai viri famosi, civis Sandomiriensis, dicti Paczonow.

[a] an outline of a bearded face with a raised hand; [b] *Xpianus*; [c] below an outline floral flourish; [d] *Xpiano*; [e] crossed out by the author of the base text; [f] the remainder of the line filled with an outline floral flourish.

Incipit de Inperio, quomodo terre Saksonie ius suum ab inicio statutum fuerit et confirmatum.

[110] | Nunc placeat audire et intelligere, quod presens scriptum informat ex relacione veridica. Primo de Imperio et quomodo terre Saksonie ius suum ab inicio statutum fuerit et confirmatum in suo iure, sicut ab antiquo tempore Babilonia tenebat. Ibi stetit Inperium et regnabat potencialiter per omnia regna, quia Nemrot gentilis rex primo Babiloniam edificavit et circu[m]cinxit civitatem [a] nimia amplitudine, et edificaverit in ea, innumerabiles ac altas municiones, unde usque in presens ius municipale nun-
f. 117 cupatur. Et ibi erat manens idem rex Nemrot ac duces | multi et ceteri viri famosi, qui nunc imperatores vocantur, et omnes uno utebantur iure, quod municipale ius appellabatur, ut bene in libro presenti patebit. Unde nomen sortiebatur absque qualibet transmutacione.

[a] erasure.

[111] De Inperio.

Nunc dicetur quamdiu {quamdiu} steterit Inperium steterit [*s*] in potencia. Potencialiter absque permutacione usque Greciam a tempore Darii Secundi, aut ultimi, quem rex Allexander maximis ac sediciosis devicit bellis. Tunc transmutatum fuit inperium a Babilonia et stetit in Constantinopolim [*s*] usque ad illud tempus, quod [*s*] se Roma de Inperio intromisit, et po|tencialiter obtinuit usque ad presens tempus ex parte beati Petri, qui caput est Cristianitatis. Cum Inperium Romam versum fuisset, ibi stetit, ut patet in premissis. Tunc Christiani absque iure fuerint, idcirco quivis pro sua in terris faciebat voluntate, aut quid facere poterat aut perficere, et hoc absque querela permansit et per iudicium inultum, quia nullum fuit ius, ubi quis iudicium consequi posset, et usque ad illud tempus perseveravit, quo se Roma de imperio intromisit. Et ipsi ibi
f. 117v venerunt et iusticiam consecuti fuerunt, et ibi exhibuerunt manus, | unde manupacem optinuimus usque in presens. Tunc Romani convenerunt et decreverunt deliberando, quomodo regna sibi subiugare possent. Et omnes unanimi consensu et pari consilio concordaverunt, quod edificarent castra in terris, unde terras sibi subiugare possent. Et cum hoc fecissent, tunc arbitrati sunt, quomodo castra confortarent, ut ipsis esset in iuvamen. Et illos acceperunt, qui nomen militale habuerunt, et eos super castra locaverunt cum tali iure, ut hucusque ius castrense tenet in castrensi feodo. Extunc delibe|raverunt, qualis statuta iuris terris constituere vellent, et terris tale ius constituerunt, quale adhuc terra Saksonie protestatur, per inperatorem Constantinum et per imperatorem Carolum. Nunc audire et intelligere potestis pro principibus ac baronibus, et hiis omnibus, qui nomen militale digne sortiuntur, quomodo ipsi cum Romanis sint arbitrati, quod scire vellent, quo iure Inperium deberet permanere. Et statuerint regi ius cum consilio, quod ipse sedem regiam Rome regere debeat ex parte beati Petri
f. 118 cum gladio temporali, unde adhuc advocatus Romanus appellatur. Idcirco | vitam

demereri non potest, nec in suo honore debilitari, nisi tribus de causis, que patebunt in sequentibus. Quorum primum est, si sedem Romanam destruere vellet. Secundum est, si contra fidem faceret Katholicam. Tercium, si legittimam sine reali causa dimitteret uxorem. Quorum horum trium, [si] de uno, quod absit, convictus fuerit, extunc deberet iudicari, caput sibi deberet amputari cum aureo dolabro, propterea quia ipse est rector gladii temporalis, cum quo habet iudicare omnes hos, qui noxam fecerint, aut qui caput demerentur. Et insuper omnibus conmisit, qui iu|dicis nomine censentur, cum eo protegere viduas et pubillos [*s*], et domos Dei, et omnes iniurias humiliare et iusticias confortare. Insuper iudicium commisit omnibus iudicibus temporalibus, sive secularibus, cum eo iudicare super omnes hos, qui in maleficiis deprehensi fuerint in facto manifesto, ad iudicium deducti et convicti fuerint, ut ius dictaverit. Ibi omnes iudices soli iudicare debent, vel preco ipsorum loco. Eodem modo ut iudices temporalem gladium habent a rege. Eodem modo sacerdotes spiritualem gladium habent
ab Apostolico. Nunc | attendatis, quis inperatorem iudicare debeat, si ex hiis tribus f. 118v
premissis in aliquo convictus fuerit. Hoc facere debet Sacri Impereii [*s*] Renensis palatinus, qui imperatori ac Inperio ex arbitrio positus fuerat. Simili modo, ut palatinus imperatorem debet iudicare, eodem modo iudicet burgravius marchionem pro suo excessu, et scultetus burgravium.

[112] De mercatoribus.

Extunc mercatores dicebant ad imperatorem, quod libenter scire vellent, in quo permanere possent. Tunc indicavit ipsos imperator ⌊ad aq⌋ cum consilio Romanorum ad aquas | navipotentes, quod edificarent ibi civitates firmas cum muris et turribus. Tunc plus dicebant imperatori, quod libenter scire vellent, quo iure stare deberent. Extunc inperator dedit ipsis tale ius, quale cottidie in sua curia habere solebat. Et hoc confirmavit eis cum consilio Romanorum et cum veridicis singnis. Et suam manum exhibuit, quam apprehendit quidam mercator, et dexteram cirotecam de manu sibi deposuit, super quo pax beati Petri ipsis firmata fuit. Quod hucusque manet in exemplum, ubi
nove civitates edificantur aut fora, quod ibi crux ponitur super forum. In eo pro | batur f. 119
et apparet, quod de voluntate regis factum sit, cum municipale ius ab antiquo tempore hucusque permansit et confirmatum ab Inperio, et nomen obtinuit usque in presentem diem.

[113] De civitate Meydeburc.

Nunc attendatis de civitate Meydeburc. Cum primo Meydeburc locatum seu fundatum fuit imperatoris Ottonis Magni consilio, et cum terre arbitrio, et stabilitum

fuit in suo iure, sicut nunc tenet in iure municipali secundum consuetudinem antiquorum, et Hallis civitas ex ea fundata est, idcirco utraque uno utitur iure. Eapropter omnes de Polonia ac de Bohemia, qui sub iu|re locati sunt Teutunico et de marchia et de Myssenensi provincia, et de marchia Luziciensi, hii omnes ius suum in Hallis recipere debent, et de civitatibus, que in hiis districtibus locati sunt. Et si sentenciam ingnoraverint aut defectum habuerint in una sentencia, hanc oportet in Meydeburc querere. Idcirco, quia omne municipale protegit, quod iure terrestri fieri non potest, quod cum reprobata sentencia de marchia ad comitatum trahi possit, quia marchio secundum suum arbitrium aut propriam graciam iudicat, quod comes non facit, sed
f. 119v iudicat sub banno | regio. Hoc idem fit in omnibus civitatibus, ubi bannum regium est, quod vir demeretur tria talenta iudici feodato sub banno regio. Sin autem iudicatur sub banno regio, tunc sculteto demerentur octo solidi de iudicio cum sentenciis scabinorum. Idem fit burgravio. Scabini undecim esse debent, et scultetus sit duodecimus, quia burgravio primam sentenciam diffinire debet. Quia burgravius nullum bannitum iudicium absque sculteto habere potest, nec scultetus absque hiis undecim scabinis in vero loco iudiciali.

[114] De civitate Hallis.

Nunc attendatis de | hiis de Hallis, ubi reprobatam sentenciam recipere debeant, si ignoraverint, aut si sentencia reprobata fuerit. Hanc in Meydeburc recipere debent et Meydeburgenses ipsis dare debent ante quatuor scampna et scabinis ipsorum ius dari debent [*s*], quia inposterum oportet ipsos esse testes, si necesse fuerit, quod sentencia rite ac racionabiliter sit data absque qualibet contradiccione. Et ibi nuncii presentes esse debent, ubi sentencia diffinitur, ex utraque parte, ubi sentencia fuit reprobata, qui audierunt et viderunt, quod utrique iusticia fiat. Iudex ipsos in expensis procurare
f. 120 debet [in] eundo et redeundo. | Si sentencia sub banno regio reprobata fuerit, tunc debet reportari infra decem et octo ebdomadas. Sin autem sub comitis banno reprobata fuerit, tunc reportari debet infra duas ebdomadas, quia scultetus habet bannum a comite et sculteciam a domino terre. Idem vero habet burgravius bannum a rege, et iudicium a domino terre.

[115] De reprobacione sentencie.

Nunc attendendum est, si in Meydeburc reprobatur sentencia, quo aut ubi eam querere aut invenire deberent. Ipsi debent se trahere in Scharthow, ultra Elbe, et ibi accipiunt quatuor seniores viros, quos ibi invenire poterint. Hoc | idcirco, quia diucius stetit, quam Meydeburc, et Cesar Otto a tempore diuturno ducatum ex eo constituit, et omnes uno eodem iure constricti sunt. Tunc trahunt cum eisdem quatuor senibus, quos de Scharchow duxerunt et invenerunt, redeunt in Meydeburc ante palaciam ad curiam, que inperatoris Octonis Ruffi fuerat[a], qui palaciam ipsis formaverat, et in summi sine[b] templi, ut in premissis patet et in sequentibus apparebit, quia continue pro reprobata sentencia ad Inperium se trahere non potuerunt.

[a] in MS *fueerat*; [b] alternative reading: *sive*.

[116] De palacia.

Nunc attendatis per quem | modum ipse palaciam fecerit. Vocavit eosdem quatuor f. 120v
senes de Scharthow, et quatuor canonicos, qui prelaturas habent in summo: primus prepositus, secundus decanus, tercius episcopi vicarius, quartus cellarius. Insuper recepit quatuor barones, ecclesie maioris feodales in Meydeburc. Unus fuit marsalcus, secundus dapifer, tercius pincerna, quartus kamerarius. Insuper recepit undecim scabinos et scultetum duodecimum. Insuper recepit tres duces laycos, qui primi sunt in eleccione inperiali, et quartus, quem accepit supremus, fuit | advocatus ecclesie maioris in Meydeburc, hoc est burgravius. Tunc inperator accepit eosdem viginti octo viros prenotatus [s] et super sedes ipsos locavit palacie, et dedit eis potestatem ex parte sui, quecumque sentencia in Meydeburc diffiniri non posset, aut reprobaretur, ibi deberet recipi, et quitquid daretur rite ac racionabiliter pro iure municipali teneri deberet. Et cum sentencia ante palaciam data fuerit, tunc debet dari in signum hiis viginti octo [s], cuilibet [eorum], solidum aureorum, et quivis solidus debet valere duodecim solidos talis pecunie aut talium denariorum, cum quibus ibidem | consuetudo fuerit forisare. f. 121
Tunc hiis quatuor dantur quatuor marce, quod quivis marca debet duodecim marcas valere argenteas. Hoc datur hiis viginti octo. Hoc illi dare tenentur, quibus sentencia ad profectum vel ad utilitatem diffinita et inventa fuerit.

[117] Nunc attendatur, quantum plus dare oportet. Dare tenetur illi scabino suam emendam, cuius sentenciam reprobavit, quam diffinierat, si iuste inventa fuerat, et iudici suam penam. Sin autem ante consensum aliorum scabinorum sentenciam reprobata fuerit, tunc cuilibet scabino datur emenda et iudici pena, et quod fuerint emende, tot erunt et pene. [a]

[a] a floral motif.

Conclusio libri.

Iste liber finitus et de Teutunico translatus in Latinum per Conradum scriptorem, notarium quondam Sandomiriensem ac civis[a] dicte civitatis, ad peticionem viri famosi, domini Nicolai dicti de Paczonow, civis supradicte civitatis, qui fuit causa inciens, in cuius nomine est inchoatus. In eiusdem vero nomine est finitus, cui laus et gloria per infinita seculorum secula, Amen. [b]

Idem vero Conradus supliciter exhortatur diligenter quemque lectorem petens, cum
f. 121v in hoc libro ipsum legere contingerit, quit sibi displiciencie fuerrint [*s*], hoc sue | non inputet ruditati. Cum tamen per inperatores ac cesares idem liber sit constitutus, ac iuris constituciones, licet conpendiose, et [per] Constantinum, Iustinianum ac Carolum confirmatus. Ac eorum peticionibus per sanctos patres Apostolicos sit sanccitus, ac sub anathemate prohibitur, ne quis augmentando vel minuendo eundem librum in aliqua sua institucione vel diffinicione transponere, aut transmutare aliquatenus presumat, sed ipsum in eo vigore inviolabili mittere permanere [*s*]. Cum [*?*] eciam per falsam gramaticam mortale peccatum non conmittatur, et ideo, si mi|nus rethorice aliquit in eodem opusculo repertum fuerit, hoc peto non nimium ponderari, nec michi propter hoc improperari.

⊦Hec autem pacta sunt sub anno Incarnacionis Domini millesimo trecentesimo quinquagesimo nono, sabbato in vigilia benedicte Trinitatis ac in festo sancti Viti gloriosi martyris.⊣

Scriptum per manus Nicolai de Thessyn.

[a] alternative reading: *curie*; [b] a floral motif.

Bibliography

Archival Sources

Archdiocesan Archives of Gniezno, Shelfmark 104.

Jagiellonian Library in Cracow, Shelfmarks 168, 169, 170a, 399, 4405.

Kórnik Library of the Polish Academy of Sciences, Shelfmarks 800, 801.

Library and Archives of the Pauline Monastery in Częstochowa, Shelfmark AJG II-3.

Library of the Diocesan Seminary in Kielce, Shelfmark RK 45/28.

Library of the Russian Academy of Sciences in St Petersburg, Shelfmark F 143.

National Library in Warsaw, Shelfmarks 3068 III, 12600 III, 12607 III, BOZ 90.

National Library of Russia in St Petersburg, Shelfmark Lat. Q II 157.

Ossoliński National Institute, Shelfmark 832/II.

Sankt-Florian Monastery Library in Austria, Shelfmark 551/II.

State Archive in Przemyśl, Archives of Przemyśl City, Shelfmark 428.

University Library in Leipzig "Albertina", Shelfmark 951b.

University of Warsaw Library, Shelfmark 5.

Wrocław University Library, Shelfmarks II F 8, II Q 4.

Jan Łaski's *Statutes* and Other Old Prints

Cervus Tucholiensis Johannes, *Farraginis Actionum Iuris Civilis et provincialis, Saxonici, Municipalisq[ue] Maydeburgensis Libri septem* ... (Cracoviae, 1546).

Cervus Tucholiensis Johannes, *Farrago actionum civilium Iuris Magdeburgensis* ... (Cracoviae, 1531, 1535).

Commune Incliti Poloniae Regni privilegium constitutionum et indultuum publicitus decretorum approbatorumque ..., ed. Jan Łaski (Cracoviae, 1506).

Jagiellonian Library in Cracow, Shelfmark St. Dr. Cim. 8002–8003, 8004–8005, 8006–8007, 8008–8009, 8470.

The National Library in Warsaw, Shelfmark SD 57, 88, 211, 335, 350, 735.

University of Warsaw Library, Shelfmark Sd.612.523.

Wrocław University Library, Shelfmark St. Dr. 401097.

The Princes Czartoryski Library in Cracow, Shelfmark 30 III Cim.

Juliusz Słowacki Public Library at Tarnów, Shelfmark. SD 173.

National Museum in Cracow, Shelfmarks VIII–XVI.134.

Ossoliński National Institute, Shelfmarks XVI.F.4320, XVI.F.4654.

Jaskier Mikołaj, *Iuris Provincialis quo Speculum Saxonum vulgo nuncupatur Libri tres* ... (Samosci, 1602).

Jaskier Mikołaj, *Iuris Municipalis Maideburgensis Liber vulgo Weichbild nuncupatur* ... (Samosci, 1602).

Johannes Andreae, *Questiones mercuriales super regulae iuris* (Venetiae, 1490).

Printed Sources

Bandtkie Jan W., *Jus Polonicum, codicibus veteribus manuscriptis et editionibus quibusque collatis* (Varsaviae, 1831).

Behrend Jacob F., *Die Magdeburger Fragen* (Berlin, 1865).

Böhme Johann E., ed., *Diplomatische Beyträge zur Untersuchung der schlesischen Rechte und Geschichte*, 2.2 (Berlin, 1775).

Bourassé Jean J., eds., *Venerabilis Holdeberti primo Cenomanensis episcopi deinde Turonensis archiepiscopo opera omnia, tam edita, quam inedita accesserunt Marboni Redonensis episcopi, ipsius Hildeberti supparis opuscula*, (Jacques P. Migne, Patrologia Latina) 171 (Paris, 1854).

Daniels Alexander v. and Gruben Franz v., *Das Saeschsische Weichbildrecht. Ius municipale Saxonum. Erster Band. Mit Weltchronik und Weichbildrecht in XXXVI mit Glosse* (Berlin, 1858).

Ebel Friedrich, ed., *Magdeburger Recht*, Vol. II: *Die Rechtsmitteilungen und Rechtssprüche für Breslau*, Part 1: Die Quellen von 1261 bis 1452 (Köln – Wien, 1989).

Eike von Repgow, *Sachsenspiegel. Die Dresdner Bilderhandschrift Mscr. Dresd. M 32. Textband*, ed. Heiner Lück, coop. Thomas Haffner, Marion Perrin, and Jörn Weinert (Graz, 2006).

Eike von Repgow, *Sachsenspiegel. Landrecht*, ed. Karl A. Eckhardt, (*Monumenta Germaniae Historica. Fontes iuris Germanici antiqui.* Nova Series) 1.1 (Göttingen-Frankfurt, 1973).

Fokt Krzysztof, Speer Christian, Mikuła Maciej, eds., *Najstarsza zgorzelecka księga miejska 1305–1416 (1423). Edycja i komentarz*, cz. 1 [The Earliest Book of Municipal Court Records of Zgorzelec (Görlitz) 1305–1416 (1423): A Critical Edition and Commentary, Part 1] (Fontes Iuris Polonici) 5 (Kraków, 2017).

Gaupp Ernst Th., *Das alte Magdeburgische und Hallische Recht. Ein Beitrag zur deutschen Rechtsgeschichte* (Breslau, 1826).

Groicki Bartłomiej, *Porządek sądów i spraw miejskich prawa majdeburskiego w Koronie Polskiej* [The Constitution of Courts and Urban Matters According to Magdeburg Law in the Kingdom of Poland], (Biblioteka Dawnych Polskich Pisarzy-Prawników) 1, ed. Karol Koranyi (Warszawa, 1953).

Groicki Bartłomiej, *Tytuły prawa majdeburskiego* [Titles of the Magdeburg Law], ed. Karol Koranyi, *Biblioteka Dawnych Polskich Pisarzy-Prawników* [Library of Ancient Polish Jurists] 3 (Warszawa, 1954).

Jurek Tomasz, ed., "Najdawniejsze zapiski z księgi miejskiej Pleszewa (1428–1444)" [The Earliest Records in the Book of Pleszew Town Council (1428–1444)], in: *Wielkopolska dawniej i dziś. Studia, źródła i materiały* [Wielkopolska in the Past and Today: Studies, Sources and Materials], ed. Andrzej Gulczyński, (*Kwartalnik Historii Kultury Materialnej*) 60/3 (2012) (Poznań, 2011).

Kozak Adam, transl. and ed., *Najstarsza pleszewska księga radziecka: zapiski z lat 1485–1519* [The Oldest Volume of the Book of Pleszew Town Council: Records 1485–1519], (Wielkopolska Dawniej i Dziś) 4 (Poznań, 2014).

Laband Paul, ed., *Magdeburger Rechtsquellen. Zum akademischen Gebrauch herausgegeben* (Königsberg, 1869).

Leman Karl Ch., ed., *Das Alte Kulmische Recht, mit einem Wörterbuche* (Berlin, 1838).

Ludovicio Jacob F., ed., *Das Sächsische Weichbild in der lateinischen und jetzo gebräuchlichen hochteutschen Sprache aus alten bewährten Codicibus …* (Halle, 1721).

Łysiak Ludwik and Nehlsen-von Stryk Karin, eds., *Decreta iuris supremi Magdeburgensis castri Cracoviensis. Die Rechtssprüche des Oberhofs des deutschen Rechts auf der Burg zu Krakau, 1456–1481; 1481–1511* (Frankfurt am Main, 1995, 1997).

Maisel Witold and Zdrójkowski Zbigniew, eds., Bzdęga Andrzej and Gaca Anna, trans., *Prawo starochełmińskie 1584 (1394)*, (Teksty Pomników Prawa Chełmińskiego w Przekładach Polskich) 2 (Toruń, 1985).

Maisel Witold, ed., *Poznańska księga prawa magdeburskiego i miśnieńskiego* [The Poznań Book of Magdeburg-Meissen Law] (Wrocław, 1964).

Michał Bobrzyński, ed., *Ortyle magdeburskie. Przedruk homograficzny z kodeksu Biblioteki Kórnickiej* [*The Magdeburg Ortyle: A Homographic Reprint of the Kórnik Library Codex*] (Poznań, 1876).

Paweł Szczerbic, *Ius Municipale, to jest prawo miejskie majdeburskie nowo z łacińskiego i z niemieckiego* na *polski język z pilnością* i *wiernie przełożone* [*Ius Municipale*, or the Magdeburg Municipal Law: A New and Meticulously Accurate Translation from the Latin and the German], ed. Grzegorz M. Kowalski, (Bibliotheca Iagellonica. Fontes et Studia) 20 (Kraków, 2011).

Paweł Szczerbic, *Speculum Saxonum, albo prawo saskie i majdeburskie, porządkiem obiecadła z łacińskich i niemieckich egzemplarzów zebrane. A na polski język z pilnością i wiernie przełożone* [Speculum Saxonum or Saxon and Magdeburg Law, in Alphabetical Order, Collected from Latin and German Copies. A New and Meticulously Accurate Translation into Polish], ed. Grzegorz M. Kowalski, 1, (Bibliotheca Iagiellonica. Fontes et Studia) 29 (Kraków, 2017).

Piirainen Ilpo Tapani, Waßer Winfried, eds., *Der Sachsenspiegel aus Oppeln und Krakau*, (Schriften der Stiftung Haus Oberschlesien. Landeskundliche Reihe) 10 (Berlin, 1996).

Reczek Józef and Twardzik Wacław, *Najstarsze staropolskie tłumaczenie ortyli* magdeburskich [The Earliest Polish Translation of the Magdeburg ortyle] 1–3 (Warszawa, 1970).

Rymaszewski Zygfryd, ed., *Nieznany spis prawa chełmińskiego z przełomu XIV i XV wieku* [A Newly Discovered Manuscript of Chełmno Law from the Late 14th–Early 15th Century] (Łódź, 1993).

Stanisław Kuraś, ed., *Zbiór dokumentów małopolskich* [Collection of Lesser-Poland Documents], 3 (Warszawa, 1969).

Thüngen Wilhelm von, ed., *Das sächsische Weichbildrecht nach dem Codex Palatinus Nro. 461. Mit einer Einleitung als Inaugural-Dissertation* (Heidelberg, 1837).

Tzschoppe Gustav Adolf, Stenzel Gustav Adolf, *Urkundensammlung zur Geschichte des Ursprungs der Städte und der Einführung und Verbreitung deutscher Kolonisten und Rechte in Schlesien und der Oberlausitz* (Hamburg, 1832).

Uruszczak Wacław, Grodziski Stanisław and Dwornicka Irena, eds., *Volumina Constitutionum*, Vol. 1: 1493–1549, vol. 1. 1493–1526 (Warszawa, 1996).

Wasserschleben Hermann, ed., *Sammlung deutscher Rechtsquellen*, 1 (Giessen, 1860).

Witold Maisel, "Prawo magdeburskie miasta Pleszewa" [The Magdeburg Lawbook of Pleszew], *Studia i Materiały do Dziejów Wielkopolski i Pomorza* 9/1 (1963).

Monographs and Articles

Adamska Anna, "Away with the Germans and Their Language?", in: *Uses of the Written Words in Medieval Towns. Medieval Urban Literacy II*, eds. Marco Mostert and Anna Adamska (Brepols: 2014).

Ameisenowa Zofia, *Rękopisy i pierwodruki iluminowane Biblioteki Jagiellońskiej* [*Manuscripts and Illuminated Incunabula in the Jagiellonian University Library*] (Wrocław – Kraków, 1958).

Bardach Juliusz, "Pojęcie recepcji i jej zakres w dziejach państwa i prawa" [The Concept of Reception and its Scope in the History of State and Law] in: *Ars historica. Prace z dziejów powszechnych i Polski ofiarowane G. Labudzie* [Ars historica: Studies in World History and the History of Poland. A Festschrift in Honour of Professor Gerard Labuda] (Poznań, 1976).

Bardach Juliusz, "Recepcja w historii państwa i prawa" [Reception in the History of State and Law], *Czasopismo Prawno-Historyczne* 29/1 (1977).

Bartoszewicz Agnieszka, "Urban Literacy in Small Polish Towns and the Process of 'Modernisation' in the Latter Middle Ages" in: *Writing and the Administration of Medieval Towns: Medieval Urban Literacy I*, eds. Marco Mostert and Anna Adamska (Turnhout, 2014).

Bartoszewicz Agnieszka, *Piśmienność mieszczańska w późnośredniowiecznej Polsce* [Burgher Writing in Late Medieval Poland] (Warszawa, 2012).

Bernd Kannowski, *Die Umgestaltung des Sachsenspiegelrechts durch die Buch'sche Glosse*, (Monumenta Germaniae Historica, Schriften) 56 (Hannover, 2007).

Bily Inge, "Der Rechtsterminus Morgengabe im deutsch-polnischen Sprachvergleich (untersucht auf der Grundlage eines frühneuhochdeutschen und eines altpolnischen Textes der Magdeburger Urteile)", in: *Deutsch-slawische Kontakte – Geschichte und Kultur. Festschrift für Mária Papsonová*, eds. Michaela Kováčová, Jörg Meier, and Ingrid Puchalová, (Acta facultatis philosophicae Universitatis Šafarikinae) 12 (Kosice, 2011).

Bily Inge, "Die Rezeption des sächsisch-magdeburgischen Rechts in Osteuropa. Zum Analyseraster der Rechtstermini am Beispiel der Lexeme Burggraf und Lehen", in: *Kanzleisprache – ein mehrdimensionales Phänomen: Tagungsband für Prof. PhDr. Zdeněk Masařík, DrSc., zum 80. Geburtstag (Beiträge zur Sprachinselforschung)*, eds. Andrea Moshövel and Libuše Spáčilová (Wien, 2009).

Bily Inge, "Neb wykpildske prawo – to gest miestczke prawo", in: *Městské právo ve střední Evropě. Sborník příspěvků z mezinárodní právnické konference Práva městská Království českého*, 19–21 září 2011, Praha [Urban Law in Central Europe: Proceedings of the International Conference on Law and History: Urban Laws of the Kingdom of Bohemia, 19–21 September 2011, Prague], eds. Karel Malý and Jiři Šouša jr. (Praha, 2013).

Bischoff Ferdinand, "Beiträge zur Geschichte des Magdeburgerrechts", *Sitzungsberichte der Kaiserlichen Akademie der Wissenschaften. Philosophisch-Historische Classe* 50/4 (1865).

Bischoff Ferdinand, "Über einen deutschen Rechtscodex der Krakauer Universitäts-Bibliothek", *Sitzungsberichte der Kaiserlichen Akademie der Wissenschaften. Philosophisch-Historische Classe* 48/1–2 (1864).

Bleskina Olga, *Katalog sobraniâ latinskih rukopisej: pravo, filosofiâ, nauka, literatura i iskusstvo / Catalogus codicum manuscriptorum latinorum, qui in Bibliotheca Publica Petropolitana asservantur: jurisprudentia, philosophia, scientia, monumenta litterarum* (Sankt-Petersburg, 2011).

Blumenstock Alfred, "Wiadomość o rękopisach prawno-historycznych Biblioteki Cesarskiej w Petersburgu. Sprawozdanie z poszukiwań" [Latest Information about Legal History Manuscripts in St Petersburg Imperial Library], in: *Archiwum Komisji Historycznej. Collectanea ex Archivo Collegii Historici*, 6 (Kraków, 1891).

Boffey Julia, "Banking on Translation: English Printers and Continental Texts", in: *In principio fuit interpres*, ed. Alessandra Petrina, (The Medieval Translator) 15 (Brepols: 2013).

Bogucka Maria and Samsonowicz Henryk, *Dzieje miast i mieszczaństwa w Polsce przedrozbiorowej* [*A History of Towns and the Urban Middle Class in Poland until 1795*] (Wrocław – Warszawa – Kraków – Gdańsk – Łódź, 1986).

Bojarski Władysław, *Jan Jelonek Cervus z Tucholi. Z dziejów prawa rzymskiego w Polsce. Prawo prywatne materialne* [Johannes Cervus of Tuchola: A Chapter in the History of Roman Law in Poland. Substantive Private Law] (Toruń, 1989).

Bojarski Władysław, Naworski Zbigniew, *Jan Jelonek Cereus z Tucholi i jego twórczość prawnicza. Ustrój sądów i prawo procesowe*, [Johannes Cervus of Tuchola and His Legal Works: The Constitution of Courts and Procedural Law] (Toruń, 1993).

Bremer Thomas, Molitor Paul, Pöckelmann Marcus, Ritter Jörg, and Schütz Susanne, "Zum Einsatz digitaler Methoden bei der Erstellung und Nutzung genetischer Editionen gedruckter Texte mit verschiedenen Fassungen. Das Fallbeispiel der Histoire philosophique des deux Indes von Guillaume-Thomas Raynal", *Editio* 29/1 (2015).

Brückner Aleksander, "Średniowieczne słownictwo prawne" [Medieval Legal Vocabulary], *Prace Filologiczne* 5 (1895).

Buchda Gerhard, "Enthält die Glosse zum sächsischen Weichbild echte Schöffensprüche?", in: *Festschrift Heinrich Demelius zum 80. Geburtstag. Erlebtes Recht in Geschichte und Gegenwart*, ed. Gerhard Frotz (Wien, 1973).

Bukowska Krystyna, "Jeszcze w sprawie rozwoju miejskiego prawa prywatnego w Polsce" [More on the Development of Urban Private Law in Poland], *Czasopismo Prawno-Historyczne* 22/1 (1970).

Bukowska Krystyna, "O wpływach obcych w dawnym prawie miast polskich" [Foreign Influences on Early Urban Law of Polish Towns], *Czasopismo Prawno-Historyczne* 17/1 (1965).

Bukowska Krystyna, *Orzecznictwo krakowskich sądów wyższych w sporach o nieruchomości miejskie (XVI–XVIII w.). Studium z historii prawa rzymskiego w Polsce* [The Caselaw of Cracow High Courts Concerning Disputes over Real Property in Towns (16th–18th Century): A Study in the History of Roman Law in Poland] (Warszawa, 1967).

Bukowska-Gorgoni Krystyna, "Das sächsisch-magdeburgische Recht und die vermogensrechtlichen Verhaltnisse in den polnischen Stadten der Renaissance", in: *Studien zur Geschichte des sächsich-magdeburgischen Rechts in Deutschland und Polen*, eds. Dietmar Willoweit and Winfried Schich, (Rechtshistorische Reihe) 10 (Frankfurt am Main, 1980).

Carls Wieland, "Das sächsisch-magdeburgische Recht – Sprach- und Rechtstransfer in Mittel- und Osteuropa. Versuch einer Bestandsaufnahme am Beispiel der heutigen Slowakei", in: *Deutsche Sprache in der Slowakei. Festschrift für Ilpo Tapani Piirainen zum 65. Geburtstag. Internationale Fachtagung, Piešťany, den 13–15 Juni 2007*, eds. Peter Ďurčo, Ružena Kozmová, and Daniela Drinková (Trnava – Bratislava, 2009).

Carls Wieland, "Hy hebit sich an magdburgisch recht: Wege eines europäischen Rechts und seiner Erforschung", *Denkströme: Journal der Sächsischen Akademie der Wissenschaften zu Leipzig* 5 (2010).

Carls Wieland, "Rechtsquellen Sächsisch-magdeburgischen Rechts", in: Inge Bily, Wieland Carls, and Katalin Gönczi, *Sächsisch-magdeburgisches Recht in Polen.*

Untersuchungen zur Geschichte des Rechts und seiner Sprache, (Ivs Saxonico-Maidebvrgense in Oriente) 2 (Berlin, 2011).

Carls Wieland, "Zur Verbreitung des Halle-Neumarkter Rechts in Schlesien", in: *Halle im Licht und Schatten Magdeburgs. Eine Rechtsmetropole im Mittelalter*, eds. Heiner Lück, (Forschungen zur hallischen Stadtgeschichte) 19 (Halle/Saale, 2012).

Celichowski Zygmunt, *Słowniczek łacińsko-polski wyrazów prawa magdeburskiego z wieku XV* [A Latin-Polish Glossary of Magdeburg Law Terms from the 15th Century] (Poznań, 1875).

Coing Helmut, *Europäisches Privatrecht*, 1: *Älteres Gemeines Recht (1500 bis 1800)* (München, 1985).

Cytowska Maria, *Bibliografia druków urzędowych XVI wieku* [Bibliography of 16th Century Legal and Government Documents] (Wrocław, 1961).

Czerny Albin, *Die Handschriften der Stiftsbibliothek St. Florian* (Linz, 1871).

Dargun Lotar, "O źródłach prawa miast polskich w wieku szesnastym. II. O źródłach porządku sądowego spraw miejskich Prawa Magdeburskiego przez Bartłomieja Groickiego" [Sources of Urban Law Used in Polish Towns in the 16th Century: II. Sources of Judicial Procedure in Urban Matters in Accordance with Bartłomiej Groicki's Magdeburg Law], *Rozprawy Akademii Umiejętności. Wydział Historyczno-Filozoficzny* 25 (1891).

Dudík Beda, "Historische Forschungen in der keiserlichen öffentlichen Bibliothek zu St. Petersburg", *Sitzungsberichte der kaiserlichen Akademie der Wissenschaften, philosophisch-historische Classe* 95/1 (1879, published 1880).

Ebel Friedrich and Schelling Renate, "Das lateinische lübische Recht in der schlesisch-polnischen Fassung des 13. Jahrhunderts", *Zeitschrift der Savigny-Stiftung für Rechtsgeschichte. Germanistische Abteilung* 110 (1993).

Ebel Friedrich and Schelling Renate, "Die Bedeutung deutschen Stadtrechts im Norden und Osten des mittelalterlichen Europa. Lübisches und Magdeburger Recht als Gegenstand von Kulturtransfer und Träger der Moderne", in: *Die Stadt im Europäischen Nordosten. Kulturbeziehungen von der Ausbreitung des Lübischen Rechts bis zur Aufklärung. Beiträge anläßlich des II. Internationalen Symposiums zur deutschen Kultur im europäischen Nordosten der Stiftung zur Förderung deutscher Kultur (Aue-Stiftung) Helsinki in Zusammenarbeit mit dem Stadtarchiv Tallinn, dem Estnischen Kunstmuseum, der Ostsee-Akademie Lübeck-Travemünde und dem Deutschen Kulturinstitut Tallinn vom 10. bis 13. September 1998 in Tallinn, Estland*, eds. Robert Schweitzer, Waltraud Bastman-Bühner, and Jörg Hackmann (collab.), (Aue-Säätiön julkaisuja / Skrifter utgivna Aue-Stiftelsen / Veröffentlichungen der Aue-Stiftung) 12 (Helsinki – Lübeck, 2001).

Ebel Friedrich, "Das spreke wy vor eyn recht … Versuch über das Recht der Magdeburger Schoppen", in: Friedrich Ebel, *Unseren fruntlichen grus zuvor: Deutsches Recht des*

Mittelalters in mittel- und osteuropäischen Raum. Kleine Schriften, eds. Andreas Fijal, Hans-Jörg Leuchte and Hans-Jochen Schiewer (Köln [u.a.], 2004).

Ebel Friedrich, "Nachträge zu Homeyer – Borchling – Gierke – Eckhardt: Die deutschen Rechtsbücher des Mittelalters und ihre Handschriften", *Zeitschrift der Savigny-Stiftung für Rechtsgeschichte. Germanistische Abteilung* 99 (1982).

Ebel Friedrich, *Über die Legaldefinitionen. Rechtshistorische Studie zur Entwicklung der Gesetzgebungstechnik in Deutschland, insbesondere über die Verhältnis von Rechtsetzung und Rechtsdarstellung*, (Schriften zur Rechtsgeschichte) 6 (Berlin, 1974).

Estreicher Karol, *Bibliografia polska* [Polish Bibliography], General Series, 21 (Kraków, 1906).

Estreicher Stanisław, "Freimarkt i Frymark", *Czasopismo Prawnicze i Ekonomiczne* 25 (1929).

Estreicher Stanisław, "Nieznane teksty ortyli magdeburskich" [Recently Discovered Texts of the Magdeburg *ortyle*], in: *Studia staropolskie. Księga ku czci Aleksandra Brücknera* [Old Polish Studies: A Festschrift in Honour of Aleksander Brückner] (Kraków, 1928).

Estreicher Stanisław, *Kultura prawnicza w Polsce XVI wieku* [Legal Culture in Poland of the Sixteenth Century] (Kraków, 1931).

Fiedlerová Naďa and Šmídová Malárová Lenka, "The Earliest Law Books of the City of Brno and Their Relation to the Contemporary Legal Practice", *Krakowskie Studia z Historii Państwa i Prawa* 10/2 (2017).

Fillipov Igor, "Vulgate versus vetus Latina: The Choices of Caesarus of Arles", in: *Translation and Authority – Authorities in Translation*, eds. Pieter De Leemans and Michèle Goyens (Brepols: 2017).

Friedrich Ebel, "Rechtsentstehung und Rechtstransfer im Spiegel der Überlieferung (Magdeburger und Lübecker Recht)", in: *Grundlagen für ein neues Europa. Das Magdeburger und Lübecker Recht in Spätmittelalter und Früher Neuzeit*, eds. Heiner Lück, Matthias Puhle, and Andreas Ranft, Quellen und Forschungen zur Geschichte Sachsen-Anhalts, 6 (Köln – Weimar – Wien, 2009).

Goerlitz Theodor, "Das flämische und das fränkische Recht in Schlesien und ihr Widerstand gegen das sächsische Recht", *Zeitschrift der Savigny-Stiftung für Rechtsgeschichte. Germanistische Abteilung* 57 (1937).

Gönczi Katalin, "Stadtbücher aus dem Königreich Ungarn im Spiegel der städtischen Schriftkultur – Überlegungen zum Stand der Forschung", *Krakowskie Studia z Historii Państwa i Prawa* 9/3 (2016).

Gönczi Katalin, "Städte des Magdeburger Rechts in Osteuropa", in: *Städtische Räume im Mittelalter*, eds. Susanne Ehrich and Jörg Oberste (Regensburg, 2009).

Grodziski Stanisław, *Z dziejów staropolskiej kultury prawnej* [From the History of the Old Polish Legal Culture] (Kraków, 2004).

Heirbaut Dirk, "Sachsenspiegel or Sassen Speyghel (Saxon Mirror)c.1220–1235, ed. pr. 1474 Eike von Repgow (c.1180–c.1235)", in: *The Formation and Transmission of Western Legal Culture. 150 Books that Made the Law in the Age of Printing*, Serge Dauchy, Georges Martyn, Anthony Musson, Heikki Pihlajamäki, Alain Wijffels, eds., coop. Naoko Seriu (Studies in the History of Law and Justice) 7, series eds. Georges Martyn, Mortimer Sellers (New York – Berlin – Heidelberg, 2016).

Helcel Antoni Z., *Starodawne prawa polskiego pomniki poprzedzone wywodem historyczno krytycznym tak zwanego Prawodawstwa Wiślickiego Kaziémirza Wielkiego w texcie ze starych rękopism krytycznie dobranym*, [Ancient Monuments of Polish Law with a Critical-Historical Introduction to the Legislation Known as Kazimerz the Great's Statute of Wiślica: A Critical Edition of Its Text Collected from Old Manuscripts] (Warszawa, 1856).

Helena Kozerska and Wanda Stummer, eds., *Katalog rękopisów Biblioteki Uniwersyteckiej w Warszawie* [A Catalogue of Manuscripts in the University Library in Warsaw], 1 (Warszawa, 1963).

Helssig Rudolf, *Die lateinischen und deutschen Handschriften der Universitätsbibliothek Leipzig*, 3: *Die juristischen Handschriften* (1926, repr. Wiesbaden, 1996).

Hermans Theo, *What is (not) Translation?*, in: *The Routledge Handbook of Translation Studies*, eds. Carmen Millán and Francesca Bartina (London – New York, 2013).

Hespanha António M., "Form and Content in Early Modern Legal Books Bridging the Gap between Material Bibliography and the History of Legal Thought", *Rechtsgeschichte* 12 (2008).

Homeyer Carl G., *Die deutschen Rechtsbücher des Mittelalters und ihre Handschriften*, New Edition, eds. Conrad Borchling, Karl A. Eckhardt and Julius von Gierke (Weimar, 1931–1934).

Homeyer Carl G., *Die Extravaganten des Sachsenspiegels* (Berlin, 1861).

Ivanusa Nataliia, *Frauen im Sächsisch-Magdeburgischen Recht. Die Rechtspraxis in kleinpolnischen Städten im 16. Jahrhundert*, (Studien zur Ostmitteleuropaforschung) 38 (Marburg, 2017).

Janicka Danuta, "Die Rezeption des Sachsenspiegels und des Magdeburger Rechts am Beispiel von Thorn im Kulmer Land", in: *Rechts- und Sprachtransfer in Mittel- und Osteuropa. Sachsenspiegel und Magdeburger Recht. Internationale und interdisziplinäre Konferenz in Leipzig vom 31. Oktober bis 2. November 2003*, eds Ernst Eichler, Heiner Lück, and Wieland Carls, (Ivs Saxonico-Maidebvrgense in Oriente) 1 (Berlin, 2009).

Janicka Danuta, "Neuere Rechtsgeschichte in Polen in den Jahren 2002–2014", *Zeitschrift für Neuere Rechtsgeschichte* 37 (2015).

Janicka Danuta, "Wkład polskich historyków prawa w badania nad prawem magdeburskim w XX w. (1945–2010)" [The Contribution of Polish Law Historians to the Study of Magdeburg Law in the 20th Century (1945–2010)], *Studia Iuridica Toruniensia* 10 (2013).

Janicka Danuta, "Zur Topographie der Städte des Magdeburger Rechts in Polen: das Beispiel Kulm und Thorn", in: *Grundlagen für ein neues Europa. Das Magdeburger und Lübecker Recht in Spätmittelalter und Früher Neuzeit*, eds. Heiner Lück, Matthias Puhle, and Andreas Ranft, Quellen und Forschungen zur Geschichte Sachsen-Anhalts, 6 (Köln – Weimar – Wien, 2009).

Janicka Danuta, *Prawo karne w trzech rewizjach prawa chełmińskiego z XVI wieku* [Criminal Law in Three Revisions of the Chełmno Law in the 16th Century] (Toruń, 1992).

Johanek Peter, "Magdeburger Rechtsbücher", in: *Die deutsche Literatur des Mittelalters: Verfasserlexikon*, eds. Kurt Ruh, Gundolf Keil, *et al.*, Supplementary 11, 2nd ed., 2004.

Johnson Tom, *Law in Common. Legal Cultures in Late-Medieval England* (Oxford, 2020).

Juliusz Bardach, "Recepcja w dziejach: harmonia i dysharmonia w spotkaniu kultur" [Reception in History: Harmony and Disharmony] in: *Pamiętnik XII Powszechnego Zjazdu Historyków Polskich, Katowice 17–20 września 1979* [Proceedings of the 12th General Congress of Polish Historians, Katowice, September 17–20, 1979], 1 (Katowice, 1979).

Kacprzak Agnieszka, Krzynówek Jerzy, and Wołodkiewicz Witold, *Regulae iuris: łacińskie inskrypcje na kolumnach Sądu Najwyższego Rzeczypospolitej Polskiej* [*Regulae iuris*: Latin Inscriptions on the Columns of the Supreme Court of the Republic of Poland], ed. Witold Wołodkiewicz (Warszawa, 2001).

Kaliszuk Jerzy and Szyller Sławomir, eds., Inwentarz rękopisów do połowy XVI wieku w zbiorach Biblioteki Narodowej [*Inventory of Manuscripts (until the Mid-16th Century) in the National Library Collections*] (*Inwentarze Rękopisów Biblioteki Narodowej) 3 (Warszawa, 2012).*

Kaliszuk Jerzy, *Codices deperditi. Średniowieczne rękopisy łacińskie Biblioteki Narodowej utracone w czasie II wojny światowej*, [*Codices deperditi*: Medieval Latin Manuscripts of the National Library Lost during World War II], Vol 1: *Dzieje i charakterystyka kolekcji* [A History and Description of the Collection]; 2.2: *Katalog rękopisów utraconych* [A Catalogue of the Lost Manuscripts] (Wrocław, 2016) [series: Dziedzictwo Kulturowe po Skasowanych Klasztorach (Cultural Heritage of the Dissolved Monasteries), ed. M. Derwich, 8/1, 8/2.2].

Kałużniacki Emil, "Die polnische Recension der Magdeburger Urtheile und die einschlägigen deutschen, lateinischen und czechischen Sammlungen", *Sitzungsberichte der phil.-hist. Classe der Kaierischer Akademie der Wissenschaften* 111 (1886).

Kamińska Krystyna, *Lokacje miast na prawie magdeburskim na ziemiach polskich do 1370 r. Studium historyczno-prawne* [Incorporation of Towns under Magdeburg Law in Poland until 1370: A Study in the History of Law] (Toruń, 1990).

Kaniewska Irena, "Kowalowski Józef", in: *Polski Słownik Biograficzny* [Dictionary of Polish Biography], 14 (Wrocław, 1968–1969).

Karpavičienė Jolanta, "Das sächsisch-magdeburgische Recht in den Kleinstädten Litauens", in: *Grundlagen für ein neues Europa. Das Magdeburger und Lübecker Recht in Spätmittelalter und Früher Neuzeit*, eds. Heiner Lück, Matthias Puhle and Andreas Ranft (Köln – Weimar – Wien, 2009).

Karplukówna Maria, *Słownik Jana Cervusa z Tucholi* [Johannes Cervus of Tuchola's Glossary] (Wrocław, 1973).

Kędelska Elżbieta, *Łacińsko-polskie słowniki drukowane pierwszej połowy XVI wieku i ich stosunek do źródeł czeskich* [Latin-Polish Printed Dictionaries of the Early 16th Century and Czech Sources] (Wrocław, 1986).

Kętrzyński Wojciech, ed., *Catalogus Codicum Manuscriptum Bibliothecae Ossolinianae Leopoliensis. Katalog rękopisów Biblioteki Zakładu Nar. Im. Ossolińskich*, 3 (Lwów, 1898).

Kiryk Feliks, "Przyczynki do dziejów szkolnictwa i stosunków kulturalnych późnośredniowiecznego Przemyśla" [Some Highlights of the History of Education and Cultural Relations in Late-Medieval Przemyśl], in: *Cracovia, Polonia, Europa: studia z dziejów średniowiecza ofiarowane Jerzemu Wyrozumskiemu w sześćdziesiątą piątą rocznicę urodzin i czterdziestolecie pracy naukowej* [Cracovia, Polonia, Europa: A Festschrift Dedicated to Professor Jan Szymczak on His 65th Birthday Anniversary and 40 Years of Academic Work], eds. Krzysztof Baczkowski, Waldemar Bukowski, Mariusz Markiewicz, Krzysztof Ożóg, Maciej Salamon, Franciszek. Sikora, and Stanisław Szczur (Kraków, 1995).

Kiryk Feliks, "Ze stosunków ustrojowych w późnośredniowiecznym Przemyślu", in: *Parlamentaryzm i prawodawstwo przez wieki*, eds. Jerzy Malec, Wacław Uruszczak (Kraków, 1999).

Kiseleva Ludmila I., *Catalogue des manuscrits médiévaux en écriture latine de la Bibliothèque de l'Académie des Sciences de Russie de Saint-Pétersbourg* (Paris, 2005).

Kitowski Piotr, "Przysięga dowodowa w polskim prawie miejskim i ziemskim w XVII–XVIII wieku" [The Evidentiary Oath in Polish Municipal Law and Polish Land Law in the 17th–18th Century], in: *Nil nisi veritas. Księga dedykowana Profesorowi Jackowi Matuszewskiemu* [Nil nisi veritas: A Festschrift in Honour of Professor Jacek Matuszewski], eds. Marcin Głuszak and Dorota Wiśniewska-Jóźwiak (Łódź, 2016).

Kitowski Piotr, *Sukcesja spadkowa w mniejszych miastach województwa pomorskiego w II połowie XVII i XVIII wieku. Studium prawno-historyczne* [Inheritance Succession in Small Towns of the Voivodship of Pomerania in the Late 17th–18th Century: A Study in Legal History] (Warszawa, 2015).

Kłoczowski Jerzy, *Młodsza Europa. Europa Środkowo-Wschodnia w kręgu cywilizacji chrześcijańskiej średniowiecza* [The Younger Europe: Central and Eastern Europe and the Civilization of the Christian Middle Ages] (Warszawa, 2003).

Kobilec'kij Mikola M., *Magdeburz'ke prawo v Ukraïnì*, [The Magdeburg Law in Ukraine (14th–early 19th Century)] (L'vìv, 2008).

Kociołek-Pęksa Anna, Pęksa Władysław, "Between History and Sociology – Remarks on Differences in Percussion 'Legal Culture', Particularly Sociology of Law and the Disciplines of the History of Law", *The Lawyer Quarterly* 4 (2016).

Koranyi Karol, "Johannes Cervus Tucholiensis i jego dzieła (z dziejów praw obcych i literatury prawniczej w Polsce)" [Johannes Cervus Tucholiensis and His Work (Chapters from the History of Foreign Laws and Legal Literature in Poland)], *Przewodnik Historyczno-Prawny* 1 (1930).

Koranyi Karol, "W sprawie genezy czterech artykułów starościńskich" [The Origin of the Four Articles That Are the Prerogative of the Captain], *Sprawozdania Towarzystwa Naukowego we Lwowie* 11/1 (1931).

Korta Wacław, "Rola kulturalna średniowiecznej kancelarii" [The Cultural Role of the Medieval Chancery], in: *Studia z dziejów kultury i ideologii ofiarowane Ewie Maleczyńskiej w 50 rocznicę pracy dydaktycznej i naukowej* [Studies in History and Ideology: A Festschrift in Honour of Professor Ewa Maleczyńska to Mark 50 Years of Her Academic and Teaching Career] (Wrocław – Warszawa – Kraków, 1968).

Koselleck Reinhart, *Warstwy czasu. Studia z metahistorii* [Sediments of Time: On Possible Histories], transl. Krystyna Krzemieniowa and Jarosław Merecki (Warszawa, 2012).

Kowalski Grzegorz M., *Bartłomiej Groicki – prawnik polskiego Odrodzenia. Wystawa w 400-setną rocznicę śmierci. Biblioteka Jagiellońska 5–29 kwietnia 2005* [Bartłomiej Groicki – A Jurist of the Polish Enlightenment: Special Exhibition 400th Anniversary of His Death, Jagiellonian Library, 5–12 April 2005] (Kraków, 2005).

Kowalski Grzegorz M., *Zwyczaj i prawo zwyczajowe w doktrynie prawa i praktyce sądów miejskich karnych w Polsce XVI–XVIII w.* [Custom and Customary Law in Legal Doctrine and Practice of Municipal Criminal Courts in Poland 16th–18th Century] (Kraków, 2013).

Kramperowa Maria and Maisel Witold, "Księgozbiory mieszczan poznańskich drugiej połowy XVI w". [Book Collections of Poznań Burghers (Late 16th Century)], *Studia i Materiały do Dziejów Wielkopolski i Pomorza* 11/1 (1960).

Krystyna Kamińska, "Communitas civium w miastach polskich rządzących się prawem magdeburskim", *Acta Universitatis Nicolai Copernici. Prawo* 30 (1990).

Krystyna Kamińska, "Prawo średzkie jako instrument polityki osadniczej i gospodarczej w Polsce od XIII do początku XVI wieku" [The Środa Law as an Instrument of Settler Policy and Economic Development in Poland in the 13th and Early 14th Century], in: *Historia integra. Księga pamiątkowa ofiarowana prof. Stanisławowi Salmonowiczowi w siedemdziesięciolecie urodzin* [Historia integra: A Festschrift in Honour of Professor Stanisław Salmonowicz on His 70th Birthday], eds. Danuta Janicka and Ryszard Łaszewski (Toruń, 2001).

Kümper Hiram, *Sachsenrecht. Studien zur Geschichte des Sächsichen Landrechts in Mittelalter und früher Neuzeit*, (Schriften zur Rechtsgeschichte) 142 (Berlin, 2007).

Kutrzeba Stanisław, "Opisy rękopisów", in: *Archiwum komisji prawniczej*, 2 (Kraków, 1921).

Kutrzeba Stanisław, *Historia źródeł dawnego prawa polskiego* [History of the Sources of Old Polish Law], 2 (Lwów – Warszawa – Kraków, [1926]).

Kwaśniewski Andrzej, "Księgozbiory prywatne zachowane w Bibliotece Kapituły Kieleckiej (XV–XVIII w.)", [Private Collections Held in the Chapter Library in Kielce (15th–18th Century)], *Biuletyn Biblioteki Jagiellońskiej* 62 (2012).

Laband Paul, "Eine bisher unbekannte Rechtshandschrift", *Zeitschrift der Savigny-Stiftung für Rechtsgeschichte. Germanische Abteilung*, 11 (1873).

"Law Books During the Transition from Late-Medieval to Early-Modern Legal Scholarship", in: *The Formation and Transmission of Western Legal Culture. 150 Books that Made the Law in the Age of Printing*, Serge Dauchy, Georges Martyn, Anthony Musson, Heikki Pihlajamäki, Alain Wijffels, eds., Naoko Seriu, coop. (Studies in the History of Law and Justice) 7, series eds. Georges Martyn, Mortimer Sellers (New York – Berlin – Heidelberg, 2016).

Lazar Marija, "Transfer des Rechts und Transfer der Rechtssprache. Sächsisch-magdeburgisches Recht und seine Verbreitung im Ostmitteleuropa nach den Hussitenkriegen", in: *Persönlichkeiten in der tschechischen Sprach- und Kulturgeschichte. Beiträge zum 8. Bohemicum Dresdense: Tomáš Garrigue Masarik (1850–1937) 07.11.2014 und 9. Bohemicum Dresdense: Jan Hus (~1370–1415) – Erbe und Bedeutung 30.10.2015*, eds. Holger Kuße and Hana Kosourová, (Specimina Philologiae Slavicae) 191 (Leipzig, 2016).

Le Goff Jacques, *Medieval Civilization*, trans. Julia Barrow (Blackwell Publishing: 1991).

Lelewel Joachim, "Słownik 87 wyrazów. Vocabula iuris Magdeburgensis koło roku 1455 spisany" [A Glossary of 87 Words – Vocabula iuris Magdeburgensis Written Down c.1455], in: *Polska wieków średnich* [Medieval Poland], 2nd ed. (Poznań, 1951).

Lesław Pauli, "Die polnische Literatur des Magdeburger Rechts im 16. Jahrhundert", in: *Studien zur Geschichte des sächsich-magdeburgischen Rechts in Deutschland und Polen*, eds. Dietmar Willoweit and Winfried Schich, (Rechtshistorische Reihe) 10 (Frankfurt am Main, 1980).

Lesław Pauli, *Jan Kirstein Cerasinus (1507–1561). Krakowski prawnik doby Odrodzenia. Studium z dziejów praw obcych i literatury prawniczej w Polsce* [Jan Kirstein Cerasinus (1507–1561): A Cracow Jurist of the Renaissance. A Study in the History of Foreign Laws and Legal Literature in Poland] (Kraków, 1961).

Lieberwirth Rolf, "Einführung oder Rezeption? Mittelalterlich deutsches Recht in slawischen Herrschaftsgebieten. Das Beispiel: Polen", in: *Rechts- und Sprachtransfer in Mittel- und Osteuropa. Sachsenspiegel und Magdeburger Recht. Internationale und interdisziplinäre Konferenz in Leipzig vom 31. Oktober bis 2. November 2003*, eds. Ernst Eichler and Heiner Lück, (Ivs Saxonico-Maidebvrgense in Oriente) 1 (Berlin, 2008).

Lieberwirth Rolf, "Magdeburger Recht", in: *Hanse, Städte, Bünde. Die sächsischen Städte zwischen Elbe und Weser um 1500*, ed. M. Puhle, 1, (Magdeburger Museumsschreiben) 4 (Magdeburg, 1996).

Lieberwirth Rolf, *Eike von Repchow und der Sachsenspiegel* (Berlin, 1982).

Łosowska Anna, *Kolekcja liber legum i jej miejsce w kulturze umysłowej późnośredniowiecznego Przemyśla* [The Liber legum MS and Its Place in the Intellectual Culture of Late-Medieval Przemyśl] (Warszawa – Przemyśl, 2007).

Lück Heiner, "Aspects of the Transfer of the Saxon-Magdeburg Law to Central and Eastern Europe", *Rechtsgeschichte – Legal History* 22 (2014).

Lück Heiner, "Das Gericht des Burggrafen von Magdeburg zu Halle an der Saale. Eine Skizze nach vorwiegend sächsichen Quellen", in: *Vertrauen in den Rechtsstaat. Beiträge zur deutschen Einheit im Recht. Festschrift für Walter Remmers*, ed. Jürgen Goydre, Dietrich Rauschning, Rainer Robra, Hans-Ludlig Schreiber, and Christian Wulff (Köln – Berlin – Bonn – München, 1995).

Lück Heiner, "Das sächsich-magdeburgische Recht als kulturelles Bindeglied zwischen den Rechtsordnungen Ost- und Mitteleuropa", in: *Rechts- und Sprachtransfer in Mittel- und Osteuropa. Sachsenspiegel und Magdeburger Recht. Internationale und interdisziplinäre Konferenz in Leipzig vom 31. Oktober bis 2. November 2003*, eds. Ernst Eichler, Heiner Lück, and Wieland Carls, (Ivs Saxonico-Maidebvrgense in Oriente) 1 (Berlin, 2008).

Lück Heiner, "Die Anfänge des Magdeburger Stadtrechts und seine Verbreitung in Europa. Strukturen, Mechanismen, Dimensionen", *Sachsen und Anhalt* 27 (2015).

Lück Heiner, "Die Rezeption des Sachsenspiegels und des Magdeburger Rechts in Ostmitteleuropa", in: *Eike von Repgow, Sachsenspiegel, Die Dresdner Bilderhandschrift Mscr. Dresd. M 32. Aufsätze und Untersuchungen*, (Codices selecti) 107 (Graz, 2011).

Lück Heiner, "Jaskier Mikołaj", in: *Handwörterbuch zur deutschen Rechtsgeschichte*, 2, 2nd ed. (Berlin, 2012).

Lück Heiner, "Prawo magdeburskie jako czynnik identyfikacji europejskiej rodziny miast", in: *Europejskie miasta prawa magdeburskiego: tradycja, dziedzictwo, identyfikacja. Sesja komparatystyczna Kraków, 13–15 października 2006. Materiały konferencyjne*, ed. Anna Biedrzycka and Agnieszka Kutylak-Hapanowicz (Kraków, 2007).

Lück Heiner, "Rechtsbücher als „private" Rechtsaufzeichnungen?" *Zeitschrift der Savigny-Stiftung für Rechtsgeschichte. Germanistische Abteilung*, 131 (2014).

Lück Heiner, "Rechtstransfer und Rechtsverwandtschaft. Zum Einfluss des Magdeburger Stadtrechts im Königreich Böhmen", in: *Městské právo ve střední Evropě. Sborník příspěvků z mezinárodní právnické konference Práva městská Království českého*, 19–21 září 2011, Praha [Urban Law in Central Europe: Proceedings of the International Conference on Law and History: Urban Laws of the Kingdom of Bohemia, 19–21 September 2011, Prague], eds. Karel Malý and Jiří Šouša jr. (Praha, 2013).

Lück Heiner, "*Sachsenspiegel* und Magdeburger Recht. Grundlagen für Europa", *Denkströme. Journal der Sächsischen Akademie der Wissenschaften zu Leipzig* 4 (2010), 81–104 (http://www.denkstroeme.de/heft-4/s_81-104_lueck, accessed 8 July 2017).

Lück Heiner, "Urban Law: The Law of Saxony and Magdeburg", in: *The Oxford Handbook of European Legal History*, eds. Heikki Pihlajamäki, Markus D. Dubber, and Mark Godfrey, Published online: August 2018, DOI: 10.1093/oxfordhb/9780198785521.001.0001.

Lück Heiner, "Wirkungen des *Sachsenspiegels* und des Magdeburger Rechts in Ostmitteleuropa", in: *Legal Transitions. Development of Law in Formerly Socialist States and the Challenges of the European Union/Rechtsentwicklung in den ehemaligen sozialistischen Staaten und die Herausforderung der Europäischen Union*, eds. Elemér Balogh, Andrea Hegedűs, Péter Mezei, Zsolt Szomora, and Julianna S. Traser, (A Pólay Elemér Alapítvány Könyvtára) 17 (Szeged, 2007).

Lück Heiner, "Zur Verbreitung des *Sachsenspiegels* und des Magdeburger Rechts in den baltischen Landern", in: *Baltische-europäische Rechtsgeschichte und Lexikographie*, eds. Ulrich Kronauer and Thomas Taterka (Heidelberg, 2009).

Lück Heiner, *Der Sachsenspiegel: Das berühmteste deutsche Rechtsbuch des Mittelalters* (Darmstadt, 2017).

Lück Heiner, *Sachsenspiegel und Magdeburger Recht. Europäische Dimensionen zweier mitteldeutscher Rechtsquellen*, (Adiuvat in itinere) 5 (Hamburg, 1998).

Lück Heiner, *Über den Sachsenspiegel. Entstehung, Inhalt und Wirkung des Rechtsbuches, mit einem Beitrag zu den Grafen von Falkenstein im Mittelalter* (Halle an der Saale, 1999).

Łysiak Ludwik, "Sąd wyższy prawa niemieckiego w Bieczu" [The Supreme Court of German Law in Biecz], *Czasopismo Prawno-Historyczne* 33/1 (1981).

Łysiak Ludwik, *Ius supremum Maydeburgese castri Cracoviensis 1356–1794. Organisation, Tätigkeit und Stellung des Krakauer Oberhofs in der Rechtsprechung Altpolens* (Frankfurt am Main, 1990).

Łysiak Ludwik, *Własność sołtysia (wójtowska) w Małopolsce do końca XVI wieku* [Property of the sołtys (wójt) in Małopolska until the End of the 16th Century] (Kraków, 1964).

Maciejowski Wacław A., *Historia prawodawstw słowiańskich* [History of Slavic Legislatures], 6 (Warszawa, 1858).

Magin Christine, *'Wie es umb der iuden recht stet'. Der Status der Juden in Spätmittelalterlichen deutschen Rechtsbüchern* (Göttingen, 1999).

Maisel Witold, "Die Quellen des deutschen Rechts im mittelalterlichen Posen", in: *Studien zur Geschichte des sächsich-magdeburgischen Rechts in Deutschland und*

Polen, eds. Dietmar Willoweit and Winfried Schich, (Rechtshistorische Reihe) 10 (Frankfurt am Main, 1980).

Maisel Witold, *Poznańskie prawo karne do końca XVI w.* [Poznań Criminal Law until the 16th Century] (Poznań, 1963).

Malicki Marian, Zwinogrodzka Ewa, eds., Malicki Marian, Gołuszka Małgorzata, Ptak-Korbiel Wanda, Wawrykiewicz Zofia, Zwinogrodzka Ewa, coop., *Katalog poloników XVI wieku Biblioteki Jagiellońskiej* [Catalogue of *Polonica* from 16th Century in Jagiellonian Library], 1: A–Ł (Kraków, 1992).

Matuszewski Józef, "Proles illegittima w polskim prawie ziemskim" [Proles illegitima in Polish Land Law], *Czasopismo Prawno-Historyczne* 18/2 (1966).

Matuszewski Józef, "Artykuły słowiańskie Zwierciadła saskiego", [Slavic Articles of the *Sachsenspiegel*], *Czasopismo Prawno-Historyczne* 1 (1948).

Matuszewski Józef, "Prawo sądowe na wsi polskiej lokowanej na prawie niemieckim" [Law in Polish Villages Founded under German Law], *Studia z Dziejów Państwa i Prawa Polskiego* 2 (1995).

Matuszewski Józef, "Rodzaje własności gruntu we wsi lokowanej na prawie niemieckim" [Types of Land Ownership in Villages Founded under German Law], in: *Parlament, prawo, ludzie. Studia ofiarowane Profesorowi Juliuszowi Bardachowi* [Parliament, the Law and the People: A Festschrift in Honour of Professor Juliusz Bardach], eds. Katarzyna Iwanicka, Maria Skowronek, Kazimierz Stembrowicz (Warszawa, 1996).

Mayenowa Maria R., *Walka o język w życiu i literaturze staropolskiej* [The Struggle for Language in Polish Life and Literature (until the 18th Century)] (Warszawa, 1955).

The Medieval Translator, 16: *Translation and Authority – Authorities in Translation*, eds. Pieter De Leemans and Michèle Goyens (Brepols, 2017).

Menzel Josef J., Review of Zygfryd Rymaszewski, *Łacińskie teksty Landrechtu Zwierciadła Saskiego w Polsce* [Lateinische Texte des Landrechts des Sachsenspiegels in Polen]: *Versio Vratislaviensis, Versio Sandomiriensis, Łaski, Zeitschrift der Savigny-Stiftung für Rechtsgeschichte: Germanistische Abteilung* 93/1 (1976).

Meuten Ludwig, *Die Erbfolgeordnung des Sachsenspiegels und des Magdeburger Rechts. Ein Beitrag zur Geschichte des sächsich-magdeburgischen Rechts* (Frankfurt am Main, 2000).

Mikołajczyk Marian, "'Stosując się do prawa wyraźnego ...' Podstawy prawne wyroków kryminalnych grodziskiego sądu miejskiego w latach 1702–1756" ['Following the Law Clearly ...' The Legal Basis of Criminal Convictions Grodzisk City Court during 1702–1756], *Studia Iuridica Lubliniensia* 19 (2013).

Mikołajczyk Marian, *Przestępstwo i kara w prawie miast Polski południowej XVI–XVIII w.* [Crime and Punishment in the Law of Southern Polish Towns in the 16th–18th Century] (Katowice, 1998).

Mikołajczyk Marian, *Proces kryminalny w miastach Małopolski XVI–XVIII wieku* [Criminal Procedure in the Towns of Małopolska in the 16th–18th Century], (Prace Naukowe Uniwersytetu Śląskiego w Katowicach) 2979 (Katowice, 2013).

Mikuła Maciej, "Czynniki ograniczające prawo retraktu w średniowiecznej Polsce" [Factors Limiting *ius retractus* in Medieval Poland], in: *Studia z dziejów państwa i prawa* [Studies in the History of the State and the Law], 9/1, ed. Jacek S. Matuszewski (Lublin – Łódź, 2006).

Mikuła Maciej, "Das Magdeburger Weichbildrecht in seiner schlesisch-kleinpolnischen Fassung. Anmerkungen zur Autorschaft und Textevolution", in: *Kulturelle Vernetzung in Europa. Das Magdeburger Recht und seine Städte. Wissenschaftlicher Begleitband zur Ausstellung »Faszination Stadt«*, eds. Gabriele Köster, Christina Link, Heiner Lück (Sandstein Kommunikation, 2019).

Mikuła Maciej, "Das sächsisch-magdeburgische Recht in den Manuskripten der Bibliothek des Priesterseminars in Kielce, Signatur RK 45/28 – Ergänzung zu Deutsche Rechtsbücher des Mittelalters", *Zeitschrift der Savigny-Stiftung für Rechtsgeschichte: Germanistische Abteilung* 1/137 (2020).

Mikuła Maciej, "Die Könige und das Reformationsverfahren des Rechts in den polnischen Städten vom 14. bis zum 16. Jahrhundert", *Beiträge zur Rechtsgeschichte Österreichs* 2/2 (2013).

Mikuła Maciej, "Die Modifizierung des Erb- und Familienrechts im Magdeburger Weichbildrecht (Einführung zum Thema)", in: *Judiciary and Society Between Privacy and Publicity*, ed. Danuta Janicka, 8th Conference on Legal History in the Baltic Sea Area, 3rd–6th September (Toruń, 2015).

Mikuła Maciej, "Edycje źródeł do dziejów prawa miejskiego w Polsce XIV–XVI w.: propozycja elektronicznej metaedycji źródeł normatywnych" [Editions of Sources for the History of Municipal Law in Poland (14th–16th Century): A Proposal for an Electronic Metaedition of Normative Source Material], *Krakowskie Studia z Historii Państwa i Prawa* 9/4 (2016), English edition: *Krakowskie Studia z Historii Państwa i Prawa*, special issue (2018).

Mikuła Maciej, "Modyfikacje łacińskich tekstów Weichbildu magdeburskiego a ewolucja prawa w średniowiecznych miastach polskich. Uwagi wstępne" [Modifications of Latin Texts of the Magdeburg *Weichbild* and the Evolution of Law in Medieval Polish Towns: An Introduction], in: *Acta Iuridico-Historica Pilsnensia*, 2012–2013 (published 2014; ed. Vilém Knoll).

Mikuła Maciej, "Niezbędnik średniowiecznego praktyka prawa miejskiego: łacińsko-polski słownik terminów prawnych w rękopisie Biblioteki Narodowej w Warszawie, sygn. 3068 III" [A Necessary Equipment of Municipal Lawyer: Latin-Polish Legal Dictionary in MSS National Library in Warsaw Sign. 3068 III], in: *Semper fidelis. Prace dedykowane pamięci Profesora Janusza Sondla legendzie krakowskiego fakultetu prawniczego* [*Semper fidelis*. Works in Honour of Prodessor Janusz Sondel], eds. Dorota Malec, Łukasz Marzec, Tomasz Palmirski (Kraków, 2017).

Mikuła Maciej, "O reformie prawa miejskiego w XVI wieku. Ciężkowicka uchwała o prawie prywatnym i administracji" [Reforms of Municipal Law in the 16th Century: A Statute concerning Private Law and Administration Adopted by the Municipality of Ciężkowice], *Krakowskie Studia z Historii Państwa i Prawa* 6/3 (2013).

Mikuła Maciej, "Statuty prawa spadkowego w miastach polskich prawa magdeburskiego (do końca XVI wieku)" [Inheritance Statutes in Polish Towns under Magdeburg Law (until the End of the 16th Century)], *Z Dziejów Prawa* 7 (15) (2014).

Mikuła Maciej, "Was Canon Law in Use in Municipal Courts in Late-Medieval Poland?", in print.

Mikuła Maciej, "*Weichbild* magdeburski w rękopisie Biblioteki Jagiellońskiej nr 4405" [The Magdeburg *Weichbild* in MS BJ 4405], in: *Nil nisi veritas. Księga dedykowana Profesorowi Jackowi Matuszewskiemu* [*Nil nisi veritas*. A Festschrift Dedicated to Professor Jacek Matuszewski], eds. Marcin Głuszak and Dorota Wiśniewska-Jóźwiak (Łódź, 2016).

Mikuła Maciej, "Wpływ 'Summa utriusque iuris' mistrza Rajmunda na regulację dziedziczenia testamentowego w Statucie litewskim I z 1529 roku" [The Impact of Master Raymund's *Summa utriusque iuris* on Testamentary Inheritance in the Lithuanian Statute of 1529], *Czasopismo Prawno-Historyczne* 60/2 (2008).

Mikuła Maciej, *Prawodawstwo króla i sejmu dla małopolskich miast królewskich (1386–1572). Studium z dziejów rządów prawa w Polsce* [Royal and Parliamentary Legislation for the Royal Towns of Małopolska (1386–1572): A Study in the History of the Rule of Law in Poland] (Kraków, 2014).

Munzel Dietlinde, "Posener Rechtbuch", in: *Handwörterbuch zur deutschen Rechtsgeschichte*, 1st ed., 3 (Berlin, 1984).

Munzinger Mark, "The Text and Textualization of Codex BJ 168: Legal Culture in Transition at the High Court of Magdeburg Law at the Castle of Kraków", *Krakowskie Studia z Historii Państwa i Prawa* 4 (2011).

Nabiałek Karol, *Starostwo olsztyńskie od XIV do połowy XVII wieku* [Captainship of Olsztyn from the 14th until the Middle of the 17th Century] (Kraków, 2012).

Nowak Elisabeth, *Die Verbreitung und Anwendung des Sachsenspiegels nach der überlieferten Handschriften*, Dissertation zur Erlangung der Doktorwürde der Philosophischen Fakultät der Universität Hamburg (Hamburg, 1965) [typescript].

Obladen Margret, *Magdeburger Recht auf der Burg zu Krakau: Die güterrechtliche Absicherung der Ehefrau in der Spruchpraxis des Krakauer Oberhofs* (Berlin, 2005).

Ogris Werner, "Auflassung", in: *Handwörterbuch zur deutschen Rechtsgeschichte*, 1st ed., 1 (1971), col. 341–342.

Oppitz Ulrich-Dieter, "Ergänzungen zu „Deutsche Rechtsbücher des Mittelalters und ihre Handschriften", *Zeitschrift der Savigny-Stiftung für Rechtsgeschichte. Germanistische Abteilung* 128 (2011).

Oppitz Ulrich-Dieter, *Deutsche Rechtsbücher des Mittelalters*, 1–3 (Köln – Wien, 1990).

Pacyna Jana, *Mittelalterliche Judenrechte. Norm und Anwendung im Magdeburger Rechtskreis (1250–1400)* (Halle/Saale, 2015).

Pałecki Krzysztof, "O użyteczności pojęcia kultura prawna" [About the Utility of the Concept of Legal Culture], *Państwo i prawo* 2 (1974).

Patkaniowski Michał, *Krakowska rada miejska w średnich wiekach* [The Cracow City Council in the Middle Ages] (Kraków, 1934).

Piirainen Ilpo Tapani, "Der *Sachsenspiegel* von Conrad von Oppeln und Rechtshandschriften in Breslau", in: *Die Anfänge des Schrifttums in Oberschlesien bis zum Frühhumanismus*, ed. Gerhard Kosellek, (Tagungsreihe der Stiftung Haus Oberschlesien) 7 (Frankfurt am Main *et al.*, 1997).

Piotr Okniński, "Uwarunkowania początków rozwoju kancelarii miejskich. Przykład Krakowa (do 1312 r.)" [The Origins of Municipal Chancelleries: The Case of Cracow (until 1312)], in: *Loca scribendi. Miejsca i środowiska tworzące kulturę pisma w dawnej Rzeczypospolitej XV–XVIII stulecia* [Loca scribendi: Sites and Communities Involved in the Creation of the Culture of Writing in the Old Polish Commonwealth in the 15th–18th Century], eds. Anna Adamska, Agnieszka Bartoszewicz, and Maciej Ptaszyński (Warszawa, 2017).

Plezia Marian, "Wstęp" [Introduction], *Słownik łacińsko-polski* [The Latin-Polish Dictionary], 1 (Warszawa, 1959).

Podgórecki Adam, *Prestiż prawa* [The Prestige of Law] (Warszawa, 1966).

Potkowski Edward, *Książka rękopiśmienna w kulturze Polski średniowiecznej* [The Hand-Written Book in the Culture of Medieval Poland] (Warszawa, 1984).

"Preface", in: *The Formation and Transmission of Western Legal Culture. 150 Books that Made the Law in the Age of Printing*, Serge Dauchy, Georges Martyn, Anthony Musson, Heikki Pihlajamäki, Alain Wijffels, eds., Naoko Seriu, coop. (Studies in the History of Law and Justice) 7, series eds. Georges Martyn, Mortimer Sellers (New York – Berlin – Heidelberg, 2016).

Regulae Iuris w kulturze prawnej dawnej Polski [*Regulae iuris* in the Legal Culture of Poland until the 18th Century], *Krakowskie Studia Prawnicze* 22 (1989), repr.: Wacław Uruszczak, *Opera historico-iuridica selecta. Prawo kanoniczne – nauka prawa – prawo wyznaniowe*, [*Opera historico-iuridica selecta: Canon Law – Legal Scholarship – Law on Religion*], eds. Maciej Mikuła *et al.* (Kraków, 2017).

Regulae iuris. Ipotesi di lavoro tra storia e teoria del dirito (Napoli, 2016).

"Relationships between Text and Translation in Medieval Europe", in: *Translation. An International Encyclopedia of Translation Studies*, 2, eds. Harald Kittel, Armin P. Frank, Norbert Freiner, Theo Hermans, Werner Koller, José Lambert, Fritz Paul (Berlin – New York, 2007).

Reszczyński Jarosław, "*Sigismundina* Macieja Śliwnickiego. Uwagi o genezie dzieła, technice wprowadzania norm i interesie państwa jako ratio legis" [Maciej

Śliwnicki's *Sigismundina*: Some Remarks about the Origin of the Treatise, Methods of Promulgating Norms and the raison d'état as *ratio legis*], in: *Honeste vivere. Księga pamiątkowa ku czci Profesora Władysława Bojarskiego* [Honeste vivere: Festschrift in Honour of the Late Professor Władysław Bojarski], eds. Ewa Gajda and Andrzej Sokala (Toruń, 2001).

Reszczyński Jarosław, *Sądownictwo i proces w kodyfikacji Macieja Śliwnickiego z 1523 roku: o wpływach prawa rzymskiego i praw obcych na myśl prawną polskiego Odrodzenia* [The Justiciary and the Trial in Maciej Śliwnicki's Draft Code of 1523: The Influence of Roman Law and Foreign Laws on the Legal Thought of the Polish Renaissance] (Kraków, 2008).

Rogatchevski Alexander, "Das Magdeburger Recht auf dem heutigen Territorium Rußlands. Forschungsstand und Forschungsperspektiven", in: *Rechts- und Sprachtransfer in Mittel- und Ostmitteleuropa. Sachsenspiegel und Magdeburger Recht. Internationale und interdisziplinäre Konferenz in Leipzig vom 31. Oktober bis 2. November 2003*, eds. Ernst Eichler and Heiner Lück, (Ivs Saxonico-Maidebvrgense in Oriente) 1 (Berlin, 2008).

Rogatchevski Alexander, "Das sächsisch-magdeburgische Rechtsdenkmäler und verwandte Quellen in den St. Petersburger Handschriftensammlungen", in: *Grundlagen für ein neues Europa. Das Magdeburger und Lübecker Recht in Spätmittelalter und Früher Neuzeit*, eds. Heiner Lück, Matthias Puhle, and Andreas Ranft, Quellen und Forschungen zur Geschichte Sachsen-Anhalts, 6 (Köln – Weimar – Wien, 2009).

Rogatchevski, *Mech Rolanda: pravovye vzgli͡ady nemet͡skikh gorozhan XIII–XVII vv.* [The Sword of Roland] (St. Petersburg, 1996).

Rył Jadwiga, "Biblioteka katedralna w Gnieźnie. Aneks" [Cathedral Chapter Library at Gniezno. Appendix], *Archiwa, Biblioteki i Muzea Kościelne* 36 (1978).

Rył Jadwiga, "Biblioteka katedralna w Gnieźnie" [Cathedral Chapter Library at Gniezno], *Archiwa, Biblioteki i Muzea Kościelne* 33 (1976).

Rymaszewski Zygfryd, "*Forum commune* a *forum liberum*", *Studia z Dziejów Państwa i Prawa Polskiego* 2 (1995).

Rymaszewski Zygfryd, "Kłopoty Gdańska z kadukami królewskimi" [Gdańsk's Problems with Royal Escheats], in: *Historia integra. Studia z historii państwa i prawa, dziejów kultury, religii i oświaty epoki nowożytnej. Księga pamiątkowa ofiarowana Prof. Stanisławowi Salmonowiczowi w siedemdziesięciolecie urodzin* [Historia integra: A Festschrift in Honour of Professor Stanisław Salmonowicz on His 70th Birthday], eds. Danuta Janicka and Ryszard Łaszewski (Toruń, 2001).

Rymaszewski Zygfryd, *Łacińskie teksty Landrechtu Zwierciadła Saskiego w Polsce. Versio Vratislaviensis, versio Sandomiriensis, Łaski* [Latin Texts of the Landrecht of the Sachsenspiegel in Poland: Versio Vratislaviensis, versio Sandomiriensis, Łaski] (Łódź, 1975).

Rymaszewski Zygfryd, *Łacińskie teksty Landrechtu Zwierciadła Saskiego w Polsce. Jaskier – tekst główny i noty marginesowe* [Latin Texts of the Sachsenspiegel Landrecht in Poland: Jaskier – The Main Text and the Marginal Glosses] (Łódź, 1985).

Schelling Renate, "Magdeburger Schöffensprüche und Magdeburger Weichbildrecht in urkundlicher und handschriftlicher Überlieferung", in: *Hanse, Städte, Bünde. Die sächischen Städte zwischen Elbe und Weser um 1500. Ausstellung Kulturhistorisches Museum Magdeburg 28. Mai bis 26. August 1996. Braunschweigisches Landesmuseum. Ausstellungszentrum Hinter Aegidien 17. September bis 1. Dezember 1996*, 1, ed. Matthias Puhle, (Magdeburger Museumsschriften) 4/1 (Magdeburg, 1996).

Schlenker Gerlinde, "Das Magdeburger Burggrafenamt und Schultheißentum zu Halle/Salle", in: *Hanse, Städte, Bünde. Die sächischen Städte zwischen Elbe und Weser um 1500. Ausstellung Kulturhistorisches Museum Magdeburg 28. Mai bis 26. August 1996. Braunschweigisches Landesmuseum. Ausstellungszentrum Hinter Aegidien 17. September bis 1. Dezember 1996*, 1, ed. Matthias Puhle, (Magdeburger Museumsschriften) 4/1 (Magdeburg, 1996).

Schmidt-Recla Adrian, *Kalte oder warme Hand? Verfügungen von Todes wegen in mittelalterlichen Referenzrechtsquelle*, Forschungen zur deutschen Rechtsgeschichte, 29 (Köln, 2011).

Schmidt-Wiegand Ruth, "*Weichbild*", in *Handwörterbuch zur Deutschen Rechtsgeschichte*, 1st ed., 5 (Berlin, 1998).

Schott Clausdieter, "Magdeburger Recht und Sachsenspiegel – Stadtrecht und Landrecht", in: *Das Burger Landrecht und sein rechtshistorisches Umfeld. Zur Geschichte der Landrechte und ihrer Symbolik im Mittelalter von Rügen bis Niederösterreich*, eds. Dieter Pötschke, Gerhard Lingelbach, Bernd Feicke, and Ulrich-Dieter Oppitz (collab.) (Berlin, 2014).

"Selected Texts Disseminated Internationally through Translation: The Bible", in: *Translation. An International Encyclopedia of Translation Studies*, 3, eds. Harald Kittel, Armin P. Frank, Norbert Freiner, Theo Hermans, Werner Koller, José Lambert, and Fritz Paul (Berlin – Boston, 2011).

Słownik łaciny średniowiecznej [A Dictionary of Medieval Latin], 3, compiled by Marian Plezia and Julia Mruk (Wrocław – Warszawa – Kraków, 1969).

Snell-Hornby Mary *et al.* eds., *Handbuch Translation* (Tübingen, 1998).

Sohm Rudolph, "Zur Geschichte der Auflassung", in: *Festgabe zum Doctor-Jubiläum des Herrn Geheimen Justizrathes Professors Dr. Heinrich Thöl* (Strassburg, 1879).

Sondel Janusz, "Ze studiów nad rolą i miejscem łaciny prawniczej w kulturze europejskiej" [Studies on the Role and Position of Legal Latin in European Culture], *Krakowskie Studia z Historii Państwa i Prawa* 7/1 (2014).

Sondel Janusz, *Słownik łacińsko-polski dla prawników i historyków* [A Latin-Polish Dictionary for Lawyers and Historians] (Warszawa, 1997).

Sondel Janusz, *Z rozważań o łacińsko-polskiej terminologii i leksykografii prawniczej* [Reflections on Latin-Polish Legal Terminology and Lexicography], in: *Parlament, prawo, ludzie. Studia ofiarowane Profesorowi Juliuszowi Bardachowi* [Parliament, the Law and the People: A Festschrift in Honour of Professor Juliusz Bardach], eds. Katarzyna Iwanicka, Maria Skowronek, and Kazimierz Stembrowicz (Warszawa, 1996).

Sowina Urszula, "Trousseau according to the *Ius municipale Magdeburgense* by Paweł Szczerbic and the position of a woman in the craftsman family at the beginning of the early modern time", *Kwartalnik Historii Kultury Materialnej* 68/4 (2020).

Starzyński Marcin, *Krakowska rada miejska w średniowieczu* [The Cracow City Council in the Middle Ages] (Kraków, 2010).

Stein Paul, *Regulae iuris. From Juristic Rules to Legal Maxims* (Edinburgh, 1966).

Stephan Dusil, *Jahr und Tag* in: *Handwörterbuch zur Deutschen Rechtsgeschichte*, 2nd ed., 2 (Berlin, 2011).

Stępień Mateusz, "Kultura prawna" [Legal Culture], in: *Lexicon of sociology of law*, eds. Anna Kociołek-Pęksa, Mateusz Stępień (Warszawa, 2013).

Suski Piotr, "Spory wokół gerady i hergewetu w polskim miejskim prawie spadkowym w XVI w." [Debates about *gerada* and *hergewet* in Polish Urban Inheritance Law in the 16th Century], in: *Prawo blisko człowieka. Z dziejów prawa rodzinnego i spadkowego* [The Law and the Ordinary People: From the History of Family and Inheritance Law], ed. Maciej Mikuła (Kraków, 2008).

Švecová Adriana, "Die Stadtrechtsbücher in der mittelalterlichen Slowakei und Ungarn als Beispiel des eigenen Selbstbewusstseins im Rahmen der europäischen Rechtskultur", *Krakowskie Studia z Historii Państwa i Prawa* 9/3 (2016).

Szczepankowska Irena, "Rola łaciny w kształtowaniu terminologii prawa polskiego w okresie od XVI do XVIII wieku. Problemy transferu pojęć i nazw" [The Role of Latin in the Development of Polish Legal Terminology in the 16th–18th Century: Problems of the Transfer of Concepts and Names], in: *Język w urzędach i w sądach* [Language in Offices and Courts], ed. Maria Lizisowa (Kraków, 2006).

Tabor Dariusz, *Malarstwo książkowe na Śląsku w XIV wieku* [The Art of Book Illustration in Silesia in the 14th Century] (Kraków, 2008).

Tafiłowski Piotr, *Jan Łaski (1456–1531) kanclerz koronny i prymas polski* [Jan Łaski (1456–1531): Grand Chancellor of Poland and Primate of Poland] (Warszawa, 2007).

"Translations and the Role of the Vernacular Languages in Medieval Europe", in: *Translation. An International Encyclopedia of Translation Studies*, 2, eds. Harald Kittel, Armin P. Frank, Norbert Freiner, Theo Hermans, Werner Koller, José Lambert, Fritz Paul (Berlin – New York, 2007).

Trzciński [Tadeusz], *Średniowieczne rękopisy biblioteki kapitulnej w Gnieźnie* [Medieval Manuscripts in the Cathedral Chapter Library at Gniezno], (Rocznik Towarzystwa Przyjaciół Nauk Poznańskiego) 35 (Poznań, 1909).

Tymieniecki Kazimierz, "Prawo czy gospodarstwo?" [The Law or the Household?], *Roczniki Dziejów Społecznych i Gospodarczych* 8/2 (1946).

Tymieniecki Kazimierz, "Prawo niemieckie w rozwoju społecznym wsi polskiej" [German Law and the Social Development of the Polish Village], *Kwartalnik Historyczny* 37 (1923).

Ulanowski Bolesław, "Opisy rękopisów" [Descriptions of Manuscripts], ed. Stanisław Kutrzeba, in: *Archiwum komisji prawniczej*, 2 (Kraków, 1921).

Uruszczak Wacław, '*Commune incliti Poloniae Regni privilegium constitutionum et indultuum*: O tytule i mocy prawnej Statutu Łaskiego z 1506 roku' [*Commune incliti Poloniae Regni privilegium constitutionum et indultuum*: The Title and Legal Validity of Łaski's *Statutes* (1506)], in: *Prace poświęcone pamięci Adama Uruszczaka* [Studies in Honour of the Late Adam Uruszczak], eds. Jan Halberda, Michał Hosowicz, and Anna Karabowicz, (Prace Instytutu Prawa Własności Intelektualnej UJ) 96 (Zakamycze, 2006).

Uruszczak Wacław, "Europejskie kodeksy prawa doby renesansu" [European Legal Codices of the Renaissance], *Czasopismo Prawno-Historyczne* 40/1 (1988).

Uruszczak Wacław, "Krakowski komentarz reguł prawa z początku XVI wieku (*Lectura super titulo de regulis iuris Libro Sexto*)" [A Cracow Commentary on the *regulae iuris* from the Early 16th Century (*Lectura super titulo de regulis iuris Libro Sexto*)], *Czasopismo Prawno-Historyczne* 25/2 (1973), repr.: Wacław Uruszczak, *Opera historico-iuridica selecta. Prawo kanoniczne – nauka prawa – prawo wyznaniowe*, [Opera historico-iuridica selecta: Canon Law – Legal Scholarship – Law on Religion], eds. Maciej Mikuła *et al.* (Kraków, 2017).

Uruszczak Wacław, "Nowelizacja Statutów Kazimierza Wielkiego w statucie warckim z 1423 roku. Z badań nad ustawodawstwem w dawnej Polsce" [Amendment of the Statutes of Kazimierz the Great in the Statute of Warta of 1423: Studies in Polish Legislation until the Late 18th Century], in: *Studia z Dziejów Państwa i Prawa Polskiego* [Studies in the History of Polish State and Law], 9/1, eds. Jacek S. Matuszewski and Wojciech Witkowski (Lublin – Łódź, 2006).

Uruszczak Wacław, "Reguła Quod omnes tangit debet ab omnibus approbari dawnego prawa kanonicznego i jej znaczenie" [The Maxim Quod omnes tangit debet ab omnibus approbari in the Old Xanon Law ant its Meaning], in: *Servabo legem Tuam in toto corde meo. Księga pamiątkowa dedykowana Księdzu Profesorowi Józefowi Krzywdzie CM, Dyrektorowi Instytutu Prawa Kanonicznego UPJPII z okazji 70. rocznicy urodzin* [*Servabo legem Tuam in toto corde meo.* A Festschrift in Honour of Professor Józef Krzywda CM, Manager of the Canon Law Institute of Pontifical University of John Paul II, on His 70th Birthday], eds. Arkadiusz Zakręta CM, Andrzej Sosnowski CR (Kraków, 2013).

Uruszczak Wacław, "Rękopisy Statutu krakowsko-warckiego z 1421/1423" [Manuscripts of the Statutes of Cracow and Warta, 1421/1423], in: *Nil nisi veritas. Księga dedykowana Profesorowi Jackowi Matuszewskiemu* [Nil nisi veritas: A Festschrift in Honour of Professor Jacek Matuszewski], eds. Marcin Głuszak and Dorota Wiśniewska-Jóźwiak (Łódź, 2016).

Uruszczak Wacław, "Wydział Prawa Uniwersytetu Jagiellońskiego i jego profesorowie w latach 1364–1780" [Faculty of Law of the Jagiellonian University and Its Professors in 1364–1780], in: Krzysztof Ożóg, Krzysztof Fokt, Maciej Mikuła, Maciej Zdanek, Dagmara Wójcik-Zega, and Katarzyna Kuras, *Profesorowie Wydziału Prawa Uniwersytetu Jagiellońskiego*, 1: *1364–1780* [Professors of the Faculty of Law of the Jagiellonian University, 1: 1364–1780], ed. Wacław Uruszczak (Kraków, 2015).

Uruszczak Wacław, "Z badań nad Statutem Warckim z 1423 roku" [Studies of the Statutes of Warta], in: *Parlamentaryzm i prawodawstwo przez wieki* [Parliamentarism and Legislation over the Centuries], eds. Jerzy Malec and Wacław Uruszczak (Kraków, 1999).

Uruszczak Wacław, *Historia państwa i prawa polskiego* [History of Polish State and Law], 1: 966–1795, 1st ed. (Warsaw, 2010).

Uruszczak Wacław, *Opera historico-iuridica selecta. Prawo kanoniczne – nauka prawa – prawo wyznaniowe* [Opera historico-iuridica selecta: Canon Law – Legal Scholarship – Law on Religion], eds. Maciej Mikuła *et al.* (Kraków, 2017).

Uruszczak Wacław, *Próba kodyfikacji prawa polskiego w pierwszej połowie XVI wieku. Korektura praw z 1532 r.* [An Attempt to Codify Polish Law in the First Half of the 16th Century: Correctura Iurium of 1532] (Warszawa, 1979).

Vetulani Adam, "Nouvelles vues sur le *Décret de Gratien*", in *La Pologne au Xe Congrès international des sciences historiques à Rome* (Warszawa, 1955; repr. Aldershot, 1990, ed. Wacław Uruszczak).

Vetulani Adam, "W sprawie prawa chłopskiego w Polsce feudalnej" [Concerning Peasant Law in Feudal Poland], *Państwo i Prawo* 10 (1956).

Wagner Anne, King Kui Sin and Le Cheng, "Cultural Transfer and Conceptualization in Legal Discourse", in: *The Ashgate Handbook of Legal Translation* (Ashgate, 2014).

Watson Allan, *Legal transplants. An Approach to Comparative Law*, 2nd ed. (Athens – London, 1974).

Weichbildrecht, Das Sächsische, "Geschichtsquellen des deutschen Mittelalters" (http://www.geschichtsquellen.de/repOpus_04593.html, accessed 8 July 2017).

Wesołowski Jacek, *Kolekcje historyczne w Polsce średniowiecznej XIV–XV wieku* [Historical Collections in Medieval Poland (14th–15th Century)] (Wrocław – Warszawa – Kraków, 1987).

Wieland Carls, "Überlieferungsgeschichtliche Beobachtungen zum Verhältnis von Schwabenspiegel und Sächsisch-magdeburgischem Recht", in: *Schwabenspiegel-Forschung im Donaugebiet. Konferenzbeiträge in Szeged zum mittelalterlichen Rechtstransfer deutscher Spiegel*, ed. Elemér Balogh, (Ivs Saxonico-Maidebvrgense in Oriente) 4 (Berlin – Boston, 2015).

Winroth Anders, *The Making of Gratians's Decretum* (Cambridge University Press: 2000).

Wisłocki Władysław, "Kodeks pilzneński ortylów magdeburskich" [The Pilzno Codex of Magdeburg *ortyle*], *Rozprawy Akademii Umiejętności* 2 (1874).

Wisłocki Władysław, *Inwentarz rękopisów Biblioteki Jagiellońskiej* [Inventory of Manuscripts in the Jagiellonian University], 1 (Kraków, 1877–1881).

Witold Maisel, "Sąd miejski prawa polskiego w Kaliszu w XVI wieku" [Sąd miejski prawa polskiego w Kaliszu w XVI wieku], *Czasopismo Prawno-Historyczne* 23/2 (1971).

Włodek Zofia, *Catalogus Codicum Manuscriptorum Medii Aevi Latinorum qui in Bibliotheca Jagellonica Cracoviae Asservantur*, 1 (Wrocław, 1980).

Wolff Adam, "Projekt instrukcji wydawniczej dla pisanych źródeł historycznych do połowy XVI w." [A Blueprint Guide to Publishing Written Historical Sources from before the Mid-16th Century], *Commentationes: Studia Źródłoznawcze* 1 (1957).

Wolny Jerzy, "Inventaire des manuscrits théologiques médiévaux de la bibliothéque du chapitre à Kielce", *Mediaevalia Philosophica Polonorum* 16 (1971).

Wyrozumska B., *Kancelaria miasta Krakowa w średniowieczu* [Chancellery of the City of Cracow in the Middle Ages] (Kraków, 1995).

Zajda Aleksander, "Deutsche Einflüße in der altpolnischen juristischen Terminologie", in: *Rechts- und Sprachtransfer in Mittel- und Osteuropa. Sachsenspiegel und Magdeburger Recht. Internationale und interdisziplinäre Konferenz in Leipzig vom 31. Oktober bis 2. November 2003*, eds Ernst Eichler, Heiner Lück, and Wieland Carls, (Ivs Saxonico-Maidebvrgense in Oriente) 1 (Berlin, 2009).

Zajda Aleksander, *Staropolska terminologia prawnicza (do 1500 r.)* [Polish Legal Terminology (until 1500)] (Kraków, 1990).

Zajda Aleksander, *Studia z historii polskiego słownictwa prawniczego i frazeologii* [Studies in the History of Polish Legal Terminology and Phraseology] (Kraków, 2001).

Zancarini Jean-Claude, "*Uno Picolo Dono*: A Software Tool for Comparing the First Edition of Machiavelli's *The Prince* to Its Sixteenth Century French Translations", in: *The Radical Machiavelli. Politics, Philosophy and Language*, eds. Filippo Del Lucchese, Fabio Frosini, and Vittorio Morfino (Leiden – Boston, 2015).

Zander Herbert, *Das Rote Buch der Stadt Gorlitz 1305–1416* (Leipzig, 1929).

Zathey Jerzy, *Katalog rękopisów średniowiecznych Biblioteki Kórnickiej* [A Catalogue of Medieval Manuscripts in Kórnik Library] (Wrocław, 1963).

Zdanek Maciej, "Jakub z Szadka h. Wieniawa (zm. 28 X 1487)" [Jakub of Szadek (Clan Wieniawa) (d. 28 October 1487)], in: Krzysztof Ożóg, Krzysztof Fokt, Maciej Mikuła, Maciej Zdanek, Dagmara Wójcik-Zega, and Katarzyna Kuras, *Profesorowie Wydziału Prawa Uniwersytetu Jagiellońskiego, 1: 1364–1780* [Professors of the Faculty of Law of the Jagiellonian University, 1: 1364–1780], ed. Wacław Uruszczak (Kraków, 2015).

Zdrójkowski Zbigniew, "Geneza prawa średzkiego i jego rola dziejowa (1223–1511)", *Acta Universitatis Wratislaviensis. Historia* 70 (1990).

Zdrójkowski Zbigniew, "Stan badań nad problematyką prawa średzkiego. Studium na 750-lecie pouczenia miasta Halle dla Środy Śląskiej (1235–1985)" [Stan badań nad problematyką prawa średzkiego. Studium na 750-lecie pouczenia miasta Halle dla Środy Śląskiej (1235–1985)], *Czasopismo Prawno-Historyczne* 37/2 (1985).

Zdrójkowski Zbigniew, "Wstęp historyczny" [A Historical Introduction], in: *Prawo starochełmińskie* [Old Chełmno Law] 1584 (1394), eds. Witold Maisel and Zbigniew Zdrójkowski, trans. Andrzej Bzdęga and Anna Gaca, (Teksty Pomników Prawa Chełmińskiego w Przekładach Polskich) 2 (Toruń, 1985).

Zientara Benedykt, "Das Deutsche Recht (*ius teutonicum*) und die Anfänge der städtischen Autonomie", in: *Autonomie, Wirtschaft und Kultur der Hansestädte*, eds. Konrad Fritze, Eckhard Mueller-Mertens, Walter Stark (Weimar, 1984).

Online Sources

Dziedzictwo kulturowe po klasztorach skasowanych na ziemiach dawnej Rzeczpospolitej oraz Śląsku w XVIII i XIX w.: losy, znaczenie, inwentaryzacja, baza danych finansowana w ramach programu Ministra Nauki i Szkolnictwa Wyższego pod nazwą "Narodowy Program Rozwoju Humanistyki" w latach 2012–2016, http://pw.kasaty.pl/rekopis/Scroll/4384.html?search=bydgoszcz (Accessed: 18 March 2015).

http://dk.bu.uni.wroc.pl/cymelia/displayDocument.htm;jsessionid=0C8E4EBBFF0E78C07ADFC0E96B1FB74B?docId=5002000234 (Accessed: 22 May 2017).

http://hyperprince.ens-lyon.fr (Accessed: 8 July 2017).

http://lera.uzi.uni-halle.de (Accessed: 8 July 2017).

https://iura.uj.edu.pl/dlibra (Accessed: 25 August 2020).

Index Auctorum

Index Personarum et Locorum

Index Operarum

www.ingramcontent.com/pod-product-compliance
Lightning Source LLC
LaVergne TN
LVHW010638300926
849161LV00005B/972